D0871242

PRENTICE HALL

MIDDLE GRADES MATH

TOOLS FOR SUCCESS

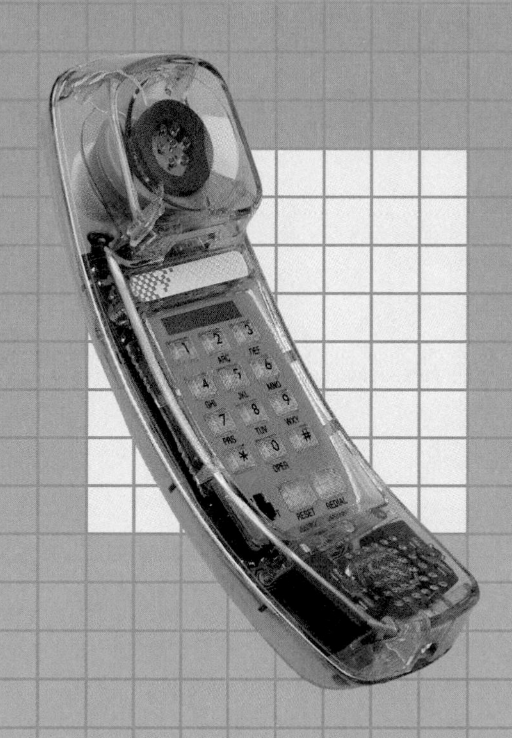

Course 3

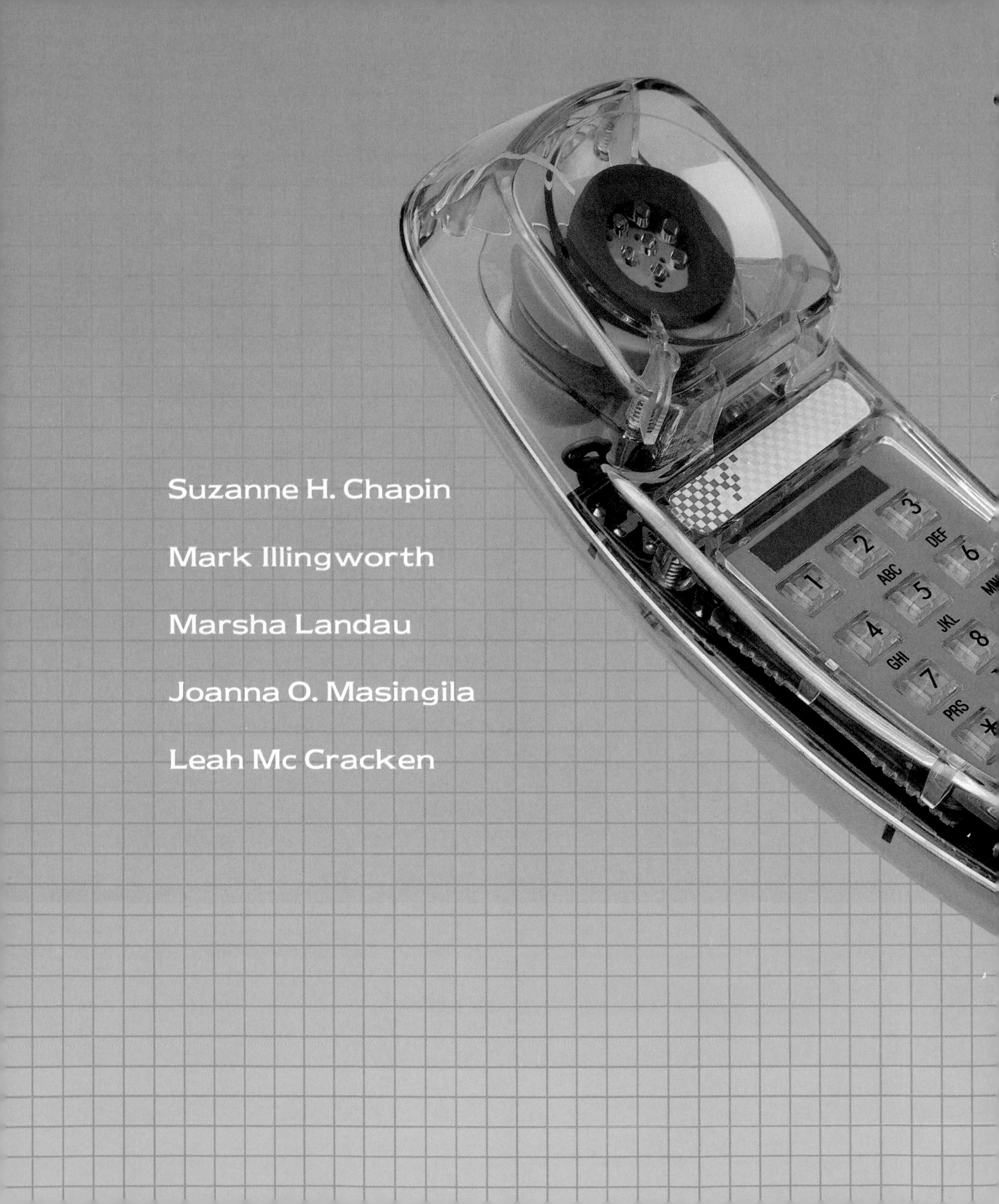
Suzanne H. Chapin
Mark Illingworth
Marsha Landau
Joanna O. Masingila
Leah Mc Cracken

PRENTICE HALL

MIDDLE GRADES MATH

TOOLS FOR SUCCESS

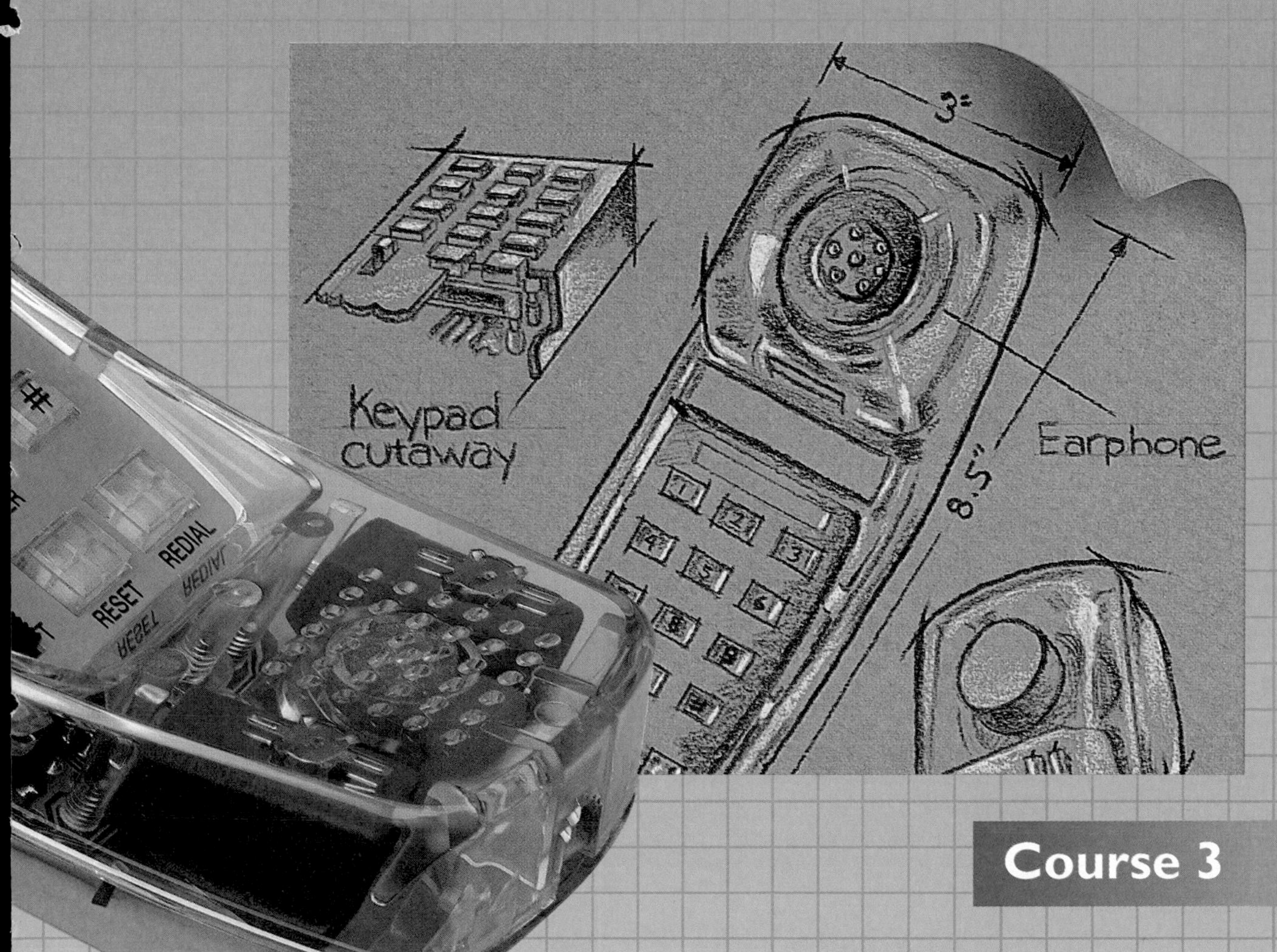

Course 3

PRENTICE HALL
Needham, Massachusetts
Upper Saddle River, New Jersey

The authors and consulting authors on *Prentice Hall Math: Tools for Success* team worked with Prentice Hall to develop an instructional approach that addresses the needs of middle grades students with a variety of ability levels and learning styles. Authors also prepared manuscripts for strands across three levels of Middle Grades Math. Consulting authors worked alongside authors throughout program planning and all stages of manuscript development offering advice and suggestions for improving the program.

Authors

Suzanne Chapin, Ed. D., Boston University, Boston MA; Proportional Reasoning and Probability strands
Mark Illingworth, Hollis Public Schools, Hollis, NH; Graphing strand
Marsha S. Landau, Ph. D., National Louis University, Evanston, IL; Algebra, Functions, and Computation strands
Joanna Masingila, Ph. D., Syracuse University, Syracuse, NY; Geometry strand
Leah McCracken, Lockwood Junior High, Billings, MT; Data Analysis strand

Consulting Authors

Sadie Bragg, Ed. D., Borough of Manhattan Community College, The City University of New York, New York, NY
Vincent O'Connor, Milwaukee Public Schools, Milwaukee, WI

PRENTICE HALL
Simon & Schuster Education Group
A VIACOM COMPANY

Printed in the United States of America.

ISBN 0-13-427691-4

3 4 5 6 7 8 9   02 01 00 99 98 97

Reviewers

All Levels

Ann Bouie, Ph. D., Multicultural Reviewer, Oakland, CA
Victoria Delgado, Director of Multicultural/Bilingual Programs, District 32, Brooklyn, NY (Spanish Edition)
Mary Lester, Dallas Public Schools, Dallas, TX
Dorothy S. Strong, Ph. D., Chicago Public Schools, Chicago, IL

Course 1

Darla Agajanian, Sierra Vista School, Canyon Country, CA
Rhonda Bird, Grand Haven Area Schools, Grand Haven, MI
Leroy Dupee, Bridgeport Public Schools, Bridgeport, CT
Ana Marina Gómez-Gil, Sweetwater Union High School District, Chula Vista, CA (Spanish Edition)
José Lalas, California State University, Dominguez Hills, CA
Richard Lavers, Fitchburg High School, Fitchburg, MA
Jaime Morales, Gage Middle School, Huntington Park, CA (Spanish Edition)

Course 2

Raylene Bryson, Alexander Middle School, Huntersville, NC
Sheila Cunningham, Klein Independent School District, Klein, TX
Eduardo González, Sweetwater High School, National City, CA (Spanish Edition)
Natarsha Mathis, Hart Junior High School, Washington, DC
Marcela Ospina, Washington Middle School, Salinas, CA (Spanish Edition)
Jean Patton, Sharp Middle School, Covington, GA
Judy Trowell, Little Rock School District, Little Rock, AR

We are grateful to our reviewers who read manuscript at all stages of development and provided invaluable feedback, ideas, and constructive criticism to help make this program one that meets the needs of middle grades teachers and students.

Course 3

Frank Acosta, Colton Junior High School, Colton, CA (Spanish Edition)
Michaele F. Chappell, Ph. D., University of South Florida, Tampa, FL
Bettye Hall, Math Consultant, Houston, TX
Joaquín Hernández, Shenandoah Middle School, Miami, FL
Dana Luterman, Lincoln Middle School, Kansas City, MO
Isabel Pereira, Bonita Vista Senior High School, Chula Vista, CA (Spanish Edition)
Loretta Rector, Leonardo da Vinci School, Sacramento, CA
Anthony C. Terceira, Providence School Department, Providence, RI

Staff Credits

Editorial: Judith D. Buice, Kathleen J. Carter, Linda Coffey, Noralie V. Cox, Edward DeLeon, Christine Deliee, Audra Floyd, Mimi Jigarjian, Lynn H. Raisman
Marketing: Bridget A. Hadley, Christina Trinchero
Production: Gabriella Della Corte, David Graham
Electronic Publishing: Joanne Hudson, Pearl Weinstein
Manufacturing: Jackie Bedoya, Vanessa Hunnibell
Design: Alison Anholt-White, Bruce Bond, Russell Lappa, Eve Melnechuk, Stuart Wallace

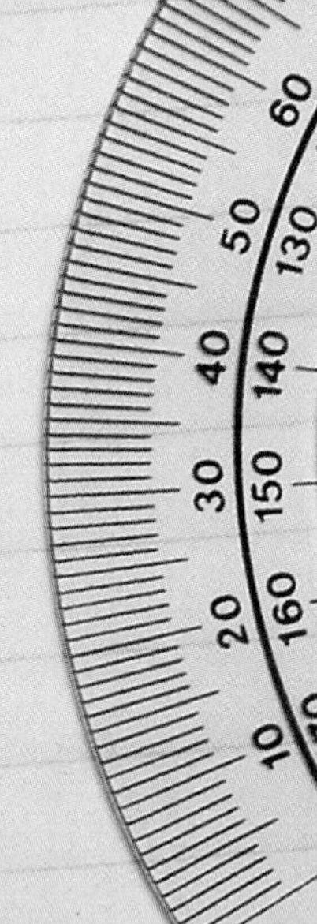

Prentice Hall dedicates this mathematics series to all middle level mathematics educators and their students.

TABLE OF CONTENTS

CHAPTER 1 Drawing Conclusions from Data

✸ ***Hot Page™ Lesson on CD-ROM***

CHAPTER 2 Patterns in Geometry

✻ ***Hot Page™ Lesson on CD-ROM***

Extra SKILLS PRACTICE

CHAPTER 3 Integers and Variable Expressions

* ***Hot Page™ Lesson on CD-ROM***

INVESTIGATION
A NEW WAY TO MEASURE

Extra SKILLS PRACTICE

CHAPTER 4 Algebraic Equations and Inequalities

✱ *Hot Page™ Lesson on CD-ROM*

INVESTIGATION
MAKING MOBILES

Extra SKILLS PRACTICE

CHAPTER 5

Graphing in the Coordinate Plane

✷ ***Hot Page™ Lesson on CD-ROM***

INVESTIGATION
THE GREAT RESCUE

Extra **SKILLS PRACTICE**

CHAPTER 6 Functions

CHAPTER 7

Rational Numbers

* *Hot Page™ Lesson on CD-ROM*

INVESTIGATION
WRITING IN CODE

Extra SKILLS PRACTICE

CHAPTER 8

Applications of Proportions

✷ *Hot Page™ Lesson on CD-ROM*

INVESTIGATION
ESTIMATING DISTANCES

CHAPTER 9 Probability

* ***Hot Page™ Lesson on CD-ROM***

INVESTIGATION
How Many Woozles?

Extra SKILLS PRACTICE

385, 389

CHAPTER 10 Applications of Percent

✱ ***Hot Page™ Lesson on CD-ROM***

INVESTIGATION
Make a Million

Extra SKILLS PRACTICE

CHAPTER 11 Geometry and Measurement

✱ *Hot Page™ Lesson on CD-ROM*

CHAPTER 1

Drawing Conclusions from Data

Data File 1

WORLD VIEW

Karl Benz built the first car with a gasoline-powered engine in Germany in 1885.

Soap box derby is a race for motorless cars. At one time most of the cars were made from wooden soap boxes. Nine to 16 year olds may enter.

Rules:

- Combined weight of car and driver cannot be over 250 lb.
- Steering wheel must be at least 6 in. in diameter.

Source: *World Book Encyclopedia*

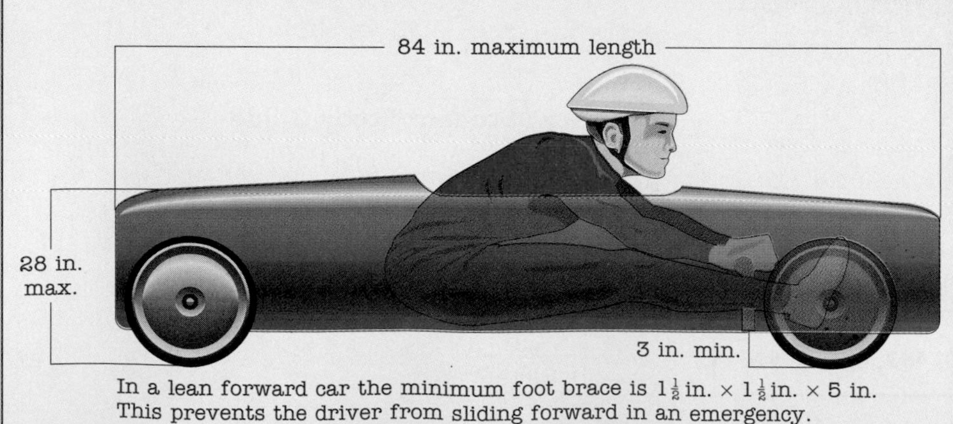

In a lean forward car the minimum foot brace is $1\frac{1}{2}$ in. × $1\frac{1}{2}$ in. × 5 in. This prevents the driver from sliding forward in an emergency.

WHAT YOU WILL LEARN

- how to make and interpret graphs
- how to plan and write survey questionnaires
- how to use technology to create scatter plots
- how to solve problems with too much or too little information

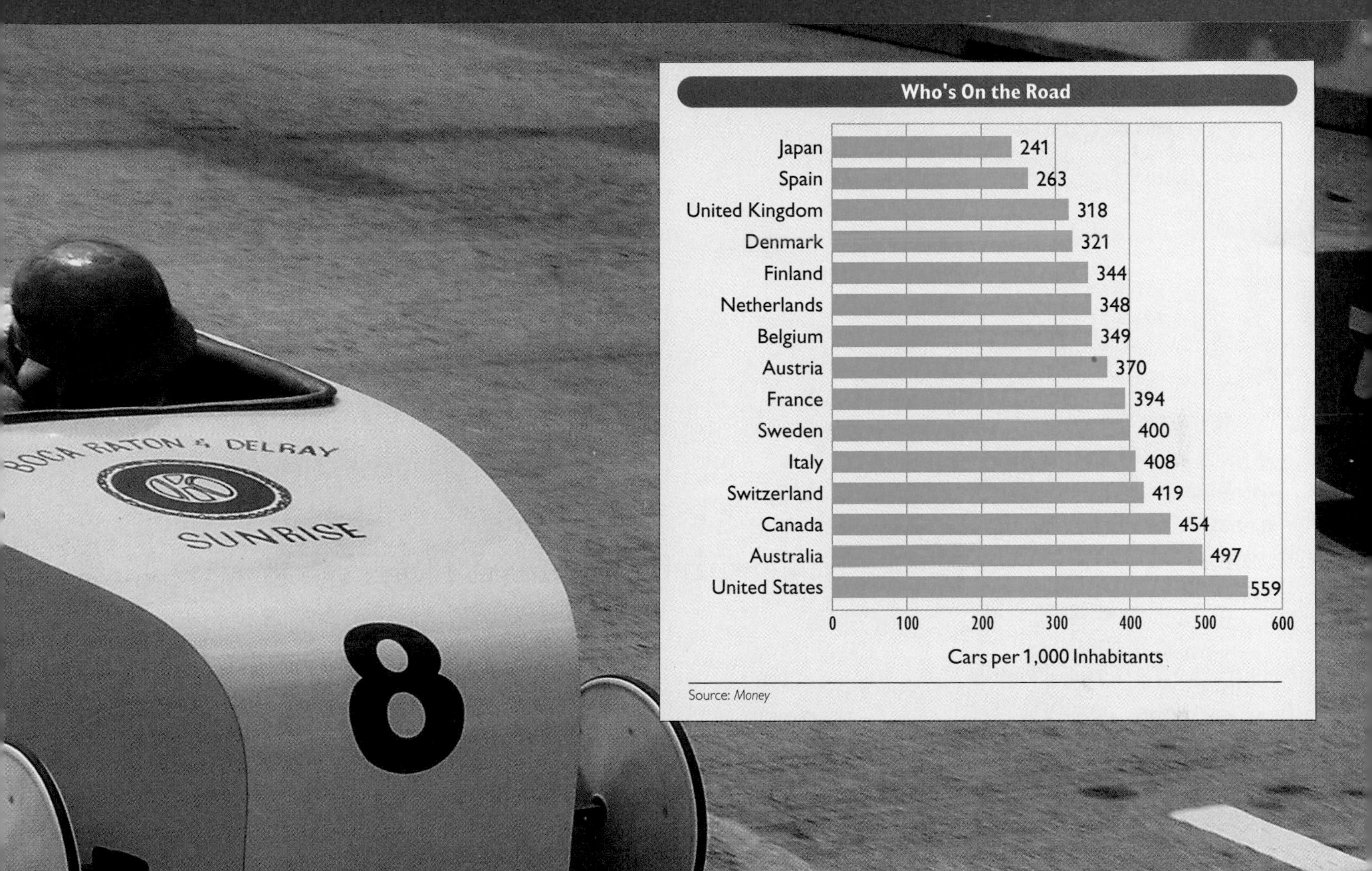

Who's On the Road

Country	Cars per 1,000 Inhabitants
Japan	241
Spain	263
United Kingdom	318
Denmark	321
Finland	344
Netherlands	348
Belgium	349
Austria	370
France	394
Sweden	400
Italy	408
Switzerland	419
Canada	454
Australia	497
United States	559

Cars per 1,000 Inhabitants (axis: 0, 100, 200, 300, 400, 500, 600)

Source: *Money*

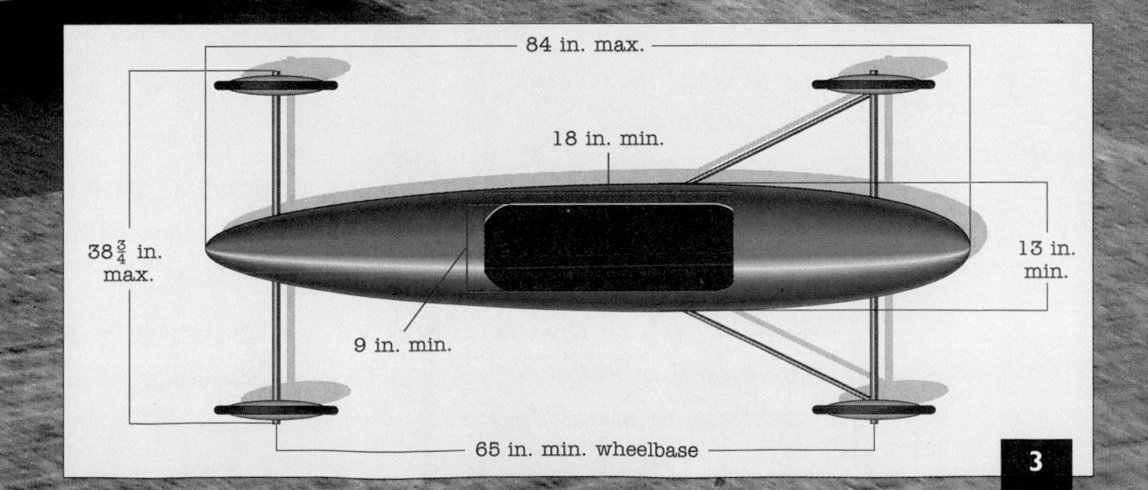

investigation

Project File

Memo

It's against the law for a company to make false claims about its products. Sometimes the line between true statements and false statements is very thin. For example, one car manufacturer claimed that 95% of the cars it manufactured in the past 20 years were still on the road. This statement was misleading even though it was true. Ninety-five percent of the cars were still on the road. However, the manufacturer had only been in business for two years. This example shows that consumers must be wary of advertising claims.

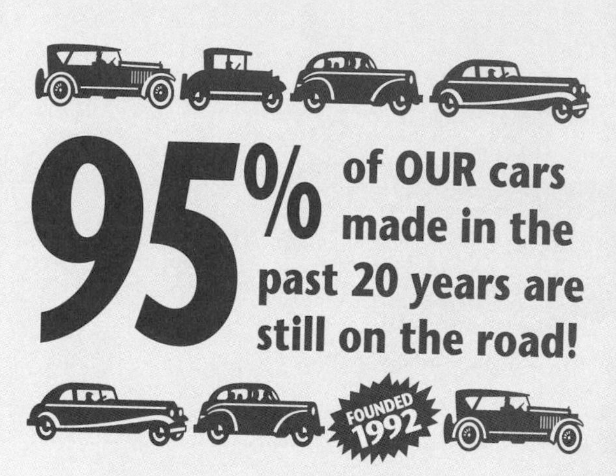

Mission: Look for a false or misleading statement in a radio or TV commercial or in a print ad. Then write a letter to the Federal Trade Commission, which regulates advertisements. In your letter, give the statement in each ad that you are questioning and tell why it makes the ad false or misleading.

- ✓ Imagine that you are an advertiser. Think of true but misleading claims you could make about a product.
- ✓ Are there types of ads that are more likely than others to bend the truth?
- ✓ Are any target audiences likely to be less critical than others?

1-1 Organizing and Displaying Data

What's Ahead

- Interpreting circle graphs
- Making stacked bar graphs, sliding bar graphs, and multiple line graphs

WHAT YOU'LL NEED

✓ Graph paper

In March 1992, the fifth Farm Aid Concert was held at Texas Stadium in Irving, Texas. 40,000 fans attended the 12-hour concert.

Source: *Rolling Stone*

Bar graphs compare amounts or frequencies.

Line graphs usually show changes over time.

Circle graphs show the parts of a whole.

THINK AND DISCUSS

Circle Graphs Is rock music everyone's favorite? You can tell by looking at a graph that displays data about music sales. The **legend**, or *key,* shows the categories used in the graph. Look at the circle graph below.

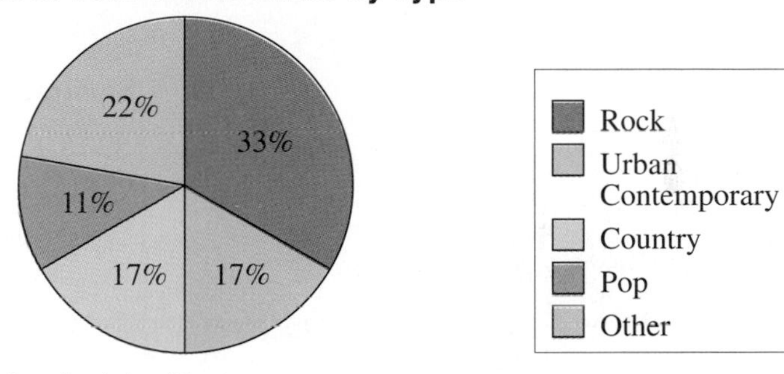

Source: *Recording Industry Association of America*

1. Which type of music had the highest percent of sales?
2. Which two types of music had the same percent of sales?
3. Which type of graph would you want to look at to answer each of the following questions, a line graph or a bar graph? Give a reason for your answer.
   a. During 1992, how much more money was spent on rock music than on each of the other types of music?
   b. Over the last ten years, how has the amount of money spent on country music changed?

Bar Graphs You can use different types of bar graphs when comparing amounts. A **stacked bar graph** has bars that are divided into categories. Each bar represents a total. A **sliding bar graph** shows only two categories as bars graphed in opposite directions.

Environmental Club Members

Grade	Girls	Boys
6	23	16
7	17	15
8	21	26

Seventy-four million people live in cities that fail to meet federal clean air standards.

Source: *The Information Please Environmental Almanac*

Example 1 The table at the left shows the number of girls and boys in the Environmental Club. Display this data in (a) a stacked bar graph and (b) a sliding bar graph.

a.

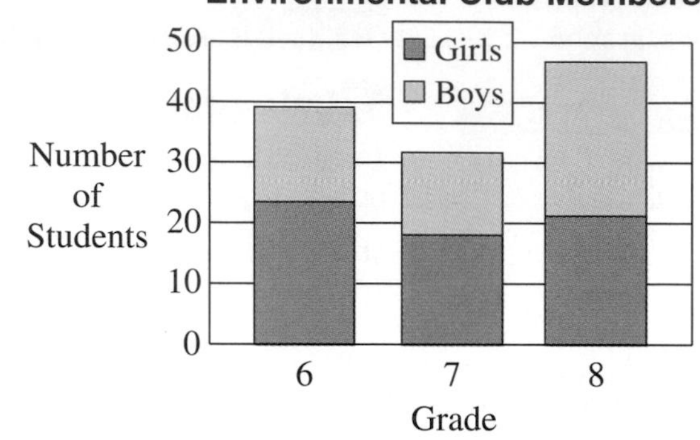

b.

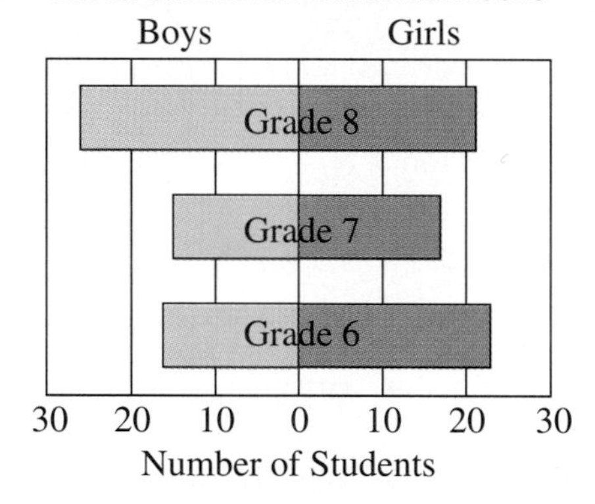

4. In which graph is it easier to see the total from each grade?

5. In which graph is it easier to compare the total number of eighth grade boys with the total number of seventh grade boys?

WORK TOGETHER

Work in your group. Record how many adults (people over the age of 17) and how many children (people age 17 or younger) live in your household. Using the data, have half your group make a stacked bar graph and the other half make a sliding bar graph. Each bar should represent one household. Compare your graphs.

Line Graphs A **multiple line graph** shows more than one category changing over time.

Example 2 Display the data in the table at the right in a multiple line graph.

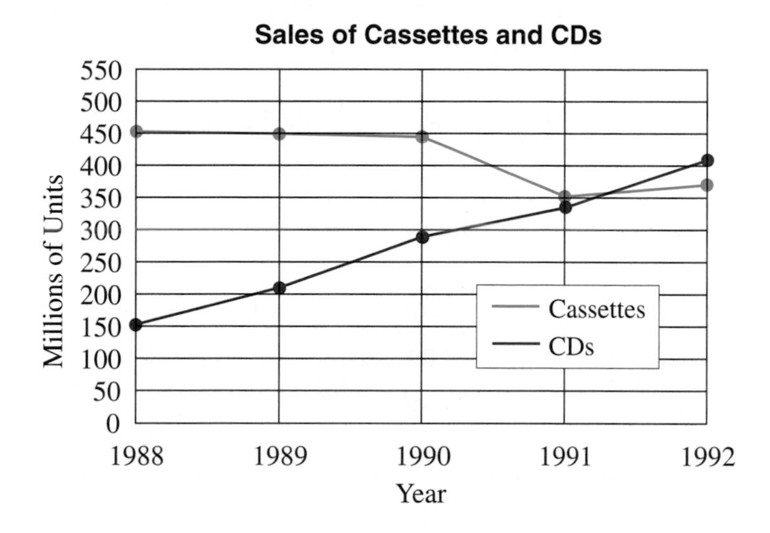

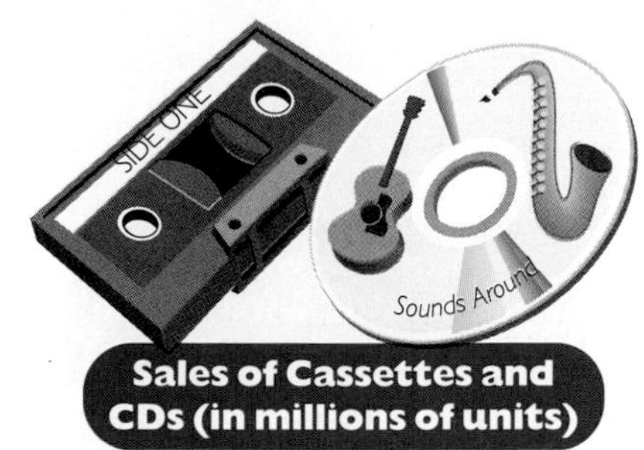

Sales of Cassettes and CDs (in millions of units)

Year	Cassettes	CDs
1988	450	150
1989	446	207
1990	442	286
1991	350	334
1992	368	407

Source: *Recording Industry Association of America*

TRY THESE

Entertainment For Exercises 6–8, use the graph and data from Example 2.

6. Describe the trend in the sale of CDs.
7. During which year were the sales of CDs and cassettes closest to being equal?
8. Display the data in a stacked bar graph and a sliding bar graph. Let each bar represent a year.
9. **Sports** The table below gives data on average annual salaries in thousands of dollars. Display the data in a multiple line graph.

Year	1987	1988	1989	1990	1991	1992
Football	203	239	295	352	415	496
Baseball	412	439	497	598	891	1,012

Sources: *USA TODAY and NFL Players Association*

Mixed REVIEW

Complete.

1. A ■ graph is used to show parts of a whole.
2. A ■ graph shows more than one category changing over time.

Estimate.

3. $685 \cdot 98$
4. $1789 \div 303$
5. It is about 840 mi from New York to Chicago. That is about $\frac{4}{5}$ of the distance from Chicago to Denver. How far is it from New York to Denver via Chicago?

Number of U.S. Households with Cable TV or VCRs (in millions)

Year	Cable	VCRs
1986	39	41
1987	42	43
1988	44	51
1989	48	58
1990	55	67
1991	55	67

Source: *Statistical Abstract of the United States*

ON YOUR OWN

Use the table at the left for Exercises 10 and 11.

10. Display the data in a multiple line graph.

11. Use the data to make a sliding bar graph where each bar represents a year.

12. **Consumer Issues** Use the table below to make a stacked bar graph showing the cost of a meal in each country. Divide each bar into three categories: burger, drink, and dessert.

Prices at an International Chain Restaurant

Country	Burger	Drink	Dessert
Japan	$1.65	$1.15	$1.80
Panama	$.70	$.70	$.80
U.S.	$1.34	$.93	$1.31

Source: *Scholastic Math*

13. **Writing** The *double bar graph* at the right displays the data for Example 1. Compare this graph to the stacked bar graph. Write a paragraph giving the advantages and disadvantages of each type of graph.

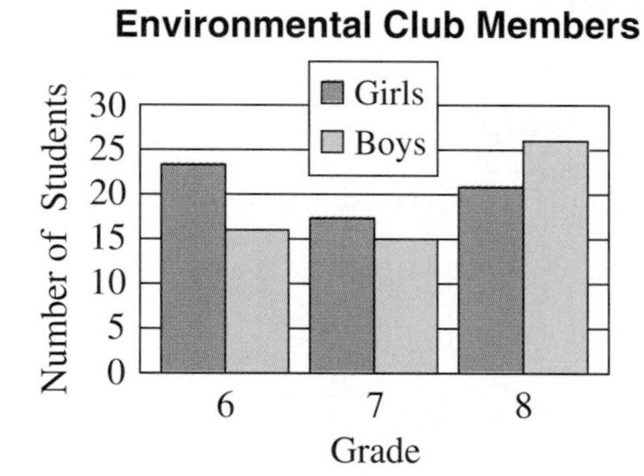

14. **Data File 11 (pp. 462–463)** How many more million tons of garbage were incinerated in 1960 than in 1990?

Number and Type of Bowling Leagues

Men 28,372

Women 36,421

Mixed 73,553

Source: *USA TODAY*

Exercises 15 and 16 refer to the circle graph at the left.

15. About how many times greater is the number of women's and mixed leagues than the number of men's leagues?

16. **Critical Thinking** The music sales circle graph at the beginning of this lesson has values expressed as percents. This graph does not. What are the advantages of giving percent values on a circle graph? the disadvantages?

What's Ahead

- Working with misleading graphs

1-2 Reading Graphs Critically

WHAT YOU'LL NEED

✓ Graph paper

THINK AND DISCUSS

Misleading Line Graphs The same data may be graphed in different ways. Look at the graphs below.

The lower graph has a ≷ symbol on the vertical axis. It shows that some of the values on the axis have been left out.

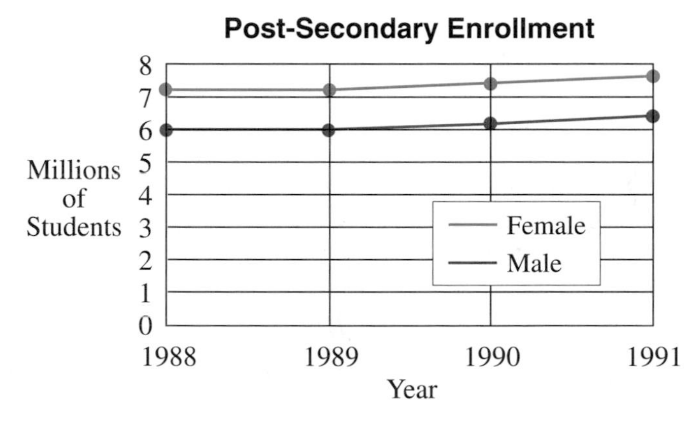

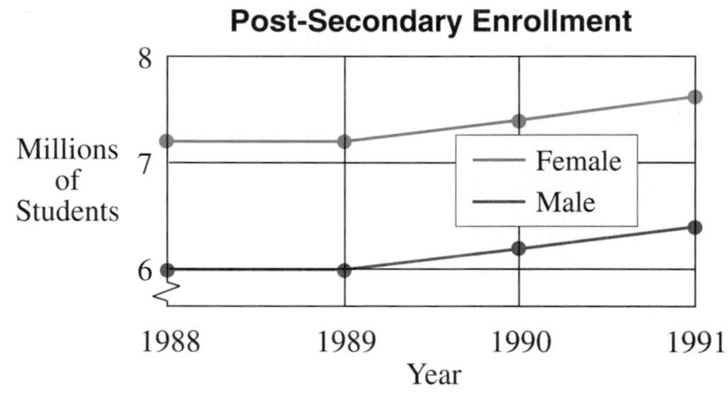

Source: *Statistical Abstract of the United States*

In 1992, almost three quarters of freshmen said that they were attending their first-choice school. Twenty percent were at their second choice and just eight percent were at their third or lesser choice.

Source: *The Wall Street Journal*

1. Both graphs display the same data, but they do not give the same impression of the data. Explain why.
2. Which graph gives the impression that there are more than twice as many female students as male students?
3. Which graph makes the difference between the number of male and female students appear small?

Misleading Bar Graphs Leaving values out of a graph is a useful way to simplify graphing. Sometimes the resulting graph gives a misleading visual impression. Consider the graph below.

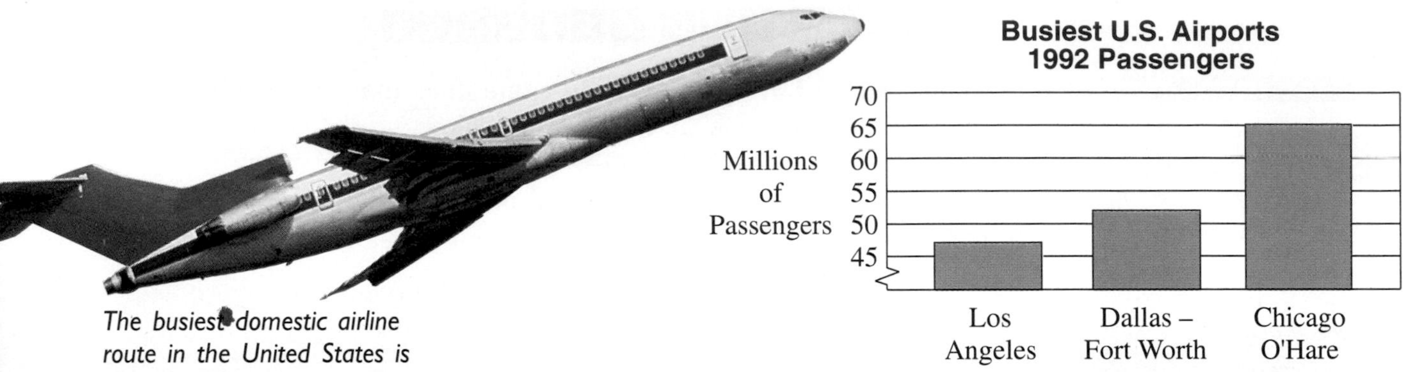

Source: *Airports Council International*

The busiest domestic airline route in the United States is between New York and Los Angeles. 2,966,690 passengers flew between these two cities in 1991.

Source: *The Universal Almanac*

4. This graph gives the visual impression that O'Hare Airport is twice as busy as Dallas–Fort Worth. Explain why this impression is incorrect.

5. Which airport manager would use this graph to support an argument to hire more workers?

6. **Discussion** You want to draw a new graph that gives a more realistic picture of traffic at Los Angeles Airport.
   a. How would you change the values on the vertical axis?
   b. How would adding data on more airports help to show that Los Angeles is a busy airport?

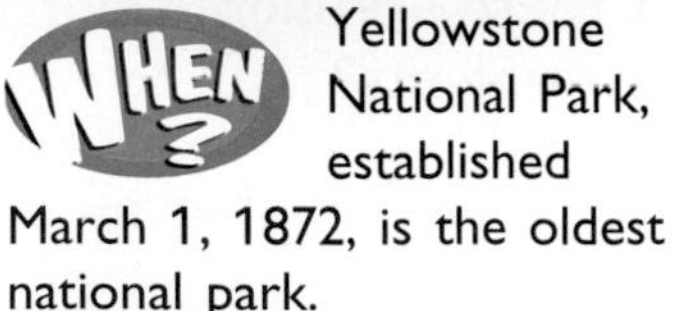

Yellowstone National Park, established March 1, 1872, is the oldest national park.

Source: *Information Please Almanac*

WORK TOGETHER

Work in your group using the data given below. You want to write to Congress about the National Park Service. Create one graph that gives the visual impression of a large annual growth in the number of visitors. Create a second graph that gives the impression of modest growth. Compare your graphs.

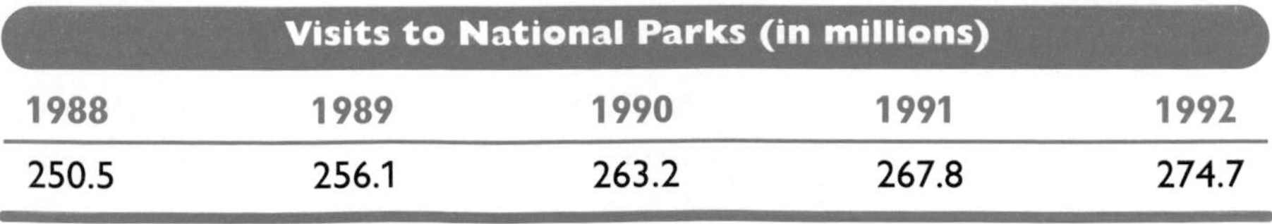

Visits to National Parks (in millions)

1988	1989	1990	1991	1992
250.5	256.1	263.2	267.8	274.7

Source: *National Park Service*

ON YOUR OWN

Use the following graph for Exercises 7–9.

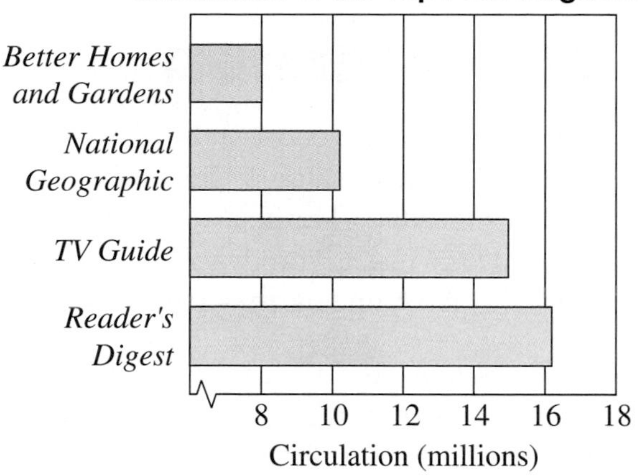

Source: *The Information Please Almanac*

7. a. Which magazine appears to have about twice the circulation of *Better Homes and Gardens*?

b. Which magazine actually has about twice the circulation of *Better Homes and Gardens*?

8. Writing Explain why the graph gives a misleading visual impression of the data.

9. Redraw the graph to give an accurate impression of the data.

10. Using the data at the right, draw a line graph that gives the visual impression of large increases in recycling.

11. Sports Use the data below to create a bar graph that gives the visual impression that Monica Seles and Stefan Edberg each earned more than twice as much as Jim Courier.

1991 Professional Tennis Winnings		
Monica Seles	Stefan Edberg	Jim Courier
$2,457,758	$2,363,575	$1,748,171

Source: *The Information Please Sports Almanac*

12. Investigation (p. 4) Find a graph that appears in an ad or article. If the graph is misleading, explain why it is. If it is not, redraw it so that it is misleading. Explain why it might be misinterpreted by someone.

Mixed REVIEW

Find each answer.

1. 374 + 213 + 875

2. 124 − 76 + 236

Use the data on calories burned during activities: sleeping—1 cal/min, walking—5 cal/min, swimming—10 cal/min, running—14 cal/min.

3. What type of graph would be best to compare the calories used during these activities?

4. Draw a graph to display the data.

5. Rob's heart rate is 72 beats/min. About how many times a week does his heart beat?

Recycling of Soft Drink Containers

Year	Percent
1989	48.7%
1990	52.4%
1991	54.1%
1992	60.0%

Source: *National Soft Drink Association*

What's Ahead

- Making frequency tables, line plots, and histograms
- Organizing data in intervals

WHAT YOU'LL NEED

✓ Graph paper

The great glory of American democracy is the right to protest for right.
—Rev. Martin Luther King, Jr. (1929–1968)

1-3 Displaying Frequency

THINK AND DISCUSS

Have you ever wondered how a secret code is broken? This is the job of a cryptographer who studies the *frequency* of letters or symbols in a coded message. The **frequency** of an item is the number of times it occurs. The cryptographer then compares these frequencies to the frequencies in an uncoded message.

Displaying Data Let's look at the frequency of vowels in the quote from Rev. Martin Luther King, Jr. A **frequency table** lists each data item with the number of times it occurs.

There is a *tally mark* for each vowel. The sum of the tally marks in each row is the frequency of the vowel.

Letter	Tally	Frequency
a	||||	4
e	卌 |	6
i	||||	4
o	卌 |	6
u		0

Data from a frequency table can be displayed in a **line plot** by placing an x for each response above the category of the response.

	x		x	
	x		x	
x	x	x	x	
x	x	x	x	
x	x	x	x	
x	x	x	x	
a	e	i	o	u

1. Cryptographers have found that the letters *e* and *t* occur with the greatest frequency.
   a. Look at the quote. Complete a new row in the frequency table for the letter *t*.
   b. Look at the quote. Choose another letter that appears to occur frequently. Create a row for this letter.
   c. Which letter or letters occur with greatest frequency in this quote?

Using Intervals The **range** is the difference between the greatest and least values in a set of numerical data. When the range of a set of data is large, it is easier to make a frequency table by dividing the data into intervals of equal size that do not overlap.

A **histogram** is a special type of bar graph used to show the frequency of data. There are no spaces between bars, and the height of each bar gives the frequency of the data.

In 1992, $437 million worth of portable tape players and $1.057 billion worth of portable CD players were sold.

Source: *Electronic Market Data Book*

Example *Dynamath* and *Scholastic Math* magazines kept track of the number of hours of battery life for different brands of personal stereos and portable CD players. Here are the results, rounded to the nearest hour.

12 9 10 14 10 11 10 18 21 10 14 22

Display this data in (a) a frequency table and (b) a histogram.

a. The range of the data is 22 − 9, or 13. To make it easy to display the data, divide the data into a convenient number of equal-size intervals. In this case, we have chosen four intervals.

Hours	Tally	Frequency
5–9	|	1
10–14	~~||||~~ |||	8
15–19	|	1
20–24	||	2

b.

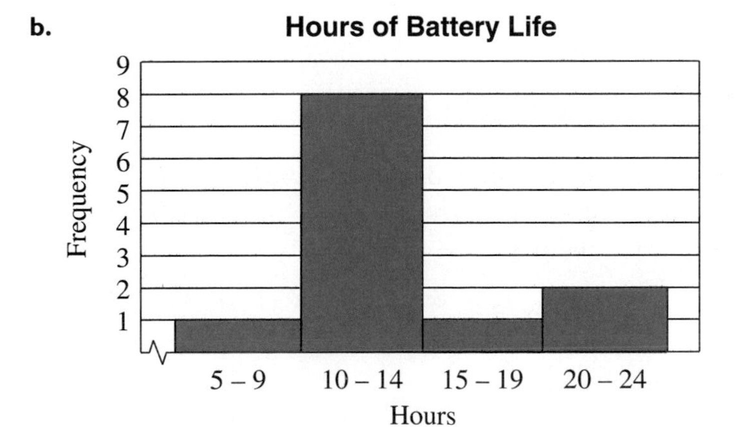

Six states have passed laws requiring that batteries be free of added mercury by 1996. These batteries will have 90 to 92 percent of the life of batteries with added mercury.

Source: *The Information Please Environmental Almanac*

TRY THESE

For Exercises 2–4, use the histogram below showing the number of students participating in the Read-a-thon according to the number of books each student read.

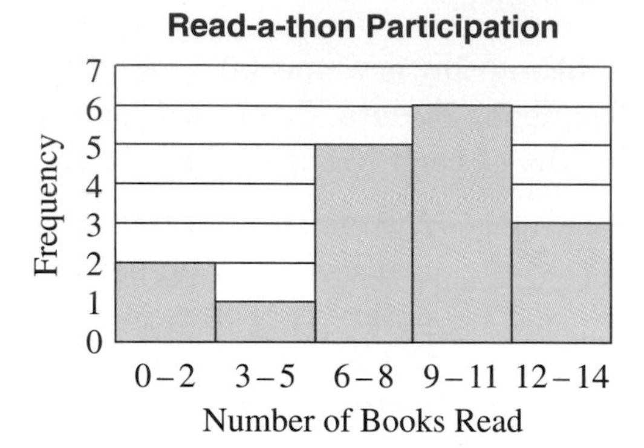

2. Which interval had the highest frequency of student participation?

3. How many students participated in the Read-a-thon?

4. Make a frequency table for the data.

5. **Sports** Use the Olympic gold medal data on the left.
   a. Find the range.
   b. Make a frequency table. Do not use intervals.
   c. Draw a line plot.

6. While shopping for school supplies, José compared the prices of nine different binders. Here are the prices he found.

   $2 $3.50 $3.50 $7.50 $7.50 $3.50 $4 $2 $2.20

   a. Find the range of the prices.
   b. Make a frequency table. Use intervals like $2.00–$2.99 or $2.00–$3.99.
   c. Use your frequency table to draw a histogram.

ON YOUR OWN

7. Mr. Eagle Feather asked his class to fill out a survey on the number of hours spent on homework each night. Here are his results.

   2 2 3 1 1 1 0 3 2 0 4 2 1 3 1 1 2 2 2 3 1 4

   a. Make a frequency table for the hours. Do not use intervals.
   b. Use your frequency table to make a line plot.

Distribution of Gold Medals 1992 Winter Olympics

Country	Medals
Germany	10
Unified Team*	9
Norway	9
Austria	6
United States	5
Italy	4
France	3
Finland	3
Canada	2
South Korea	2
Japan	1
Holland	1
Sweden	1
Switzerland	1

* The Unified Team included Belarus, Kazakhstan, Russia, Ukraine, and Uzbekistan.
Source: *The Information Please Sports Almanac*

8. **Critical Thinking** The frequency table at the right shows the size of art classes at a middle school. What is wrong with the table?

Size of Class		
Interval	Tally	Frequency
0–10	|	1
10–20	𝍸	5
20–30	𝍸 𝍸 𝍸	15
30–40	||	2

9. The ages of the members of the Seniors Hiking Club are given below.

   58 73 80 66 67 59 60 73 76 82 78 78 60 57 75 62

   a. Find the range of the ages.

   b. Display the data in a frequency table. Use the range to help you choose intervals.

   c. Use the frequency table to draw a histogram.

10. **Data File 1 (pp. 2–3)**

   a. Using intervals, make a frequency table of the number of cars per 1,000 inhabitants in industrialized countries.

   b. Display the data in a histogram.

11. **Writing** Write a paragraph about how the appearance of a histogram will change if you choose many small intervals instead of a small number of large intervals.

12. **Research** Choose a famous quotation of between 10 and 20 words. Make a frequency table for the occurrence of vowels.

Find each answer.

1. 348 ÷ 12
2. 1380 ÷ 15

Use the data on winning speeds for the Indianapolis 500: 1988—144.8 mi/h, 1989—167.6 mi/h, 1990—186.0 mi/h, 1991—176.5 mi/h.

3. Draw a graph that appears to exaggerate the 1990 winning speed.
4. Redraw the graph to give a more accurate visual impression of the data.

5. The mean of Leta's three test scores is 90. What must she get on the next test to raise the mean to 92?

CHECKPOINT

1. The table at the right shows how two students spend their weekly leisure time. Display the data in a stacked bar graph and a sliding bar graph.

2. **Writing** Write a paragraph describing how data can be graphed in a misleading way.

Below are the scores on a math test. For Exercises 3–4, choose intervals and display the data in the forms listed.

93 75 87 83 99 75 80 90 72 77 95 98 82 87 100 91 68

3. a frequency table

4. a histogram

Activity	Tobi	Nicole
Reading	10 h	8 h
Listening to music	12 h	6 h

What's Ahead

- Determining whether mean, median, or mode best represents a set of data

1-4 Analyzing Measures of Data

WHAT YOU'LL NEED

✓ Calculator 

✓ Stopwatch 

FLASHBACK

To find the mean of a set of numbers, find the sum of the numbers and divide the sum by the number of items.

The median is the middle value in an ordered set of numbers.

The mode is the data item that occurs most often. A set of data may have no mode, one mode, or more than one mode.

In 1991, the average hourly wage for people working in service industries was $10.24.

Source: *Statistical Abstract of the United States*

THINK AND DISCUSS

Taisha's Juice Stand hires students for the summer. Taisha says the average hourly wage is $5.50. Some students disagree. They say most students make an hourly wage of $4.25.

Central Tendency Tasha and the students are using different *measures of central tendency.* **Measures of central tendency** are statistics that describe data. Three familiar measures of central tendency are mean, median, and mode. Here are the students' hourly wages in dollars.

4.25 4.25 4.25 4.25 4.25 5.00 5.00
5.00 5.25 6.00 6.00 6.00 12.00

1. Which measure of central tendency are the students using to describe the data?
2. Which measure of central tendency is Taisha using to describe the data?
3. Find the value of a third measure of central tendency that you could use to describe the data.
4. The student manager makes $12.00 per hour. She leaves and is replaced by a student who makes $6.00 per hour.
   a. **Calculator** Find the new mean, median, and mode.
   b. **Discussion** How does the change in this one data item affect the mean, median, and mode?

Mean, Median, Mode If one data item is much higher or lower than most of the data, it is called an **outlier.** The $12.00 hourly rate is an example of an outlier. One outlier can affect the sum of the data. The mean becomes distorted and is not a good representation of the data.

The median is not distorted by an outlier since half of the data is above the median and half of the data is below it. If there is an even number of data items, there are two middle numbers. To find the median, add the two middle numbers and divide by 2.

Example 1 Find (a) the mean, (b) the median, and (c) the mode of the temperature data shown at the right.

Normal Daily Temperature in San Francisco, CA	
Month	Temperature °F
January	56
February	59
March	60
April	61
May	63
June	64
July	64
August	65
September	69
October	68
November	63
December	57

Source: The Information Please Almanac

a. The mean is the sum of all of the temperatures divided by the number of months.

749 [÷] 12 [=] 62.416667

The mean is $62.41\overline{6}$.

b. To find the median, first arrange the data in numerical order.

56 57 59 60 61 63 63 64 64 65 68 69

Since there are an even number of data items, the median is the sum of the two middle numbers, divided by 2. In this case, both middle numbers are 63, so the median is 63.

c. Two numbers, 63 and 64, are listed twice. Therefore, there are two modes, 63 and 64.

Example 2 Isao did a survey on the number of pets in each apartment in his building. He displayed his results in the line plot at the lower right. Find (a) the mean, (b) the median, and (c) the mode of his data.

a. To find the mean, multiply each number of pets by its frequency. Add the results and divide by the total of the frequencies.

$$\frac{0(5) + 1(6) + 2(3) + 3(0) + 4(1)}{5 + 6 + 3 + 0 + 1} = \frac{16}{15} = 1.0\overline{6}$$

The mean is $1.0\overline{6}$.

b. To find the median, list each number according to its frequency.

0 0 0 0 0 1 1 1 1 1 1 2 2 2 4

The median is the middle number, 1.

c. The number 1 occurs with the greatest frequency. The mode is 1.

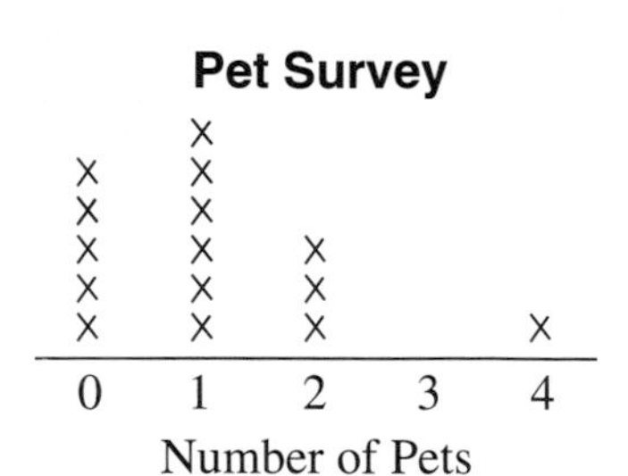

Making Choices Sometimes your data may not be numerical. If you ask ten people for their first names, the set of names is your data. The only measure of central tendency that describes nonnumerical data is the mode.

Mixed REVIEW

Use the data: 30, 34, 33, 33, 35, 30, 31, 33, 32, 34, 29, 35.

1. Find the range.

2. Make a frequency table.

3. Draw a line plot.

4. Draw a histogram.

5. Kerry's license plate has two letters followed by three digits. The letters are A and C and the digits are 8, 3, and 2, but not necessarily in that order. How many different combinations of letters and numbers are there?

Example 3 Is the mean, median, or mode the best measure of central tendency for each situation? Explain.

a. the favorite music video of your class

Mode; the mode is used when the data are not numerical.

b. the ages of the students in your class

Mean or median; the mean is useful when there are no outliers to distort the data.

c. the number of days absent from school

Median; the median is used when an outlier may distort the data. One student may have a high number of absences.

WORK TOGETHER

Use a stopwatch to time each member of your group estimating when a minute has elapsed. Record the number of seconds from when you say "go" until the student being timed says "stop." Find the mean, median, and mode of your group's data.

World Series Games Played 1983 – 1992

			x
	x		x
x	x		x
x	x	x	x
4	5	6	7

Number of Games

Source: *The World Almanac*

TRY THESE

Choose Use a calculator, paper and pencil, or mental math to find the mean, median, and mode.

5. hits per game 0 0 0 0 1 1 2 2 3

6. test scores 70 80 84 90 92 100

7. cost of lunch ($) 1.25 1.75 1.25 1.75 1.35 1.25 1.75 1.35

What is the best measure of central tendency for each type of data? Explain.

8. allowance

9. favorite cereal

10. hours in school each day

11. spelling test scores

12. **Sports** The number of games played in each World Series from 1983 to 1992 is displayed in the line plot at the left. Find the mean, median, and mode of the data.

ON YOUR OWN

Choose Use a calculator, pencil and paper, or mental math to find the mean, median, and mode of each of the following.

13. hours of sleep 7 8 8 9 9 9 9 10 10

14. rainy days per month 2 1 3 0 2 3 4 6 5 4 1 2

15. body temperature (°F) 98.7 99.3 98.2 97.9 98.6 98.7 99.0

16. The *Student News* rates movies by giving them one to five stars. Find the mean, median, and mode of the ratings data in the line plot at the right.

This Week's *Student News* Movie Ratings

```
          X
          X
          X    X
          X    X
X         X    X    X
-------------------------
1    2    3    4    5
    Number of Stars
```

What is the best measure of central tendency for each type of data? Explain.

17. eye color **18.** new car cost **19.** indoor temperature

20. Writing Write a paragraph describing three situations in which the mean, the median, or the mode would each be the most appropriate measure of central tendency.

21. You have one more math test. Here are your present scores.

89 92 78 83 83

a. What score must you get to raise the mean to 87?

b. What score must you get to raise the median to 85?

SAT Scores

Imagine taking a multiple-choice test that lasts for three hours. Every year thousands of college-bound high school students do just that when they take the Scholastic Aptitude Test, known as the SAT.

The test results are sent to the colleges where a student applies. Divided into math and verbal sections, each section of the test is graded on a scale from 200 to 800. Look at the table to find the mean scores from 1985 to 1992.

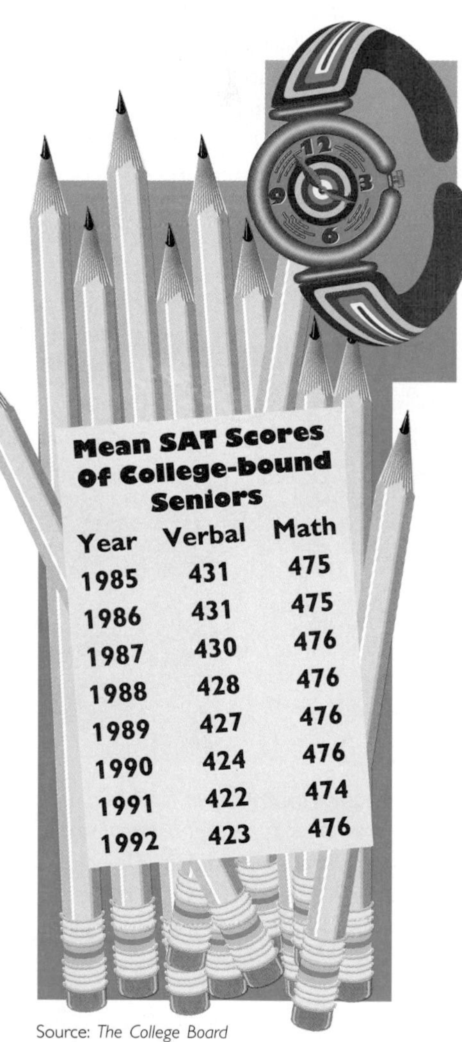

Mean SAT Scores of College-bound Seniors

Year	Verbal	Math
1985	431	475
1986	431	475
1987	430	476
1988	428	476
1989	427	476
1990	424	476
1991	422	474
1992	423	476

Source: *The College Board*

22. Find the mean, median, and mode of the verbal SAT scores.

Problem Solving Practice

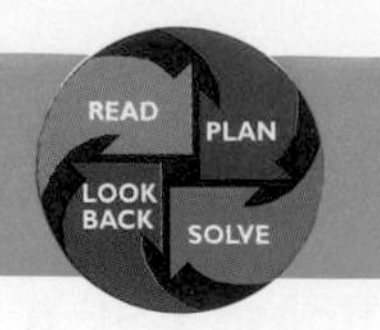

PROBLEM SOLVING STRATEGIES

Make a Table
Use Logical Reasoning
Solve a Simpler Problem
Too Much or Too Little Information
Look for a Pattern
Make a Model
Work Backward
Draw a Diagram
Guess and Test
Simulate a Problem
Use Multiple Strategies
Write an Equation
Use a Proportion

Solve. The list at the left shows some possible strategies you can use.

1. How many squares are in the diagram at the right?

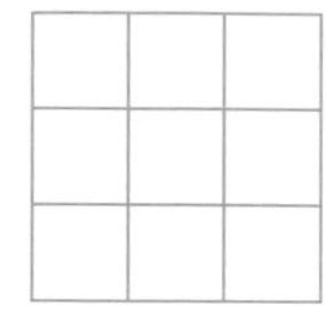

2. The sum of three integers is 193. The smaller two are consecutive integers and the larger two are consecutive even integers. What are the three integers?

3. Find the missing number.

   3, 4, 6, 9, 13, 18, ■

4. A maintenance person is putting numbers on the mail boxes in an apartment building. She uses one stick-on number for each digit in the box number. How many 3's will she need to number boxes 1–343?

5. A town with a population of 28,000 people discards an average of 4 lb of waste per person each day. About how many tons of waste does the town discard in a week?

6. An art teacher is purchasing sketch paper for his students. He can buy a 12-package box with 300 sheets per package for $72.00, or a 6-package box with 200 sheets of paper per package for $30.00. Which is the better buy?

7. After three games, Elena's bowling average is 105. Her first two scores were 112 and 96. What was her score on the third game?

8. Ted, Yolanda, Uyen, and Pat weigh themselves with two on a scale at a time. Together Ted and Yolanda weigh 160 lb. Yolanda and Uyen weigh in at a total of 180 lb. Uyen and Pat total 200 lb. What do Ted and Pat weigh together?

9. How many two-digit numbers have two different even digits?

Many communities have set up programs for composting leaves. One such program in Quincy, MA has saved the city more than $200,000 in landfill costs.

Source: *The Information Please Environmental Almanac*

1-5 Conducting a Survey

What's Ahead

- Writing and analyzing survey questions
- Conducting a survey

In a national survey, 46,800 students were asked if they agreed with the statement "My parents attend meetings or events at school." The sample was heavily Midwestern. Here are the percents of students who agreed with the statement.

Grade	6th	9th	12th
Percent	41	36	32

Source: *The New York Times*

THINK AND DISCUSS

Using a Sample What sport do you play? How much do you exercise? Questions like these are often asked in surveys. Statisticians collect information about specific groups. Any group of objects or people is called a **population**.

A **sample** is a small subset of the population. The **sample size** is the number of objects in the sample. A sample is a **random sample** if each object in the population has an equal chance of being included.

1. Refer to the survey at the left. The population chosen for this survey is sixth, ninth, and twelfth grade students in the United States.
   a. What is the sample size?
   b. Is the sample a random sample? Explain.
   c. What trend do you see in the responses?
   d. Can you conclude that the same trend exists in the population chosen for this survey?

Analyzing Questions Survey questions can be closed-option or open-option. **Closed-option** questions, such as multiple-choice questions, limit you to listed choices. **Open-option** questions allow you to answer freely. "What do you like to do on vacation?" is an open-option question.

2. Describe the student survey as closed-option or open-option.

Unfair questions are **biased questions.** They can make assumptions about you that may or may not be true. Biased questions can also make one answer seem better than another.

Explain why each of the following questions is biased.

3. How do you like your eggs cooked?
4. Do you like the luxurious car A, or the cheaper version, car B?

Mixed REVIEW

Use the list of class test scores: 100, 93, 73, 63, 98, 68, 88, 73, 73, 78, 83, 88, 78, 73, 99, 92.

1. Find the range.
2. Find the mean.
3. Find the median.
4. Find the mode.

5. On Saturday the softball team practices at 9:00 A.M. It takes Jodie 35 min to get dressed and have breakfast, 1 h 25 min to do her paper route, and $\frac{3}{4}$ h to get from home to the softball field. For what time must Jodie set her alarm?

A good survey uses a random sample that is large enough to represent the population. Statisticians avoid using biased questions. They sometimes use closed-option questions when they want to make it easier to analyze their data.

WORK TOGETHER

In your group, decide on a topic for a survey at your school.

5. Define the population you want to study. Does it include just students? Is it limited to certain classes?
6. Decide on a random sample of your population. What is the sample size?
7. Write two unbiased survey questions. Make one question closed-option and the other open-option.

ON YOUR OWN

Explain why the following survey questions are biased.

8. Is your brother one of your closest friends?
9. Do you think that warm, cuddly, little kittens are nicer than puppies?

DECISION MAKING

Every year the entertainment industry gives awards to the best movies, videos, recordings, and performers. Now it is your chance to conduct a survey, analyze the data and determine your own winner.

COLLECT DATA

1. Design a survey to find the best female recording star. Decide what population you will study. Will you include adults or just people your age?
2. Decide how you will choose your sample. Try to make the sample a random one.

10. **Consumer Issues** Consider the survey at the right.
   a. Define the sample. What is the sample size?
   b. Can you tell if the sample is random?
   c. Is the question open-option or closed-option?

263,000 consumers 14 years and older were surveyed. They were asked, "How often do you buy products from TV shopping shows?" Here is how they responded.

Source: *USA TODAY*

11. You think that your school bus stops are too far apart. You want to see if other bus riders agree. Does a random survey of 50 students entering the building represent a good sample? Explain.

12. A researcher in Dallas is investigating the type of music people prefer. She surveys people at random in a local museum. Is this a good sample? Explain.

13. **Writing** Give an example of a closed-option, biased survey question. Rewrite the question to ask for the same information in an unbiased way.

14. **Investigation (p. 4)** The president of Dazzle Toothpaste Company phoned 30 dentists and asked if they knew of anything wrong with Dazzle. Twenty hung up. Eight said as far as they knew, Dazzle was fine. Two said Dazzle was dangerous. Create a misleading slogan for Dazzle based on the president's survey.

3. Write your survey question. It can be either open-option or closed-option.

4. Conduct your survey.

ANALYZE DATA

5. Make a frequency table and a line plot to display data on the most frequently chosen stars.

MAKE DECISIONS

6. Determine the winner. Describe what population your award represents.

The album Into the Light *by Gloria Estefan and the Miami Sound Machine was awarded platinum album status after 1 million copies were sold.*

TECHNOLOGY

1-6 Scatter Plots

What's Ahead

- Using scatter plots to see if two sets of data are related
- Using computers to display data

WHAT YOU'LL NEED

✓ Computer 

✓ Statistics or spreadsheet software 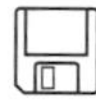

A spreadsheet is a tool for organizing and analyzing data. The data are arranged in rows and columns.

THINK AND DISCUSS

Is the amount of TV you watch related to your grades? If a music company spends more on a video, will it sell more copies of the CD? Does the length across your outstretched arms have anything to do with your height? Computers can help us decide whether one thing is related to another.

Making Scatter Plots This *spreadsheet* shows height and arm-span measurements for members of a family of six.

	A	B	C
1	Name	Height (cm)	Arm Span (cm)
2	Manuel	192	191
3	Ana	157	160
4	Luis	178	180
5	Rena	157	156
6	Roberto	142	142
7	Felicia	119	116

One way to explore how two sets of data are related is to make a *scatter plot.* In a **scatter plot,** related data from two different sets are graphed as ordered pairs. A computer creates a scatter plot from data entered on a spreadsheet. If you don't have a computer, you can make a scatter plot by graphing the points by hand.

Height vs. Arm Span

Arm Span (cm): 100, 125, 150, 175, 200

Height (cm): 100, 125, 150, 175, 200

W

In the scatter plot at the left, each of the six points represents an ordered pair: (height, arm span). Notice that a computer-drawn graph may not include the ≶ symbol.

1. Point W represents Luis. If (x, y) is the ordered pair for point W, what is the value of x? the value of y?

2. Describe the point that represents Felicia.

3. **Discussion** What trend do you see in the scatter plot?

4. **Choose A, B, or C.** Which statement best describes the relationship?

   A. As height increases, arm span increases.

   B. As height increases, arm span decreases.

   C. Height and arm span are not related.

Looking for Trends If the points on a scatter plot show a trend, sometimes you can draw a straight line that closely fits the points. This line is called a **fitted line.** The scatter plot on the right shows a fitted line.

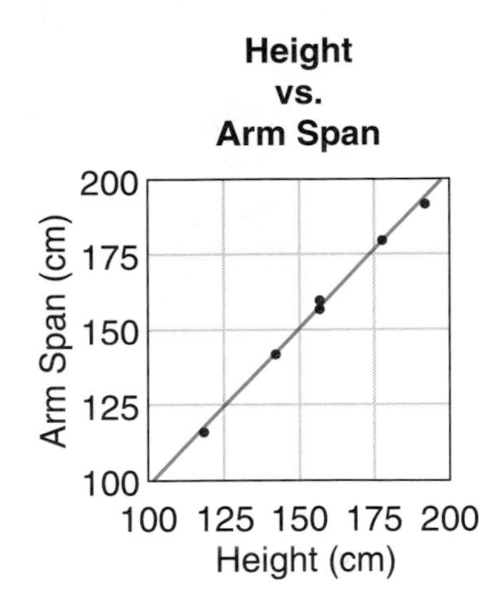

5. **Discussion** Do you think everyone would draw exactly the same line to fit the points? Why or why not?

Is the temperature of a city related to its location? The table at the right lists latitude and the mean April temperature for 15 U.S. cities. The data are displayed below in a scatter plot with a fitted line.

City	Latitude (° North)	Mean April temp. (°F)
Albuquerque	35	55
Atlanta	34	62
Baltimore	39	54
Boston	42	49
Buffalo	43	45
Charlotte	35	61
Chicago	42	49
Columbus	40	51
Dallas	33	66
Denver	40	47
Detroit	42	47
Honolulu	21	76
Houston	30	69
Indianapolis	40	52
Juneau	58	39

Source: *The Information Please Almanac*

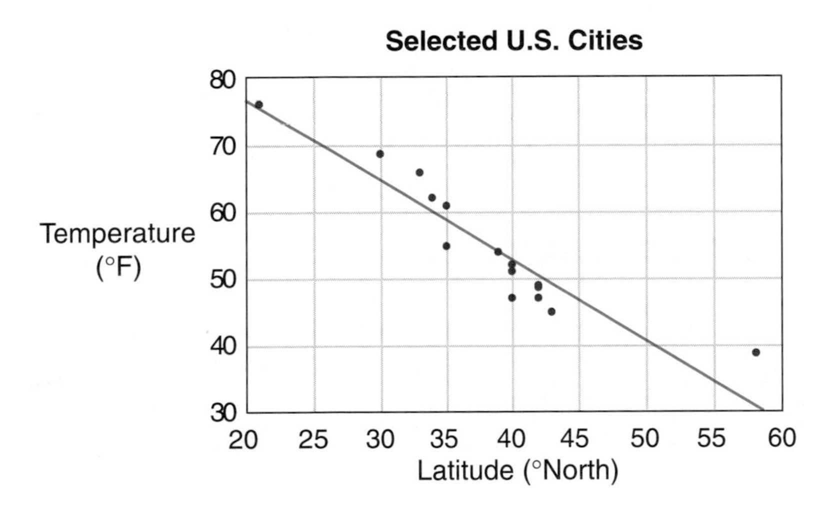

6. Describe the trend in the data.

7. Which shows the trend better, the scatter plot or the table?

8. Which point fits the trend the least?

A fitted line can be used to make predictions. If you know the latitude of a city, you can predict its mean April temperature.

9. Do you think that predictions made from a fitted line will always be accurate? Why or why not?

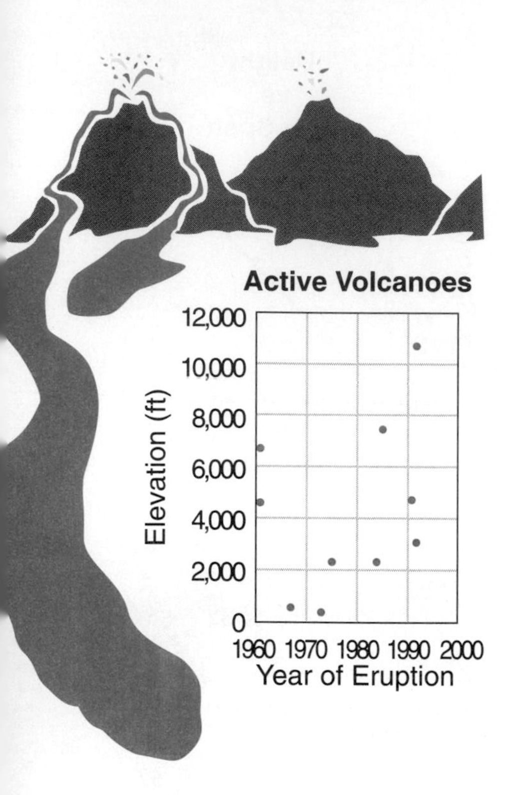

10. **Earth Science** The scatter plot at the left below gives data on active volcanoes in Europe and the Atlantic Ocean.

a. Does this scatter plot show a clear trend? Explain.

b. Does it make sense to try to fit a line to the data points? Why or why not?

These three scatter plots summarize the types of relationships two sets of data may have.

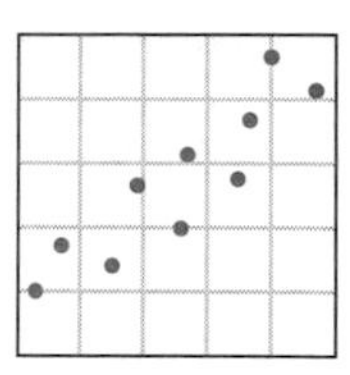

Positive correlation
As the value of one variable increases, the other increases also.

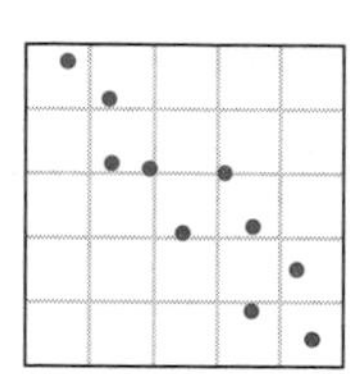

Negative correlation
As the value of one variable increases, the other decreases.

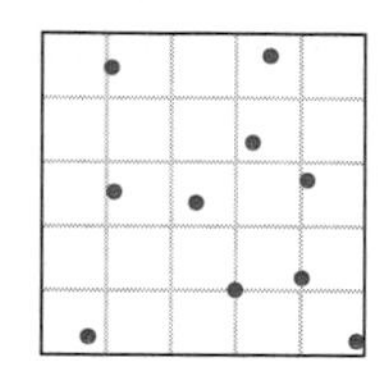

No correlation
There is no line that closely fits the points.

11. Tell whether each scatter plot discussed so far shows positive correlation, negative correlation, or no correlation.

WORK TOGETHER

Computer Work in a group of at least five people. Estimate the number of hours each of you slept last night and the number of minutes of homework each of you did yesterday. Make a scatter plot of your group's data. If a correlation exists, draw a fitted line.

ON YOUR OWN

Tell whether a scatter plot of the data in Exercises 12–15 would likely show positive, negative, or no correlation.

12. grades and study time

13. temperature and layers of clothing

14. age and number of pets

15. age of a car and its value

Mixed REVIEW

You are conducting a survey of favorite TV programs.

1. Write an open-option, unbiased survey question.

2. Write a closed-option, biased survey question.

For Exercises 3 and 4, use the following data: 9, 5, 5, 7, 5, 5, 7, 6, 7, 9, 7, 5.

3. Display the data in a line plot.

4. Find the mean, median, and mode.

5. Together, Kim and Al earned \$22.50 ironing. Kim earned \$5.50 less than Al. How much did Kim earn?

Computer For the scatter plots in Exercises 16 and 17, use a computer or graph the points by hand.

16. **Farming** Use the farm data at the right. Make a scatter plot showing the number of farms on one axis and the average number of acres on the other axis. If the data show a positive or negative correlation, draw a fitted line.

17. **Sports** In 1992, the Chicago Bulls won the National Basketball Association Championship. The table below gives data for the championship series. Display the data in a scatter plot. If a correlation exists, draw a fitted line.

Player	Jordan	Pippen	Paxson	Grant	Cartwright
Average Points per Game	35.8	20.8	10.3	9.2	6.3
Most Points in One Game	46	26	16	18	10

Source: *Sports Illustrated Sports Almanac and Record Book*

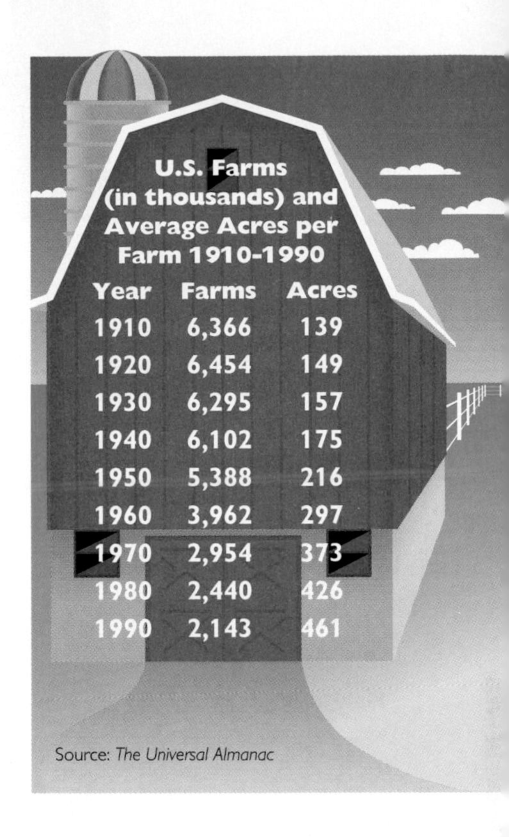

U.S. Farms (in thousands) and Average Acres per Farm 1910–1990

Year	Farms	Acres
1910	6,366	139
1920	6,454	149
1930	6,295	157
1940	6,102	175
1950	5,388	216
1960	3,962	297
1970	2,954	373
1980	2,440	426
1990	2,143	461

Source: *The Universal Almanac*

18. **Writing** Give examples of data sets with positive, negative, or no correlation. Write a paragraph explaining your choices.

19. **Critical Thinking** As the number of women holding jobs increased, the record time in the women's 200 m run decreased. Does this negative correlation mean that there was a cause and effect between the sets of data?

CHECKPOINT

Find the mean, median, and mode of each of the following sets of data.

1. 6 7 10 8 5 9 2 7 7
2. 44 45 55 46 48 53

What is the best measure of central tendency for each type of data? Explain.

3. favorite color
4. annual salaries
5. Write an unbiased survey question about alarm clocks.
6. The table at the right gives the percent of eye-chart symbols that could be identified at different distances. Display this data in a scatter plot.

Distance (m)	Percent Identified
100	2
93	4
82	6
68	8
60	10
48	12

What's Ahead

- Making and interpreting stem-and-leaf plots and back-to-back stem-and-leaf plots

1-7 Stem-and-Leaf Plots

Northeastern States

Percent of People Age Five and Older who Speak a Foreign Language at Home

State	Percent
Connecticut	15
Massachusetts	15
Maine	9
New Hampshire	9
New Jersey	20
New York	23
Pennsylvania	7
Rhode Island	17
Vermont	6

Source: *USA TODAY*

English is spoken by about one third of the people of the world, although it is the native tongue of only about five to eight percent of the world's population.

Source: *The Universal Almanac*

THINK AND DISCUSS

Do you speak a language other than English when you are at home? Have you ever wondered how many people do?

Making Stem-and-Leaf Plots Look at the table at the left. Using a *stem-and-leaf plot* can make working with the data easier. A **stem-and-leaf plot** shows data in order. The choice of *stems* and *leaves* depends upon the type of data.

To choose the **stems,** look at the ten's place of the greatest and least numbers. The greatest value is 23; the least value is 6. Use stems 0, 1, and 2 to represent the tens' places. In this case, the **leaves** are the one's digits. The **key** explains what the stems and leaves represent.

```
stems → 0 | 6 7 9 9 ← leaves
        1 | 5 5 7
        2 | 0 3
```

key: 1 | 7 means 17

1. What number has stem 0 and leaf 7? stem 2 and leaf 0?
2. Why are there two 5's as leaves with the stem 1?

Because a stem-and-leaf plot displays each data item in numerical order, it is easy to find the median and mode. The median is represented by the middle leaf. The mode is represented by the greatest number of repeated leaves.

3. For the data displayed above, find the median and the mode.
4. **Discussion** If you want to find the median or the mode of a set of data, why is a stem-and-leaf plot a better way to display the data than a frequency table with intervals?

A stem can be more than one digit. It can be any number that helps you to organize your data. A leaf is always one digit.

Example 1 Here are the finishing times (in seconds) for the 100 m at a recent middle school track meet.

13.7 14.2 13.9 15.7 13.6 13.9 15.2 14.8

Display this data in a stem-and-leaf plot and find the median and the mode.

Stem	Leaves
13	6 7 9 9
14	2 8
15	2 7

14 | 2 means 14.2

To find the median, average the two middle scores, 13.9 and 14.2. The median is 14.05. The mode is 13.9.

American Jean Driscoll has four consecutive Boston Marathon records. In four years, she has reduced her winning time by 8 min 27 s.

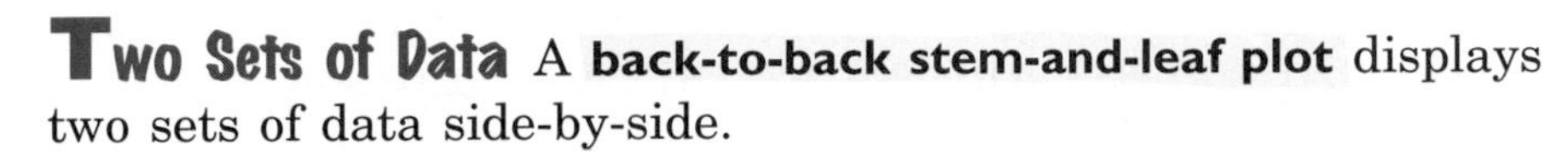

Two Sets of Data

A **back-to-back stem-and-leaf plot** displays two sets of data side-by-side.

Example 2 Display the data in the table at the right in a back-to-back stem-and-leaf plot.

Men		Women
6 2	8	
6 1 0	9	5 7
3	10	3 3
6	11	0
	12	
	13	1
	14	0

means 116 ← 6 | 11 | 0 → means 110

Boston Marathon Wheelchair Division Winning Times (rounded to the nearest minute)

Year	Men	Women
1993	82	95
1992	86	97
1991	91	103
1990	90	103
1989	96	110
1988	103	131
1987	116	140

Source: *Boston Athletic Association*

TRY THESE

Use the stem-and-leaf plot below for Exercises 5–7.

5. What numbers make up the stems?
6. What are the leaves for the first stem?
7. Find the median and the mode.

Stem	Leaves
20	0 0 0 7
21	2 3 3 6 9
22	2 7

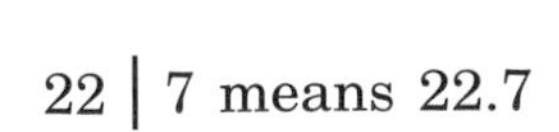

22 | 7 means 22.7

Top 10 Cities in Recycling Solid Waste

City	Percent Recycled
Honolulu, HI	72
Jacksonville, FL	35
Los Angeles, CA	20
Minneapolis, MN	27
Newark, NJ	51
Portland, OR	38
St. Paul, MN	39
Seattle, WA	40
Virginia Beach, VA	22
Washington, DC	20

Source: *The Information Please Environmental Almanac*

8. Make a stem-and-leaf plot for the recycling data at the left.

9. Make a back-to-back stem-and-leaf plot for the following data. Find the median and mode for each set of data.

Set A: 175 186 169 180 178 183 176 184 179
Set B: 191 175 178 187 180 180 186 182 163

ON YOUR OWN

Make a stem-and-leaf plot for each set of data, then find the median and mode.

10. 6 13 30 2 27 17 19 13 24 35 27 26 18 32 9

11. 3.7 5.0 6.9 3.2 4.5 6.3 6.7 5.8 5.2 6.9 5.0 4.3

12. 875 920 900 883 915 899 921 873 917 920 908 881

13. Writing A set of data contains numbers in the 30's, 40's and 60's only. Is it necessary to put a 5 on the stem of a stem-and-leaf plot? Write a sentence justifying your answer.

The plot below shows the city and highway mi/gal for one manufacturer's cars. Use this for Exercises 14–16.

14. Find the range for highway driving.

15. Find the median for highway driving.

16. Find the mode for city driving.

City		Highway
9 8 8	1	
7 4 2	2	7 8
0	3	3 3 5
	4	0

means 27 ← 7 | 2 | 8 → means 28

For each of the following exercises, display the data in a back-to-back stem-and-leaf plot.

17. Median age at first marriage for the census years 1910–1990:

Females: 21.6 21.2 21.3 21.5 20.3 20.3 20.8 22.0 23.9
Males: 25.1 24.6 24.3 24.3 22.8 22.8 23.2 24.7 25.9

Source: *The Universal Almanac*

18. Height in inches:

Girls: 58 62 63 60 60 59 63 58 61 61
Boys: 65 63 59 61 62 60 64 65 59 63

Mixed REVIEW

For Exercises 1–3, use the following data: 95, 85, 65, 100, 55, 90, 60, 80, 65, 65, 70, 75, 80, 70, 65, 95.

1. Find the range.

2. Make a frequency table, using intervals.

3. Draw a histogram.

4. Complete the sentence. On a scatter plot, if one variable decreases as the other increases, the correlation is ■.

5. Mel bought three T-shirts for $6.95 each and one tape for $5.75. How much change did he receive from $30?

Practice

1. In physical education class students chose either tennis or aerobics. Ten girls and eight boys chose tennis and six girls and seven boys chose aerobics. Display this data in a stacked bar graph and a sliding bar graph where each bar represents an activity.

Find the mean, median, mode, and range for each of the following sets of data.

2. 1 1 2 2 3 3 4 4 4 4 4 5 7 7
3. 67 48 56 85
4. $6.50 $8.00 $5.75 $7.50 $6.50
5. 92 92 92 92 92
6. 8.9 9.2 8.7 8.8 8.2 8.9 8.8
7. 6.2 5.7 3.1 8.9 5.3 7.4

Arrange each set of data in a frequency table. Do not use intervals. Draw a line plot for each set of data.

8. 4 1 3 0 5 0 1 3 2 2 4 3 1
9. 18 15 17 17 19 16 16 16 20

Choose appropriate intervals and display the following data in a histogram.

10. 293 320 285 275 315 290 305 316 296 328 318
11. $9.60 $4.75 $1.25 $3.75 $8.55 $2.67 $2.98 $1.98 $2.35 $3.85

Which measure of central tendency would you use for each situation: mean, median, or mode? Explain.

12. favorite fruit juice
13. test scores for a term
14. heights of students in a class

Make a stem-and-leaf plot for each set of data.

15. 217 225 219 190 207 210 198 222 215 216 229 210
16. 61.5 61.8 60.6 60.4 59.5 62.2 61.8 61.8 62.4 62.0 59.1

Make a back-to-back stem-and-leaf plot for each of the following sets of data.

17. Set A: 23 34 15 23 12 25 22 33 Set B: 22 19 25 17 5 21 25 2
18. Set A: 6.4 5.1 6.5 7.1 5.3 6.9 8.7 Set B: 5.8 6.7 5.1 5.2 6.3 4.2 4.0

What's Ahead

- Making box-and-whisker plots

1-8 Box-and-Whisker Plots

WHAT YOU'LL NEED

✓ Metric Ruler 

Average Amount of Money Spent per Person by Foreign Visitors to the United States	
Country	**Dollars**
Australia	2,279
Canada	330
France	1,703
Germany	1,778
Italy	1,973
Japan	2,381
Mexico	592
Netherlands	1,422
New Zealand	2,181
United Kingdom	1,596
Other Countries	1,038

Source: *The World Almanac*

THINK AND DISCUSS

Making Box-and-Whisker Plots The table at the left gives data on the average amount of money spent by visitors. You can make a *box-and-whisker plot* to display the data.

A **box-and-whisker plot** shows the distribution of data in each **quartile,** that is, in each 25% of the data.

To find the median, first arrange the data in numerical order. The median is also called the **second quartile.** Next, find the median of the lower half of the data and the upper half of the data. These are called the **first** and **third quartiles.**

330 592 1038 1422 1596 1703 1778 1973 2181 2279 2381

(1038: **first quartile**; 1703: **second quartile median**; 2181: **third quartile**)

To draw a box-and-whisker plot, first draw a number line. Below it, mark each of the following with a dot: the lowest value, the first quartile, the median, the third quartile, and the highest value. Then draw a box from the first to the third quartiles. Next, mark the median with a vertical line through the box. Finally, draw whiskers from the box to the highest and lowest values.

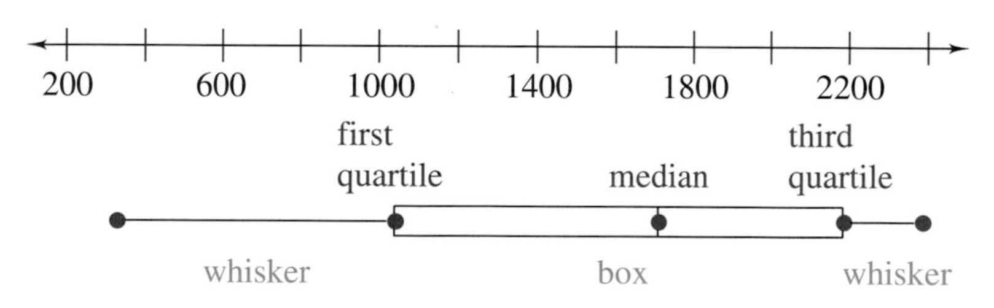

1. Why is the median not exactly in the middle of the box?
2. When a box-and-whisker plot has a long box like the one shown above, what does that indicate about the data?
3. Would the box change if the numbers 2,279 and 2,381 were replaced by greater numbers? Explain.

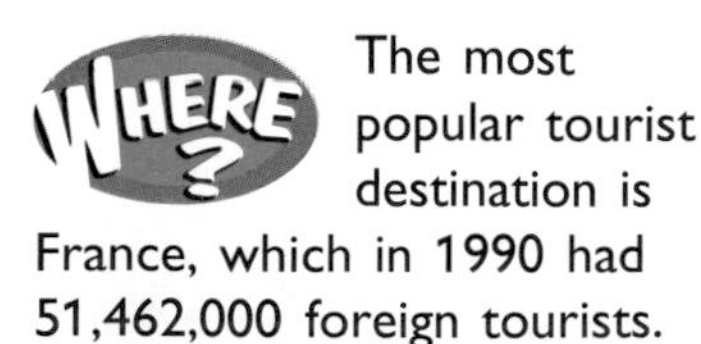

The most popular tourist destination is France, which in 1990 had 51,462,000 foreign tourists.

Source: *The Guinness Book of Records*

4. If you have an even number of pieces of data in the lower half of your data, how would you find the first quartile?

5. By looking at a box-and-whisker plot, which of the following can you determine: mean, median, mode, range?

Unlike stem-and-leaf plots, box-and-whisker plots do not display every piece of data. Because box-and-whisker plots summarize data, they are useful for recognizing trends.

Example 1 Describe the data in the plot below.

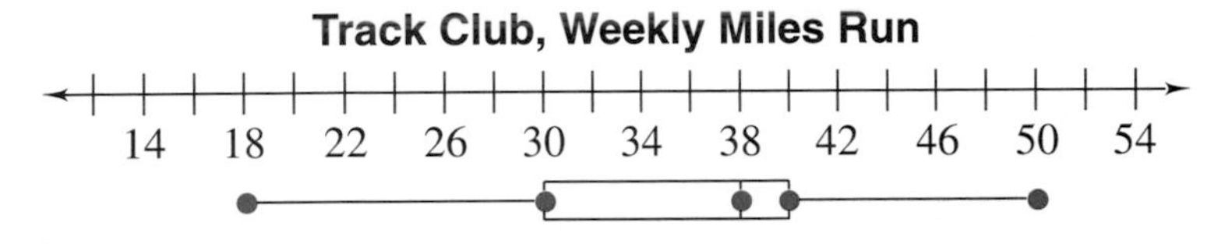

The highest mileage is 50. The lowest is 18. The first quartile is 30 and the third quartile is 40. The plot has a small box, indicating that about half of the scores are clustered around the median, which is 38.

Two Sets of Data

You can use box-and-whisker plots to compare two sets of data.

Example 2 The box-and-whisker plots below compare women's and men's NCAA, Div. 1, basketball scores. In each case, the scores are the highest single game scores of the top eleven scorers. Compare the sets of data.

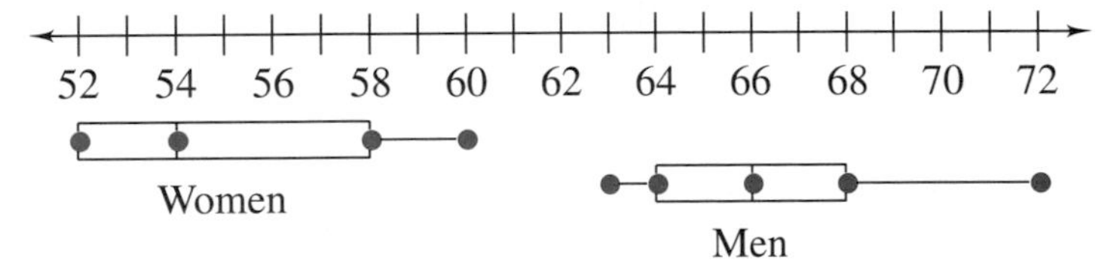

Source: *Sports Illustrated Sports Almanac*

The median is 54 for women and 66 for men. In each case, the scores cluster around the median. The range for the men's scores is 9 and for the women's is 8. There is no left whisker on the women's scores. This indicates that each score in the bottom quarter of the data is 52, the same as the first quartile score.

Mixed REVIEW

For Exercises 1–4, use the following data: 31, 45, 50, 52, 45, 32, 33, 45, 50, 38.

1. Make a stem-and-leaf plot.
2. Find the range.
3. Find the median.
4. Find the mode.

5. Find five consecutive whole numbers whose sum is 50.

In February, 1992, 14,500 fans attended a home game of the University of Maryland women's basketball team. Their number-one ranking created a big surge in attendance. During the previous year, their *total* attendance for 13 home games was only 11,385.

Source: *Sports Illustrated Sports Almanac*

WORK TOGETHER

Measure the span of your hand to the nearest half of a centimeter. One student should record the measurement for each group member, making separate lists for boys and for girls. Combine data with other groups to make a list for the whole class. Using a number line with decimal intervals, make box-and-whisker plots displaying boys' and girls' data. Use the box-and-whisker plots to compare the sets of data.

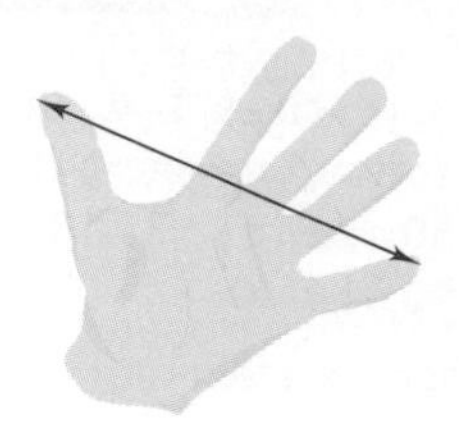

Extra SKILLS PRACTICE

1. Make a box-and-whisker plot for: 45, 60, 32, 48, 50, 55, 48, 37, 43, 54, 44, 57, 46, 51, 53, 58, 47, 38, 41.

Use the plot to find each of the following.

2. the median
3. the first quartile
4. the third quartile
5. the lowest score
6. the highest score
7. the range

Average Miles per Hour of Daytona 500 Winners

Year	Average mi/h
1982	154
1983	156
1984	151
1985	172
1986	148
1987	176
1988	138
1989	148
1990	166
1991	148
1992	160

Source: *Sports Illustrated Sports Almanac*

TRY THESE

Use the box-and-whisker plot below to find each of the following.

Test Scores

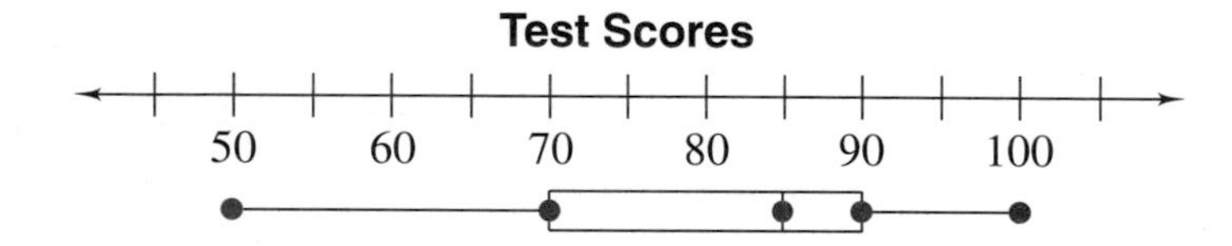

6. the median
7. the first quartile
8. the third quartile
9. the highest score
10. the lowest score
11. the range
12. Make a box-and-whisker plot for the data below.

    1 5 7 2 2 4 3 4 5 3 1

13. The data below shows the number of home runs hit by the league leaders of the American League and the National League in the 1992 baseball season. Make a box-and-whisker plot for each league's data. Use a single number line.

    AL: 43 42 35 34 34 32 32 27 26 26 26
    NL: 35 34 33 27 27 26 23 22 21 21 20

ON YOUR OWN

Make a box-and-whisker plot for each set of data.

14. 9 7 12 15 11 11 13 8 9 8 7 13 8 14 6
15. the Daytona 500 data at the left

Writing For Exercises 16 and 17, make a box-and-whisker plot for each set of data. Use a single number line. Write a paragraph comparing the two sets of data.

16. Set 1: 4 8 10 13 3 2 7 6 5 4 8 1 14 9 2
Set 2: 10 9 2 8 7 4 8 10 9 7 5 8 9 10 11

17. the data on college costs at the right

18. Does a box-and-whisker plot tell you how many data items are included? Explain.

19. Is it possible for the median and first quartile of a set of data to be the same? Explain.

20. **Data File 4 (pp. 142–143)** Make a box-and-whisker plot for the percent of students sent to college in various countries.

21. **Choose A, B, C, or D.** Identify the box-and-whisker plot for the data given below.

70 76 80 74 78 56 86 80 80 81 40 75 98 101 103

A.

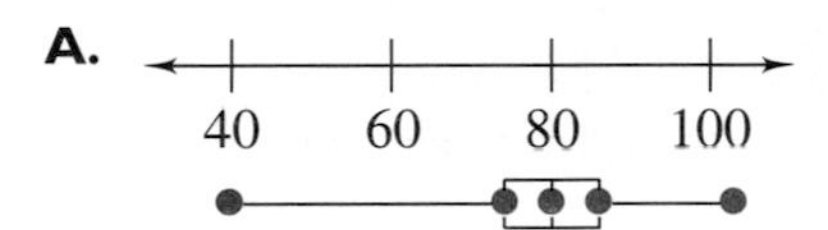

B.

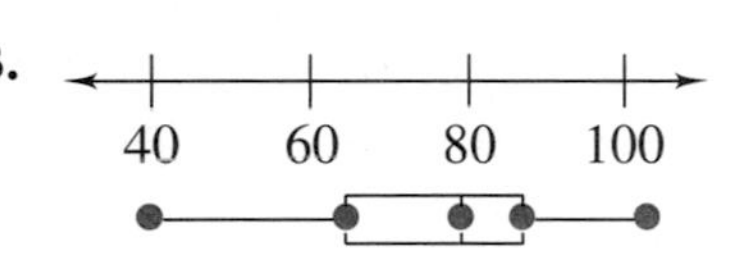

C.

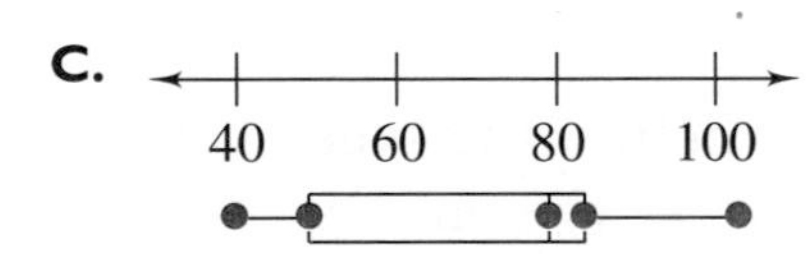

D. none of these

Are We Living Longer?

The average age of the U.S. population has been increasing steadily since the beginning of the century.

The aging of the Baby Boom generation of the 1950s and a lower birthrate since that time have significantly impacted the average. Another major factor in this trend is the increased life expectancy for older people.

22. Make a box-and-whisker plot to display the data at the right showing the percent of the population age 65 and older.

Average Cost (in dollars) of 4-Year Colleges (tuition and fees, per year)

Year	Public	Private
1981	909	3,617
1982	1,031	4,639
1983	1,148	5,093
1984	1,228	5,556
1985	1,318	6,121
1986	1,414	6,658
1987	1,537	7,116
1988	1,646	7,722
1989	1,781	8,446
1990	1,908	9,340
1991	3,137	10,017

Source: *The Universal Almanac*

Percent of the Population Age 65 and Older (rounded to the nearest percent)

Year	Percent
1930	6
1940	7
1950	8
1960	9
1970	10
1980	11
1990	13
2000	13
2010	14
2020	17
2030	21

Note: Figures for 1990 through 2030 are Census Bureau projections based on their "most likely" series of estimates.
Source: *The Universal Almanac*

What's Ahead

- Determining an appropriate graph for a set of data

1-9 Choosing an Appropriate Graph

New England H.S. Graduation Rates

State	Percent
Massachusetts	72
Vermont	81
Rhode Island	72
New Hampshire	74
Maine	78
Connecticut	83

Source: *The Information Please Almanac*

THINK AND DISCUSS

Once you have gathered data, you must decide how to display the data. The type of graph you choose depends on the type of data you have collected and the idea you want to communicate.

1. Explain why the graph below is not an appropriate display of the data.

Graduation Rates for New England

83% 72% 81% 72% 74% 78%

Massachusetts
Vermont
Rhode Island
New Hampshire
Maine
Connecticut

2. What type of data should be displayed in a circle graph?

For each of the following, explain whether the type of graph would be an appropriate way to display the data on New England high school graduation rates.

3. a bar graph
4. a line graph
5. a scatter plot
6. a stacked bar graph

Data may be displayed appropriately in more than one type of graph.

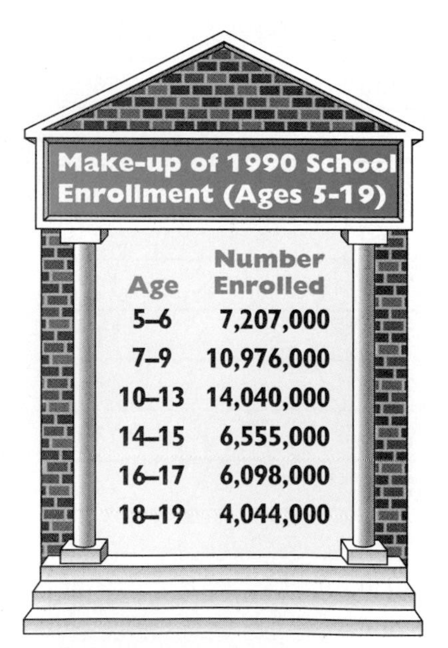

Make-up of 1990 School Enrollment (Ages 5-19)

Age	Number Enrolled
5–6	7,207,000
7–9	10,976,000
10–13	14,040,000
14–15	6,555,000
16–17	6,098,000
18–19	4,044,000

Source: *The Information Please Almanac*

Example 1 Use the data at the left on the make-up of school enrollment by age. For each of the following, decide whether the type of graph is appropriate for the data. If it is appropriate, draw the graph.

a. a bar graph **b.** a circle graph **c.** a scatter plot

a. It is easy to compare amounts on a bar graph.

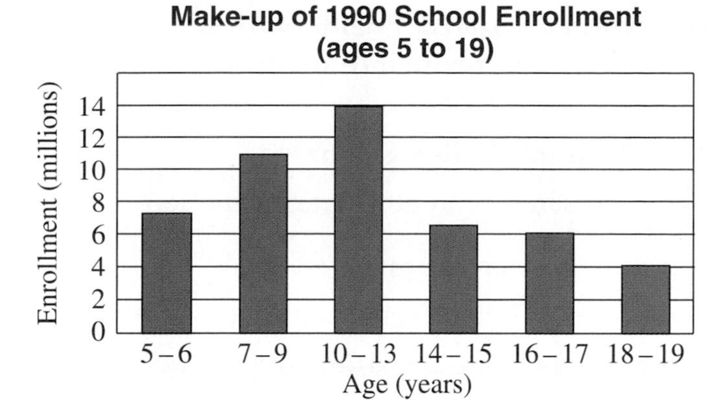

b. It is easy to see parts of a whole on a circle graph.

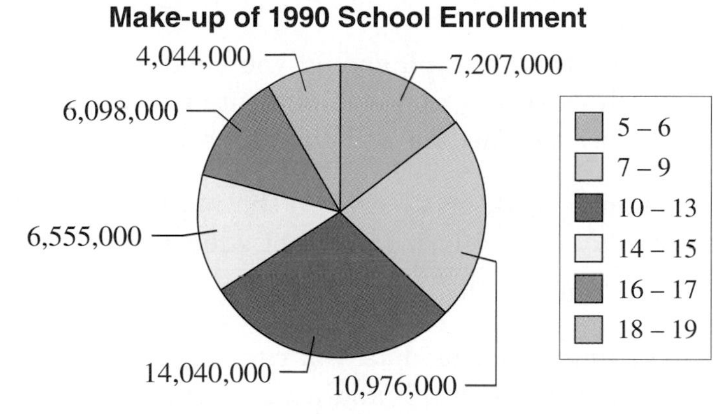

c. A scatter plot is not appropriate. A scatter plot is used to see if a correlation exists between two related sets of data.

TRY THESE

Decide which of the two types of graphs is an appropriate display for the data given. Explain your choice.

7. line graph or circle graph?

percent of city dwellers in the U.S. by year for 1980 to 1993

8. bar graph or scatter plot?

life spans of selected animals

9. scatter plot or histogram?

inches of rain vs. high temperature for each day in May

Mixed REVIEW

For Exercises 1–5, use the following data: 80, 83, 88, 88, 90, 106, 100, 101, 110, 109, 85.

1. Find the range.

2. Find the mean.

3. Find the median.

4. Find the mode.

5. Draw a box-and-whisker plot.

6. Brenda received a gift certificate for $34. If she also has $8.50 cash, how many $9 tapes can she buy?

Extra SKILLS PRACTICE

Use the circle graph on page 36.

1. What percent of the students in Vermont graduate?

2. What percent graduate in Connecticut?

3. Which state has the highest graduation rate?

4. Which states have the lowest rate?

Use the circle graph on this page.

5. Which group has the largest enrollment?

6. Which group has the smallest enrollment?

7. How many students ages 14–15 are enrolled?

8. How many students ages 7–9 are enrolled?

Percent of U.S. Homes with Personal Computers

Year	Percent
1985	13.6
1986	16.6
1987	19.4
1988	22.4
1989	24.0
1990	25.4
1991	26.6
1992	29.6
1993 (projected)	32.7

Source: *The Boston Globe*

ON YOUR OWN

For Exercises 10–12, decide which of the two types of graphs is an appropriate display for the data given. Then, draw the graph.

10. circle graph or line graph?

the personal computer data at the left

11. scatter plot or bar graph?

daily temperature and number of students wearing jackets

temp. (°F): 55, 57, 63, 68, 70; jackets: 10, 11, 8, 5, 4

12. bar graph or line graph?

test scores: Amy 93, Joy 87, Tran 91, Leah 82, Jeb 78

13. What type of graph should you choose when you have too much data to graph each data item, but you want to display the median and the highest and lowest data items?

14. **Choose A, B, or C.** Choose the most appropriate graph to display data relating years of education to median income.

A. a line graph **B.** a bar graph **C.** a scatter plot

15. **Writing** Describe data you can collect that can be displayed in both a bar graph and a circle graph.

16. **Investigation (p. 4)** Find an ad or article that contains a graph. Display the data in a different type of graph. Decide which graph displays the data more appropriately.

Typical Heights of Trees after 15 Years

Type of Tree	Heights in Feet
Holly	10
Oak	25
Poplar	30
Juniper	10
Douglas fir	40
Yew	12
Weeping willow	30

CHECKPOINT

1. Make a back-to-back stem-and-leaf plot for the data below.

Set A: 116 115 120 125 132 117 129 135 110 129 135
Set B: 128 129 138 118 145 143 130 127 141 119 112

2. Make a box-and-whisker plot for the following set of data.

26 39 15 21 42 19 26 38 11 6 39 28 19 24 40 21

3. **Choose A, B, C, or D.** Select the appropriate type of graph for the tree height data at the left. Then, make the graph.

A. a scatter plot **B.** a circle graph

C. a line graph **D.** a bar graph

PROBLEM SOLVING

1-10 Too Much or Too Little Information

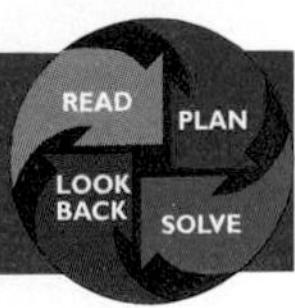

What's Ahead

- Working with problems with too much or too little information

Sometimes you cannot solve a problem because you do not have enough information. Other times you may be given more information than you actually need. In either case, you need to decide which facts are important before you begin any calculations.

In 1992, 24.9% of all recorded music was purchased by people age 19 or under.

Source: *Recording Industry Association of America*

During the first week in October, 28 students at Gates Middle School were surveyed. They were asked, "Rounding to the nearest hour, how many hours a week do you spend listening to music?" Their responses are summarized in the box-and-whisker plot below.

Hours of Music Listening per Week

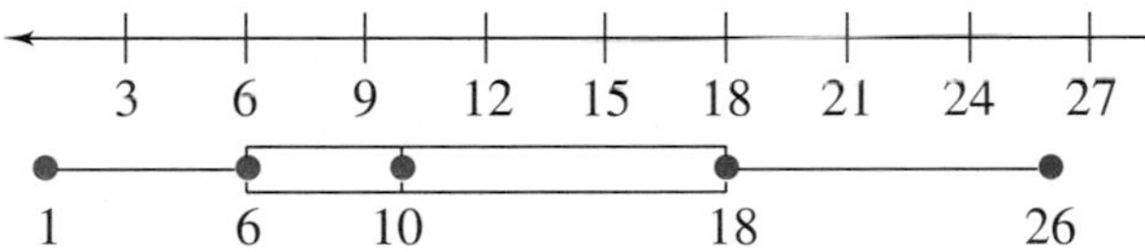

Find the mode and median of the student responses.

READ

Read and understand the given information. Summarize the problem.

Read the problem carefully.

1. What is the problem about?
2. What information are you asked to find?

PLAN

Decide on a strategy to solve the problem.

Look at the information in the problem and decide whether you have too much or too little information.

3. What information is given in the problem that will help you find each of the following?

   a. the mode

   b. the median

4. What information is given that is not necessary for solving the problem?

SOLVE

Try out the strategy.

You cannot find the mode. Because individual data items are not listed, you cannot tell which data item occurs most frequently.

The median is indicated by the dot on the vertical line in the box. The median number of hours is 10.

LOOK BACK

Think about how you solved the problem.

5. How could the data have been presented differently so that you could find the mode?

TRY THESE

Solve if possible. If not possible, tell what needed information is missing.

6. Maria left her home at 8:20. She took a fifteen-minute bus ride, stopped at a bakery, and then walked to the library. If she spent twice as long walking as she did at the bakery, what time did she arrive at the library?

7. **Sports** In 1992, Juan Gonzales and Fred McGriff led the major leagues in home runs. Their combined total of 78 homers equaled the number of bases stolen by the National League stolen base leader, Marquis Grissom. If Gonzales hit eight more homers than McGriff, find the number of homers McGriff hit.

8. **Consumer Issues** Dan bought four packages of hot dogs on sale at $1.99 per package. They regularly sold for $2.49 per package. Rolls were on sale at two packages for one dollar. Don bought four packages of rolls. How much did he save by buying the sale items?

***The remaining ruins** of the Theater of Dionysus in Athens, Greece, are shown above. Originally a circular theater, it seated between 6,000 and 12,000 people. The theater took approximately 75 years to be built and was completed about 300 B.C.*

Source: *Theater by Jacques Burdick and the Encyclopedia Britannica*

ON YOUR OWN

Use any strategy to solve each problem. Show all your work.

9. You are planning to set up chairs for the class play. The front row will have eight chairs. Each row thereafter will have three more chairs than the row in front of it. You know that there will be twelve rows. How many chairs will you need?

10. In a collection of dimes and quarters, there are three more dimes than quarters. If the collection is worth $3.45, how many dimes and quarters are there?

11. The sum of five consecutive numbers is 415. Find the numbers.

12. The length of a rectangle is 12 more than the width. The perimeter is 100. Find the length and width.

13. **Sports** Eight teams are playing in a soccer tournament. Once a team loses a game, it is eliminated. If a team wins, it plays again. Each game consists of a ten-minute warm-up, two 30-minute halves, and a five-minute half-time. What is the latest time the tournament can start if it must end by 4:00 P.M. and there is only one field available?

14. A truck driver plans to take 9 h to drive 805 km. After 5 h, she has traveled 470 km. If she continues driving at this rate, will she arrive within 9 h of her starting time?

15. A drill team director wanted to arrange the team members in pairs. She found that she was one person short. She tried to arrange by fives and was still one person short. She finally arranged the team members by sevens. What is the least number of people on the drill team?

16. The sum of two numbers is 15. Twice the greater subtracted from three times the lesser equals five. What are the numbers?

17. Sarah is choosing her outfit for the day. She has four pairs of jeans, three sweaters, and five hats. How many different three-piece outfits can she choose?

18. Examine the pattern below. In which row will the number 100 appear?

1	row 1
2 3	row 2
4 5 6	row 3
7 8 9 10	row 4

19. **Money** In how many different ways can you give change from a $100 bill for a $79 purchase if the customer will not accept coins or more than six $1 bills?

Mixed REVIEW

For Exercises 1–3, choose the appropriate type of data display: (A) circle graph, (B) line graph, or (C) scatter plot.

1. percent of students in each grade at a school
2. points vs. rebounds for each member of a basketball team
3. daily high temperatures during May in Phoenix
4. Write a closed-option survey question about favorite movies.
5. A baby-sitter earned $4.25 per hour plus $7 for cab fare. He started working at 10 A.M. At what time did he finish if he received $41?

The first jeans were made by Levi Strauss in 1873. In 1975, Calvin Klein began the era of designer jeans.

Source: *The Information Please Kids Almanac*

CHAPTER 1

Wrap Up

Organizing and Displaying Data 1-1, 1-2

A ***stacked bar graph*** has bars that are divided into categories and each bar represents a total. A ***sliding bar graph*** shows two categories as bars graphed in opposite directions. A ***multiple line graph*** shows more than one category changing over time.

School Chorus Members

Year	Girls	Boys
1989	35	41
1990	32	40
1991	35	43
1992	34	37
1993	32	39

1. Make a stacked bar graph and a sliding bar graph using the 1992 and 1993 data shown at the right. Let each bar represent a year.

2. Use the data at the right to draw a multiple line graph which appears to exaggerate the difference between the number of boys and the number of girls.

Frequency and Measures of Central Tendency 1-3, 1-4

A ***frequency table*** lists each data item with the number of times it occurs. Data from a frequency table can be displayed in a ***line plot*** or a ***histogram.*** The ***range*** of a set of numbers is the difference between the greatest and the least values in the set.

The ***mean*** of a set of numbers is the sum of the numbers divided by the number of data items. The ***median*** is the middle number in a set of numbers in numerical order. The ***mode*** is the data item that occurs most often. An ***outlier*** is a data item that is much higher or lower than most of the data.

For Exercises 3 and 4, use the following data on the ages of members of the Over 50 Bowling League.

53 57 78 64 68 72 77 58 60 78 80 81 55 70 52 63 65 79

3. Choose intervals and make a frequency table and a histogram.

4. Find the mean, median, and mode.

Conducting a Survey 1-5

A survey studies a ***population*** by studying a ***sample,*** or subset, of the population. A sample is a ***random sample*** if each object in the population has an equal chance of being selected. Survey questions can be ***closed-option*** questions which limit you to choices listed or ***open-option*** questions which allow you to answer freely. ***Biased*** questions are unfair questions.

5. **Writing** Write an open-option, unbiased survey question to determine people's favorite type of fruit. Rewrite the question as a closed-option question.

Scatter Plots, Stem-and-Leaf Plots, Box-and-Whisker Plots 1-6, 1-7, 1-8

In a ***scatter plot,*** related data from two sets are graphed as ordered pairs. If the points on a scatter plot show a trend, you can draw a ***fitted line.*** A ***stem-and-leaf plot*** displays each data item in order. A ***back-to-back stem-and-leaf plot*** displays two sets of data side-by-side. A ***box-and-whisker plot*** shows the distribution of data in each quartile (25% of the data).

For Exercises 6 and 7, use the data listed below showing juice prices (in cents) at various stores.

89 79 85 79 85 67 75 99 79 63 90 72 78 65 78

6. Make a stem-and-leaf plot.

7. Make a box-and-whisker plot.

Appropriate Graphs, Problem Solving 1-9, 1-10

The type of graph you choose depends on the type of data you have collected and the idea you want to communicate.

Some problems may have too much or too little information.

8. **Choose A, B, or C.** Choose the most appropriate graph to display data on changes in a child's height over a ten-year period.

   A. circle graph **B.** line graph **C.** scatter plot

Solve the following problem. If there is too little information, describe the information that is needed.

9. Enid left home at 6:45 A.M. and drove for 2 h 10 min. She stopped for breakfast then drove for 3 h 5 min before stopping for gas. At what time did she stop for gas?

GETTING READY FOR CHAPTER 2

To find the area of a circle, use the formula $A = \pi r^2$.

Find the area of each circle. Use $\pi \approx 3.14$ or $\pi \approx \frac{22}{7}$.

1. $r = 3$ in.
2. $r = 4.2$ cm
3. $r = 0.45$ m
4. $r = \frac{3}{4}$ in.

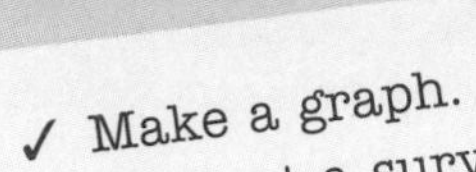

Follow Up

Misleading Ads

In this chapter you learned to analyze and display data accurately. Earlier you drew up a list of statements appearing in ads or commercials that you thought were false or misleading. Now review your list based on your study of the chapter. Revise your letter to the Federal Trade Commission. Use the following suggestions to help support the claims in your letter.

✓ Make a graph.
✓ Conduct a survey of students' opinions about truth in advertising.
✓ Design an ideal ad for a product.

The problems preceded by the magnifying glass (p. 11, # 12; p. 23, # 14; and p. 38, # 16) will help you complete your investigation.

False or misleading claims are all around you from the headlines in supermarket tabloids to statements made by celebrities and politicians. Read and listen with an open but critical mind.

Excursion: The following statement can be interpreted in several possible ways. Give as many interpretations as you can.

Happy Hank is America's largest joke-book publisher.

A Statistical Slip Up

The 1948 presidential election was a low point for poll takers and political experts. As usual, every poll and expert predicted the winner. The morning after the election the Chicago Daily Tribune newspaper announced in banner headlines that the favored candidate had won. It was too soon to tell!

Investigate the 1948 presidential election. Prepare a newspaper editorial that includes discussion of the following:

- Who were the candidates?
- Who won? Who lost?
- What was unusual about the 1948 election?
- Why, in your opinion, were the experts wrong? What did statistics have to do with their mistakes?
- Do you think an incorrect headline would ever be published after an election today? Why or why not?

Pen Names, Pseudonyms, and People

Everyone has heard of Stephen King. But who is Richard Bachman? Easy—he's Stephen King too! Stephen King is a *pseudonym,* or pen name, that Richard Bachman used for some of his books. Other famous writers have adopted pen names from time to time. Benjamin Franklin wrote as himself and as Poor Richard. Do authors write differently under different names? Let's find out.

- Choose a writer who has used a pen name. Select a passage written under the writer's real name and another written under the pen name.
- Look for similarities and differences between the two passages. For example, consider the number of syllables in the words of the passages. Calculate the percent of 1, 2, and 3-syllable words.
- Show your data in a chart, table, or graph.

A BLAST FROM THE PAST

Imagine...searching through ruins in the year 2112, an archeologist unearths this graph:

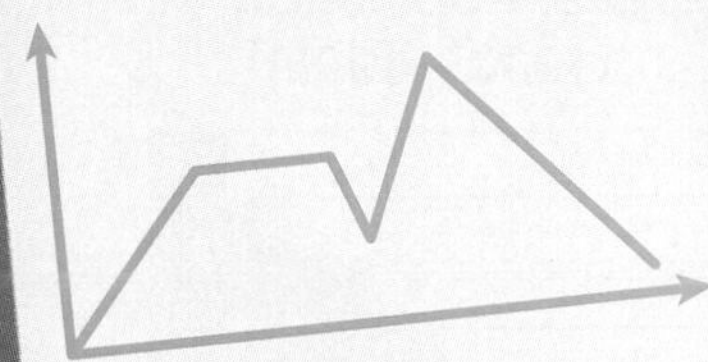

By analyzing the paper, the archeologist determines that the graph was drawn during the 1990's. Unfortunately, any words that might once have appeared on the graph have disappeared.

Create a story, song, or play about what the graph shows. Who drew it? How was it used? Why was it drawn?

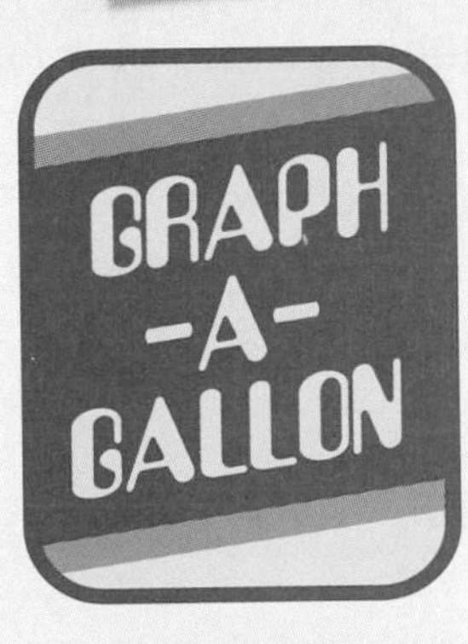

A car's gas mileage is the average number of miles the car travels on one gallon of gas. The Environmental Protection Agency evaluates and publishes the gas mileage of all models of cars.

- Research the gas mileage and prices of several new cars.
- Graph your data.
- Is there a relationship between a car's price and its gas mileage?

Excursion: Create a statistic comparing a car's cost to its gas mileage. An inexpensive car with high mileage per gallon should rate a higher statistic than an expensive car with low mileage per gallon. Why?

Assessment

1. In what year was the population of the United States about twice that of 1930?

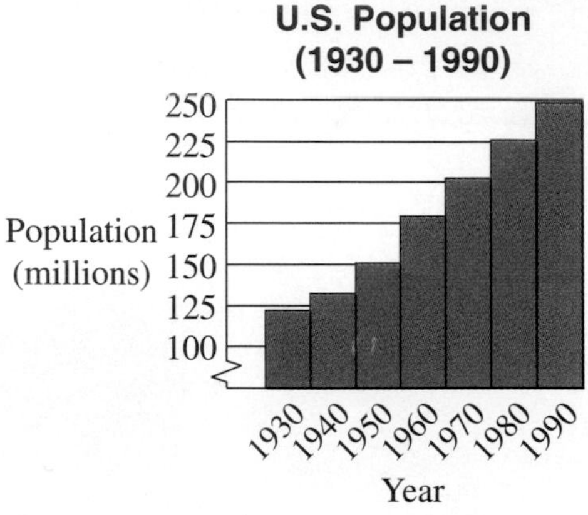

Source: *The Universal Almanac*

2. Decide whether a scatter plot, a bar graph, or a line graph would be the best way to display the data below. Explain your reasoning and draw your graph.

   Average daily water use in gallons per person per day:

   U.S.A.: 188, Canada: 142, Japan: 114, Spain: 102, France: 84, Germany: 50

   Source: *The Information Please Environmental Almanac*

3. Make a frequency table and line plot for the following data:

   Subscribers (in millions) of the top 10 cable television networks:

   59 59 58 58 57 56 56 55 55 55

   Source: *The Universal Almanac*

4. Display this data, using a back-to-back stem-and-leaf plot.

   Career earnings in millions of dollars of the top male and female golfers:

   M: 7.1 5.9 5.7 5.4 5.3 5.1 5.1 4.8 4.7
   F: 4.2 3.5 3.4 3.3 3.2 2.8 2.5 2.5 1.9

   Source: *The Universal Almanac*

5. Use the data from Exercise 4 to find the mean, median, and mode of the top female golfers' career earnings.

6. **Writing** Write a closed-option, unbiased survey question to find the favorite subject of students in your school.

7. Lee's first five test scores are 78, 86, 88, 95, and 97. What score must he get on his next test to have a mean of 90?

8. You have a set of data with five data items. The median is 23, the mean is 23, the mode is 26, and the range is 7. Find the five data items.

9. **Choose A, B, C, or D.** Which one of the following values can be determined using the box-and-whisker plot shown below.

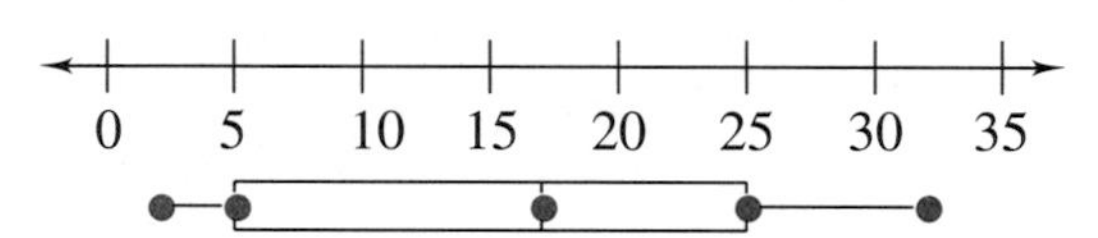

   A. the sample size **B.** the mean
   C. the third quartile **D.** the mode

10. Use the scatter plot below to determine if a correlation exists between hours of TV viewing and math quiz scores. If a correlation exists, draw a fitted line.

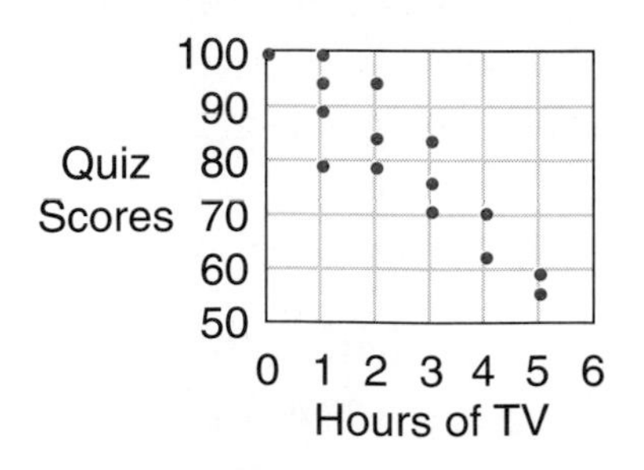

Cumulative Review

Choose A, B, C, or D.

1. Find the median and the mode of the data in the line plot at the right.

	×		
	×		×
	×	×	×
×	×	×	×
6	7	8	9

A. 7 and 8 **B.** 8 and 9
C. 7.5 and 7 **D.** 7.5 and 8

2. Which measure of central tendency would you use to describe data on your classmates' favorite brand of sneakers?

A. mode **B.** median
C. mean or median **D.** mean

3. What are the missing numbers in the pattern below?

2, 3, 5, 8, 12, ■, 23, ■, . . .

A. 18 and 28 **B.** 17 and 30
C. 15 and 26 **D.** 19 and 26

4. On one day of Megan's beach vacation, high tide occurred at 11:36 A.M., and low tide occurred at 6:39 P.M. How much time elapsed between high and low tide?

A. 7 h 3 min **B.** 7 h 15 min
C. 6 h 15 min **D.** 6 h 39 min

5. At a middle school gymnastics competition, the scores for the floor exercises were 5.1, 5.6, 5.3, 5.1, 4.8, 4.6, and 5.2. Find the mean and median.

A. 5.1 and 5.3 **B.** 5.15 and 5.2
C. 5.2 and 5.1 **D.** 5.1 and 5.1

6. At the Armstrong School, the student-teacher ratio is 12 : 1. If there are 30 teachers in the school, how many students are there?

A. 42 **B.** 360
C. 300 **D.** 250

7. Describe the relationship in the scatter plot shown below.

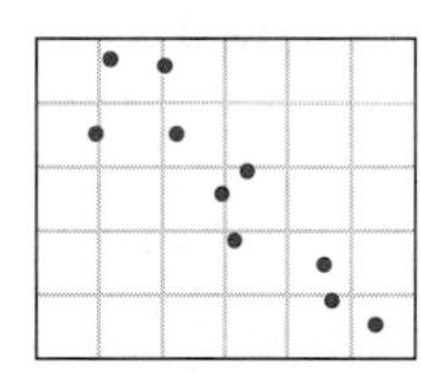

A. positive correlation
B. negative correlation
C. no correlation
D. positive and negative correlation

8. In a stem-and-leaf plot, which of the following can a stem represent?

A. a units' digit **B.** a tens' digit
C. a tenths' digit **D.** any of these

9. Which type of graph shows different items changing over time?

A. stacked bar **B.** sliding bar
C. line **D.** multiple line

10. Find two numbers whose sum is 10 and whose product is 24.

A. 5 and 6 **B.** 3 and 8
C. -2 and 12 **D.** 6 and 4

CHAPTER 2 Patterns in Geometry

THE HUMAN MACHINE

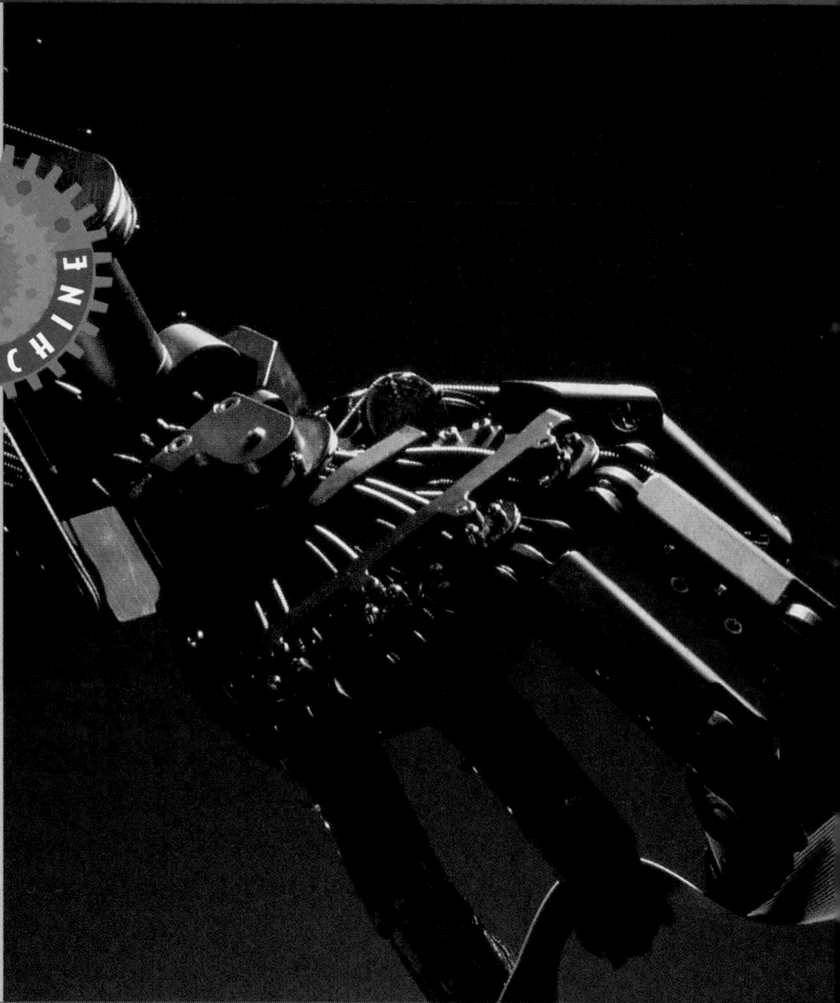

To measure your pulse, place your forefinger and middle finger on either the inside of your wrist or on your neck just below your jawbone. Count the number of beats for 10 s and multiply by 6.

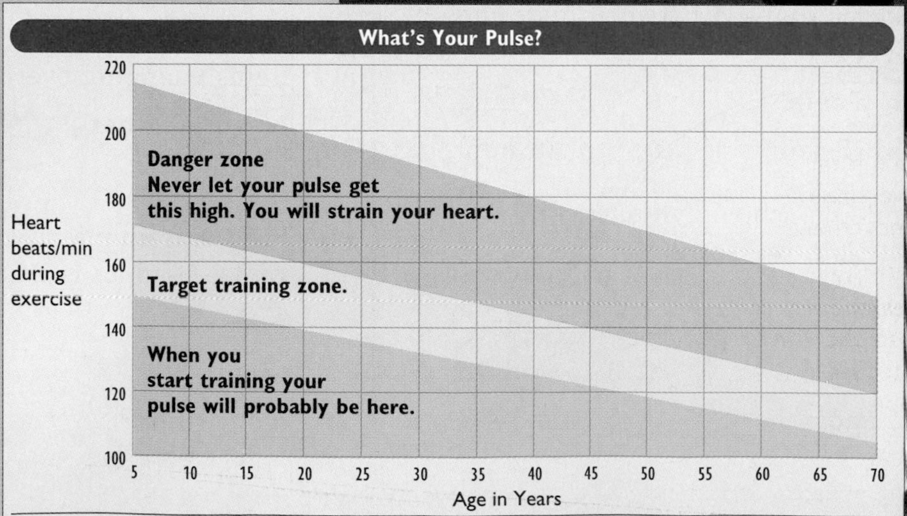

What's Your Pulse?

Heart beats/min during exercise: 100, 120, 140, 160, 180, 200, 220

Age in Years: 5, 10, 15, 20, 25, 30, 35, 40, 45, 50, 55, 60, 65, 70

Danger zone
Never let your pulse get this high. You will strain your heart.

Target training zone.

When you start training your pulse will probably be here.

Source: *The USBORNE Book of Food, Fitness, and Health; Prentice Hall Health*

Data File 2

WHAT YOU WILL LEARN

- how to find patterns in geometric figures
- how to use tools to construct geometric figures
- how to use technology to explore parallel lines
- how to solve problems by looking for a pattern

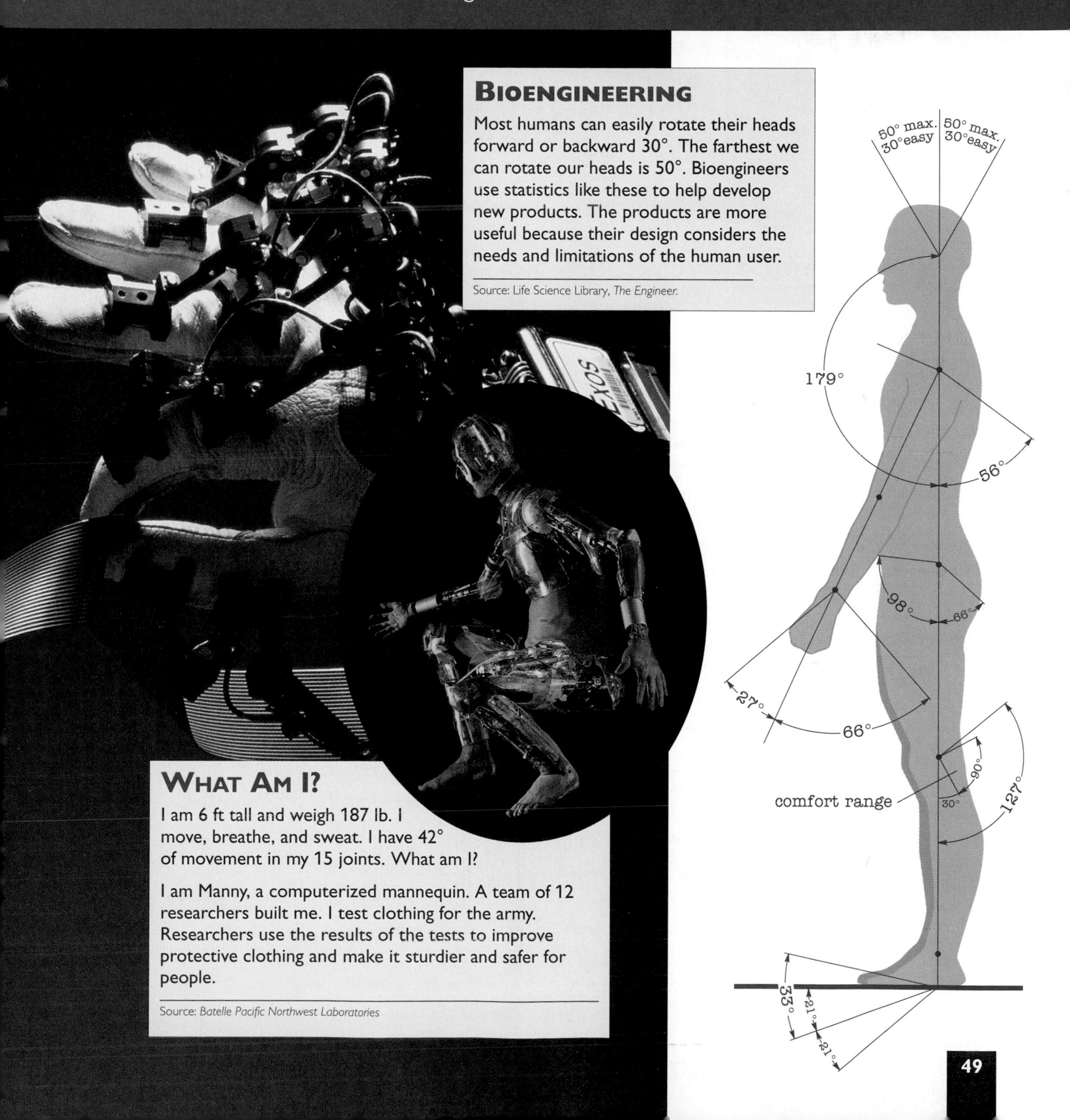

BIOENGINEERING

Most humans can easily rotate their heads forward or backward 30°. The farthest we can rotate our heads is 50°. Bioengineers use statistics like these to help develop new products. The products are more useful because their design considers the needs and limitations of the human user.

Source: Life Science Library, *The Engineer.*

WHAT AM I?

I am 6 ft tall and weigh 187 lb. I move, breathe, and sweat. I have 42° of movement in my 15 joints. What am I?

I am Manny, a computerized mannequin. A team of 12 researchers built me. I test clothing for the army. Researchers use the results of the tests to improve protective clothing and make it sturdier and safer for people.

Source: *Batelle Pacific Northwest Laboratories*

investigation

Project File

Memo

The shortest distance between two points is a straight line. But what is the shortest route when there are 3, 4, 5, or 100 points? This is a common problem in today's world. The local post office needs to know the shortest routes for carriers to follow on their rounds. The sanitation department needs the shortest routes for its trucks to follow when picking up trash in order to save gas. To be more efficient, the telephone company tries to route its long-distance calls along the shortest possible network of lines.

Mission: Use a street map of your city or sketch a map showing the streets in your neighborhood. Mark your home and five places you might visit on a weekend. None of the places should be on the same street. Find the shortest route that begins and ends at your home and that takes in all five places. Then find the fastest route.

LeADS tO FOLLoW

- ✓ What factors might cause a shorter route to take more time to travel than a longer route?
- ✓ How can you tell if one route is shorter than another route without measuring their lengths?

What's Ahead

- Identifying and working with central angles and inscribed angles of a circle

2-1 Angles of Circles

WHAT YOU'LL NEED

✓ Compass 

✓ Protractor 

FLASHBACK

A chord is a segment with both endpoints on a circle.

WORK TOGETHER

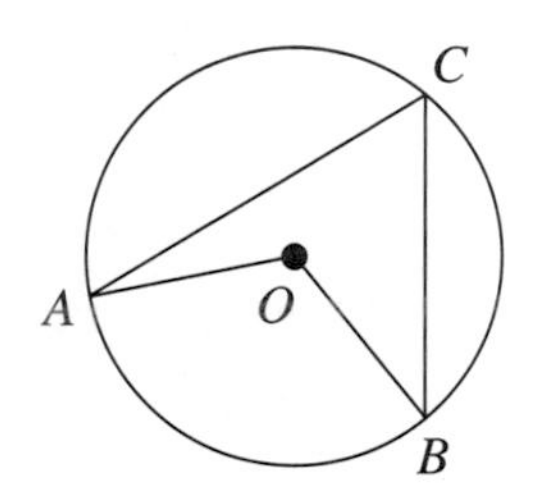

An angle like $\angle AOB$ that has its vertex at the center of a circle is a **central angle** of the circle. An angle like $\angle ACB$ that has its vertex on a circle and whose sides contain chords of the circle is an **inscribed angle** of the circle.

1. Estimate the measures of $\angle AOB$ and $\angle ACB$. Then use a protractor to measure the angles. Record the measures in a table with the headings Central Angle and Inscribed Angle.

2. $\angle AOB$ and $\angle ACB$ have the same **intercepted arc**, $\widehat{AB}$.
   - Use a compass to draw a circle.
   - Draw a central angle and an inscribed angle that have the same intercepted arc.
   - Measure each angle and record its measure in your table.
   - Repeat for a second circle.

3. In your group, compare the measures of each central angle and inscribed angle that have the same intercepted arc. Describe the relationships between the measures.

FLASHBACK

Angles are congruent if they have the same measure. Segments are congruent if they have the same length.

THINK AND DISCUSS

In each circle, the non-overlapping central angles are congruent.

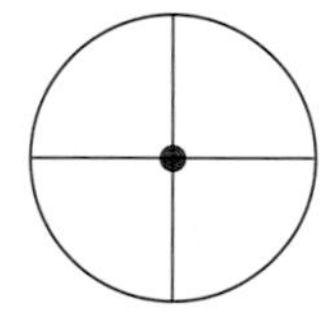
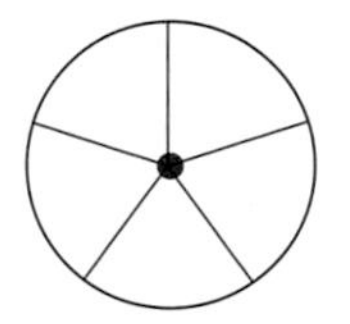
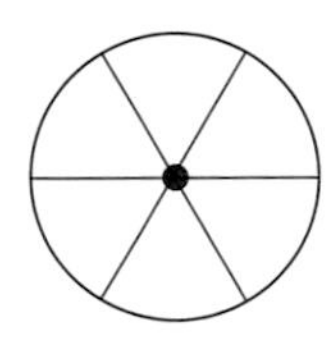

4. What is the sum of the measures of the non-overlapping central angles in each circle?

5. For each circle, find the measure of a central angle.

From noon to midnight how many times do the hands of a clock form a 180° angle?

One kind of *arc* is a *semicircle*. $\overset{\frown}{XWY}$ and $\overset{\frown}{XZY}$ are semicircles of circle O. Points X and Y are endpoints of both semicircles.

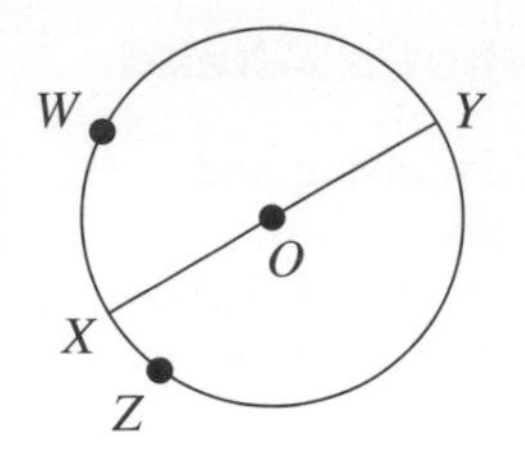

6. How would you define a semicircle?

7. Why do you need to use three letters to name a semicircle?

You can use two letters to name an arc like $\overset{\frown}{XW}$ that is shorter than a semicircle.

8. Name four more arcs of circle O that are shorter than a semicircle.

In the Work Together activity you discovered the following:

If a central angle and an inscribed angle have the same intercepted arc, the measure of the central angle is twice the measure of the inscribed angle.

9. If $m\angle RST = 52°$, what is $m\angle RPT$?

10. If $m\angle RPT = 98°$, what is $m\angle RST$?

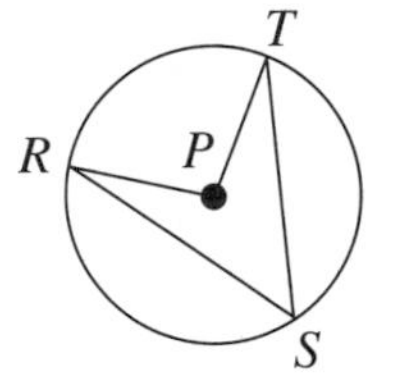

ON YOUR OWN

Identify the following parts of circle *A*.

11. the center

12. four radii

13. a diameter

14. three chords

15. a central angle

16. an inscribed angle

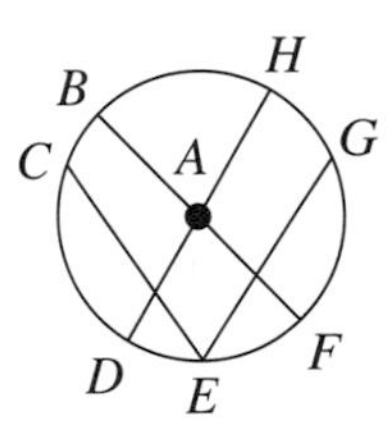

Find the measure of each numbered angle.

17.

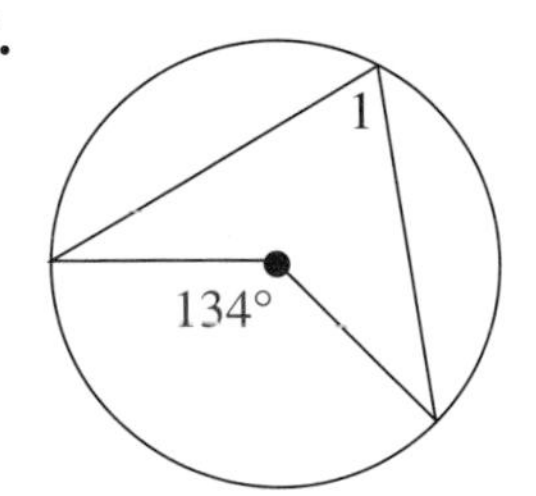

18.

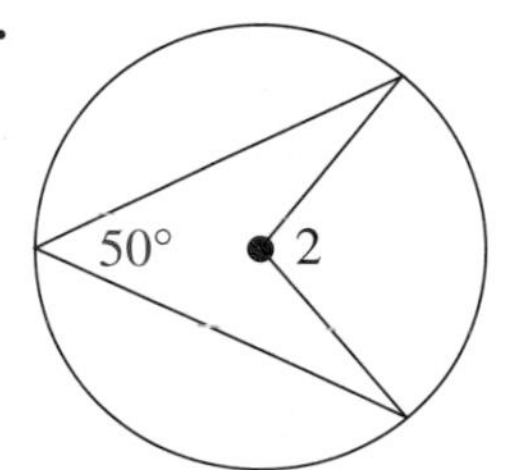

19.

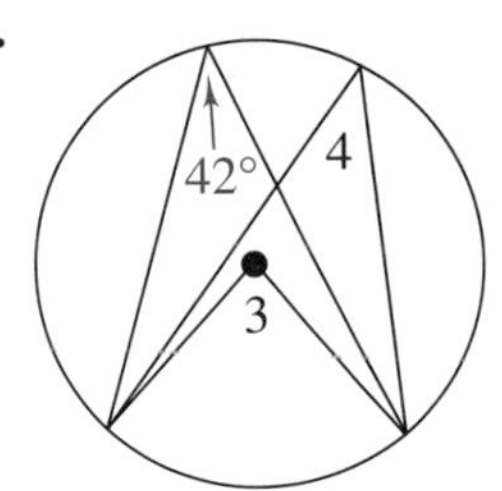

20. a. **Estimation** Estimate the measure of each central angle.

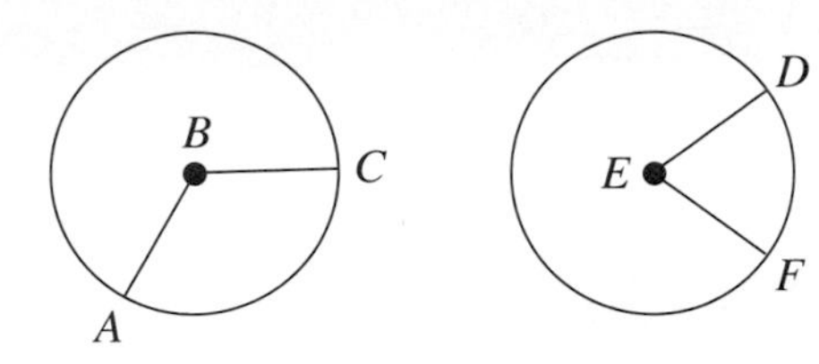

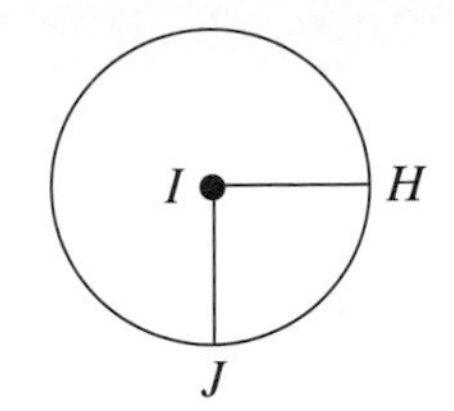

b. Measure each central angle.

c. What kind of angle is $\angle HIJ$?

d. What fraction of the circumference of circle I is $\overset{\frown}{HJ}$?

21. Draw a circle O and a central angle with measure 55°.

22. Draw a circle P and an inscribed angle with measure 78°.

23. a. What is $m\angle ROT$?

b. What is $m\angle RST$?

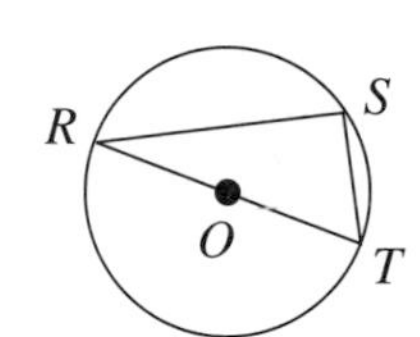

24. **Data File 2 (pp. 48–49)** Through what angle measure can a person comfortably move his or her wrist?

25. **Critical Thinking** The measure of $\angle AOB$ is 110°. Must the measure of $\angle ADC$ be 55°? Why or why not?

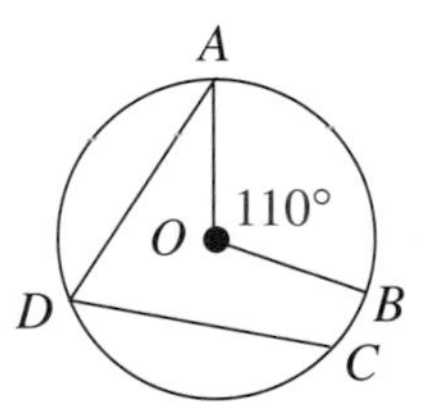

Complete with always, sometimes, or never.

26. A chord is ■ a diameter.

27. A radius is ■ a chord.

28. An inscribed angle ■ has a greater measure than a central angle.

29. A diameter is ■ a chord.

30. **Investigation (p. 50)** The Investigation lists reasons why the post office, sanitation department, and phone company might be interested in finding shortest routes. List other people, agencies, or businesses that might also be interested. For each one, tell why.

Mixed REVIEW

Use the following data: 22, 26, 25, 25, 27, 22, 23, 25, 24, 26, 23, 27.

1. Make a frequency table. Do not use intervals.

2. Draw a line plot.

3. Data File 9 on pages 378–379 shows the results of a smoking survey of 9,965 teens. What type of graph would best show the data? Why?

Find each answer.

4. $\frac{3}{16} \cdot 11$

5. $\frac{18}{5} \cdot 6$

6. Six students are running for class president. How many different ways can they be listed on the ballot?

What's Ahead

- Finding the area and circumference of a circle

2-2 Measuring Circles

WHAT YOU'LL NEED

✓ Calculator 

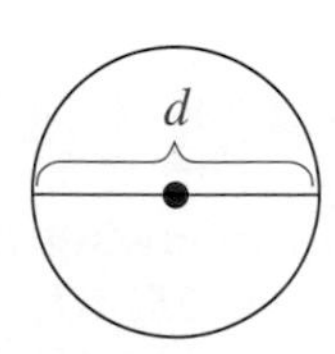

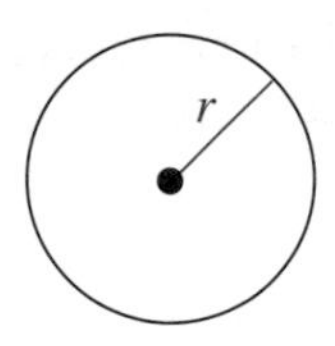

THINK AND DISCUSS

Using Formulas The distance around a polygon is the *perimeter*. **Circumference** is the distance around a circle.

The circumference is a little more than three times the diameter. **Pi** (π) is the special name for the ratio of the circumference (C) to the diameter (d).

$$\pi = \frac{C}{d}$$

If you solve this equation for C, you get a formula for finding the circumference of a circle.

$$C = \pi d$$

1. Another formula for finding the circumference is $C = 2\pi r$, where r is the radius of the circle. Why is πd equivalent to $2\pi r$?

You also use π when you find the area (A) of a circle.

$$A = \pi r^2$$

2. a. Explain the difference between the circumference and area of a circle.
   b. Are the circumference and area measured in the same units? Explain.

Pi is actually an infinite string of nonrepeating digits. On November 19, 1989, the University of Tokyo calculated π to 1,073,740,000 decimal places using a computer.

Source: *The Guinness Book of Records*

Computing with Pi You can use $\frac{22}{7}$ or 3.14 as an approximation for π. Many calculators have a π key.

Example 1 The diameter of a circle is 8 cm. Find the circumference and area.

- To find the circumference, use $C = \pi d$.

The circumference is about 25 cm.

- To find the area, first find the radius and then use $A = \pi r^2$.

  $r = \frac{d}{2} = \frac{8}{2} = 4$

  π × 4 x^2 = 50.265482

  The area is about 50 cm^2.

3. a. Use a calculator to find the circumference and area of the circle in Example 1. Use 3.14 for π instead of the π key.
   b. Why do you think we rounded the circumference and area in Example 1 to the nearest unit?

The circles on the Olympic flag represent the continents of Africa, America, Asia, Australia, and Europe.

Source: *Troll's Student Handbook*

You can find the area of a circle if you know the circumference.

Example 2 Kathy wants to determine how much water it will take to fill a circular swimming pool to different depths. She knows she can do that if she finds the area of the bottom of the pool. She measured the circumference of the pool and found that it was about 63 ft. What is the area of the bottom?

- Use $d = \frac{C}{\pi}$, $r = \frac{d}{2}$, and $A = \pi r^2$.

  63 ÷ π (→ d)   (→ r)    = 315.84298

  The area is about 316 ft^2.

WORK TOGETHER

Give lengths and areas to the nearest tenth.

4. Find the circumference of circle O.
5. $\angle DOE$ is a right angle. What fraction of the circle is the intercepted arc, $\widehat{DE}$? Find the length of $\widehat{DE}$.
6. Find the area of circle O.
7. Find the area of the shaded wedge.

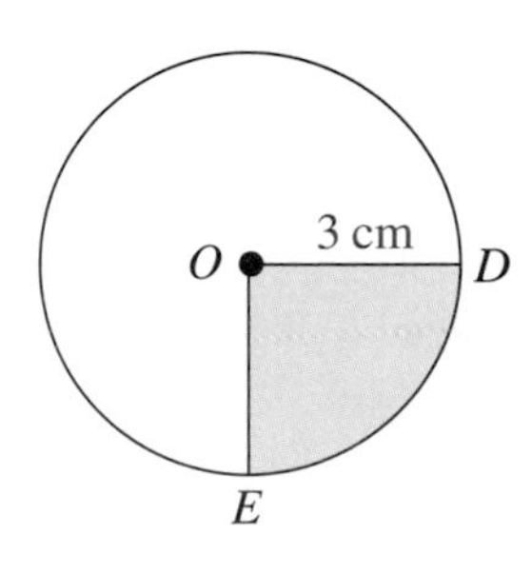

If you slice** a cantaloupe in half you will see three congruent central angles.* ***What is the measure of each angle?

Extra SKILLS PRACTICE

Find the circumference of each circle.

1. $d = 5$ cm
2. $d = 6$ ft
3. $d = 25$ in.
4. $d = 3.2$ m
5. $d = 70$ mm
6. $r = 100$ mm
7. $r = 2.5$ m
8. $r = 14$ yd
9. $r = 9.25$ km

Find the area of each circle.

10. $r = 4$ yd
11. $r = 10$ ft
12. $r = 16$ in.
13. $r = 0.3$ m
14. $r = 2.2$ km
15. $d = 20$ in.
16. $d = 1.2$ km
17. $d = 27$ ft
18. $d = 3.5$ m

8. In circle P with radius 6 cm, $\angle FPG$ is a central angle with measure 60°.

- **a.** Find the length of the intercepted arc, $\overset{\frown}{FG}$.
- **b.** Find the area of the wedge formed by $\angle FPG$ and the circle.

9. In circle Q with radius 10 in., $\angle JQK$ is a central angle with measure 120°.

- **a.** What is the length of the intercepted arc, $\overset{\frown}{JK}$?
- **b.** Find the area of the wedge formed by $\angle JQK$ and the circle.

TRY THESE

10. $C \approx$ ■

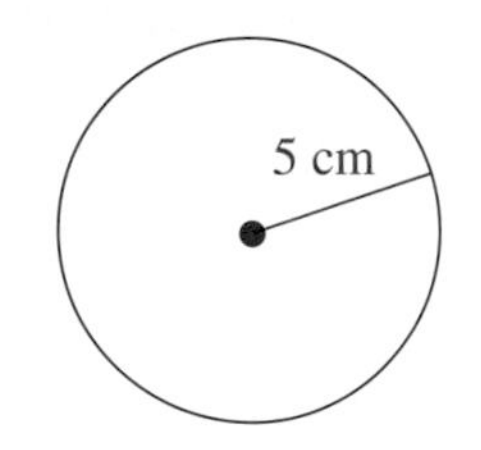

11. $A \approx$ ■

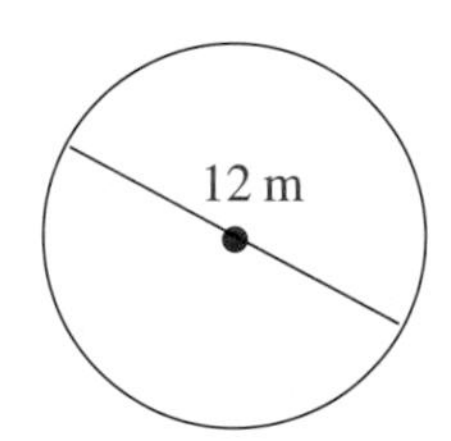

12. A circle has diameter 7 in. Find the circumference and area.

13. Find the diameter and radius of a circle with a circumference about 12.6 m.

ON YOUR OWN

Find the circumference and area of each circle.

14.

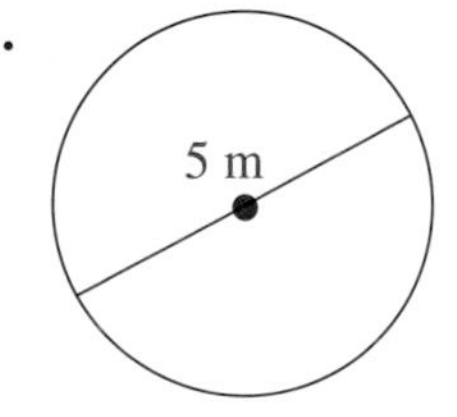

15.

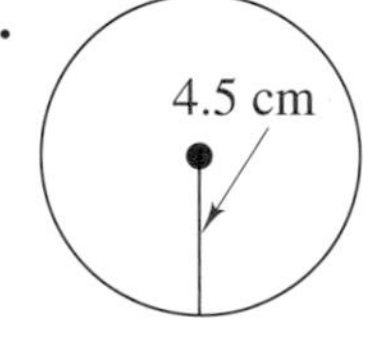

16. Use $\frac{22}{7}$ for π.

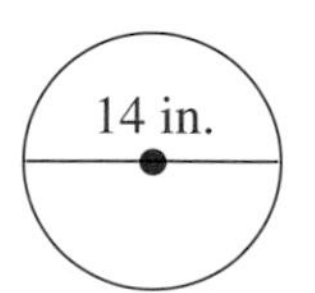

Mental Math Find the circumference and area of each circle.

17. $d = 2$ cm

18. $r = 10$ in.

19. If the circumference of a circle is 132 cm, what is the diameter? What is the radius?

20. If the circumference of a circle is 226 in., what is the radius? What is the radius in feet? in yards?

21. $\angle EOD$ is a central angle with measure 45°. The radius of circle O is 3 cm.

a. Find the length of $\widehat{ED}$.

b. Find the area of the shaded wedge.

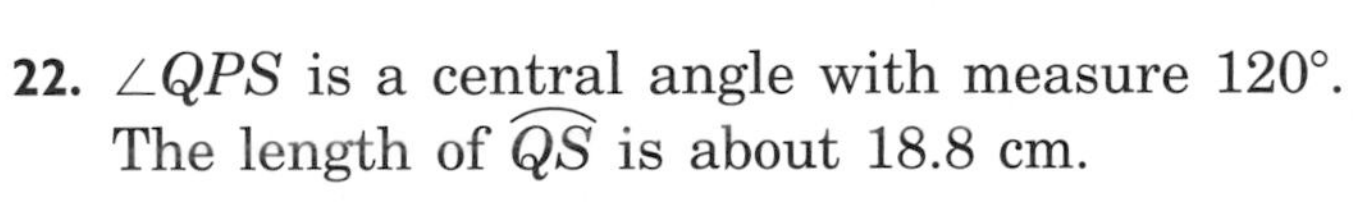

22. $\angle QPS$ is a central angle with measure 120°. The length of $\widehat{QS}$ is about 18.8 cm.

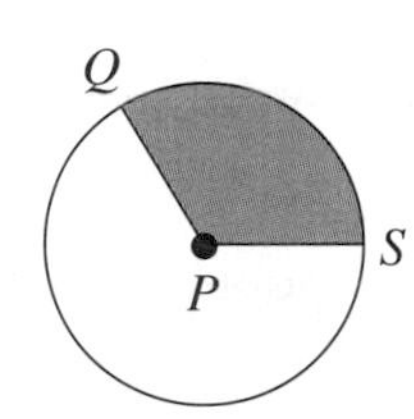

a. Find the radius of circle P.

b. Writing Explain how you found the length of the radius of circle P.

23. Choose A, B, C, or D. Which of the following figures has a perimeter that is about the same as the circumference of a circle of radius 10?

A. square with sides 10, 10, 10, 10

B. square with sides 20, 20, 20, 20

C. rectangle with sides 20, 10, 20, 10

D. rectangle with sides 12, 5, 12, 5

24. Data File 3 (pp. 100–101) About how many people standing 3 ft apart would it take to surround the world's largest pizza?

2 cm

3 cm

25. a. Find the area of the outer ring.

b. Explain how you found the area.

26. Gardening A circular garden with radius 3 ft is surrounded by a path 3 ft wide. It is 10 ft from the center of this garden to the outside of the outer garden shown. What is the combined area of the two gardens?

1. Use the following data on U.S. population to create a bar graph giving the impression that the population doubled from 1970 to 1990. 1970: 203.3 million; 1980: 226.5 million; 1990: 249.6 million.

2. Redraw the graph to give an accurate impression of U.S. population growth.

3. Draw a circle and a central angle with measure 85°.

4. Draw a circle and an inscribed angle with measure 53°.

5. What is the date when the month of October is 20,000 minutes old?

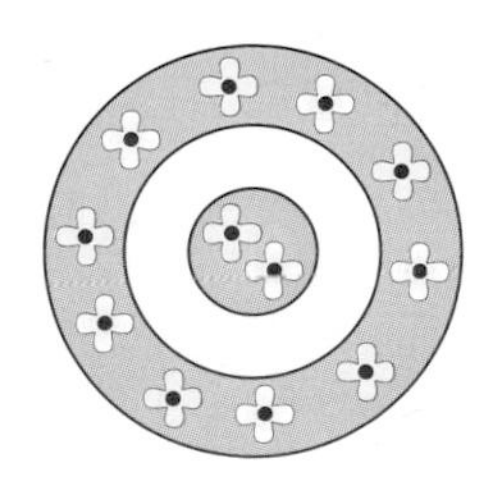

PROBLEM SOLVING

2-3 Look for a Pattern

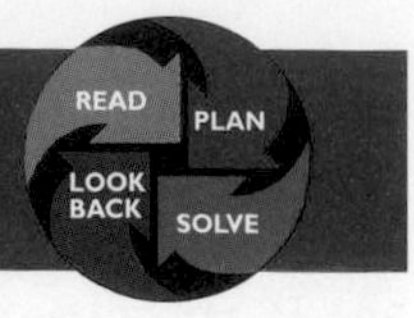

What's Ahead

- Solving a problem by looking for a pattern

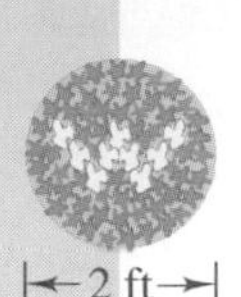

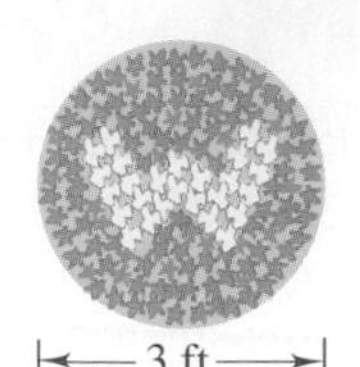

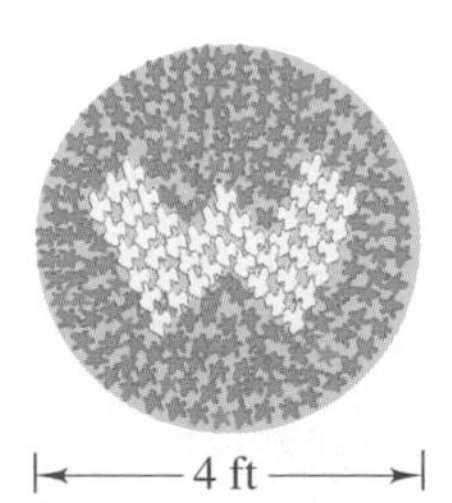

Sometimes the best way to solve a problem is to look for a pattern.

> The eighth grade students at Woodlawn Middle School voted to hire a landscaper to decorate the front lawn of the school with a large circular floral design. The landscaper's most popular sizes include a 2 ft diameter that costs $36, a 3 ft diameter for $81, and a 4 ft diameter for $144. Other sizes are available on request. The class has $500 in the treasury for a gift to the school. What is the largest size flower bed they can afford?

READ

Read and understand the given information. Summarize the problem.

1. Think about the information you are given and what you are asked to find.
   a. **Discussion** Do you think the landscaper sets prices of circular designs based on the *circumference* or the *area* of each circle?
   b. Why isn't the cost of the 4 ft size twice the cost of the 2 ft size?

PLAN

Decide on a strategy to solve the problem.

Look for a Pattern is a good strategy to use here. There is a relationship between the cost and the area of the circular design. Looking for a pattern can help you identify that relationship.

SOLVE

Try out the strategy.

2. Make a table that shows the diameter, radius, square of the radius, and the cost.

Diameter	2 ft	3 ft	4 ft
Radius	■	■	■
Square of the Radius	■	■	■
Cost	$36	$81	$144

3. Look for a pattern. How is the cost related to the square of the radius?

4. Continue the table. What is the largest size available for $500?

5. Does your solution fit the pattern you found?

LOOK BACK

Think about how you solved this problem.

TRY THESE

Look for a pattern to solve each problem.

6. The first four *triangular numbers* are 1, 3, 6, and 10. What is the tenth triangular number? What is the forty-fifth triangular number? Describe how you found it.

7. Keith found a box that increased his money magically. The first night he put $2 in the box and found $5 in the morning. The second night he put $3 in the box and found $7.50 in the morning. He put $4 in the box on the third night and found $10 in the morning. How much money would be in the box in the morning if he put $6 in the night before?

A human pyramid** is really a triangle. The highest human pyramid was nine levels high.* ***How many people were in the pyramid?

Source: *The Guinness Book of Records*

ON YOUR OWN

Use any strategy to solve each problem. Show all your work.

8. Jaleesa's mother gave her a number puzzle. She told Jaleesa to pick a number, add 7 to it, multiply the sum by 3, and then subtract 6. Jaleesa did this and ended up with 45. What number did she start with?

9. You are offered a job with an unusual pay rate. Your pay is $.15 for the first day. Each day after that you earn twice as much as you did the day before. If you take the job, how many days will it take to earn more than $5 a day? more than $20 a day?

> *The world is round and the place which may seem like the end may also be only the beginning.*
>
> —*Ivy Baker Priest (1905–1975)*

10. The houses on the north side of Hall Avenue are numbered in order with even numbers from 140 to 224. How many houses have at least one 6?

11. Find the next three numbers in the pattern.

1, 2, 3.5, 5.5, 8, ■, ■, ■

12. **Sports** By 4 P.M. Velvet had made twice as many free throws as Kris. During the next game, Velvet made 2 free throws and Kris made 5. In the following game Kris made 3 free throws and Velvet made none. At that point the girls had made the same number of free throws. How many free throws had each player made before the last two games?

13. Juan uses his paper route money to buy baseball cards for his collection. One week he bought 5 cards. The next three weeks he bought 8, 14, and 23 cards, respectively. How many cards will Juan buy next week if this pattern continues?

14. Draw the sixth figure in the pattern.

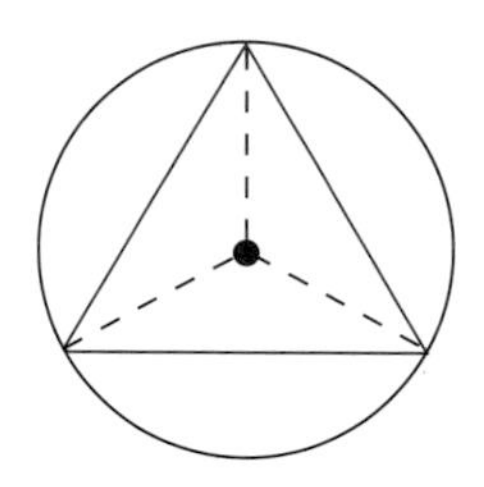
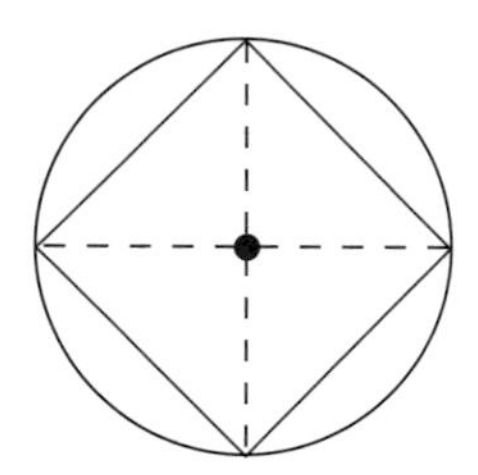
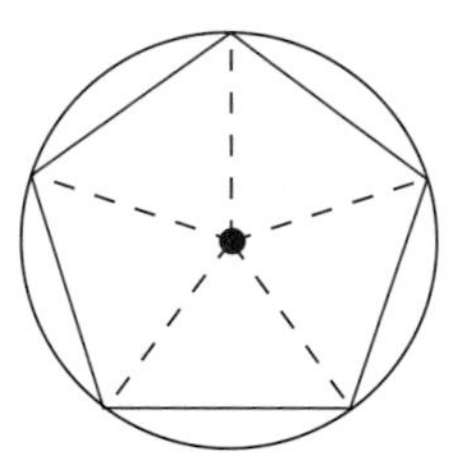

15. Walter rides the bus to go shopping every sixth day, while Jack rides the bus to go shopping every eighth day. On what day will Walter and Jack both ride the bus to go shopping?

16. **Money** A local restaurant offers a breakfast buffet. The restaurant charges \$8 for one person, \$16 for two people, \$23 for three, \$29 for four, and so on.

a. How much does a buffet breakfast for 7 cost? How much does the group save by eating together rather than alone?

b. The buffet costs the restaurant \$5 per person. What size group can the restaurant serve without losing money?

17. **Investigation** **(p. 50)** On a map of your town find a route that curves. Estimate the length of the curve. Explain how you made your estimate.

Use the data: −10.3, 5.6, −4.1, 7.5, 6.4, −4.6.

1. Find the median.

2. Find the mean.

Find the circumference of each circle.

3. $r = 8$ cm

4. $d = 7$ in.

Use a protractor to draw the following angles.

5. $m\angle P = 55°$

6. $m\angle Q = 100°$

7. When Yoshi was 8, her mother was 30. Now Yoshi's mother is twice as old as she is. How old is Yoshi?

What's Ahead

- Determining when two triangles are congruent

2-4 Exploring Congruent Triangles

WORK TOGETHER

WHAT YOU'LL NEED

✓ Protractor

✓ Metric Ruler

✓ Toothpicks

Draw and label the first two triangles described below. Use toothpicks to form the third triangle. Compare your results with those of your group. Are your triangles all the same size and shape?

- Draw $\triangle ABC$ with $AB = 5$ cm, $m\angle A = 45°$, $m\angle B = 40°$.
- Draw $\triangle DEF$ with $m\angle D = 35°$, $DE = 4$ cm, $DF = 3$ cm.
- Use 11 toothpicks to form a triangle with sides 2, 4, and 5 toothpicks long.

THINK AND DISCUSS

***The Eiffel Tower** weighs almost 8,000 tons. It is made almost entirely of triangles. Builders often use the triangle in construction because its rigid shape makes a structure very strong.*

Objects that have the same size and shape, such as the footprints shown below, are **congruent.**

1. Name some everyday objects that are congruent.

Identifying Corresponding Parts Two *polygons* are congruent if there is a correspondence between their vertices so that corresponding sides and angles are congruent. Marks like those in this diagram show congruent parts.

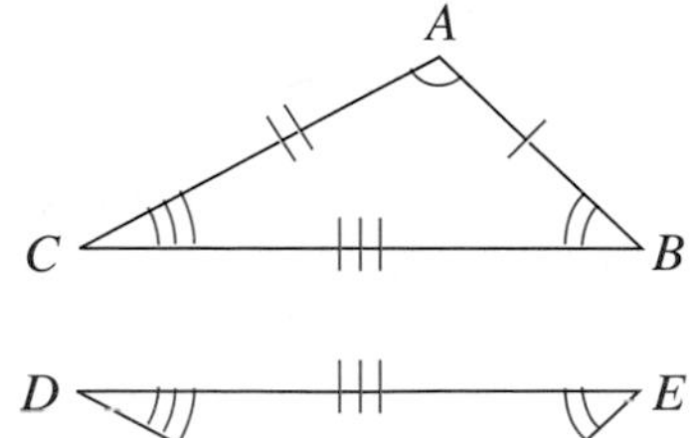

$\angle A \cong \angle F$ $\quad \overline{AB} \cong \overline{FE}$

$\angle B \cong \angle E$ $\quad \overline{BC} \cong \overline{ED}$

$\angle C \cong \angle D$ $\quad \overline{CA} \cong \overline{DF}$

$$\triangle ABC \cong \triangle FED$$

The *tribar* is an impossible figure. The sides seem to form a triangle, but the measure of each angle is 90°.

Source: *The Joy of Mathematics*

Note that you name the corresponding vertices in the same order.

2. The polygons are congruent.

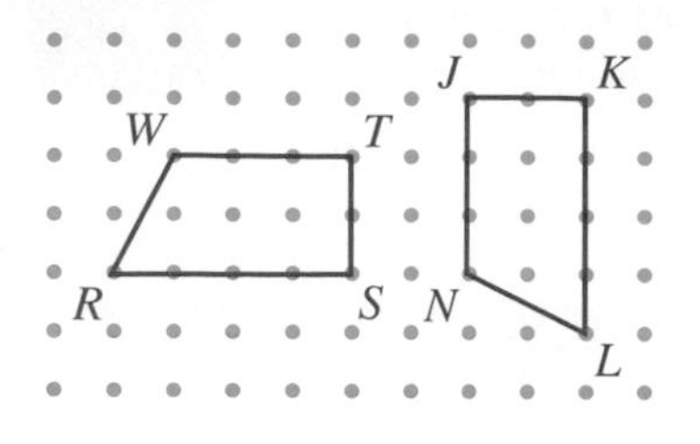

a. Which vertex corresponds to vertex R? to S? to T?

b. Complete: $RSTW \cong$ ■.

c. Name eight congruences between corresponding sides and angles of the polygons.

Identifying Congruent Triangles Two polygons are congruent when there is a correspondence between them such that all corresponding parts are congruent. In the Work Together activity you discovered that, for *triangles,* you do not have to show that *all* corresponding parts are congruent.

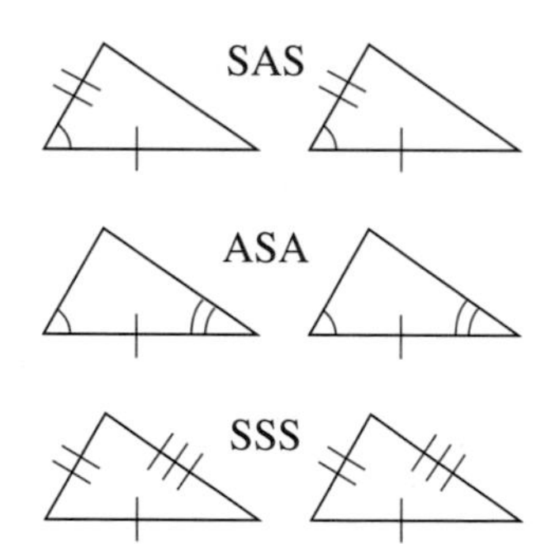

Congruent Triangles

Two triangles are congruent if the following parts of one triangle are congruent to the corresponding parts of the second triangle.

- two sides and the *included* angle **(SAS)**
- two angles and the *included* side **(ASA)**
- three sides **(SSS)**

The following facts will help you show that two triangles are congruent.

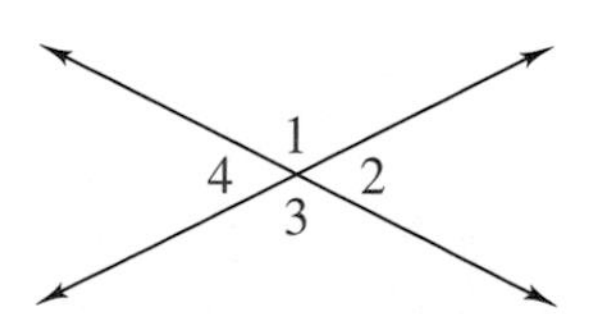

- *Vertical angles* are congruent. For example, $\angle 1 \cong \angle 3$ and $\angle 2 \cong \angle 4$.
- A segment is congruent to itself. This fact is helpful when a segment is a side of both triangles.

3. Which of SAS, ASA, or SSS, if any, could you use to show that the triangles are congruent?

a.

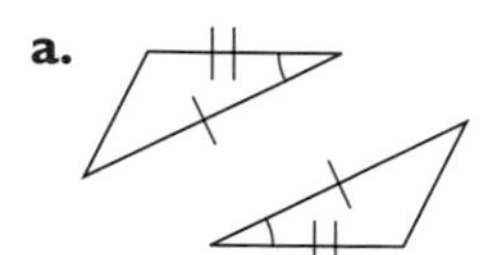

b.

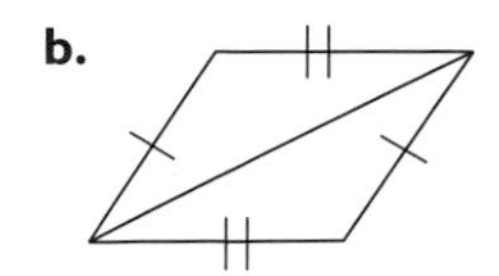

c.

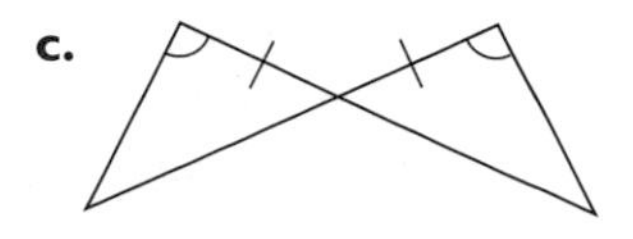

One way you can show that two angles or two segments are congruent is to show that they are corresponding parts of congruent triangles. You can give the following reason.

Corresponding parts of congruent triangles are congruent.

Rafael wanted to find the distance from A to B across the pond. He walked 70 yd on a path perpendicular to $\overline{AB}$ and put a stake at point C. He walked 70 yd on the same path and turned right 90° at point D. Then he walked until he could see point A and the post at C in a straight line. This final point, E, is 82 yd from D.

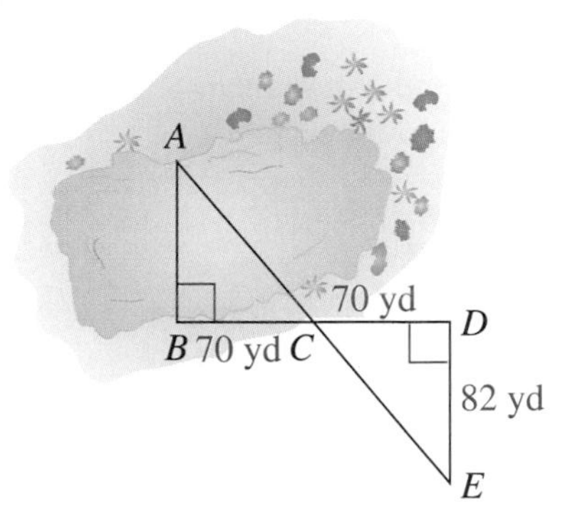

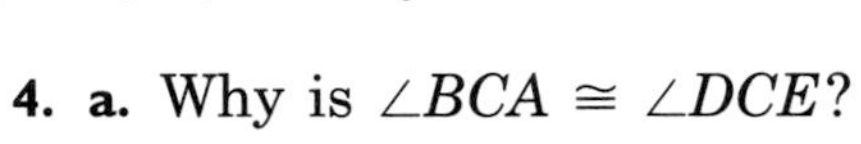

4. a. Why is $\angle BCA \cong \angle DCE$?

b. Why is $\triangle BCA \cong \triangle DCE$?

c. Why is $\overline{AB} \cong \overline{ED}$?

d. What is the distance from A to B?

ON YOUR OWN

Must the triangles be congruent? If so, write a congruence and tell why they are congruent.

5.

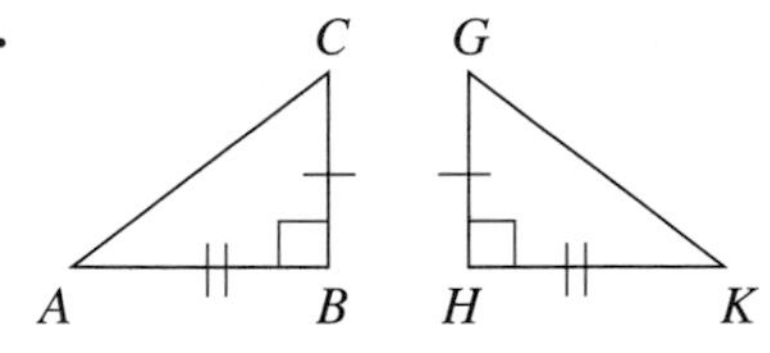

6.

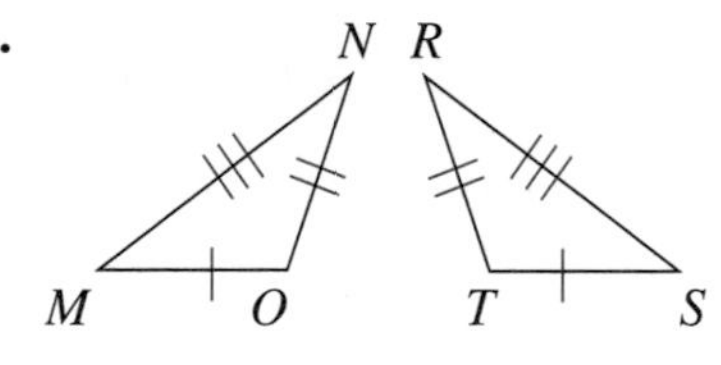

7.

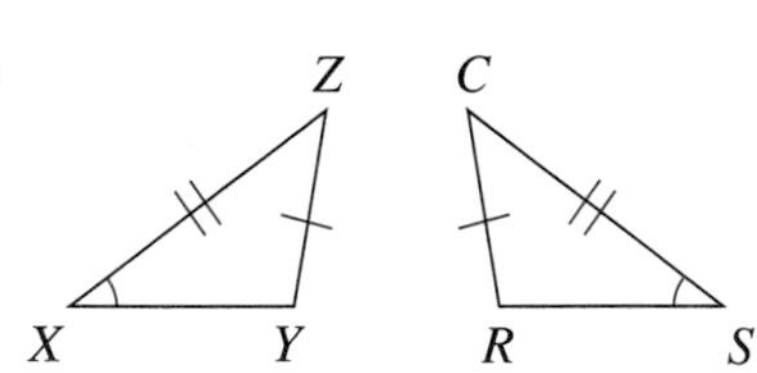

8.

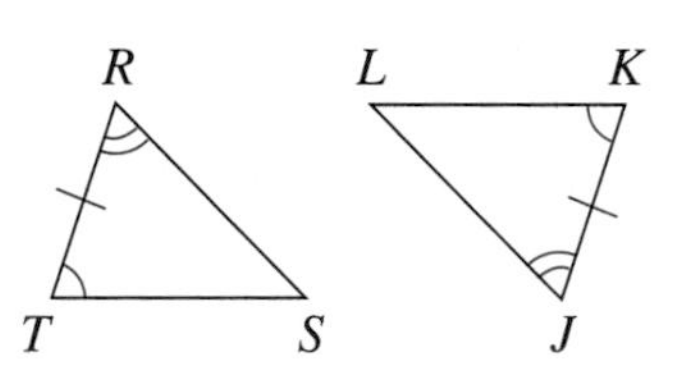

9.

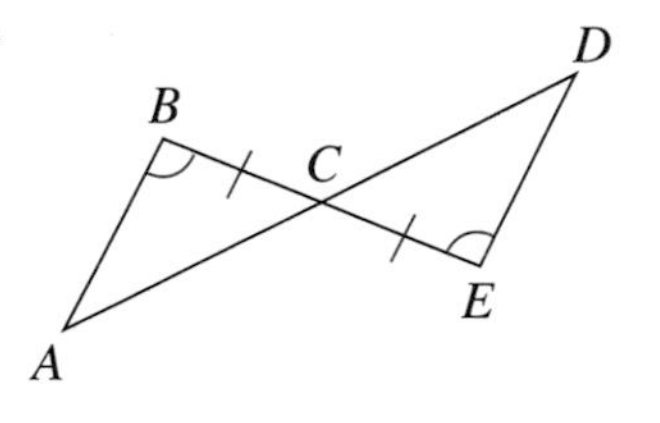

10.

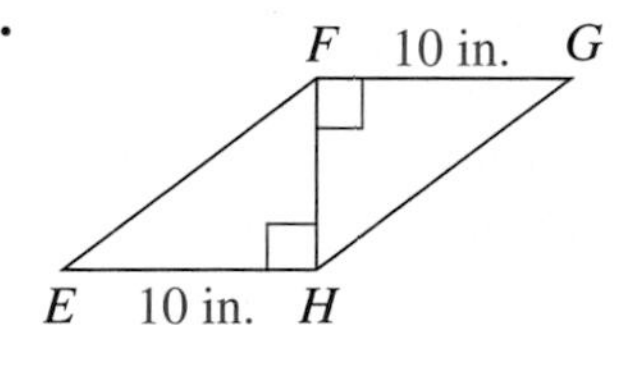

11. Writing How are congruent triangles used in this swing set? Why do you think it is important to the manufacturer that the triangles have exactly the same dimensions each time a swing set is produced?

Mixed REVIEW

Use the data: 55, 65, 45, 47, 36, 39, 52, 57, 64, 63, 63, 63.

1. Make a stem-and-leaf plot.

2. Find the median and the mode.

Complete each sentence.

3. A quadrilateral is a polygon with ■ sides.

4. A ■ is a polygon with 3 sides.

5. Jorge is working on his family tree. He has 2 parents, 4 grandparents, and 8 great-grandparents. How many ancestors are in the 8th generation back?

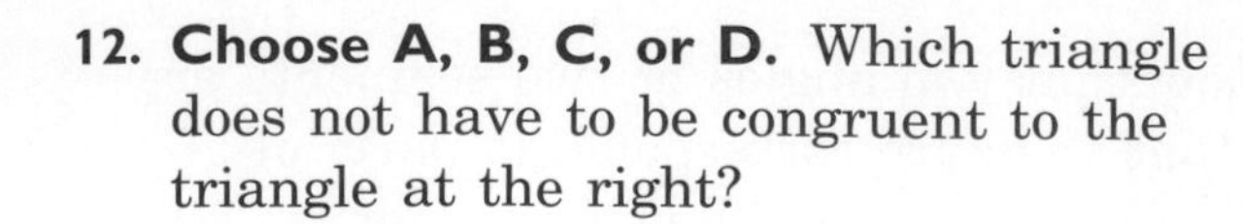

12. Choose A, B, C, or D. Which triangle does not have to be congruent to the triangle at the right?

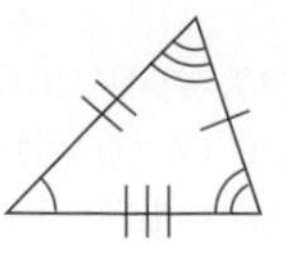

A. 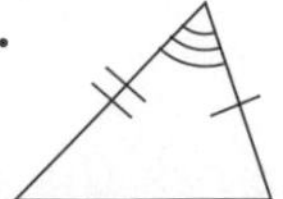 **B.** 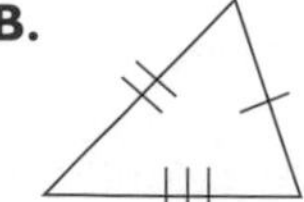 **C.** 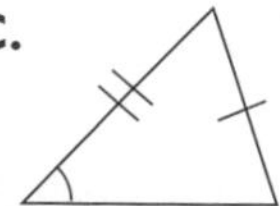 **D.** 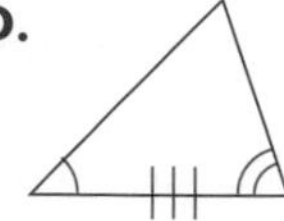

13. a. Critical Thinking What additional congruence would you need to know in order to use ASA to show that the triangles are congruent?

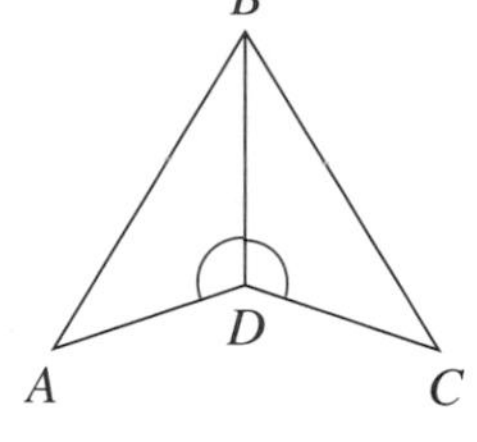

b. What additional congruence would you need to know in order to use SAS to show that the triangles are congruent?

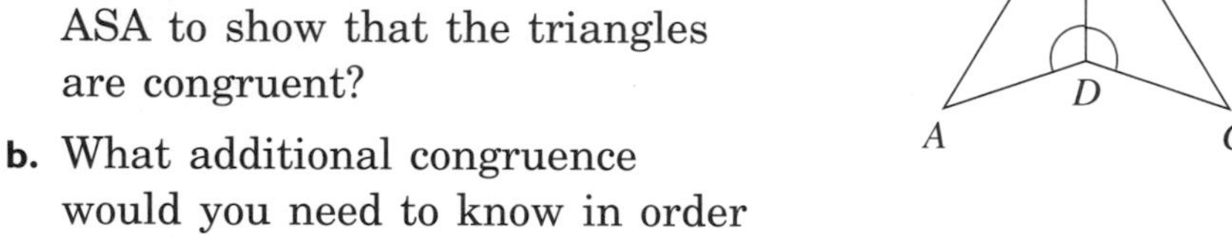

14. a. Complete: $\triangle RST \cong$ ■ by ■.

b. Find the missing measures.

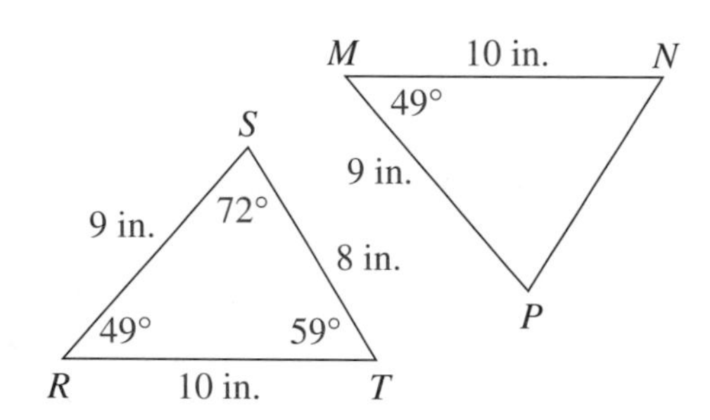

CHECKPOINT

Identify the following parts of circle Q.

1. all inscribed angles

2. all central angles

3. the arc intercepted by $\angle P$

4. a semicircle

5. $PQ = 6.5$ cm. Find the area and circumference of the circle.

6. Andrea jogged 3 blocks the first day. She increased her distance 4 blocks every day. How far did she jog on the sixth day?

7. Choose A, B, C, or D. Which figure does not appear to be congruent to the others?

A.  **B.**  **C.**  **D.** 

What's Ahead

- Classifying quadrilaterals
- Classifying triangles by sides and by angles

2-5 Quadrilaterals and Triangles

FLASHBACK

Two lines are parallel if they lie in the same plane and do not intersect. Segments are parallel if they lie in parallel lines.

THINK AND DISCUSS

Classifying Quadrilaterals Some quadrilatrals have special names.

1. List all the quadrilaterals that satisfy each definition.

A **trapezoid** has exactly one pair of parallel sides.

A **parallelogram** has both pairs of opposite sides parallel.

A **rectangle** is a parallelogram with four right angles.

A **rhombus** is a parallelogram with four congruent sides.

A **square** is a parallelogram with four right angles and four congruent sides.

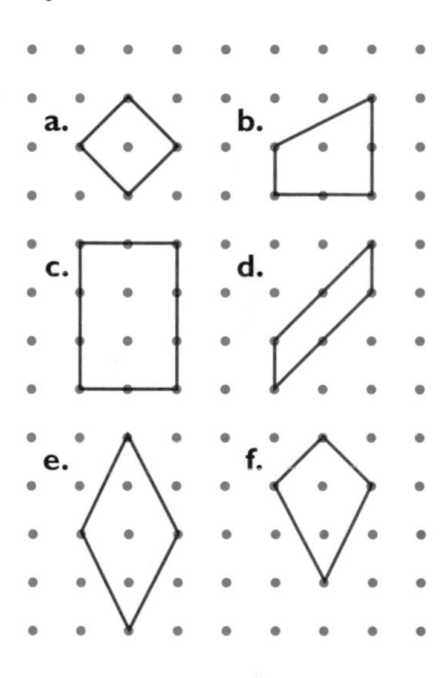

2. For each quadrilateral (a) through (e), give the best name.

3. Describe quadrilateral (f). What name would you give to this type of quadrilateral?

***For centuries** artists and architects have used the golden* rectangle. *The ratio of its length to its width is about 1.6. The Parthenon in Athens, as originally built, fit almost perfectly into a golden rectangle.*

When you draw one diagonal of any parallelogram, the result is a pair of congruent triangles.

4. Complete.

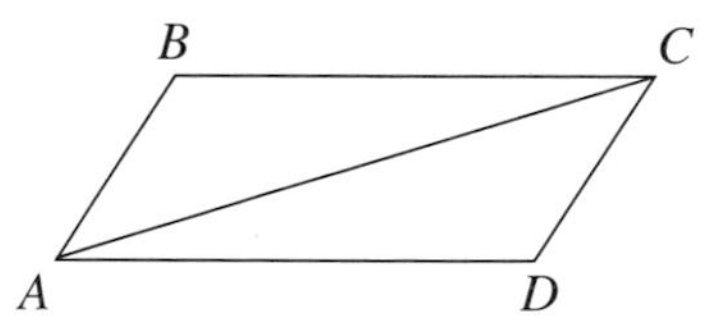

a. $\triangle ABC \cong$ ■ **b.** $\overline{AB} \cong$ ■

c. $\overline{BC} \cong$ ■ **d.** $\angle B \cong$ ■

5. a. What is true of the opposite sides and opposite angles of a parallelogram?

b. Is this also true for trapezoids, rectangles, rhombuses, or squares? Why or why not?

6. One special kind of trapezoid is an *isosceles* trapezoid like *TRAP*. What property makes a trapezoid an *isosceles* trapezoid?

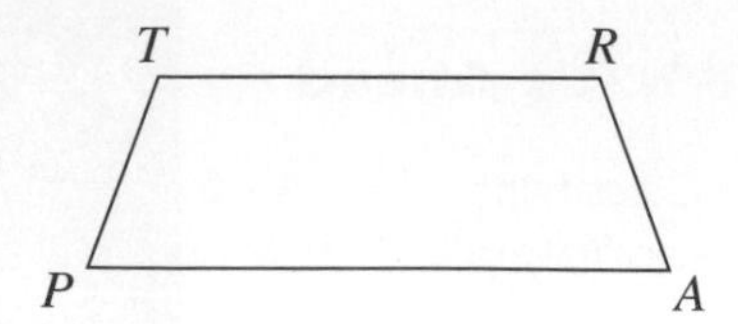

Classifying Triangles You can classify triangles by angle measures or by the number of congruent sides.

An acute angle measures less than 90°.

A right angle measures 90°.

An obtuse angle measures greater than 90° and less than 180°.

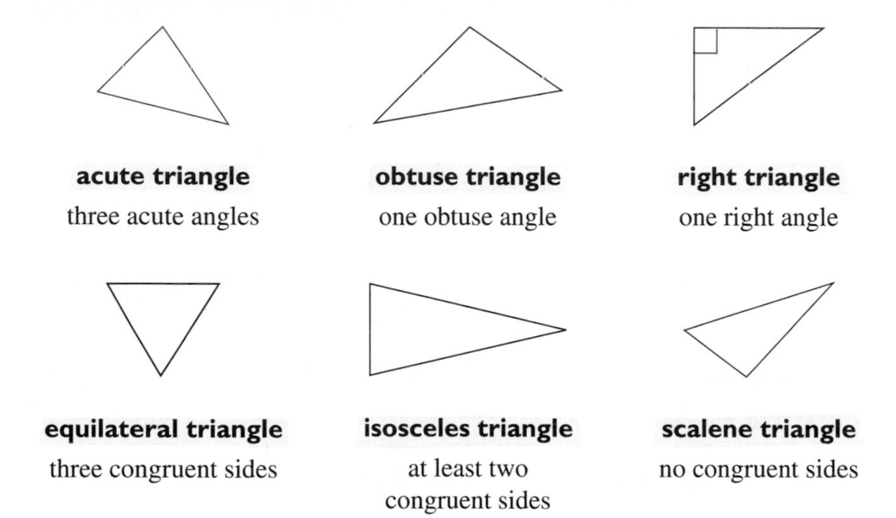

7. What is the relationship between equilateral triangles and isosceles triangles? Explain.

8. Draw each figure.
   a. a scalene right triangle
   b. an isosceles obtuse triangle

WORK TOGETHER

Work with your group. Investigate the kinds of triangles that result when you draw one diagonal in each of the following types of special quadrilaterals. For each quadrilateral describe as completely as you can all the types of triangles that might be formed.

- rectangle
- rhombus
- square
- parallelogram

Be prepared to share your descriptions with the class.

ON YOUR OWN

Judging by appearance, classify each quadrilateral. Name the congruent sides and angles.

9.

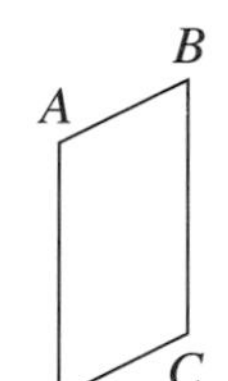

10.

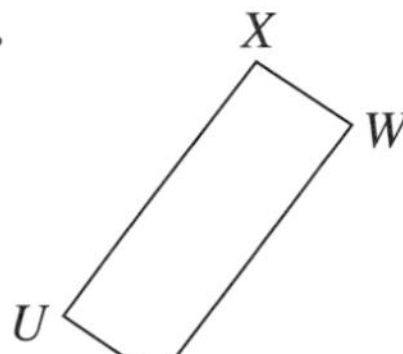

11.

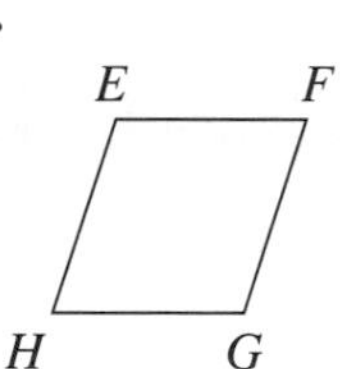

12.

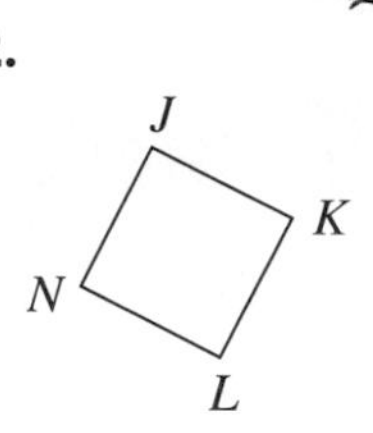

The greatest distance** flown in a glider is 303.35 mi.* ***What kinds of quadrilaterals do you see in this glider?

Source: The Guinness Book of Records

Draw and label a figure to fit each description.

13. an isosceles trapezoid

14. a scalene obtuse triangle

15. an equilateral triangle

16. an isosceles right triangle

17. a trapezoid with a right angle

18. a rhombus that is not square

Judging by appearance, name all the polygons shown that fit each description.

19. parallelogram

20. isosceles triangle

21. right triangle

22. obtuse triangle

23. scalene triangle

24. acute triangle

25. rectangle

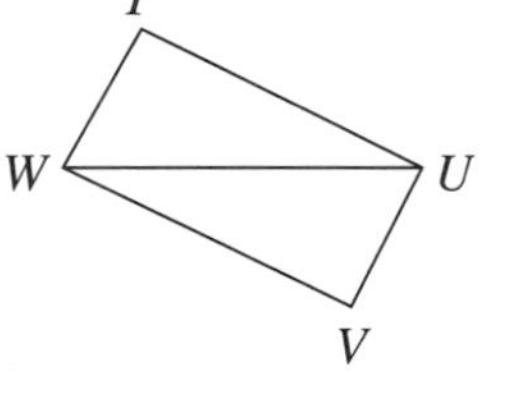

R
S
P
T

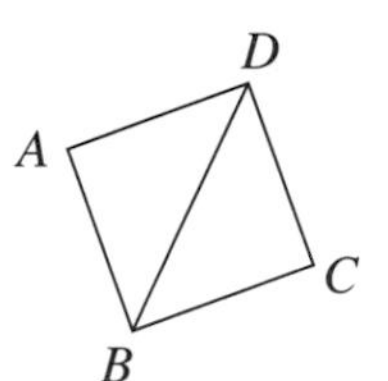

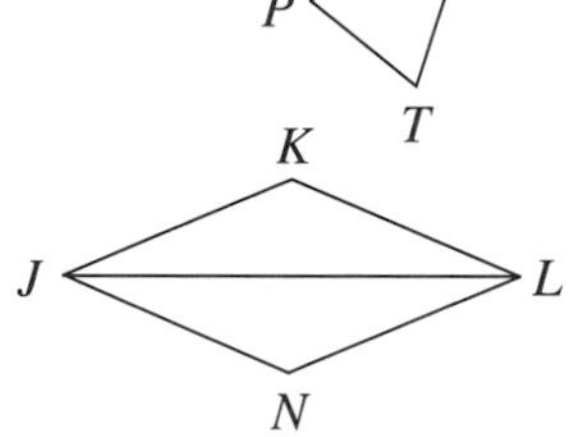

26. Choose A, B, C, or D. For which special quadrilateral is it possible for a diagonal to form two equilateral triangles?

A. square **B.** rectangle

C. rhombus **D.** trapezoid

27. Writing Explain the relationship between rectangles, rhombuses, and squares. Use words like *all, some,* and *no.*

Mixed REVIEW

Use the data: 22, 19, 26, 37, 29.

1. Make a stem-and-leaf plot.

2. Find the median and the mode.

True or false?

3. If $\triangle LMN \cong \triangle RST$, then $\angle L \cong \angle T$.

4. If $\triangle EFG \cong \triangle UVW$, then $\overline{FG} \cong \overline{VW}$.

5. A triangle has three diagonals.

6. What three consecutive whole numbers have a sum of 702?

What's Ahead

- Finding the sum of the measures of the angles of a polygon
- Finding the angle measure of each angle of a regular polygon

2-6 Angles of Polygons

WORK TOGETHER

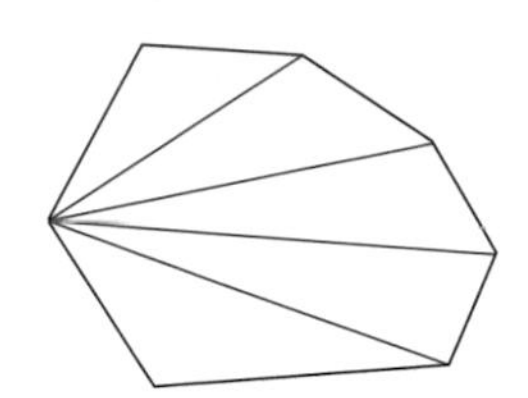

If you draw all the diagonals from one vertex of a polygon, non-overlapping triangles are formed. Then you can use the sum of the angle measures of each triangle to find the sum of the angle measures of the polygon.

FLASHBACK

The sum of the measures of the angles of a triangle is 180°.

1. Work in a group to determine the results when you draw all the diagonals from one vertex of a quadrilateral, pentagon, and hexagon. Complete a table like the one shown below.

Polygon	Number of Sides	Number of Triangles Formed	Sum of Angle Measures
Triangle	3	1	180°

2. What happens to the sum of the angle measures as the number of sides of a polygon increases by 1? Why?

3. What relationship do you notice between the number of sides of a polygon and the number of triangles that are formed when you draw all the diagonals from one vertex?

Polygon	Number of Sides
Pentagon	5
Hexagon	6
Heptagon	7
Octagon	8
Nonagon	9
Decagon	10

THINK AND DISCUSS

Angles and Polygons Apply what you have learned to find the sum of the angle measures of *any* polygon.

4. a. When you draw all the diagonals from one vertex of a *heptagon* (a seven-sided polygon), how many triangles are formed?

b. What is the sum of the measures of the angles of a heptagon?

5. a. When you draw all the diagonals from one vertex of a polygon with 100 sides, how many triangles are formed?
   b. What is the sum of the measures of the angles of a polygon with 100 sides?

6. What is the sum of the measures of the angles of a decagon? Explain how you found the answer.

If you know the measures of all but one angle of a polygon, you can find the measure of that angle.

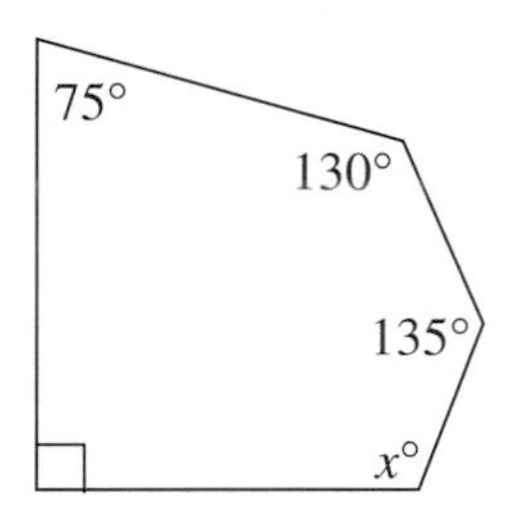

Example 1 Find the missing angle measure.

- The polygon is a pentagon, so the sum of the angle measures is 540°.
- $90° + 75° + 130° + 135° = 430°$

$x° = 540° - 430°$
$x° = 110°$

A regular polygon is a polygon with all the sides congruent and all the angles congruent.

Regular Polygons You can find the measure of each angle of a regular polygon by dividing the sum of the angle measures by the number of angles.

Example 2 Find the measure of each angle of a regular polygon with 12 sides.

- If you draw all the diagonals from one vertex of a polygon with 12 sides, 10 triangles are formed.
- Multiply the number of triangles by 180°.

$$10 \cdot 180° = 1800°$$

- Divide the sum of the angle measures by the number of angles in the polygon.

$$1800° \div 12 = 150°$$

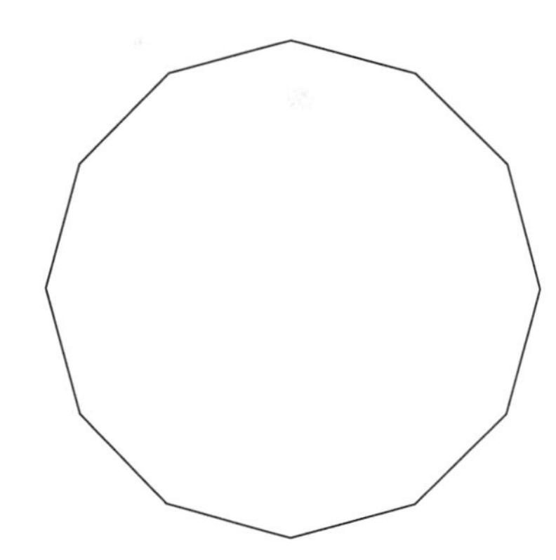

Each angle of a regular polygon with 12 sides has measure 150°.

7. a. What is the measure of each angle of a regular triangle?

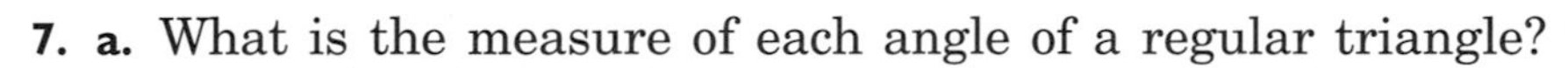

   b. What is another name for a regular triangle?

8. a. What is the measure of each angle of a regular quadrilateral?
   b. What is the special name for a regular quadrilateral?

TRY THESE

9. Two angles of a triangle have measures of 48° and 65°. What is the measure of the third angle?

10. When you draw all the diagonals from one vertex of a polygon with 14 sides, how many triangles are formed?

11. Find the sum of the measures of the angles of a *nonagon* (a polygon with 9 sides).

12. Find the measure of each angle of a regular pentagon.

What kind of ***polygons*** *do you see in the design of this kite?*

ON YOUR OWN

Classify each polygon by the number of its sides.

13. 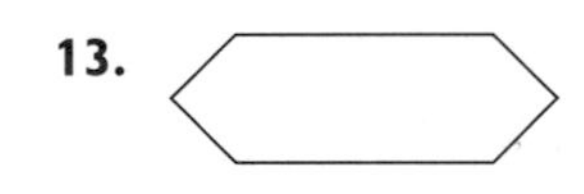

14. 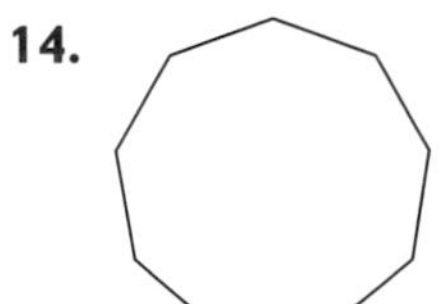

15. 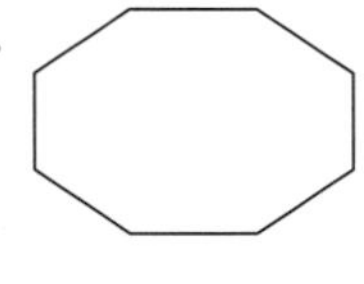

16. a polygon with 7 sides

17. a polygon with 10 sides

Find the measure of the third angle of each triangle. Then classify the triangle as acute, obtuse, or right.

18. $\triangle ABC,\ m\angle A = 79°,\ m\angle C = 23°,\ m\angle B = ■$

19. $\triangle JKL,\ m\angle K = 45°,\ m\angle L = 90°,\ m\angle J = ■$

20. $\triangle TRS,\ m\angle T = 68°,\ m\angle R = 15°,\ m\angle S = ■$

21. a. Find the sum of the measures of the angles of an octagon.
    b. Find the measure of each angle of a regular octagon.

22. Find the measure of each angle of a regular decagon.

23. What kind of triangle has two complementary angles?

24. **Writing** Explain why you cannot find the measure of each angle in a *nonregular* polygon by dividing the sum of the measures of the angles by the number of angles.

FLASHBACK

Two angles are complementary if the sum of their measures is 90°.

25. The measures of five angles of a hexagon are 145°, 115°, 152°, 87°, and 150°. Find the measure of the sixth angle.

26. Draw a large pentagon. Measure all the angles, and find the sum. Compare this to the sum of the angle measures of the pentagon that you found in the Work Together activity. If there is any difference between the sums, explain what might account for the difference.

27. **Choose A, B, C, or D.** A polygon has n sides. Which of the following represents the sum of the measures of the angles of the polygon?

A. $180°n$ **B.** $180°(n - 2)$ **C.** $180°$ **D.** $\frac{180°(n - 2)}{n}$

28. The measure of each angle of a regular polygon is 120°. Classify the polygon.

29. **Research** What is the shape of home plate in baseball? Draw a diagram of home plate and give the measure of each angle.

30. The measures of three angles of a quadrilateral are 50°, 100°, and 138°. Both Saba and Wendie used calculators to find the measure of the fourth angle.

Saba

360 [−] 50 [−] 100 [−] 138 [=] 72

Wendie

50 [+] 100 [+] 138 [=] 288

360 [−] 288 [=] 72

Whose method do you prefer? Why?

31. **a.** Draw a circle. With the same compass opening, mark six points consecutively around the circle. Connect the points to form the polygon shown.

b. Connect the vertices of the polygon to the center of the circle. Describe the triangles formed. Find the measure of each angle of each triangle.

c. Describe the original polygon. Explain your answer.

If you cut open an apple you will see that the seeds are arranged in a pentagonal pattern.

Mixed REVIEW

Make a box-and-whisker plot for each set of data.

1. 7, 9, 55, 41, 9, 52, 36, 33

2. 40, 98, 79, 77, 65, 74, 55, 90

True or false?

3. A square is always a rhombus.

4. A parallelogram is always a rectangle.

5. Two corn muffins and a glass of milk cost $1.80. One corn muffin and a glass of milk cost $1.25. What is the cost of a glass of milk?

MATH AND ART

2-7 Polygons and Tessellations

What's Ahead

- Working with tessellations

WHAT YOU'LL NEED

✓ Congruent copies of each of the following regular polygons: triangles, squares, pentagons, hexagons, octagons, decagons

WORK TOGETHER

A **tessellation** is a repeated geometric design that covers a plane with no gaps and no overlaps.

1. Use congruent copies of each regular polygon listed at the left to determine whether the polygon can tessellate the plane. Record your results in a table like the following.

Regular Polygon	Measure of Each Angle	Number of Polygons Sharing Each Vertex	Tessellation?
Triangle	■	■	■

2. Look for a pattern involving the regular polygons that can form a tessellation.

THINK AND DISCUSS

Dutch artist M. C. Escher (1898–1972) was famous for using tessellations in his art. Many of his designs used geometric figures like parallelograms, equilateral triangles, and regular hexagons that tessellate. Escher used *translations, rotations,* and *reflections* to modify each figure so that it would still tessellate.

One of Escher's woodcuts consists of 12 parts that flow into each other. In one part, black and white parallelograms alternate. Then the top of each parallelogram is changed. The change at the top is translated to the bottom of the parallelogram. Next, the right side of the parallelogram is modified. This change is translated to the left of the parallelogram.

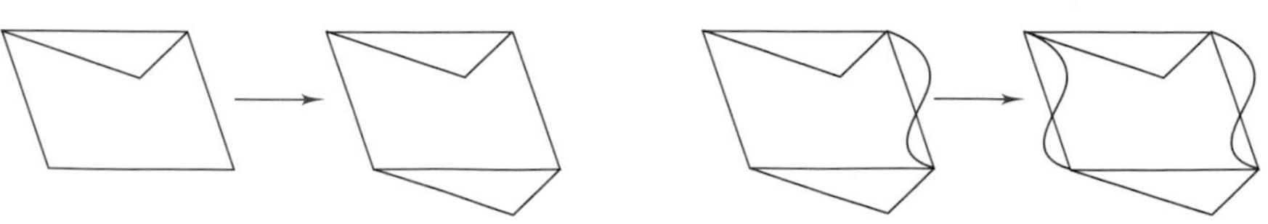

In 1960 Escher *designed this tiled facade for the hall of a school in The Hague. It was made in concrete in two colors.*

Later in the woodcut, each modified parallelogram becomes a bird and then a fish.

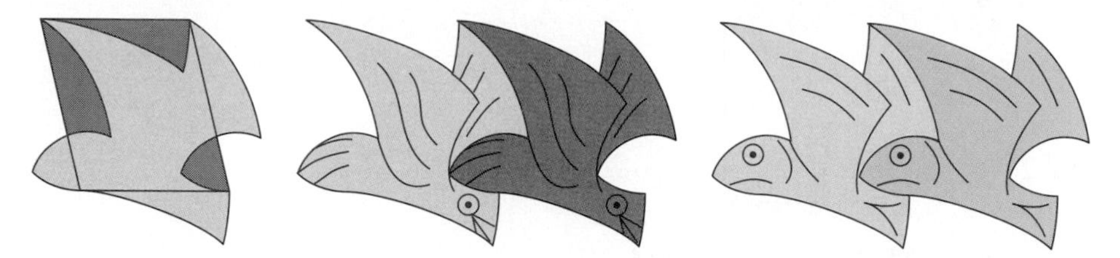

To develop the pattern for the tessellation at the right, begin with an equilateral triangle and use rotations.

3. Describe how the design is related along sides $\overline{BA}$ and $\overline{BC}$. (*Hint*: What is the center of rotation?)

4. Describe how the design is related along $\overline{AD}$ and $\overline{DC}$.

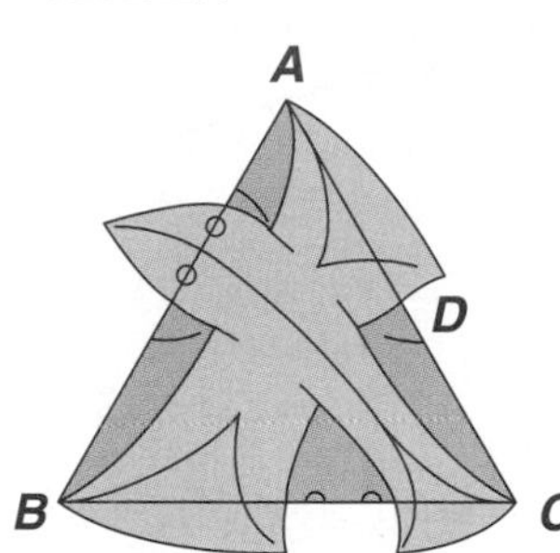

Another famous tessellating design is a reptile. It is based on a regular hexagon and rotations. First, three sides of the hexagon are modified, as shown at the left below. Then each modified side is rotated to an adjacent side, as shown at the right below.

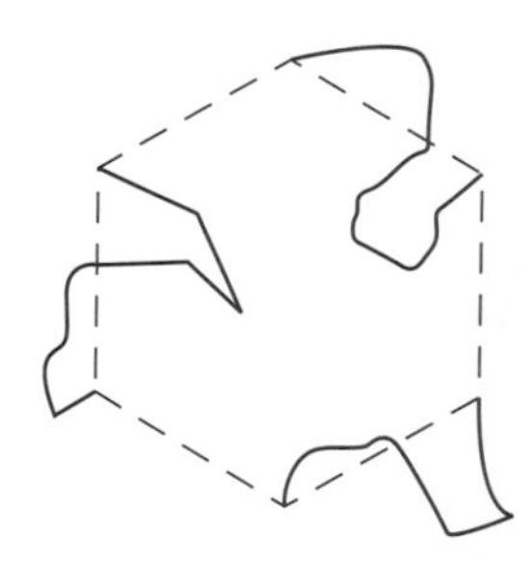

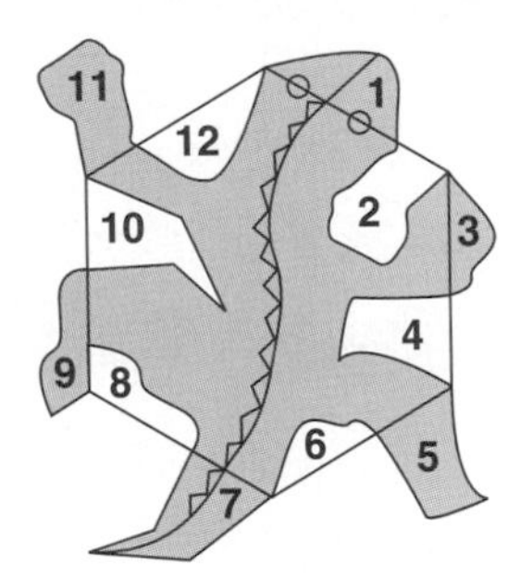

5. List pairs of congruent numbered regions.

ON YOUR OWN

6. a. Copy the design on graph paper. Use it to form a tessellation.

b. Modify the design on the top and bottom. Use the modified design to form a tessellation.

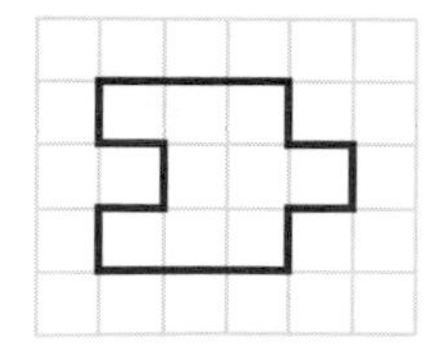

Trace each design. Use it to form a tessellation.

7.

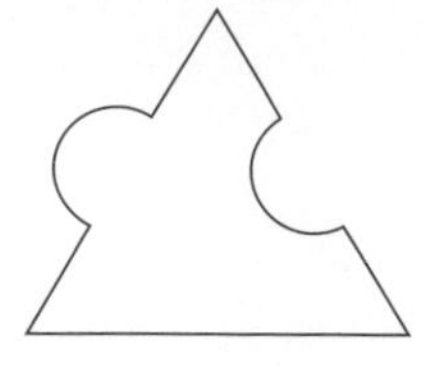

8.

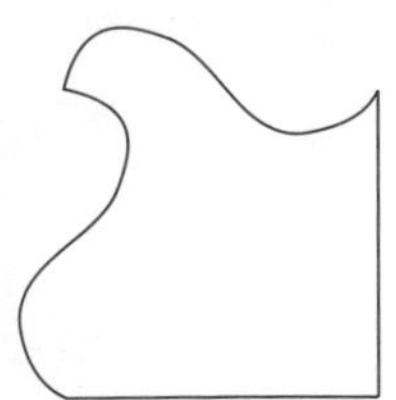

Draw each figure on graph paper. Make congruent copies to use to determine how the figure tessellates. Then draw the tessellation on graph paper.

9.

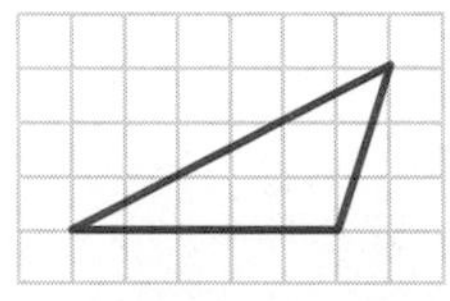

10.

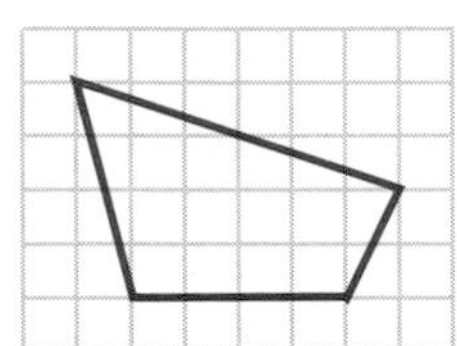

11.

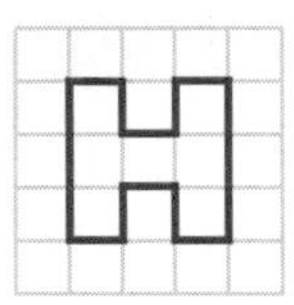

12.

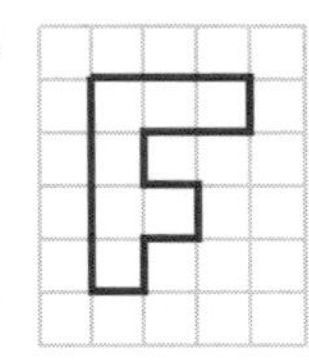

13.

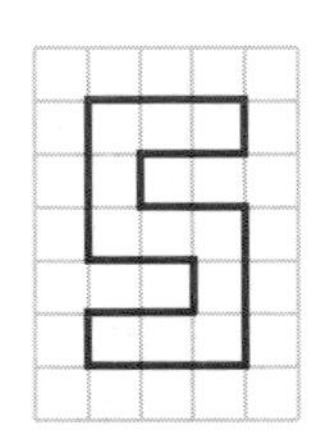

GREAT EXPECTATIONS

Paleontologist

When I grow up I would like to be a paleontologist. A paleontologist is a person who studies dinosaurs. My favorite dinosaur is Tyrannosaurus Rex. I would like to go places and look for bones and put them together in museums. I would like this career because I would like to know more about when and how they lived. My interest in this career developed when I was little and found a rabbit skeleton in the dirt in my backyard. I also build models and in a way that would be like putting together dinosaur bones.

Ken Sharkey

14. Create your own tessellation. See how interesting you can make it.

15. **Writing** Explain why a regular pentagon cannot form a tessellation.

16. **Choose A, B, C, or D.** Which of the following figures could you use to form a tessellation?

A. 

B. 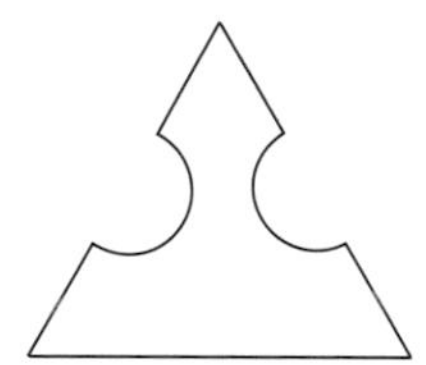

C. 

D. 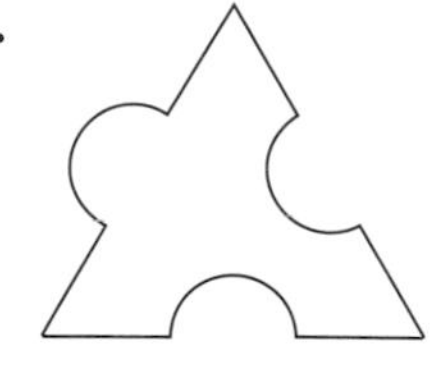

17. Trace the reptile in the Think and Discuss section. Show how it forms a tessellation.

Mixed REVIEW

1. The radius of circle O is 6 cm. $\angle POQ$ is a central angle with measure 45°. Find the length of the intercepted arc, $\overset{\frown}{PQ}$.

2. The sum of the measures of the angles of a polygon is 900°. Classify the polygon.

3. The sum of the measures of the angles of a regular polygon is 1,080°. What is the measure of each angle?

4. Toni has \$6.00, made up of equal numbers of quarters, dimes, and nickels. How many of each coin does she have?

Dear Ken,

A paleontologist is a scientist who collects and studies fossils. Fossils are the remains or traces of ancient animals and plants that are preserved in the rocks of the Earth.

Computers help us store and use huge amounts of information. We can measure dinosaur bones or the wings of flying reptiles, the pterosaurs, or any other parts of the skeletons of ancient animals. With the help of mathematics, we can compare the differences and similarities among animals. We learn more about the stresses placed on different parts of their skeletons by using mathematical formulas. Mathematics can be used to understand how an animal's shell, such as a snail shell, grew and coiled. The more we understand, the better we can recreate what these wondrous creatures did when they were alive.

Donald L. Wolberg, Paleontologist

What's Ahead

- Constructing perpendicular lines

2-8 Constructing Perpendicular Lines

WHAT YOU'LL NEED

✓ Tracing paper 

✓ Compass 

✓ Straightedge

FLASHBACK

Perpendicular lines are lines that intersect to form right angles. A line that is perpendicular to a segment at its midpoint is the perpendicular bisector of the segment.

WORK TOGETHER

Use a straightedge to draw a long segment, $\overline{XY}$, on tracing paper. Discuss with a partner how to do each of the following.

1. Fold the paper so that the foldline is the perpendicular bisector of $\overline{XY}$.

2. Label a point, P, on $\overline{XY}$ that is not the midpoint of $\overline{XY}$. Fold the paper to make a line through P that is perpendicular to $\overline{XY}$.

3. Label a point, Q, not on $\overline{XY}$. Fold the paper to make a line through Q that is perpendicular to $\overline{XY}$.

THINK AND DISCUSS

Constructing Perpendicular Lines You can use a compass and straightedge to *construct* perpendicular lines.

4. Draw $\overleftrightarrow{ST}$ and label a point, R, on $\overleftrightarrow{ST}$. Then follow the steps described below.

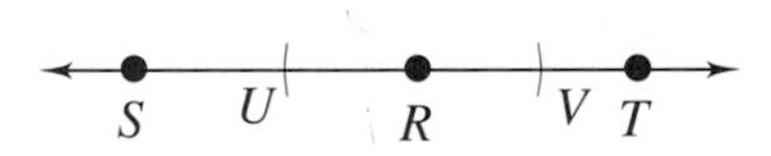

Step 1 Put the tip of the compass at R. Draw arcs intersecting $\overleftrightarrow{ST}$ in two points. Label the points as U and V.

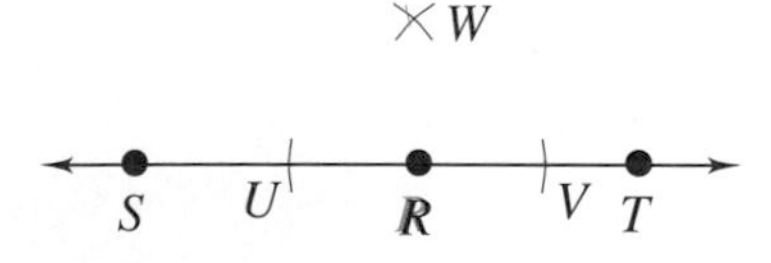

Step 2 Open the compass to more than half the length of $\overline{UV}$. Put the tip of the compass first at U and then at V, and draw arcs. Label the point where the arcs intersect as W.

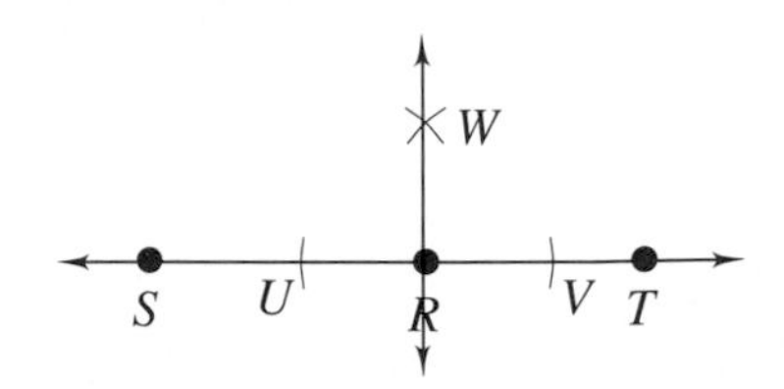

Step 3 Draw $\overleftrightarrow{WR}$. $\overleftrightarrow{WR}$ is perpendicular to $\overleftrightarrow{ST}$.

You can construct a perpendicular to a line from a point not on the line.

5. Draw $\overleftrightarrow{JK}$ and label a point, L, not on $\overleftrightarrow{JK}$. Then follow the steps described below.

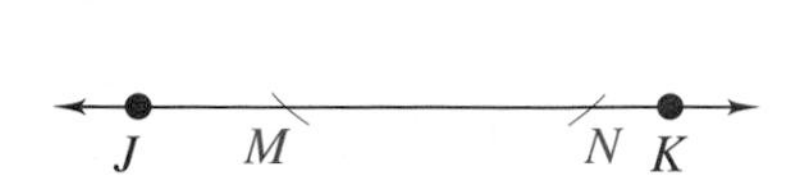

Step 1 Put the tip of the compass at L. Draw arcs intersecting $\overleftrightarrow{JK}$ in two points. Label the points as M and N.

Step 2 Keeping the compass open to the same width, put the tip first at M, and then at N, and draw intersecting arcs. Label the point where these arcs intersect as O.

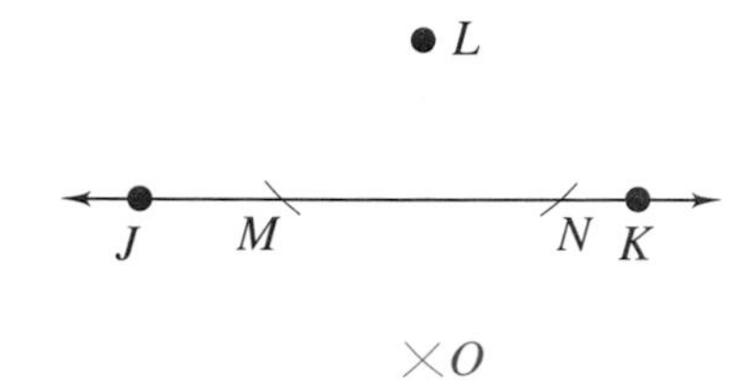

Step 3 Draw $\overleftrightarrow{LO}$. $\overleftrightarrow{LO}$ is perpendicular to $\overleftrightarrow{JK}$.

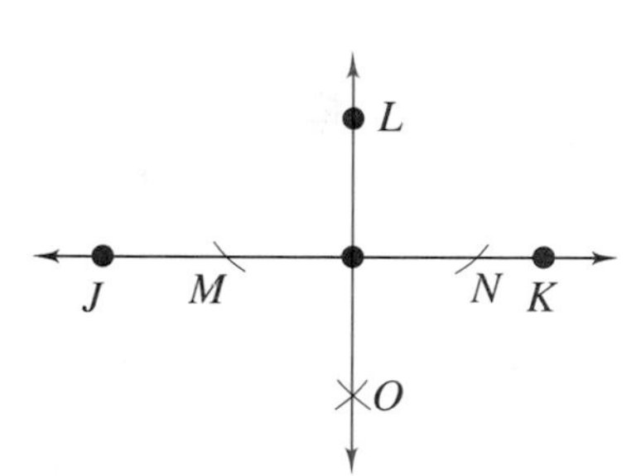

Using Perpendicular Lines

You can apply what you know about triangle congruence to prove that a construction works.

6. Critical Thinking To see why the construction above works, draw $\overline{LM}$, $\overline{LN}$, $\overline{MO}$, and $\overline{NO}$. Label the intersection of $\overleftrightarrow{JK}$ and $\overleftrightarrow{LO}$ as P.

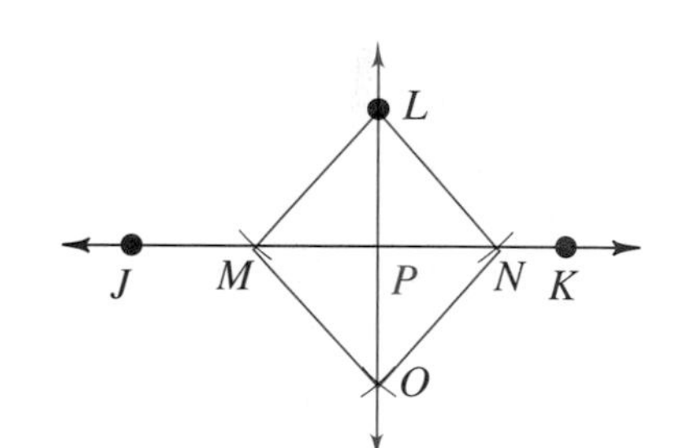

a. Why is $\triangle LMO \cong \triangle LNO$?

b. Why is $\angle MLP \cong \angle NLP$?

c. Why is $\triangle MLP \cong \triangle NLP$?

d. Why is $\angle MPL \cong \angle NPL$?

e. What are $m\angle MPL$ and $m\angle NPL$? How do you know?

7. In 6(c) you explained why $\triangle MLP \cong \triangle NLP$. Use this fact to complete each statement.

a. P is the ■ of $\overline{MN}$. **b.** $\overleftrightarrow{LO}$ is a ■ of $\overline{MN}$.

8. Critical Thinking Describe how you would construct the perpendicular bisector of $\overline{AB}$.

*The **T-square,** together with a triangle, are tools used by designers and artists to make accurate right angles. Vertical, angled, or horizontal lines can also be drawn.*

ON YOUR OWN

9. Draw a line. Label a point not on the line. Then construct a perpendicular to the line from the point.

10. Draw a line. Label a point on the line. Then construct a perpendicular to the line through the point.

11. Draw a segment about 6 cm long. Construct its perpendicular bisector.

12. **Choose A, B, or C.** Which figure shows how to construct an angle bisector?

A.

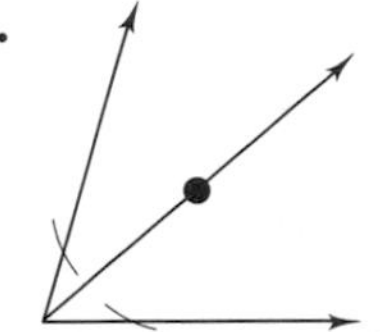

B.

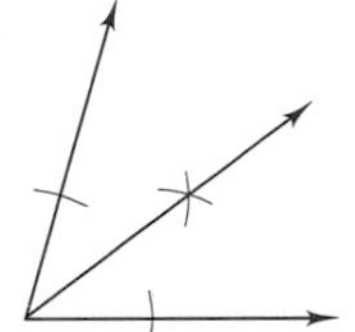

C.

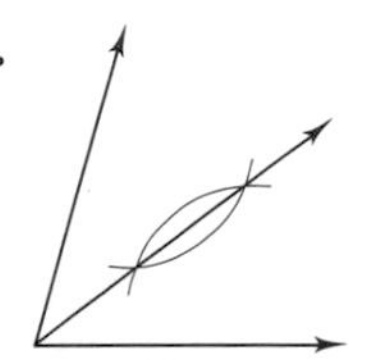

13. Draw $\overline{PQ}$ about 6 cm long. Then construct a square with sides congruent to $\overline{PQ}$.

14. Draw a segment like $\overline{CD}$ below. Construct a rectangle with $\overline{CD}$ as one side and with a second side half the length of $\overline{CD}$.

15. a. An *altitude* of a triangle is a perpendicular segment from a vertex to the line containing the opposite side. Draw a large triangle like $\triangle XYZ$. Construct the altitude of $\triangle XYZ$ from Y.

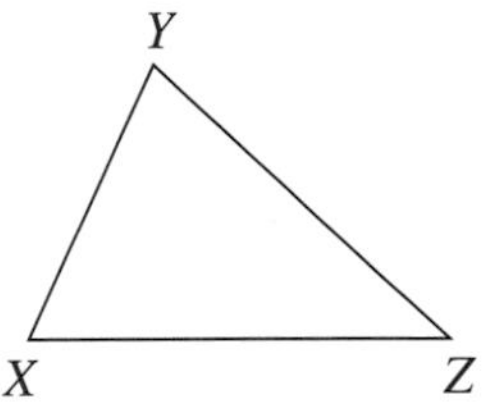

b. **Writing** If $\overline{XZ}$ is the base of the triangle, the *height* of the triangle is the length of the altitude from vertex Y. Explain how you would find the area of $\triangle XYZ$.

16. **Critical Thinking** Answer the following questions to explain why the construction in Question 4 works.

a. Why is $\triangle URW \cong \triangle VRW$?

b. Why is $\angle URW \cong \angle VRW$?

c. Why is $\overleftrightarrow{WR}$ perpendicular to $\overleftrightarrow{ST}$?

Mixed REVIEW

1. One of the acute angles of a right triangle measures 32°. What is the measure of the other acute angle?

2. Draw and label an acute scalene triangle.

3. Define *tessellation* in your own words.

4. Name two polygons that form tessellations.

5. A clock has a minute hand 8 in. long. What is the distance traveled by the tip of the minute hand in one day?

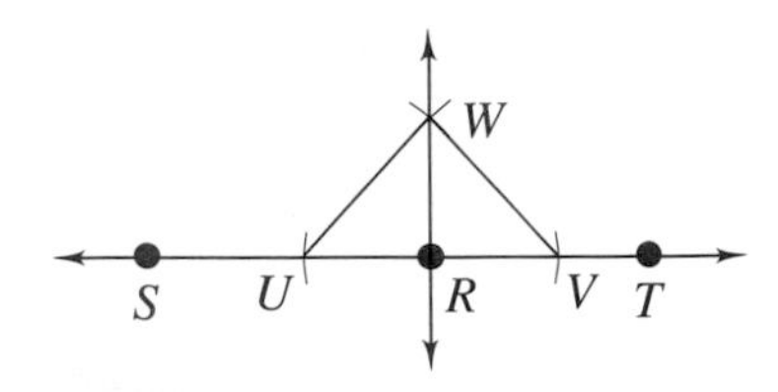

TECHNOLOGY

What's Ahead

- Working with angles formed by two lines and a transversal

2-9 Parallel Lines

WHAT YOU'LL NEED

✓ Computer 

✓ Geometry software 

✓ Protractor 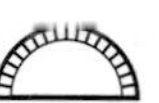

WORK TOGETHER

You don't have to be 7 ft tall or have springs in your feet to slam dunk a basketball. Some poles and backboards let you move the hoop down so that you can play above the rim. Designers often use computers to design sports equipment like this.

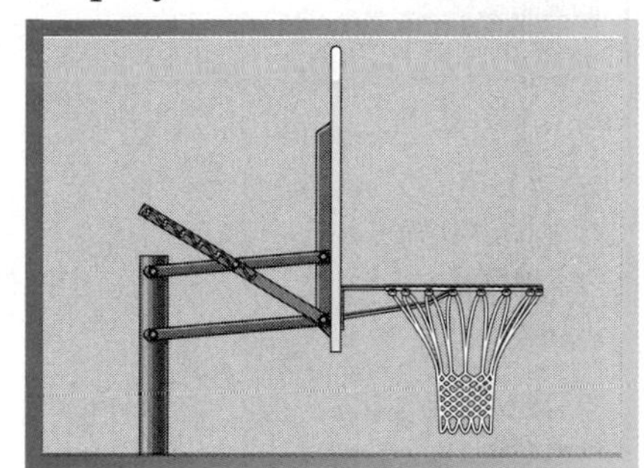

The photograph shows different positions of an adjustable backboard. The drawing shows one position of the backboard.

1. What parallel lines do you see in the drawing above?

A **transversal** is a line that intersects two other coplanar lines in different points.

2. What transversals do you see in the drawing above?

The figure shows two parallel lines and a transversal.

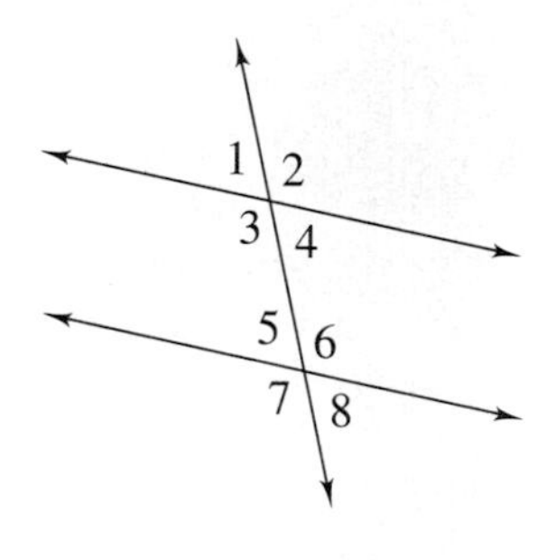

3. Name some pairs of angles that appear to be congruent.

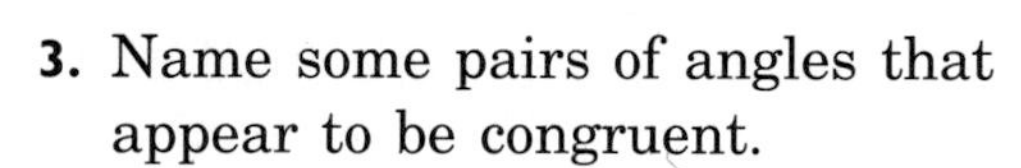

4. Name some pairs of angles that appear to be supplementary.

FLASHBACK

Two angles are supplementary if the sum of their measures is 180°.

5. a. **Computer** Create other sets of two parallel lines and a transversal. Check which angles are congruent and which are supplementary.

   b. **Writing** Summarize your results about the angles formed by two parallel lines and a transversal. Use diagrams to show which angles you are describing. Compare your summary with others in your group.

THINK AND DISCUSS

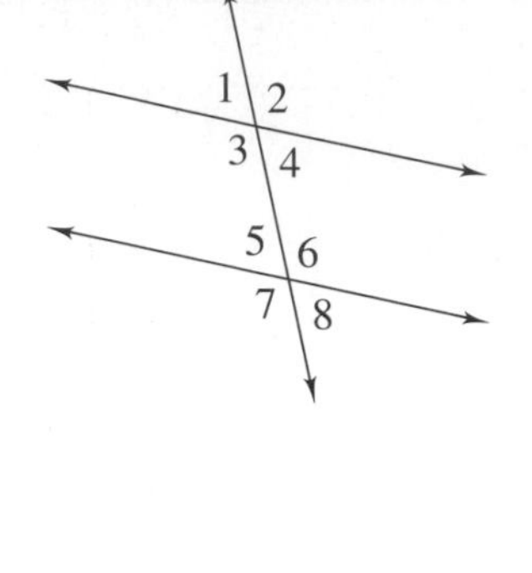

Types of Angles Some pairs of angles have special names.

Corresponding angles: $\angle 1$ and $\angle 5$
$\angle 2$ and $\angle 6$
$\angle 3$ and $\angle 7$

6. Name another pair of corresponding angles.

Alternate interior angles: $\angle 3$ and $\angle 6$
$\angle 4$ and $\angle 5$

7. Discussion Explain why these names are appropriate.

Adjacent angles share a vertex and a side, but have no interior points in common. $\angle 1$ and $\angle 3$ are adjacent.

8. Name another pair of adjacent angles.

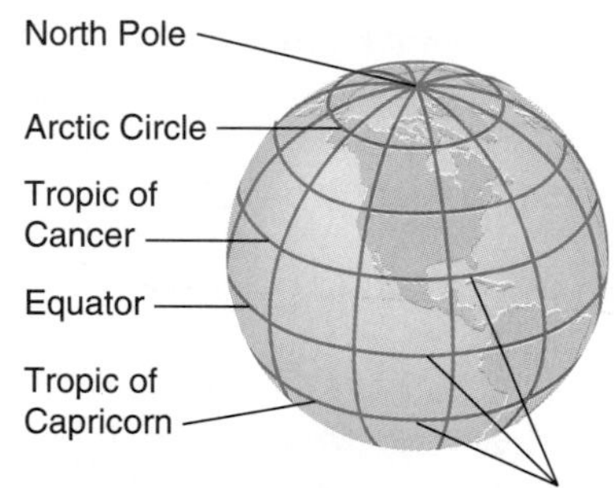

Points with the same latitude form circles. **Why do you think these circles are called *parallels* of latitude?**

These pairs of angles exist whenever two lines and a transversal intersect. The lines do not have to be parallel.

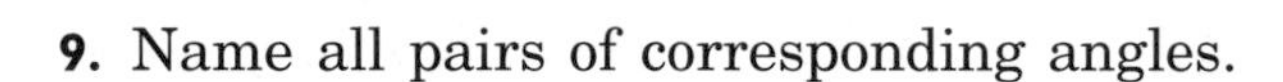

9. Name all pairs of corresponding angles.

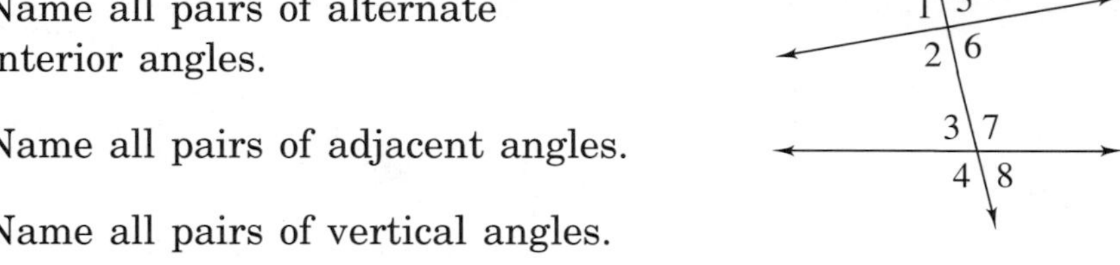

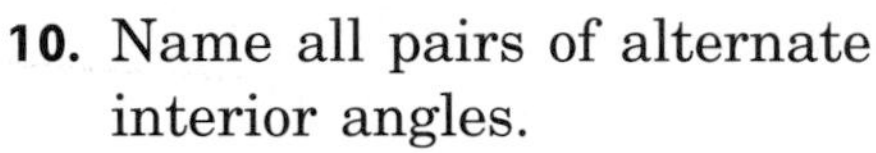

10. Name all pairs of alternate interior angles.

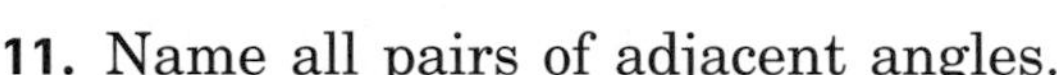

11. Name all pairs of adjacent angles.

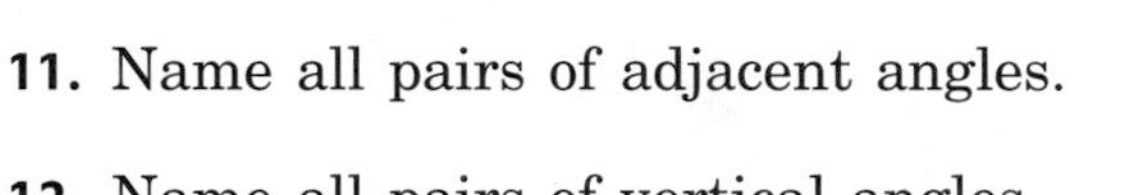

12. Name all pairs of vertical angles.

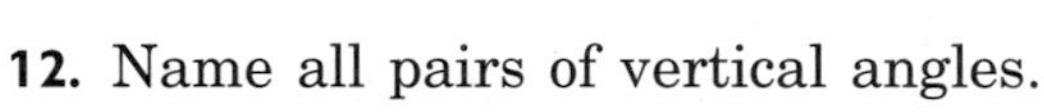

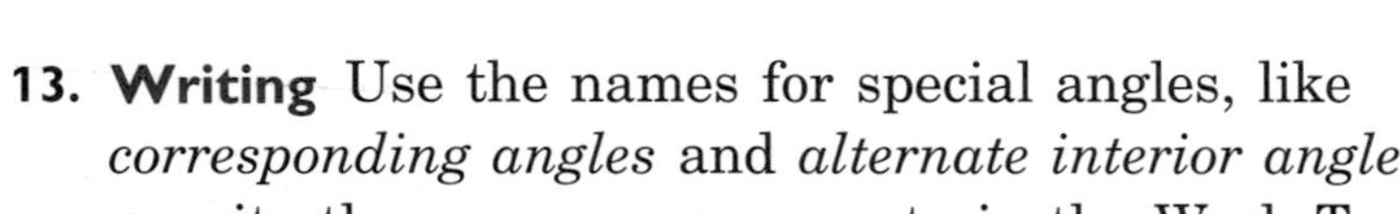

13. Writing Use the names for special angles, like *corresponding angles* and *alternate interior angles,* to rewrite the summary you wrote in the Work Together activity.

Angle Measures Use what you know about special angles to figure out the size of an angle without measuring it.

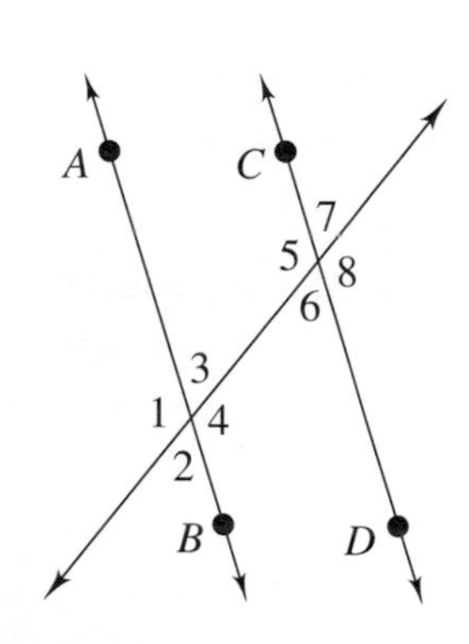

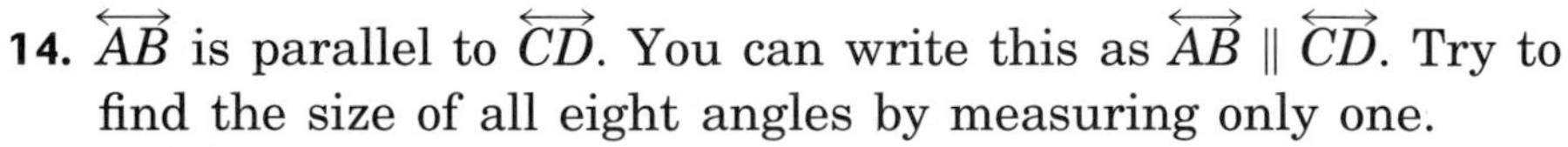

14. $\overleftrightarrow{AB}$ is parallel to $\overleftrightarrow{CD}$. You can write this as $\overleftrightarrow{AB} \parallel \overleftrightarrow{CD}$. Try to find the size of all eight angles by measuring only one.

a. Measure $\angle 3$ with a protractor.

b. How can you find $m\angle 1$, $m\angle 2$, and $m\angle 4$ without measuring?

c. What is $m\angle 5$? How do you know?

d. What are $m\angle 6$, $m\angle 7$, and $m\angle 8$?

You know that when a transversal crosses two parallel lines, certain pairs of angles are congruent. The *converses* are also true.

- If a pair of corresponding angles are congruent, then the lines are parallel.
- If a pair of alternate interior angles are congruent, then the lines are parallel.

Example $m\angle 1 = 65°$, $m\angle 2 = 65°$, and $m\angle 3 = 65°$. What kind of quadrilateral is *ABCD*?

- $\angle 1$ and $\angle 2$ are corresponding angles. Each has measure 65°, so $\overleftrightarrow{AB}$ must be parallel to $\overleftrightarrow{CD}$.
- $\angle 1$ and $\angle 3$ are alternate interior angles. Each has measure 65°, so $\overleftrightarrow{AD}$ must be parallel to $\overleftrightarrow{BC}$.

Both pairs of opposite sides of *ABCD* are parallel, so *ABCD* is a parallelogram.

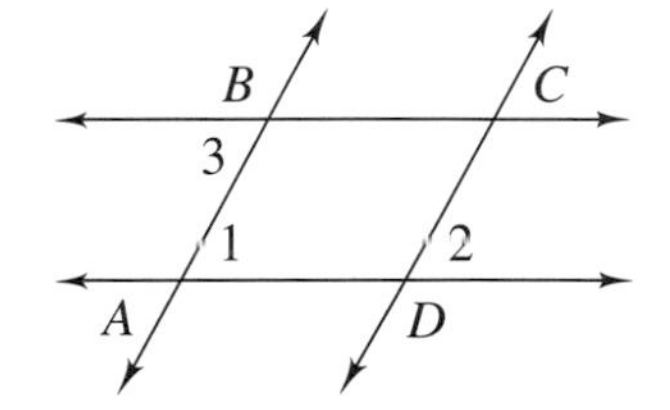

TRY THESE

15. Sports A football player runs diagonally as shown so that $m\angle 1 = 70°$. What is $m\angle 2$?

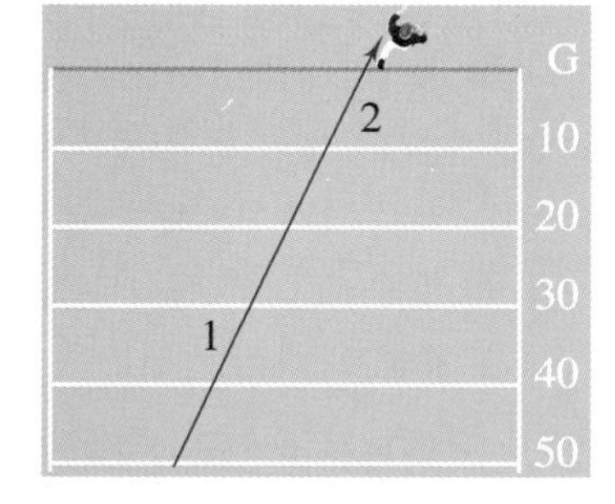

16. *QRST* is a parallelogram. If $m\angle Q = 60°$, what are the measures of the other three angles in *QRST*?

17. Critical Thinking Suppose a line intersects two parallel lines and is perpendicular to one of them. Why must it also be perpendicular to the other one?

ON YOUR OWN

Describe the angles as vertical, adjacent, corresponding, alternate interior, or none of these. Then tell whether they are congruent, supplementary, or neither.

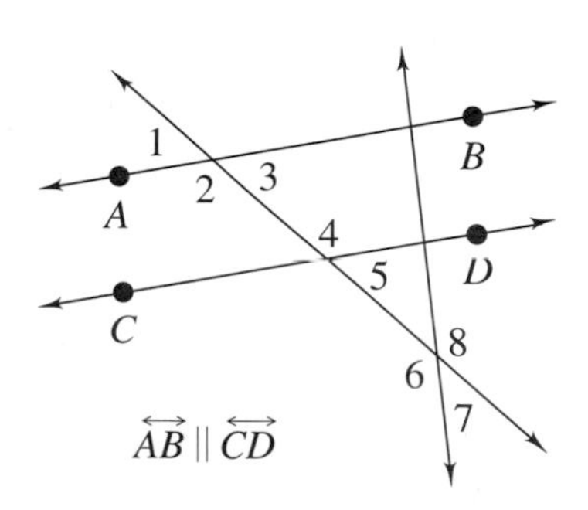

18. $\angle 6$, $\angle 7$

19. $\angle 6$, $\angle 8$

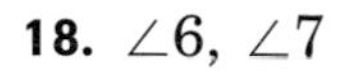

20. $\angle 2$, $\angle 4$

21. $\angle 3$, $\angle 5$

22. $\angle 1$, $\angle 7$

23. $\angle 1$, $\angle 5$

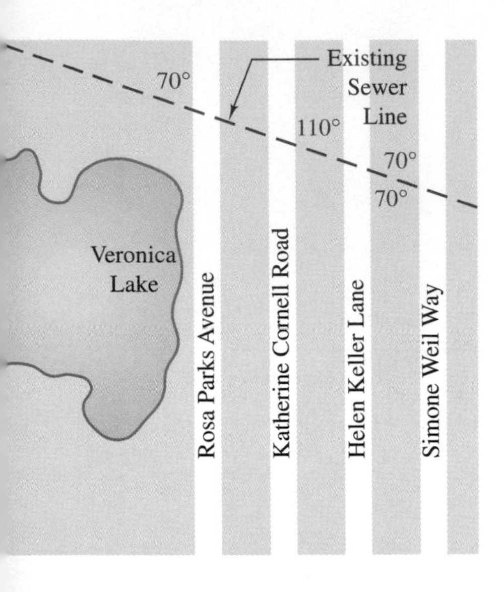

Subdivision Approved

Want to live near the lake? Now may be your chance. The town has just approved the construction of a new subdivision near Veronica Lake. The subdivision, Lakeside Estates, will consist of forty house lots situated on four parallel streets.

According to the town engineer, Beth Michael, special attention will have to be paid to the drainage system of the development. "We don't want to pollute the lake with waste from the project. Town specifications require an additional sewer line."

24. Use the plan to verify that the streets are parallel.

25. The new sewer line must be parallel to the existing sewer line and not pass through the lake. Find two possible locations for the new sewer line.

26. Aviation Four jets in an air show leave vapor trails. The trails that look parallel are. The trails that look perpendicular are. Find each measure given that $m\angle 1 = 50°$.

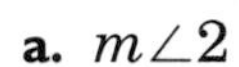

a. $m\angle 2$ **b.** $m\angle 3$

c. $m\angle 4$ **d.** $m\angle 5$

27. a. What is $m\angle EBC$? What is $m\angle C$? How do you know?

b. Writing What kind of quadrilateral is $ABCD$? How do you know?

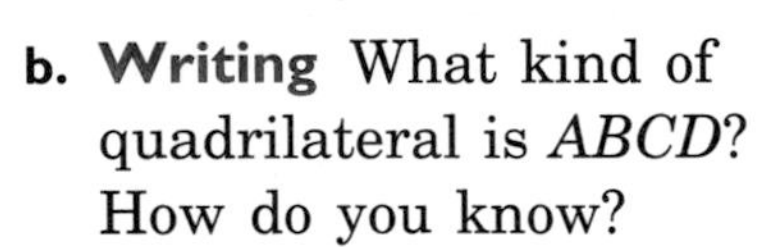

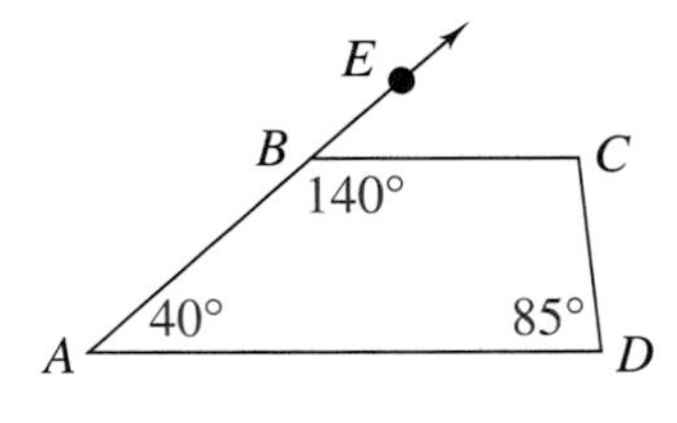

28. Computer Investigate the diagonals of parallelograms, rectangles, rhombuses, and squares. Which of these special quadrilaterals have each of the following properties?

a. The diagonals are bisectors of each other.

b. The diagonals are congruent.

c. The diagonals are perpendicular.

29. Investigation (p. 50) Study a street map of your town or city. Describe any patterns in perpendicular lines and parallel lines that you observe.

Mixed REVIEW

1. The diameter of a circle is 5 cm. Find the circumference.

2. The circumference of a circle is about 44 in. Find the radius.

3. Draw a segment about 5 in. long. Construct its perpendicular bisector.

4. Construct a line parallel to the perpendicular bisector you constructed in Exercise 3.

5. How long is the day if the sun rises at 5:42 A.M. and sets at 8:17 P.M.?

Problem Solving Practice

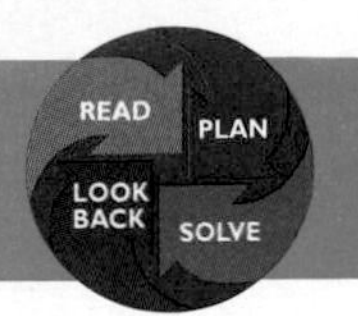

PROBLEM SOLVING STRATEGIES

Make a Table
Use Logical Reasoning
Solve a Simpler Problem
Too Much or Too Little Information
Look for a Pattern
Make a Model
Work Backward
Draw a Diagram
Guess and Test
Simulate a Problem
Use Multiple Strategies
Write an Equation
Use a Proportion

Solve. The list at the left shows some possible strategies you can use.

1. A junior high school student council has 6 members. The council wants to form a committee of 2 members to plan assemblies. How many committees of 2 people can be formed from the council of 6?

2. What is the area of the largest circle that can be drawn on a square piece of paper that is 32 in. on a side?

3. Daniel, David, and Matthew are saving all their quarters to buy baseball cards. Daniel has three times as many quarters as David. Matthew has three more quarters than David. Together they have $9.50. How many quarters does each boy have?

4. A clown was giving away balloons at a county fair. In the first half hour she gave away five more than half of the balloons. In the next 30 minutes, she gave away five more than half of the balloons she had left. At the end of one hour, the clown had only five balloons left. With how many balloons did the clown start?

5. The perimeter of a rectangle is 20 cm. Find the possible integer values for the length and width of the rectangle.

6. The Kim family is returning home after a three-week vacation. They began 2,815 km from home. After driving one day, they were 2,265 km from home. After another day of driving, they still had 1,615 km to go. After driving for a third day, they were 865 km from home. If they continued this same pattern, would they make it home on the fourth day?

7. Colleen spent $3.45 to mail a total of 15 postcards and letters. It costs $.19 to mail each postcard and $.29 to mail each letter. How many postcards and how many letters did she mail?

The biggest stamp in the world is the 75¢ stamp issued by the Marshall Islands. It measures 6.3 in. × 4.33 in.

Source: *The Guinness Book of Records*

What's Ahead

- Constructing parallel lines

2-10 Constructing Parallel Lines

WHAT YOU'LL NEED

✓ Compass 

✓ Straightedge

THINK AND DISCUSS

Our everyday world contains many representations of parallel lines: lines on a highway, opposite sides of window panes, ladder rungs.

1. What are some representations of parallel lines in your classroom?

You can use what you learned about corresponding angles to construct parallel lines.

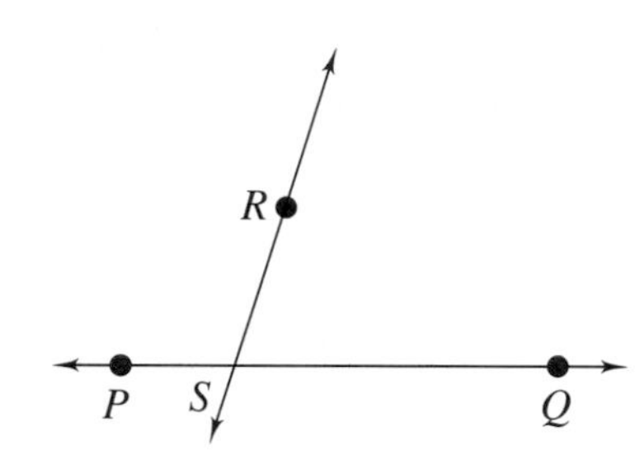

2. Draw $\overleftrightarrow{PQ}$, and label a point, R, not on $\overleftrightarrow{PQ}$. Then follow the steps described below.

Step 1 Draw a line through R that intersects $\overleftrightarrow{PQ}$. Label the point of intersection as S.

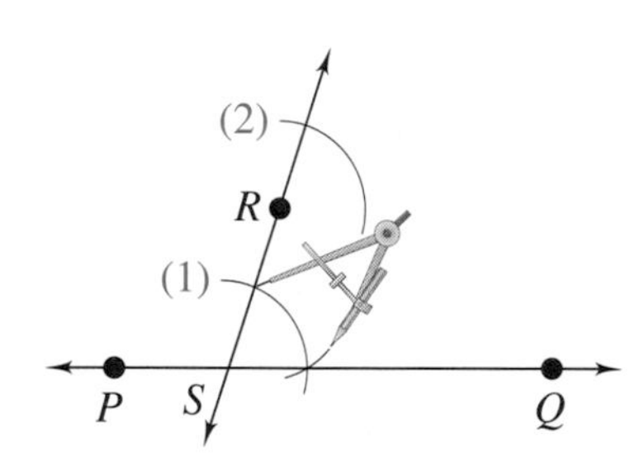

Step 2 At vertex R, construct an angle congruent to $\angle RSQ$. To do so, follow these steps:

- First put the compass tip at S. Draw arc (1). Keep the compass open to the same width. Put the tip at R. Draw arc (2).
- Open the compass as shown so that it measures the distance between the points where arc (1) intersects $\overleftrightarrow{SR}$ and $\overleftrightarrow{SQ}$.

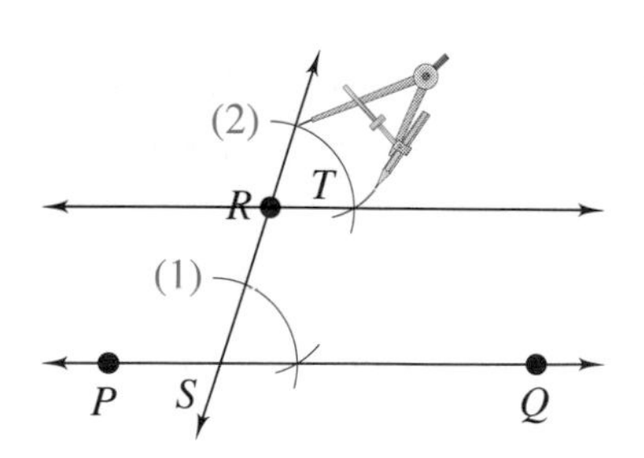

- Without changing the width of the compass, put the compass tip on the point where arc (2) and $\overleftrightarrow{SR}$ intersect. Draw an arc that intersects arc (2). Label the point where the two arcs intersect T.
- Draw $\overleftrightarrow{RT}$.

3. Explain why $\overleftrightarrow{RT}$ is parallel to $\overleftrightarrow{SQ}$.

WORK TOGETHER

A number of special quadrilaterals have parallel sides. Work with your group to construct the following quadrilaterals. Begin by drawing large figures like those shown.

4. a rhombus $ABCD$ with $\overline{AD}$ on $\overleftrightarrow{AE}$

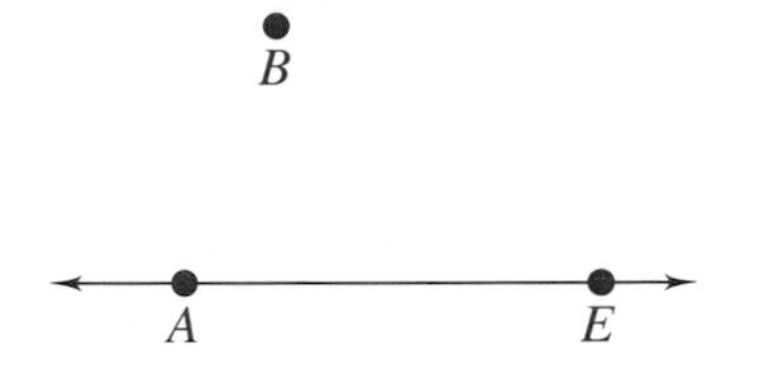

5. a parallelogram $HIJK$

ON YOUR OWN

For Exercises 6 and 7, begin by drawing a large figure like the one shown.

6. Construct a line through D that is parallel to $\overleftrightarrow{EF}$.

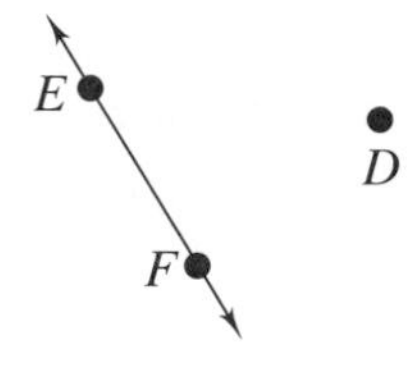

7. Construct a line through X that is parallel to $\overleftrightarrow{YZ}$.

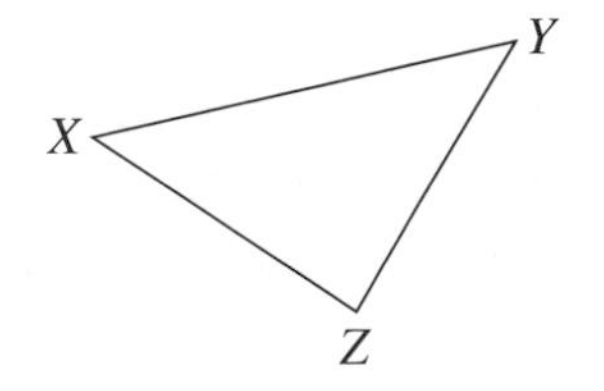

For Exercises 8–10, copy the diagram below.

8. Construct a trapezoid $RSTU$ with $\overline{SR} \parallel \overline{TU}$. Make the length of $\overline{SR}$ half the length of $\overline{TU}$.

R

T U

9. Writing Construct a line through R that is parallel to $\overline{TU}$. Use congruent alternate interior angles instead of corresponding angles. Write out all the steps.

10. Construct parallelogram $RSTU$ without constructing any congruent angles.

Mixed REVIEW

Complete each sentence.

1. A ■ has 6 sides.

2. A decagon has ■ sides.

Use the diagram. $\overleftrightarrow{EF}$ is parallel to $\overleftrightarrow{GH}$.

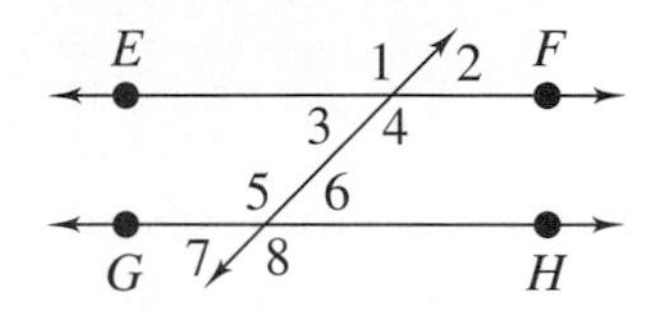

3. Name four pairs of corresponding angles.

4. Name two pairs of alternate interior angles.

5. How many of the whole numbers between 100 and 1,000 contain only 3, 4, or 5 as digits?

What's Ahead

- Finding the square roots of numbers

2-11 Square Roots

WHAT YOU'LL NEED

✓ Square tiles

✓ Calculator  

WORK TOGETHER

Work with a partner. Find the number of tiles along each side of the following squares.

- Use 16 square tiles to form a square as large as possible.
- Use 28 square tiles to form a square as large as possible.
- Use 38 square tiles to form a square as large as possible.

THINK AND DISCUSS

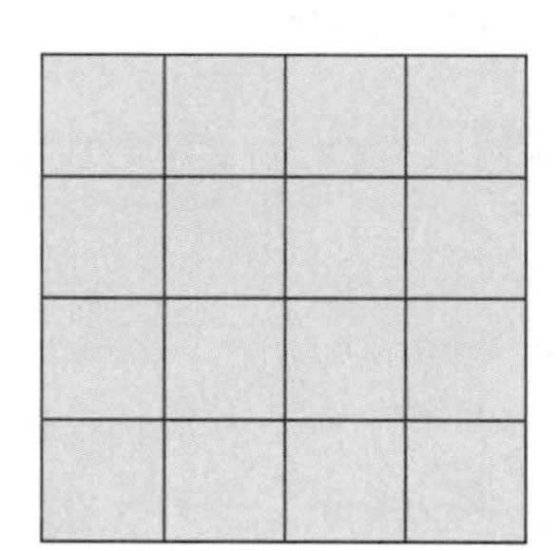

Sixteen square tiles can form a square with 4 tiles on each side.

$$16 = 4^2$$

A number like 16 that is the square of a whole number is a **perfect square.**

The opposite of squaring a number is finding its **square root.** Because $16 = 4^2$, the square root of 16 is 4. You can use the square root symbol, $\sqrt{\ }$, to write this as $\sqrt{16} = 4$.

1. What is $\sqrt{25}$?

2. Complete: $49 = \blacksquare^2$.

3. What are the squares of the first 10 counting numbers?

Mathematicians of the 1500s were the first to use the square root symbol. They chose this symbol because it looks like an *r*, the first letter of the word *radix*, Latin for *root.*

Source: *The History of Mathematics*

In the Work Together activity you found that you could not use all 28 tiles to form a square. So 28 is not a perfect square.

Example 1 **Estimation** Find two consecutive whole numbers that $\sqrt{28}$ lies between.

- The consecutive perfect squares that 28 lies between are 25 and 36.
- $\sqrt{25} = 5$ and $\sqrt{36} = 6$

$5 < \sqrt{28} < 6$

4. **Estimation** Find two consecutive whole numbers that $\sqrt{38}$ lies between.

You can use a calculator to find square roots.

Example 2 Find $\sqrt{47}$ and $\sqrt{75}$ to the nearest tenth.

- 47 $\sqrt{x}$ 6.8556546
- 75 $\sqrt{x}$ 8.660254

$\sqrt{47} \approx 6.9$ and $\sqrt{75} \approx 8.7$

5. Calculator Find $\sqrt{28}$ to the nearest tenth.

Because $(-4)^2 = 16$, another square root of 16 is -4. You can write this as $-\sqrt{16} = -4$, read as "the negative square root of 16 is negative 4." The positive square root is sometimes called the *principal square root.*

6. What are two square roots of 81?

You're a jet pilot *cruising at 40,000 ft. How far can you see? The distance to the horizon in miles is 1.23 times the square root of the altitude in feet.* ***Calculate the distance to the horizon.***

Source: *Discover*

TRY THESE

Find the square roots of the following perfect squares.

7. 100 **8.** 64 **9.** 400

Find two consecutive whole numbers that each of the following is between.

10. $\sqrt{56}$ **11.** $\sqrt{94}$ **12.** $\sqrt{125}$

Calculator Find each square root to the nearest tenth.

13. $\sqrt{56}$ **14.** $\sqrt{94}$ **15.** $\sqrt{125}$

ON YOUR OWN

Choose Use mental math, pencil and paper, or a calculator to find the length of a side of a square with the given area.

16. $A = 36$ in.^{2} **17.** $A = 100$ yd^2 **18.** $A = 144$ ft^2

19. $A = 121$ cm^2 **20.** $A = 0.01$ km^2 **21.** $A = 0.64$ m^2

22. $A = 2.25$ in.^{2} **23.** $A = \frac{9}{16}$ in.^{2} **24.** $A = \frac{49}{100}$ ft^2

Extra SKILLS PRACTICE

Find each square root to the nearest tenth.

1. $\sqrt{49}$ **2.** $\sqrt{900}$
3. $\sqrt{81}$ **4.** $\sqrt{256}$
5. $\sqrt{7}$ **6.** $\sqrt{72}$
7. $\sqrt{40}$ **8.** $\sqrt{6.4}$
9. $\sqrt{2.89}$
10. $\sqrt{170}$
11. $\sqrt{800}$
12. $\sqrt{3{,}025}$

Find the area of a square with the given side length.

25. $s = 7.5$ m　**26.** $s = \frac{1}{4}$ in.　**27.** $s = \frac{2}{3}$ yd

Find two consecutive whole numbers that each of the following is between.

28. $\sqrt{54}$　**29.** $\sqrt{148}$　**30.** $\sqrt{250}$

Find each square root. If a number is not a perfect square, approximate the square root to the nearest tenth.

31. $\sqrt{169}$　**32.** $\sqrt{53}$　**33.** $\sqrt{89}$　**34.** $\sqrt{0.27}$

35. $\sqrt{2{,}704}$　**36.** $\sqrt{3{,}481}$　**37.** $-\sqrt{289}$　**38.** $-\sqrt{191}$

39. The area of a circle is about 804 m^2. What is the radius of the circle?

40. Find the area of the smaller square in the figure. The area of the larger square is 49 $in.^2$

2 in.
2 in.　2 in.
2 in.

41. Writing Explain why you cannot find the square root of a negative number.

CHECKPOINT

Use the diagram for Exercises 1–4. Name all pairs of:

1. corresponding angles

2. alternate interior angles

3. adjacent angles

4. vertical angles

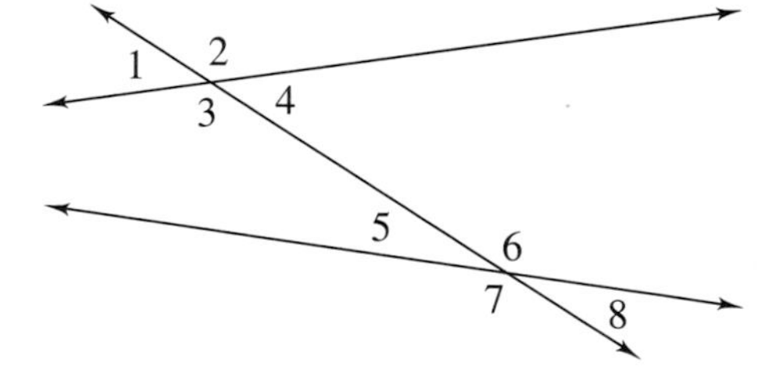

5. Construct a rectangle $HIJK$. Make the length of $\overline{HI}$ twice the length of $\overline{IJ}$.

Find each square root.

6. $\sqrt{16}$　**7.** $\sqrt{4{,}900}$　**8.** $\sqrt{0.25}$　**9.** $-\sqrt{256}$

10. Find the measure of each angle of a regular pentagon.

Mixed REVIEW

Find the circumference and area of each circle. Use 3.14 for π.

1. $r = 15$ in.

2. $d = 11$ cm

3. Draw a segment $\overline{DE}$. Construct a square $DEFG$ that has $\overline{DE}$ as one of its sides.

Find the square of each number.

4. 8　**5.** 5

6. A painter needs 15 gal of violet paint. The formula for mixing violet paint is 3 parts blue to 2 parts red. How many gallons of blue paint does the painter need?

What's Ahead

- Using the Pythagorean Theorem and its converse

WHAT YOU'LL NEED

✓ Geoboard

✓ Dot paper

✓ Calculator

2-12 The Pythagorean Theorem

WORK TOGETHER

Work with a partner.

- On a geoboard, make a right triangle with an area of $\frac{1}{2}$ square unit.
- Make squares on each side of the triangle as shown.

1. What is the area of each square?

2. **Critical Thinking** Write an equation that shows the relationship between the areas of squares I, II, and III.

On dot paper, draw a right triangle with an area of 1 square unit. Draw squares on each side of the triangle. (If you have trouble drawing a square on the longest side, model the triangle and the square on your geoboard.)

3. What is the area of each square?

4. **Critical Thinking** Write an equation that shows the relationship between the areas of the squares that you drew on the sides of the triangle.

THINK AND DISCUSS

FLASHBACK

The side opposite the right angle is the *hypotenuse*. The other sides are the *legs* of the right triangle.

Finding Side Lengths In the Work Together activity you investigated some cases of the Pythagorean Theorem.

The Pythagorean Theorem

In any right triangle, the square of the length of the hypotenuse is equal to the sum of the squares of the lengths of the legs.

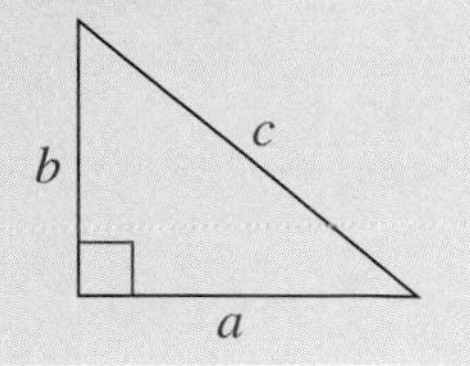

$$c^2 = a^2 + b^2$$

More proofs of the Pythagorean Theorem have been published than any other theorem. One book alone contains 370 proofs of this theorem, including one by President Garfield.

Source: *The Guinness Book of Records*

5. **a.** Which side is the hypotenuse of $\triangle RST$?
   b. Which sides are the legs?

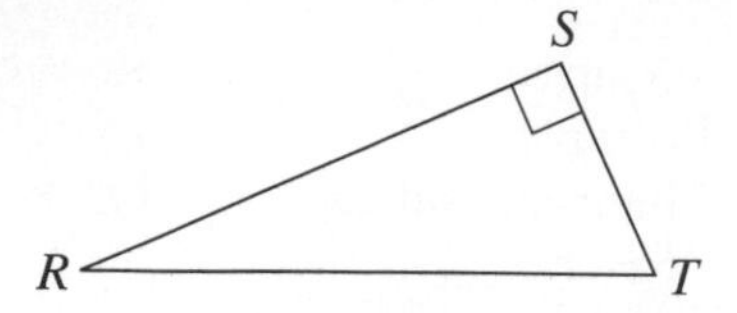

$RS = 12$ in. and $ST = 5$ in. Find the length of $\overline{RT}$.

6. **a.** What side of a right triangle is always the longest side?
   b. If 10 m, 26 m, and 24 m are the lengths of the sides of a right triangle, which is the length of the hypotenuse?

You can use a calculator to find a missing length in a right triangle.

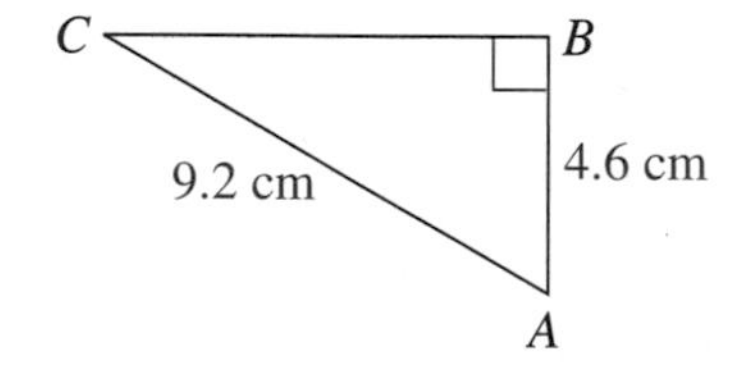

Example 1 Find BC to the nearest tenth of a centimeter.

$$AB^2 + BC^2 = AC^2$$
$$4.6^2 + BC^2 = 9.2^2$$
$$BC^2 = 9.2^2 - 4.6^2$$
$$BC = \sqrt{9.2^2 - 4.6^2}$$

9.2 [x^2] [−] 4.6 [x^2] [=] [$\sqrt{x}$] 7.9674337

$BC \approx 8.0$ cm

Finding Right Triangles If the lengths of the sides of a triangle satisfy $a^2 + b^2 = c^2$, the triangle is a right triangle.

Example 2 Is a triangle with sides 6, 11, and 9 a right triangle?

- $a^2 + b^2 \stackrel{?}{=} c^2$
- $6^2 + 9^2 \stackrel{?}{=} 11^2$ — Substitute 11 for c, the length of the longest side.

$$36 + 81 \stackrel{?}{=} 121$$
$$117 \neq 121$$

The triangle is not a right triangle.

TRY THESE

Name the hypotenuse and the legs of each right triangle.

7. 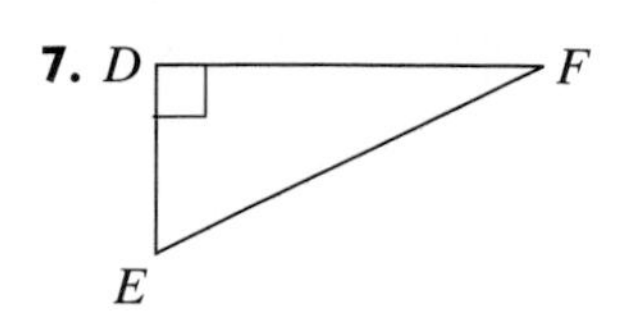

8. 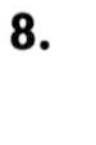 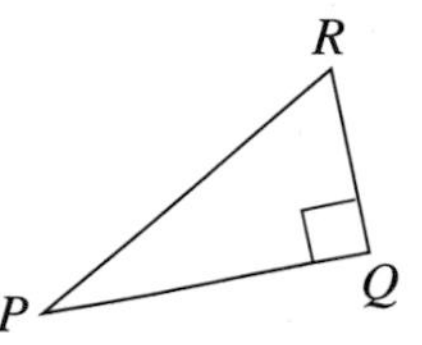

Is a triangle with the given side lengths a right triangle? Explain.

9. 4 cm, 5 cm, 3 cm

10. 8 in., 9 in., 10 in.

Calculator The lengths of two sides of a right triangle are given. Find the length of the third side to the nearest tenth of a unit.

11. legs: 7 m and 4 m

12. leg: 3 ft; hypotenuse: 8 ft

Pythagoras was a Greek mathematician born about 550 B.C. He traveled to Egypt, and spent more than 20 years there studying astronomy and mathematics. He founded a school to promote the study of philosophy, mathematics, and natural science.

ON YOUR OWN

Find the missing side length to the nearest tenth of a unit.

13.

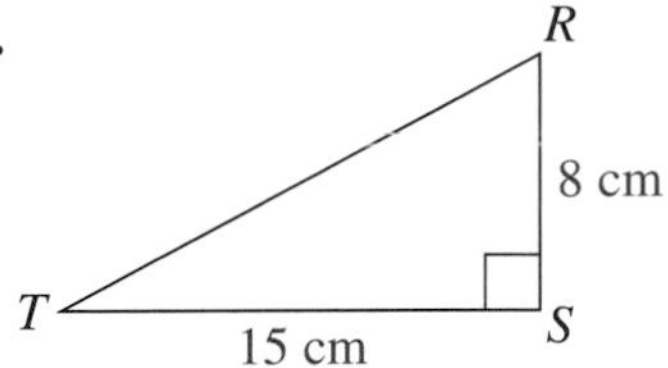

14.

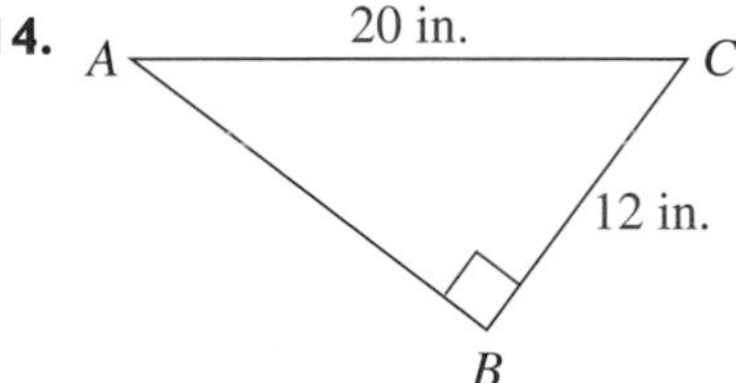

15.

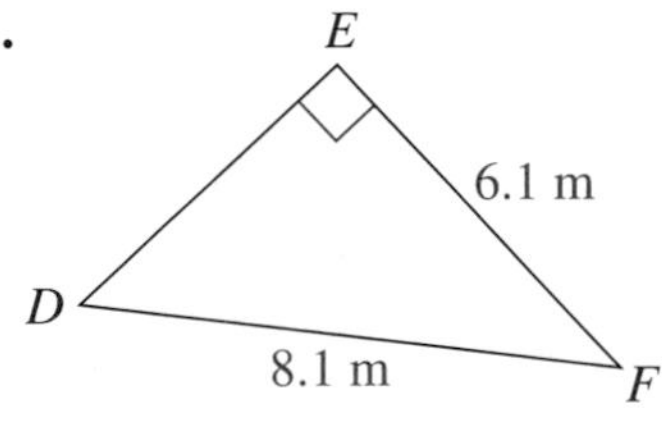

16.

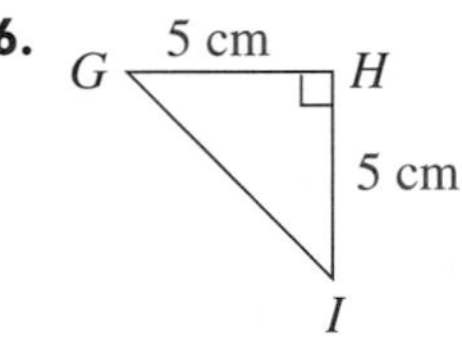

Is a triangle with the given side lengths a right triangle? Explain.

17. 16 in., 63 in., 65 in.

18. 15 cm, 35 cm, 40 cm

19. 7 ft, 12 ft, 9 ft

20. 2.9 m, 2.0 m, 2.1 m

21. 2.8 cm, 5.3 cm, 4.5 cm

22. $\sqrt{56}$ m, 9 m, 5 m

23. Each side of a square is 17 cm long. Find the length of a diagonal to the nearest tenth.

24. **Writing** Describe a situation in your everyday life where you could use the Pythagorean Theorem to find a length or distance.

Problem Solving Hint

Draw a diagram.

Extra SKILLS PRACTICE

The hypotenuse and one side of a right triangle are given. Find the length of the other side to the nearest tenth.

1. 5 cm, 2 cm
2. 10 m, 7 m
3. 20 ft, 12 ft
4. 11 yd, 4 yd
5. 41 m, 27 m
6. 80 ft, 45 ft
7. 7.2 cm, 3.4 cm
8. 26.4 m, 18.3 m
9. 31.4 m, 10.2 m
10. 78.6 m, 32.1 m

25. Measure a, b, and c to the nearest 0.1 cm.

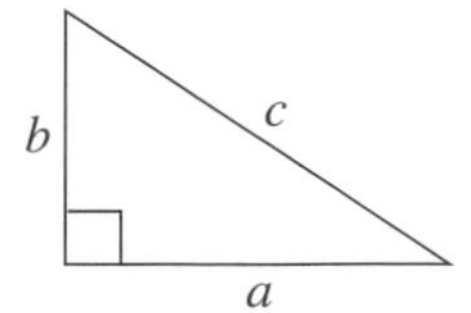

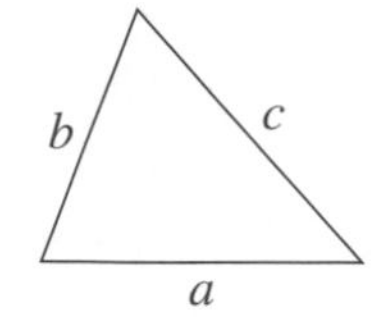

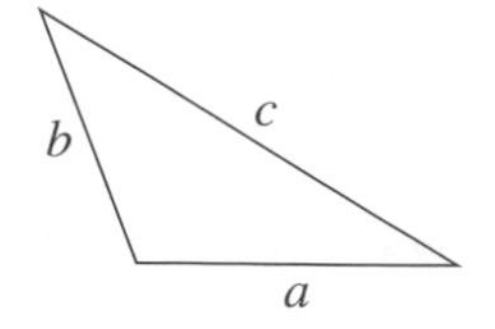

a. **Critical Thinking** How do $a^2 + b^2$ and c^2 compare for an acute triangle?

b. **Critical Thinking** How do $a^2 + b^2$ and c^2 compare for an obtuse triangle?

26. Oceanography A diver swims 20 m underwater to the place where a buoy is anchored 10 m below the surface of the water. How far is the buoy on the surface located from the place where the diver started?

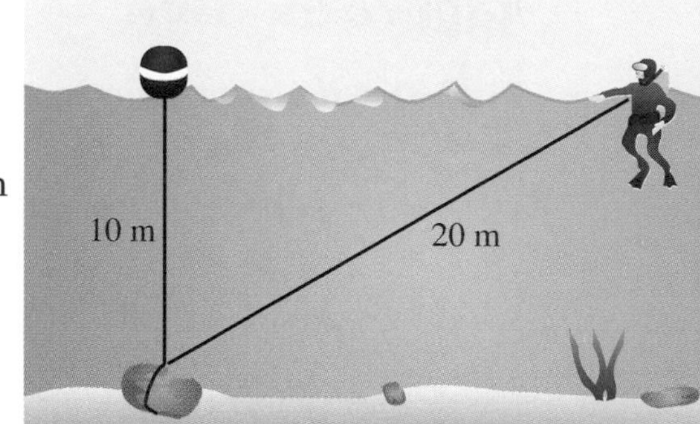

27. Hobbies Two hikers started their trip from base camp by walking 15 m due east. They then turned due north, walking 17 m to a large pond. How far is the pond from the base camp, to the nearest tenth of a meter?

28. Janet walked 110 m north on Walnut Street. Then she turned east and walked another 75 m. Pearl left from the same place as Janet, but she cut across the block on a diagonal and met Janet. Who walked farther? How much farther, to the nearest meter?

29. Choose A, B, C, or D. The length of each side of a regular hexagon is 1 unit. What is the length of a perpendicular segment that joins opposite sides of the hexagon?

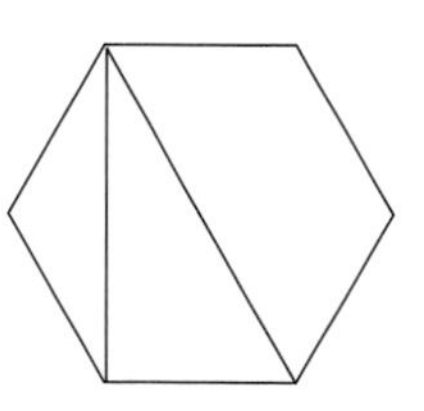

A. 1 **B.** 2 **C.** about 2.2 **D.** about 1.7

30. Any three counting numbers that satisfy $a^2 + b^2 = c^2$ form a *Pythagorean triple.* For example, 3, 4, 5 is a Pythagorean triple. Find at least five more Pythagorean triples.

31. Investigation (p. 50) Use a street map of your city or town. Show how to use the Pythagorean Theorem to find the distance between two important points on the map.

Mixed REVIEW

Complete each sentence with mean, median, or mode.

1. The ■ is the data item that occurs most often.
2. The middle value in a set of data is the ■.

Find each square root.

3. $\sqrt{81}$ 4. $\sqrt{121}$

5. Sandy earns $40 for an 8-hour workday. How many hours does she have to work to earn enough to buy a $7.50 movie ticket?

Practice

Use circle E at the right for Exercises 1–8.

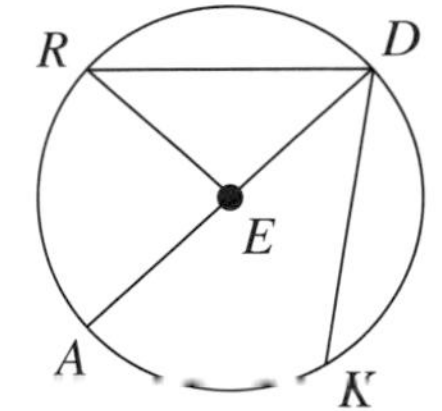

1. Name all radii.
2. Name an inscribed angle.
3. Name all chords.
4. Name a central angle.
5. If $m\angle AER = 80°$, find $m\angle ADR$.
6. If $m\angle ADR = 45°$, find $m\angle AER$.
7. If circle E has a diameter of 1.5 m, find its area and circumference. Use $\pi \approx 3.14$.
8. If circle E has a circumference of 314 ft, find its area.

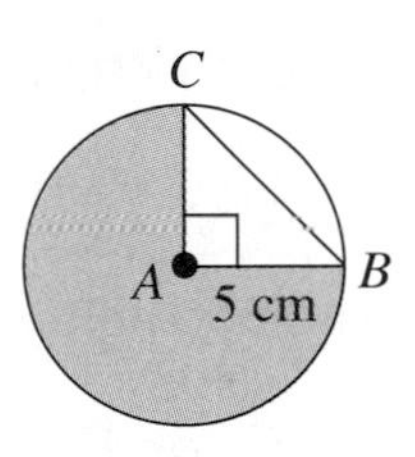

9. Find the area of the shaded region in circle A at the right.
10. Find BC to the nearest tenth of a centimeter.

$\triangle HLQ \cong \triangle DBF$. Find each measure.

H
10 70° 11.3
60°
L Q
12.3

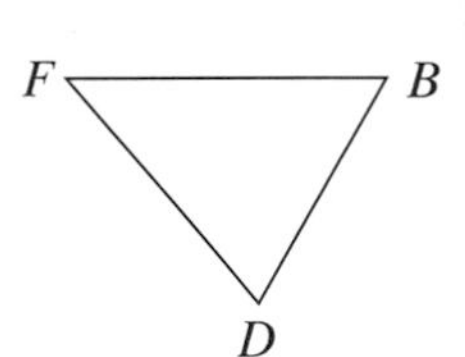

11. $m\angle B$
12. $m\angle F$
13. DF

Write *true* or *false*. Draw a figure to justify your answer.

14. Every rhombus is a square.
15. A trapezoid can have three right angles.
16. Every square is a rectangle.

Find the measures of the numbered angles.

17.

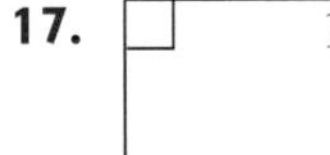
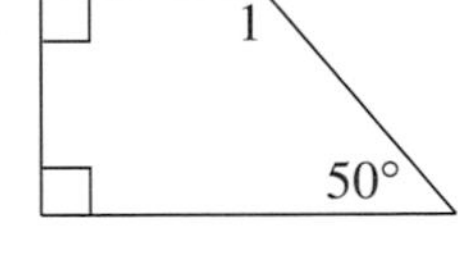

18.

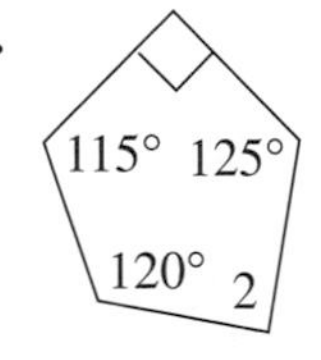

19.

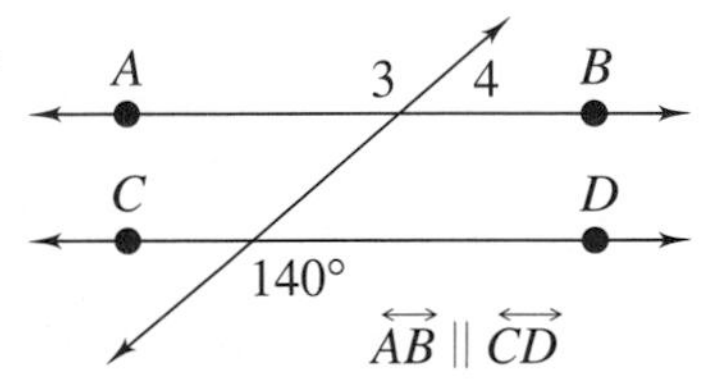

20. Draw $\overline{AB}$. Construct its perpendicular bisector.
21. Is a triangle with sides 15, 20, and 25 a right triangle? Explain.

Wrap Up

Circles 2-1, 2-2

An angle that has its vertex at the center of a circle is a ***central angle*** of the circle. An angle that has its vertex on a circle is an ***inscribed angle*** of the circle. If a central angle and an inscribed angle have the same intercepted arc, the measure of the central angle is twice the measure of the inscribed angle.

The distance around a circle is the ***circumference of the circle;*** $C = \pi d$.

To find the ***area of a circle,*** use the formula $A = \pi r^2$.

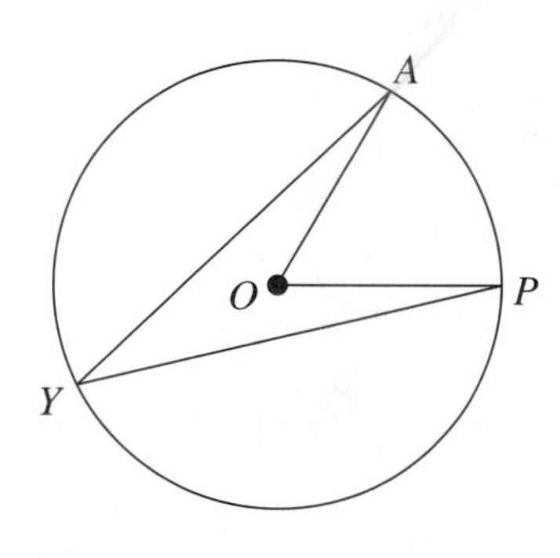

1. If $m\angle AOP = 60°$, what is $m\angle AYP$?

2. Find the circumference and area of circle O if $AO = 6$ cm.

3. Choose A, B, C, or D. If $m\angle AYP = 30°$ and $OP = 3.5$ in., find the length of $\widehat{AP}$.

A. 7.0 in. **B.** 3.7 in. **C.** 1.8 in. **D.** 6.4 in.

Polygons 2-4, 2-5, 2-6

Polygons that have the same size and shape are ***congruent.*** You can use SAS, ASA, or SSS to show that two triangles are congruent. You can classify triangles by angles and by sides. Some types of quadrilaterals have special names.

To find the sum of the measures of the angles of a polygon, subtract 2 from the number of sides, and multiply the result by 180°. To find the measure of each angle of a regular polygon, divide the sum of the angle measures by the number of angles.

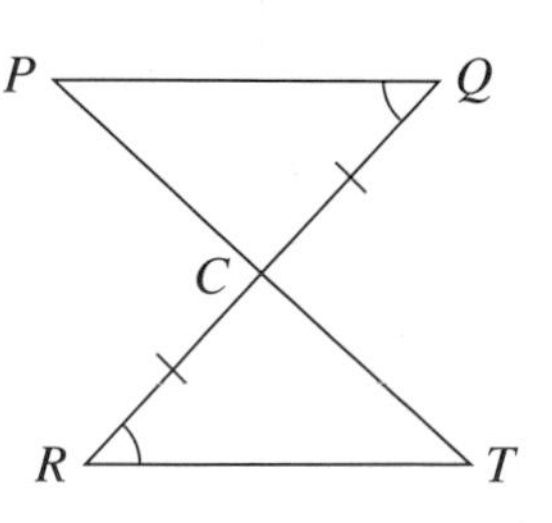

4. Are the triangles in the figure congruent? If so, write a congruence and tell why they are congruent.

5. If $m\angle R = 48°$, and $m\angle T = 42°$, find $m\angle PCQ$.

6. Writing Explain why a square is a rectangle.

7. Find the sum of the measures of the angles of an octagon.

8. Find the measure of each angle of a regular hexagon.

Perpendicular and Parallel Lines — 2-8, 2-9, 2-10

If two parallel lines are cut by a transversal, ***corresponding angles*** and ***alternate interior angles*** are congruent. You can use this information to construct perpendicular and parallel lines.

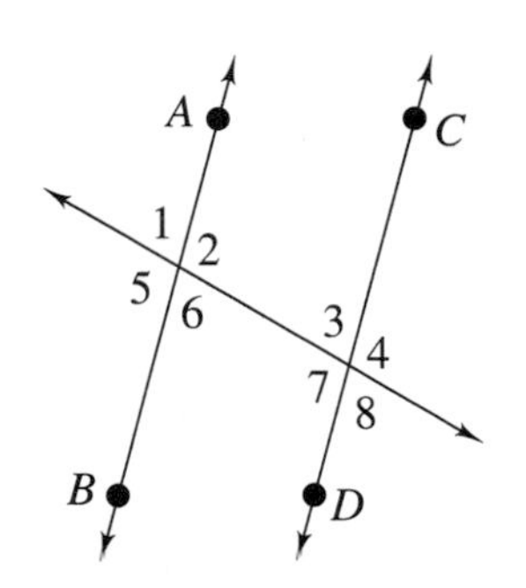

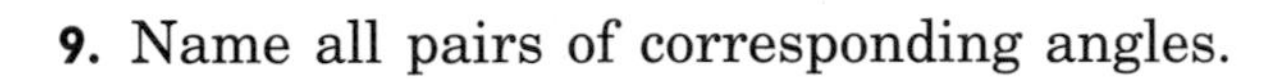

9. Name all pairs of corresponding angles.

10. $\overleftrightarrow{AB} \parallel \overleftrightarrow{CD}$. Which angles are congruent to $\angle 3$?

11. $\overleftrightarrow{AB} \parallel \overleftrightarrow{CD}$, and $m\angle 6 = 75°$. Find $m\angle 7$.

12. Draw $\triangle PQR$. Construct a line through Q parallel to $\overline{PR}$.

Square Roots and the Pythagorean Theorem — 2-11, 2-12

The inverse of squaring a number is finding its ***square root.*** You can use the ***Pythagorean Theorem*** to find unknown parts of a right triangle: If a and b are the lengths of the legs, and c is the length of the hypotenuse, then $c^2 = a^2 + b^2$.

Find each square root.

13. $\sqrt{81}$ **14.** $\sqrt{0.64}$ **15.** $-\sqrt{121}$ **16.** $\sqrt{225}$

17. The foot of a 20-ft ladder is 12 ft from the base of a house. How far up the side of the house does the ladder reach?

Patterns — 2-3, 2-7

A ***tessellation*** uses geometric figures to cover a plane with no gaps or overlaps.

18. Copy the figure on graph paper and use it to form a tessellation.

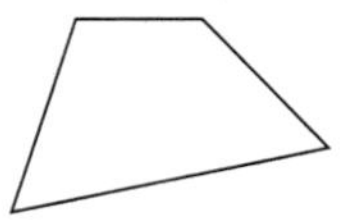

Identifying patterns can be helpful in solving problems.

19. A telephone call costs 25¢ for 1 min, 34¢ for 2 min, and 43¢ for 3 min. How much will a 6-min call cost?

GETTING READY FOR CHAPTER 3

To evaluate a variable expression, substitute numbers for the variables and follow the order of operations.

Evaluate each expression for $a = 3$, $b = 5$, and $c = 10$.

1. $8b$ **2.** $a + c$ **3.** $4 \cdot b - 2 \cdot a$ **4.** $\frac{6b}{ac}$ **5.** $a(b + c)$ **6.** $a \cdot b + c$

The Shortest Route

The City Transportation Commission is looking for people who can help map out efficient routes for commuters. The commission has heard about the routes you worked out to connect your home and five weekend destinations. Look again at those routes. Revise them based on your study of the chapter. Then write a letter to the commission describing your findings. Explain the reasoning that led you to choose the shortest route and the fastest route.

The problems preceded by the magnifying glass (p. 53, # 30; p. 60, # 17, p. 82, # 29; and p. 92, # 31) will help you prepare your letter.

Excursion: The map shows seven bridges connecting the city of Kaliningrad, Russia, with two islands in the Pregel River. Is it possible to take a walk and cross each bridge exactly once?

This is a 4-hexagon by 4-hexagon game board for a 2-person game of HEX. Players alternate marking single hexagons. Players X and Y try to build an unbroken chain of x's and y's between their sides. Corner hexagons belong to both players. When playing, a player may mark any hexagon on the board except one already marked.

- Play HEX several times. There is a winning strategy for the first player. Can you find it?
- The standard HEX board measures 11 hexagons by 11 hexagons. Draw a standard board.
- Play the game with a friend at home.

Y X X Y

PYTHAGOREAN BASEBALL

Baseball statistician Bill James has found a Pythagorean relationship among several variables in baseball.

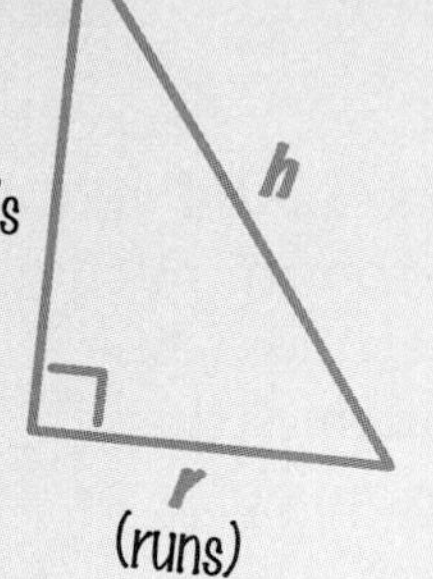

- Choose a baseball team. In an almanac find r, the number of runs the team scored last season.
- Find o, the number of runs all the team's opponents scored last season. If the almanac does not give o, you can use the team's pitchers' earned run average (ERA) and number of innings pitched (IP) to find o:

$$o = \frac{\text{ERA} \times \text{IP}}{9}$$

- Use the Pythagorean theorem to find h. ($h^2 = r^2 + o^2$).
- James discovered that the value $\left(\frac{r}{h}\right)^2 \times 162$ (there are 162 games in a season) estimates the number of games won by a team during any season. Calculate the value for the team you chose and compare with others. What do you notice?

This design was constructed with a compass and straightedge.

Create your own geometric designs by using a compass and straightedge. For each design, write a list of directions that explains how to create the design. Share your directions with a friend. Can your friend follow your directions to make the same design?

***Excursion** Describe how the design shown was created.*

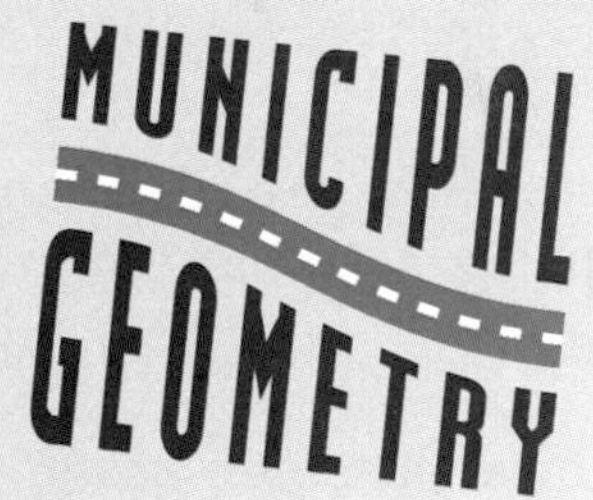

Some cities' streets and transportation routes appear random, while others' are organized. The winding streets of Boston are said to have been laid out to follow the meandering cow paths that preceded them. At the other extreme, the subway routes of Washington, D.C. form a precise pattern of wheel spokes overlying a regular checkerboard of intersecting streets.

- Choose a city. Get maps of the city's streets and transportation networks.
- How does the layout of the street map compare with the transportation network? Is it more like Boston's or Washington, D.C.'s?
- Describe any geometric patterns in the network.
- Tell how these patterns contribute to the efficiency of the network.

Assessment

1. Draw $\triangle ABC$ like the one shown, but larger. Construct a line through A that is perpendicular to $\overline{BC}$.

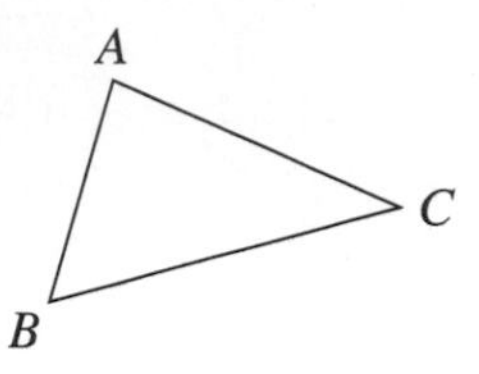

2. **Choose A, B, C, or D.** In $\triangle LMC$, $LM = 6$, $MC = 8$, and $LC = 10$. Which phrase best describes $\triangle LMC$?

   A. right isosceles **B.** right scalene

   C. acute scalene **D.** obtuse isosceles

3. Circle K has a radius of 5.8 cm. Find the:

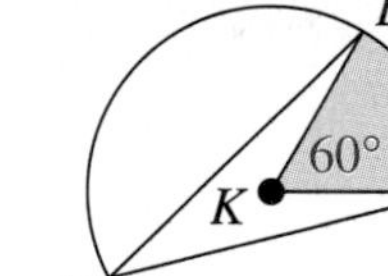

   a. area of circle K.

   b. circumference of circle K.

   c. length of $\widehat{AE}$.

   d. area of the shaded region.

   e. $m\angle EDA$.

4. **Writing** How are a rectangle and a parallelogram alike? How are they different?

5. To run a classified ad for 7 days costs \$28 for 4 lines. Each additional line costs \$6.50. What is the cost of a 10-line ad?

6. Write *true* or *false*.

   a. An equilateral triangle is always isosceles.

   b. An obtuse triangle can be a right triangle.

   c. A scalene triangle can be obtuse.

7. Find the sum of the measures of the angles of a decagon.

8. Can a triangle with sides 2 cm, 4 cm, and 5 cm long be a right triangle? Explain.

9. Find each square root.

   a. $\sqrt{169}$ b. $\sqrt{1.21}$ c. $-\sqrt{400}$

10. Each side of a square is 10 cm long. Find the length of a diagonal to the nearest hundredth.

11. Determine whether each pair of triangles must be congruent. If so, write a congruence and tell why they are congruent.

   a.

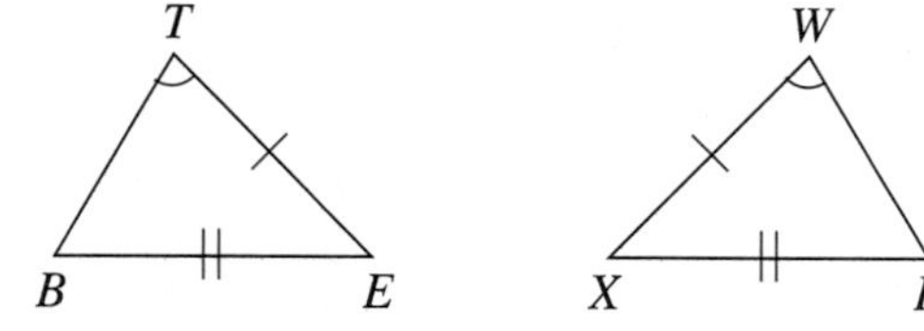

   b.

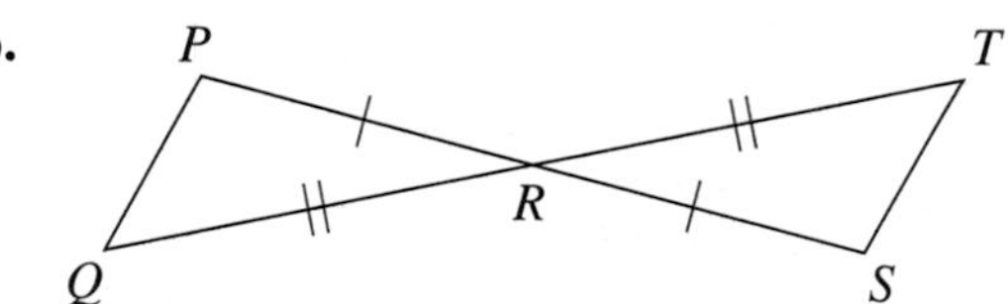

12. Describe the pairs of angles as alternate interior, corresponding, adjacent, or none of the above.

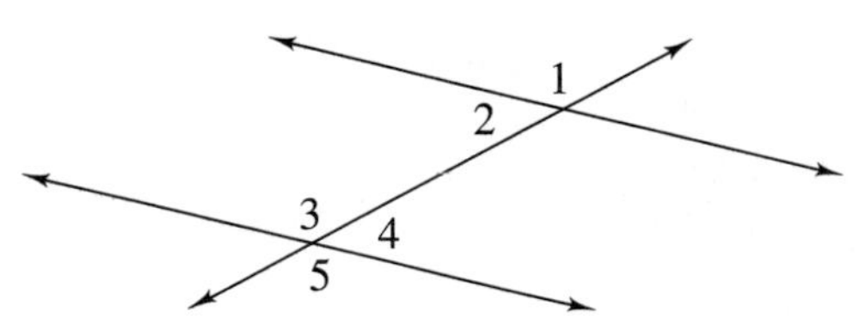

   a. $\angle 2$, $\angle 4$ b. $\angle 1$, $\angle 5$

   c. $\angle 1$, $\angle 3$ d. $\angle 3$, $\angle 4$

Cumulative Review

Choose A, B, C, or D.

1. Which triangle does not have to be congruent to the triangle shown?

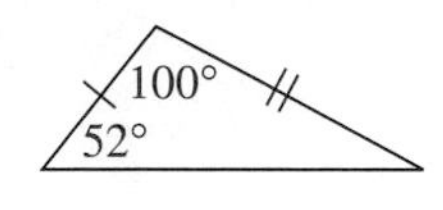

A.  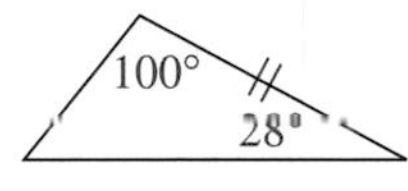

B. 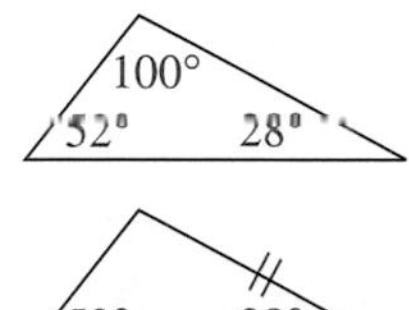

C. 100° 52°

D. 52° 28°

2. Which survey question is an example of a non-biased, closed-option question?

   A. What is your favorite TV show?

   B. Are you under voting age or are you old enough to vote?

   C. Do you like your popcorn with or without butter?

   D. Are you in 7th or 8th grade?

3. Ervin has art class every 6th day of school. How often does he have art class on Monday?

   A. every week **B.** every 5th week

   C. every 6th week **D.** every 7th week

4. Which square root lies between the whole numbers 11 and 12?

   A. $\sqrt{135}$ **B.** $\sqrt{144}$ **C.** $\sqrt{120}$ **D.** $\sqrt{101}$

5. Which pairs of angles are corresponding angles?

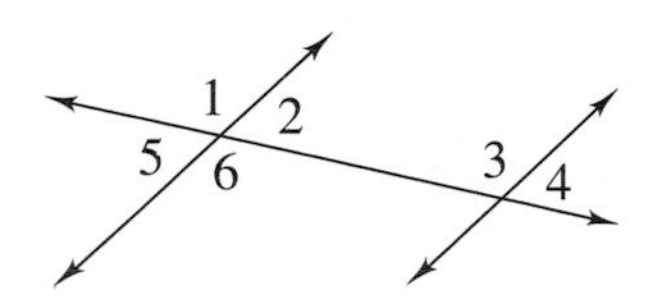

   A. $\angle 1$ and $\angle 6$ **B.** $\angle 3$ and $\angle 6$

   C. $\angle 1$ and $\angle 4$ **D.** $\angle 2$ and $\angle 4$

6. Which conclusion is correct?

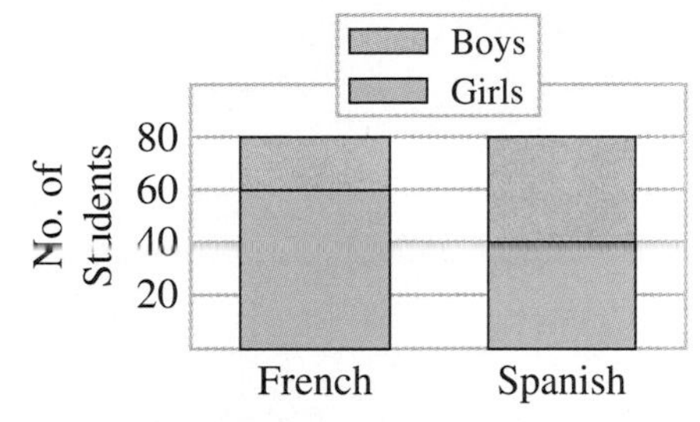

   A. 80 boys take French.

   B. More boys than girls take Spanish.

   C. More girls take French than Spanish.

   D. The total number of students studying Spanish and French is 80.

7. What is the circumference of a circle whose area is 36π square inches?

   A. 12π inches **B.** 18π inches

   C. 36π inches **D.** 6π inches

8. Althea has $3.50 to spend for lunch each week. She always buys milk, which costs $.25. A full lunch (including milk) costs $1.35. How many days a week can she buy a full lunch?

   A. 1 **B.** 2 **C.** 3 **D.** 4

9. Each angle of a regular polygon has measure 140°. Find the number of sides.

   A. 7 **B.** 8 **C.** 10 **D.** 9

10. For the school bottle-and-can drive, the class officers brought in the following number of cans: 36, 40, 85, 63. Find the average (mean) number of cans.

    A. 40 **B.** 51.5 **C.** 56

    D. There is no mean.

CHAPTER 3

Integers and Variable Expressions

WORLD VIEW The Himalaya-Karakoram mountain range in Central Asia is the world's greatest. It includes 96 of the world's 109 peaks that are over 24,000 ft high.

Most caves are formed when surface water trickles down through tiny cracks in the rock. This water slowly dissolves the rock and eventually passages and chambers are formed. This can take thousands of years.

Notice the spectacular stalactites and stalagmites at Blanchard Springs Caverns, in the Arkansas Ozarks.

Source: *World Book Encyclopedia*

Data File 3

Caves

Characteristic	Name and Location	Size
Deepest descent in the world	Gouffre Jean Bernard, France	5,256 ft deep
Deepest in the United States	Lechugilla Cave, New Mexico, USA	1,565 ft deep
Longest in the world	Mammoth Cave, Kentucky, USA	348 mi long
Largest chamber in the world	Sarawak Chamber, Malaysia	2,300 ft long, average width 980 ft, more than 230 ft high
Longest underwater	Nohoch Na Chich, Mexico	43,600 ft long

Source: *Guinness Book of Records*

WHAT YOU WILL LEARN

- how to understand and apply integer concepts
- how to model, write, and simplify expressions
- how to use technology to evaluate expressions
- how to solve problems by using guess and test

stalactites

the longest free standing stalactite in the world is 21 ft 6 in.

Highest Mountains

Name and Location	Height
Everest, Nepal/China	29,028 ft
K2, Kashmir	28,250 ft
Kanchenjunga, Nepal/India	28,208 ft
Lhotse I, Nepal/China	27,923 ft
Makalu I, Nepal/China	27,824 ft

Source: *World Almanac*

stalagmites

the tallest free standing stalagmite in the world is 105 ft tall.

THE LARGEST...

- **hamburger** weighed 5,520 lb. It was made at the Outdamie County Fairgrounds in Seymour, WI on August 5, 1989.
- **lasagna** weighed 3,609.6 lb and measured 50 ft x 5 ft. It was made in the Republic of Ireland on May 11, 1990.
- **omelet** was made in a skillet with a diameter of 41 ft 1 in. The staff and students of Municipal School for Special Education created it in Opwijk, Belgium on June 10, 1990.
- **paella** was made by Josep Gruges on August 25, 1987 in Spain. The diameter measured 52 ft 6 in.
- **pancake** was 32 ft 11 in. in diameter, 1 in. deep, and weighed 2,866 lb. It was made at Dijkerhoek, Holten, Netherlands on May 13, 1990.
- **pizza** was baked at the Norwood Hypermarket, in Norwood, South Africa, on Dec. 8, 1990. Its diameter measured 122 ft 8 in.

Source: *Guiness Book of Records*

investigation

Project File

Memo

The word *measurement* usually calls to mind length or distance. But we also measure time, weight, capacity, speed, and many other things. Each type of measurement has its own carefully defined units such as feet, seconds, or degrees. Usually you can convert between similar units (1 yd = 3 ft; 12 in. = 1 ft). Some systems such as temperature involve negative as well as positive numbers.

Time, weight, capacity, speed.... Is there anything we don't have a system for measuring?

Mission: Brainstorm with your group to create a system for measuring memory. Your system should have well defined units and should include negative numbers. You may want to create a tool for measuring units in your system and formulas for converting your units into other units.

Leads to Follow

- ✓ Why do some systems of measurement have negative numbers while others do not?
- ✓ How are units defined in measurement systems with which you are familiar?

What's Ahead

- Comparing and ordering integers
- Finding the absolute value of an integer

3-1 Graphing Integers on the Number Line

WORK TOGETHER

Work with a group. Make a list of examples of real world uses of negative numbers. Compare it with the other groups' lists.

THINK AND DISCUSS

Positive and Negative Numbers You can use integers to record money. Think of earning \$6 as the positive integer 6, and spending \$6 as the negative integer -6.

FLASHBACK

Positive integers: 1, 2, 3, . . .

Negative integers: -1, -2, -3, . . .

The integer 0 is neither positive nor negative.

You can graph 6 and -6 on the number line.

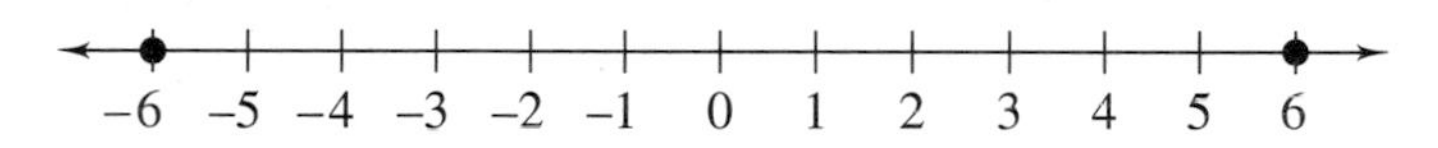

1. a. Where is the set of positive integers graphed on the number line?
   b. Where is the set of negative integers graphed on the number line?
   c. What do the arrows on both ends of the number line indicate?

Earnings		Expenses	
\$12	\$9	\$3	\$8
\$15	\$8	\$12	\$19

2. a. Draw a number line and graph as integers the earnings and expenses listed in the table at the left.
   b. Which pairs of numbers of your graph are the same distance from zero?

The integers 9 and -9 are *opposites.* Numbers that are the same distance from zero on the number line but in opposite directions are called **opposites.**

3. What is the opposite of -5?
4. Make a number line and graph three pairs of opposites.
5. How far from zero is 2? How far is -2?

A number's distance from zero on the number line is called its **absolute value.** You write the "absolute value of -4" as $|-4|$. Since -4 is 4 units from zero, $|-4| = 4$.

6. What does $|12|$ represent? What is its value?

7. **Writing** Can the absolute value of a number be negative? Explain your answer.

8. Name all the integers with an absolute value less than 4.

Element	Boiling Point*
Chlorine	−30°F
Helium	−452°F
Hydrogen	−423°F
Nitrogen	−320°F
Oxygen	−297°F

* Rounded to the nearest degree.

The elements in the chart are gases at room temperature. Water, which is a compound, has a boiling point of 212°F.

Comparing and Ordering Integers You can use the number line to compare and order positive and negative integers. Numbers increase from left to right on a number line.

The table at the left shows the boiling points of several elements. The boiling point of oxygen is -297°F and the boiling point of nitrogen is -320°F. To compare these temperatures you can graph the integers -297 and -320 on a number line.

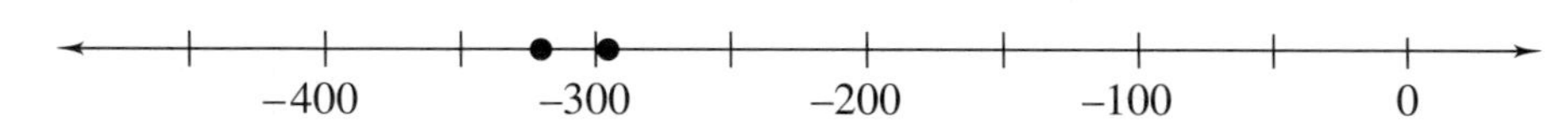

The integer -297 is to the right of -320, so $-297 > -320$. Therefore, the boiling point of oxygen is higher than the boiling point of nitrogen.

9. Which element in the table has the highest boiling point? Explain your answer.

10. Order all the elements in the chart from highest to lowest boiling point.

Mixed REVIEW

Find the mean.

1. 4, 5, 9, 2, 2, 3
2. 98, 95, 91, 98, 95, 95

Use the Pythagorean theorem to find the hypotenuse of a right triangle with the following legs:

3. 7, 24
4. 9, 12

5. Mallory catalogued 24 shelves of books. Each shelf held 47 books. How many books did she catalogue?

ON YOUR OWN

Write an integer to represent each situation.

11. **Weather** The lowest outdoor temperature ever recorded was 129°F below zero, in Vostok, Antarctica, in 1983.

12. **Geography** The lowest point in Africa, Lake Assal in Djibouti, is 571 ft below sea level.

13. **Money** The QRS Corporation made \$2 million last year.

Use the information in the graph at the right to answer the questions.

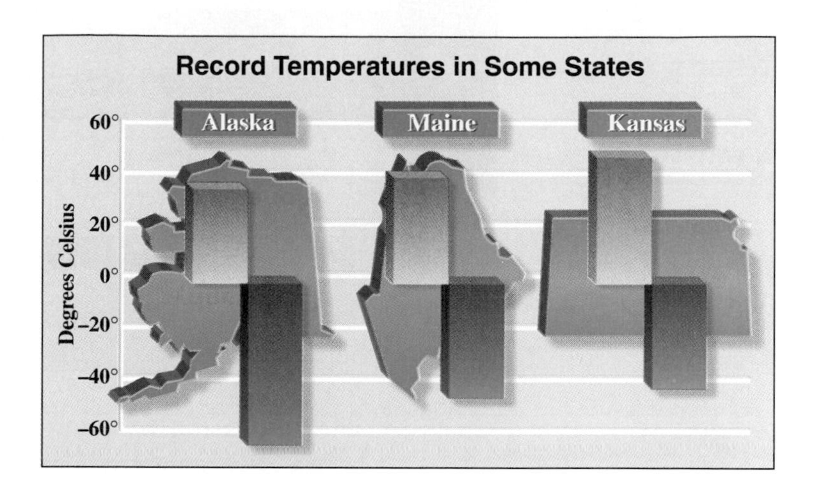

14. **Weather** The lowest outdoor temperature ever recorded in Texas, $-31°C$, occurred on February 8, 1931. Was it ever that cold in Kansas? Explain.

15. Which state on the graph had a temperature of 48°C below zero at some time?

16. **Choose A, B, C, or D.** Which of the following contains only integers?

A. $-6, 0, \frac{1}{2}, 3, |-16|, 2$ **B.** $-3.2, -5, -1, -0.1, -4$

C. $2, -2, 2.5, -2.5, 3, -3$ **D.** $-9, 0, 2, -3, 1, 100, -8$

Weather **Match each record low temperature with its letter on the number line.**

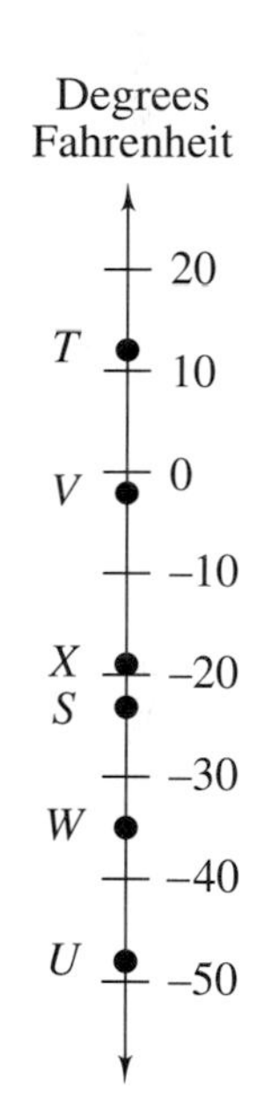

17. Van Buren, ME
Jan. 19, 1925: $-48°F$

18. Tallahassee, FL
Feb. 13, 1899: $-2°F$

19. Mauna Kea, HI
May 17, 1979: 12°F

20. Greensburg, IN
Feb. 2, 1951: $-35°F$

21. Corinth, MI
Jan. 30, 1966: $-19°F$

22. Seminole, TX
Feb. 8, 1933: $-23°F$

Compare. Write >, <, or =.

23. $|-14|$ ■ $|14|$

24. 3 ■ -4

25. $|-3|$ ■ $|-6|$

26. 6 ■ 0

27. $|-25|$ ■ $|-1|$

28. 0 ■ $|-5|$

29. $|75|$ ■ $|-210|$

30. $|1|$ ■ 0

31. 28 ■ -35

32. -13 ■ -16

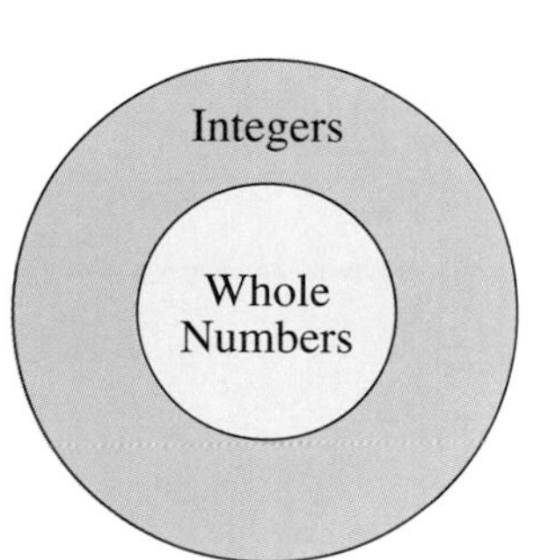

33. **Writing** Explain how the set of whole numbers {0, 1, 2, . . . } is related to the set of integers. Use the Venn diagram.

What's Ahead

- Writing variable expressions for word phrases

3-2 Writing Variable Expressions

THINK AND DISCUSS

Writing Expressions Raquel's after-school job pays \$6 an hour. She works a different number of hours every week.

The *expression* $6h$ shows her weekly earnings. The number of hours is represented by the h. It is a *variable* because its value can vary. A **variable expression** contains a variable.

FLASHBACK

$27 \cdot 8$, 5×6, and $12 + 17 - 9$ are numerical expressions.

$6h = 6 \cdot h$

1. If Raquel gets a raise and now earns \$6.50 an hour, what variable expression would she write for the amount she earns in h hours?

2. a. At the ball game, hot dogs cost \$2. Write a variable expression for the cost of n hot dogs.
   b. A carton of juice costs \$.75. Write a variable expression for the cost of x cartons of juice.

Evaluating Expressions When you substitute a number for the variable, you **evaluate** an expression. If Raquel works 12 hours, then $h = 12$, and $6h = 6 \cdot 12 = 72$. She earns \$72.

3. a. Evaluate the expression you wrote in Question 2 part (a) for $n = 5$.
   b. Evaluate the expression you wrote in Question 2 part (b) for $x = 8$.

> *Language is the archives of history.*
> —Ralph Waldo Emerson (1803–1882)

You've often heard word phrases such as "twice as much," "three times as long," "half as heavy." Mathematics is a language, too. You can translate word phrases into variable expressions and vice versa. Here are some examples.

Word Phrase	Variable Expression
a number plus negative 3	$n + (-3)$
the quotient of a number and 8	$k \div 8$
6 less than a number	$y - 6$
15 minus a number	$15 - b$

4. The variable expressions in the table on page 106 can represent word phrases other than those given. Write another word phrase for each variable expression.

5. Write a variable expression for each phrase.
   a. 27 plus a number
   b. 13 less than a number
   c. the quotient of a number divided by negative 10
   d. the product of 17 and a number

Sometimes variable expressions contain more than one mathematical operation.

Example You can represent the cost of a trip with Rod's Limo by the expression $1.5 + 2n$, where n is the number of miles you travel. How much does a 12-mile trip cost?

Evaluate $1.5 + 2n$ for $n = 12$.

$1.5 + 2(12) = 1.5 + 24$ — Substitute 12 for *n*.

$= 25.5$ — Compute.

A 12-mile trip costs $25.50.

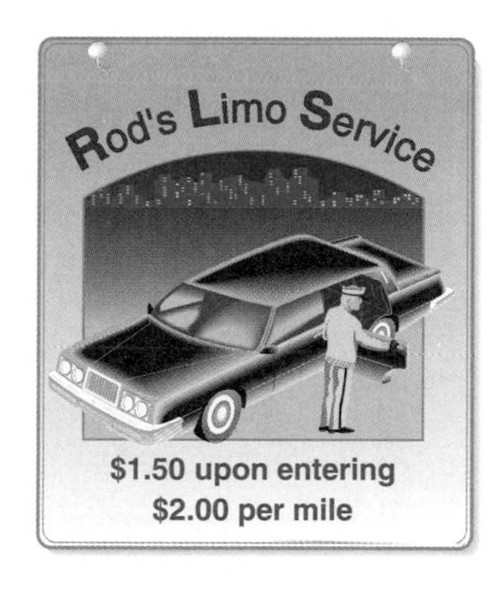

6. a. What mathematical operations are used in $1.5 + 2n$?
   b. Write a word phrase for the variable expression $1.5 + 2n$.

TRY THESE

Write a variable expression for each quantity. Explain what the variable represents.

7. Kim's height if she is 6 inches shorter than her mother
8. the number of calories in three slices of bread
9. Mike's age if Mike is 3 years older than Jill
10. the number of months old Eric is on his birthday

Write a variable expression for each phrase.

11. twice a number
12. sum of -12 and a number
13. product of -4 and y
14. quotient of 3 divided by w
15. 18 more than a
16. 17 less than n

Mixed REVIEW

Find the mode.

1. 14, 31, 33, 14, 50
2. 8, 17, 34, 17, 19

Compare. Use >, <, or =.

3. -7 ■ 7
4. $|-32|$ ■ 32
5. The attendance at a medical lecture was 342 on Monday and 1257 on Tuesday. Find the total attendance.
6. It takes Cara 12 min to walk to school. She needs to get to school 15 min early to meet with the swim coach. What time should she leave her house if school starts at 8:00?

Extra SKILLS PRACTICE

Write a variable expression for each phrase.

1. 7 times a number
2. double a number
3. the product of a number and -7
4. a number increased by 10
5. the product of 45 and a number
6. the sum of a number and -3
7. the quotient of a number and -2
8. a number decreased by -5
9. 14 more than 3 times a number

In 1960, it was estimated that the number of motor vehicles in Tokyo was increasing at a rate of 10,000 each month. ***If the rate didn't change, about how many more vehicles would there be in 1994 than in 1960?***

Source: *Japan, Life World Library*

ON YOUR OWN

Write a variable expression for each phrase.

17. 6 less than a number

18. 7 more than the absolute value of a number

19. the product of the absolute value of a number and 9

Evaluate each expression for the value given.

20. $12x + 4$ for $x = \frac{1}{2}$

21. $17 - n$ for $n = 12.5$

22. $(30 \div z) + 19$ for $z = 6$

23. $52y - 16$ for $y = 1\frac{1}{2}$

Match each sentence with its expression.

a. $35 - 7$ **b.** $35x$ **c.** $m - 35$ **d.** $n + 35$ **e.** $35(7)$

24. A car was traveling 35 mi/h for a number of hours.

25. Jayda ran 7 times a week for 35 weeks.

26. The plumber added an extra $35 to her bill because she worked overtime.

27. Thirty-five fewer people came than the number expected.

28. Mark is 7 years younger than his 35-year-old sister.

Writing Create a word phrase that can be represented by each variable expression.

29. $n \div 3$ **30.** $3 + a$ **31.** $-(-x)$ **32.** $7w - 5$

33. Data File 1 (pp. 2–3)

a. Write an expression to show the number of cars owned by n thousand inhabitants in Japan.

b. Use the information in the chart to write a variable expression of your own. Write a word phrase to describe it.

34. Choose A, B, or C. Which word phrase best describes the variable expression $6 - n$?

A. 6 fewer than n eggs

B. the number of eggs in 6 cartons

C. n fewer eggs than 6

What's Ahead

- Adding integers

MATH AND LEISURE

3-3 Adding Integers

WORK TOGETHER

The home team has the football on their 20-yd line. They have 4 downs to move the ball forward 10 yd toward the opponents' goal line. Does the ball always move forward? No! On the first down, the quarterback hands the ball to a running back who is tackled for a 5-yd loss. They lose 7 yd on the second down.

Charting plays in a football game is similar to adding integers. The number line shows the home team's total loss in yards.

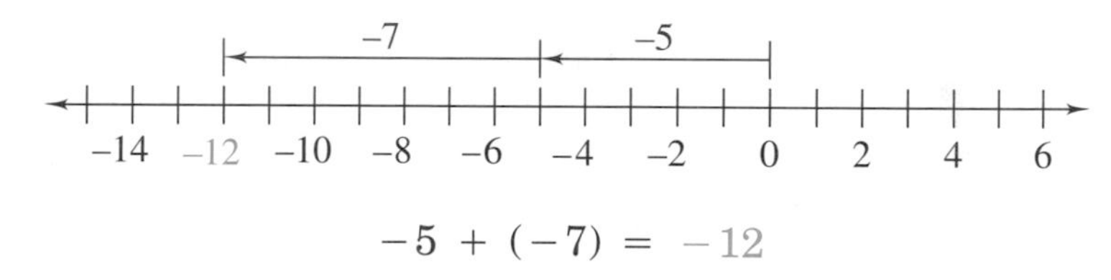

$$-5 + (-7) = -12$$

The home team lost 12 yd.

1. Work with a group. Use the number line to find each sum.

   a. $-9 + (-3)$ b. $6 + (-13)$ c. $9 + 16$

   d. $-3 + 7$ e. $0 + 2$ f. $17 + (-8)$

2. When you have finished, write a rule for adding integers. Use your rule to do the additions above. Does it work? Discuss your rule with other groups. Do they agree?

The Chrysler Building** in New York City has 77 floors and stands 1,046 ft tall. Suppose your office is on the 34th floor. You take the elevator down 8 floors and then take the elevator up 15 floors to the mail room. **On what floor is the mail room? How do you get back to your office?

Refer to the additions above to answer the questions.

3. a. For 1(a), what is the absolute value of each addend?

   b. What is the sign of the sum?

4. a. For 1(f), what is the absolute value of each addend?

   b. What is the difference of the absolute values?

   c. What is the sign of the sum?

Mixed REVIEW

Find the square root of each number.

1. 16 **2.** 49

Write a variable expression for each quantity.

3. Tim is 7 years older than his brother.

4. Dale is 6 in. shorter than his father.

Find the opposite of each number.

5. 9 **6.** -2

7. Ms. Klauss gives her students 3 points for every correct answer. At the end of class Ken has 21 points. How many correct answers did Ken have?

You probably found these rules.

Adding Integers

To add two integers with the same sign, add their absolute values and use the same sign.

To add two integers with different signs, find the difference of their absolute values. The sum has the sign of the integer with the greater absolute value.

Example 1 Complete: $-6 + (-15) = \blacksquare$

$|-6| + |-15| = 21$ ← **Add the absolute values.**

$-6 + (-15) = -21$ ← **Both addends have the same sign; use that sign for the sum.**

Example 2 Complete: $6 + (-15) = \blacksquare$

$|-15| - |6| = 15 - 6 = 9$ ← **Subtract the absolute values.**

$|-15| > |6|$ ← **Use the sign of the integer with the greater absolute value.**

$6 + (-15) = -9$

GREAT EXPECTATIONS

Park Ranger

The career I am looking toward is something along the line of United States history. National parks, forests, and historical places interest me. I love our natural history and I am also interested in mountains and rivers. I would like to learn more about the Revolutionary and Civil Wars. My interest in this career developed from all the trips and vacations my family and I have taken. One time when I was in a national park, someone was lost on one of the trails and I directed them back to their car. A park ranger told me that I had done a good job of explaining things to them. He said that I should work there.

Benji Zimmerman

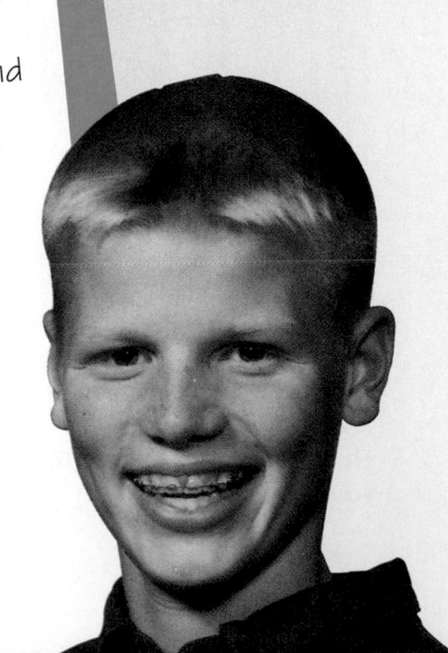

If a football team loses 12 yards (-12) and then gains 12 yards ($+12$), the team is back where it started. $12 + (-12) = 0$. Because -12 and $+12$ are opposites and their sum is 0, they are called **additive inverses** of each other.

5. What is the additive inverse of 6? Justify your answer by writing an equation.

TRY THESE

6. **Sports** In golf, the lowest score wins. Each stroke is one point. The goal of a golfer is to keep the number of strokes *at* or *under* par. The integer $+2$ means 2 above par; -2 means 2 under par.
   a. What is the player's score on each hole?
   b. How many strokes above or below par is this player so far?
   c. Par for the fifth hole is 4. How many strokes must this player take at Hole 5 for her total score to be at par for the first five holes?

Hole	Par	Number of Strokes Above or Below
1	3	$+2$
2	4	-1
3	5	-2
4	4	$+3$

Par is the number of strokes by a skillful player for a particular hole or course.

Dear Benji,

Your interest in learning more about the Revolutionary and Civil wars is commendable. Park rangers must possess a variety of skills. They need good verbal and written communication skills, and an understanding of the park's history. Math and science play an important part in the daily life of today's park ranger. Park rangers determine how many people can be accommodated on walks, hikes, and talks. Too many people in a group could cause damage to a resource such as a historical battleground or an old bridge. Taking inventory of flora and fauna at a site requires math and science. We use surveys to find out how our visitors feel about our park. Some of the reports I prepare show percentage and contain data that were derived from equations.

Patricia A. Ruff, Chief Park Ranger at
Cowpens National Battlefield

Extra SKILLS PRACTICE

Find each sum.

1. $9 + (-4)$
2. $-1 + (-6)$
3. $2 + (-6)$
4. $-14 + (-7)$
5. $5 + (-10)$
6. $-6 + 4$
7. $-8 + (-5)$
8. $-2 + 6$
9. $-4 + (-5)$
10. $15 + (-8)$
11. $-9 + 0$
12. $-2 + (-2)$
13. $6 + (-6)$
14. $-7 + 11$

Find each sum.

7. $13 + (-12)$
8. $12 + (-4)$
9. $-4 + 6 + 4$
10. $-45 + (-67)$
11. $-13 + (-4)$
12. $14 + (-62)$

Sports **Write a sum for each situation.**

13. Maria was 2 points below par on the first hole, and 3 points above par on the second hole.
14. The hot air balloon rose 1,800 ft and then descended 750 ft.
15. The scuba diver went down 53 ft and then rose 28 ft.

ON YOUR OWN

Find each sum.

16. $9 + (-3)$
17. $-9 + 3$
18. $-9 + (-3)$
19. $9 + 3$
20. $-8 + 0$
21. $-8 + 8$
22. $-11 + (-9)$
23. $11 + (-9)$
24. $-23 + 15$
25. $-17 + 18$
26. $|-13| + (-13)$

Round	Points
1	−37
2	33
3	−32
4	29
5	18

27. a. Entertainment To win a computer game, the total of the points scored must be positive. The chart at the left shows the points scored in each round. Did the player win?
    b. By how many points did the player win or lose?
    c. **Writing** Explain how you could use mental math or estimation to answer part (a).

Downs	Team A	Team B
1	+30	+4
2	−40	−40
3	−15	−9

Sports **Use the chart at the left to answer the questions.**

28. Which football team had a net loss of 45 yards after its third down?
29. How many yards must this team gain in order to make the needed 10-yard gain at the 4th down?

30. **Investigation (p. 102)** Make a list of things that can be measured using negative numbers. Describe why it makes sense to use negative numbers in each case.

What's Ahead

- Subtracting integers

3-4 Subtracting Integers

WHAT YOU'LL NEED

✓ Calculator 

FLASHBACK

3 and −3 are called opposites. The opposite of an integer is also called its additive inverse.

WORK TOGETHER

Exploring Subtracting Integers Work with a partner. One person uses a calculator, the other records the expressions. Find each difference. Remember: To input a negative number, use the change sign key, +/-.

1. Compute each difference.

a. $9 - 10$	**b.** $-27 - (-8)$	**c.** $15 - (-6)$
d. $-35 - 12$	**e.** $-7 - (-18)$	**f.** $10 - 12$
g. $22 - (-4)$	**h.** $15 - (-10)$	**i.** $-15 - 10$

Now switch jobs with your partner.

2. Compute each sum.

a. $9 + (-10)$	**b.** $-27 + 8$	**c.** $15 + 6$
d. $-35 + (-12)$	**e.** $-7 + 18$	**f.** $10 + (-12)$
g. $22 + 4$	**h.** $15 + 10$	**i.** $-15 + (-10)$

3. Look at both lists of expressions. What do you notice about them?

4. What is the relationship between the numbers you subtracted in the first list and the numbers you added in the second list? Write a rule for subtracting integers. Discuss your conclusions with your classmates.

Spanish, the official language of 20 nations, territories, and colonies, is spoken by 125–320 million people.

Source: *The Universal Almanac*

THINK AND DISCUSS

Applying a Rule The Spanish Club has \$55 for its end-of-school party. The decorations cost \$15. How much is left for refreshments and a door prize?

$$55 - 15 = 40$$

The club has \$40 left.

Extra SKILLS PRACTICE

Find each difference.

1. $6 - 8$
2. $2 - (-8)$
3. $5 - 11$
4. $-4 - 5$
5. $-7 - (-5)$
6. $-1 - 8$
7. $-3 - (-8)$
8. $7 - 9$
9. $-4 - (-2)$
10. $6 - (-3)$
11. $4 - (-4)$
12. $-2 - 6$
13. $8 - (-17)$

The club decides to buy a more expensive door prize, and spends \$52 in all on refreshments and the prize. What is left in the treasury?

You can write a subtraction equation to find the amount in the treasury.

$$40 - 52 = 40 + (-52)$$
$$= -12$$

5. Explain what an amount of $-\$12$ means.

Some of the parents donated \$10 to the club. You can think of it as removing, or taking away, \$10 of debt:

$$-12 - (-10) = -12 + 10$$
$$= -2$$

The debt is now \$2. The treasury contains $-\$2$.

6. If the parents had donated \$15 instead of \$10, how much money would be in the treasury?
7. Suppose that you owe your brother \$7. Now you pay back \$4. How much do you still owe him? (Think of a debt of \$7 as -7.)
8. If you borrowed \$4 more instead of paying back \$4, how much would you owe your brother?

Mixed REVIEW

True or False?

1. Parallel lines sometimes intersect.
2. Parallel lines are not perpendicular.

Find each sum.

3. $-5 + 2$
4. $-7 + (-3)$

Find each product or quotient.

5. 927×63
6. $23{,}868 \div 52$
7. Additional prints in a film developing store cost \$.07. What is the cost if Brenda orders 12 additional prints?

ON YOUR OWN

Find each difference by writing an equivalent addition.

9. $9 - (-1)$
10. $5 - 8$
11. $6 - 9$
12. $-16 - (-2)$
13. $27 - 52$
14. $19 - (-12)$
15. $-10 - (-8)$
16. $11 - (-25)$
17. $|-12| - 17$
18. $-28 - 28$
19. $-28 - (-28)$
20. $|-17| - |-12|$
21. $-36 - |29|$
22. $10 - (-14)$

Write the next four numbers in each pattern.

23. 27, 20, 13, ■, ■, ■, ■

24. 8, 5, 2, −1 ■, ■, ■, ■

25. 14, 7, 0, −7, ■, ■, ■, ■

26. 3, 5, 2, 4, 1, 3, 0, ■, ■, ■, ■

Complete each sentence.

27. To subtract an integer, add its ■.

28. The opposite of a negative integer is a ■ integer.

29. **Writing** Explain the relationship between adding a positive integer and subtracting a negative integer. Give examples.

Evaluate each expression for $x = 4$, $y = -7$, and $z = -3$.

30. $x + y$

31. $10 - z$

32. $y - z$

33. $x + y - z$

34. $y - 20 + x$

35. $35 - z + x$

36. $|y| - |z|$

37. $z + |y|$

38. $y - (-z)$

The graph at the right shows temperature at various altitudes. Use the graph to answer the questions.

39. As the altitude increases, what happens to the temperature?

40. When you climb from sea level to 1,500 m, by how much does the temperature change?

41. What would be the approximate temperature at a height of 10,000 m?

42. **Data File 3 (pp. 100–101)** About how many feet separate the top of the highest mountain and the bottom of the deepest cave?

43. **Investigation (p. 102)** Make a list of systems of measurement that you've studied. For each system, give three examples of how you convert from one unit to the other within the system.

Mt. Everest, with an altitude of over 29,000 ft, is the highest mountain in the world. The first woman to reach the summit was Junko Tabei of Japan on May 16, 1975. The oldest person to reach the summit was an American, Richard Daniel Bass, on April 30, 1985. He was 55 years 130 days old.

Source: *The Guinness Book of Sports Records*

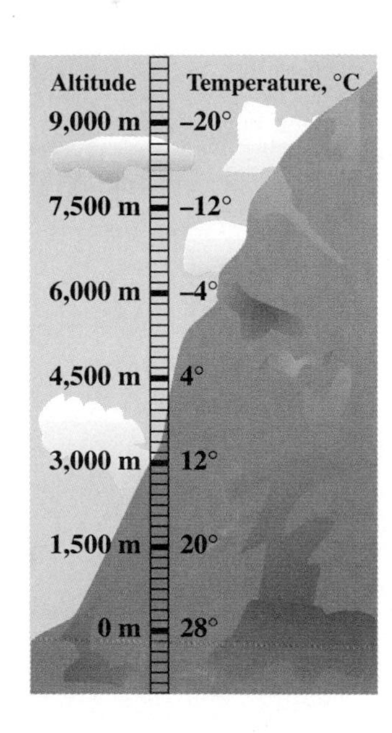

Problem Solving Practice

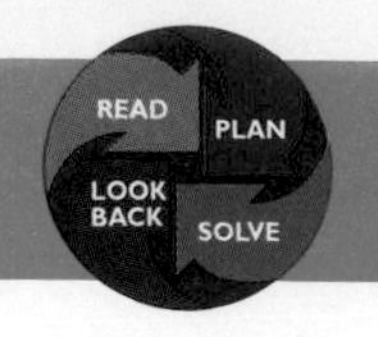

PROBLEM SOLVING STRATEGIES

Make a Table
Use Logical Reasoning
Solve a Simpler Problem
Too Much or Too Little Information
Look for a Pattern
Make a Model
Work Backward
Draw a Diagram
Guess and Test
Simulate a Problem
Use Multiple Strategies
Write an Equation
Use a Proportion

Solve if possible. If not, tell what information is needed.

1. Al, Barbara, Carla, and Dan have different vehicles: a sports car, a van, a pick-up truck, and a convertible. Use the clues to tell who owns each vehicle.
   a. Barbara went for a ride in her friend's convertible on Saturday and another friend's sports car on Sunday.
   b. Carla does not own a sports car.
   c. Dan's name rhymes with his vehicle.

2. During a five day work week, Ace Truckers delivered 40 more crates of pineapples each day than they did on the day before. If they delivered 600 crates on Friday, how many did they deliver on Monday?

3. In math class each girl drew a triangle and each boy drew a rectangle. If there were 92 sides in all, how many girls and how many boys are in the class?

4. A parking garage had 460 empty spaces at 8:00 A.M. By 11:00 A.M., 324 cars had entered the garage and none had left. Then every 15 minutes, an average of 6 cars left and 14 more cars came in. By what time did the garage fill up?

5. **Hobbies** Jake's little sister collects stickers. She started her collection with 10 stickers. By the end of the first week she had 12. The following week her collection was up to 16, and by the end of the third week she had 22. If she continues adding to her collection following the same pattern, how many stickers will she have at the end of the eighth week?

6. **Cars** Mr. Juarez leased a car for 3 years. The terms of the lease were $900 down and $198 per month during the term of the lease. The lease also stated that Mr. Juarez would pay $.12 per mile for every mile over 45,000 mi on the odometer. If the odometer read 52,193 mi when he turned it in, how much did Mr. Juarez pay to lease the car, including the extra miles?

WHAT? The greatest recorded mileage for a car is 1,402,515 mi for a 1963 Volkswagen "Beetle."

Source: *The Guinness Book of Records*

What's Ahead

- Multiplying and dividing integers
- Evaluating expressions by applying the order of operations

WHAT YOU'LL NEED

✓ Calculator 

3-5 Multiplying and Dividing Integers

THINK AND DISCUSS

Multiplying Integers The fastest domestic passenger elevator in the world is in Tokyo, Japan. Its average speed is a little more than 30 feet per second (30 ft/s). Suppose you ride down in the elevator for 4 seconds at this rate. To find the number of feet you descend you can multiply integers.

FLASHBACK

3×2 is also written as $3 \cdot 2$ or $3(2)$.

Represent a descent of 30 ft/s as -30. For every second you travel, you go down 30 ft.

$$\begin{aligned} 4 \cdot (-30) &= (-30) + (-30) + (-30) + (-30) \\ &= -120 \end{aligned}$$

In 4 seconds you go down 120 feet.

1. **Calculator** Make up several multiplications that have one positive and one negative integer as factors. What do you notice about the product in each case?

Factor		Factor		Product
-30	•	3	=	-90
-30	•	2	=	-60
-30	•	1	=	-30
-30	•	0	=	0
-30	•	(-1)	=	30
-30	•	(-2)	=	60

2. a. Look at the multiplications at the left. What is the pattern in the *factors* and *products*?
   b. What does the pattern show about the product of two negative integers?
   c. Using the pattern, predict the product of -30 and (-3).
   d. **Calculator** Try several multiplications on your calculator to test your theory.

FLASHBACK

$0 \cdot n = 0$

Multiplying Integers

To multiply two integers, multiply the absolute values of the integers.

- If the signs are the same, the product is positive.
- If the signs are different, the product is negative.

3. **Mental Math** Without computing, tell whether the product $(-2) \cdot 3 \cdot (-5)$ is positive, negative, or zero. Explain your answer.

Dividing Integers You know that division and multiplication are inverse operations. Since $-7 \cdot 5 = -35$, you know that $(-35) \div (-7) = 5$ and $(-35) \div 5 = -7$.

4. Write two related division sentences for each multiplication.

a. $9 \cdot 12 = 108$ **b.** $-30 \cdot 5 = -150$

c. $25 \cdot (-10) = -250$ **d.** $-13 \cdot (-4) = 52$

5. What is the sign of the quotient when

a. a negative number is divided by a negative number?

b. a positive number is divided by a negative number?

c. a negative number is divided by a positive number?

The rule for dividing integers is similar to the rule for multiplying integers.

Dividing Integers

To divide two integers, find the quotient of the absolute values of the integers.

- If the signs are the same, the quotient is positive.
- If the signs are different, the quotient is negative.

Order of Operations

1. Work inside grouping symbols.
2. Multiply and divide from left to right.
3. Add and subtract from left to right.

When you evaluate numerical expressions, you need to follow the order of operations.

Example Find the value of $4 + 5 \cdot (-3) - (6 - 2) \div 2$.

$4 + 5 \cdot (-3) - (6 - 2) \div 2$

$= 4 + 5 \cdot (-3) - 4 \div 2$ ← **Work inside grouping symbols.**

$= 4 + (-15) - 2$ ← **Multiply and divide.**

$= -11 - 2$ ← **Add and subtract.**

$= -13$

TRY THESE

Write two related division sentences for each multiplication.

6. $18 \cdot (-3) = -54$ **7.** $-12 \cdot 4 = -48$

Evaluate.

8. $-6(-9)$ 9. $(-5 \cdot 6) \div (-5)$ 10. $48 \div (-8)$

Explain how to apply the order of operations. Then evaluate.

11. $-5 \cdot (-4 - 2)$ 12. $48 \div (-19 + 11)$

13. $-3 \cdot 2 \cdot (-4) + (-6)$ 14. $-32 + (-8) \cdot 4$

ON YOUR OWN

Write two related division sentences for each multiplication.

15. $3 \cdot (-4) = -12$ 16. $-7 \cdot (-2) = 14$

Evaluate.

17. $-5 \cdot 8$ 18. $-12 \cdot (-2)$ 19. $-56 \div (-7)$ 20. $-210 \div 15$

Tell what you should do first to evaluate the numerical expression. Then evaluate.

21. $-4 \cdot (-6) \cdot 7 \cdot 2$ 22. $3 + 3 \cdot (-4)$ 23. $-84 \div (-3 \cdot 4)$

24. **Writing** How can you predict the sign of a product when there are more than two factors? Use examples.

Find two integers that fit the given description.

25. sum: -5
product: 4

26. sum: -5
product: -6

27. sum: 0
product: -4

Calculator Evaluate.

28. $-14 \cdot (-327)$ 29. $-448 \div 14$

30. $1134 \div (-54)$ 31. $23 \cdot (-212) \cdot 43$

32. $712 - [83 \cdot (-2)]$ 33. $-786 \cdot [-567 - (-489)]$

34. **Choose A, B, C, or D.** Suppose you borrow \$8 from each of 6 friends. Which number sentence best represents your debt?

A. $-6 \cdot 8 = -48$ B. $-8 \cdot 6 = -48$

C. $-48 \div 6 = -8$ D. $-8 + 6 = -2$

Mixed REVIEW

Can you use the figure to form a tessellation?

1. hexagon
2. circle

Evaluate each expression for $x = 2$ and $y = 4$.

3. $19 - x - y$
4. $y - 10 - (-x)$

Evaluate mentally.

5. $199 + 1 - 60$
6. $17 - 10 \div 2$

7. Sue sleeps about 7 h each night. At the end of a year, about how many hours has she slept?

Extra SKILLS PRACTICE

Evaluate.

1. $-3 \cdot 6$
2. $-50 \div 5$
3. $-7 \cdot 10$
4. $6 \cdot (-7)$
5. $-3 \cdot (-4)$
6. $-12 \div (-3)$
7. $-6 \cdot (-9)$
8. $-32 \div 4$
9. $-18 \div 6$
10. $-5 \cdot 12$
11. $-45 \div 9$
12. $3 \cdot (-15)$
13. $-64 \div 8$
14. $-54 \div (-9)$
15. $-2 \cdot (-8)$
16. $-28 \div (-7)$

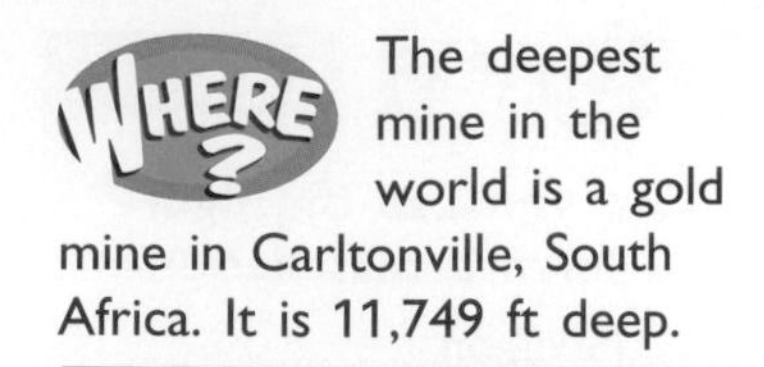

The deepest mine in the world is a gold mine in Carltonville, South Africa. It is 11,749 ft deep.

Source: *The Guinness Book of Records*

35. To explore the Earth's crust, scientists began drilling in Zapolarny in the Kola Peninsula of Arctic Russia on May 24, 1970, and by April, 1992, had reached a depth of 40,230 ft.

a. How do you represent this depth as an integer?

b. What is the depth in yards?

The Mahi wreck** was Hawaii's first planned artificial reef. About 20 min away from the Mahi is the wreck of a small plane. The plane is located at a depth of about 75 ft. **How much deeper is the Mahi than the plane?

Source: *Diving and Snorkeling Guide to the Hawaiian Islands*

Check the Wreck

The wreck of the *Mahi* is a favorite site for divers in Oahu, Hawaii. The *Mahi* is a 165-ft minesweeper that was sunk purposely in 1983. It is located 95 ft below the surface in Waianae Harbor. A diver can explore the interior of the ship, which houses many different moray eels—some 6 ft long—and a variety of tropical fish.

Use the article to answer Exercises 36–38.

36. What integer represents the depth of the *Mahi*?

37. What integer represents a descent of 20 ft/min?

38. If a diver descends at a rate of 20 ft/min, does she reach the ship in 5 min? Explain.

CHECKPOINT

Compare. Use >, <, or =.

1. $|76| \blacksquare 76$ **2.** $-19 \blacksquare |-23|$ **3.** $|-2| \blacksquare 1$

Write a variable expression for each phrase.

4. the product of -3 and some number

5. some number divided by 12

Find each sum or difference.

6. $-7 + (-12)$ **7.** $-15 + 8$ **8.** $-32 - (-11)$

Evaluate each expression for $a = 19$ and $b = -3$.

9. $-a + (-b)$ **10.** $-2a - 13$ **11.** $-15b + (-1)$

What's Ahead

- Using properties for mental math shortcuts

3-6 Mental Math

THINK AND DISCUSS

Using Whole Numbers Maybe you've heard a friend say something like this: "Let's see, I need 4 pencils at \$.89 each, so that's \$3.56 and I'll get \$1.44 change from my \$5."

What, no calculator? Chances are your friend knows how to use mathematical properties to make these calculations simple enough to do mentally.

A few rare people are able to perform amazing calculations. Thomas Fuller, born in Africa in 1710, grew up as a slave in Virginia. He never learned how to read or write, but he could calculate mentally the product of two 9-digit numbers.

Source: *The World of Mathematics*

Properties of Addition and Multiplication

Arithmetic	Algebra
Commutative Property	
$3 + 2 = 2 + 3$	$a + b = b + a$
$3(2) = 2(3)$	$ab = ba$
Associative Property	
$(2 + 3) + 4 = 2 + (3 + 4)$	$(a + b) + c = a + (b + c)$
$(2 \cdot 3) \cdot 4 = 2 \cdot (3 \cdot 4)$	$(a \cdot b) \cdot c = a \cdot (b \cdot c)$
Identity Property	
$6 + 0 = 6$	$a + 0 = a$
$6(1) = 6$	$a(1) = a$

You may be disappointed if you fail, but you are doomed if you don't try.
—Beverly Sills (1929–)

1. Is the equation $0 + a = a$ true? How do you know?

When you add or multiply groups of numbers, look for combinations that equal 10 or multiples of 10.

Example 1

Addition		Multiplication
$23 + 16 + 37 =$ $23 + 37 + 16 =$	**Commutative Property**	$5 \cdot 7 \cdot 8 =$ $5 \cdot 8 \cdot 7 =$
$(23 + 37) + 16 =$ $60 + 16 = 76$	**Associative Property**	$(5 \cdot 8) \cdot 7 =$ $40 \cdot 7 = 280$

In 1887, Herman Hollerith won a U.S. Census Bureau competition for a device that would speed up computation of census information. In 1924, his Tabulating Machine Company became known as IBM.

Source: *The Universal Almanac*

Using Integers When working with integers, group positive numbers and negative numbers. Then look for opposites.

Example 2 Evaluate $(-6) + 46 + 17 + (-11)$.

$$\begin{aligned} & (-6) + 46 + 17 + (-11) & \\ &= 46 + 17 + (-11) + (-6) & \text{Commutative Prop.} \\ &= 46 + 17 + [(-11) + (-6)] & \text{Associative Property} \\ &= 46 + 17 + (-17) & \\ &= 46 + 0 = 46 & \text{Identity Property} \end{aligned}$$

$(-6) + 46 + 17 + (-11) = 46$

2. How was each property used in the steps above?

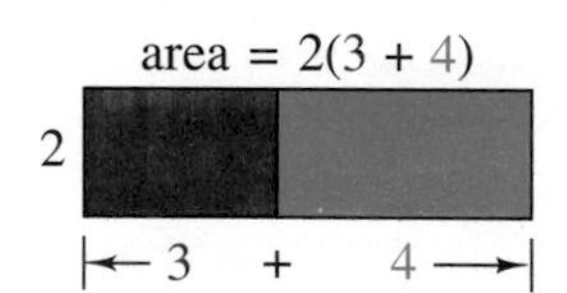

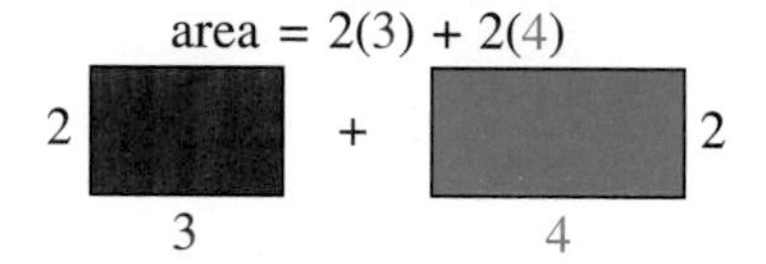

The **distributive property** combines addition and multiplication, and combines subtraction and multiplication.

Distributive Property

Arithmetic	Algebra
$2(3 + 4) = (2 \cdot 3) + (2 \cdot 4)$	$a(b + c) = ab + ac$
$9(15 - 3) = (9 \cdot 15) - (9 \cdot 3)$	$a(b - c) = ab - ac$

3. Is the equation $(b + c)a = ba + ca$ true? Explain.

You can use the distributive property to multiply mentally.

Example 3 Evaluate 4(8.9) mentally.

$$\begin{aligned} 4(8.9) &= 4(9 - 0.1) & \leftarrow 8.9 = 9 - 0.1 \\ &= 4(9) - 4(0.1) & \leftarrow \text{Distribute 4.} \\ &= 36 - 0.4 & \leftarrow \text{Multiply and subtract.} \\ 4(8.9) &= 35.6 & \end{aligned}$$

WORK TOGETHER

Work with a partner to figure out a method to solve the following problem mentally. Write down the steps you use.

> There was a big sale at Green's Department Store. Mr. Lacey bought three sweaters at $14.95 each. He gave the clerk $50. How much change should he get?

Make up your own problem and exchange it with your partner.

TRY THESE

4. **Writing** How do ordering and grouping numbers help you find sums or products mentally?

Explain how to evaluate each expression mentally. Name the property or properties you would use.

5. $-3 + 14 + (-7) + 6$
6. $4 \cdot 356 \cdot 25$
7. $(32 + 87) + 13$
8. $2(13 + 50)$

ON YOUR OWN

Evaluate each expression mentally. Explain the method you use.

9. $4 + (-3) + 6 + (-7)$
10. $-2 \cdot 34 \cdot (-5)$
11. $-2(5 \cdot 46)$
12. $-5 + 2 + 18 + (-45)$

Rewrite each product so you can use the distributive property. Evaluate mentally.

13. $25(-198)$
14. $1.8(-5)$
15. $4 \cdot \$1.99$
16. $103 \cdot \$22$

Critical Thinking **Decide whether the statement is *true* or *false*. Explain why.**

17. $7 \cdot 6 + 4 = 7 \cdot 4 + 6$
18. $-6(9 - 2) = 6(11)$
19. $13 \cdot 9 = 10 \cdot 9 + 3 \cdot 3$
20. $10 + (-12) = 12 + (-10)$

21. **Mental Math** **Use the table at the right.**
    a. If the temperature was 32°F on Sunday, what was it by the end of the day on Thursday?
    b. Which properties helped you solve this problem mentally?

22. **Investigation (p. 102)** Lumber is measured in *board feet.* Type widths are measured in *ems.* Find other examples of unusual systems of measurement. Define the units used in each.

Mixed REVIEW

Find the circumference of a circle with the following radius.

1. 9 in.
2. 4 cm

Find each product or quotient.

3. $8 \cdot (-4) \cdot (-10)$
4. $-(-30) \div 6$

5. Bart saves a nickel every five days and a penny every two days. At the end of 30 days, how much money will he have?

The Nambiquara of northwest Matto Grosso in Brazil have no system of numbers. They do have a verb that means "they are alike."

Source: *The Guinness Book of Records*

Day	Change in Temperature
Mon	+11
Tues	−14
Wed	+9
Thurs	−6

PROBLEM SOLVING

What's Ahead

- Learning and applying the strategy of guess and test

3-7 Guess and Test

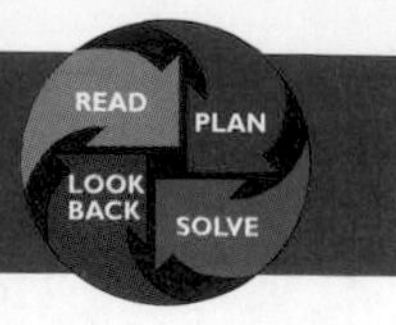

While searching through some computer bulletin boards late one evening, Nita noticed this intriguing clipping.

> Eighty-nine scientists of the planet Leggus held a meeting to study a strange creature discovered on the planet Earth.
>
> "It seems strange," the Centaurians said, "that this creature can maneuver on only two legs, when using four legs like we do is so much better."
>
> "Indeed," the three-legged Tripodians replied. "It's a wonder they don't fall without a third leg for balance."
>
> The 89 Centaurian and Tripodian scientists at this gathering had a total of 319 legs. Now, all you fine detectives out there, how many were Centaurians and how many were Tripodians?

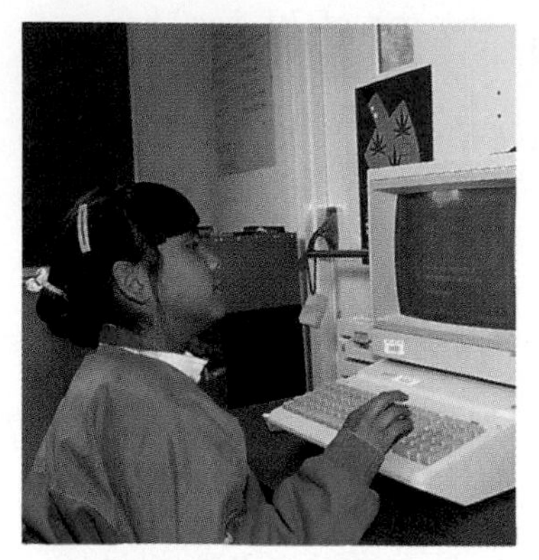

The Internet *is a computer network connecting over 2 million computers. It reaches 15 to 20 million users in over 100 different countries and it is growing at an amazing rate of 20% per month.*

Source: *The New York Times*

Nita was fascinated by the question, but had no idea of how to answer it. She could have used the strategy *guess and test.*

To *guess and test* means you begin with a guess. Even a wild guess. Then you test the guess to see if it gives you an answer that fits the problem. If your first guess does not solve the problem, you can use the results to help you make a better guess the next time. Then continue to guess and test until you find the answer.

READ

Read and understand the given information. Summarize the problem.

1. Read the problem again. Think about the information.
   a. What is the total number of scientists?
   b. How many legs does a Centaurian have? a Tripodian?
   c. What is the total number of legs?
   d. Summarize what the problem is about and what it is asking you to find.

Guess and test is a good strategy to use in this problem.

- By guessing the number of scientists in one group you will have a starting point for solving the problem.
- By comparing the total number of scientists and the number of legs they represent, you will be able to guess more accurately each time.

PLAN

Decide on a strategy to solve the problem.

First try 45 Centaurians (about half the scientists).

SOLVE

Try out the strategy.

2. a. How many Tripodians would there be?
   b. How many legs would all the Centaurians have?
   c. How many legs would all the Tripodians have?
   d. Does it satisfy the conditions of the problem?
3. Should your next guess be more or fewer Centaurians? Explain.

Try another number for the Centaurians.

4. a. How many Tripodians would there be?
   b. What is the sum of the two numbers?
   c. Using your guess, how many legs will the creatures have altogether?
   d. Does it satisfy the conditions of the problem? Why or why not?

If you did not get the correct answer the second time, keep on trying until you do. You may find it helpful to use a table to keep track of your guesses.

LOOK BACK

Think about how you solved the problem.

5. Discuss any pattern you found or shortcut you used that helped you solve the problem.

TRY THESE

Use the Guess and Test strategy to solve each problem.

6. On the two days before a swim meet, Jesse swam a total of 2,050 m. The second day she swam 250 m more than the first day. How many meters did she swim on each day?

In 1990, the cat population in the United States was approximately 63.2 million. Almost one third of all American households included at least one cat.

Source: *Collier's Encyclopedia Yearbook*

Mixed REVIEW

1. Give a real life example of perpendicular lines.
2. Give a real life example of parallel lines.

Evaluate mentally.

3. 12 + (−1) + 8 + (−9)
4. 20 • 6 • 5
5. William's brother is half his father's age. William's father is three times as old as William. How old is William's brother if William is 16?

7. The Paws and Claws Grooming Salon has a busy weekend. The groomer must clip nails for a total of 40 birds and cats. There are 110 animal feet in all.
   a. How many birds are there? How many cats?
   b. **Discussion** Discuss how you solved this problem. Explain how you knew when a guess was not the answer.

ON YOUR OWN

Use any strategy to solve each problem. Show all your work.

8. Two integers have a sum of −9 and a difference of 5. What are the integers?
9. Rosa drove a total of 1,000 mi during three days. On the second day she drove the same number of miles as she did on the first and third days combined. How many miles did she drive on the second day?
10. At a nearby hospital, 40 of the babies born this year were members of either triplets or twins.
    a. Could there have been only one set of triplets and all the rest twins? Explain your answer.
    b. How many different combinations of twins and triplets could there be?
11. A sporting goods store manager ordered twice as many basketball sneakers as tennis sneakers. He ordered 96 pairs of sneakers in all. How many pairs of each kind did he order?
12. Shigechiyo Izumi of Japan lived to be the oldest authenticated centenarian (100 or more years old). The oldest known person in the United States (Carrie White) lived 4 years less than Izumi. If the sum of their ages is 236 years, how old did each person live to be?
13. **Sports** Clorae defeated six opponents to become the class tennis champion. At each level the loser of the match dropped out of the competition. The winner moved on to the next level. How many players were in the games?

What's Ahead

- Simplifying and evaluating expressions with exponents

WHAT YOU'LL NEED

✓ Calculator 

3-8 Exponents and Multiplication

THINK AND DISCUSS

Using Exponents Einstein's equation, $E = mc^2$, is a formula in physics. The variable c represents the speed of light. You read c^2 as "c to the *second power*" or "c *squared.*"

base → c^2 ← exponent

The **base** is the number that is used as a factor. The **exponent** tells how many times the base is used as a factor. The *exponent* 2 means that c is used as a factor two times, or $c^2 = c \cdot c$.

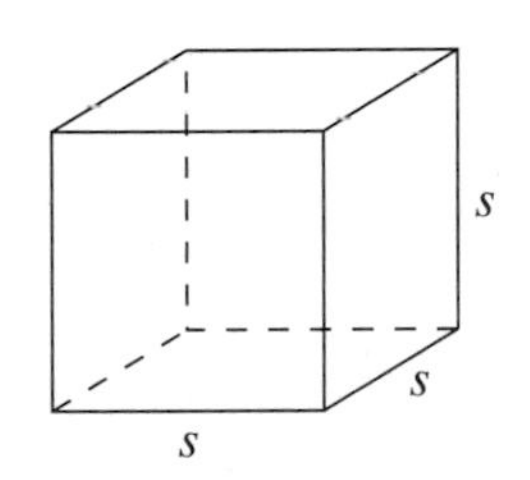

Exponents are used in many formulas. In the formula for the volume of a cube, for example, s is the base and 3 is the exponent.

$$V = s^3 \text{ or } s \cdot s \cdot s$$

1. What is the volume of a cube with sides 5 cm long?

Sometimes you use an exponent with a negative number as the base. When you do, it is important to use grouping symbols to avoid confusion.

$$(-4)^4 = (-4)(-4)(-4)(-4) = 256$$
$$-4^4 = -(4 \cdot 4 \cdot 4 \cdot 4) = -256$$

2. **Discussion** Explain the difference between $(-4)^4$ and -4^4.

3. Find the value of $(-2)^3$ and -2^3.

You can use the y^x key on your calculator to find the value of a number raised to a power.

Example 1 Use a calculator to evaluate.

a. 17^3 17 [y^x] 3 [=] 4913

b. $(-8)^5$ 8 [+/-] [y^x] 5 [=] − 32768

4. List the keystrokes you would use to evaluate -5^4.

When a ball is packed in a cubical box, almost 50% of the volume of the box is air! A standard basketball has a diameter of approximately 10 in. ***If a basketball is packed inside a box, what is the approximate volume of air in the box (not counting the air in the ball)?***

Describe the pattern.

1. 100, 50, 25, 12.5, . . .
2. 1, 11, 21, 31, . . .

Find the circumference of a circle with the given radius.

3. 19 ft 4. 3 yd

5. Refreshments are being sold at a school play. A small juice is $.50, a large is $.75. On Saturday, $103 was collected by selling 162 juice drinks. How many large juice drinks and how many small juice drinks were sold?

A *googol* is the number 1 followed by 100 zeros or 10^{100}. The number 1 followed by a googol of zeros is called a *googolplex.* The name was invented by the 9-yr-old nephew of the American mathematician Edward Kasner.

5. a. Use a calculator to evaluate 12^0, $(-15)^0$, and 3^0

b. Make a statement about the value of any nonzero number raised to the 0 power.

The *standard form* of 7^2 is 49. The *exponential form* of 49 is 7^2.

6. Write 2^3 in standard form.

7. The number 16 can be written in exponential form as 2^a or as 4^b. Find a and b.

Grouping symbols can make a difference when you work with exponents and variables. Compare, for example, $5x^3$ and $(5x)^3$.

$$5x^3 = 5(x)(x)(x) \quad \text{and} \quad (5x)^3 = (5x)(5x)(5x)$$

8. a. Evaluate $5x^3$ for $x = 2$.

b. Evaluate $(5x)^3$ for $x = 2$.

9. a. Write $6 \cdot a \cdot a \cdot a \cdot a$ in exponential form.

b. Write $6a \cdot 6a \cdot 6a \cdot 6a$ in exponential form.

Multiplying Powers When you multiply numbers that have the same base, a pattern develops. Look at the exponents and the number of factors in each expression.

$$3^1 \cdot 3^2 = 3 \cdot (3 \cdot 3) = 3^3$$
$$3^2 \cdot 3^2 = (3 \cdot 3)(3 \cdot 3) = 3^4$$
$$3^2 \cdot 3^3 = (3 \cdot 3)(3 \cdot 3 \cdot 3) = 3^5$$
$$3^3 \cdot 3^3 = (3 \cdot 3 \cdot 3)(3 \cdot 3 \cdot 3) = 3^6$$
$$3^4 \cdot 3^3 = (3 \cdot 3 \cdot 3 \cdot 3)(3 \cdot 3 \cdot 3) = 3^7$$

10. a. What do you notice about the exponents in each pair of factors shown above and the exponent of the product?

b. Write $3^5 \cdot 3^5$ as a base with a single exponent.

Multiplying Powers

To multiply numbers or variables with the same base, add the exponents.

Arithmetic	Algebra
$3^2 \cdot 3^5 = 3^7$	$n^a \cdot n^b = n^{a+b}$

Example 2 Simplify $n^5 \cdot n^7$.

$n^5 \cdot n^7 = n^{5+7} = n^{12}$

11. List factors to show why $n^5 \cdot n^7 = n^{12}$.

When a numerical expression has both exponents and grouping symbols, you have to follow the order of operations carefully.

Example 3 Evaluate $3^2 - 5(6 - 4)^4 + 14 \div 7$.

$3^2 - 5(6 - 4)^4 + 14 \div 7$
$= 3^2 - 5(2)^4 + 14 \div 7$ ← Work inside grouping symbols.
$= 9 - 5(16) + 14 \div 7$ ← Evaluate powers.
$= 9 - 80 + 2$ ← Multiply and divide.
$= -71 + 2$ ← Add and subtract.
$= -69$

FLASHBACK

Order of Operations

1. Work inside grouping symbols.
2. Evaluate powers.
3. Multiply and divide from left to right.
4. Add and subtract from left to right.

TRY THESE

12. a. Write $a \cdot a \cdot a \cdot a \cdot a$ in exponential form. What is the base? the exponent?

b. What is the value of the expression if $a = 2$?

Evaluate.

13. $(-3)^2$ **14.** 6^0 **15.** -8^2 **16.** 1^{15} **17.** 7^3

Write each expression using a single exponent.

18. $4^4 \cdot 4^2$ **19.** $a^3 \cdot a^5$ **20.** $1^2 \cdot 1^7$ **21.** $(-5)^2 \cdot (-5)^7$

Evaluate.

22. $(3 \cdot 2)^2 + 5$ **23.** $3^2 \cdot 2 + 5$ **24.** $-4^2 + 6 \cdot 3^2$

ON YOUR OWN

Write each expression using exponents.

25. $7 \cdot 7 \cdot 7 \cdot 7$ **26.** $(-5)(-5)(-5)$ **27.** $(-x)(-x)(-x)(-x)$

28. Which number is larger, 3^4 or 4^3?

Extra SKILLS PRACTICE

Evaluate.

1. -4^3
2. $(-6)^2$
3. 1.5^3
4. 2^7
5. -15^1
6. 8^0
7. $12 + 7^2$
8. $-15 + 4^3$
9. $10^3 + 5^3$
10. $-9^2 - (-30)$
11. $-3^4 + 40 - 2^5$
12. $12^1 \cdot 30 - 8^2$
13. $6^2 - 50 \cdot 3^3$
14. $(14 + 5^2) \cdot 7^0$
15. $23 + (9 - 14)^2$
16. $(14 - 16)^3 + 10$
17. $-4 \cdot (2 - 8)^2$
18. $(-7 - 8)^2 \cdot 20$

WHAT ? Computers store information in *bits.* 2^3 bits are equal to 1 *byte.* A *kilobyte* is defined as 2^{10} bytes. **How many bits are in a kilobyte?**

Choose **Use a calculator, paper and pencil, or mental math to evaluate each expression.**

29. -4^3 **30.** 1^8 **31.** 9^0 **32.** $(-5)^2$ **33.** 5^3

34. Choose A, B, C, or D. Which of the following number sentences are true?

I. $2^4 \cdot 2^3 = 2^{12}$ **II.** $2^3 \cdot 3^2 = 6^6$

III. $2^7 \cdot 2^0 = 2^7$ **IV.** $2^4 \cdot 3^3 = 6^7$

A. III only **B.** I only **C.** I and III **D.** II and IV

Evaluate.

35. $4 + (8 - 6)^2$ **36.** $4 + 8 - 6^2$

37. $(-3)^2 + 4^3 - 4$ **38.** $-3^2 + 4^3 - 4$

39. Writing Estimate the value of $(2.3)^2$. Explain the method you used. Find the exact value using a calculator or pencil and paper to see how close your estimate was.

Find the value of each expression if $b = 3$.

40. $(b + 5)^2$ **41.** $b^2 + 5^2$ **42.** $b^2 + 5b + 5^2$

CHECKPOINT

Evaluate.

1. $13 \cdot (-32)$ **2.** $-4 \div (-1)$ **3.** $-90 \div (-3 \cdot 10)$

4. $-17 \cdot (-12) - 3 \cdot (-18)$ **5.** $5 \cdot 19 \cdot (-10) \cdot 7$

Choose **Use calculator, paper and pencil, or mental math to evaluate.**

6. $5^5 \cdot 3^2$ **7.** $(-15 \div 3)(-12)$ **8.** $3 + (-7)^4$

9. $(-6 + 5)^3$ **10.** $8[5 + (-4)]^3$ **11.** $(-6)^2 + (9 - 7)^3$

12. Choose A, B, or C. Six friends have five marbles each. Which expression represents the total number of marbles?

A. 6^5 **B.** $5 \cdot 6$ **C.** $6 + 5$

Practice

Compare. Write $>$, $<$, or $=$.

1. -7 ■ 7
2. 3 ■ -8
3. $|-9|$ ■ 3
4. $|-8|$ ■ $|-6|$

Write a variable expression for each phrase.

5. 18 less than n
6. product of 5 and x
7. 10 more than a number

Find each sum.

8. $-7 + 4$
9. $8 + 5$
10. $-6 + (-2)$
11. $41 + (-26)$

Find each difference by writing an equivalent addition.

12. $8 - (-1)$
13. $9 - 11$
14. $-15 - (-5)$
15. $|-1| - |17|$

Evaluate each expression for $x = 5$, $y = -9$, and $z = -1$.

16. $x + y$
17. $x - z$
18. $z - (-y)$
19. $|y| - |x|$

Find each product or quotient.

20. $-8(-7)$
21. $36 \div (-9)$
22. $(-3 \cdot 8) \div (-4)$
23. $6 \div (-2) \cdot (-2)$

Evaluate each expression mentally. Explain the method you use.

24. $5 + (-2) + 5 + (-8)$
25. $(-2) \cdot 43 \cdot (-5)$

Rewrite each product so you can use the distributive property. Evaluate each expression mentally.

26. $50(-97)$
27. $17(-3)$
28. $6 \cdot \$2.99$
29. $98 \cdot \$20$

Write each expression using exponents.

30. $(-1)(-1)(-1)$
31. $5 \cdot 5 \cdot 5 \cdot 5$
32. $(-y)(-y)$
33. $-(4 \cdot 4 \cdot 4)$

Evaluate.

34. $(-2)^3$
35. $(-3)^2 + 5^2 - 5$
36. $(3^2 + (6 - 2)) \cdot 5 - 4^3 - 7$
37. $x + 5$ for $x = -8$
38. $5n - 11$ for $n = -3.2$
39. $a^2 + 4a - 3$ for $a = 0.3$

TECHNOLOGY

3-9 Evaluating Variable Expressions

What's Ahead

- Evaluating variable expressions with integers and decimals
- Using technology to explore variable expressions

WHAT YOU'LL NEED

✓ Computer 

✓ Spreadsheet software 

THINK AND DISCUSS

Using Integers As you read this your hair is growing. Does it seem to grow too quickly sometimes? Not quickly enough?

Some scientists have found that typical human hair grows at a rate of about 0.0165 in. per day, although it does grow faster in the summer than in the winter.

Do you think that the figure of 0.0165 inches per day makes sense? To find out, you can see if this rate describes the way your own hair grows.

You can write the number of inches hair grows in a period of time as a variable expression:

$$0.0165n$$

1. What does n stand for in the expression?

FLASHBACK

To evaluate an expression, replace each variable with a number. Then compute, following the order of operations.

You have learned that to evaluate an expression you replace each variable with a number. Then you compute, following the order of operations.

Let's evaluate the expression for a convenient period of time—like 3 months, or 90 days. To find how many inches your hair would grow in 90 days, you substitute 90 for n:

$$(0.0165)(90)$$

2. **Estimation** Estimate the value of (0.0165)(90). Explain the method you used.
3. **Discussion** Based on your own experience, is the growth rate given above reasonable?
4. **Calculator** Use a calculator to find the exact value of the expression $0.0165n$ for $n = 90$.

In 1992, a woman from Worcester, MA, Diane Witt, had hair that measured 12 ft 2 in. long.

Source: *The Guinness Book of Records*

Using Exponents Some expressions contain exponents. When solving equations containing exponents and decimals: (a) estimate the answer (b) calculate the exact answer, or (c) create a computer spreadsheet.

A spreadsheet will instantly evaluate an expression for many values. You can see how the value of an expression changes using different numbers for the variables.

***The minimum** chute-opening altitude for U.S. skydiving competition is 670 m. This allows time to open the auxiliary chute if the main chute fails.*

Source: *Collier's Encyclopedia*

Example The distance a skydiver falls before she opens her parachute depends on how long she waits. If you ignore air resistance, the formula that relates distance to time is:

$d = 4.9t^2$ d = distance in meters
t = number of seconds in free fall

How far does a skydiver fall in 2.5 s?

Method 1 Estimate.

- $4.9t^2 = 4.9(2.5)^2$ **Replace t with 2.5**
- $(2.5)^2$ is between $2^2 = 4$ and $3^2 = 9$. So, let's say $(2.5)^2 \approx 6$.
- $4.9(2.5)^2 \approx 5(6) = 30$

The skydiver would fall about 30 m in 2.5 s.

Method 2 Use a calculator.

- 4.9 [×] 2.5 [y^x] 2 [=] 30.625

The skydiver falls 30.625 m in 2.5 s.

Method 3 Create a computer spreadsheet.

- Set column A equal to t.
- Set column B equal to:

$$4.9 * t * t$$

The table at the right shows a sample spreadsheet for 9 values of t. According to this spreadsheet, the skydiver falls 30.6 m in 2.5 s.

	A	B
1	TIME	DISTANCE
2	0.0	0.0
3	0.5	1.2
4	1.0	4.9
5	1.5	11.0
6	2.0	19.6
7	2.5	30.6
8	3.0	44.1
9	3.5	60.0
10	4.0	78.4

5. **Discussion** Look at the spreadsheet. Describe how the distance changes as the time increases.

One cup of orange juice *contains 27 g carbohydrates, 0 g fat, and 78 mg vitamin C.*

A variable expression can contain more than one variable. For example, when you run, you burn about 14 calories per minute. Fresh orange juice has 110 calories per cup. Suppose you run for a while and then drink some fresh orange juice. The net calories taken in would be given by $-14m + 110n$, where m is the number of minutes you run and n is the number of cups of juice you drink.

6. What would be your net amount of calories if you run for 45 minutes and drink $2\frac{1}{2}$ cups of juice?

WORK TOGETHER

	A	B
1	A	A*A – 4*A
2	–5	■
3	–4	■
4	–3	■

7. a. Computer Create a spreadsheet to evaluate the expression $a^2 - 4a$ for $a = -5$, $a = -4$, $a = -3$, and so on up to $a = 5$.

b. Writing What happens to the value of $a^2 - 4a$ as a increases from -5 to 5?

c. Critical Thinking Suppose you evaluated the expression $r^2 - 4r$ for $r = -5$ up to $r = 5$. How do you think your results would compare to your results for $a^2 - 4a$? Why?

TRY THESE

Choose Use a calculator or mental math. Evaluate each expression for $a = 2.45$, $b = -5$, and $c = 5$.

8. $b + 5$ **9.** $b - 5$ **10.** $5 - b$ **11.** $5a - 5$

12. $20ab$ **13.** abc **14.** $(b \div c)^3$ **15.** $b^2 + b + 5$

16. Which expressions in Exercises 8–15 did you evaluate using mental math? Explain.

x	$10 - x$
–1	■
0	■
1	■
2	■
3	■

17. Copy and complete the table at the left.

a. How does the value of $10 - x$ change as the value of x increases?

b. Does the value of $10 + x$ increase or decrease as the value of x increases?

c. Can $10 + x$ ever be negative? Explain.

18. **Money** A phone call costs \$1.50 for the first minute plus \$.65 for each additional minute. Let t stand for the total number of minutes the call lasts.

a. Write an expression for the number of *additional* minutes.

b. Write an expression for the cost in dollars of the *additional* minutes.

c. Write an expression for the cost in dollars of the *entire* call.

d. Evaluate the expression in part (c) for $t = 10$. What does your result mean?

e. How much will an 11-minute call cost? A 1-hour call?

ON YOUR OWN

Evaluate each expression for the given values of the variables.

19. $3n + 5$ for $n = -2$

20. $x - 8$ for $x = -4$

21. $-10c$ for $c = 6$

22. $-3t$ for $t = -7$

23. $-2xy$; $x = 5$ and $y = 11$

24. $7a + b$; $a = -3$ and $b = 2.5$

25. $p + q + r + 3$; $p = -5$, $q = -4$, $r = 6$

Estimation **Estimate the value of each expression for the given value of the variable. Then find the exact value using a calculator or pencil and paper.**

26. $3 + 2p$ for $p = 4.3$

27. $m^2 + 3$ for $m = 1.7$

28. $5r - 4r$ for $r = 0.874$

29. $z^2 - 4z + 3$ for $z = 5.1$

30. **Music** Zip Code Music charges \$8.95 for each cassette they mail to you plus a single shipping charge of \$2.95, no matter how many cassettes you order.

a. Write an expression for the total charge in dollars if you order n cassettes.

b. Evaluate your expression for $n = 5$.

c. What does your result in part (b) mean?

Extra SKILLS PRACTICE

Evaluate each expression.

1. $-6b$ for $b = -2$
2. $12 - g$ for $g = -4$
3. $3c + 7$ for $c = -1$
4. $-12 - 2w$ for $w = 3$
5. $7d$ for $d = 0$
6. $-1.5y$ for $y = 6$
7. $-2p - 6$ for $p = 5$
8. $13 - z$ for $z = -11$
9. $4k^2$ for $k = 3$
10. $15 - a^3$ for $a = 2$
11. $-3m + 6n$ for $m = 1$ and $n = -5$
12. $6w^3 - 2x^2$ for $w = -2$ and $x = -6$

Mixed REVIEW

Find the missing angle for each triangle.

1. 65°, 90°
2. 22°, 68°

Evaluate.

3. -5^2
4. 8^4

5. An investor purchased a 2.5-oz gold ingot for \$1,710. Find the price per ounce.

CHAPTER 3

Wrap Up

Negative Integers 3-1

A number on the number line is greater than any number to its left. The ***absolute value*** of a number is its distance from zero on the number line. Two numbers on opposite sides of zero and the same distance from zero on the number line are ***opposites.***

Compare. Write >, <, or =.

1. -8 ■ -1
2. -7 ■ 2
3. $|-3|$ ■ 1
4. $|-4|$ ■ $|4|$

Adding and Subtracting Integers 3-3, 3-4

To add integers with the *same* sign, *add* the absolute values of the integers. The sum has the same sign as the addends.

To add integers with *unlike* signs, *subtract* their absolute values and keep the sign of the integer with the greater absolute value. To subtract an integer you add its opposite.

Find each sum or difference.

5. $(-9) + (-3)$
6. $8 + (-3)$
7. $(-11) - (-5)$
8. $(-9) - 2$

Multiplying and Dividing Integers 3-5, 3-6

The product or quotient of two integers with the *same* sign is *positive.* The product or quotient of two integers with *different* signs is *negative.*

To evaluate an expression, you may find the commutative property, associative property, and distributive property helpful.

Evaluate.

9. $-3 \cdot 18$
10. $(-34) \div (-2)$
11. $-1260 \div 45$
12. $-15 \cdot (-4) \div (-12)$

13. **Writing** Explain how you would use the distributive property and the commutative and associative properties of addition to simplify $-8(99) + (-7) + (-93)$.

14. **Choose A, B, C, or D.** Which has a value of 1?

    A. $-15 \div (-3) - 6$ B. $2 - 3(4 - 5)$ C. $-2 + (-1)(-3)$ D. $-4 + 3(-5 + 4)$

Strategies and Applications 3-7

Sometimes the best way to solve a problem is to guess, test your guess, and make a better guess. Making a table is a good way to organize your guesses so that you can look for a pattern.

15. The length of a rectangle is 6 m greater than the width, and the area is 55 m^2. What are the dimensions?

16. A box contains 30 cardboard models of triangles and squares. There are 103 sides altogether. How many models of each figure are there?

Exponents 3-8

An exponent indicates repeated multiplication. For example, in 2^3 the exponent 3 means use the base 2 as a factor 3 times: $2^3 = 2 \cdot 2 \cdot 2 = 8$. Any nonzero number raised to the 0 power equals 1. To multiply powers of the same base, add the exponents.

Evaluate.

17. $3^4 + (-11)^0$

18. $2^3 \cdot 2^2$

19. $(6 - 8)^4$

20. $-4^2 + 1^3$

Variable Expressions 3-2, 3-9

A variable is a letter that represents a number. A ***variable expression*** contains a variable.

To evaluate a variable expression, you replace the variable with a number and then compute, following the order of operations.

Write a variable expression for each phrase.

21. the sum of b and 7

22. 8 less than w

23. 3 more than twice y

24. the quotient of x divided by 5

Evaluate each expression for $x = -2.5$.

25. $6 \cdot (x - 1)^2$

26. $40 \div x + 7.5$

27. $40 \div (x + 7.5)$

28. $x^2 - 7x$

GETTING READY FOR CHAPTER 4

Solve.

1. $a + 7 = 12$

2. $5b = 35$

3. $\frac{c}{9} = 7$

4. $17 - d = 5$

5. If $x > -4$, what do you know about $-x$?

PUTTING IT ALL TOGETHER

A New Way to Measure

The National Institute of Standards and Technology oversees systems of measurement in the United States. The institute has heard about your new system and would like to know more. Review your system. If you wish, make changes based on your study of the chapter. Then write a letter to the institute describing your system. Here are suggestions to help you convince the institute that your system should be adopted nationwide.

- ✔ Make a display illustrating uses of your system.
- ✔ Make a table comparing your system with others.
- ✔ Create a tool for making measurements in your system.

The problems preceded by the magnifying glass (p. 112, # 30; p. 115, # 43; and p. 123, # 22) will help you complete the investigation.

Excursion: Make up math problems involving your system of measurement. Show how one of them can be solved using a calculator.

Bouncing Around

You and a partner will conduct an experiment that investigates the physical movement of a bouncing ball. You need a ball and measuring stick.

- *Drop the ball.*
- *Measure the height that the ball rebounds on each of its first five bounces.*
- *Record the total height of each bounce. Also show the height of each bounce as a fraction of the previous bounce.*
- *Describe your results.*
- *Use a spreadsheet or graph to display your data.*

THE GAME OF EXPONENTS

- Any number can play. Each player needs a scientific calculator.
- One player chooses a number between 1 and 20. A second player names a random number with 4 to 8 digits.
- All players write these numbers as an equation with a question mark for an exponent. Example: $12^? = 23,777,619$.
- Each player estimates the value of the question mark.
- Players use calculators to evaluate the exponential expression shown on the left side of the equation.
- The player with the closest estimate to the value shown on the right side of the equation scores 1 point.
- The first player to score 10 points wins the game.

Little Miss ...Who?

Do you remember *Little Miss Muffett?* Now meet Little Miss Bottenoose:

Little Miss Bottenoose
Squared the
hypotenuse,
Certain that she would
gain fame.
Each leg she did square,
Then she added the pair
And cried out, "The
results are the
same!"

Write a nursery rhyme based on a math concept. Illustrate it to make your rhyme suitable for framing.

THAT'S PAR FOR THE COURSE!

A golf score is the number of strokes a player takes to get the golf ball from the tee to the hole. Each golf course has an average number of strokes for each hole. This is called par. Here are other golf terms.

Term	Score	Meaning
eagle (e)	-2	2 strokes under par
birdie (b)	-1	1 stroke under par
par (p)	0	average for that hole
bogey (B)	+1	one stroke over par
double bogey (D)*	+2	two strokes over par

(*There are triple bogeys (T), quadruple bogeys (Q), and so on.)

✓ How do the number of eagles, birdies, pars, and bogies that you score determine the number of strokes you need for par?

✓ Write a variable expression that explains your reasoning.

CHAPTER 3

Assessment

1. Compare. Write >, <, or =.

   a. $-12 \blacksquare 12$ b. $|-4| \blacksquare -4$

   c. $0 \blacksquare -1$ d. $-(-2) \blacksquare |-2|$

2. Perform the indicated operations.

   a. $-15 + (-11)$ b. $26 - (-14)$

   c. $-9(-6)$ d. $|-21| \div (-3)$

3. **Writing** Explain the difference between the *opposite* of a number and the *absolute value* of a number.

4. Write a variable expression for each phrase.

   a. a number y increased by 15

   b. the quotient of 6 and a number c

   c. 7 less than twice a number n

   d. the product of x and -13

5. Evaluate.

   a. $-8(15) + 12 \div (-4)$

   b. $(-14) \div 2 - (-5) \cdot (-10)$

   c. $3^2 + 6 \div (-2)$

   d. $(-24) \cdot 2 - (-13) \cdot 2$

6. Use the distributive property to complete. Then evaluate mentally.

   a. $28 \cdot (-6) = (30 + \blacksquare)(-6)$

   b. $15 \cdot 1.97 = 15(2 - \blacksquare)$

7. Write each expression using exponents.

   a. $(-7)(-7)(x)(x)(x)$

   b. $8 \cdot 8 \cdot 8 \cdot 8 \cdot y \cdot y$

   c. $(a)(a)(a)(a)(-2)(-2)(-2)$

8. Write each expression using a single exponent.

   a. $t^2 \cdot t^3 \cdot t$

   b. $2^5 \cdot 2^6 \cdot 2^4$

9. **Choose A, B, C, or D.** Which of the following equations are true?

   I. $8^5 \cdot 8^4 = 8^{20}$

   II. $(-1)^3 \cdot 1^2 = 1$

   III. $(-5)^2 - |-5| = 10^2 \div 5$

   IV. $3^4 \cdot 3^5 = 3^9$

   A. I only   **B.** II and III

   C. III and IV   **D.** I, II, III, IV

10. Evaluate each variable expression for the given values of the variables.

    a. $-19b$ for $b = -3$

    b. x^3 for $x = 10$

    c. $|-5 - t|$ for $t = -6$

    d. $-b^2 - 4b$ for $b = -3$

    e. $-8abc$ for $a = -5$, $b = 7$, $c = -4$

11. A department store was selling ten-speed bikes at $120 each, CDs at $10 each and backpacks at $12 each. During the first five minutes of their opening day sale, 12 of these items were sold. The total cost of these items was $680. How many bikes, CDs, and backpacks were sold?

12. **Writing** Explain how to determine the *sign* of the product of a string of positive and negative integers without computing the product.

CHAPTER 3

Cumulative Review

Choose A, B, C, or D.

1. Which has the same value as $8 - 11$?

A. $8 - (-11)$ **B.** $|8 - 11|$

C. $-8 + 11$ **D.** $8 + (-11)$

2. What is the first step in constructing a line through P perpendicular to $\overleftrightarrow{XY}$?

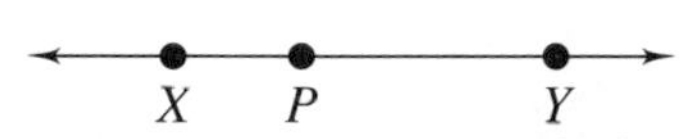

A. Pick a point Q not on $\overleftrightarrow{XY}$.

B. Bisect $\overline{XY}$.

C. Put the compass tip at P and draw arcs intersecting $\overleftrightarrow{XY}$ in two points.

D. Put the compass tip first at X, then at Y, and draw two intersecting arcs.

3. What information *cannot* be determined from the box-and-whisker plot shown?

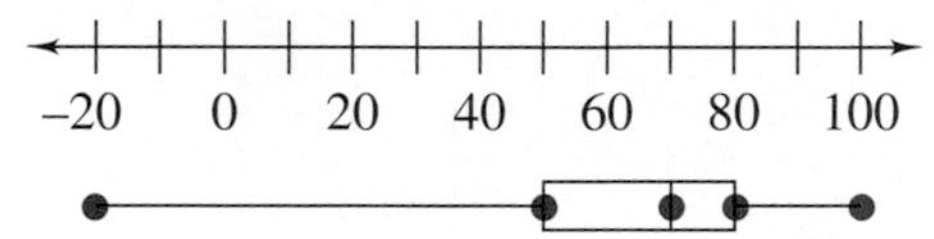

A. the median **B.** the range

C. the quartiles **D.** the outliers

4. What special quadrilateral *cannot* have four congruent sides?

A. rectangle **B.** rhombus

C. parallelogram **D.** trapezoid

5. Which expression does *not* equal 5(2.99)?

A. $5(3) - 0.01$ **B.** $5(3) - 5(0.01)$

C. $5(2) + 5(0.99)$ **D.** $\frac{10(2.99)}{2}$

6. How many integers are there whose absolute value is less than 3?

A. 4 **B.** 5 **C.** 6 **D.** 83

7. What could the expression $12k$ represent?

A. the cost (in cents) of a dozen cans of juice if each can costs 12 cents

B. the cost (in cents) of k photocopies if each photocopy costs 12 cents

C. the time it took Alana to run 1 mi if she ran 12 mi in k min

D. Darrin's age, if Darrin is k years older than his brother and his brother is 12

8. When did the stock fund earn the most?

A. the 1st year **B.** the 2nd year

C. the 3rd year **D.** none of the above

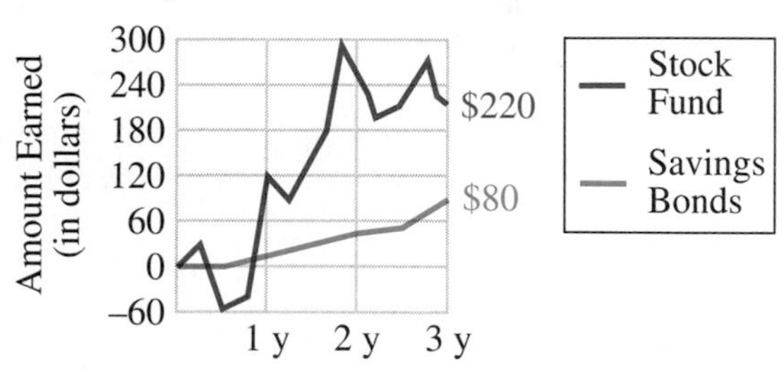

9. Which could be sides of a right triangle?

A. 15, 12, 9 **B.** 9, $\sqrt{15}$, 10

C. 8, 14, 22 **D.** 28, 6, 30

10. Find the area of the shaded region.

A. $4\pi - (\sqrt{2})^2$

B. $2 - \pi$

C. $\pi - (\sqrt{2})^2$

D. $4\pi - 4$

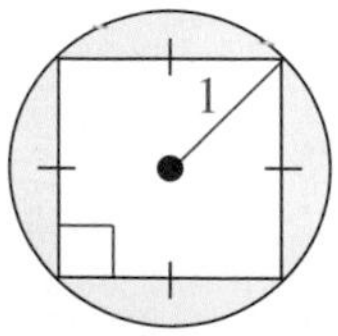

CHAPTER 4

Algebraic Equations and Inequalities

Most of the world's college graduates speak at least two languages. In Scandinavia, most college graduates speak three languages. In the U. S., most students study only English.

School Work

Many businesses provide opportunities for college students through internship programs. College students receive on-the-job training while working on their degree.

For some students this preview can help them make career decisions.

College Enrollment for 20–24-year olds

Country	Percent
Canada	62
United States	60
Finland	40
France	35
Belgium	33
Netherlands	32
Spain	32
West Germany	32
Austria	31
Denmark	31
Sweden	31
Japan	30
Australia	29
Italy	26
Switzerland	25
United Kingdom	23

Source: *Money*

WHAT YOU WILL LEARN

- how to model equations
- how to write and solve equations and inequalities
- how to use spreadsheets to evaluate formulas
- how to solve problems by writing an equation

investigation

Project File

Memo

Around 1930 the sculptor Alexander Calder invented a new art form called the mobile. A mobile consists of shapes hanging from wires. The shapes balance so perfectly that even the slightest air currents cause the shapes to move continuously. Many of Calder's mobiles are beautiful and graceful works of art. All of them exhibit the principle of balance we use to solve equations.

Mission: Investigate the principles that govern the construction of mobiles. Use string, wires, or plastic soda straws, and identical shapes cut from cardboard. Use the mobile illustrated to get started. The number in the shape tells you how many shapes to use.

4 in. | 3 in.
6 in. | 3 in.
1 2 4

Leads to Follow

- ✓ How much weight do you need on one side to balance a given weight on the other side?
- ✓ How far from a support string must you hang a given weight to balance a different weight on the other side?
- ✓ How can you add rows to a mobile to make a more complex sculpture?

What's Ahead

- Simplifying variable expressions

4-1 Simplifying Variable Expressions

WHAT YOU'LL NEED

✓ Algebra tiles 

$\blacksquare$ represents x

represents 1

represents -1

Researchers in Japan have come up with a unique idea: a paper bike! The bicycle weighs only 4 lb and is made from handmade paper and glue. Covered with a plastic coating to keep it from falling apart when wet, the bicycle is sturdy, fast, and recyclable.

Source: 3-2-1 *Contact Magazine*

Distributive Property

$a(b + c) = ab + ac$

and

$(b + c)a = ba + ca$

THINK AND DISCUSS

Reading and Writing Expressions Six students from San Jose Middle School bicycled to the game; the rest came in three buses. Seven students from Mission Hill School bicycled, the rest came in two buses. If each bus carried the same number of students, you can use algebra tiles for modeling.

San Jose Middle School

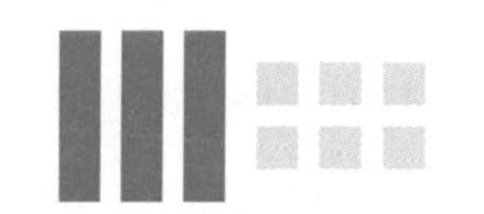

Mission Hill School

1. How many buses were there in all? How many students bicycled in all?
2. Write a variable expression that represents the total number of students who came by bus.
3. Write a variable expression that represents the total number of students who came to Band Day.

A **term** is part of a variable expression. For example, the expression $-3x + 5y + 10$ has three terms: $-3x$, $5y$, and 10.

A term that does not contain a variable is called a **constant.** In the expression $-3x + 5y + 10$, the constant term is 10. When a term does contain a variable, the number that is multiplied by the variable is called the **numerical coefficient** of the term. The numerical coefficients of $-3x$ and $5y$ are -3 and 5, respectively.

Terms with the same variable(s) are called **like terms.** You can add or subtract like terms by using the distributive property.

Example 1 Add like terms: $5m + 9m$

$5m + 9m = 5 \cdot m + 9 \cdot m$

$= (5 + 9)m$ **Add numerical coefficients.**

$= 14m$

Things should be as simple as possible, but no simpler.
—Albert Einstein
(1879–1955)

Simplifying Expressions

When you add or subtract like terms, you are **combining like terms.** You can **simplify** an expression, by performing as many of the operations within the expression as possible.

Example 2

Simplify $7c + 8 - 3c$.

$7c + 8 - 3c = 7c - 3c + 8$ — Commutative Property
$= (7c - 3c) + 8$ — Associative Property
$= (7 - 3)c + 8$ — Distributive Property
$= 4c + 8$ — There are no more like terms to combine.

Example 3 shows a different way of using the distributive property to simplify an expression.

Example 3

Simplify $2(x + 3)$.

$2(x + 3) = 2(x) + 2(3)$ — Distributive Property
$= 2x + 6$ — Unlike terms

4. Explain how the tiles below are a model of Example 3.

Sometimes you must use the distributive property more than once in simplifying an expression.

Example 4

Simplify $2k + 7(k - 4)$.

$2k + 7(k - 4)$
$= 2k + 7(k) - 7(4)$ — Distributive Property
$= 2k + 7k - 28$ — Simplify.
$= (2k + 7k) - 28$ — Associative Property
$= (2 + 7)k - 28$ — Distributive Property
$= 9k - 28$

You can also simplify expressions involving different variables.

Example 5

Simplify $3s + 4t + 5s - 8t - 6$.

$3s + 4t + 5s - 8t - 6$
$= 3s + 5s + 4t - 8t - 6$ — Commutative Property
$= (3s + 5s) + (4t - 8t) - 6$ — Associative Property
$= (3 + 5)s + (4 - 8)t - 6$ — Distributive Property
$= 8s - 4t - 6$

TRY THESE

Combine like terms using algebra tiles as a model.

5. $x + 4x$ **6.** $3y + 5 + 2y - 3$

$a \cdot 1 = a$ and $a = a \cdot 1$

Simplify each expression.

7. $-5s + 2s$ **8.** $7q - 6q$ **9.** $8n - n$ **10.** $-2j - 7j$

Complete with the appropriate numbers or variables.

11. $5(h + 12) = \blacksquare \cdot h + 5 \cdot \blacksquare = 5h + \blacksquare$

12. $(\blacksquare - 3)\blacksquare = \blacksquare \cdot 6 - \blacksquare \cdot 6 = 6z - \blacksquare$

Simplify each expression.

13. $12(d - 6)$ **14.** $3 + 5(a - 4)$

15. $(2x + 1) + 3x$ **16.** $4 + 3p - 9q + q - 2p$

17. Kia, Dave, and Mika each have two boxes of pencils and five more pencils. Each box contains the same number of pencils.

a. Work in pairs. Model this situation using algebra tiles.

b. Which of these variable expression(s) can represent the situation above: $3(2x + 5)$, $6x + 5$, or $6x + 15$?

Some bakers** give an extra roll with every dozen sold. This is called a baker's dozen.* ***How many more rolls would you have if you receive x baker's dozens rather than x regular dozens?

ON YOUR OWN

Simplify each expression.

18. $3a + 2 + a$ **19.** $9(m - 7)$

20. $n + 4n - 3n$ **21.** $(q + 1)5$

22. $4(z - 3) - 8$ **23.** $-6 + 5(1 + r)$

24. $5n - 6 + 4n + 3 - 2n$ **25.** $3(g + 5) + 2 + 3g$

26. **Art** A neon sign is made from bended lengths of glass tubes filled with gas. The kind of gas inside a tube determines its color. Write a simplified variable expression that represents the perimeter of the rectangular neon sign at the right.

Mixed REVIEW

Estimate the value of each square root.

1. $\sqrt{133}$ 2. $\sqrt{226}$

Evaluate for $h = 17$.

3. $(6h + 50) \div 8$
4. $h^2 (371 - 6h)$

Find each answer.

5. $542.8 + 53.7$
6. $8092.43 - 413.85$
7. A 14-in. length of chain sells for \$8.50. At this rate, what should be the price of a 10-in. chain?

Extra SKILLS PRACTICE

Simplify each expression.

1. $-7n + 5n$
2. $-10g - g + 5g$
3. $-4(6t - 2)$
4. $(p - 1)12$
5. $-2(-x + 3)$
6. $5c + 3(c - 6)$
7. $-4(1 - m) - 5$
8. $-5 - 3(-z - 1)$

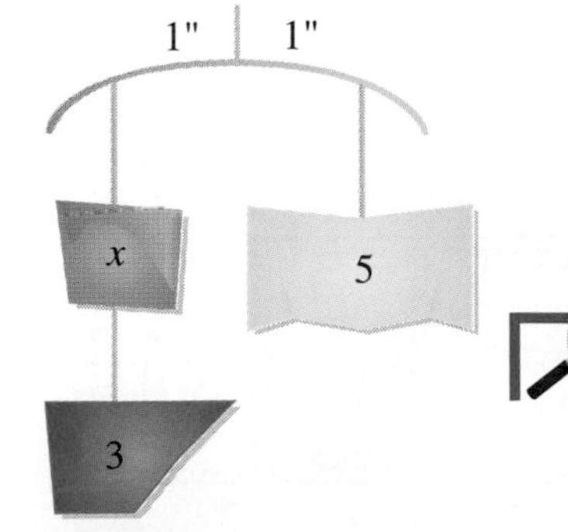

27. **Writing** Your best friend was absent when the distributive property was explained in class. Write out an explanation you might give to her over the telephone. Your friend is still confused. Write out another explanation. Give examples.

28. **Money** Martin bought three folders priced at x cents each, two report covers priced at y cents each, and one binder priced at \$1.89. Write an expression that represents the total price of these items.

Choose Use a calculator, paper and pencil, or mental math. Simplify each expression.

29. $1.07(y - 4.2)$
30. $34 + 14p - 18 + 47p$
31. $9.2b + 5c + 1.2b + 1.8c$
32. $19k + 24(5 + k)$
33. $-5u + 6 + u + 4u$
34. $(5.1r + 2.4) - 1.009r$

35. Try this number trick with a friend.

Step 1 Choose a number.
Step 2 Double the chosen number.
Step 3 Add 3 to the result.
Step 4 Multiply the result by 5.
Step 5 Subtract 6 from the result.

a. If your friend tells you the result of Step 5, how can you tell what number your friend chose in Step 1?

b. Let n represent the number chosen in Step 1. Write a simplified expression that represents what happens at each step. Record your expressions in a table like the one at the right.

Step	Expression
1	n
2	$2n$
3	$2n + 3$
4	■
5	■

c. Using the expressions, explain why the trick works.

36. **Critical Thinking** Write two different expressions that are equivalent to $3m + 8$. One expression should have three terms, and the other should have four terms.

37. **Investigation (p. 144)** You want to construct the mobile shown at the left. Experiment to find the weight x which will make the mobile balance. Write and solve an equation to represent your conclusion.

What's Ahead

- Solving one-step equations using addition and subtraction

4-2 Addition and Subtraction Equations

WHAT YOU'LL NEED

✓ Algebra tiles 

THINK AND DISCUSS

An **equation** is a mathematical sentence with an equal sign. In an equation like $x + 2 = 5$, a value of the variable that makes the equation true is called a **solution** of the equation. You can solve $x + 2 = 5$ using this model made of algebra tiles.

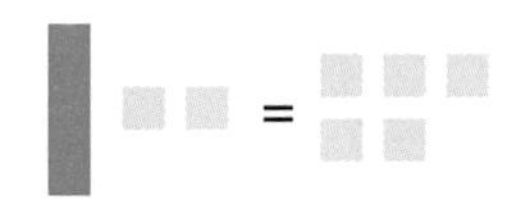

1. What is the result if you remove two yellow tiles from each side of the equation?
2. What is the solution of the equation?
3. Model $x + 5 = 7$. Use your model to solve the equation.

Equivalent equations are equations that have the same solution.

Addition Equations To solve equations using algebra, you use the fact that addition and subtraction are inverse operations. You can use subtraction to "undo" addition, and the result is an *equivalent equation.*

Subtraction Property of Equality

If you subtract the same number from each side of an equation, the results are equal.

Arithmetic	Algebra
$9 = 9$	$a = b$
$9 - 4 = 9 - 4$	$a - c = b - c$

The use of two short parallel lines to represent equality, =, was first proposed in 1557 by Robert Recorde (1510–1558), Royal Court Physician.

Source: *The VNR Concise Encyclopedia of Mathematics*

Example 1 Solve $n + 3.4 = 8$. Check the solution.

$n + 3.4 = 8$

$n + 3.4 - 3.4 = 8 - 3.4$ **Subtract 3.4 from each side.**

$n = 4.6$

Check $n + 3.4 = 8$

$4.6 + 3.4 = 8$ **Replace *n* with 4.6.**

$8 = 8$ ✓

Extra SKILLS PRACTICE

Solve each equation.

1. $b + 15 = 8$
2. $-2 = 0.5 - c$
3. $-7 + h = 1$
4. $p - 2 = -4$
5. $0 = -15 + n$
6. $g - 11 = 5$
7. $3 = t - 6$
8. $1.2 - r = 8.4$
9. $6 = e + 14$
10. $25 + d = -10$
11. $20 - a = 32$
12. $-5 = w + 9$
13. $m + 3.5 = 9$
14. $3.5 = y - 2.5$
15. $-8 = 12 + q$
16. $7 = -3 - k$

Subtraction Equations

Addition undoes subtraction.

Addition Property of Equality

If you add the same number to each side of an equation, the results are equal.

Arithmetic	Algebra
$9 = 9$	$a = b$
$9 + 4 = 9 + 4$	$a + c = b + c$

Example 2 Solve $t - 3 = -7$. Check the solution.

$$t - 3 = -7$$
$$t - 3 + 3 = -7 + 3 \quad \text{Add 3 to each side.}$$
$$t = -4$$

Check

$$t - 3 = -7$$
$$-4 - 3 = -7 \quad \text{Replace } t \text{ with } -4.$$
$$-7 = -7 \checkmark$$

If you remember that the sum of a number and its opposite is zero, then you can solve equations in a different way.

FLASHBACK

$a + (-a) = 0$ and $-a + a = 0$

Example 3 Solve $c + 14 = 5$ using opposites.

$$c + 14 = 5$$
$$c + 14 + (-14) = 5 + (-14) \quad \text{Add } -14 \text{ to each side.}$$
$$c + 0 = -9$$
$$c = -9$$

WORK TOGETHER

- Work with a partner. Write an equation for each model.
- Devise a way to use the model to solve the equation. (*Hint:* You may have to add "zero pairs" before you can take away.)
- Write the steps you take to solve the equation using algebra.

FLASHBACK

is a zero pair.

4. =

5. =

6. =

7. =

Sometimes you can use an equation to help you solve an everyday problem.

Example 4 Vida deposited \$7.50 in her savings account. The new balance was \$43.25. What was the previous balance?

Use the variable p to represent the previous balance.

previous balance	plus	deposit	equals	new balance
p	$+$	7.50	$=$	43.25

$$p + 7.50 = 43.25$$
$$p + 7.50 - 7.50 = 43.25 - 7.50$$ Subtract 7.50 from each side.
$$p = 35.75$$

The previous balance in Vida's account was \$35.75.

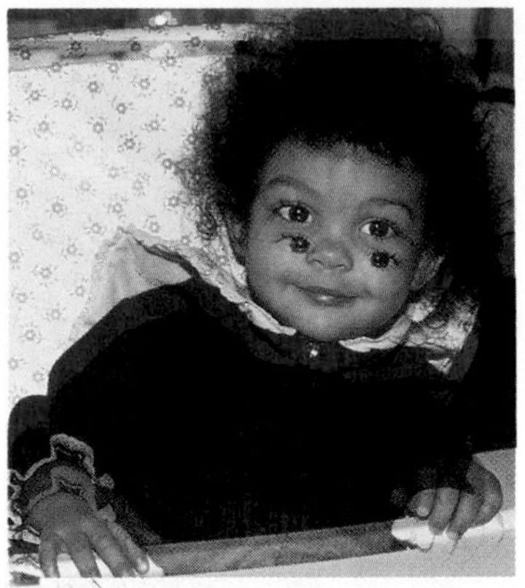

***\$1,000 deposited** in a bank at 7% annual interest on the day a baby is born is worth \$2,759.03 on her fifteenth birthday.*

TRY THESE

8. Explain why these four equations are equivalent.
   $t + 7 = 4$ $\quad 7 + t = 4$ $\quad 4 = t + 7$ $\quad 4 = 7 + t$
9. Explain why subtracting 8 from each side of $b + 8 = 17$ is equivalent to adding -8 to each side.

Mental Math Solve each equation. Check the solution.

10. $y + 7 = 12$
11. $n - 8 = -2$
12. $20 = -7 + k$
13. $7 = d - 1.4$
14. $g - \frac{1}{2} = \frac{1}{4}$
15. $6 + q = -8$

Solve each equation. Check the solution.

16. $a - 15 = -9$
17. $64 = n + 34$
18. $x - 3.66 = -4.1$
19. **Discussion** When do you think you would use a calculator to help you solve an equation?
20. **Choose A, B, C, or D.** José sold one of his baseball cards for \$9.30. This was \$3.75 more than he originally paid for the card. If a represents the amount José originally paid, which equation *cannot* be used to find this amount?

    A. $a + 3.75 = 9.30$ **B.** $9.30 - a = 3.75$
    C. $9.30 = 3.75 + a$ **D.** $a - 3.75 = 9.30$

Mixed REVIEW

Compare. Use $>$, $<$, or $=$.

1. -8 ■ -6
2. $|15|$ ■ $|-15|$

Simplify each expression.

3. $8 + 6r + 47 - 4r$
4. $3.4(s + t) + 12s - t$
5. $1.7(z + 15)$
6. $(164 + b)22 - 6b$
7. Three children inherited a sum of money. The oldest received $\frac{2}{5}$ of the money. The middle child received $\frac{1}{3}$ of the money. The youngest child received the remainder, \$24,000. What was the total amount of money inherited by the three children?

ON YOUR OWN

Choose Use a calculator, paper and pencil, or mental math. Solve each equation. Check the solution.

21. $z - 4 = -11$ 22. $-15 = 6 + m$ 23. $3.15 + w = 12.09$

24. $f + \frac{1}{2} = \frac{3}{5}$ 25. $7 + b = -13$ 26. $x - 1.75 = 19$

For Exercises 27–29, write an equation for the problem. Solve the equation. Then give the solution.

27. Yesterday Jena mailed some invitations for a party. Today she mailed eight more invitations. If Jena mailed 52 invitations in all, how many did she mail yesterday?

28. After Darnel spent \$8.13 on a cassette tape, he had \$6.87 left. How much money did he have before buying the tape?

29. The temperature at 6:00 P.M. was 12°F. At 6:00 A.M. it was 15°F cooler. What was the temperature at 6:00 A.M.?

30. **Data File 4 (pp. 142–143)** In 1990, how much more money did a person with four years of college earn than a person with fewer than four years of high school?

In 1991, the United States was the number one country in sales of recorded music, with purchases totaling \$7.8 billion. Japan was second with sales of \$3.4 billion.

Source: *International Federation of the Phonographic Industry*

Estimation Estimate the solution of each equation.

31. $r + 8.019 = -11.57$ 32. $-3.9004 = y - 61.41$

33. $j - 0.0155 = 3.029$ 34. $-14.8 + p = 2.03$

Critical Thinking Choose from −3, −2, −1, 0, 1, 2, and 3. Find *all* the numbers that are solutions of each equation.

35. $n = 3$ 36. $|n| = 3$ 37. $|n| = -3$

38. $|n| = 0$ 39. $|n| + 1 = 2$ 40. $|n + 1| = 2$

$|n|$ means the absolute value of n.

41. **Writing** Write a problem that you can solve using the equation $a + 8.40 = 11.55$.

42. **Investigation (p. 144)** To construct a mobile, you hang one medallion five inches from the main support wire. You want to hang two medallions together on the other side. Experiment to find out how far away from the support wire they should be for the mobile to balance. Write an equation to represent your conclusion.

Problem Solving Practice

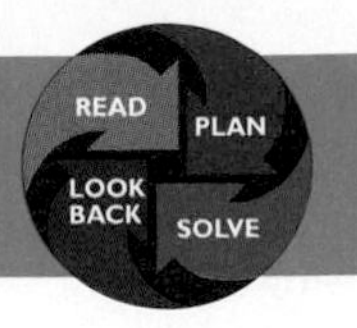

PROBLEM SOLVING STRATEGIES

Make a Table
Use Logical Reasoning
Solve a Simpler Problem
Too Much or Too Little Information
Look for a Pattern
Make a Model
Work Backward
Draw a Diagram
Guess and Test
Simulate a Problem
Use Multiple Strategies
Write an Equation
Use a Proportion

Solve. The list at the left shows some possible strategies you can use.

1. A four-digit number contains the digits 1, 4, 7, and 9, but not necessarily in that order. Is the number divisible by 4?

2. If you add 10 to one third of a number, the result is 20 less than the number. What is the number?

3. A pair of pants and a sweater together cost \$75. The sweater costs \$15 more than the pants. How much do the pants cost?

4. Find three consecutive integers such that the sum of the smallest and largest is 36.

5. Nathan has an after-school job delivering groceries. He usually works 15 h per week and earns \$4 per hour. When he works more than 15 h in a week, he earns \$6 per hour for each hour of overtime. How many hours must Nathan work in one week to earn at least \$100 in that week?

6. **Calculator** The population of Centerville is 10,000. Suppose that the population begins to increase by 3% each year. In how many years will the population be greater than 12,000?

7. A large wooden cube is painted red. Then it is cut into 27 small cubes of equal size, as shown in the figure at the left. How many small cubes have exactly two faces painted red?

8. The length of a board is 48 in. Dyani cuts the board into two pieces so that one piece is 8 in. longer than the other. How long is each piece?

9. **Calculator** Use each of the digits from 1 to 5 exactly once. Find the two numbers made from these digits that give you the greatest possible product. Explain why you believe you have found the greatest product.

10. A math contest consists of ten problems. Three points are given for each correct answer. One point is deducted for each incorrect answer. Estelle answers all the problems and scores 18 points. How many correct answers does she have?

What's Ahead

- Using multiplication and division to solve one-step equations
- Using equations to solve problems involving savings

WHAT YOU'LL NEED

✓ Algebra tiles 

MATH AND SAVINGS

4-3 Multiplication and Division Equations

THINK AND DISCUSS

Save your pennies! You have only three weeks to save $27 for a ticket to the big concert. How much must you save per week?

1. Explain how the tiles below are a model of this situation. What do the green tiles represent? the yellow tiles?

2. What is the result if you divide the tiles on each side of the equal sign into three equal groups?
3. How much money must you save per week?
4. What equation do the tiles represent? What is the solution?

More than 250 billion Lincoln pennies have been minted since the coin was first issued in 1909. If all the pennies were stacked in a pile, they would reach 220,851 mi into space.

Source: *The Guinness Book of Records*

Multiplication Equations

Multiplication and division are inverse operations. Use division to "undo" multiplication.

Division Property of Equality

If you divide both sides of an equation by the same nonzero number, the results are equal.

Arithmetic	Algebra
$7 = 7$	$a = b$
$\frac{7}{3} = \frac{7}{3}$	$\frac{a}{c} = \frac{b}{c} \quad c \neq 0$

Example 1 Solve $2n = -18$. Check the solution.

$$2n = -18$$
$$\frac{2n}{2} = \frac{-18}{2} \qquad \text{Divide each side by 2.}$$
$$n = -9$$

Check

$$2n = -18$$
$$2(-9) = -18 \qquad \text{Replace } n \text{ with } -9.$$
$$-18 = -18 \checkmark$$

Division Equations To solve an equation involving division, you can multiply each side by the same number.

Multiplication Property of Equality

If you multiply both sides of an equation by the same number, the results are equal.

Arithmetic	**Algebra**
$7 = 7$	$a = b$
$7(3) = 7(3)$	$ac = bc$

Example 2 Solve $\frac{z}{9} = 1.4$. Check the solution.

$$\frac{z}{9} = 1.4$$

$$9\left(\frac{z}{9}\right) = 9(1.4) \quad \text{Multiply each side by 9.}$$

$$z = 12.6$$

Check

$$\frac{z}{9} = 1.4$$

$$\frac{12.6}{9} = 1.4 \quad \text{Replace } z \text{ with 12.6.}$$

$$1.4 = 1.4 \checkmark$$

TRY THESE

Write and solve an equation using each model.

5. 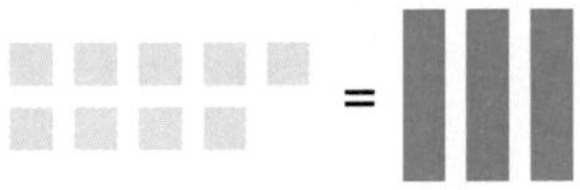

6. 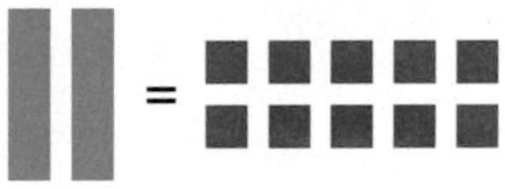

Solve each equation. Check the solution.

7. $24 = -3s$ **8.** $\frac{c}{-4} = -64$ **9.** $30 = \frac{w}{1.5}$ **10.** $1.6a = 4.96$

11. Money The cost of a bicycle is $150. Write and solve an equation for each problem. Then give the solution of the problem.

a. Tran plans to buy the bicycle eight weeks from now. He wants to know how much money he must save per week.

b. Anica knows she can save $7.50 per week. She wants to know how many weeks it will take to save the $150.

Extra SKILLS PRACTICE

Solve each equation.

1. $-4b = 76$
2. $\frac{m}{-1.5} = -10$
3. $426 = -3d$
4. $\frac{h}{-7} = 6$
5. $7w = 280$
6. $5 = \frac{x}{4.2}$
7. $-2 = \frac{d}{5}$
8. $0.4 = \frac{a}{-3}$
9. $6p = -30$
10. $-3.2 = -8k$
11. $\frac{m}{8} = -4$
12. $-5.6 = 0.8y$

The first major bicycle innovation in 70 years is a "two-wheel drive" bike invented by Billie Joe Becoat of Illinois. His company holds the patent rights on the bike in 32 countries.

Source: *EBONY*

ON YOUR OWN

Mental Math Is -5 a solution of each equation?

12. $25v = -5$ **13.** $\frac{15}{m} = -3$ **14.** $-15 = \frac{d}{-3}$ **15.** $10 = -2t$

Choose Use a calculator, paper and pencil, or mental math. Solve each equation. Check the solution.

16. $\frac{b}{-4} = 20$ **17.** $35 = \frac{y}{3.5}$ **18.** $270 = 1.35j$

19. $-352 = -32h$ **20.** $0 = \frac{n}{24}$ **21.** $0.3z = -1.86$

Write an equation for each problem. Solve the equation. Then give the solution of the problem.

22. Eight pens cost \$9.84 in all. What is the price of one pen?

23. The temperature at noon in Fairbanks, Alaska, was 0°F. It then began to drop at a steady rate of 2°F per hour. At what time did the temperature reach -14°F?

In 1867, U.S. Secretary of State, William H. Seward, purchased Alaska from the Russians for \$7.2 million. People who did not realize the bargain the United States had gotten referred to Alaska as "Seward's Folly."

Source: *The World Almanac*

GREAT EXPECTATIONS

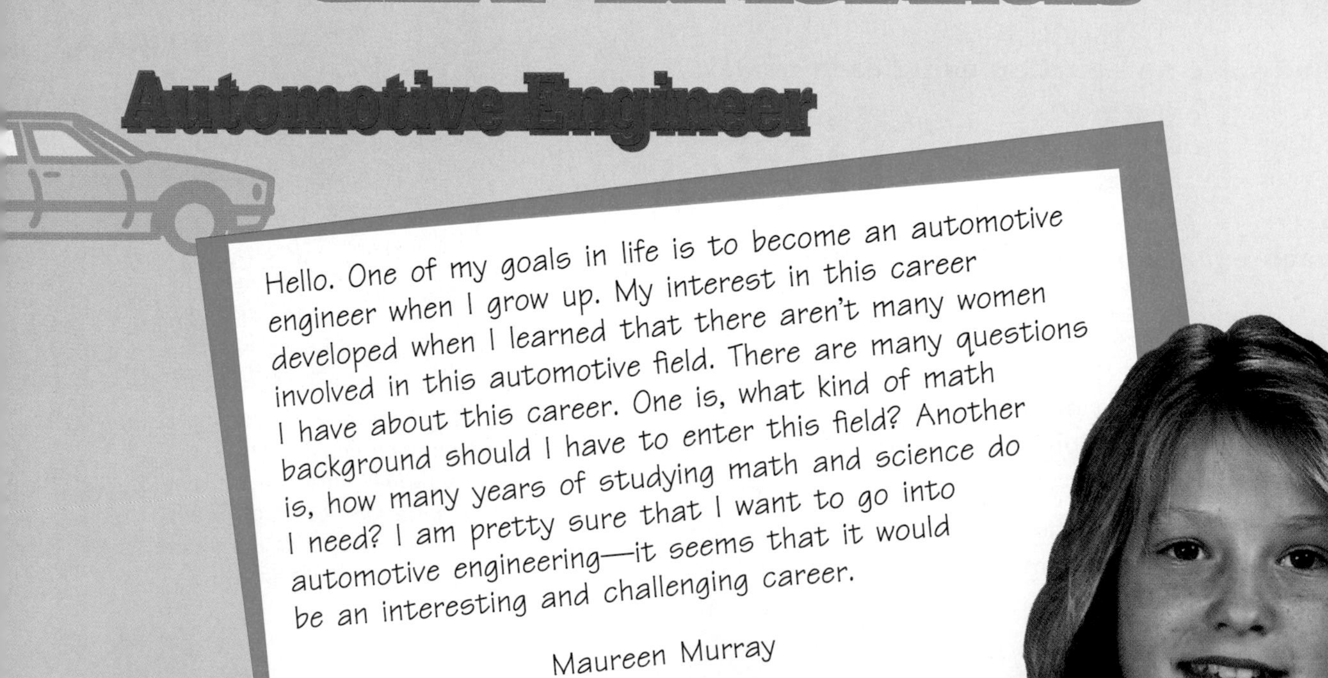

Automotive Engineer

Hello. One of my goals in life is to become an automotive engineer when I grow up. My interest in this career developed when I learned that there aren't many women involved in this automotive field. There are many questions I have about this career. One is, what kind of math background should I have to enter this field? Another is, how many years of studying math and science do I need? I am pretty sure that I want to go into automotive engineering—it seems that it would be an interesting and challenging career.

Maureen Murray

Critical Thinking Choose from −8, −4, −2, 0, 2, 4, and 8. Find *all* the numbers that are solutions of each equation.

24. $2|n| = 4$

25. $-2|n| = -4$

26. $|2n| = 4$

27. $\frac{|n|}{2} = 4$

28. $\frac{|n|}{2} = -4$

29. $|\frac{n}{2}| = 4$

30. Writing Write a paragraph that compares the process of solving $6a = -42$ to the process of solving $a + 6 = -42$. What are the similarities? What are the differences?

31. How would you solve the equation $\frac{-7}{r} = 1$?

Estimation Write an equation for each problem. Estimate the solution of the equation. Then answer the question.

32. Lisa earns \$3.75 per hour. The amount on her paycheck this month was \$69.38. About how many hours did she work?

33. A MegaSonic radio costs \$46.99. You and two friends plan to share the cost equally. About how much will you each pay?

Mixed REVIEW

Find each answer.

1. 23 • (−15)
2. 213 • 12
3. 192 ÷ (−12)
4. 5,684 ÷ 98

Solve each equation.

5. $22 = f - 17.6$
6. $k + 76 = 283$
7. If a new dollar bill is 0.1 mm thick, how high can you stack 10,000 dollar bills?

Dear Maureen,

I'm always happy to learn of a student who is interested in an engineering career. You won't be spending all of your days working out math or science problems. The problem solving techniques you are learning in school now will help you to anticipate and solve a variety of problems before they affect the customer. In an automotive company, we need each part of the car to get to the factory on time and work the way it should after it is installed. It is the engineer's job to solve any technical problems along the way.

I hope you stay interested in an engineering career. Try to find an opportunity to talk to some engineers in person. Ask your counselor about programs where professionals come in to your schools and give practical examples of your school work being applied in the real world.

Deborah Meagher, Automotive Product Engineer

What's Ahead

- Solving two-step equations

4-4 Solving Two-Step Equations

WHAT YOU'LL NEED

✓ Algebra tiles 

FLASHBACK

Subtracting an integer is the same as adding its opposite.

$a - b = a + (-b)$

Truth is the only safe ground to stand upon.
—Elizabeth Cady Stanton (1815–1902)

THINK AND DISCUSS

Using Tiles These tiles are a model of $2x + (-3) = 7$.

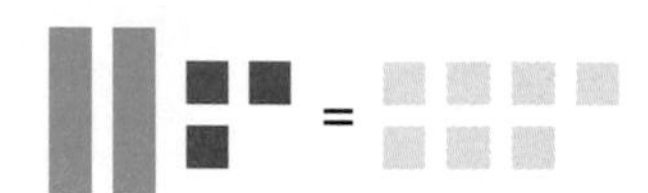

1. Write the equation a different way using subtraction.
2. What happens if you add three yellow tiles to each side of the equal sign? Write an equation to represent the result.
3. What happens if you now divide the tiles on each side of the equal sign into two groups of equal size?
4. What is the solution of the equation?

Using Two Operations Many equations involve two operations. To solve equations like these using algebra, you must use two properties of equality.

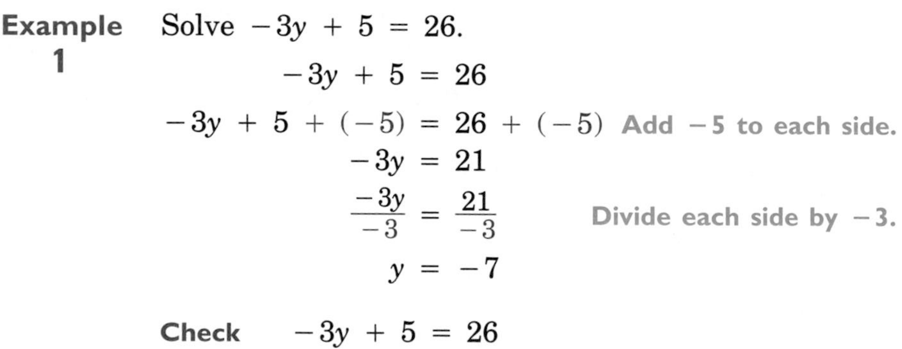

Example 1 Solve $-3y + 5 = 26$.

$$-3y + 5 = 26$$
$$-3y + 5 + (-5) = 26 + (-5) \quad \text{Add } -5 \text{ to each side.}$$
$$-3y = 21$$
$$\frac{-3y}{-3} = \frac{21}{-3} \quad \text{Divide each side by } -3.$$
$$y = -7$$

Check
$$-3y + 5 = 26$$
$$-3(-7) + 5 = 26 \quad \text{Replace } y \text{ with } -7.$$
$$26 = 26 \checkmark$$

The equation $-3y + 5 = 26$ is a simple *two-step equation.* To solve equations like these, you can use this method.

How to Solve a Simple Two-Step Equation

1. Undo addition or subtraction.
2. Undo multiplication or division.

You can use two-step equations to solve everyday problems.

Example 2 Three friends shared equally the cost of renting a canoe. Each person rented a paddle for $4 and paid $20 in all. What was the cost of renting the canoe?

Use the variable c to represent the cost of the canoe.

cost of canoe shared by 3	plus	cost of a paddle	equals	cost per person
$\frac{c}{3}$	$+$	4	$=$	20

$$\frac{c}{3} + 4 = 20$$

$$\frac{c}{3} + 4 - 4 = 20 - 4 \quad \text{Subtract 4 from each side.}$$

$$\frac{c}{3} = 16$$

$$3\left(\frac{c}{3}\right) = 3(16) \quad \text{Multiply each side by 3.}$$

$$c = 48$$

The cost of renting the canoe was $48.

WORK TOGETHER

- Work with a partner. Outline a method for using algebra to solve a two-step equation in the form $ax + b = c$.
- Show how to use your method to solve the following equations.

5. $2x + 8 = -6$ **6.** $3x - 8 = 10$ **7.** $9 = 4x + 17$

TRY THESE

Show how to model and solve each equation with algebra tiles.

8. $4x - 2 = -6$ **9.** $5 = 3x + 8$

Solve each equation. Check your solution.

10. $3s - 4 = 8$ **11.** $\frac{k}{5} + 1.5 = 6.5$ **12.** $-7 = 9 + 2g$

13. Kyle ordered four tapes by mail. Each tape cost the same amount. With a $5 shipping charge, the total cost was $33. Show how to find the cost of one tape by using an equation.

Extra SKILLS PRACTICE

Solve each equation.

1. $-2 = 10d - 3$
2. $\frac{h}{-3} - 6 = 8$
3. $7 = -2 + 3b$
4. $-8 + 2g = 4$
5. $\frac{k}{5} + 11 = -4$
6. $-12 = \frac{m}{4} - 9$
7. $7 + \frac{c}{-6} = -3$
8. $-3 - 5n = -1$
9. $-1 = -4 + \frac{e}{8}$
10. $8 + \frac{a}{-1.2} = 0.7$
11. $4.8 = 4p + 1.6$
12. $3.5 = -6m - 0.1$

WHAT? Any method that follows a set procedure to solve a certain type of problem is called an *algorithm*. This term can be traced back to a 9th century Moslem mathematician, Mohammed ibn-Musa al-Khwarizmi. Through a translation of his work on algebra, Arabic numerals became generally known in Europe.

Source: *Word Mysteries and Histories*

ON YOUR OWN

Mental Math Solve each equation.

14. $2j - 7 = 11$
15. $\frac{x}{2} - 3 = 9$
16. $15 = -2x - 5$
17. $4m + 8 = 4$
18. $-11 = 1 + 3n$
19. $3 + \frac{m}{-10} = 6$

Choose Use a calculator, paper and pencil, or mental math. Solve each equation. Check the solution.

20. $5 + \frac{k}{9} = -31$
21. $30 = 18 + 2b$
22. $1.2z - 0.6 = 32.4$
23. $\frac{x}{-8} - 7 = -9$
24. $1.2 = 3s - 1.8$
25. $\frac{y}{4.5} - 9 = 3.5$

26. **Writing** Describe how the process of solving $3v - 9 = 12$ is different from solving $3v = 12$. For each equation, describe a real situation that it can represent.

The Franchise Boom

Franchising—operating a store or service that is part of a chain—is a rapidly expanding part of the US economy. Sales at franchise outlets increased from \$232 billion* in 1991 to \$248 billion in 1992. In the same time period, the number of franchise outlets grew from 408 thousand to 428 thousand. The International Franchise Association reports that about 11 percent of all retail sales are made at franchise outlets.

** All figures exclude gasoline stations, auto dealers, and bottlers.*

27. **Calculator** There were 408 thousand franchise outlets in 1991. In 1992, there were 428 thousand. To find the percent of increase in the number of franchise outlets, you can solve the equation $428 = 408p + 408$. To the nearest whole percent, what was the percent of increase?

28. **Investigation (p. 144)** You are constructing a mobile. You hang a 2-ounce clay bird six inches from the main support wire. You want to hang a clay cat four inches away on the other side of the support wire. Experiment to find out how much the cat should weigh for the mobile to balance. Write an equation to represent your conclusion.

Mixed REVIEW

Use mental math to evaluate.

1. $20 \cdot 9 \cdot 5$
2. $15 + 42 + 35$

Solve each equation.

3. $18m = 162$
4. $27 = \frac{x}{5.6}$
5. $-241.93 = -13z$
6. $\frac{173.7}{c} = 19.3$
7. Jodie spent $\frac{1}{3}$ of her money at the amusement park and $\frac{1}{2}$ of the remainder on a new shirt. She had \$15 left. How much money did she start out with?

To write decimals as percents, multiply by 100 and write the percent sign.

What's Ahead

- Solving problems by writing and solving equations

PROBLEM SOLVING

4-5 Write an Equation

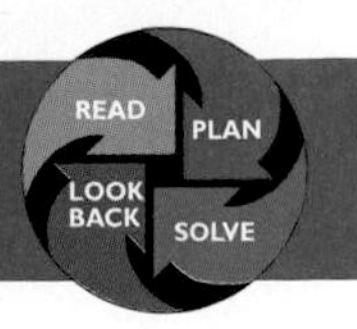

You can solve many types of problems using equations.

> Leroy wants to buy a camera that costs $269.95. He plans to make a down payment of $100. He will pay the rest of the cost in five equal payments over the next five months. How much will each payment be?

READ

Read and understand the given information.

1. Think about the information you are given and what you need to find.
   a. What is the cost of the camera that Leroy wants to buy?
   b. What does it mean to make a "down payment" of $100?
   c. What is Leroy's plan for paying for the camera?
   d. Summarize the goal of the problem in your own words.

PLAN

Decide on a strategy to solve the problem.

Writing an equation is an appropriate strategy for this problem. The amount of each payment is the *unknown,* so use a variable such as p to represent it. Then translate the important words and phrases of the problem into the symbols of an equation.

down payment	plus	5 equal payments	equals	total cost
100	$+$	$5p$	$=$	269.95

SOLVE

Try out the strategy.

2. What operation(s) will you use to solve the equation?
3. What is the solution of the equation?
4. What is the solution of the problem?

LOOK BACK

Think about how you solved this problem.

5. Check your solution of the *equation.* (Replace p in the original equation with the value you found.)
6. Check your solution of the *problem* by using estimation.

TRY THESE

7. Look back at the problem about Leroy and the camera.
   a. Suppose that Leroy made three equal payments instead of five. What would be the amount of each payment?
   b. Suppose that Leroy made five equal payments, but his down payment was $125. What would be the amount of each payment?
   c. Suppose that Leroy made a down payment of $100, but could only afford payments of $20 each month. About how many months would it take to pay for the camera?

8. **Choose A, B, C, or D.** Isabel had $185 in her bank account. She withdrew $15 each week to pay for a guitar lesson. She now has $110. Which equation can you use to find the number of weekly withdrawals that she made?

   A. $185 - 15 = 110n$ **B.** $\frac{185}{n} + 15 = 110$

   C. $185 - 15n = 110$ **D.** $185 + 15n = 110$

> *You say you've got a real solution.*
> *Well, you know,*
> *We'd all love to see the plan.*
> —John Lennon (1940–1980)

Write an equation to solve each problem. Check the solution.

9. **Jobs** Asheesh and two friends shoveled snow for three hours yesterday. They divided their total earnings equally. Asheesh spent $11 of his share on a CD, then deposited the remaining $15 in his savings account. What was the total amount the friends earned shoveling snow?

10. **Money** The cost of a long-distance telephone call to your friend is 35¢ for the first minute and 14¢ for each additional minute. What was the total length of a call that cost $2.59?

ON YOUR OWN

Use any strategy to solve each problem. Show all your work.

11. The product of the page numbers on two facing pages of a book is 4,160. What are the page numbers?

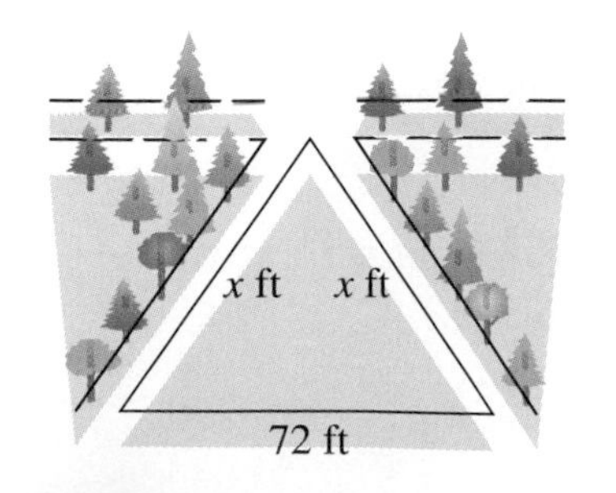

12. The perimeter of the park shown at the left is 67 yd. What are the unknown lengths of the sides?

13. When 18 gal of water are poured into an empty tank, the tank is filled to three fourths of its capacity. What is the total number of gallons that the tank can hold?

14. If you add 2.36 to half a number, the result is 9.5. What is the number?

15. The student council's budget for a party is shown at the right. They need to increase the amount for music to $725, but they must keep the same total amount. They want to decrease the amount for each of the other items equally. Make a revised budget for the party.

Item	Amount
Music	$500
Refreshments	$750
Decorations	$325
Supplies	$120

16. In 1991, the total population of Pennsylvania was 11,961,000. Of that number, 27% were between 5 and 24 years old. How many people were in that age group?

17. In a music poll of 25 students, 15 liked rock, 9 liked jazz, and 12 liked rap. Four students liked all three types of music, 4 liked only rock and jazz, and 5 liked only rock and rap. If no students liked only jazz and rap, how many students didn't like any of these types of music?

Pittsburgh residents are conservation minded. Residential water use in the city of Pittsburgh is a low 41 gallons per person per day compared to an average usage in other U.S. cities of approximately 90 gallons per person per day.

Source: *The Information Please Environmental Almanac*

CHECKPOINT

Simplify each expression.

1. $9(4 + d)$
2. $-3m + 4 - 5m$
3. $2h + 4(h - 5)$

Solve each equation. Check the solution.

4. $-7 + q = 4$
5. $16 = -2v$
6. $x - 7.8 = 13.75$
7. $2s + 5 = 12$
8. $\frac{b}{-12} = -3$
9. $49 = 3.7z - 25$

10. Julio bought pencils that cost 39¢ each and a notebook that cost $1.19. The total cost was $3.92. Write and solve an equation to find the number of pencils Julio bought.

11. Write two different equations for which -2 is the solution. One should be a one-step equation and the other should be a simple two-step equation. Describe a situation that can be represented by each equation.

Mixed REVIEW

Graph on a number line.

1. -8
2. 3
3. 0

Solve each equation.

4. $80 - \frac{b}{5} = 20$
5. $158 = 86 + 12a$

6. Find the next number in the following sequence: 7, 8, 10, 13, 17, 22, ■

What's Ahead

- Combining like terms and using the distributive property to solve equations
- Solving equations with variables on both sides of the equal sign

WHAT YOU'LL NEED

✓ Algebra tiles 

4-6 Simplifying and Solving Equations

THINK AND DISCUSS

Combining Like Terms These tiles model $4x + (3 + x) = 18$.

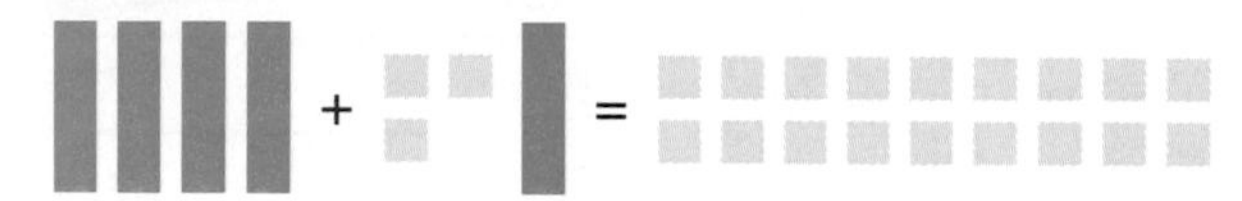

1. How is this equation different from the simple one-step and two-step equations you have studied so far in this chapter?

2. Regroup the tiles at the left of the equal sign so all the green tiles are together. Write an equation for the regrouped tiles.

3. What is the solution of your new equation?

Some equations have like terms on one or both sides of the equal sign. The first step in solving equations like these is to simplify each side by combining the like terms.

Example 1 Solve $3n + 9 + 4n = 2$.

$$3n + 9 + 4n = 2$$
$$3n + 4n + 9 = 2 \quad \leftarrow \text{Use the commutative property.}$$
$$7n + 9 = 2 \quad \text{Combine like terms.}$$
$$7n + 9 - 9 = 2 - 9 \quad \text{Subtract 9 from each side.}$$
$$7n = -7$$
$$\frac{7n}{7} = \frac{-7}{7} \quad \text{Divide each side by 7.}$$
$$n = -1$$

Check $3n + 9 + 4n = 2$

$$3(-1) + 9 + 4(-1) = 2 \quad \text{Replace } n \text{ with } -1.$$
$$2 = 2 \checkmark$$

4. a. Solve the equation modeled below using algebra tiles.

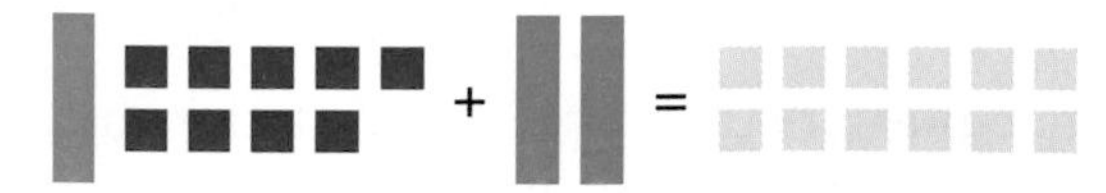

b. Show how the solution is represented using algebra.

Knowing when to use a calculator can make solving equations easier.
Use a calculator to solve:
$\mathbf{8.4x + 2 - 6.74x = 7.229}$

Using the Distributive Property

Sometimes you must first use the distributive property to remove parentheses.

To follow, without halt, one aim: There's the secret of success.

—Anna Pavlova (1881–1931)

Example 2 Solve $-7 = 2(r + 1) + 3$.

$$
\begin{aligned}
-7 &= 2(r + 1) + 3 \\
-7 &= 2r + 2 + 3 && \leftarrow \text{Use the distributive property.} \\
-7 &= 2r + 5 && \text{Combine like terms.} \\
-7 - 5 &= 2r + 5 - 5 && \text{Subtract 5.} \\
-12 &= 2r \\
\frac{-12}{2} &= \frac{2r}{2} && \text{Divide each side by 2.} \\
-6 &= r
\end{aligned}
$$

Check

$$
\begin{aligned}
-7 &= 2(r + 1) + 3 \\
-7 &= 2(-6 + 1) + 3 && \text{Replace } r \text{ with } -6. \\
-7 &= -7 \checkmark
\end{aligned}
$$

5. Explain how the tiles below are a model of Example 2.

The equations in Examples 1 and 2 are *multi-step equations.* Here is one method for solving such equations.

How to Solve a Multi-Step Equation

1. Remove parentheses using the distributive property.
2. Combine like terms.
3. Undo addition or subtraction.
4. Undo multiplication or division.

WORK TOGETHER

- Work with a partner. Let x represent any integer. Write expressions that represent the next two consecutive integers.
- Translate the following sentence into an equation.
  The sum of three consecutive integers is some number n.
- Use your equation to find three consecutive integers with the given sum.

FLASHBACK

You get consecutive integers when you count by ones from any given integer.

6. 27 **7.** -48 **8.** 0 **9.** 123

Mixed REVIEW

Simplify.

1. $13x + 4x + 7x$
2. $18(3h + 11h)$
3. $6(n + 6) + 4n$
4. $12(-8u) + 13 - 7$

5. Four ounces of XtraGreen fertilizer mixed with 1 gal of water will fertilize 400 ft^2 of lawn. If there are 32 oz of fertilizer in a box, how many boxes must you buy to fertilize 6,000 ft^2 of lawn?

You can also use the properties of algebra to solve equations with variables on both sides of the equal sign.

Example 3 Solve $3h + 7 = 5h - 1$.

$$\begin{aligned} 3h + 7 &= 5h - 1 && \text{Subtract } 3h \text{ from} \\ 3h + 7 - 3h &= 5h - 1 - 3h && \text{each side.} \\ 7 &= 2h - 1 && \text{Combine like terms.} \\ 7 + 1 &= 2h - 1 + 1 && \text{Add 1 to each side.} \\ 8 &= 2h && \\ \frac{8}{2} &= \frac{2h}{2} && \text{Divide each side by 2.} \\ 4 &= h && \end{aligned}$$

Check

$$\begin{aligned} 3h + 7 &= 5h - 1 && \\ 3(4) + 7 &= 5(4) - 1 && \text{Replace } h \text{ with 4.} \\ 19 &= 19 \checkmark && \end{aligned}$$

TRY THESE

10. **a.** Explain how the tiles below are a model of the equation $4x - 8 = x + 7$.

    b. Explain how to solve the equation using the tiles.

Solve each equation. Check the solution.

11. $-8 = z + 3z$
12. $-5y = 12 - 9y$
13. $2(z - 1) = 16$
14. $6d + 1 = 15 - d$
15. $8 - 3(p - 4) = 2p$
16. $19 = 4(k + 1) - k$
17. The length of a rectangle is 7 cm more than its width. The perimeter is 38 cm. Find the length and width.

Perimeter of a rectangle = $l + l + w + w$, or $2l + 2w$.

ON YOUR OWN

18. **a.** Draw a model for $2(x + 4) = 12$ and a model for $2x + 4 = 12$. How are they different?

    b. Show how to solve each equation using algebra.

Choose Use a calculator or paper and pencil. Solve each equation. Check the solution.

19. $2(1.5a + 4) - 6a = -7$

20. $5y = y - 40$

21. $5(r + 3) = 2r + 6$

22. $0.5x + 4 + 2x = 14$

23. $15 = -3(c - 1) + 9$

24. $7m = 9(m + 4)$

25. $0.3t + 1.4 = 4.2 - 0.1t$

26. $5s - 2 + 3(s - 11) = 5$

Write an equation for each problem. Solve the equation. Then give the solution of the problem.

27. A computer store received a shipment of 36 monitors. There were three times as many color monitors as black-and-white. How many of each type were in the shipment?

28. Eight less than twice a number is sixteen less than three times the number. What is the number?

For Exercises 29 and 30, write an equation for the given diagram. Then find the unknown lengths.

29.

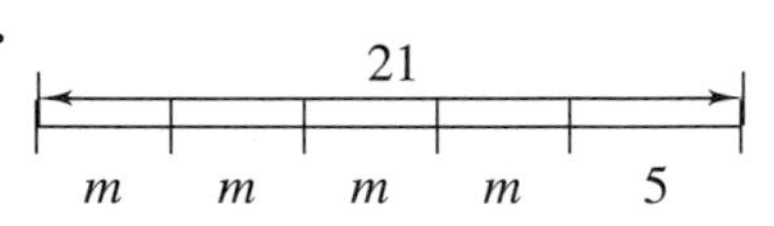

30.

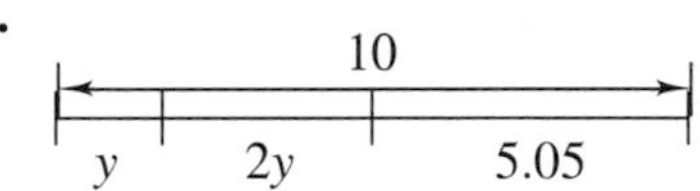

31. **Writing** Write a summary of the methods you have learned for solving equations. Be sure to include examples.

32. a. **Computer** Make a spreadsheet like the one below.

	A	B	C
1	x	3(4x − 55)	9(2x + 15)
2	■	■	■
3	■	■	■

b. Enter −5, −4, −3, −2, −1, 0, 1, 2, 3, 4, and 5 in Column A.

c. For the given values of x, what is the relationship between the number in Column B and the number in Column C?

d. Enter additional values of x until you find a value for which the numbers in Columns B and C are equal.

e. What equation have you solved?

f. Use a spreadsheet to solve $2(4x - 5) - 2 = 3(2x + 14)$.

Extra SKILLS PRACTICE

Solve each equation.

1. $9p - 6 = 3p$
2. $4m - 7 = 3m$
3. $5h - 2 = 28 - h$
4. $8t - 1 = 23 - 4t$
5. $5c - 2 = 6 + c$
6. $2a - 1 = 4 + a$
7. $5y + 3 = 2y + 15$
8. $6w + 3 = 2w + 11$
9. $3(2g - 3) = 27$
10. $4(2m - 3) = 28$
11. $9 = 3(5z - 2)$
12. $40 = 5(3d + 2)$
13. $3(5 + 3q) - 8 = 88$
14. $6x - (3x + 8) = 16$
15. $2(3 + 4d) - 9 = 45$
16. $5b - (2b + 8) = 16$
17. $3s - 3 = 3(7 - s)$
18. $9(n + 2) = 3(n - 2)$
19. $10 - 3e = 2e - 8e + 40$
20. $5 - 2k = 3k - 7k + 25$
21. $5 + 4r - 7 = 4r + 3 - r$
22. $4 + 3a - 6 = 3a + 2 - a$
23. $5(w + 4) = 3(w - 2)$
24. $8(3g - 2) = 4(7g - 1)$

What's Ahead

- Using formulas to solve problems
- Transforming formulas to solve for the unknown value

4-7 Formulas

THINK AND DISCUSS

Using Formulas A **formula** is an equation that shows a relationship between two or more quantities. You can represent the quantities by variables.

1. Write a formula for finding the number of inches, i, in f feet.
2. From your everyday experiences, describe two other quantities that you can relate by a formula. Choose variables to represent the quantities and write a formula.

FLASHBACK

The perimeter of a figure is the distance around it. For rectangles and squares, you can find perimeter using a formula.

- rectangle: $P = 2l + 2w$
- square: $P = 4s$

You can solve many measurement problems by using formulas.

Example 1 How many feet of fencing will Jorge need to enclose a rectangular garden that is 24 ft long and 15 ft wide?

- Jorge wants to find the distance around a rectangle. Use the perimeter formula for rectangles.

$$P = 2l + 2w$$
$$P = 2(24) + 2(15)$$
$$P = 48 + 30$$
$$P = 78$$

Jorge needs 78 ft of fencing.

FLASHBACK

The area of a figure is the amount of space that it encloses. Below are some common formulas for area.

- square: $A = s \cdot s = s^2$
- rectangle: $A = lw$
- parallelogram: $A = bh$
- triangle: $A = \frac{1}{2}bh$
- trapezoid: $A = \frac{1}{2}h(b_1 + b_2)$

You can use formulas to find *areas* of geometric figures.

Example 2 Find the area of the trapezoid shown at the right.

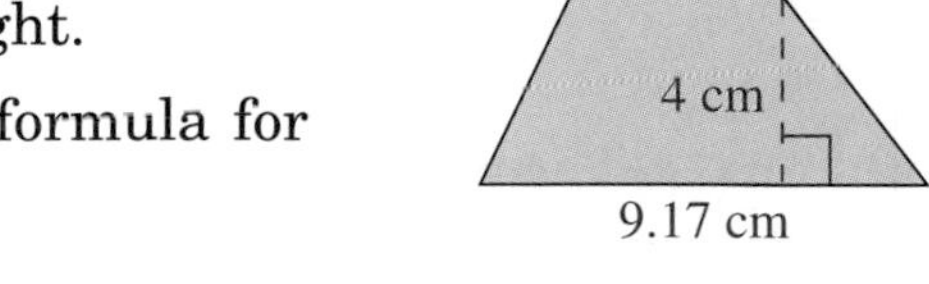

- Use the area formula for trapezoids.

$$A = \frac{1}{2}h(b_1 + b_2)$$
$$A = \frac{1}{2}(4)(4.35 + 9.17)$$
$$A = \frac{1}{2}(4)(13.52) = 2(13.52) = 27.04$$

The area of the trapezoid is 27.04 cm^2.

To use a formula, you may need to apply properties of equality.

Example 3 Rae drove 198 mi in 4 h. Find her average speed.

- Use the formula for distance. Replace d with 198, replace t with 4, and solve for r.

$$d = rt$$
$$198 = r \cdot 4$$
$$\frac{198}{4} = \frac{r \cdot 4}{4} \quad \text{Divide each side by 4.}$$
$$49.5 = r$$

Rae drove at an average speed of 49.5 mi/h.

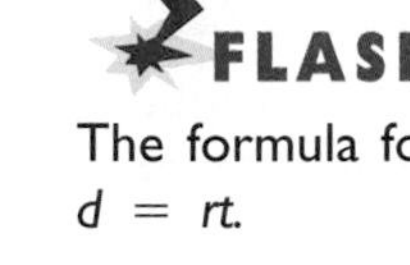

FLASHBACK

The formula for distance is $d = rt$.

d: distance traveled
r: rate of travel
t: time spent traveling

Transforming Formulas

Example 4 Write a formula for finding the width of a rectangle when the length and perimeter are known.

- Use the formula $P = 2l + 2w$. Apply the properties until w is alone on one side of the equal sign.

$$P = 2l + 2w$$
$$P - 2l = 2l + 2w - 2l \quad \text{Subtract } 2l \text{ from each side.}$$
$$P - 2l = 2w$$
$$\frac{P - 2l}{2} = \frac{2w}{2} \quad \text{Divide each side by 2.}$$
$$\frac{P - 2l}{2} = w \quad \text{This is the new formula.}$$

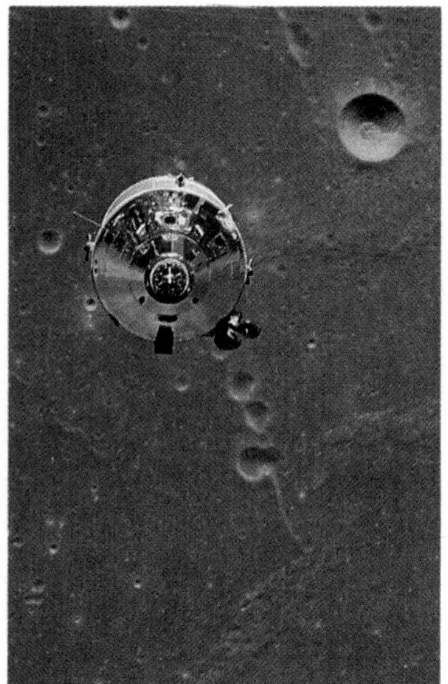

On May 26, 1969, the Apollo 10 spacecraft, carrying three astronauts, reached a speed of 24,791 mi/h. This is the fastest speed at which humans have ever traveled.

Source: *The Guinness Book of Records*

TRY THESE

Find the area of each figure.

3. 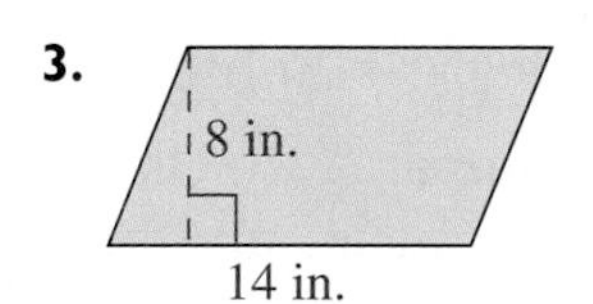

4. 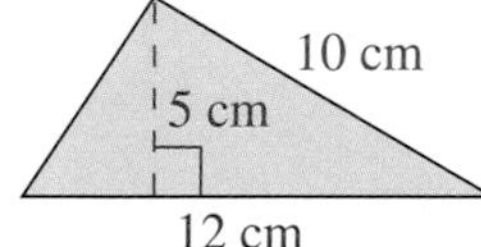

5. 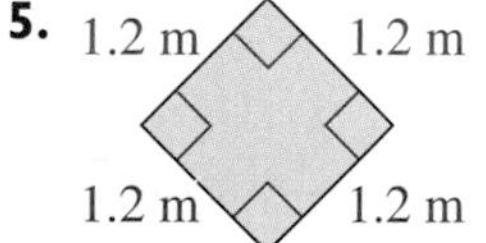

6. a. Write a formula for finding the height of a trapezoid, h, when the area and the lengths of the bases are known.

b. The area of a trapezoid is 133 ft^2. The bases are 11 ft and 17 ft long. Use your formula to find the height.

7. Aviation An airplane flew for 90 min at an average speed of 475 mi/h. How far did it fly?

ON YOUR OWN

Find the perimeter and the area of each figure.

8.

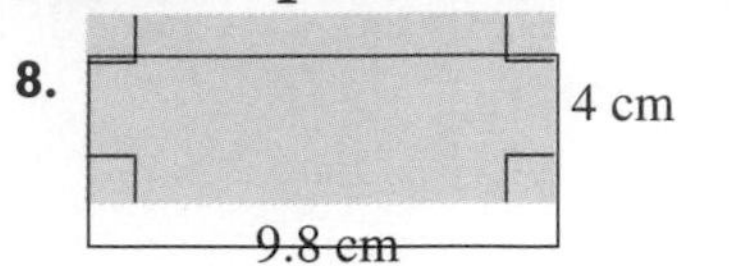

9.

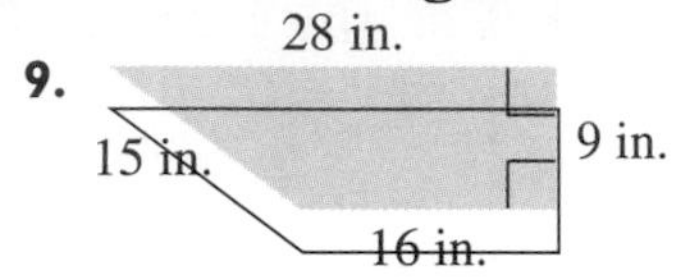

10. The perimeter of a rectangular picture frame is 48 in. The width is 10 in. Find the length.

11. What is the length of one side of a square with area $0.64\ m^2$?

12. The Jacksons left home at 7:00 A.M. and drove directly to their vacation spot 240 mi away. They arrived at noon.

a. What was their average speed?

b. Three days later, the Jacksons began the return trip at 4:00 P.M. They drove at an average speed of 40 mi/h and made a 30-min rest stop. When did they arrive home?

Find the area of each figure.

13.

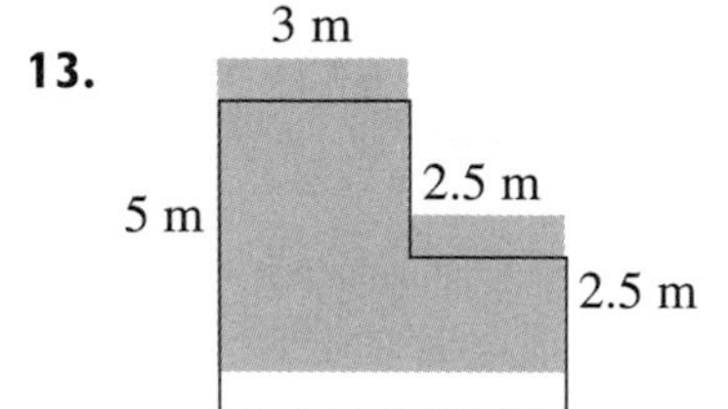

14.

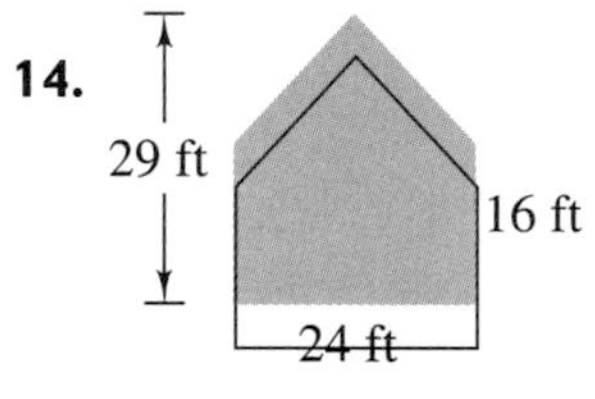

15. You use the formula $F = \frac{9}{5}C + 32$ to find a temperature in degrees Fahrenheit, F, given degrees Celsius, C.

a. Write a formula for finding the temperature in degrees Celsius when given a temperature in degrees Fahrenheit.

b. Use your formula to find the Celsius temperature that corresponds to a comfortable room temperature of 68°F.

16. Discussion The perimeter of a rectangular garden is to be 24 ft. What is the greatest possible area for the garden?

17. Writing Describe the method you would use to find the area of the irregular figure drawn at the left. Find the area, then explain why you think your method is the best solution.

Mixed REVIEW

Find the circumference and area of each circle.

1. d = 7.5 in.

2. r = 12 cm

Solve each equation.

3. $3x + 15 - x + 5 = 4$

4. $(7 + t)6 = 3t + 6$

5. Emilia has the same number of sisters as brothers. Her brother Oscar has twice as many sisters as brothers. How many children are in the family?

Extra SKILLS PRACTICE

Find each area.

1. rectangle: 8 m by 2.5 m
2. square: side = 6.25 cm
3. triangle: b = 3ft, h = 7 ft
4. trapezoid: b_1 = 12 cm, b_2 = 20 cm, h = 8.5 cm

Find each perimeter.

5. rectangle: 1.2 m by 5 m
6. square: side = 8.1 cm
7. triangle: each side = 9 in.

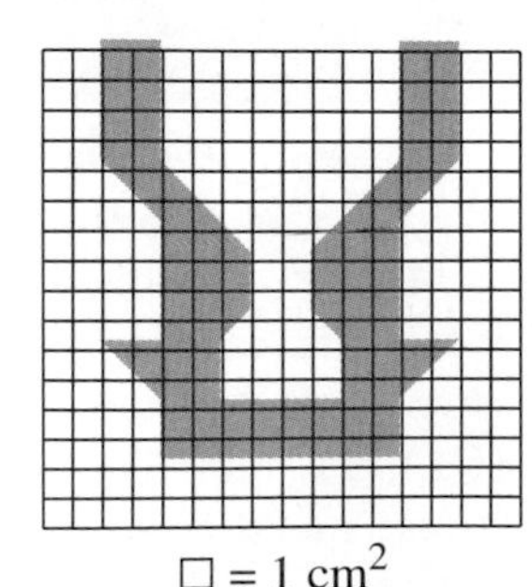

□ = 1 cm²

Practice

Simplify each expression.

1. $-3(x + 5)$ **2.** $4n - 5 - 12n$ **3.** $3h + 2(h + 1)$

4. $(3s + 2) + s$ **5.** $4j - 5j + 2j$ **6.** $9q - 2 + 4p - q + 7p$

Choose **Use a calculator, pencil and paper, or mental math. Solve each equation. Check the solution.**

7. $r - 4.5 = 12$ **8.** $\frac{x}{4.5} = 12$ **9.** $4m + 3m = 49$

10. $3c + 5 = 2c - 1$ **11.** $8 - 2(p + 3) = 4$ **12.** $-3 = 5a - 22$

13. $\frac{t}{3} - 15.7 = 12.2$ **14.** $2(v - 6) = 18$ **15.** $15 = (x - 2) - 5$

16. $2g + 7 = 8g$ **17.** $b - \frac{1}{2} = \frac{3}{4}$ **18.** $4.5w = 9$

Find the area of each figure.

19.

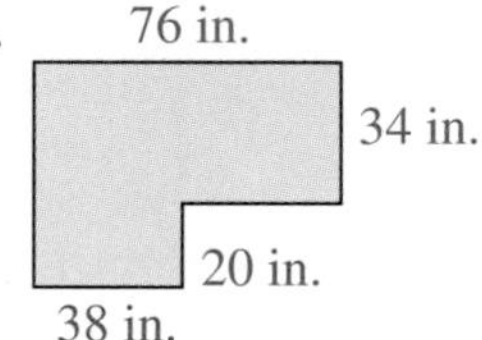

20.

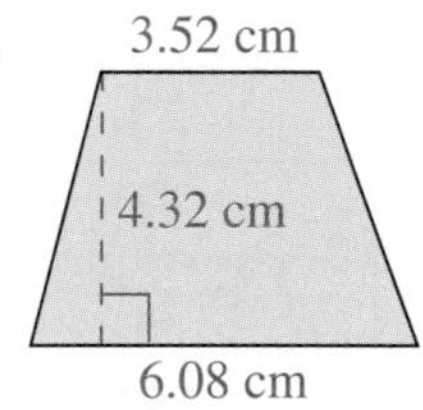

21.

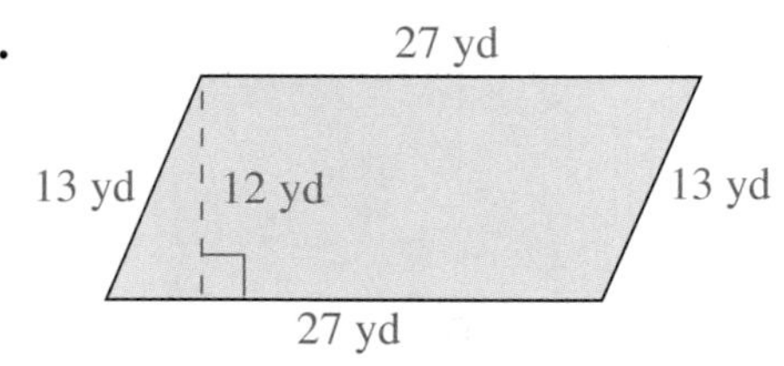

Write an equation to find the solution for each problem. Solve the equation. Then give the solution of the problem. Check the solution.

22. The perimeter of a rectangle is 64 ft, and the length is 12 ft. Find the width of the rectangle.

23. A camcorder costs \$995. Linda plans to make a down payment of \$150, then make weekly payments of \$50. How many weeks will it take her to complete the purchase?

24. When a cricket chirps n times per minute, you can find the temperature in degrees Fahrenheit, F, by using the formula $F = \frac{n}{4} + 37$. Write a formula to find the number of times a cricket chirps per minute when you know the temperature.

TECHNOLOGY

4-8 Formulas in Spreadsheets

What's Ahead

- Using a spreadsheet to evaluate formulas

WHAT YOU'LL NEED

✓ Computer 

✓ Spreadsheet software 

THINK AND DISCUSS

When a roller coaster car gets to the top of the first hill, it stops for a moment. Then it soars down the track, giving its passengers a thrilling ride. To achieve this effect safely, the engineers who design the rides use a variety of mathematical formulas. Here is one formula that relates the speed of the car at the bottom of the hill to the height of the hill.

$$v = 8\sqrt{h}$$

In the formula, v is the speed in feet per second, and h is the height in feet. (We will ignore the effect of air resistance.)

The symbol $\sqrt{h}$ means *the square root of h.*

1. Copy the table below. Then complete the table using a calculator or mental math.

h	$8\sqrt{h}$
25	■
64	■
96	■
150	■

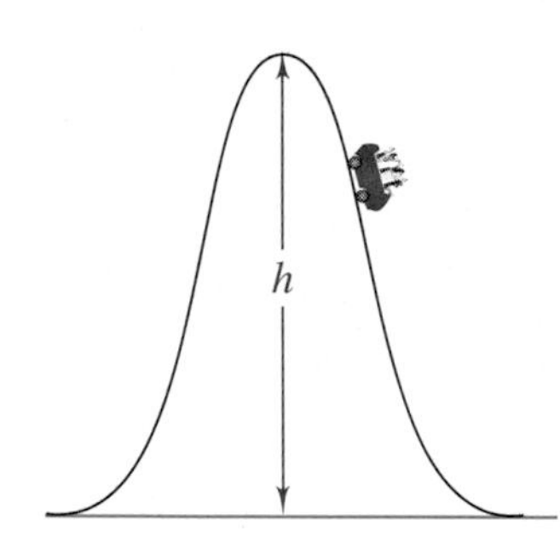

An electronic spreadsheet can help you to study the relationship between height and bottom speed more closely.

2. a. Make a spreadsheet table like the one shown below.

	A	B
1	HEIGHT (h)	BOTTOM SPEED (v)
2	■	■
3	■	■
4	■	■

b. In the HEIGHT column, enter 5, 10, 15, . . . , 100.

c. In the BOTTOM SPEED column, enter $8\sqrt{h}$.

d. Describe how v changes as h increases.

e. When the value of h doubles, does the value of v double?

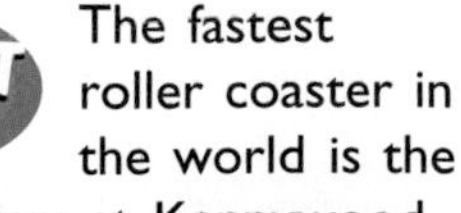

The fastest roller coaster in the world is the *Steel Phantom* at Kennywood Amusement Park, West Mifflin, PA. It reaches a speed of 80 mi/h.

Source: *The Guinness Book of Records*

Sometimes the designer places a loop at the bottom of a hill. This formula gives the speed of the car at the top of a loop.

$$s = 8\sqrt{h - 2r}$$

In this formula, h is the height of the hill in feet and r is the radius of the loop in feet. The variable s is the speed of the car at the top of the loop, in feet per second. A spreadsheet can help you see the effect on s when h increases and r remains constant.

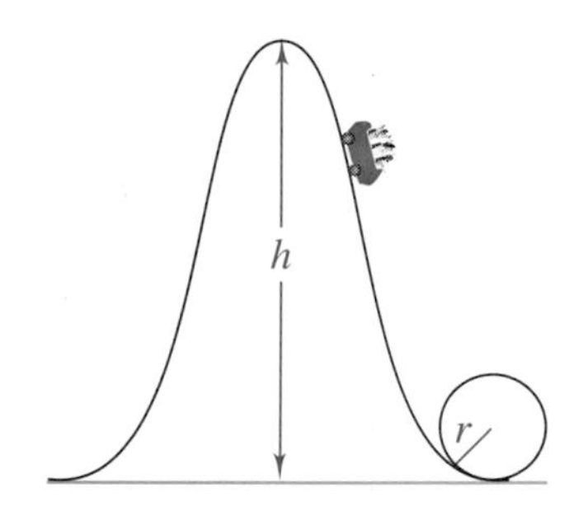

3. a. Make a spreadsheet table like the one shown below.

	A	B	C
1	HEIGHT (h)	RADIUS (r)	TOP SPEED (s)
2	■	■	■
3	■	■	■

b. In the HEIGHT column, enter 80, 85, 90, . . . , 160.

c. In the RADIUS column, enter 40 in each cell.

d. In the TOP SPEED column, enter $8\sqrt{h - 2r}$.

e. Describe how s changes as h increases.

You also can use the spreadsheet to see the effect on s when r increases and h remains the same.

4. a. Make a spreadsheet table for HEIGHT, RADIUS, and TOP SPEED like the one shown above.

b. In the HEIGHT column, enter 160 in each cell.

c. In the RADIUS column, enter 20, 25, 30, . . . , 60.

d. In the TOP SPEED column, enter $8\sqrt{h - 2r}$.

e. Describe how s changes as r increases.

Here is the view of the first drop on the Cyclone at Coney Island, Brooklyn, NY. When the Cyclone opened in 1927, you could ride for a quarter. In 1992, the price was $3.00.

Source: *Astroland Amusement Park*

WORK TOGETHER

- Work with a partner. Choose one of the formulas for the area of a geometric figure. Make a spreadsheet for the formula.
- Each should choose a different variable from the formula. Investigate the effect on the area as that variable remains constant and the other variable(s) increase or decrease.
- Compare your findings.

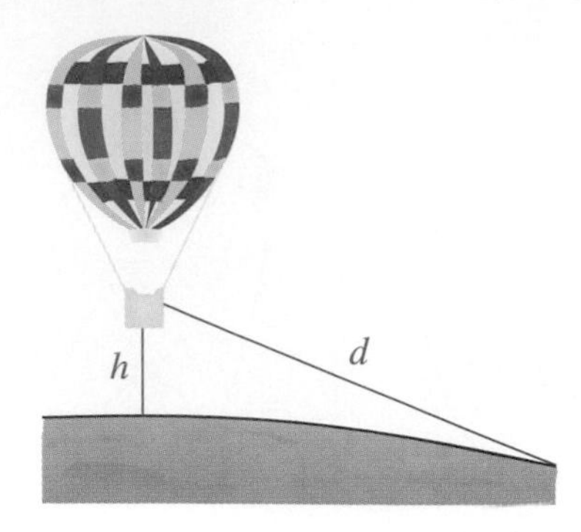

ON YOUR OWN

5. The formula $d = \sqrt{1.5h}$ gives the distance d in miles you can see to the horizon from a height of h feet above Earth.
   a. Make a spreadsheet with headings HEIGHT and DISTANCE.
   b. In the HEIGHT column, enter 100, 200, 300, . . . , 1,000.
   c. In the DISTANCE column, enter $\sqrt{1.5h}$.
   d. From the output, describe how d changes as h increases.

$r^2 = r \cdot r$

6. **Physics** When a driver traveling at r miles per hour applies the brakes, it takes a while for the car to stop. The braking distance d in feet is given by $d = 0.055r^2 + 1.1r$.
   a. Make a spreadsheet with headings SPEED and DISTANCE.
   b. In the SPEED column, enter 0, 5, 10, . . . , 60, 65.
   c. In the DISTANCE column, enter $0.055r^2 + 1.1r$.
   d. How does the braking distance for a car traveling at 30 mi/h compare to the braking distance for a car traveling at 60 mi/h?

7. **Money** Suppose that you deposit P dollars in a savings account that pays annual interest at rate r (expressed as a decimal). After t years you will have an amount A given by $A = P(1 + rt)$.
   a. Make a spreadsheet with the headings DEPOSIT, RATE, TIME, and AMOUNT.
   b. Enter a deposit of $1,000 and a rate of 0.05.
   c. In the TIME column, enter 1, 2, 3, . . . , 10.
   d. In the AMOUNT column, enter $P(1 + rt)$.
   e. Describe how A changes as t increases.

8. a. **Physics** Suppose you throw a ball straight up into the air at 40 mi/h. The height h in feet of the ball after t seconds is given by $h = -16t^2 + 58.67t$. Use a spreadsheet to analyze how the height changes over time.
   b. What is the greatest height the ball will reach?

9. **Writing** Describe some advantages of using a spreadsheet to evaluate a formula.

Mixed REVIEW

Write an expression for each situation.

1. Tim's father is 5 years older than 3 times Tim's age.
2. For the picnic, Melissa bought 3 packages each containing x spoons and 4 packages each containing y forks.

Find the perimeter and area of each figure.

3. a rectangle with length 5.3 cm and width 3 cm
4. a square with sides 4.7 in.
5. an equilateral triangle with base 6 in. and height 5.2 in.

6. How can a ten-dollar bill be changed into the same number of nickels, dimes, and quarters?

What's Ahead

- Graphing simple inequalities on a number line
- Writing simple inequalities in one variable

4-9 Inequalities

THINK AND DISCUSS

1. Tell whether each statement is *true* or *false*.

   a. $-6 < -4$ **b.** $9 > -2$ **c.** $5 \le 5$ **d.** $-5 \ge -3$

$<$ is less than
$>$ is greater than
$\le$ is less than or equal to
$\ge$ is greater than or equal to

Writing Inequalities

An **inequality** is a statement that compares two expressions. Some inequalities contain a variable, like $y \ge -3$. A **solution** of an inequality like this is any value of the variable that makes the inequality true.

2. Tell whether each number is a solution of $y \ge -3$.

   a. -4 **b.** -1 **c.** -3 **d.** 0 **e.** $\frac{1}{2}$ **f.** 4.2

3. How many solutions of $y \ge -3$ are there?

On a horizontal number line, numbers greater than a given number are to the right of the number. Numbers less than the number are to the left.

Graphing Inequalities

The solutions of $y \ge -3$ are -3 and any real number greater than -3. It is not possible to make a list of all the solutions. So, you use a number line to show the graph of the inequality. You graph -3 and all the numbers to the right of -3 as shown below.

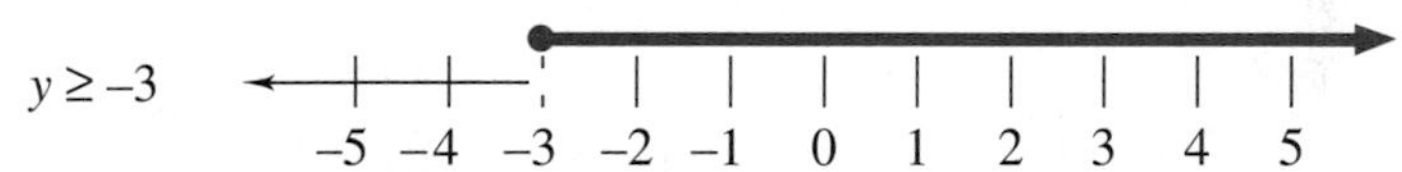

The closed dot on the number line above shows that -3 is a solution of $y \ge -3$. Suppose that you must graph $y > -3$. Then you place an *open* dot above -3 to show that -3 is *not* a solution.

$y > -3$

−5 −4 −3 −2 −1 0 1 2 3 4 5

4. According to the weather forecast, the temperature today will be greater than -4°F.

   a. Graph the possible temperatures on a number line.

   b. Write an inequality for the possible temperatures.

   c. Is -3.5°F a possible temperature for this day? Explain.

   d. How would the graph and the inequality be different if the forecast were for a temperature no less than -4°F?

The record low temperature in the United States, -79.8°F, was recorded at Prospect Creek, Alaska, on January 23, 1971.

Source: *The Guinness Book of Records*

Windchill temperature is the temperature your body feels because of the added chilling effect of the wind. If the temperature is 0°F and the wind is blowing at 30 mph, the windchill temperature is -49°F.

5. This graph shows the possible temperatures for tomorrow, given in degrees Fahrenheit.

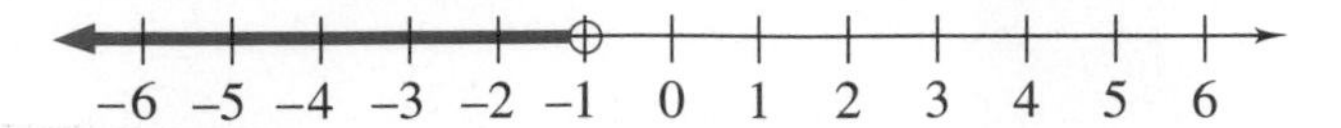

a. Write an inequality to represent the possible temperatures.

b. Write two different word descriptions of the possible temperatures.

c. Is -3.5°F a possible temperature for this day? Explain.

Sometimes a variable is on the right side of an inequality symbol.

6. List six integers that are solutions of $-4 < m$.

7. Graph all the solutions of $-4 < m$ on a number line.

8. **Choose A, B, C, or D.** Which inequality is equivalent to $-4 < m$?

A. $m < -4$ **B.** $m > -4$ **C.** $m \geq -4$ **D.** $m \leq -4$

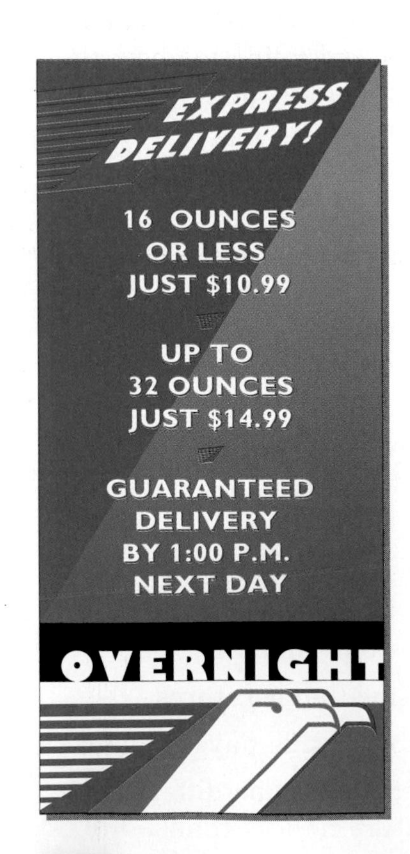

WORK TOGETHER

Work with a partner. Use the information in the sign at the left.

9. a. On a number line, graph all the weights of packages that cost $10.99. Does your graph include any negative numbers? Does it include zero? Explain why or why not.

b. On a different number line, graph all the weights of packages that cost $14.99.

c. Devise a way to write an inequality for each graph.

ON YOUR OWN

Write an inequality for each graph.

10. 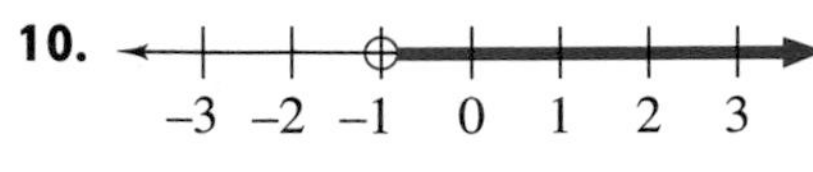

11. 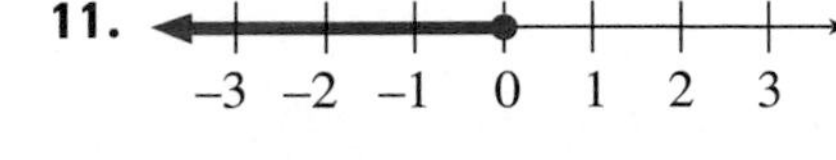

12. 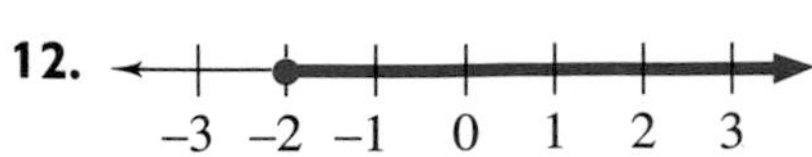

13. 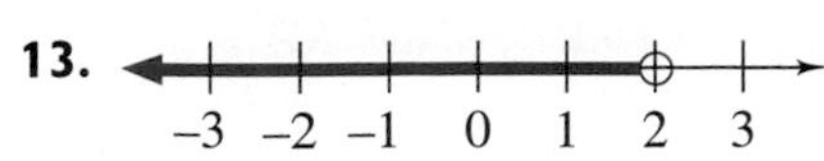

Graph each inequality on a number line.

14. $c \leq -4$ **15.** $z > -6$ **16.** $-5 > n$

17. $r \geq -1$ **18.** $0 \leq z$ **19.** $q < 3$

Write an inequality for each sentence.

20. A number k is not positive.

21. The hourly wage, w, must be no less than \$8.75.

Critical Thinking Write > or < to make a true statement.

22. If $a > b$, then b ■ a.

23. If $x > y$ and $y > z$, then x ■ z.

24. **Data File 1 (pp. 2–3)** Write an inequality to represent each of these measurements of the "lean forward" car.

a. the minimum distance off the ground

b. the maximum length of the car

25. **Writing** Describe how the solution of an inequality and the solution of an equation are alike. How are they different?

Use the following article to answer the exercises below.

Summer Heat and Exercise

When is it too hot to exercise safely? The graph at the right shows that the danger zone begins at about 82°F and 78% humidity. When conditions are in that zone, exercising increases your chances of heat exhaustion and heat stroke.

When weather conditions are in the danger or emergency zones, you are advised *not* exercise. Wait until conditions have improved.

If conditions are in the alert zone, exercise with caution.

26. The temperature is 85°F. Write an inequality to represent the humidity levels, h, at which it is safe to exercise.

27. The humidity level is 70%. Write an inequality to represent the temperatures, t, at which exercise is dangerous.

Mixed REVIEW

Compare. Use >, <, or =.

1. $5(2)^3$ ■ $(5 \cdot 2)^3$

2. $(-6)^5$ ■ -6^5

3. The formula for converting temperatures in degrees Celsius (C) to degrees Fahrenheit (F) is:

$F = (C \cdot 1.8) + 32$

Make a spreadsheet for the formula. Use it to find the temperature at which $F = C$.

4. Keith asked 30 people whether they knew how to play whist or dominoes. Twenty of them knew how to play whist and 25 knew how to play dominoes. Five people did not know how to play either game. How many knew how to play both games?

Temperature–Humidity Chart

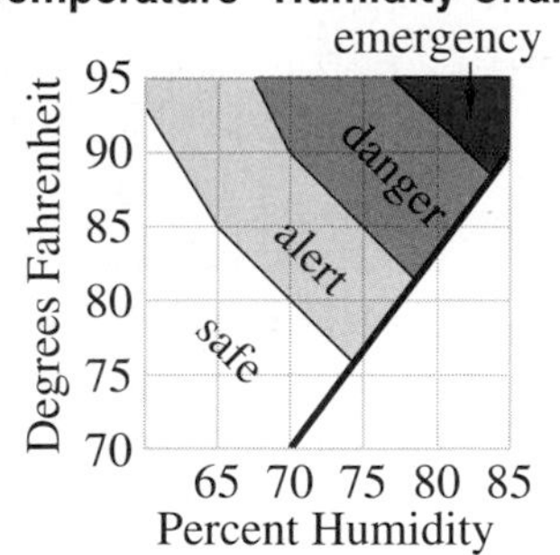

What's Ahead

- Solving one-step inequalities and graphing the solutions
- Writing one-step inequalities with one variable

4-10 Solving One-Step Inequalities

THINK AND DISCUSS

Tell whether each statement is true or false.

1. a. $10 > 8$
   b. $10 + 2 > 8 + 2$
   c. $10 - 9 > 8 - 9$
   d. $10(3) > 8(3)$
   e. $10(-3) > 8(-3)$
   f. $10 \div 2 > 8 \div 2$
   g. $10 \div (-2) > 8 \div (-2)$
2. a. $-9 < -6$
   b. $-9 + 4 < -6 + 4$
   c. $-9 - 1 < -6 - 1$
   d. $-9(2) < -6(2)$
   e. $-9(-2) < -6(-2)$
   f. $-9 \div 3 < -6 \div 3$
   g. $-9 \div (-3) < -6 \div (-3)$
3. What patterns do you observe in Questions 1 and 2?

To ensure that** manufactured parts are uniform in size and shape, they have tolerance limits on their dimensions. **If the length of a part is 2.03 cm with a tolerance limit of 0.005 cm, write and solve an inequality to find the length of the smallest acceptable part.

Using Addition and Subtraction You can add or subtract the same number from each side of the inequality.

Addition Properties for Inequalities

Arithmetic	Algebra
$7 > 3$, so $7 + 5 > 3 + 5$	If $a > b$, then $a + c > b + c$.
$2 < 9$, so $2 + 6 < 9 + 6$	If $a < b$, then $a + c < b + c$.

Example 1 Solve $q - 6 \geq -5$. Graph the solution.

$$q - 6 \geq -5$$
$$q - 6 + 6 \geq -5 + 6 \quad \text{Add 6 to each side.}$$
$$q \geq 1 \quad \text{The direction stays the same.}$$

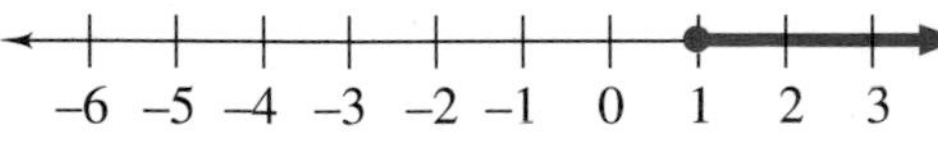

Subtraction Properties for Inequalities

Arithmetic	Algebra
$12 > 8$, so $12 - 4 > 8 - 4$	If $a > b$, then $a - c > b - c$.
$6 < 11$, so $6 - 2 < 11 - 2$	If $a < b$, then $a - c < b - c$.

Example 2 Solve $7 > k + 9$. Graph the solution.

$7 - 9 > k + 9 - 9$ — **Subtract 9 from each side.**

$-2 > k$ — **The direction stays the same.**

$k < -2$ ← **$k < -2$ is the same as $-2 > k$.**

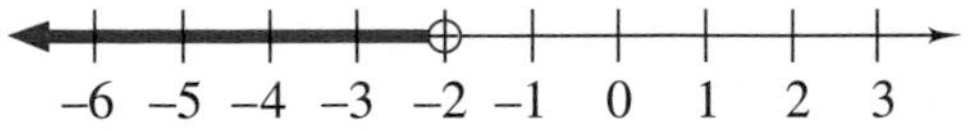

Using Multiplication and Division When you multiply each side of an inequality by the same positive number, the direction remains the same. If you multiply each side by the same *negative* number, *reverse* the direction of the inequality.

Multiplication Properties for Inequalities

Arithmetic	Algebra
$5 > 3$, so $5(7) > 3(7)$	If $a > b$ and $c > 0$, then $ac > bc$.
$4 < 8$, so $4(7) < 8(7)$	If $a < b$ and $c > 0$, then $ac < bc$.
$8 > 2$, so $8(-5) < 2(-5)$	If $a > b$ and $c < 0$, then $ac < bc$.
$6 < 7$, so $6(-3) > 7(-3)$	If $a < b$ and $c < 0$, then $ac > bc$.

Example 3 Solve $\frac{s}{-2} < 1$. Graph the solution.

$\frac{s}{-2} < 1$

$-2\left(\frac{s}{-2}\right) > -2(1)$ ← **Multiply each side by -2, and reverse the direction of the inequality.**

$s > -2$

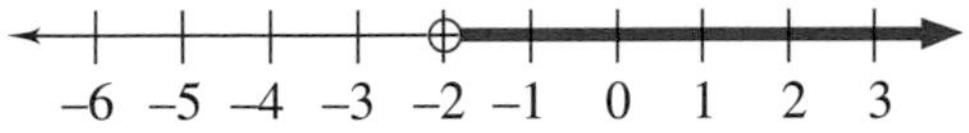

The division properties for inequalities are similar to the multiplication properties.

Division Properties for Inequalities

Arithmetic	Algebra
$12 > 9$, so $\frac{12}{3} > \frac{9}{3}$	If $a > b$ and $c > 0$, then $\frac{a}{c} > \frac{b}{c}$.
$6 < 14$, so $\frac{6}{2} < \frac{14}{2}$	If $a < b$ and $c > 0$, then $\frac{a}{c} < \frac{b}{c}$.
$16 > 8$, so $\frac{16}{-4} < \frac{8}{-4}$	If $a > b$ and $c < 0$, then $\frac{a}{c} < \frac{b}{c}$.
$10 < 15$, so $\frac{10}{-5} > \frac{15}{-5}$	If $a < b$ and $c < 0$, then $\frac{a}{c} > \frac{b}{c}$.

Mixed REVIEW

Find each answer.

1. $1914 \div 33$
2. 55×171

True or false?

3. $18 \leq -18$
4. $14 > 12$

Graph on a number line.

5. $6 \geq m$
6. $k < 5$

7. The largest possible circle is drawn on an $8\frac{1}{2}$ in. $\times$ 11 in. sheet of notebook paper. What is the area of the paper *not* covered by the circle?

Example 4 Solve $3a \leq -12$. Graph the solution.

$$3a \leq -12$$
$$\frac{3a}{3} \leq \frac{-12}{3} \quad \leftarrow \text{Divide each side by 3. The direction stays the same.}$$
$$a \leq -4$$

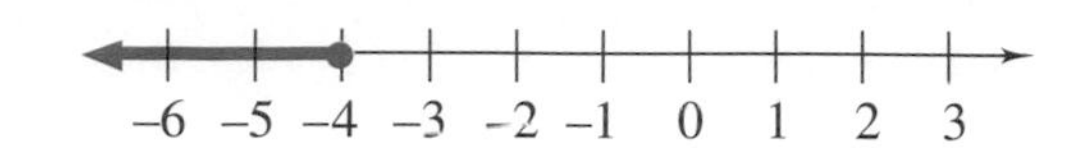

TRY THESE

Tell whether -3 is a solution of each inequality.

4. $p + 2 > -1$
5. $18 > 6j$
6. $-2x \leq -14$
7. $z - 4 > -5$
8. $-1 \leq \frac{r}{-3}$
9. $5c < -10$

Solve each inequality. Graph the solution.

10. $m - 4 < -2$
11. $3q > -15$
12. $\frac{y}{-4} \geq -2$
13. $9 > d + 4$
14. $2.75x \leq 22$
15. $x - 3.4 \geq 2.6$

16. Three friends washed cars together and shared their total earnings equally. Each earned no more than \$60.
    a. Write an inequality that you can solve to find the greatest possible amount of their total earnings.
    b. Is \$140 a possible amount for their total earnings? Explain.

ON YOUR OWN

Tell whether each number is a solution of $5 - x \geq 3$.

17. 2
18. 3
19. 1
20. -5
21. -2

Solve each inequality. Graph the solution.

22. $-4t > 20$
23. $-1 < \frac{y}{3}$
24. $4 + f \geq -1$
25. $r - 5 < -5$
26. $3 \leq 0.5c$
27. $w + 1.5 \leq 2.5$

28. **Writing** How are the properties of inequalities that you studied in this lesson similar to the properties of equality you studied earlier in this chapter? How are they different?

Extra SKILLS PRACTICE

Solve each inequality.

1. $4 > 7 + d$
2. $-5y < 35$
3. $b + 12 \leq 5$
4. $-1.5 \geq \frac{r}{5}$
5. $-3 < t + 7$
6. $g + 9 < 2$
7. $\frac{7}{2} < 8z$
8. $-6n \leq -30$
9. $m - 3 > -8$
10. $\frac{e}{-4} < -3.5$
11. $3x \geq -42$
12. $18 > -2a$
13. $\frac{d}{8} \geq 3$
14. $-6 \leq s - 13$
15. $8 < \frac{h}{-2}$
16. $-6 > \frac{c}{3}$
17. $p + 4 \leq -6$
18. $q - 0.8 > 3.6$
19. $7.2 < w + 1.6$
20. $-4.1 \geq k + 1.7$

FLASHBACK

$-x = (-1)x$

Write an inequality for each problem. Solve the inequality. Then give the solution of the problem.

29. The temperature has increased 17°F since 8:00 A.M. It is now above 65°F. What was the temperature at 8:00 A.M.?

30. When a number is divided by -3, the result is not more than 15. What is the number?

31. A perfect score on a spelling test is 10. Amy scored 9, 8, 10, and 9 on her first four tests. What score must she get on the fifth test to have a total of at least 45 points?

32. **Critical Thinking** If $a > b$, which of these statements is always true?

I. $b < a$ II. $a + c > b + c$ III. $ac > bc$

A. I only **B.** I and II only

C. II and III only **D.** None of the statements is true.

33. **Estimation** You have $37.85, and you want to buy some tapes that each cost $4.95. Write and solve an inequality to estimate the greatest number of tapes that you can buy.

The lowest possible temperature referred to as absolute zero, is about -273.15°C. Although they have come within a few thousandths of a degree of it, scientists feel that absolute zero can never be reached.

Source: *Prentice Hall Chemistry, The Study of Matter*

CHECKPOINT

Simplify each expression.

1. $-5(w + 7)$ **2.** $6y + 4z - y$ **3.** $r + 4(2 + r)$

Solve each equation. Check your solution.

4. $-1 = 4 + x$ **5.** $-8a = 2a - 30$ **6.** $-16 = 5(g - 2) + 1$

Solve each inequality. Graph the solution.

7. $n - 8 < -3$ **8.** $-6d \geq 18$ **9.** $-4 < \frac{h}{2}$

10. A car rental agency charges $27.95 per day plus 14¢ per mile. Dan's bill for one day was $45.73. Show how to write and solve an equation to find the number of miles he drove.

11. **Data File 5 (pp. 192–193)** Write an inequality to find how much a woman's running speed would have had to increase to exceed a man's speed in the 1,500 m race in 1975.

What's Ahead

- Solving two-step inequalities and graphing the solutions
- Writing two-step inequalities with one variable

4-11 Solving Two-Step Inequalities

THINK AND DISCUSS

1. a. Solve: $-2n = 14$
   b. Solve: $-2n - 5 = 9$
   c. Describe how you solved the equations in parts (a) and (b).
   d. When solving a simple two-step equation, how do you know which operation to perform first?

Graphing Inequalities The equation $-2n - 5 = 9$ is a two-step equation. It involves two operations. You can solve a two-step equation using two properties of equality. The process is similar when solving the *inequality* $-2n - 5 < 9$.

FLASHBACK

If you multiply or divide each side of an inequality by the same negative number, you reverse the order of the inequality.

Example 1 Solve $-2n - 5 < 9$. Graph the solution.

$$-2n - 5 < 9$$
$$-2n - 5 + 5 < 9 + 5 \quad \text{Add 5 to each side.}$$
$$-2n < 14 \quad \text{The order stays the same.}$$
$$\frac{-2n}{-2} > \frac{14}{-2} \quad \leftarrow \text{Divide each side by } -2. \text{ Reverse the order.}$$
$$n > -7$$

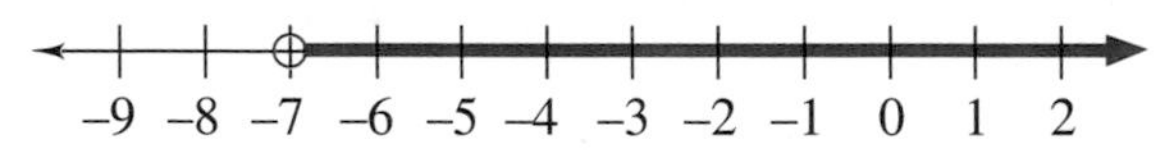

2. How would the solution of Example 1 be different if the inequality were $2n - 5 < 9$?

The inequality $-2n - 5 < 9$ is an example of a simple *two-step inequality*. To solve these inequalities, you use the method below.

How to Solve a Simple Two-Step Inequality

1. Undo addition or subtraction.
2. Undo multiplication or division. Remember to reverse the order of the inequality if you multiply or divide by a negative number.

You also can solve an inequality like $7 - v \geq 4$ in two steps.

Example 2 Solve $7 - v \geq 4$. Graph the solution.

$$7 - v \geq 4$$
$$7 - v - 7 \geq 4 - 7 \quad \text{Subtract 7 from each side.}$$
$$-v \geq -3 \quad \text{The order stays the same.}$$
$$(-1)(-v) \leq (-1)(-3) \quad \text{Multiply each side by } -1.$$
$$v \leq 3 \quad \text{Reverse the order.}$$

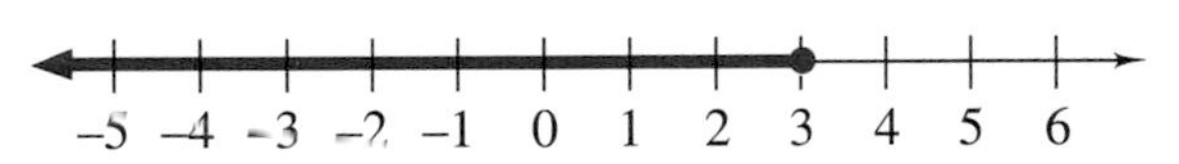

3. In the solution of Example 2, why do you multiply both sides of the inequality $-v \geq -3$ by -1?

Using Inequalities

Use inequalities to solve problems.

Example 3 Fasul wants to buy a \$14 belt he saw at the mall. He also wants to buy some T-shirts priced at \$9 each. He has \$50. How many T-shirts can he buy?

Use s to represent the number of T-shirts.

cost of belt	plus	cost of s T-shirts	is less than or equal to	total amount
14	$+$	$9s$	$\leq$	50

$$14 + 9s \leq 50$$
$$14 + 9s - 14 \leq 50 - 14 \quad \text{Subtract 14 from each side.}$$
$$9s \leq 36 \quad \text{The order stays the same.}$$
$$\frac{9s}{9} \leq \frac{36}{9} \quad \text{Divide each side by 9. The order stays the same.}$$
$$s \leq 4$$

Fasul can buy 0, 1, 2, 3, or 4 T-shirts.

4. a. Is -2 a solution of $s \leq 4$? Is 1.5 a solution?

b. Why are -2 and 1.5 *not* in the solution of Example 3?

WORK TOGETHER

5. Work in groups. Each group member should solve one of these inequalities and graph the solution. Compare results.

a. $-3n + 2 > -10$, where n is any number

b. $-3n + 2 > -10$, where n is a positive number

c. $-3n + 2 \geq -10$, where n is a positive integer

d. $-3n + 2 \leq -10$, where n is a negative integer

Mixed REVIEW

Use mental math to evaluate.

1. $65 + 17 + 35 + 3$

2. $5(220)$

Solve. Check your solution.

3. $n + 9 > -3$

4. $48 = 14(s + 3) - 36$

5. A car going 55 mi/h travels 968 in. in 1 s. How many inches per second are traveled by a car going 35 mi/h?

***The West Edmonton Mall** is in Alberta, Canada. It covers 5.2 million square feet, and includes more than 800 stores, 110 restaurants, a skating rink, the world's largest indoor roller coaster, and the world's largest indoor wave pool.*

Extra SKILLS PRACTICE

Solve each inequality.

1. $4z + 7 > -9$
2. $7 \geq -2 - 3h$
3. $13 < -2 + \frac{a}{-4}$
4. $\frac{m}{5} - 6 \geq 3$
5. $-1 + 5p < 8$
6. $10 > \frac{w}{2} - 6$
7. $20 < -5b - 1$
8. $-6 + 2y \leq 4$
9. $5 + \frac{k}{-3} < -8$
10. $-3 \leq 7 - 2d$

The greatest recorded snowfall from one storm was 189 in. at Mt. Shasta, Ski Bowl, California, February 13–19, 1959.

Source: *The Guinness Book of Records*

TRY THESE

Tell whether -1 is a solution of each inequality.

6. $-4d + 8 \leq 15$
7. $3z - 6 > -9$
8. $3 - k < 5$
9. $8 - 2p \geq 10$

Tell what was done to each side of the first inequality to obtain the second inequality.

10. $5t - 3 \leq -2$; $5t \leq 1$
11. $-b > 1$; $b < -1$
12. $16 \geq -8z - 8$; $24 \geq -8z$
13. $4 + \frac{m}{4} < 16$; $\frac{m}{4} < 12$

14. The sum of two consecutive integers is greater than 55.
    a. Let n represent the smaller of the two integers. Write an expression to represent the larger integer.
    b. Write an expression to represent the sum of the integers.
    c. Write an inequality that describes the sum of the integers.
    d. Solve the inequality you wrote in part (c).
    e. What is the smallest integer that is a solution of the inequality? What is the next consecutive integer?

Solve each inequality. Graph the solution.

15. $-3q + 4 < -2$
16. $9 - 2x > 15$
17. $\frac{a}{-4} - 3 > 0$
18. $-0.5 \leq \frac{w}{5} + 0.5$

19. **Jobs** Three students collected more than \$180 clearing snow from sidewalks and driveways. They used \$24 of that money to pay for the rental of a snow blower. They shared the remaining money equally. Write and solve an inequality to find the amount each earned.

ON YOUR OWN

Solve each inequality. Graph the solution.

20. $6 - 4r \leq -2$
21. $\frac{y}{5} - 1 \geq -1$
22. $-11 > -4c - 7$
23. $4 - j > -6$
24. $1 > 8 + \frac{n}{5}$
25. $1.5p - 9 \leq -3$

Write an inequality for each problem. Solve the inequality. Then give the solution of the problem.

26. A number is multiplied by -2, and the product is decreased by 4. The result is at least 10. What could the number be?

27. **Savings** Ken wants to buy a CD player for $150. He received $40 of this amount as a gift. He plans to earn the rest baby-sitting at $4.25 per hour. What is the least number of full hours he must baby-sit in order to earn enough money?

28. **Sales** Tanya earns a salary of $1,050 per month, plus a commission of 2% of sales. What must be the amount of her sales to earn a total of at least $1,800 in one month?

29. What are the two greatest consecutive *odd* integers whose sum is less than -11?

30. **Writing** Think about the methods you learned for solving equations and inequalities. Why do you think you add or subtract before performing multiplications or divisions?

During 1992, *consumers in the United States bought 56% of their recorded music on CDs, but country music star Waylon Jennings is not wild about CDs. He feels that analog recorded vocals are "much warmer sounding" than CD digital recordings.*

Source: *USA TODAY and The Recording Industry Association of America*

31. **Critical Thinking** Compare expression I and expression II. Which of the statements that follow is true?

I. $3y + 5$ II. $y - 7$

A. I is always greater than II.

B. I is greater than II when the value of y is greater than -6.

C. The expressions are always equal.

D. No relationship can be determined.

32. **a.** **Computer** Make a spreadsheet like the one at right.

b. Enter $-5, -4, -3, -2, -1, 0, 1, 2, 3, 4,$ and 5 in Column A.

	A	B	C
1	x	$3.1x + 8.4$	$5.3x - 9.2$
2	■	■	■

c. For the given values of x, what is the relationship between the number in Column B and the number in Column C?

d. Enter additional values of x until you find a value for which the order of the relationship changes.

e. What is the solution of $3.1x + 8.4 \leq 5.3x - 9.2$?

f. Use a spreadsheet to solve $4(1.8x - 9) > 6(1.7x + 4)$.

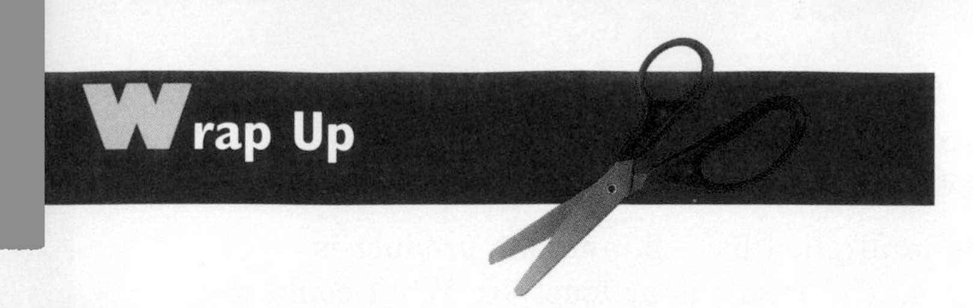

Simplifying Variable Expressions 4-1

The parts of a variable expression are ***terms.*** A term that does not contain a variable is a ***constant.*** A number multiplied by a variable is a ***numerical coefficient*** of that variable. ***Like terms*** are terms with the same variables. To simplify an expression, like terms should be combined and constants should be combined.

You can use the *distributive property* to remove parentheses around terms so that like terms can be combined.

Simplify the following.

1. $8x + 3(x - 4)$
2. $3(a + 2) + 5(a - 1)$
3. $4(x - 3) - 3(x - 1)$
4. $-2(3x - 1) + 5(x - 2)$

Writing Equations 4-5

Sometimes you can write an equation to solve a problem.

Write an equation and solve.

5. Randall bought bagels at 55¢ each and some cream cheese for $1.60. He spent $6.00. How many bagels did he buy?
6. Doreen gets her hair cut once every 4 weeks. She spends a total of $156 a year on haircuts. How much is one haircut?

Solving Equations 4-2, 4-3, 4-4, 4-6

An equation can be simplified by adding the same quantity to both sides, or by subtracting the same quantity from both sides.

Solve.

7. $x - 7 = 23$
8. $x + 3.1 = 4.6$
9. $x + 8.4 = -1.2$
10. $-14 + x = -5$

An equation can also be simplified by multiplying or dividing both sides by the same quantity.

Solve.

11. $-1.7y = -34$
12. $\frac{z}{4} = -2.1$
13. $2.5x = -8$
14. $\frac{w}{3.7} = 20$

To solve *two-step equations,* do the addition or subtraction first. Then do the multiplication or division.

Solve.

15. $2x - 5 = 19$ **16.** $4 + 3q = -6.8$ **17.** $-1 = \frac{a}{5} + 2$ **18.** $\frac{c}{-3} - 1.6 = 2$

Before attempting to solve an equation, simplify each side, and get the variable on one side only.

19. Writing Briefly describe the first three steps, in order, for solving the equation $4(x - 1) - 2x = 3(2x + 3)$.

Formulas 4-7

A ***formula*** is an equation that shows the relationship between two or more quantities.

20. Find the area of a trapezoid with bases 3 ft and 11 ft, and height 5 ft.

21. Find the average rate of travel (mi/h) if a car goes 270 mi in 6 h.

Sometimes a formula is more useful if you change its form by using the same techniques that are used in solving equations.

22. Choose A, B, C, or D. Choose the formula that is equivalent to $A = \frac{1}{2}bh$.

A. $b = \frac{2A}{h}$ **B.** $h = \frac{b}{2A}$ **C.** $h = A - 2b$ **D.** $b = h - 2A$

Solving Inequalities 4-9, 4-10, 4-11

If you multiply or divide both sides of an inequality by the same negative number, remember to reverse the order of the inequality.

Solve.

23. $5t - 1 \geq 3(t + 7)$ **24.** $-3(2b - 5) \geq 4(b - 1) + 2$

GETTING READY FOR CHAPTER 5

Subtract.

1. $2 - (5)$ **2.** $-3 - (8)$ **3.** $6 - (-2)$ **4.** $-5 - (-4)$

5. Why is $\frac{3 - 7}{5 - 2}$ equal to $\frac{7 - 3}{2 - 5}$?

Follow Up

Making Mobiles

In this chapter you began your investigation of the principles that govern the construction of mobiles. The Museum of Mathematical Art has heard about your investigation and would like to purchase one of your mobiles for its permanent collection. Construct your masterpiece, based on your study of the chapter. Prepare an explanation of the mathematical principles behind your work. This will appear with your mobile so that viewers can better understand it.

The problems preceded by the magnifying glass (p. 148, # 37; p. 152, # 42; and p. 160, # 28) will help you construct your mobile and prepare your explanation.

Although Alexander Calder was a sculptor, he received early training in mathematics and engineering. This combination of art and mathematics led him to create his first mobiles. He was born in Lawton, Pennsylvania in 1898 and died in 1976.

Excursion: Find out what you can about tessellations, the golden rectangle, and other ways that artists have combined mathematics and art.

Who to Talk To:

- an art teacher

Going 1st Class

For the right price you can send any size envelope through the mail. But for the price of a first class stamp, you can send only certain sizes allowed by the post office.

- Research the size limitations on 1-oz first-class envelopes.
- Use inequalities to express your findings.
- Use graph paper to construct a template for checking whether an envelope falls within the acceptable size range. Remember, to use a template, the postal clerk aligns the lower left corner of an envelope with a corner of the template. If the upper right corner of the envelope falls inside the template, it is acceptable.

Excursion: Describe a template to test envelope thickness.

MATHCOUNTS®

WHO THOUGHT OF THAT?

James Watt conducted a series of experiments with horses. He calculated that, on average, a horse can use his back to lift 550 lb 1 ft off the ground in 1 s. He used the term **horsepower** (hp) to describe his findings. One horsepower became the standard unit for expressing power, with 1 hp equal to 550 ft-lb/s.

So much for horsepower. But what about carats, furlongs, cubits, and all the other curious units in the world of measurement? Research the history of a measurement unit. Prepare a report that tells what you discovered.

Everyday Equations

President Promises to Reduce Deficit by $400 Billion Over 5 Years

Newspapers are full of mathematical statements that omit important information. An alert reader of this headline is certain to ask, "But what is the size of *today's* deficit?"

- Find examples of mathematical statements in newspapers that omit important information.
- Write equations or variable expressions to represent the statements. An example is shown.

Let x = the amount of today's deficit
Then, x - $400,000,000,000 = the promised deficit in 5 years

Work with a partner.

- Write simple equations for each other to solve.
- Practice using your calculator to help find the solutions for the equations your partner gives you.
- Brainstorm to work out a set of steps to follow to solve equations with a calculator.
- Make a checklist entitled *How to Use a Calculator to Solve Equations.*

Assessment

1. Simplify each expression.
   a. $9 + 4r - 7$ b. $5 + (-12t) + 8t$
   c. $2(3m - 5) + 6$ d. $-4(7f + 2g) - 5$
2. **Writing** What are the advantages of using a spreadsheet program to work with formulas? What are the drawbacks?
3. Write a problem that can be solved using the equation $3k - 12 = 4$.
4. Solve each equation.
   a. $4m - 9 = 27$
   b. $-3(h + 7) = -18$
   c. $\frac{r}{-5} - 3 = 14$
   d. $6 + 2d = 3d - 4$
5. **Choose A, B, C, or D.** Which of the following are equivalent to the equation $13s - 3 = 4s + 15$?
   I. $3y = 6$ II. $p - 2 = 0$ III. $17k = 18$
   A. I only **B.** II and III
   C. I and III **D.** I and II
6. Harvey lives 3.5 mi away from school, and can walk 1 mi every 14 min. Write an inequality that expresses the time it might take him to get home from school.
7. **Choose A, B, C, or D.** Which inequality is represented by the graph below?

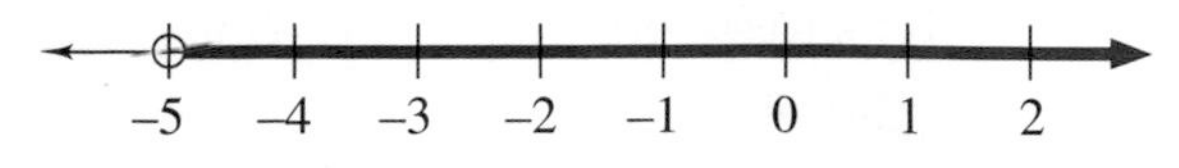

   A. $25 > -5w$ **B.** $3x \geq -15$
   C. $-4y > -20$ **D.** $2z < -10$
8. Write and solve the equations that describe these relationships.
   a.

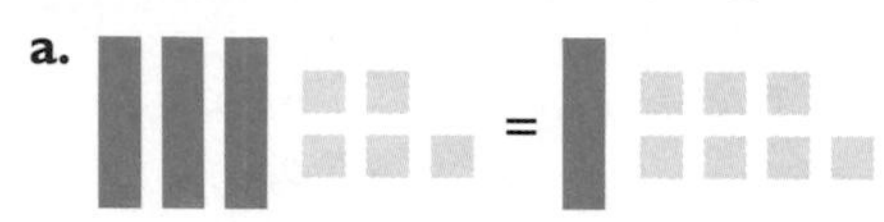

   b. You buy 15 apples and a \$2.75 block of cheese, and the bill is \$6.20. How much did each apple cost?
   c. 15
   4.5 | $3 + d$ | $3 + d$
9. Solve each inequality. Graph the solutions.
   a. $18 > \frac{w}{-9} + 3$ b. $16y - 12 > -4y$
   c. $\frac{z}{3} - 7 \leq 5$ d. $-3 + 4s \geq 4$
10. Write a formula that expresses the relationship between A, B, and C in this spreadsheet.

	A	B	C
1	1	5	11
2	−2	1	0
3	12	−7	−2
4	0	−3	−6
5	5	10	25

11. Choose a new set of values for A, B, and C that fits your formula from Exercise 10.
12. Figure out how long it takes to bicycle 30 mi at 12 mi/h, using the formula *distance* = *rate* • *time.*
13. Name a career in which people use formulas to do their jobs. Explain.

CHAPTER 4

Cumulative Review

Choose A, B, C, or D.

1. Which variable expression is not equivalent to $2(y + 3)$?

A. $2(y) + 2(3)$ B. $(y + 3) + (y + 3)$

C. $2y + 3$ D. $2(3 + y)$

2. You want to tessellate a plane using a regular octagon and one other regular polygon. What other regular polygon can you use?

A. triangle B. pentagon

C. hexagon D. square

3. What is the value of $3 + 2b^2$ when $b = -3$?

A. 45 B. -15 C. 21 D. 39

4. Karen swam for a half hour on Monday. She increased her workout by the same number of minutes each day. On Friday, she swam for one hour. Which equation describes the number of minutes she increased her daily workout?

A. $30 + 4m = 60$ B. $\frac{60}{m} = 4$

C. $30 + 5m = 60$ D. $5m = 60$

5. Which equation does *not* have the solution $w = -1.5$?

A. $\frac{9}{w} = -6$ B. $-10w = 15$

C. $4 - 3w = 8.5$ D. $-1 - 2w = -4$

6. Which sum is greatest?

A. $-15 + 7$ B. $22 + (-19)$

C. $-8 + (-16)$ D. $|-11| + (-12)$

7. Which is *not* a 30° angle?

A. $\angle CAB$

B. $\angle BCA$

C. $\angle OBA$

D. $\angle BDC$

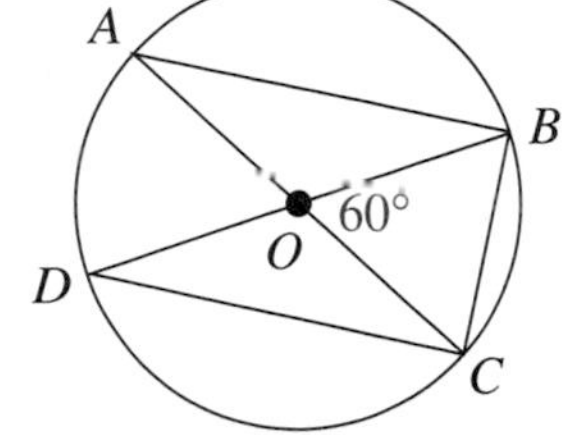

8. How much can you save on your grocery bill if you have 3 coupons, each for \$1.00 off and 2 coupons, each for \$2.00 off?

A. \$3.00 B. \$4.00

C. \$5.00 D. \$7.00

9. What can you conclude if you know that $x > y$ and $y > z$? (x, y, and z are all integers other than zero.)

A. $z > x$ B. $z < x$

C. $x > y + z$ D. $\frac{x}{y} > \frac{y}{z}$

10. To construct a line through X parallel to $\overleftrightarrow{PQ}$, what should you do first?

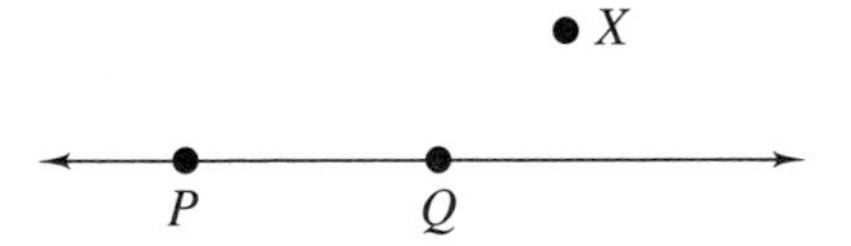

A. Draw $\overline{XP}$.

B. Open the compass to the length of $\overline{PQ}$.

C. Draw a line through X that intersects $\overleftrightarrow{PQ}$.

D. Put the compass tip at X and draw an arc passing through P or Q.

CHAPTER 5 Graphing in the Coordinate Plane

survival OF THE Fittest

The solid lines show the graphs of men's and women's speeds in different events. Some physiologists note that the slope of the women's graph is much steeper than that of men. The physiologists extended each graph (the dashed lines) and projected that women's speeds may one day meet or exceed those of men.

Source: *Science World*

WORLD VIEW In 1992 Manon Rheaume from Montreal became the first woman to play in a professional sports league. She played for the Tampa Bay Lightning in a National Hockey League exhibition game.

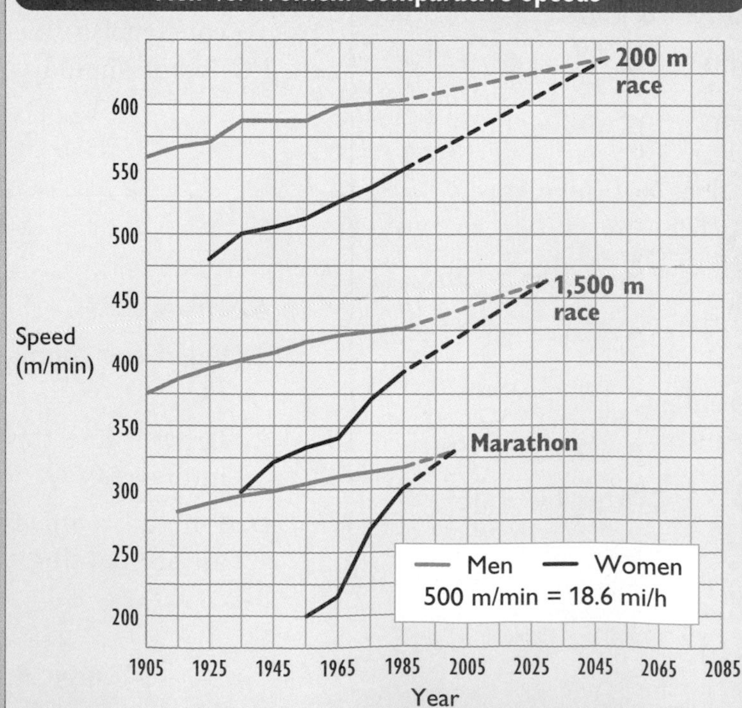

Data File 5

WHAT YOU WILL LEARN

- how to use slopes and intercepts
- how to solve problems using systems of equations
- how to use technology to explore graphs of equations
- how to solve problems by drawing a diagram

The graph shows the average weekly swimming distances of Olympic swimmers during the 26-week period before the Olympics. Training helps athletes store more food energy. Intense training also uses up this energy. Swimmers try to do less training in the weeks before a meet so their bodies will have plenty of stored energy.

Source: *Science World*

investigation

Project File

Memo

While descending a mountain, a 200-lb climber found he was unable to climb down from the top of the cliff. He attached his 150-ft elastic rope to a tree at the top of the cliff. Then he lowered himself down. The rope stretched 18 ft due to his weight but he was still 64 ft above the base of the cliff. He climbed back up the rope, filled his pack with rocks, and lowered himself again. With the added weight, he was able to reach the ground. The climber untied the rope and walked home. Do you believe the story?

Mission: Model the situation using a rubber band and a paper cup. Attach the cup to the rubber band and place paper clips, pennies, or other objects in the cup to represent the climber's weight. Use a ruler to measure the stretch. Estimate the weight of the rocks needed to stretch the rope to the bottom of the cliff. Is the story true?

Leads to Follow

- ✓ How far does the rubber band extend with no weight attached?
- ✓ What weight does each object in the cup represent?
- ✓ What marks on the ruler represent the top and bottom of the cliff?

What's Ahead

- Graphing points in the coordinate plane
- Finding coordinates of a point

5-1 Graphing Points in All Four Quadrants

THINK AND DISCUSS

Identifying Ordered Pairs Computer programmers and artists create the graphic images you see on computer screens and video games. The spaceships below were drawn by instructing the computer to color specific points called *pixels.* The graph shows one spaceship made up of colored pixels.

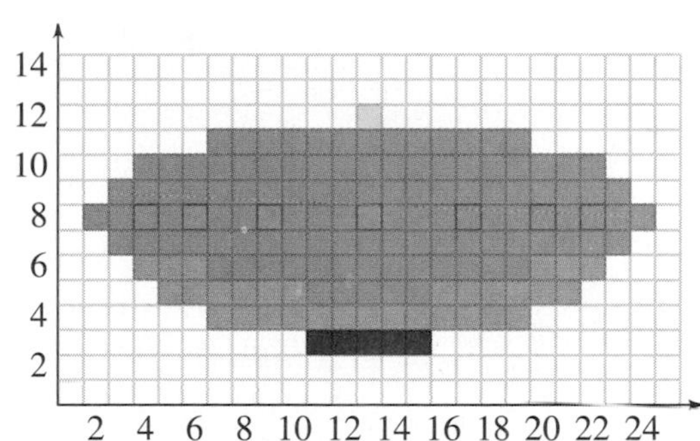

An **ordered pair** describes the location of each pixel. The ordered pair (13, 12) describes the location of the pixel on top of the spaceship. This pixel is the thirteenth space in the horizontal direction and the twelfth space in the vertical direction.

This page was edited on a computer screen that is 640 pixels long by 480 pixels high. **How many pixels did the computer have to track?**

1. What color is the pixel at (11, 3)? the pixel at (8, 4)?
2. List the ordered pairs that describe the locations of the orange pixels. What do these ordered pairs have in common?

We call the two values in an ordered pair the **coordinates** of the point they describe. The coordinates of the pixel at the far left edge of the spaceship are (2, 8).

3. What are the coordinates of the pixel at the far right edge?
4. To move the spaceship, the computer clears the screen and then draws the spaceship in another position. Find the new coordinates of the yellow light after the spaceship moves exactly one spaceship-length to the right.

Identifying Quadrants This grid is called a **coordinate plane.** A horizontal number line, the **x-axis,** intersects a vertical number line, the **y-axis,** at a point called the **origin.** The x- and y- axes divide the coordinate plane into four **quadrants.**

The first number in an ordered pair is the **x-coordinate** and the second is the **y-coordinate.**

5. Describe how to locate the point whose coordinates are $(-3, 2)$. Name the point.

6. What is the point whose coordinates are $(4, -3)$? $(0, -2)$?

7. What are the coordinates of point P? of point Q? of the origin?

8. **Mental Math** Without graphing, state in which quadrant or on which axis you would find the points with these coordinates.

   a. $(-11, -7)$ **b.** $(18.5, -9)$ **c.** $(0, -8)$ **d.** $(-2, 0)$

WORK TOGETHER

The rotating blade of a milling machine cuts a path in a sheet of metal, wood, or plastic.

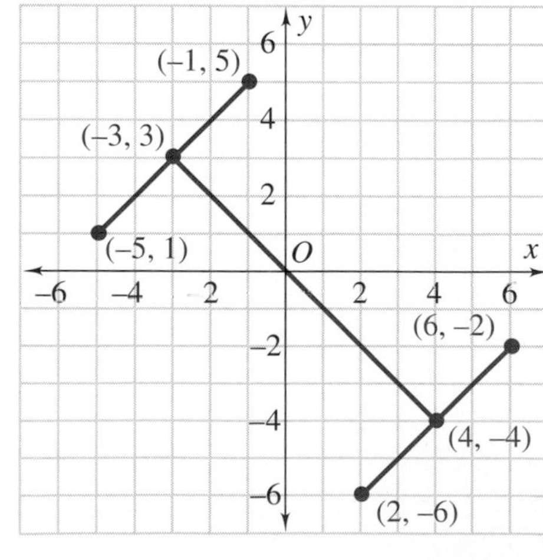

9. Use the coordinate system on the sheet of metal to write step-by-step instructions for cutting the letter I.

10. **Discussion** Compare your list of instructions with that of another group. Is there more than one way to give the instructions? Explain.

ON YOUR OWN

Name the point with the given coordinates.

11. $(2, 1)$ 12. $(-5, -2)$

13. $(0, 2)$ 14. $(2, -4)$

Name the coordinates of each point.

15. J 16. A

17. K 18. G

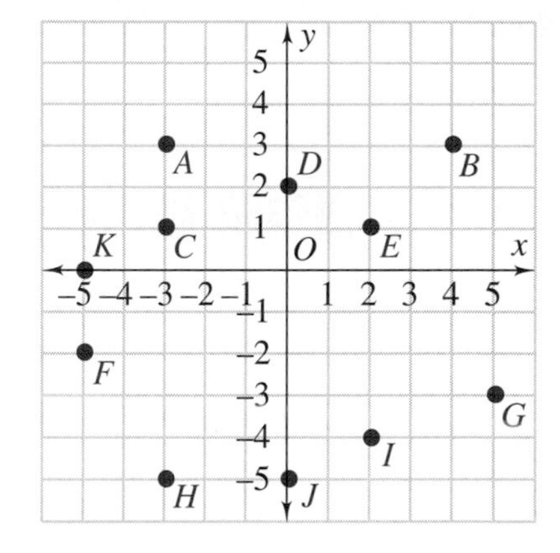

In which quadrant or on which axis would you find the points with the given coordinates?

19. $(12, 11)$ 20. $(-3, -2.71)$ 21. $(112, 0)$

22. (x, y) if $x > 0$ and $y < 0$ 23. (x, y) if $x < 0$ and $y > 0$

24. a. Use graph paper. Draw the shape that a milling machine would make given these instructions: Go to $(-7, 7)$. Lower blade. Cut to $(-7, 1)$. Raise blade. Go to $(-4, 7)$. Lower blade. Cut to $(-4, 1)$. Raise blade. Go to $(-7, 4)$. Lower blade. Cut to $(-4, 4)$. Raise blade. What is the shape?
    b. **Writing** Write directions to cut the same shape in Quadrant IV.

25. **Choose A, B, C, or D.** The coordinates of three vertices of a rectangle are $(1, -1)$, $(9, -1)$, and $(1, -10)$. What are the coordinates of the fourth vertex?

    A. $(9, 1)$ **B.** $(1, -9)$ **C.** $(9, -10)$ **D.** $(-10, -9)$

26. **Geography** Degrees of *longitude* and *latitude* give locations of places on a map. For example, the longitude of the city of Chicago is about 87° and the latitude is about 42°. Find the longitude and latitude of St. Paul and Lincoln.

27. Locate four points that are exactly 5 units from the origin. Are there any others? If so, what shape would they describe?

28. **Investigation (p. 194)** Draw sketches to represent the climber's descent from the top of the cliff. Label all distances.

Mixed REVIEW

1. Each side of a regular hexagon has length 7 in. Find the perimeter.

Solve.

2. $3x + 4 \geq 10$
3. $-x - 5 \leq -5$

Solve for y in terms of x.

4. $6x + 3y = 9$
5. $5y - 2x = 10$
6. The length of a rectangle is twice the width. The perimeter is 84 cm. Find the length and width.

Problem Solving Hint

For Exercises 22–23, try guess and test. Pick a point in a quadrant and test to see if its coordinates meet the conditions described.

How is locating a point on a map like locating a point on a coordinate plane?

What's Ahead

- Finding solutions of linear equations
- Graphing linear equations

5-2 Equations in Two Variables

THINK AND DISCUSS

Suppose your neighbor offers you a baby-sitting job and gives you a choice of two payment plans.

BABYSITTING SALARY OPTIONS

PLAN A: $3.00 per hour

PLAN B: A base salary of $3.00 plus $2.00 per hour

1. How much will you make under each plan if you work for two hours? for five hours?
2. Which do you think is the better plan? Is there information besides rate of pay that you might want to consider? Justify your answer.

Plan A Equation

total earned → $y = 3x$ ← hours worked; 3 = hourly wage

Plan B Equation

total earned → $y = 2x + 3$ ← hours worked; 2 = hourly wage; 3 = base salary

Solving Equations The equations at the left describe each payment plan. They are *equations in two variables.* An ordered pair that makes an equation a true statement is a **solution**.

Example 1 Tell whether (3, 9) and (8, 20) are solutions of the Plan B equation, $y = 2x + 3$.

Substitute the first number of each ordered pair for x and the second number of each ordered pair for y.

$y = 2x + 3$	$y = 2x + 3$
$9 = 2(3) + 3$	$20 = 2(8) + 3$
$9 = 9$ ✓	$20 = 19$ ✗
True, so (3, 9) is a solution.	False, so (8, 20) is not a solution.

3. Look at the Plan B equation and the solution (3, 9).
   a. What does the x-coordinate 3 represent?
   b. What does the y-coordinate 9 represent?
4. If you work for 8 h under Plan B, would you expect to make $20? Why or why not?
5. Suppose you work for 4 h under Plan B. What would you expect to earn?
6. Do the Plan A and Plan B equations have more than one solution? Explain.

Graphing Equations You can make a table when you need to find several solutions of an equation in two variables. Choose values for x. Substitute the values in the equation to find y. Write the solutions as ordered pairs.

Example 2 Find several solutions of the equation $y = 2x + 3$. Graph the ordered pairs.

- Make a table.

x	$2x + 3$	y	(x, y)
-2	$2(-2) + 3$	-1	$(-2, -1)$
-1	$2(-1) + 3$	1	$(-1, 1)$
0	$2(0) + 3$	3	$(0, 3)$
1	$2(1) + 3$	5	$(1, 5)$
2	$2(2) + 3$	7	$(2, 7)$

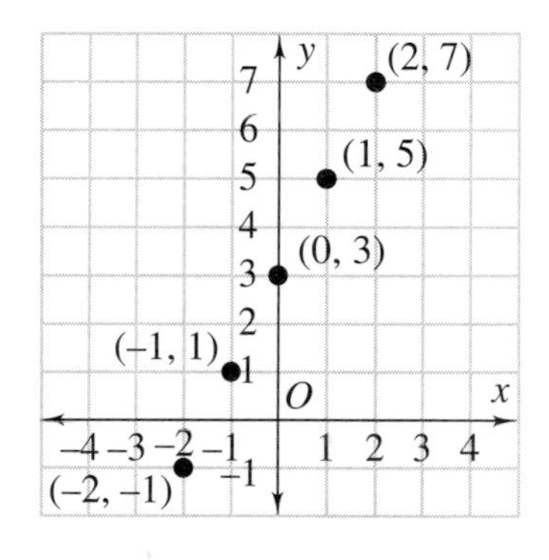

- Several solutions of the equation $y = 2x + 3$ are $(-2, -1)$, $(-1, 1)$, $(0, 3)$, $(1, 5)$, and $(2, 7)$. The graph is shown at the right.

7. Critical Thinking Think of $y = 2x + 3$ as the Plan B baby-sitting equation.

a. Does $(-2, -1)$ make sense as a solution? Why or why not?

b. Which ordered pairs make sense as solutions? Explain.

8. Study the pattern of the points on the graph in Example 2. What appears to be true?

An equation like $y = 2x + 3$ is a *linear equation* because the graph of its solution consists of points that lie on a line.

9. How could you show that $y = 3x$ is a linear equation?

10. Discussion How many solutions do you think a linear equation has? How do you know?

11. Here are more examples of linear equations. What would you have to do to these equations so that you could make a table of solutions like the one in Example 2?

$3x + 5y = 8$ $\qquad\qquad$ $x - 2y = 6$

Extra SKILLS PRACTICE

Solve for y in terms of x. Then graph each equation.

1. $2x + y = -5$
2. $-3x - 2y = 12$
3. $6x + 2y = -16$
4. $-10x - 5y = 35$
5. $6x + 3y = 18$
6. $x + 3y = -12$
7. $24x - 4y = -16$
8. $-50x + 10y = -5$

You can show all the solutions of a linear equation by graphing several solutions and then drawing a line through the points.

Example 3 Graph the linear equation $2x + 4y = 8$.

- Solve for y in terms of x.

$$2x + 4y = 8$$

$$2x + 4y - 2x = 8 - 2x \quad \text{Subtract } 2x \text{ from both sides.}$$

$$4y = -2x + 8$$

$$\frac{4y}{4} = \frac{-2x + 8}{4} \quad \text{Divide both sides by 4.}$$

$$y = -\frac{1}{2}x + 2$$

- Make a table of solutions.

x	$-\frac{1}{2}x + 2$	y	(x, y)
-2	$-\frac{1}{2}(-2) + 2$	3	$(-2, 3)$
0	$-\frac{1}{2}(0) + 2$	2	$(0, 2)$
2	$-\frac{1}{2}(2) + 2$	1	$(2, 1)$
4	$-\frac{1}{2}(4) + 2$	0	$(4, 0)$
6	$-\frac{1}{2}(6) + 2$	-1	$(6, -1)$

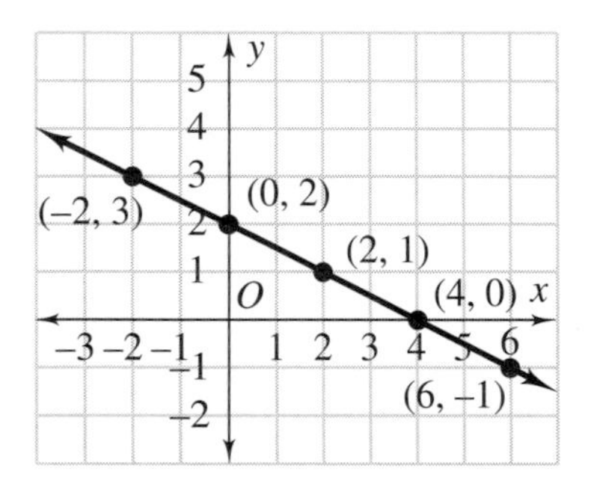

- Graph the ordered pairs and draw a line through the points. The graph is shown at the left.

12. Why do you think only even numbers were substituted for x?

TRY THESE

13. Choose the equation that describes the cost of renting videos. Graph the equation. Which solutions make sense?

    $y = 12x$ $\qquad$ $y = 12x + 3$ $\qquad$ $y = 3x + 12$

14. Is $(4, -21)$ a solution of $y = 3x + 9$? Explain.

15. Make a table of ordered pairs that are solutions of the equation $y = \frac{3}{4}x - 1$. Then graph the equation.

16. Solve for y in terms of x: $12x + 3y = 3$

17. a. Work with your group. For each linear equation, make a table of solutions. Then graph the equation.

$0x + y = 3$ $\qquad$ $x + 0y = 3$

b. Describe the graph of the equation in which x is multiplied by zero; in which y is multiplied by zero.

ON YOUR OWN

Which ordered pairs are solutions of $y = -7x + 10$?

18. $(-3, 31)$ $\quad$ 19. $(7, 59)$ $\quad$ 20. $(0, 10)$ $\quad$ 21. $(8, 46)$

Solve for y in terms of x. Then graph each equation.

22. $3x + y = -5$ $\quad$ 23. $-6x + 2y = -8$

24. $-3x + 2y = 10$ $\quad$ 25. $-20x + 5y = 30$

26. The graphs of the linear equations below form the sides of a polygon. Name the polygon.

$y = x + 3;\quad y = -\frac{1}{4}x + 3;\quad y = x - 2;\quad y = -2x - 6$

27. **Writing** Four of these ordered pairs are solutions of the same linear equation. Which one is not? Explain why.

$A(2, 1)$, $B(0, -4)$, $C(1, -2)$, $D(4, 4)$, $E(3, 2)$

28. **Design** This design consists of squares that enclose a row of 3 circles. The design takes 12 squares.

a. Use graph paper. Find the number of squares it takes to enclose rows of 1, 2, 3, 4, 5, and 6 circles. Keep track of your data in a table like the one shown.

b. Graph the ordered pairs from your table on a coordinate plane. Draw a line through all 6 points.

c. Use your graph and your table to find the number of squares it would take to enclose a row of 15 circles.

29. **Investigation (p. 194)** Suppose x represents the weight on the rope and y represents the distance from the top of the cliff to the end of the rope. What points could you graph to model the rescue?

Evaluate. Let $a = 7$ and $b = -3$.

1. b^3 $\quad$ 2. $-2a - b$

In which quadrant or on which axis would you find the points with the given coordinates?

3. $(0, -3)$ $\quad$ 4. $(5, -3)$

Solve.

5. Note pads are sold in sealed packages of 12. An office manager needs 50 note pads. How many packages must be ordered?

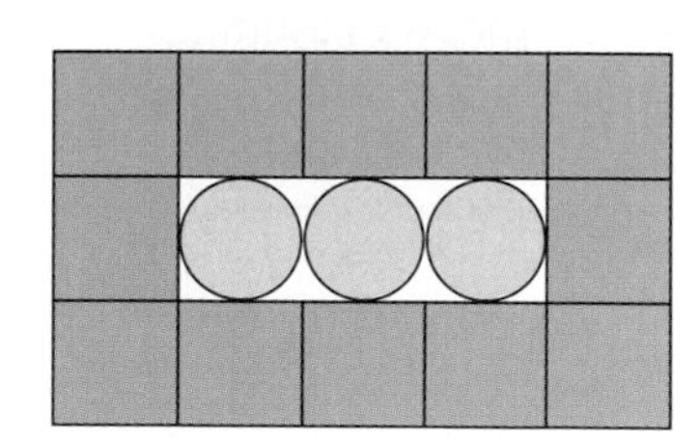

Number of circles (x)	Number of squares (y)	(x, y)
3	12	(3, 12)
■	■	■

What's Ahead

- Exploring $y = mx + b$
- Using technology to explore graphs

WHAT YOU'LL NEED

✓ Computer 

✓ Software 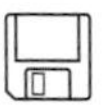

TECHNOLOGY

5-3 The Graph of $y = mx + b$

THINK AND DISCUSS

In basketball, you can score 1, 2, or 3 points for a basket. These tables show the total number of points you could score based on the type of shot and the number of baskets you make.

Foul Shots	
Baskets	Points
0	0
1	1
2	2
3	3
4	4

2-Point Shots	
Baskets	Points
0	0
1	2
2	4
3	6
4	8

3-Point Shots	
Baskets	Points
0	0
1	3
2	6
3	9
4	12

1. a. **Discussion** What patterns do you see in the tables?
   b. **Critical Thinking** In each table, describe what you must do to the number in the first column to get the number in the second column.
   c. What is the next pair of numbers, or ordered pair, in each table?

In NBA, college, and some high school games, a basket counts 3 points if it is made from behind the 3-point line. Other baskets count 2 points. Foul shots are free throws resulting from a penalty and count 1 point.

Source: *World Book Encyclopedia*

The equations $y = 3x$, $y = 2x$, and $y = x$ can each be used to describe the pattern in one of the tables.

2. Which equation matches which table? Why?

3. What do x and y represent in the three equations?

4. How are the equations alike? How are they different?

5. If you graph the equations as shown at the left, you get three lines in the first quadrant.
   a. Which line is the graph of which equation? How do you know?
   b. **Discussion** How do the graphs show the same patterns as the tables?

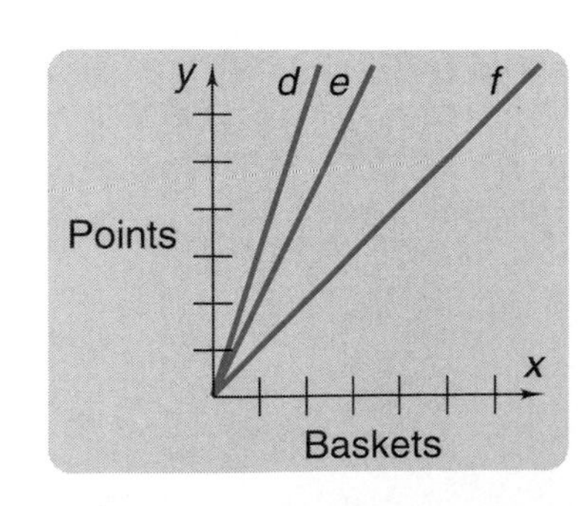

All three basketball-shot equations have the form $y = mx$. What is the value of m in each equation?

$x = 1 \cdot x$

6. $y = 2x$ **7.** $y = 3x$ **8.** $y = x$

9. The coordinate plane at the right shows the graph of the same three equations. What happens to the graph of $y = mx$ as m decreases?

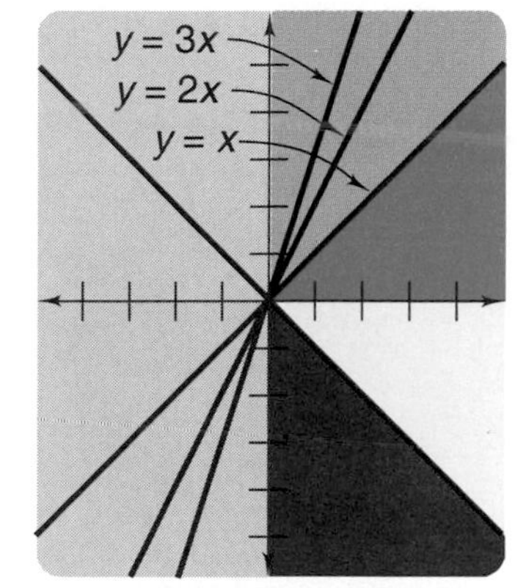

10. Computer The graphs of $y = 3x$ and $y = 2x$ go through the blue section of the plane. How can you change m so that when you graph $y = mx$ the line will go through a different color? Explore by graphing equations in the form $y = mx$. Try different positive, negative, and fractional values for m.

11. What kinds of values of m will make the line go through

a. the green section of the plane?

b. the red section?

c. the yellow section?

12. Discussion How does the graph of $y = mx$ change as values of m change

a. from positive numbers downward to zero?

b. from zero downward to negative numbers?

Some amusement parks charge an admission fee in addition to the cost of the rides. At Big Scream Amusement Park, admission is free on Mondays. On Tuesdays, Wednesdays, and Thursdays, the admission is \$1.00. On Fridays, Saturdays, and Sundays, the admission is \$2.00. Rides cost \$1.00 each regardless of the day. The tables below show your total costs for different numbers of rides on different days of the week.

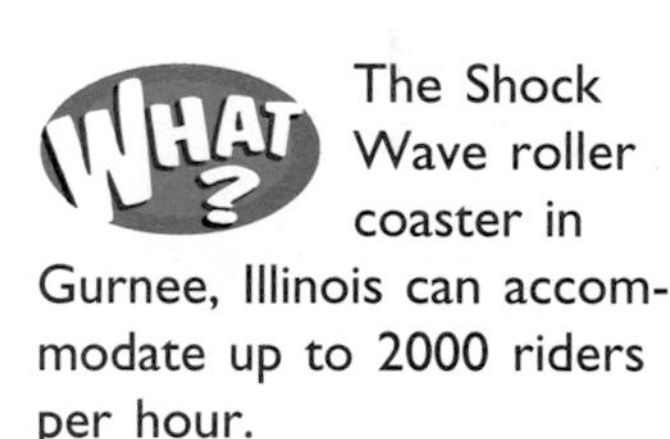

The Shock Wave roller coaster in Gurnee, Illinois can accommodate up to 2000 riders per hour.

Source: *Six Flags Great America News Fact Sheet*

Monday	
Number of rides	Final cost($)
0	0
1	1
2	2
3	3
Admission is free.	

Tuesday – Thursday	
Number of rides	Final cost($)
0	1
1	2
2	3
3	4
Admission = \$1.00	

Friday – Sunday	
Number of rides	Final cost($)
0	2
1	3
2	4
3	5
Admission = \$2.00	

13. **a.** For each table, describe what you must do to the number in the first column to get the corresponding number in the second column.

   b. Each row in each table represents an ordered pair of numbers. What is the next ordered pair in each table?

14. The equation $y = x + 1$ fits the values in the table for Tuesday–Thursday.

   a. What do x and y represent?

   b. What equations fit the values in the other two tables?

   c. All three equations can be written in the form $y = x + b$. What is the value of b in each equation?

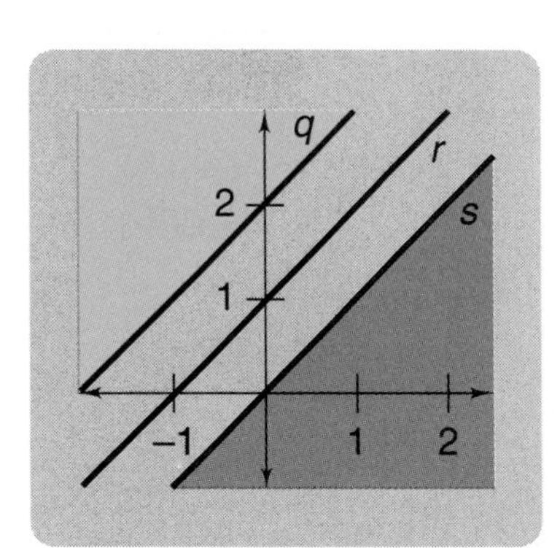

$y = x + 0$
$y = x + 1$
$y = x + 2$

15. Match each line in the graph at the left with its equation.

16. **Computer** Explore equations of the form $y = x + b$. How can you change b so the graph of $y = x + b$ will be in the green section? in the red section?

17. **Discussion** What happens to the graph of $y = x + b$ as b changes?

WORK TOGETHER

18. The equation $y = 2x + 1$ is in the form $y = mx + b$.

   a. What are the values of m and b in $y = 2x + 1$?

   b. **Computer** Make and test conjectures about what happens to the graph of $y = mx + b$ as m changes and as b changes. (Hint: First change m only. Then change b only. Then change both.)

   c. Compare your conjectures with those of another group.

ON YOUR OWN

19. **Money** Bianca gets \$1.00 plus \$3.00/h for baby-sitting. Her friend Trevor gets \$3.00 plus \$1.00/h. Which graph represents Bianca's payment plan? which represents Trevor's? Explain.

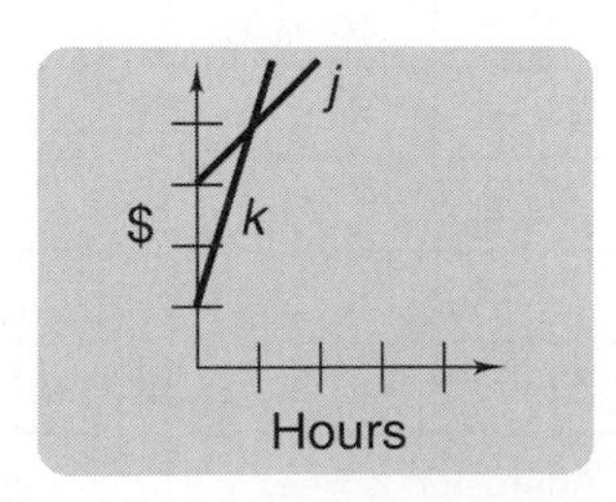

20. Identify the value of m in each equation. Then match each equation with its graph.

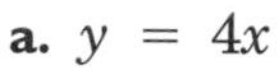

a. $y = 4x$

b. $y = -2x$

c. $y = \frac{1}{2}x$

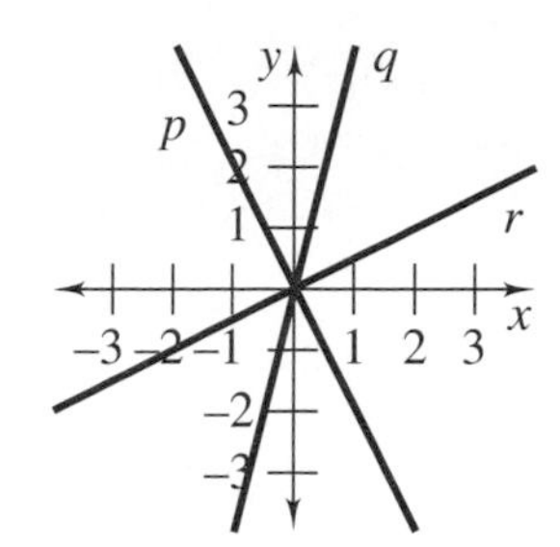

21. Identify the value of b in each equation. Then match each equation with its graph.

a. $y = x - 3$

b. $y = x + 4$

c. $y = x - \frac{1}{2}$

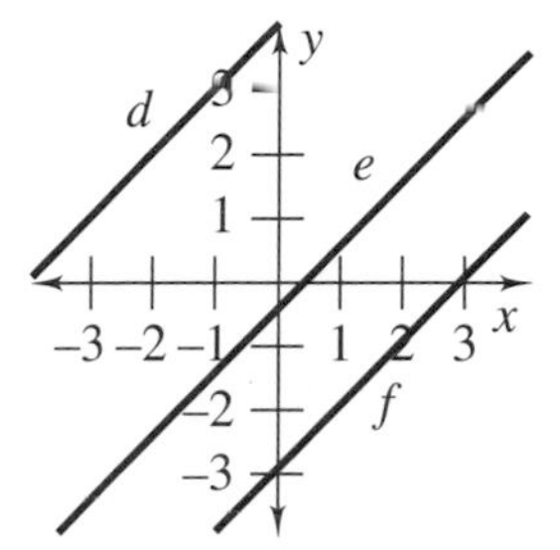

22. Identify the value of m and b in each equation. Then match each equation with its graph.

a. $y = 2x + 3$

b. $y = 2x - 3$

c. $y = -2x + 3$

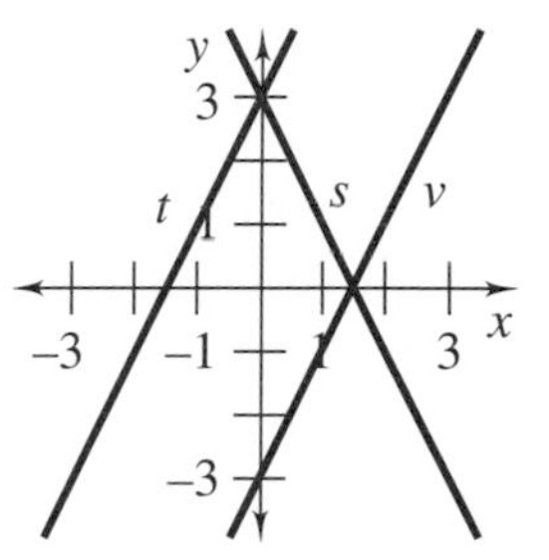

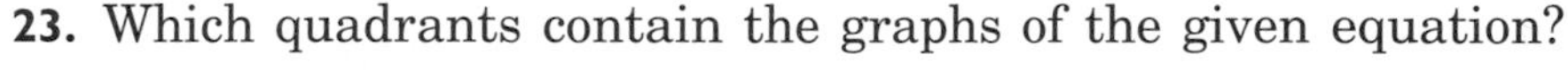

23. Which quadrants contain the graphs of the given equation?

a. $y = mx$ with m positive

b. $y = mx$ with m negative

c. $y = mx + b$ with m positive and b negative

d. $y = mx + b$ with m negative and b positive

24. **Writing** In the graph of $y = mx + b$, how is the effect of changing b different from the effect of changing m? Use examples to illustrate your answer.

25. **Data File 5 (pp. 192-193)** In what year are men and women projected to run the marathon in the same time?

26. **Investigation (p. 194)** Let x represent the weight in the paper cup. Let y represent the length of the rubber band. Draw a graph showing the results of your experiment modeling the rescue.

Mixed REVIEW

Use a calculator to find each square root.

1. $\sqrt{95}$ 2. $\sqrt{28}$

Make a table of solutions for each equation. Then graph the equations.

3. $y = -4x - 3$

4. $-3x + 2y = 18$

Solve.

5. Kelly has equal numbers of pennies, nickels, dimes, and quarters. The total is $6.15. How many of each type of coin does Kelly have?

A person weighing 120 lb burns about 7.3 calories per minute while jogging and about 11.3 calories per minute while running.

Source: *The World Almanac and Book of Facts*

What's Ahead

- Finding the slope of a line

5-4 Understanding Slope

WHAT YOU'LL NEED

✓ Graph paper

✓ Ruler

✓ Scissors

WORK TOGETHER

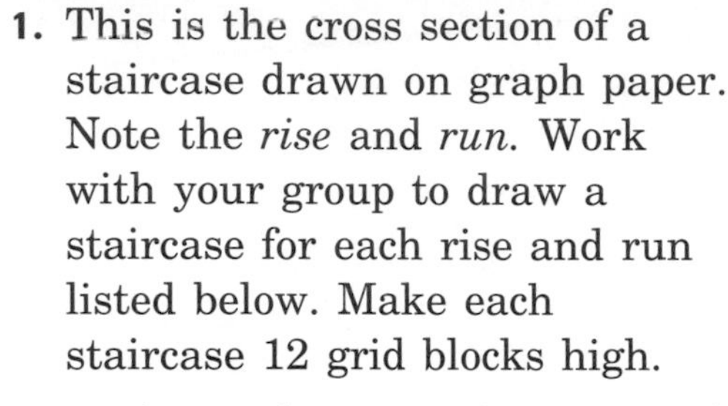

1. This is the cross section of a staircase drawn on graph paper. Note the *rise* and *run*. Work with your group to draw a staircase for each rise and run listed below. Make each staircase 12 grid blocks high.

   a. rise = 1, run = 1
   b. rise = 4, run = 2
   c. rise = 2, run = 1
   d. rise = 2, run = 2
   e. rise = 3, run = 2
   f. rise = 2, run = 3

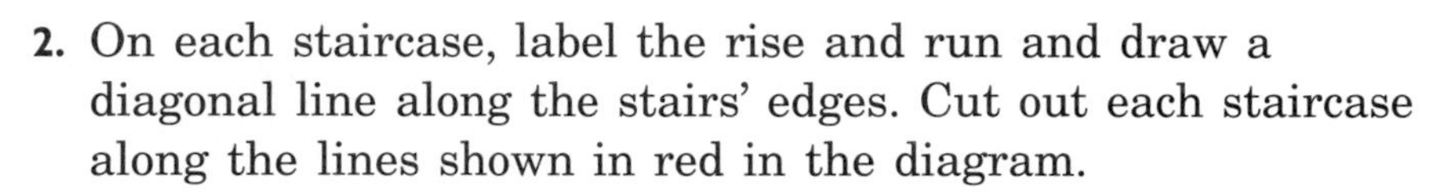

2. On each staircase, label the rise and run and draw a diagonal line along the stairs' edges. Cut out each staircase along the lines shown in red in the diagram.

3. **Discussion** Order the staircases according to steepness.

   a. Which staircase would be hardest to climb? Why?
   b. How do the values of the rise and run affect the steepness of a staircase?
   c. What do you notice about the values of the rises and runs of the staircases that are equally steep?

The stepped roofs** of the homes in Bermuda slow down the flow of rain water. Residents collect the rain water and use it for drinking.* ***What adjustment could be made to the steps to speed up the flow?

THINK AND DISCUSS

Identifying Slope *Slope* is a number indicating steepness. The slope of a staircase is the ratio of the rise to the run.

$$\textbf{slope} = \frac{\text{rise}}{\text{run}}$$

4. A staircase has risers that are 20 cm high and treads that are 24 cm deep. Express the slope in lowest terms.

5. How would you change the rise in order to increase the slope of a staircase?

6. How would you change the run to increase the slope of the staircase?

7. What changes could you make to decrease the slope of the staircase?

Slope also describes the steepness of lines in the coordinate plane.

slope of a line $= \dfrac{\text{vertical change}}{\text{horizontal change}}$ ← **rise or fall**
← **run**

To find the slope of a line, choose two points on the line. Then count the units of vertical change and the corresponding units of horizontal change. Then write the ratio of the number of vertical units to the number of horizontal units.

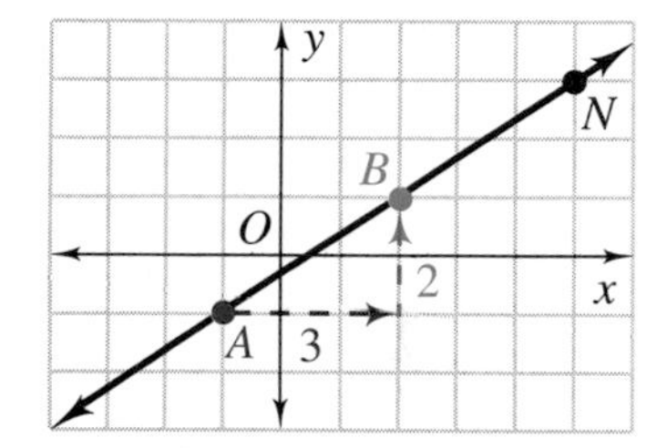

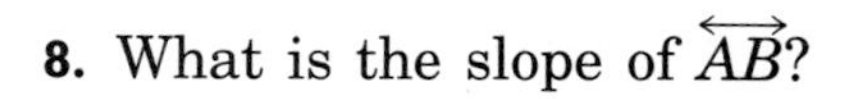

8. What is the slope of $\overleftrightarrow{AB}$?

9. Now use points A and N to find the slope of $\overleftrightarrow{AB}$. Is the slope the same?

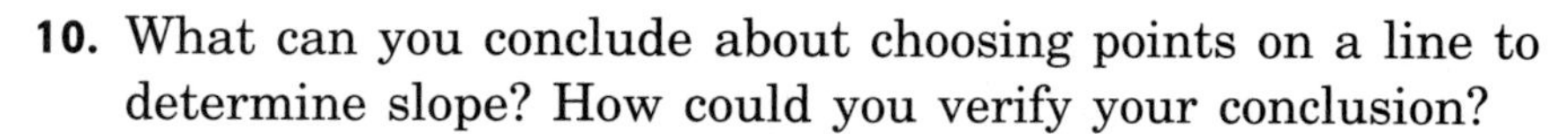

10. What can you conclude about choosing points on a line to determine slope? How could you verify your conclusion?

11. Explain why line $\overleftrightarrow{CD}$ has a slope of $-\frac{3}{4}$.

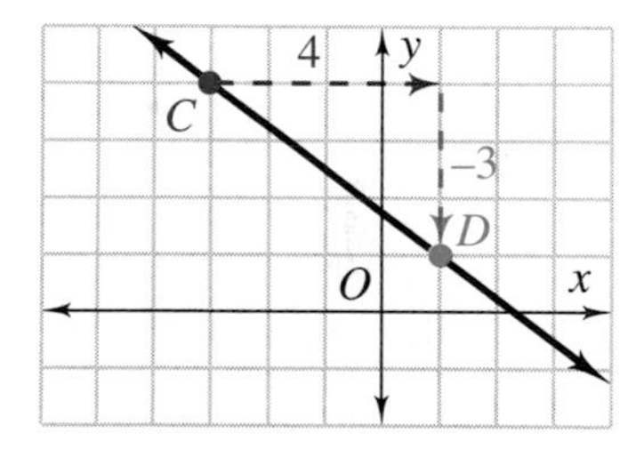

Finding Slope You can subtract to find the vertical change between two points on a line. Subtract the y-coordinate of one point from the y-coordinate of the other point. You can find the horizontal change in a similar way. Subtract the x-coordinates in the same order as the y-coordinates.

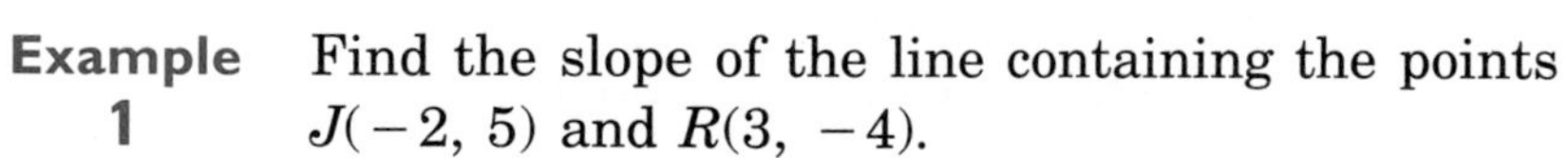

Example 1 Find the slope of the line containing the points $J(-2, 5)$ and $R(3, -4)$.

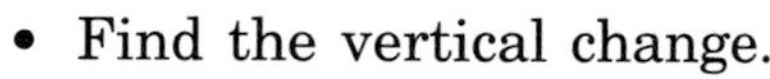

- Find the vertical change.

  $5 - (-4) = 9$ Subtract the y-coordinate of R from the y-coordinate of J.

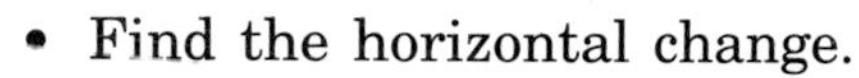

- Find the horizontal change.

  $-2 - 3 = -5$ Subtract the x-coordinate of R from the x-coordinate of J.

- slope of $\overleftrightarrow{JR} = \dfrac{\text{vertical change}}{\text{horizontal change}} = \dfrac{9}{-5}$, or $-\dfrac{9}{5}$.

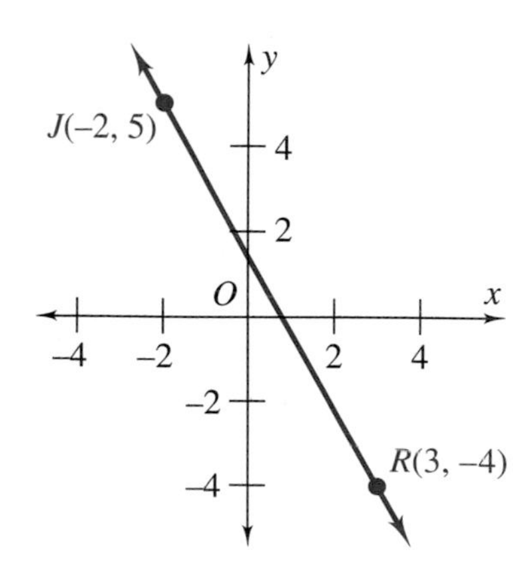

Extra SKILLS PRACTICE

Find the slope of the line that contains each pair of points.

1. $X(4, -1), Y(-3, 0)$
2. $A(3, -1), B(4, 2)$
3. $H(-5, 2), K(0, 2)$
4. $B(4, 7), C(4, -2)$
5. $S(3, -1), T(-2, 0)$
6. $P(-1, 6), Q(-1, -3)$
7. $F(2, -2), G(1, -7)$
8. $R(-3, 2), S(3, -1)$
9. $M(0, -4), N(2, -4)$
10. $D(-6, -2), E(-2, -1)$

12. Critical Thinking In Example 1, the horizontal change was calculated by subtracting the x-coordinate of R from the x-coordinate of J. Could you reverse the subtraction and still get the correct value for the slope? Explain.

Example 2 Find the slope of the line containing the points $P(-3, 2)$ and $S(4, 2)$. Then graph the line.

- slope $= \frac{2 - 2}{-3 - 4}$

  $= \frac{0}{-7}$

  $= 0$

- The slope of $\overleftrightarrow{PS}$ is zero.

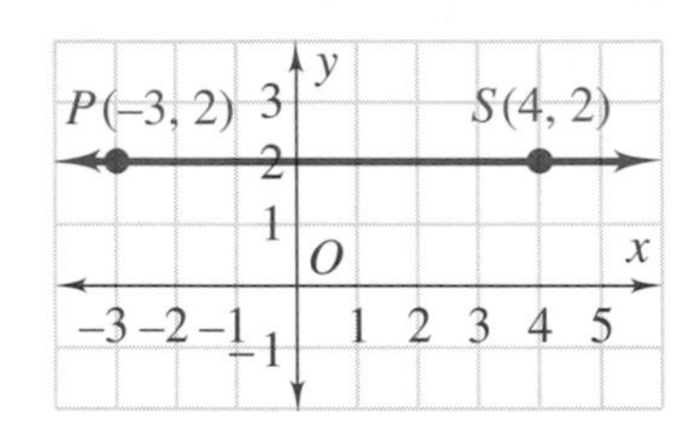

13. What appears to be true about a line whose slope is zero? Explain your answer in terms of the rise and run of the line.

FLASHBACK

Division by zero is not defined.

TRY THESE

14. **a.** Find the slope of the line containing $J(3, 4)$ and $K(3, -3)$.
    b. Graph $\overleftrightarrow{JK}$. Describe the line.

15. How can you tell from a graph whether a line has a positive slope or a negative slope?

16. **Discussion** In the previous lesson, you saw how changing the value of m in $y = mx + b$ affects the graph of the equation. What do you think m represents? Explain.

Choose Use a calculator, paper and pencil, or mental math to find the slope of the line that contains the given points.

17. $A(0, 1), B(8, 5)$

18. $C(-1, 5), D(-4, -4)$

The steepest street** in the world is Filbert Street in San Francisco. It rises 25 ft for every 79 ft of run. **What is the slope of Filbert Street?

ON YOUR OWN

19. **Choose A, B, C, or D.** A line contains the points with coordinates (3, 5) and (4, 6). Which expression can you use to find the slope of the line?

A. $\frac{3 - 4}{5 - 6}$ **B.** $\frac{5 - 6}{4 - 3}$ **C.** $\frac{5 - 6}{3 - 4}$ **D.** $\frac{6 - 5}{3 - 4}$

Use the graph to find the slope of each line.

20. line a **21.** line f

22. line c **23.** line d

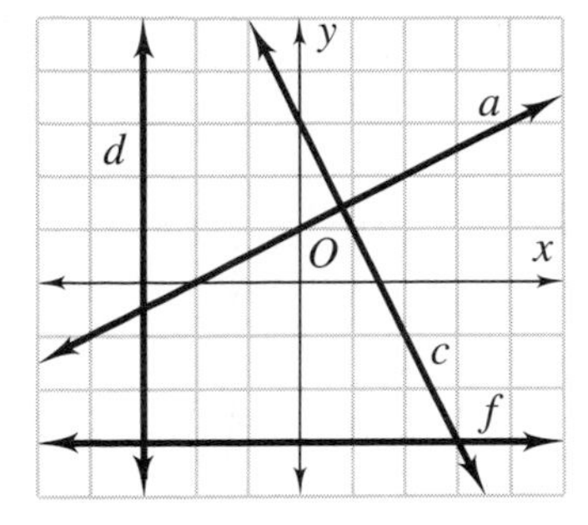

24. Writing Explain which is safer: walking on a roof with a rise of 5 and a run of 3 or a roof with a rise of 8 and a run of 5.

Choose Use a calculator, paper and pencil, or mental math to find the slope of the line that contains the given points.

25. $G(2, 0)$, $H(10, -4)$ **26.** $I(6, -5)$, $J(6, 5)$

27. $M(-3, 6)$, $N(-6, 1)$ **28.** $P(3, -7)$, $K(2, -7)$

Ramps Mean Access for All

Last night, local officials mandated that all public buildings have wheelchair accessibility. According to federal guidelines, no ramp may have a slope greater than 1 to 12. Townspeople have until the last day of the year to comply with this new ordinance.

29. a. Does a ramp with a slope of 1 to 14 comply with federal guidelines? Explain.

b. If the ramp in part (a) reaches a doorway 2 ft above ground, how far from the building does it begin?

30. Activity Measure the rise and run of some actual staircases. Find the slopes. Use your findings to report on how slope indicates how easy a staircase is to climb.

CHECKPOINT

Make a table of solutions. Then graph the equation.

1. $y = 2x - 6$ **2.** $y - 2 = -3x$

3. Find the value of m and b in $y = -2x + 4$.

Mixed REVIEW

Find the mode if it exists.

1. 7, 5, 2, 8, 6, 5, 1, 9

2. 8, 7, 6, 5, 4, 3, 2, 1

Name the coordinates of the point where the graph of the equation intersects the y-axis.

3. $y = 3x - 5$

4. $y = \frac{2}{5}x + 8$

Solve for y in terms of x.

5. $3x + y = \frac{1}{3}$

6. $4 + y = 3x$

Solve.

7. Stuart types 40 words/min. How many words does he type in $\frac{3}{4}$ h?

How would you measure the run to find the slope of this spiral staircase?

Practice

Name the point with the given coordinates.

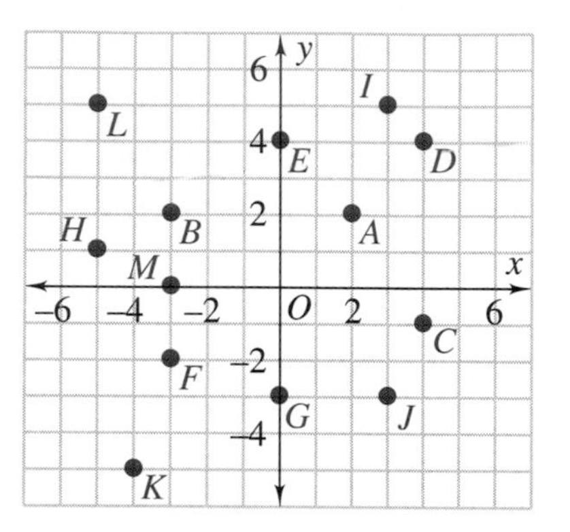

1. $(3, 5)$ 2. $(-4, -5)$ 3. $(3, -3)$

4. $(4, 4)$ 5. $(2, 2)$ 6. $(0, -3)$

Name the coordinates of each point.

7. H 8. F 9. E

10. C 11. B 12. L

Tell whether the ordered pair is a solution of the equation.

13. $(2, 3);\ y = 2x + 1$ 14. $(-6, 2);\ \frac{1}{2}x + 2y = 1$ 15. $(-2, -4);\ y = x - 6$

Make a table of solutions and graph each equation.

16. $y = 3x - 2$ 17. $y = \frac{1}{4}x + 4$ 18. $2x + y = 5$ 19. $y = -2x$

Write the values of m and b in each equation.

20. $y = x + 9$ 21. $y = -2x + 5$ 22. $y = 3x$ 23. $2x + 4y = 12$

24. $y = 7$ 25. $y = -\frac{5}{6}x - 9$ 26. $3y = 9 - 3x$ 27. $\frac{1}{2}y + 6 = 2x$

Match each equation with its graph.

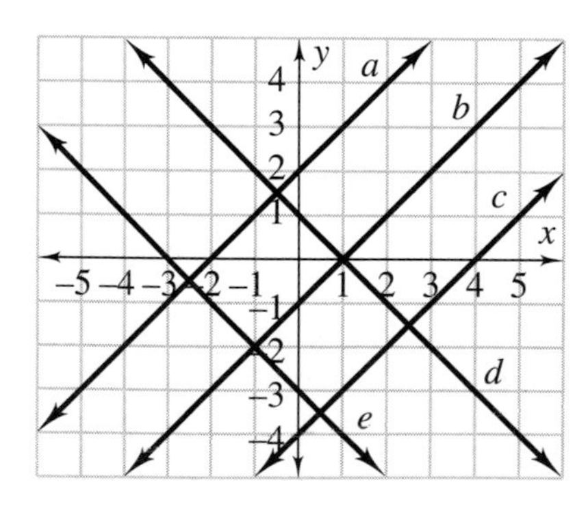

28. $y = x - 1$

29. $y = x + 2$

30. $y = x - 4$

31. $y = -x - 3$

32. $y = -x + 1$

Find the slope of the line containing the given points.

33. $(2, 1), (3, 4)$ 34. $(-5, 2), (3, -2)$ 35. $(0, 2), (0, 3)$ 36. $(6, -3), (-3, 6)$

37. $(4, 4), (-3, 4)$ 38. $(8, 2), (-2, 3)$ 39. $(5, 6), (-10, 3)$ 40. $(-2, -2), (0, -1)$

What's Ahead

- Finding x- and y-intercepts
- Using slope and the y-intercept to graph lines

In the 1993 Super Bowl, the Dallas Cowboys beat the Buffalo Bills by a score of 52-17. Dallas intercepted 4 of Buffalo's pass attempts. Buffalo committed 9 turnovers. ***What percent of the turnovers were interceptions?***

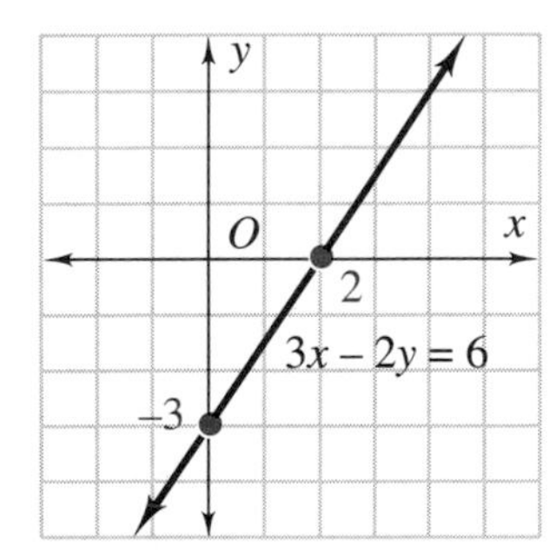

5-5 Using Slope and Intercepts

THINK AND DISCUSS

1. What does it mean to *intercept* a pass in football?
2. Think of the path of the football as a line. What happens to the path when the ball is intercepted?
3. Think of points and lines on the coordinate plane. What are some ways you could apply the word *intercept*?

Intercepts The **x-intercept** is the x-coordinate of the point where the line crosses the x-axis. The **y-intercept** is the y-coordinate of the point where the line crosses the y-axis.

Example 1 Find the x-intercept and the y-intercept of the line $3x - 2y = 6$. Use the intercepts to graph the equation.

To find the x-intercept, substitute 0 for y.

$$\begin{aligned} 3x - 2y &= 6 \\ 3x - 2(0) &= 6 \\ 3x - 0 &= 6 \\ 3x &= 6 \\ \frac{3x}{3} &= \frac{6}{3} \\ x &= 2 \end{aligned}$$

The x-intercept is 2.

To find the y-intercept, substitute 0 for x.

$$\begin{aligned} 3x - 2y &= 6 \\ 3(0) - 2y &= 6 \\ 0 - 2y &= 6 \\ -2y &= 6 \\ \frac{-2y}{-2} &= \frac{6}{-2} \\ y &= -3 \end{aligned}$$

The y-intercept is -3.

Draw a line through the points with coordinates $(2, 0)$ and $(0, -3)$.

4. How does the slope of $3x - 2y = 6$ relate to the intercepts?
5. Draw a line that has a y-intercept but no x-intercept. Describe the line. What is its slope?
6. Draw a line that has an x-intercept but no y-intercept. Describe the line. What is its slope?

In an earlier lesson, you explored the graphs of equations that were in the form $y = mx + b$. You discovered that m tells you how steep the line is and b tells you where the line crosses the y-axis. Since m is the slope and b is the y-intercept, we call $y = mx + b$ the **slope-intercept form** of an equation.

$y = mx + b$ (slope: m; y-intercept: b)

7. Identify the slope and y-intercept of the line whose equation is $y = -\frac{1}{2}x + 6$.

8. What is the slope of the graph of $y = x$? of $y = -x$? Explain.

9. What is the y-intercept of the graph of $y = x$? of $y = -x$? Explain.

Using Graphs An equation in slope-intercept form provides you with all the information you need to graph an equation.

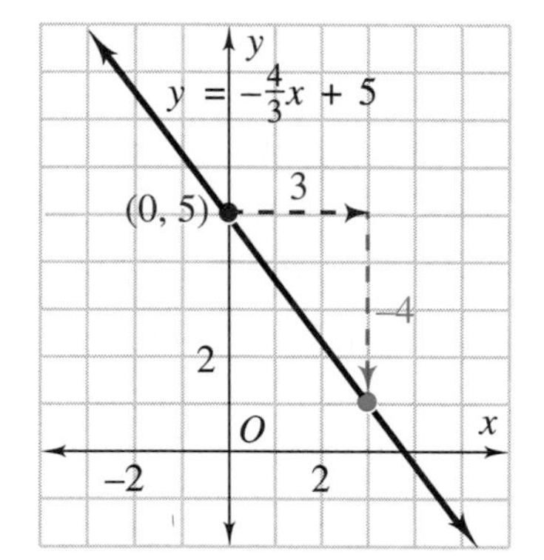

Example 2 Graph the equation $y = -\frac{4}{3}x + 5$.

- Since the y-intercept is 5, graph (0, 5).

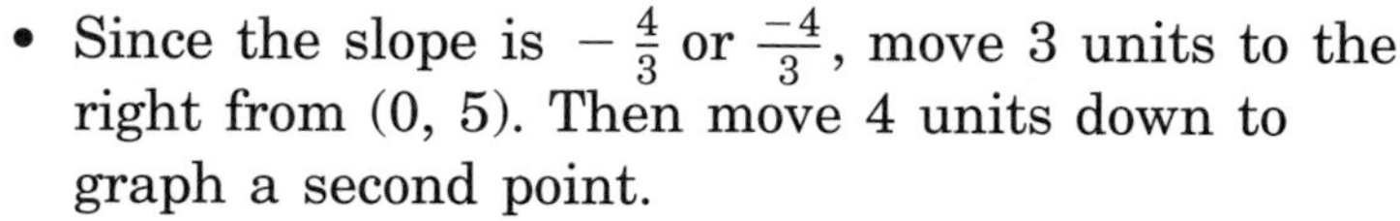

- Since the slope is $-\frac{4}{3}$ or $\frac{-4}{3}$, move 3 units to the right from (0, 5). Then move 4 units down to graph a second point.
- Draw a line through the points. Label the graph with the equation.

TRY THESE

Find the x-intercept and y-intercept. Use the intercepts to graph each equation.

10. $5x + 6y = 30$ **11.** $4x - 6y = 12$ **12.** $6x + 2y = 8$

Identify the slope and y-intercept.

13. $y = x - 2$ **14.** $y = 1.3x + 5$ **15.** $y = -8$

Graph each equation.

16. $y = -\frac{1}{3}x + 5$ **17.** $y = 4x + 7$

18. Graph $y = \frac{1}{2}x + 3$ and $y = \frac{1}{2}x - 4$ on the same coordinate plane. Compare the values of m. Compare the graphs. What appears to be true?

19. Work with your group to make a list of the techniques you have learned for graphing equations. Give each technique a name and write a set of instructions for each in the form of steps to follow, a recipe, a script, or other form of directions.

If these two jet streams were graphed as lines, how would the equations of the lines compare?

ON YOUR OWN

Find the x- and y-intercepts. Use the intercepts to graph each equation.

20. $4x - 7y = -28$

21. $-6x - 3y = 18$

22. $x + y = 8$

23. $6x + 2y = 3$

24. What do the graphs of these equations have in common? Explain.

$y = \frac{1}{2}x - 6$ $\quad$ $y = -2x - 6$ $\quad$ $y = 10x - 6$

Graph each equation.

25. $y = \frac{2}{5}x + 1$

26. $y = 0.8x - 4$

27. $y = -x - 1$

28. **Weather** The formula for converting Celsius degrees to Fahrenheit degrees is an equation in slope-intercept form:

$$F = \frac{9}{5}C + 32$$

a. Identify the slope and the y-intercept.

b. Graph the equation.

29. **Choose A, B, C, or D.** Which equation has a graph that passes through the origin?

A. $y = 7x + 1$ $\quad$ **B.** $y = 7$ $\quad$ **C.** $y = 7x$ $\quad$ **D.** $y = x - 7$

30. **Writing** Explain why it is impossible for any point to lie on both $y = 3x + 5$ *and* on $y = 3x - 2$. Use a graph to illustrate your explanation.

Use a term from geometry to describe the graphs of the pairs of lines.

31. two lines with the same slope but different y-intercepts

32. two lines with the same y-intercept but different slopes

Mixed REVIEW

Solve.

1. $3x - 5 = 7$

2. $-2x < 6$

Find the slope of the line that contains these points.

3. $P(5, 0)$, $M(0, -5)$

4. $H(9, 7)$, $G(4, 3)$

Make a table of ordered pairs, then graph each equation.

5. $y = -5x + 8$

6. $-3x + y = 0$

Solve.

7. Leslie's scores on a series of 10-question quizzes are 5, 7, 7, 8, 9, 10, and 10. If there is one quiz left, can she achieve a median score of 8.5? Explain.

PROBLEM SOLVING

What's Ahead

- Solving problems by drawing a diagram

5-6 Draw a Diagram

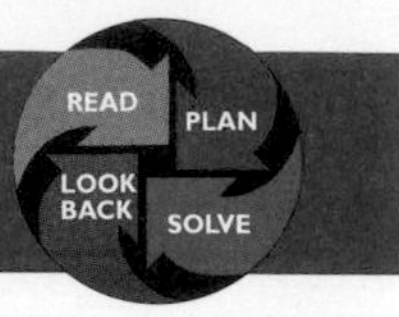

Diagrams can help you to picture the facts in problems involving distances and lengths.

> Calvin and Shawn are 200 ft apart. A flagpole is halfway between them. Both boys begin walking at the same speed toward one another. Halfway to the flagpole, Calvin realizes he dropped his key at his starting point. He goes back, picks up his key, and walks toward the pole again. How far are Calvin and Shawn from the flagpole when they finally meet?

READ

Read and understand the given information. Summarize the problem.

1. Think about what you know and what you need to find out.
   a. How far apart are the boys at the start?
   b. How far from the flagpole is each boy at the start? How do you know?
   c. Is it important to know that the boys walk at the same speed? Why or why not?
   d. Summarize the problem.

PLAN

Decide on a strategy to solve the problem.

The problem involves movement and distances, so drawing a diagram might be a good strategy. Since Calvin and Shawn are walking along the same line, the diagram can involve a line. Since the boys do not always move in the same direction, the diagram should show the changes in direction.

SOLVE

Try out the strategy.

Draw a line. Show the starting positions, the position of the flagpole, and the distance apart at the start.

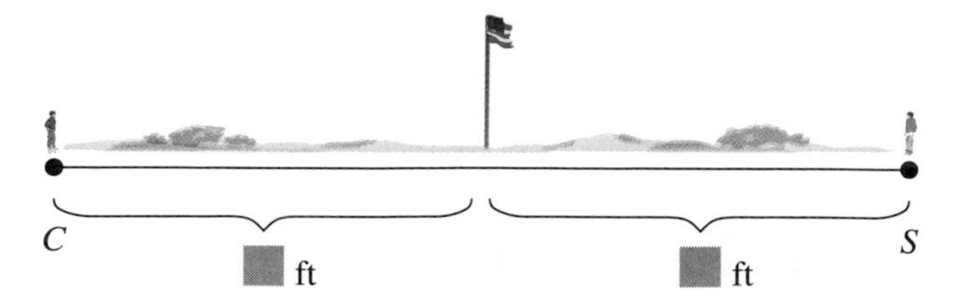

Draw Calvin's and Shawn's movements in the order taken.

(1) They walk halfway to the flagpole.

(2) Calvin returns. Shawn continues toward Calvin.

(3) Calvin starts again. Shawn continues.

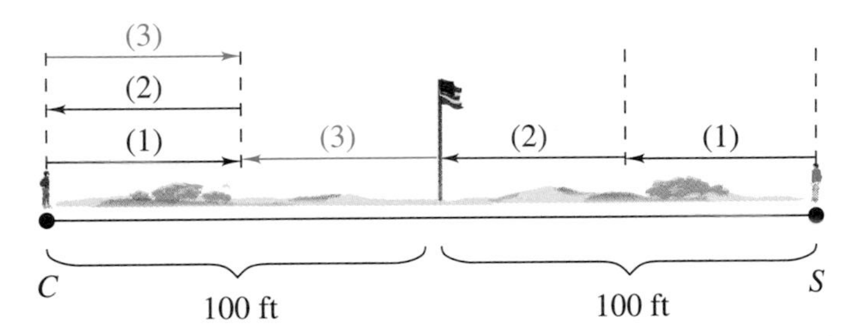

2. How far are the boys from the flagpole when they meet?

3. What if Calvin and Shawn were 400 ft apart at the beginning of the problem. How would the outcome change?

LOOK BACK

Think about how you solved the problem.

TRY THESE

Use diagrams to solve each problem.

4. Two 24-gal water tanks are next to each other. Tank A is half full, and tank B is one-third full. A pump transfers water from tank A to tank B at the rate of 8 gal/min. Another pump transfers water from tank B back to tank A at the rate of 6 gal/min.

- **a.** How many gallons of water are in each tank at the start of the problem? Draw and label the tanks.
- **b.** Draw and label arrows to represent the pumps and their rates.
- **c.** Which tank is losing water? Which tank is gaining?
- **d.** How many gallons per minute are being added to the tank that is being filled?
- **e.** **Discussion** Which tank will be empty or full first? Explain how you solved this problem. In addition to drawing the diagram, did you use any other strategies? If so, which ones did you use?

5. Jane leaves New York on a cross-country car trip at 7 A.M. She averages 40 mi/h. Alice plans to take exactly the same route but does not leave until 8 A.M. She averages 50 mi/h. At what time will she pass Jane?

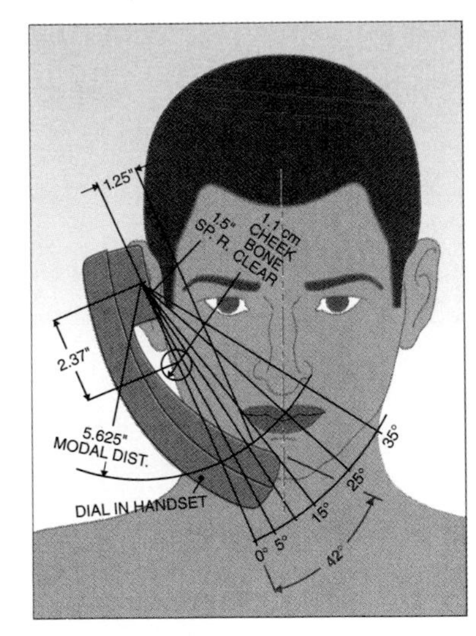

Engineers used complicated diagrams to help them keep track of the many factors involved in developing a new telephone handset.

Source: *The Engineer,* Life Science Library

Find the slope and y-intercept.

1. $y = 3x - 7$

2. $y = -\frac{5}{9}x$

Graph the equations on the same coordinate plane. Name the coordinates of the point of intersection.

3. $y = x$
   $y = -3x + 4$

Find the missing length.

4.

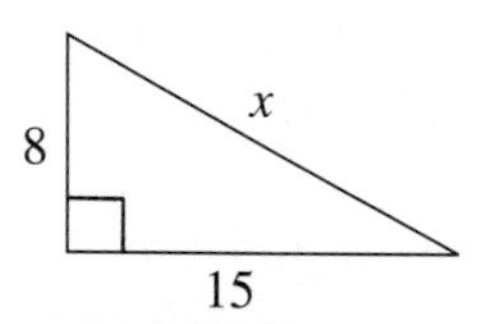

5. Supply the next three terms in the pattern:
1, 4, 13, 40, 121, ...

6. Snoozles are always born as twins, and each snoozle always moves in the opposite direction from its twin. A pair of snoozles are both at the origin. One follows the path (0, 0) to (1, 3) to (2, 2) to (4, 7). What path will its twin follow?

ON YOUR OWN

Use any strategy to solve each problem. Show all your work.

7. A ball is dropped from a height of 64 ft. With each bounce, the ball reaches a height that is half the height of the previous bounce. After how many bounces will the height of the ball be only 6 in.?

8. Alicia has started a Saturday business of making toy trucks. She employs 10 friends who work on the trucks in 3 steps: sanding, attaching the wheels, and painting. One person can sand 30 trucks per day; one person can attach wheels to 12 trucks per day; and one person can paint 20 trucks per day.
   a. How many employees should Alicia assign to each step?
   b. How many finished trucks can they produce in one day?
   c. Can all 10 friends work the same shift? Explain.

9. A delivery truck leaves a warehouse and travels in the following directions: 6 km east, then 4 km south, then 2 km west, and 7 km north. How far is the truck from the warehouse at the end of the trip?

10. Eddie failed to study for his first quiz of the marking period, and he got only 1 point out of 10. If he gets a perfect 10 on all the other quizzes, how many more quizzes will it take him to bring his mean score up to a 9?

11. In an eighth grade class, 10 students take Spanish and 12 students take algebra. Seven students take both Spanish and algebra, and half the students take neither. How many students are in the class?

12. Could you restack these blocks to form a cube? If so, how many blocks will there be along each edge of the cube?

What's Ahead

- Solving systems of linear equations by graphing

5-7 Systems of Linear Equations

THINK AND DISCUSS

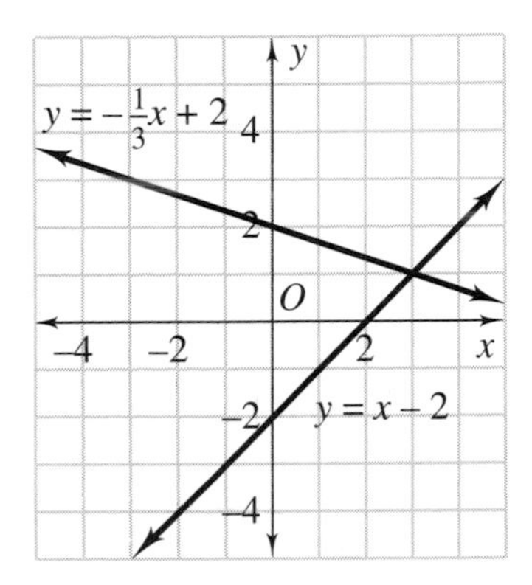

1. How many solutions does the linear equation $y = x - 2$ have? Explain.
2. How many solutions does the linear equation $y = -\frac{1}{3}x + 2$ have? Explain.
3. How many solutions do $y = x - 2$ and $y = -\frac{1}{3}x + 2$ have in common?
4. Can two linear equations ever have exactly two solutions in common? Explain.

Finding Solutions Two or more linear equations using the same variables form a **system of linear equations.** A **solution of a system of linear equations** is any ordered pair that makes all the equations true.

WHO? People have used coordinate graphing to solve problems since the 17th century. The French mathematician René Descartes (1596-1650) is considered the inventor of the coordinate plane.

Example 1 Tell whether $(1, -2)$ is a solution of the system of linear equations:

$$y = -2x \text{ and } 2x - y = 4$$

Substitute the coordinates of the ordered pair in each equation.

$$\begin{aligned} y &= -2x \\ -2 &= -2(1) \\ -2 &= -2 \checkmark \end{aligned} \qquad \begin{aligned} 2x - y &= 4 \\ 2(1) - (-2) &= 4 \\ 2 + 2 &= 4 \\ 4 &= 4 \checkmark \end{aligned}$$

Since $(1, -2)$ makes both equations true, $(1, -2)$ is a solution of the system of linear equations.

Graphing Equations You can solve a system of linear equations by graphing. The solution is the coordinates of the point of intersection of the lines.

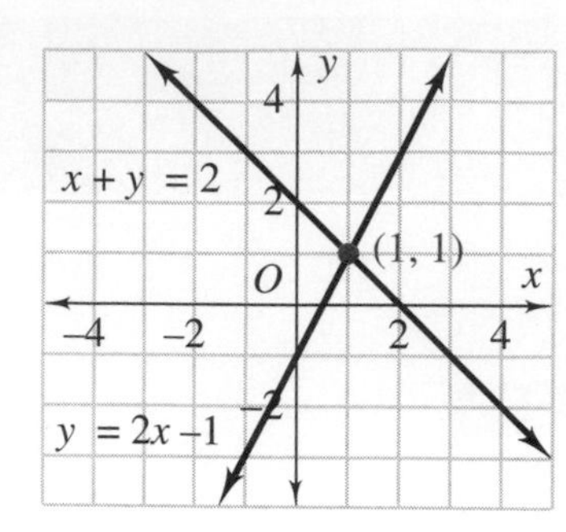

Example 2 Solve the system of linear equations by graphing.

$$x + y = 2 \text{ and } y = 2x - 1$$

- Write each equation in slope-intercept form.

$$y = -x + 2 \text{ and } y = 2x - 1$$

- Graph each equation on the same coordinate plane.
- Find the point where the lines intersect, (1, 1).

The solution of the system is (1, 1).

LOOK BACK How could you check that (1, 1) is the solution of the system in Example 2?

SALES HELP No exp. nec.; eves and Sat.; $3/h to start

MAIL ROOM Part time; $4 per day base + $2/h

You can solve systems of equations to solve word problems.

Example 3 Nabil takes the sales job, and Karen takes the mail room job. After how many hours will they earn the same amount?

- Let x represent the number of hours worked and y represent the amount of money earned. Write a system of equations.

$y = 3x$ ← sales help

$y = 2x + 4$ ← mail room

- Graph the equations on the same coordinate plane.
- The lines intersect at (4, 12).

After 4 h, both will have earned $12.

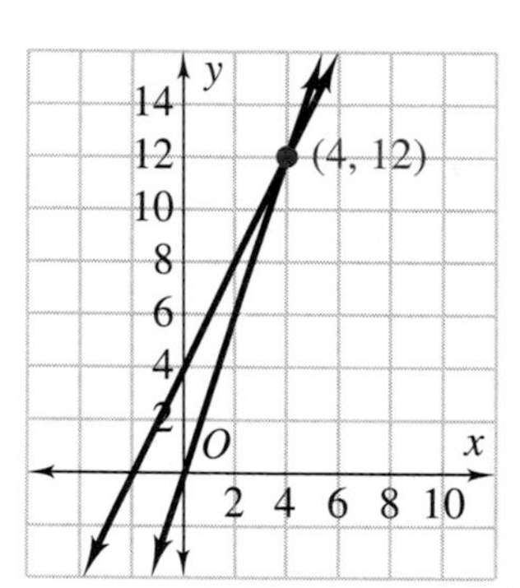

WORK TOGETHER

5. **Choose** Use pencil and paper, a computer, or a graphing calculator to graph each system.

   a. $y = \frac{1}{2}x + 3$ and $-3x + 6y = -12$

   b. $3y = 3x - 6$ and $2y = 2x - 4$

6. How many solutions does the first system have?

7. How many solutions does the second system have?

8. **Critical Thinking** Compare each system to its graph.
   a. What patterns do you see in the equations of each system?
   b. Work with your group to formulate a rule for deciding whether a system has one solution, no solution, or infinitely many solutions.

TRY THESE

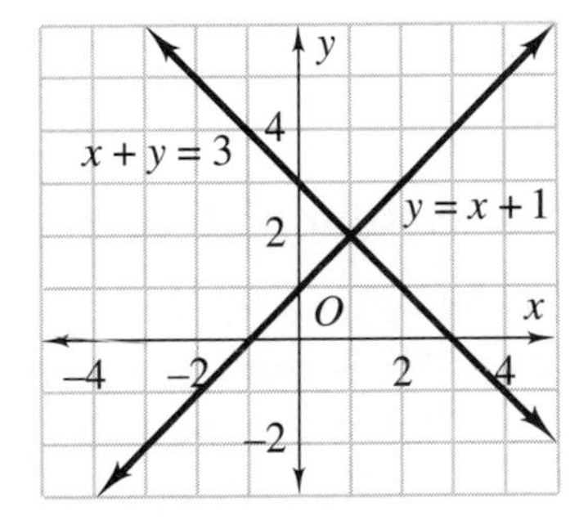

9. Use the graph to find the solution of the system of equations $y = x + 1$ and $x + y = 3$.
10. Find a solution of $y = x + 1$ that is not a solution of $x + y = 3$.
11. Find a solution of $x + y = 3$ that is not a solution of $y = x + 1$.
12. Tell whether the ordered pair (3, 1) is a solution of the system of equations $-x + y = -2$ and $x + 3y = 6$.

Work with your group. Write a system of equations to solve the problem below.

13. a. One weight lifter starts with a 3 lb dumbbell and increases the weight by 1 lb per month. Another starts with a 5 lb dumbbell and increases the weight by $\frac{1}{2}$ lb per month. After how many months will they be lifting the same amount? (Let x represent the number of months. Let y represent the amount of weight lifted.)
    b. Will they ever be lifting the same amount again? Explain.

Fifteen percent of females who exercise regularly include some kind of weight training. Such training may include low impact aerobics that utilize light hand or ankle weights.

Source: *University of California, Berkeley, Wellness Letter*

ON YOUR OWN

Tell whether the ordered pair is a solution of the system.

14. $y = -2x + 3$
    $x - y = 6$
    (3, −3)

15. $-3x + y = -2$
    $x - y = 4$
    (1, −5)

16. $x + 2y = 4$
    $x = -3y - 2$
    (16, −6)

Mixed REVIEW

Write an equation in two variables.

1. Myra's salary is equal to a base of \$4 plus \$5/h.

2. The cost of decorated badges is \$10 for supplies and \$.50 for each badge.

3. Two lines have the same slope. How are their graphs related?

4. Two lines have different slopes. How are their graphs related?

Solve.

5. Starting at the same point, Chris swims east at a rate of 2 mi/h, and Kia swims west at a rate of 4 mi/h. They begin swimming at 1 P.M. When will they be 9 mi apart?

Solve each system of linear equations by graphing.

17. $-3x + y = 2$
$y = 3x - 1$

18. $-x + y = 4$
$x + 2y = 8$

19. $x - 2y = 4$
$2x - 4y = 8$

20. Use the graph to explain why this system of three equations has no solution.

$y = -x + 3$

$y = \frac{1}{3}x + 3$

$y = 2x$

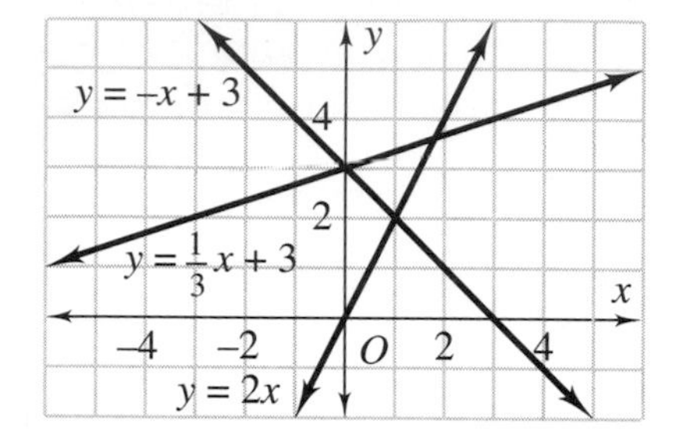

Write a system of linear equations. Solve by graphing.

21. Fitness Jan is adding 1 km/wk to her jogging distance of 2 km. Ali is adding 0.5 km/wk to her distance of 5 km. When will they jog the same distance? What is the distance? (Let w represent the number of weeks and d represent distance.)

22. Data File 6 (pp. 244–245) How much would 18.5 gal of gas cost in Japan?

23. Writing Write a word problem that can be solved by graphing a system of linear equations. Then solve it.

24. Investigation (p. 194) Suppose one point of the mountain climber's rescue graph represents the rope hanging 150 ft down the cliff with no weight attached. Suppose another point represents the rope stretched to 168 ft with 200 lb attached. How could you find the amount of weight needed to stretch the rope to the bottom of the cliff?

CHECKPOINT

1. Choose A, B, C, or D. Which equation has a graph that is a horizontal line?

A. $y = 2x - 5$ **B.** $y = -3x$

C. $y = -3$ **D.** $6y = 3x$

2. Jar x can hold three times as much water as jar y. Jar y is full of water and jar x is half full. Suppose you pour half of the water in jar y into jar x. How full will jar x be?

What's Ahead

- Using graphs to make business decisions

5-8 Using Graphs of Equations

WORK TOGETHER

When you buy a product, you are telling the manufacturer and the seller that you are willing to pay their price. If you think the price is unfair, you can cast your vote for lowering the price by not buying the product. Estimate the price you would expect to pay for each item. Then indicate what you feel is a fair price. Combine your results with those of other groups. How could you display the combined data?

a. a movie **b.** a CD **c.** a can of juice

EXPENSES
$20 to set up and decorate sales booth
$1 to make each cake
Expense equation: $y = x + 20$
INCOME
$2 each cake sold
Income equation: $y = 2x$

THINK AND DISCUSS

The student council needed to decide if it was worthwhile to hold a bake sale. The council first calculated the expenses. Then they decided on a price to charge for each cake and calculated the income. They graphed the expense and income equations as shown below.

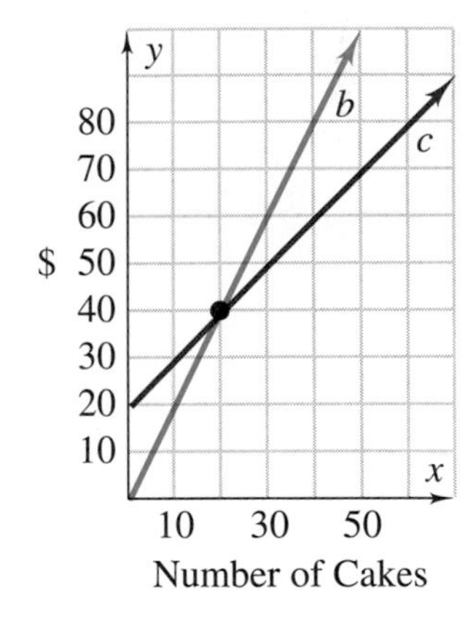

1. Which line is the graph of the expense equation? How do you know?
2. Which line is the graph of the income equation? How do you know?
3. Suppose members of the council make 10 cakes to sell. What are the total expenses?
4. Use the graph to determine the income from the sale of 10 cakes.
5. Which is greater, the total expenses for making 30 cakes or the income from the sale of 30 cakes?

There is a *profit* when income is greater than expenses. There is a *loss* when expenses are greater than income. The *break-even point* occurs when income equals expenses.

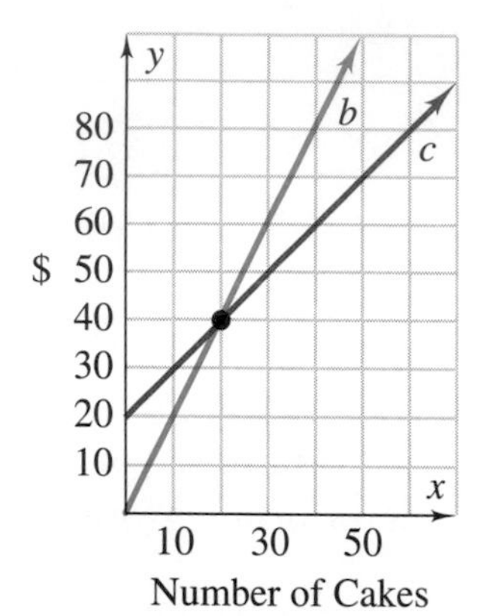

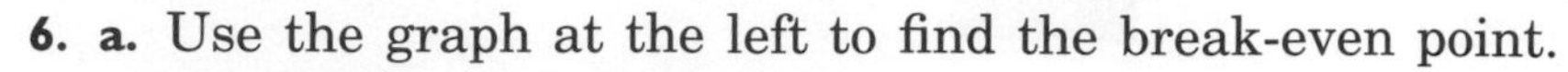

6. a. Use the graph at the left to find the break-even point.
   b. Interpret the x- and y-coordinates of the break-even point.
   c. Use the graph to describe when the cake sale would make a profit. Describe when it would lose money.
7. **Critical Thinking** What are some strategies that the student council could use in order to have the break-even point occur with the sale of fewer cakes?
8. **Critical Thinking** Would doubling the selling price guarantee a greater profit? Explain.
9. **Discussion** Should the student council proceed with plans for the bake sale? Why or why not?

DECISION MAKING

Before you manufacture a product, you should find out how many people might buy your product. You should also find out how much people are willing to spend.

COLLECT DATA

1. a. With your group, design a T-shirt you think your classmates would buy. Develop a design that requires inexpensive materials.
   b. Assume that a plain T-shirt costs $5.00. Based on the decorating materials you've chosen, estimate the cost of making one shirt.
   c. Design a survey to see what people will pay for your shirts. Include about five prices that are whole-dollar amounts. Make a colorful sketch of the design to show to the people you survey.
   d. Survey at least 25 people.
   e. **Critical Thinking** Why would you want to find out how many people will pay only $5.00 for a decorated T-shirt?

ON YOUR OWN

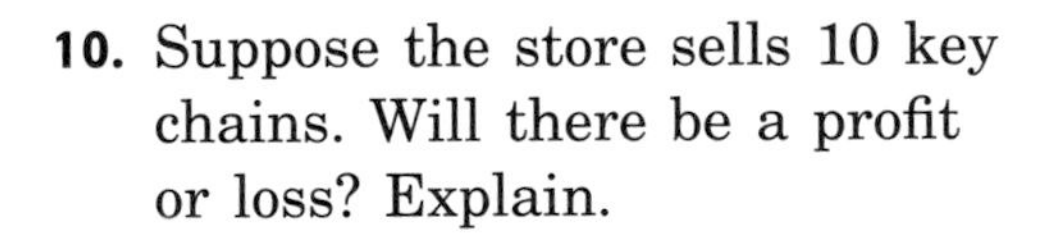

Here are the graphs of the expense and income equations for a key chain sale at a school store.

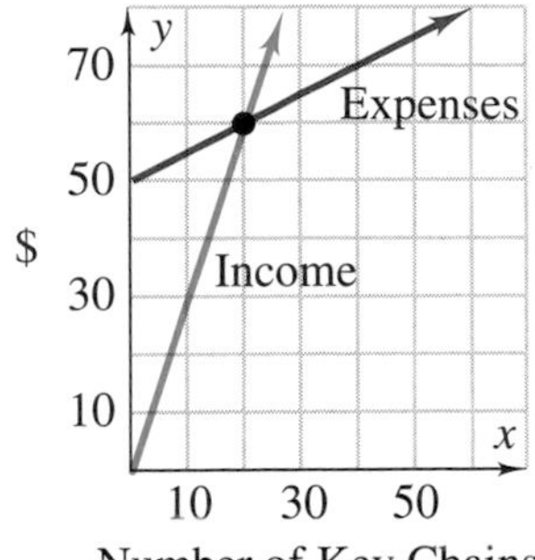

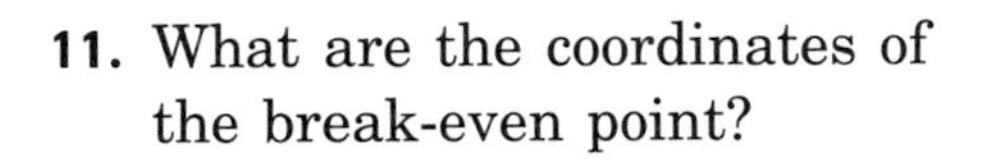

10. Suppose the store sells 10 key chains. Will there be a profit or loss? Explain.

11. What are the coordinates of the break-even point?

12. How many key chains must the store sell to break even?

13. Suppose the store sells 40 key chains. What is the profit?

14. **Writing** Explain how to tell from the graph when there is a profit and when there is a loss. Use the key chain graph to illustrate your explanation.

Mixed REVIEW

Solve for y in terms of x.

1. $8x + 2y = 10$

Solve the system of equations.

2. $y = 3x + 2;\ y = x$

3. Point $C(2, 5)$ moves up 3 units and then moves 8 units to the left. What are the new coordinates?

Solve.

4. Suppose you double the length and width of a rectangle. What happens to the area?

ANALYZE DATA

2. Write an expense equation based on the cost of materials and the price of a plain T-shirt. For example, if you spend \$30 on decorating material and \$5 for each plain T-shirt, the equation is $y = 5x + 30$.

3. Based on your survey results, write an income equation for each of the three most popular prices. For example, if the selling price is \$7, the income equation is $y = 7x$.

4. Make three graphs on separate coordinate planes. Each graph should show the expense equation and one of the three income equations. Compare the break-even points.

MAKE DECISIONS

5. What selling price will you set for the shirts? Why?

6. How many shirts are you going to manufacture? Why?

7. Design an advertisement to help boost sales of your shirts. What are some other strategies that might improve sales?

A T-shirt is an inexpensive way to promote a cause, advertise a product, or express an opinion. This T-shirt won first place in the annual Runner's World T-shirt design contest.

Source: *Runner's World*

Problem Solving Practice

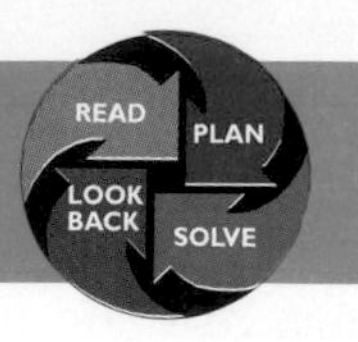

PROBLEM SOLVING STRATEGIES

Make a Table
Use Logical Reasoning
Solve a Simpler Problem
Too Much or Too Little Information
Look for a Pattern
Make a Model
Work Backward
Draw a Diagram
Guess and Test
Simulate a Problem
Use Multiple Strategies
Write an Equation
Use a Proportion

Solve. The list at the left shows some possible strategies you can use.

1. Peggy wants to cover the floor of her 12 ft-by-12 ft room with black and white tiles in a checkerboard pattern. Each tile is a 9 in.-by-9 in. square.
   a. How many tiles will Peggy need to order?
   b. Tiles come in boxes that contain a dozen tiles of one color. How many boxes of each color will Peggy need to order?
   c. Tiles cost $17.95 per box. How much will Peggy spend on tiles to cover her floor?

2. Find three numbers that have a range of 8 and a mean of 7.

3. The long way from Hereville to Thereville is twice as long as the shortcut. If a traveler takes the long way in one direction and the shortcut in the return direction, he travels 183 mi. How long is the shortcut between the two towns?

4. One angle of a triangle is three times as great as the smallest angle. The biggest angle is five times as great as the smallest angle. What are the measures of the three angles of the triangle?

5. Find the year of this 21st-century diary entry.

   Dear Diary,

   Thanks to my good eating habits and the medical miracles of the 21st century, I am now 145 years old. I feel great! While eating my spinach salad today, I realized that in exactly 400 years, my age (in that year) plus the year will equal 3,000!

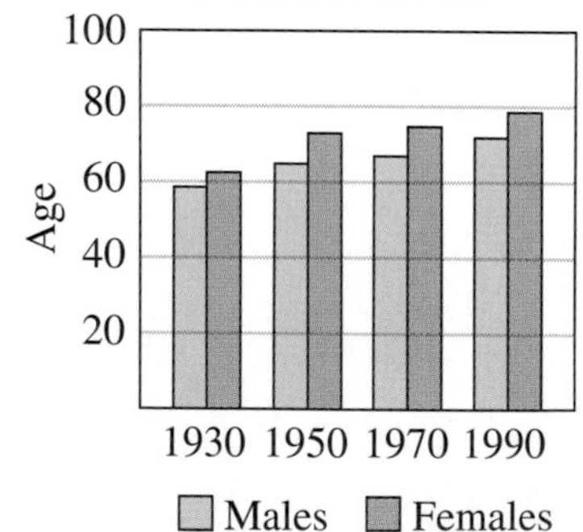

Do you think that people will live 145 years in the 21st century? Why or why not?

6. Duncan is building cubical birdhouses that each require six 8 in.-by-8 in. sides. How many birdhouses can he cut out of a sheet of plywood that is 4 ft by 8 ft?

7. What shape is formed by the lines whose equations are $y = 5$, $y = -5$, $x = 5$, and $x = -5$?

What's Ahead

- Graphing translations

5-9 Translations

WHAT YOU'LL NEED

✓ Ruler

✓ Protractor

✓ Graph paper

FLASHBACK

A tessellation covers a plane with no gaps and no overlaps.

THINK AND DISCUSS

Movements of points, lines, or figures on a plane are **transformations.** A transformation can be a slide, a flip, or a turn.

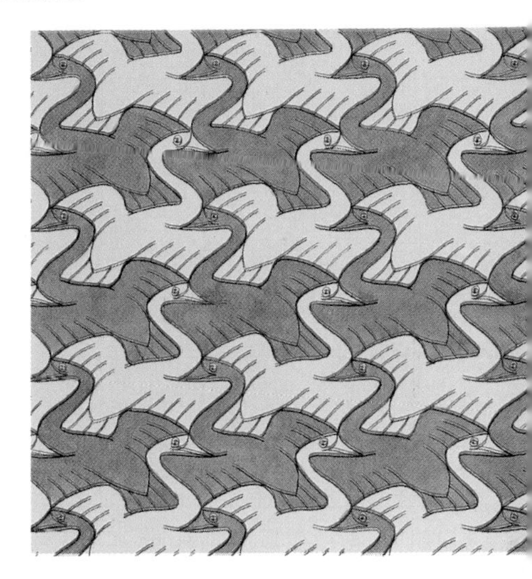

1. a. Describe a slide, a flip, and a turn in your own words.
   b. Where in real life have you seen a slide? a flip? a turn?
2. The Dutch artist M. C. Escher created this *tessellation* of birds. Explain how he used slides, flips, and turns.

Describing Translations Another name for a slide is a **translation.** After a transformation the figure is the **image** of the original figure. Prime notation (A') identifies an image.

3. Point $B(3, 2)$ has been translated up 4 units.
   a. What point is the image of point B?
   b. What are the coordinates of the image?
4. Suppose that point B had been translated to the left 4 units. What would be the coordinates of its image?

To translate geometric figures, first slide the vertices of the figure. Then connect the vertices to form the image.

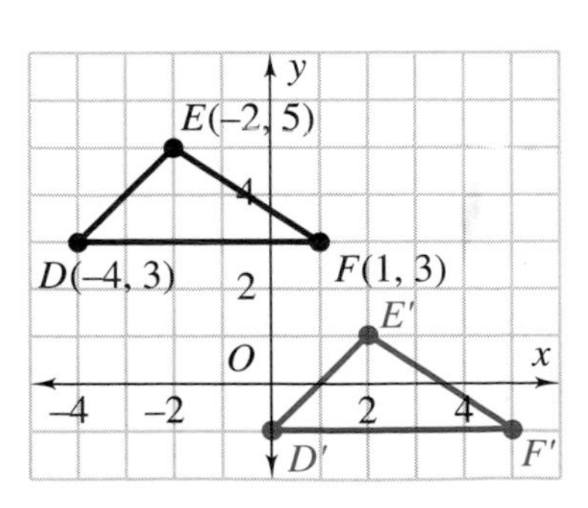

5. $\triangle DEF$ has been translated to $\triangle D'E'F'$. How far and in which directions has $\triangle DEF$ moved? Explain.
6. What are the coordinates of the vertices of $\triangle D'E'F'$?
7. To show a translation, you can use arrow notation. You write point $A \rightarrow$ point A'. You read this as "point A goes to point A'." Show the translation of $\triangle DEF$ using arrow notation.

Graphing Images To find the coordinates of an image after a translation, you can graph the image and read them from a grid. Another way is to add or subtract the amount of movement from the coordinates of the original figure.

8. Does moving a point up and down affect the *x-coordinate* or the *y-coordinate*? Explain.

9. Does moving a point left and right affect the *x-coordinate* or the *y-coordinate*? Explain.

10. Suppose that you translate a point to the left 1 unit and down 3 units. What would you do to the coordinates of the original point to find the coordinates of the image?

11. Suppose that you translate a figure to the right 4 units and up 5 units. Complete the general rule to show how to find the images: $(x, y) \rightarrow (x + ■, y + ■)$.

12. Suppose point $Q(3, 9) \rightarrow$ point $Q'(5, -2)$. How far and in which directions has point Q moved?

You can translate lines on the coordinate plane.

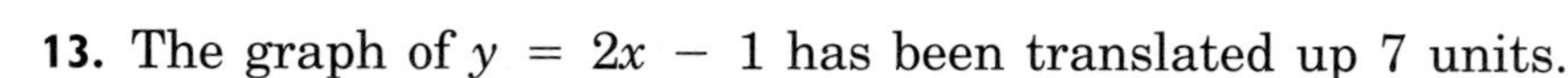

13. The graph of $y = 2x - 1$ has been translated up 7 units.

a. What is the y-intercept of the image?

b. What is the slope of the image? How did you find it?

c. What is the equation of the image line?

d. How does the equation of the image line relate to the equation of the original line?

WORK TOGETHER

14. A honeycomb is a tessellation of a regular polygon. Name the polygon.

15. Choose any two repeated polygons in the photo. Use terms such as up, down, and across to describe a translation that would make one of the polygons the image of the other.

16. Measure the sides and angles of several polygons in the honeycomb. How are the polygons alike or different?

17. a. Graph a triangle and a rectangle on separate coordinate grids. Translate each figure to another place on the grid.

b. Make a conjecture about the size and shape of a figure and its image after a translation.

c. Measure the sides and the angles of the triangle and its image. How are they alike or different?

d. Measure the sides and the angles of the rectangle and its image. How are they alike or different?

e. Compare your results with the results of your group. Do your results support your conjecture? If not, revise your conjecture.

ON YOUR OWN

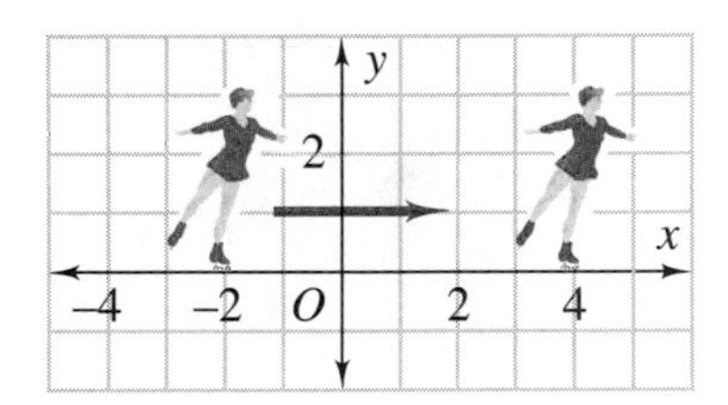

18. The graph shows an ice skater moving along the ice. How far and in what direction has the skater moved?

Describe the translation shown on each graph.

19.

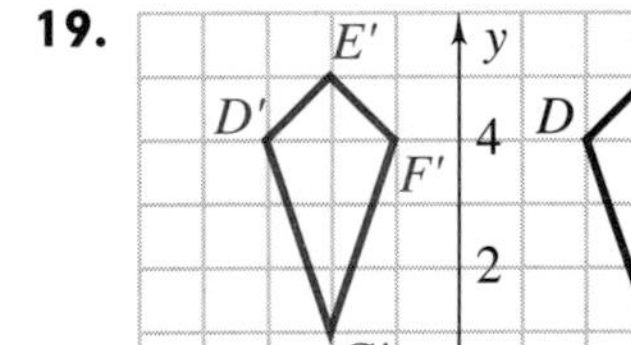

20.

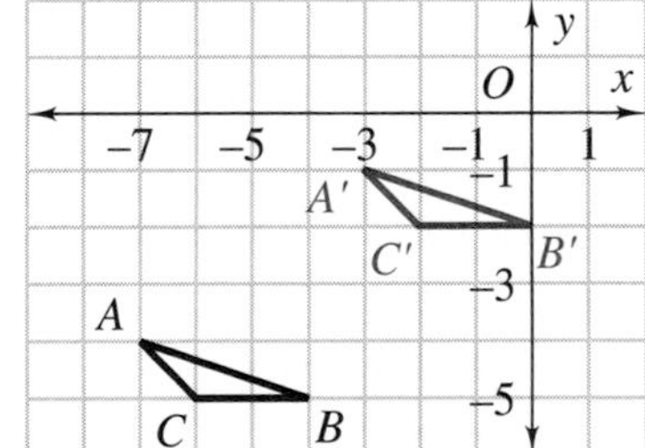

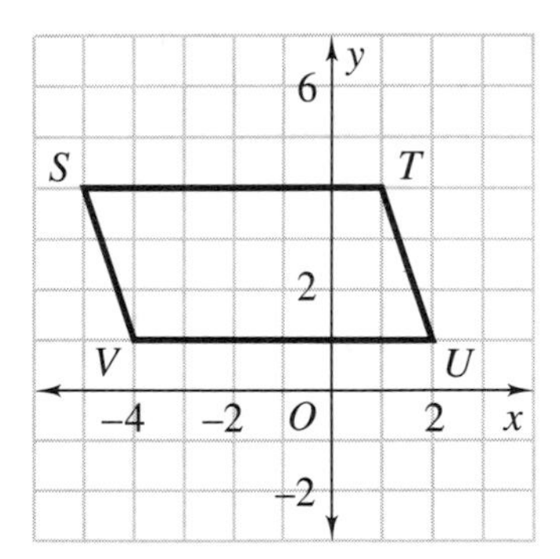

Use graph paper to graph the image of ▱ *STUV* after each translation. Name the coordinates of *S'*, *T'*, *U'*, and *V'*.

21. down 6 units

22. left 3 units, up 4 units

23. The vertices of $\triangle MNP$ are $M(-4, 1)$, $N(-2, 4)$, and $P(-1, -1)$. The triangle is translated to the right 5 units and down 2 units. How would you find the coordinates of M', N', and P'?

24. Suppose point $L(0, -4) \rightarrow$ point $L'(7, 7)$. How far and in which direction has point L moved?

25. **Mental Math** Translate point $T(1, 5)$ right 3 units and up 7 units. Translate its image, point T', left 3 units and down 7 units. What are the coordinates of the image of point T''?

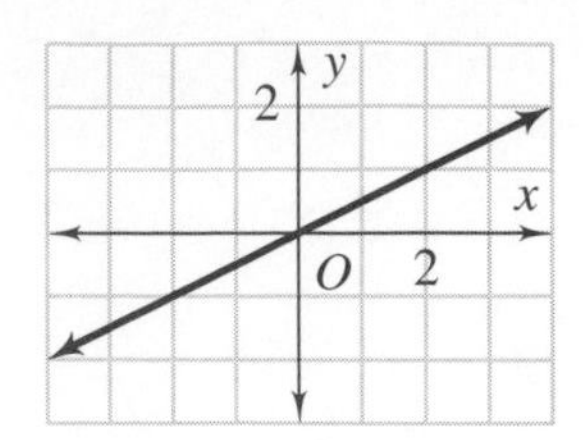

26. **a.** The coordinate plane shows the graph of the equation $y = \frac{1}{2}x$. Translate the line to the right 2 units and up 5 units. Graph its image.

b. Find the equation of the image line.

c. **Critical Thinking** Describe another translation that produces the same image line.

27. **a.** The vertices of rectangle $GHJK$ are $G(-2, -3)$, $H(-4, 0)$, $J(2, 4)$, and $K(4, 1)$. Graph the rectangle.

b. Rectangle $GHJK$ is translated so that the image of point G is the origin. Describe the translation.

c. Graph the image of rectangle $GHJK$. Name the coordinates of its vertices.

28. **a.** A checkerboard is a tessellation of regular polygons. Identify the polygon.

b. **Research** Find out the rules for moving the playing pieces in checkers. How many different types of moves can you make? Describe each move as a translation.

29. **Art** You can use translations to draw 3-D figures.

Step 1	*Step 2*	*Step 3*	*Step 4*
Draw a figure on graph paper.	Translate the figure to the right and up.	Connect each vertex with its image.	Use dashes for sides that aren't visible.

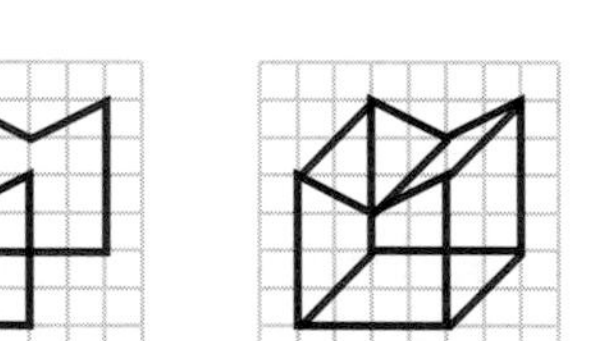

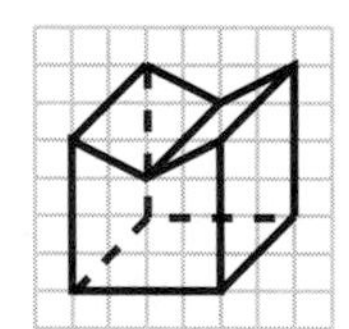

Draw a rectangular prism. Draw your initials as 3-D figures.

30. A shape is translated three times to form an image. The first translation is right 3 units and up 5 units. The second translation is right 7 units and up 11 units. The third is left 4 units and down 2 units. What shortcut can you use to form the same image in only one translation?

31. **Writing** Explain how a translation affects the coordinates and the size of a figure.

Mixed REVIEW

1. Draw $\overline{AB}$. Construct its perpendicular bisector.

2. Draw $\overleftrightarrow{XY}$. Construct a line that is parallel.

3. On the line $y = 4$, name the point that is the same distance from the y-axis as (9, 4).

Solve.

4. One square has sides four times as long as the sides of a second square. The combined area of the squares is 272 ft^2. Find their dimensions.

What's Ahead

- Graphing reflections of geometric figures
- Identifying lines of symmetry

WHAT YOU'LL NEED

✓ Tracing paper

✓ Ruler

✓ Marker

5-10 Reflections and Symmetry

WORK TOGETHER

1. a. Work with your partner. Fold a piece of tracing paper in half. Then unfold the paper and label the halves I and II. On half I, draw trapezoid *DEFG*.
   b. Refold the paper. On the back of half II, trace the trapezoid. Unfold the paper and trace this trapezoid onto the front of half II. Label the vertices of the last trapezoid D', E', F', and G' to correspond to the vertices of *DEFG*.

FLASHBACK

A trapezoid is a quadrilateral that has exactly one pair of parallel sides.

2. a. Compare the distances of D and D' from the fold. Do the same for the other vertices. What appears to be true?
   b. Draw $\overline{DD'}$, $\overline{EE'}$, $\overline{FF'}$, and $\overline{GG'}$. How is each segment related to the fold line?
   c. Is $DEFG \rightarrow D'E'F'G'$ a slide, a flip, or a turn? Explain.

THINK AND DISCUSS

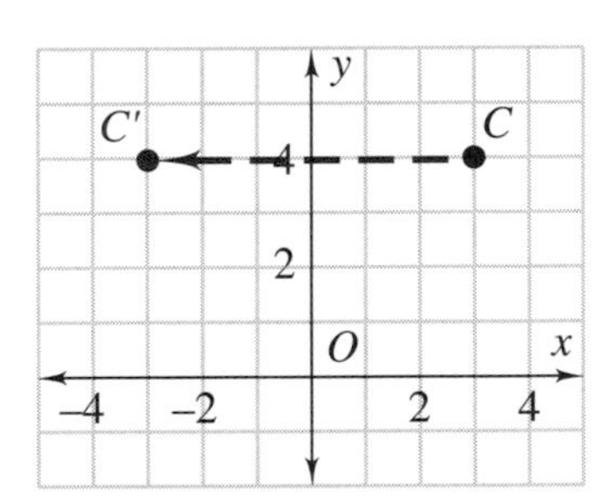

Graphing Reflections A flip is called a *reflection*. Point C' is the *image* of point C after a reflection over the y-axis. (Arrow notation: $C \rightarrow C'$). The y-axis is the *line of reflection*.

3. How many units are points C and C' from the y-axis?
4. What is the relationship between $\overline{CC'}$ and the y-axis?
5. **Critical Thinking** Use your answers to Questions 3 and 4 to describe what a reflection is.
6. **Discussion** How do reflections in a coordinate plane compare with reflections in a mirror?

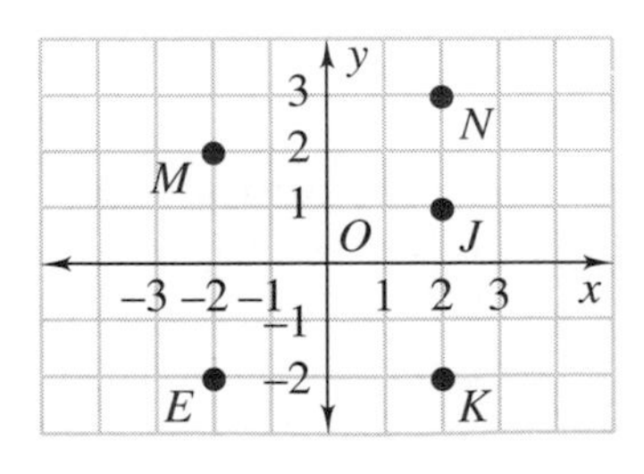

7. For which two points is the x-axis the line of reflection? Explain.
8. Point M is *not* the image of N over the y-axis. Why?
9. Points J and K are *not* reflections over the x-axis. Why not?

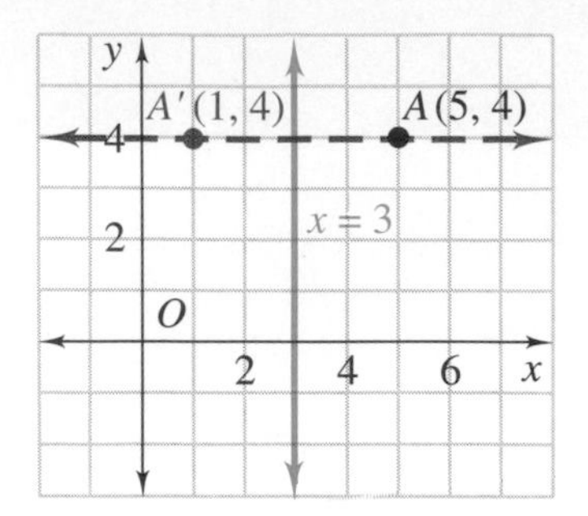

Example 1 Graph the image of $A(5, 4)$ after it is reflected over the line $x = 3$. Name the coordinates of A'.

- A' lies on a line through A that is perpendicular to the line $x = 3$.
- Since A is 2 units to the *right* of the graph of $x = 3$, A' is 2 units to the *left* of $x = 3$.
- Point $A \rightarrow$ point A'. The coordinates of A' are $(1, 4)$.

To reflect a polygon over a line, first reflect the vertices of the polygon. Then connect the image points.

What reflections can you see in the design of these Native American head bands?

Example 2 Graph the image of $\triangle BCD$ after a reflection over the line $y = -1$. Name the coordinates of the vertices of $\triangle B'C'D'$.

- Draw dashed lines from B, C, and D that are perpendicular to the graph of $y = -1$.
- Since B is 3 units above the line $y = -1$, locate B' 3 units below.
- Reflect the other vertices.
- Draw $\triangle B'C'D'$.

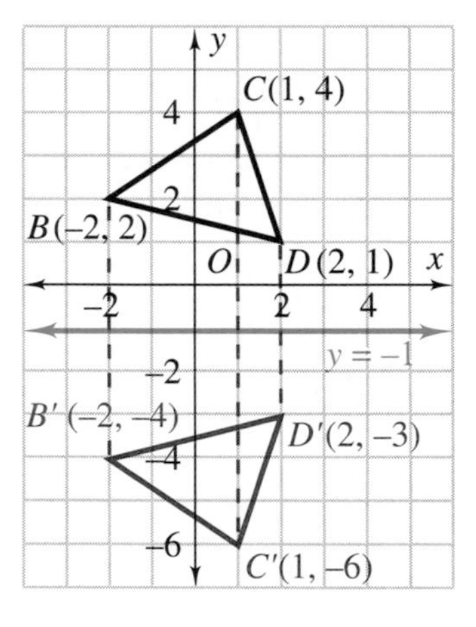

$\triangle BCD \rightarrow \triangle B'C'D'$. The coordinates of the vertices are $B'(-2, -4)$, $C'(1, -6)$, and $D'(2, -3)$.

10. a. What do you notice about the x-coordinate of each vertex of $\triangle BCD$ and its image?

b. What do you notice about the mean of the y-coordinate of each vertex of $\triangle BCD$ and its image?

11. a. How does the length of $\overline{BC}$ compare to the length of $\overline{B'C'}$?

b. How does $m\angle BCD$ compare to $m\angle B'C'D'$?

c. Compare the size and shape of $\triangle BCD$ and its image $\triangle B'C'D'$. Make a conjecture about the size and shape of a figure and its image after a reflection.

12. Suppose you reflect square *JKLM* over the *x*-axis. What is image of *J*? of *K*? of *L*? of *M*?

13. How does square *JKLM* compare with its image?

Identifying Lines of Symmetry When the reflection of a figure coincides with the original figure, the line of reflection is a **line of symmetry.** The *x*-axis is one of the lines of symmetry for square *JKLM*. Imagine folding the figure. If the part on one side of the fold coincides with the part on the other side, then the fold is a line of symmetry.

14. $\overleftrightarrow{MK}$ is another line of symmetry for square *JKLM*. Why?

15. In addition to the *x*-axis and $\overleftrightarrow{MK}$, square *JKLM* has two more lines of symmetry. What are they?

TRY THESE

Graph the image point after each reflection. Name the coordinates of the image.

16. $H(-3, 4)$ over the *x*-axis **17.** $G(2, 7)$ over the *y*-axis

18. $O(0, 0)$ over the line whose equation is $y = 4$

19. a. How do the signs of the coordinates change when you reflect a point over the *y*-axis?

b. How do the signs of the coordinates change when you reflect a point over the *x*-axis?

20. Discussion Suppose $T'(0, 6)$ is the reflection of $T(6, 0)$.

a. How would you find the line of reflection?

b. What is the line of reflection?

21. a. Graph these ordered pairs and connect the points in order: $(-3, -3)$, $(-4, -1)$, $(-1, 2)$, $(1, 1)$, $(2, 5)$, and $(4, 4)$

b. These segments form half a figure whose line of symmetry has the equation $y = x$. Complete the figure.

The Rorschach test uses inkblot designs for personality analysis. **How do you think this design was made?**

Mixed REVIEW

Simplify.

1. $(-6^3)^2$
2. $m \cdot m^2 \cdot m^3$

Find the coordinates of the image point.

3. $P(7, -1)$ is translated 4 units down.
4. $Q(-3, 4)$ is translated 2 units up and 3 units to the left.

Solve.

5. Harry started with $480. In the first week he withdrew half the money. In the second week he withdrew half of what was left. If he continued this pattern, in what week did he withdraw $15?

Tiger! Tiger! burning bright
In the forest of the night,
What immortal hand or eye
Could frame thy fearful symmetry?

ON YOUR OWN

Graph the image point after each reflection. Name the coordinates of the image.

22. $(3, -2)$ over the line whose equation is $y = -1$

23. $(-4, 10)$ over the line whose equation is $x = -2$

$\triangle MPS$ has vertices $M(4, 5)$, $P(1, 2)$, and $S(5, 1)$. Graph $\triangle MPS$ and its image after a reflection over each line.

24. the x-axis
25. $y = 3$
26. the y-axis
27. $x = 1$

28. The vertices of $\triangle RST$ are $R(0, 4)$, $S(0, 0)$, and $T(-4, 0)$.
    a. Graph $\triangle RST$ on a coordinate plane.
    b. Reflect $\triangle RST$ over the y-axis. Then reflect the image over the x-axis. Then reflect the second image over the y-axis.
    c. Describe the figure formed by $\triangle RST$ and its images.

Trace each figure and draw the line(s) of symmetry.

29. 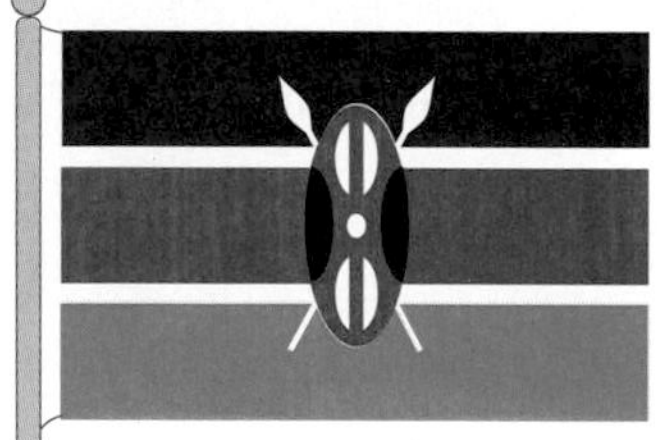

30. 

Design **Draw four 6 × 6 squares on a piece of graph paper. Color the boxes in each square to make designs with the given number of lines of symmetry.**

31. only 1
32. exactly 2
33. no lines
34. exactly 4

35. **Writing** How many lines of symmetry do you think a circle has? Explain.

36. **Literature** *Tiger! Tiger! burning bright* was written by an English poet named William Blake (1757-1827). What symmetry do you see in a tiger?

What's Ahead

- Recognizing and drawing rotations of polygons

5-11 Exploring Rotations

WHAT YOU'LL NEED

✓ Graph paper

✓ Ruler 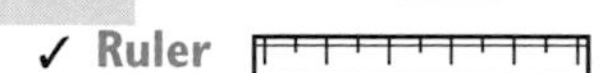

THINK AND DISCUSS

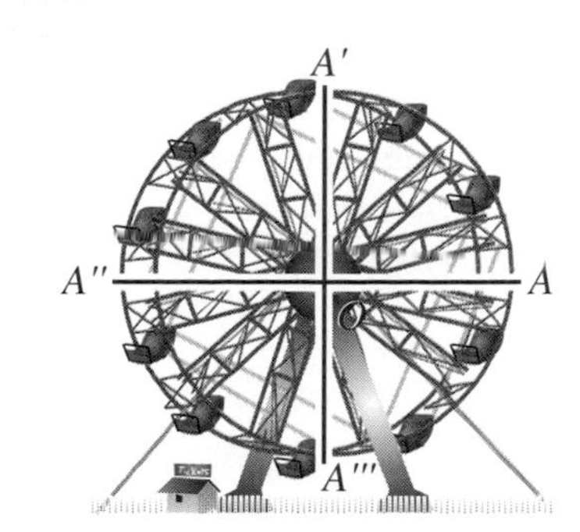

Exploring Rotations If this wheel moves in a counterclockwise direction, one full turn would bring the car at point A back to its original position.

1. How much of a turn would bring the car at position A to the A' position? the A'' position? the A''' position?

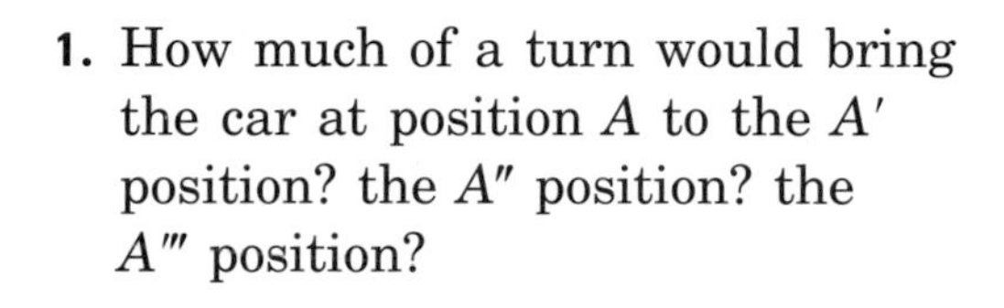

2. **Discussion** Draw the angle formed by A, vertex O, and A'. How many degrees is the turn from position A to A'? Repeat this procedure to describe, in degrees, the turn from A to A''; the turn from A to A'''.

A **rotation** is a transformation that turns a figure about a fixed point. In this text, rotations are counterclockwise. Using arrow notation, rectangle $PQRS \rightarrow$ rectangle $P'Q'R'S'$ after a 90° rotation about point O. Point O is the *center of rotation.* The *angle of rotation* is 90°.

Example 1 Draw the image of rectangle $PQRS$ after a rotation of:

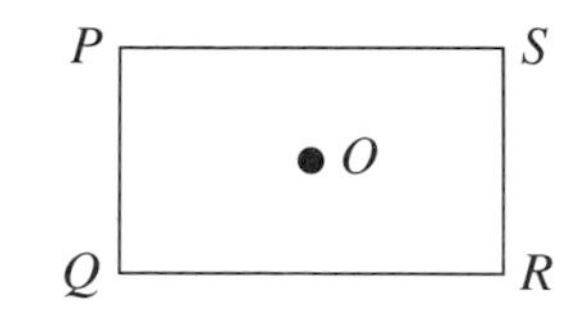

a. 180° about O.

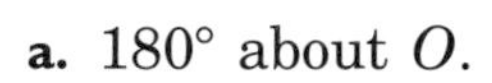

b. 270° about O.

a.

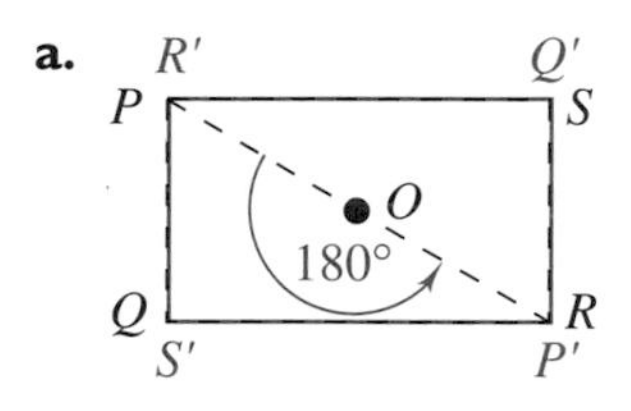

b.

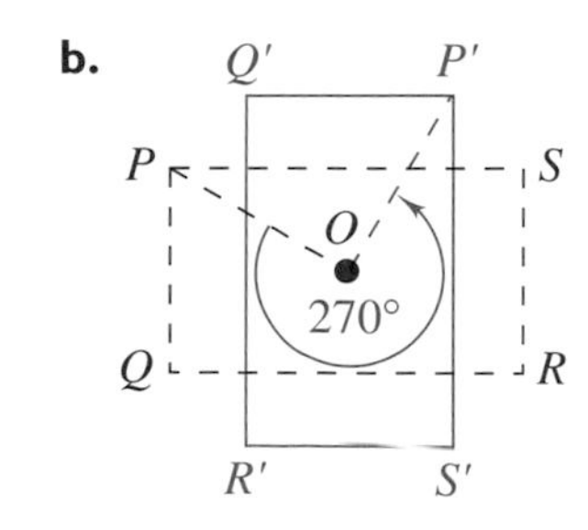

3. How does the image of $PQRS$ compare with the original figure after a 180° rotation about O?

Rotational symmetry occurs in nature. ***What are the rotational symmetries in this flower?***

A figure has **rotational symmetry** when an image after a rotation coincides with the original figure. $PQRS$ has 180° rotational symmetry.

4. What are the rotational symmetries of a square?

Graphing Rotations You can use a center of rotation that lies outside a figure. Rectangle $ABCD \rightarrow$ rectangle $A'B'C'D'$ after a 90° rotation about the origin.

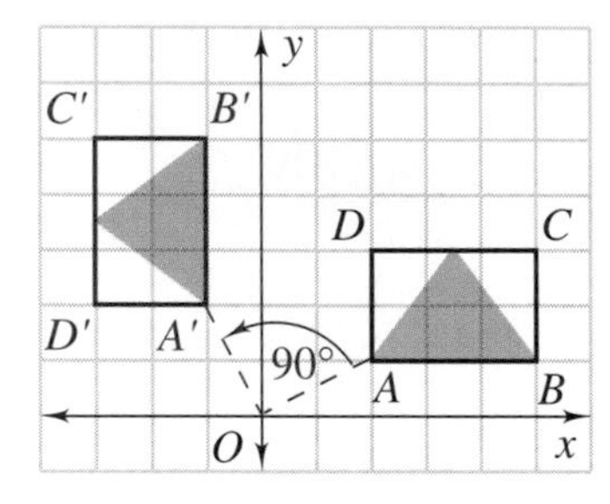

5. **Discussion** Compare the coordinates of the vertices of $ABCD$ with those of its image. How are they alike? How are they different?
   a. Describe a pattern for finding the coordinates of a point after a 90° rotation about the origin.
   b. How do you think you could use the pattern for a 90° rotation to find the coordinates of an image after a 180° rotation? after a 270° rotation?

Example 2 $\triangle DEF$ has vertices $D(1, 1)$, $E(4, 1)$, and $F(4, 3)$. Draw the image of $\triangle DEF$ after each rotation.

a. 90° **b.** 180° **c.** 270°

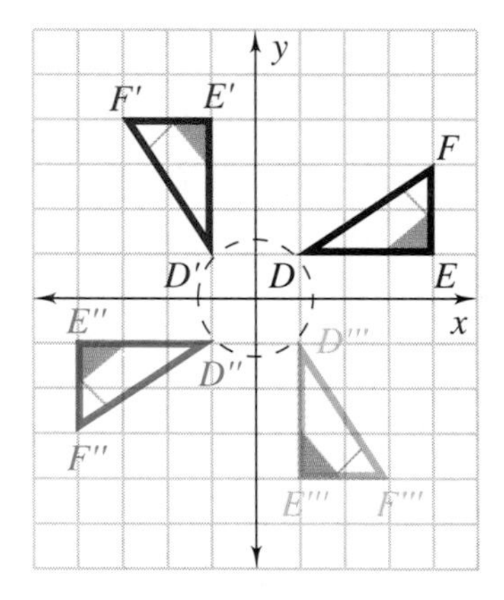

a. $\triangle DEF \rightarrow \triangle D'E'F'$. The coordinates of the vertices of $\triangle D'E'F'$ are $D'(-1, 1)$, $E'(-1, 4)$, and $F'(-3, 4)$.

b. Rotate $\triangle D'E'F'$ 90° to find $\triangle D''E''F''$. $\triangle DEF \rightarrow \triangle D''E''F''$ after a 180° rotation about the origin. The coordinates of $\triangle D''E''F''$ are $D''(-1, -1)$, $E''(-4, -1)$, and $F''(-4, -3)$.

c. Rotate $\triangle D''E''F''$ 90° to find $\triangle D'''E'''F'''$. $\triangle DEF \rightarrow \triangle D'''E'''F'''$ after a 270° rotation about the origin. The coordinates of $\triangle D'''E'''F'''$ are $D'''(1, -1)$, $E'''(1, -4)$, and $F'''(3, -4)$.

6. **Critical Thinking** Compare the coordinates of the vertices of $\triangle DEF$ with those of its image after a 180° rotation and after a 270° rotation.
   a. Describe a pattern for finding the coordinates of a point after a 180° rotation about the origin.
   b. Describe a pattern for finding the coordinates of a point after a 270° rotation about the origin.

WORK TOGETHER

7. Graph $\triangle QRS$ with $Q(-5, -2)$, $R(-1, -5)$, and $S(-5, -5)$. Graph $\triangle Q'R'S'$ with $Q'(3, 0)$, $R'(6, -4)$, and $S'(6, 0)$.
   a. Work with your partner to make a list of instructions using translations, reflections, and/or rotations for $\triangle QRS \rightarrow \triangle Q'R'S'$. Graph each step in the instructions.
   b. Compare your list and graph with those of other groups to see who wrote the easiest instructions.

TRY THESE

Each figure is an image formed by rotating the figure at the right. What is the angle of rotation of each?

8. 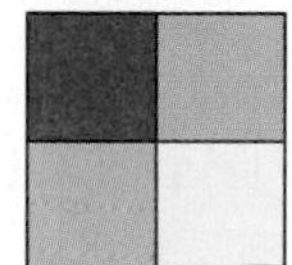

9. 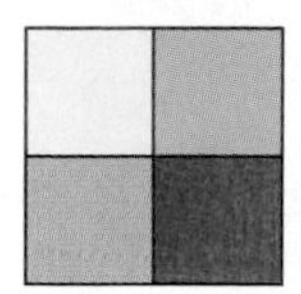

10. 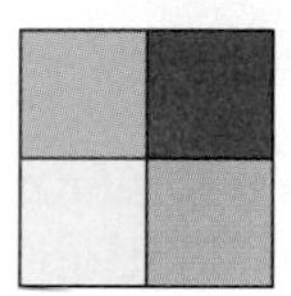

Draw the image of each figure after a rotation of 90°, 180°, and 270° about point *O*. Name any rotational symmetries.

11. 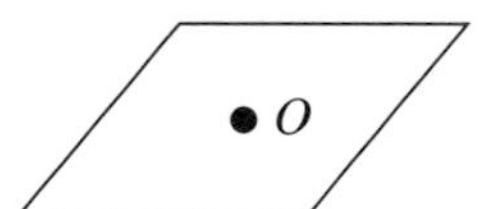

12. 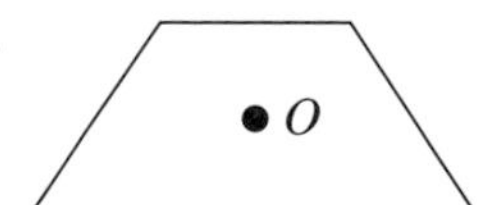

13. 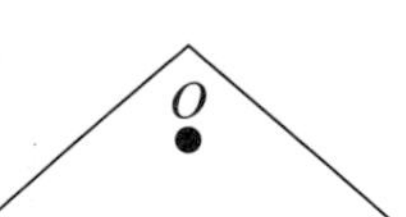

14. A figure with 180° rotational symmetry has **point symmetry.** With your group make a list of the seven upper case letters of the alphabet that have point symmetry.

Architecture is geometry made visible in the same sense that music is number made audible.

—Claude Bragdon (1866–1946)

ON YOUR OWN

Rotate each point the given number of degrees about the origin. Give the coordinates of each image point.

15. $L(3, 3)$; 90°
16. $M(-4, -2)$; 270°
17. $N(3, -5)$; 180°

18. Which figures could be a rotation of the figure at the right?

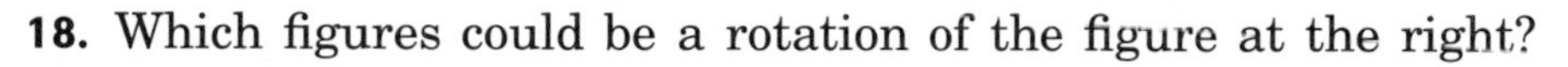

A. 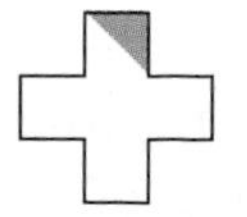

B. 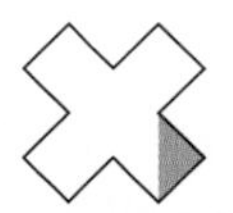

C. 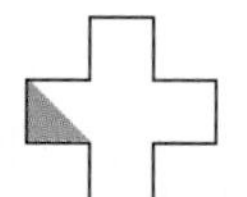

D. 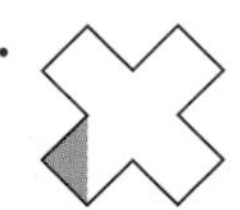

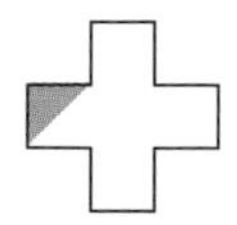

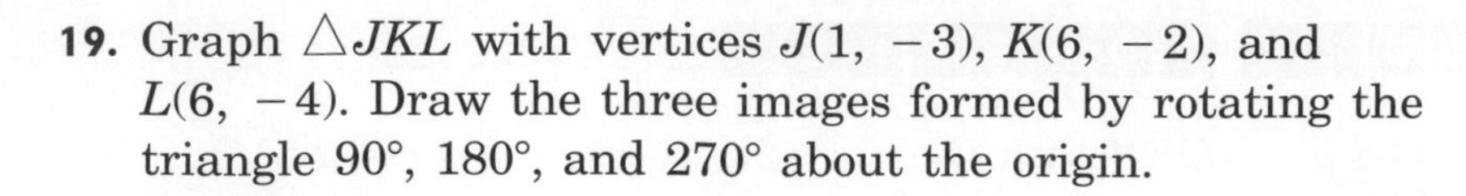

19. Graph $\triangle JKL$ with vertices $J(1,\ -3)$, $K(6,\ -2)$, and $L(6,\ -4)$. Draw the three images formed by rotating the triangle 90°, 180°, and 270° about the origin.

FLASHBACK

A hexagon is a polygon with six sides.

20. **Art** On graph paper, create a hexagonal design in the first quadrant. Draw its image after 90°, 180°, and 270° rotations about the origin.

Estimation Rotations other than 90°, 180°, and 270° are also possible. Each figure below is an image formed by rotating the figure at the left. Estimate each rotation.

21.

22.

23.

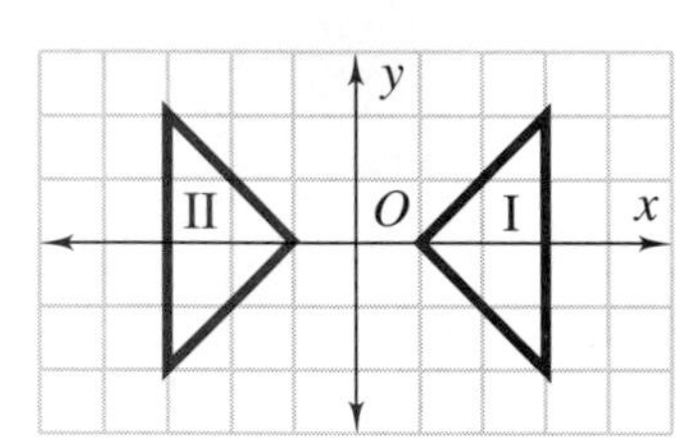

24. **Writing** Explain why triangle II is an image of triangle I after a rotation *or* after a reflection.

Tell whether triangle II is an image of triangle I after a translation, reflection, or rotation.

25.

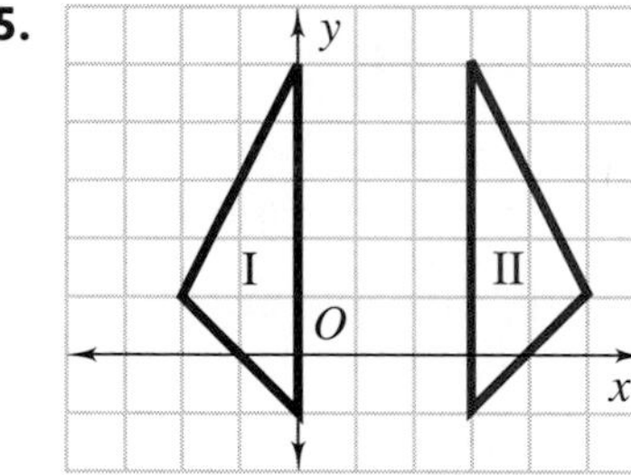

26.

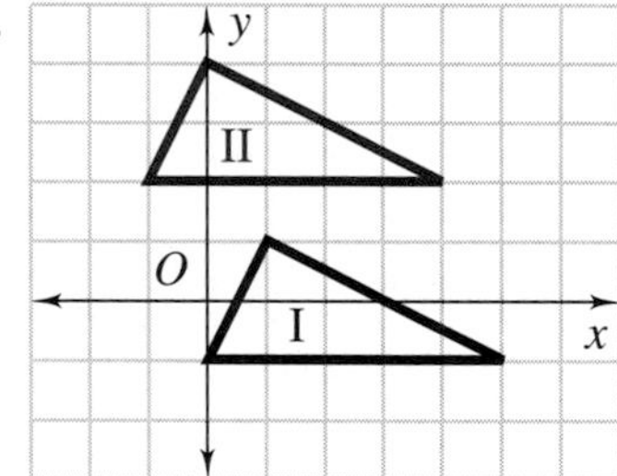

27.

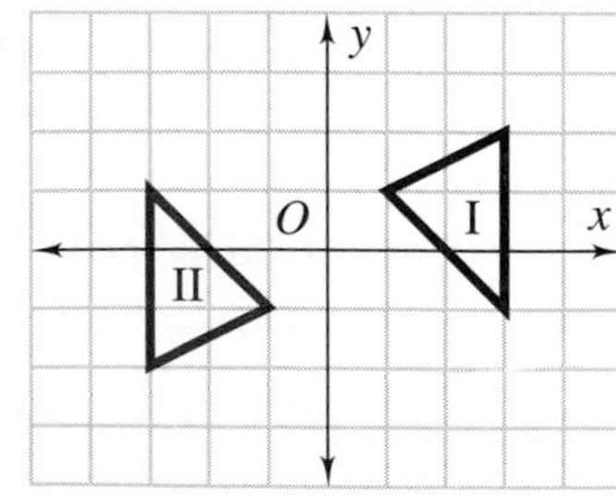

28.

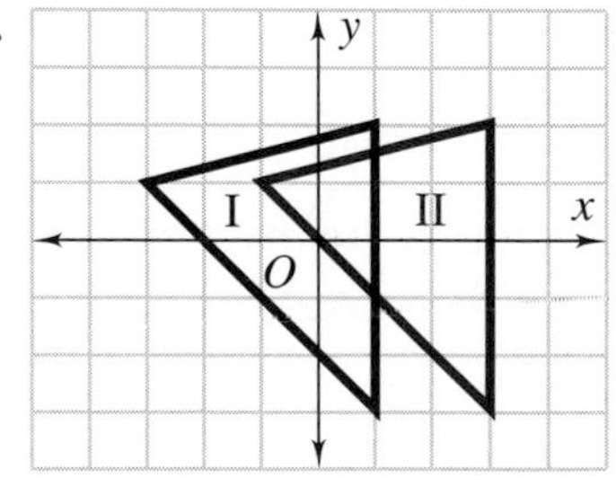

29. Rectangle $R'S'T'V'$ is the image of $RSTV$ after a rotation of 180° about the origin. The coordinates of the vertices of $R'S'T'V'$ are $R'(-4,\ -5)$, $S'(-7,\ -2)$, $T'(-5,\ 0)$, and $V'(-2,\ -3)$. Find the coordinates of the vertices of $RSTV$.

Big Birthday For Landmark

The famous architect Louis H. Sullivan created a new style of American architecture when he designed the Guaranty Building in Buffalo, NY in 1895. Now named the Prudential, this 12-story building is one of the finest examples of late 19th-century architecture in the United States.

Sullivan added visual interest to this design by decorating the terra cotta facade with flower-like patterns. It is interesting to compare those designs to the ones found on today's modern office buildings.

30. What translations, reflections, and rotations can you find in this detail from the facade of the Guaranty Building?

CHECKPOINT

The garden club is selling hanging baskets to raise funds. Setting up a table at the fair costs $50.00, and the cost to make each basket is $5.00. They will sell the baskets for $10.00 each.

1. Identify the expense equation and the income equation. Explain.

a. $y = 10x$ **b.** $y = 5x + 50$

2. Graph the equations on the same coordinate plane.

3. What is the break-even point? What does it mean?

4. **Choose A, B, C, or D.** $T'(-1, 1)$ is the image point after a translation of 6 units to the left and 3 units up. What are the coordinates of the original point?

A. $(-7, 4)$ **B.** $(5, -2)$ **C.** $(5, 4)$ **D.** $(-4, 7)$

5. Draw the image of this figure after a 180° rotation. Does the figure have 180° rotational symmetry? Explain your answer.

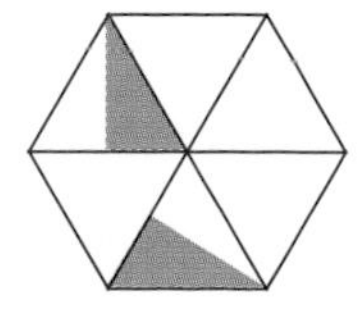

Mixed REVIEW

Simplify.

1. $6x + 3x + 2$

2. $8(z + 7) + 3z$

Draw a figure with the given number of lines of symmetry.

3. three lines **4.** no lines

Solve.

5. Tina and Tim each have $.49. They also each have 12 coins. Tina has a coin that Tim doesn't have. What coins does each have?

Wrap Up

Graphing and Equations — 5-1, 5-2, 5-3

An ***ordered pair*** describes the location of a point on a coordinate plane. The ***x-*** and ***y-axes*** divide the plane into four ***quadrants.*** A ***solution*** of an equation in two variables is an ordered pair that makes the equation a true statement. To graph a linear equation, graph several solutions and draw a line through the points.

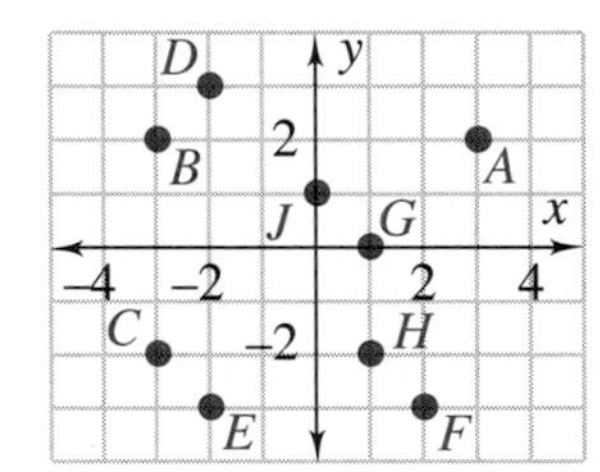

Name the point with the given coordinates.

1. $(3, 2)$
2. $(2, -3)$
3. $(1, 0)$
4. $(-3, 2)$

Name the coordinates of each point.

5. C
6. D
7. H
8. E

9. In which quadrant would you find the point $M(7, -4)$?

10. Solve $2x + y = 3$ for y. Then graph the equation.

11. **Writing** How can you tell if the graph of $y = -7x - 3$ is above or below the graph of $y = -7x + 1$?

Slopes and Intercepts — 5-4, 5-5

The slope of a line is the ratio of vertical change to horizontal change. ***slope*** $= \frac{\text{rise}}{\text{run}}$

The ***y-intercept*** is the y-coordinate of the point where the line crosses the y-axis. The ***x-intercept*** is the x-coordinate of the point where the line crosses the x-axis.

12. Find the slope of the line that contains $(4, 2)$ and $(3, 5)$.

Identify the slope and y-intercept. Then graph each.

13. $y = \frac{3}{4}x + 6$
14. $y = -5$

15. **Choose A, B, or C.** A line on the coordinate plane falls from left to right. Which could *not* be the equation of the line?

 A. $x + y = 7$ **B.** $y = -2x + 5$ **C.** $y - 2x = 1$

Systems of Linear Equations 5-7, 5-8

A ***solution of a system of linear equations*** is any ordered pair that makes the equations true.

16. Charlene sells decorated barrettes. She spends \$10 to start and \$2 per barrette. She charges \$4 per barrette.

a. Graph the system that consists of the expense equation, $y = 2x + 10$, and the income equation, $y = 4x$.

b. Solve the system and interpret the break-even point.

Transformations and Symmetry 5-9, 5-10, 5-11

You can transform figures in a plane by a ***translation,*** a ***reflection,*** or a ***rotation.*** When the reflection of a figure coincides with the original figure, the line of reflection is a ***line of symmetry.***

Figure II is the image of Figure I. Describe the transformation.

17.

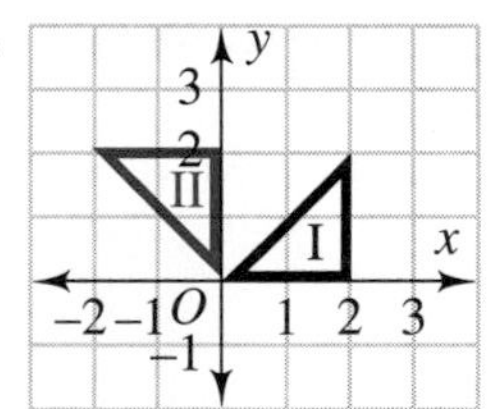

18.

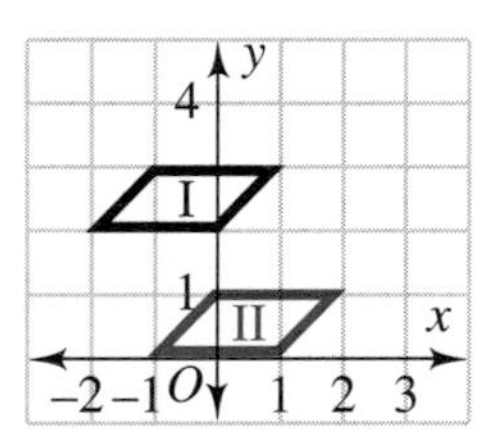

19.

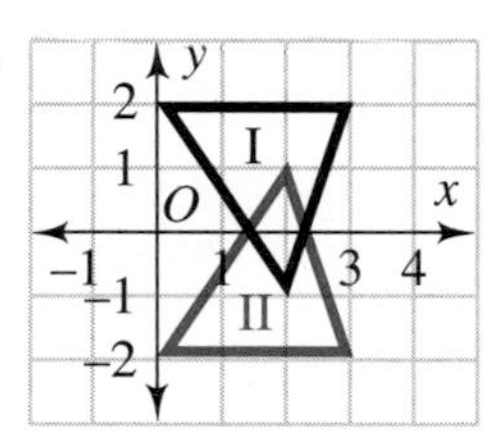

20.

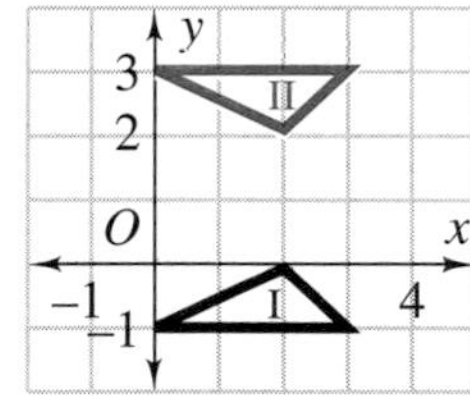

21. Draw a triangle that has exactly one line of symmetry.

22. What are the rotational symmetries of a rectangle?

Strategies and Applications 5-6

Drawing diagrams can help you solve problems.

23. A dog owner has 12 sections of fence, each 1 yd long. How many different rectangular dog pens can she build?

GETTING READY FOR CHAPTER 6

To graph an equation that is not linear, graph several solutions and try to draw a smooth curve through the points.

Graph each equation.

1. $y = x^2$ **2.** $y = 3x^2$ **3.** $y = -2x^2$ **4.** $y = 7x^2$ **5.** $y = 2x^2 + 3$

Follow Up

The Great Rescue

On page 194 you used a rubber band, some weights, and a paper cup to estimate the weight of rocks needed to stretch the rope to the bottom of the cliff. Now you can use what you have learned about graphing in this chapter to find the weight of rocks more accurately. Draw a graph modeling the climber's rescue attempt.

The problems preceded by the magnifying glass (p. 197, # 28; p. 201, # 29; p. 205, # 26, and p. 220, # 24) will help you draw the graph. Use your graph to find the weight of the rocks. Explain your method. Then tell whether you think the climber's story was true or just a tall tale.

Excursion: Suppose a 250-lb climber lowered himself down the rope with an empty pack. Use your graph to find how far above the base of the cliff the climber would find himself.

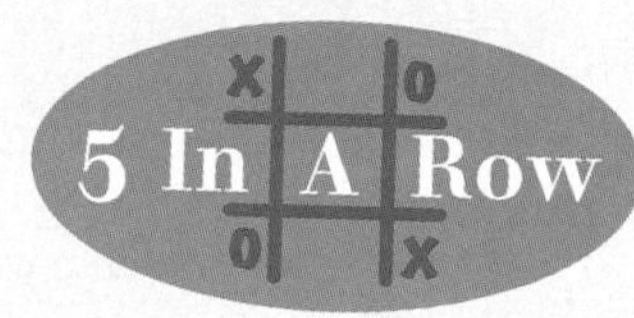

You play this game like tic-tac-toe on an xy-coordinate graph.

Directions:

- X begins the game by naming the coordinates of a point on his or her grid. If the correct coordinates are named, then he or she marks X at that point on the grid. If incorrect coordinates are named, no mark is made.
- Player O takes a turn. Play continues back and forth between the two players.
- The first player to mark five points in a diagonal, vertical, or horizontal line is the winner.

LOGO HUNT

A *logo* is a design used by an organization to identify itself or its products.

- Cut examples of logos from magazines and catalogs. Draw logos you see on signs.
- Classify each logo according to its symmetry.
- Draw lines that show symmetry on the logos.
- Glue your sorted logos into a scrapbook or on poster board.
- Share your project with other groups.

Excursion Think of a business you would like to start. Then design a logo that has both line and rotational symmetry for your business.

City Graph

The annual convention of the Coordinate Geometry Association is just around the corner. Members of the association hope to take in some of the sights of the host city. They do not like to be told that Home Run Stadium, for example, is located at the corner of Ruth Street and Aaron Avenue. Rather, they would like to be told that the stadium is at (-43, 12). They do not want to go looking for Broadway but would be happy to search for the street with the equation $y = 3x - 17$.

- Choose a city where the convention will be held.
- On a map of that city, draw a coordinate grid dividing the city into four quadrants.
- Prepare a **Visitor's Guide** to the city for members of the association. Use coordinates and equations of lines to identify the locations of the city's main attractions.

MYSTERY SQUARE

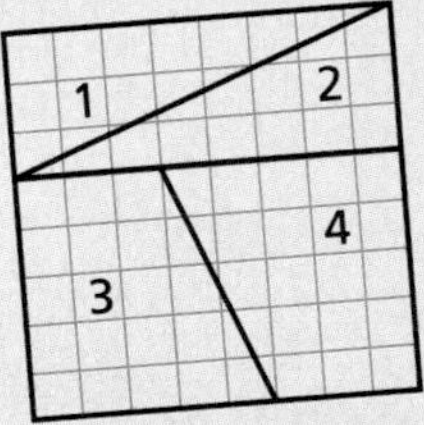

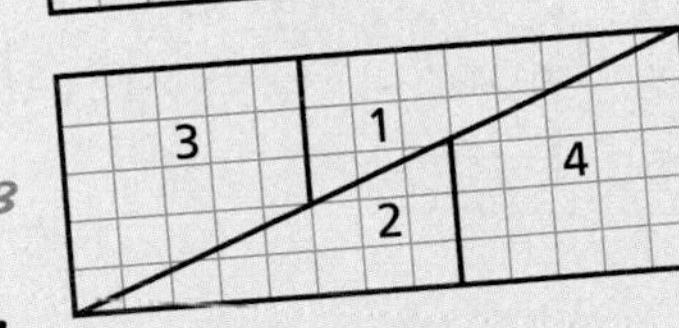

- *Draw figure A on an 8 x 8 grid.*
- *Cut out the pieces and rearrange them to form figure B.*
- *Find the area of each shape.*
- *Why are the areas of the shapes made from the same pieces different? (Hint: Calculate the slope of the diagonal between shapes 1 and 2 in figure A and of the diagonal in figure B.)*

Assessment

1. Find the slope and y-intercept. Graph each equation.

   a. $y = 3x - 5$ b. $2x - 4y = 12$

2. **Choose A, B, C, or D.** The coordinates of three vertices of a parallelogram are $(-6, 8)$, $(-4, -3)$, and $(1, 8)$. What are the coordinates of the fourth vertex?

   A. $(-1, 8)$ B. $(6, 3)$

   C. $(4, 8)$ D. $(3, -3)$

3. Find the slope of the line containing points $A(-4, 5)$ and $B(8, -1)$.

Match each equation with its graph.

4. $y = 3x + 2$
5. $3x + y = -2$
6. $y = -2$
7. $x = 2$

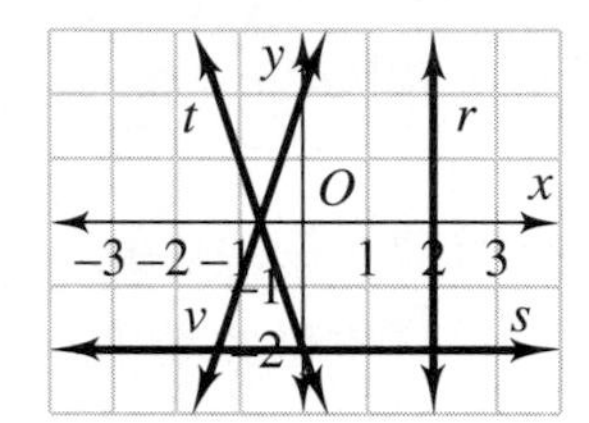

Tell whether the ordered pair $(-5, 8)$ is a solution of the system.

8. $x + y = 3$
   $2x - 10 = -2y$

Solve the system by graphing.

9. $x + 2y = 4$
   $2y = 3x - 12$

10. Give an example of a system of equations that has no solution. Describe the graph of the system.

11. Draw and describe a figure that has exactly three lines of symmetry.

12. A plank of wood is cut into thirds. Then each piece is cut into thirds. How many cuts were made?

13. **Writing** Explain the difference between a line with a slope that is undefined and a line with a slope of zero.

14. Income and expense equations for a baseball cap business are graphed at the right. Find the break-even point and tell what it means.

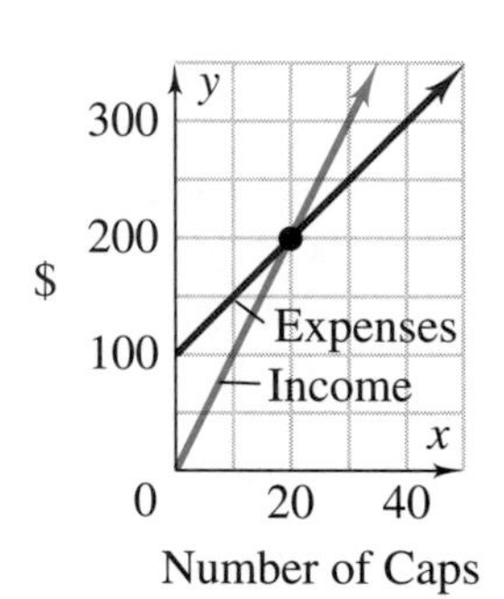

Quadrilateral $WBKJ$ has vertices $W(4, 5)$, $B(6, 3)$, $K(3, 2)$, and $J(2, 3)$.

15. Graph $WBKJ$ and its image after a translation 9 units right and 8 units down.

16. Graph $WBKJ$ and its image after a reflection over the x-axis.

17. Graph $WBKJ$ and its image after a $90°$ rotation about the origin.

18. $\triangle RWD$ has vertices $R(-4, -5)$, $W(-4, -1)$, and $D(-1, -1)$. Graph $\triangle RWD$ and its image after each rotation about the origin on the same set of axes.

    a. $180°$ b. $270°$

19. **Writing** Describe a real-life situation for which you could use the equation $y = 1.25x + 0.50$.

CHAPTER 5

Cumulative Review

Choose A, B, C, or D.

1. Which set of numbers satisfies the inequality $2x - 3 < -1$?

A. $-2, -1, 0$ **B.** $-1, 0, 1$

C. $0, 1, 2$ **D.** $1, 2, 3$

2. Which expression is *not* equivalent to $(2^3)^4$?

A. 2^{12} **B.** $(2^3)(2^3)(2^3)(2^3)$

C. $(2^4)^3$ **D.** $(6)^4$

3. "A rectangle has perimeter 28 cm. Its length is 10 cm more than its width. What are its dimensions?"
Which equation could be used to solve this problem?

A. $w + (w + 10) = 28$

B. $2w + 2(w + 10) = 28$

C. $w(w + 10) = 28$

D. $2w(w + 10) = 28$

4. Which of the following is an equation of a line with a positive slope?

A. $-3x - 4y = 1$ **B.** $2x - 3y = -6$

C. $5x + 14 = 0$ **D.** $y + 4x = 9$

5. How are x and y related?

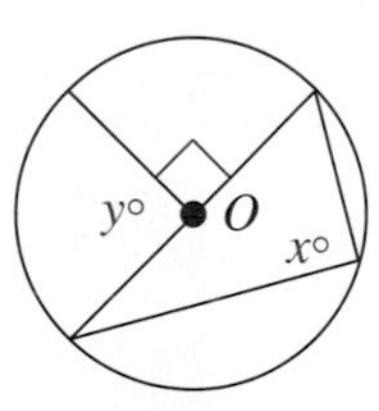

A. $x > y$ **B.** $x = y$

C. $x < y$ **D.** $x + y = 270$

6. A sales manager must prepare a report for the president of her company. The report must compare the monthly sales of the current year with the monthly sales of the previous year. What would be the best way for her to display the data?

A. A circle graph

B. A line plot

C. A multiple line graph

D. A box-and-whisker plot

7. Under a certain reflection, the image of $P(3, -1)$ is $P'(-1, -1)$. What are the coordinates of the image of $Q(-2, 4)$ under the same reflection?

A. $(-2, -5)$ **B.** $(-6, 4)$

C. $(-2, -4)$ **D.** $(4, 4)$

8. Which polygon *cannot* be used by itself to make a tessellation of the plane?

A. right scalene triangle

B. rectangle

C. regular pentagon

D. regular hexagon

9. Which numbers, when included in the set $\{8, 8, 9, 12, 13\}$, will raise the values of *both* the mean and the median?

A. 5, 8 **B.** 7, 15

C. 10, 15 **D.** 9, 10

CHAPTER 6

Functions

MONEY TALK

The money the United States spends is called "public funds". Each year about 35% of the public funds raised by the United States government come from personal income tax. Only 7% comes from corporate income tax.

TIPS FOR SAVERS

If your money is in a savings account growing at x % per year, it will double in about $72 \div x$ years. It will triple in approximately $110 \div x$ years.

WORLD VIEW

A \$ .93 soda in the United States costs \$ .27 in China, \$ .50 in Saudi Arabia, and \$ .70 in Panama. In Japan, the same soda costs \$1.15.

Source: *Zillions*

Data File 6

WHAT YOU WILL LEARN

- how to recognize sequences and functions
- how to interpret graphs for functions
- how to use technology to explore families of graphs
- how to solve problems by using a simpler problem

How Do Teens Feel About Money?

	% Who Agree
It's important to save money for the future.	91
Kids worry that they won't have enough money as adults.	75
Kids today are too greedy	65
The more money you have, the happier you will be.	48
My parent(s) usually give me money when I need it.	46
If I had to choose between a job that is satisfying and one that pays well, I'd choose the one that pays well.	44

Source: *Seventeen*

Prices Around the World

	United States	Germany	Japan
Gasoline (per gallon)	$ 1.33	$ 3.07	$ 3.80
Compact disc	$18.01	$15.02	$16.43
Daily newspaper	$ .35	$ 1.10	$ .73
Movie ticket	$ 6.00	$ 6.96	$11.68
Cup of coffee	$ .50	$ .70	$ 1.83
Ground beef (per pound)	$ 1.18	$ 2.61	$ 6.15
Eggs (per dozen)	$ .79	$ 1.67	$ 2.00

Source: *Money*

investigation

Project File

Memo

Merchants use numerous methods to determine the prices they will charge for their products. Some set prices based on what they feel customers will pay. Others take a completely scientific approach, analyzing prices mathematically and working out formulas for figuring new prices. Mr. Zorella sells pizzas at his restaurant. He is planning to add both 6-inch and 18-inch pizzas to his menu. He has hired you to calculate prices for the new items using a scientific approach.

ZORELLA PIZZA

DIAMETER	PRICE
9 in.	$ 4.00
12 in.	$ 6.00
15 in.	$ 9.00
20 in.	$15.00

Mission: Decide on prices for the two additions to the menu. Explain the reasoning behind your recommendation. Because you have been hired by Mr. Zorella only temporarily, you must be careful to take his needs into consideration if you hope to work for him again.

- ✓ What factors should you consider before making your recommendation?
- ✓ Mr. Zorella favors the scientific approach. How will that influence how you work?

What's Ahead

• Writing rules for arithmetic and geometric sequences

6-1 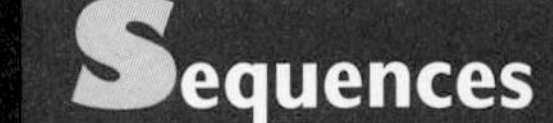 Sequences

WORK TOGETHER

Work with a partner. Suppose you've just paid $25 to join a baseball card club for a year. You are asked to choose one of the three options below to determine how you will receive your cards from the club.

Option A	Option B	Option C
Receive 230 cards the first month, 250 the second month, 270 the third month, and so on for 12 months.	Receive 1 card the first month, 2 cards the second month, 4 cards the third month, 8 cards the fourth month, and so on for 12 months.	Receive a total of 4,000 cards when you join.

1. How many cards would you receive in one year if you choose Option A? Option B? Option C?

2. Which option would you choose? Explain your answer. Compare your answer with other teams in your class.

***Honus Wagner** was a non-smoker who played for Pittsburgh in the early 1900s. When he was shown on a tobacco card in 1909, he sued the company. There are fewer than 50 cards in existence.*

Source: *The Saturday Evening Post*

THINK AND DISCUSS

Exploring Sequences Each term of an **arithmetic sequence** is found by *adding* a fixed number (called the **common difference**) to the previous term.

A sequence in which each term is found by *multiplying* the previous term by a fixed number (called the **common ratio**) is a **geometric sequence.**

FLASHBACK

A *sequence* is a set of numbers arranged according to some pattern. Each number is called a *term* of the sequence.

3. a. Which option above represents an arithmetic sequence? What is the common difference?
   b. Which option represents a geometric sequence? What is the common ratio?
   c. Which option represents neither an arithmetic sequence nor a geometric sequence? Explain your answer.

Extra SKILLS PRACTICE

Find the next three terms in each sequence.

1. 0.004, 0.04, 0.4, 4, . . .
2. 11, 15, 19, 23, . . .
3. 45, -39, 33, -27, . . .
4. 606, 6006, 6,006, . . .
5. 20, 12, 4, -4, . . .
6. 6, 4, 2, 0, . . .
7. 3.02, 3.022, 3.0222, . . .
8. 4.5, 4.2, 3.9, 3.6, . . .
9. 750, 75, 7.5, 0.75, . . .
10. 800, 400, 200, 100, . . .
11. 0.12, -0.36, 1.08, . . .
12. -60, -49, -38, -27,...

In the 1957 movie *The Incredible Shrinking Man* the main character mysteriously starts shrinking. Suppose the man's original height is 6 ft and he shrinks 3 in. every day.

a. How tall is the man at the end of one week?

b. How many days would it take for the man to shrink to half his original height?

c. Does this represent an arithmetic or geometric sequence?

d. Describe one way the man's height would have to change to describe a geometric sequence.

Using Formulas Consider the sequence 7, 11, 15, 19, . . . If k is the value of the 20th term, then the 21st term is $k + 4$. You can find the actual value of the 20th term by continuing the sequence or you could use this formula.

$k = a + d(n - 1)$ $\quad a$ = first term

$\quad d$ = common difference

$k = 7 + 4(20 - 1)$ $\quad n$ = number of term in sequence

5. Find the value of k in the equation above. Verify that the formula works for other terms in the sequence.

6. **Choose A, B, C, or D.** Myra is beginning an exercise program. She starts by walking 2 mi the first day and increases her distance by 0.3 mi each day. Which expression represents her distance on the sixth day?

A. $2(0.3)^6$ **B.** $2 + (0.3)^6$

C. $2 + (0.3)5$ **D.** $0.3 + (2)^5$

ON YOUR OWN

7. Find the next three terms in each sequence. Identify each as arithmetic, geometric, or neither. For each arithmetic or geometric sequence, find the common difference or ratio.

a. 2.0, 2.3, 2.6, 2.9, ■, ■, ■

b. 2, 5, 10, 17, ■, ■, ■

c. 21, 15, 9, 3, ■, ■, ■

d. 2, -6, 18, -54, ■, ■, ■

e. 1.1, 1.01, 1.001, 1.0001, ■, ■, ■

f. 0.5, -1, 2, -4, ■, ■, ■

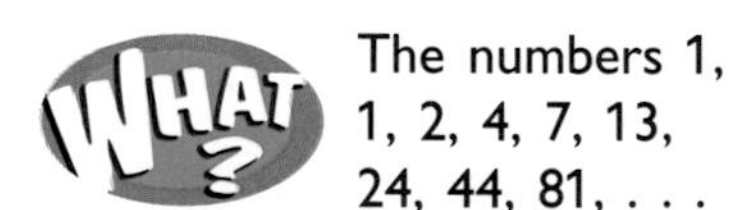

The numbers 1, 1, 2, 4, 7, 13, 24, 44, 81, . . . are called Tribonacci numbers. They were named by a 14-year-old mathematician, Mark Feinberg, who wrote about them in the October, 1963, issue of The Fibonacci Quarterly. **What is the next number in the sequence?**

Source: *Mathematical Circus*

8. Write the first five terms of each sequence.

   a. arithmetic; first term = 10; common difference = 2.4

   b. geometric; first term = 2; common ratio = 3

   c. arithmetic; first term = 23; common difference = −5

   d. geometric; first term = −4; common ratio = −3

9. **Writing** Describe a situation that represents a geometric sequence. Write a sequence of numbers and identify the first term and the common ratio.

10. Tell whether each situation produces an arithmetic sequence, a geometric sequence, or neither.

    a. The temperature falls at the rate of 0.5°F per hour.

    b. The number of bacteria in a lake doubles every day.

    c. The number of minutes a person exercises each day varies between 30 and 45.

    d. A baby gains 2 oz every day.

11. a. Find the eighth term in the sequence 5, 10, 20, 35, . . .

    b. Is this sequence arithmetic, geometric, or neither?

12. A clock gains 3 min every day. How many minutes fast will the clock be at the end of 60 days?

13. Consider the sequence 17, 18.5, 20, 21.5, . . . Find the value of the 40th term using the formula $k = a + d(n - 1)$.

14. Look at the pattern below created by making a row of pentagons with each side one unit in length.

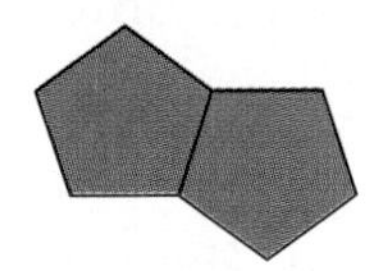
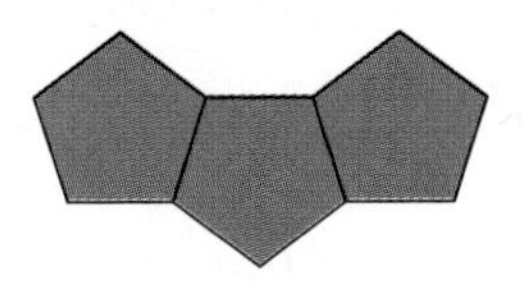

    a. Write a sequence of numbers showing how the perimeter of the figure changes.

    b. What is the perimeter of a row of ten regular pentagons? hexagons? Explain how you found your answer.

    c. **Critical Thinking** Is there a general rule that describes the relationship between the number of sides of a polygon and the perimeter of a row of polygons? Explain.

Write the coordinates of the point after each rotation about the origin.

1. $P(-5, 3)$; rotation of 90°

2. $A(7, -6)$; rotation of 270°

Find the measure of each angle of the polygon.

3. a regular octagon

4. a regular decagon

Simplify.

5. $-4(-8 - 5) - 10$

6. $-9 + 6(-8) + 4$

WHAT? In 1930, a dance marathon that lasted more than 5,000 h was held in Chicago's Merry Garden Ballroom. The rest periods were progressively cut from 20 to 10 to 5 to 0 min/h. **Does this change represent an arithmetic sequence, a geometric sequence, or neither?**

Source: *The Guinness Book of Records*

What's Ahead

- Representing functions with rules and tables of values

6-2 Function Rules

THINK AND DISCUSS

Identifying Functions Many states require a nickel deposit on drink containers to encourage recycling. The total deposit you pay, d, is a *function* of the number of containers, n, you buy. This relationship can be expressed as an equation.

$$d = \$.05n$$

WHAT? Beverage containers made of Lexan can have up to 100 lives. Users expect to reduce land fill costs by thousands of dollars.

Source: *Garbage*

You can also describe a *function rule* using *function notation.*

$$f(n) = 0.05n$$

You read this as "f of n equals 0.05 times n."

1. a. What does n represent in the function rule $f(n) = 0.05n$?
   b. Evaluate the function for $f(6)$, $f(12)$, and $f(24)$.

2. State whether the first quantity depends on the second.
   a. the total cost of tickets; the number of tickets you buy
   b. the time you get to school; the amount of your allowance
   c. the cost per gallon of paint; the total cost of paint

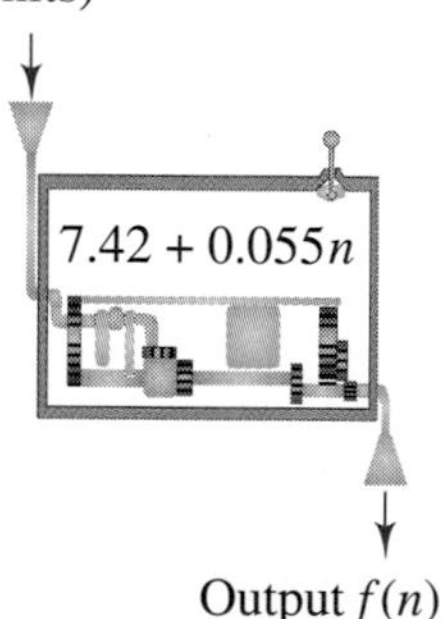

Input n (units)	Output $f(n)$ (dollars)
100	12.92
200	18.42
500	34.92

Using Rules and Tables

Example 1 The rate for basic phone service in one area is \$7.42 plus \$0.055 per message unit.

a. Let n represent the number of message units. Write a function rule to represent the monthly bill as a function of the number of message units.

$$f(n) = 7.42 + 0.055n$$

b. Make an input/output table.

- Choose several values such as $f(100)$, $f(200)$, and $f(500)$. Substitute in the function rule.

$$f(100) = 7.42 + 0.055(100)$$
$$= 7.42 + 5.5$$
$$= 12.92$$

The table at the left represents the function.

3. **Writing** Choose one of the real-life situations below, or make up a situation that represents a function. Make an input/output table and write the function rule.
   - the amount of money you can make washing cars at \$5.50 per car
   - changing temperature in degrees Celsius to degrees Fahrenheit
   - the distance you can walk at 3 mi/h

In 1980, Terry Fox began a walk across Canada to raise money for cancer research. Although Terry had to stop two-thirds of the way to his goal, his efforts raised \$24 million.

WORK TOGETHER

Work with a partner to play *What's My Rule*?

- Decide on a rule that describes what happens to the input number to get the output number.
- Write a function rule to represent the function.

Input n	Output $f(n)$
1	4
2	8
3	12
4	16

Input n	Output $f(n)$
1	3
2	5
3	7
4	9

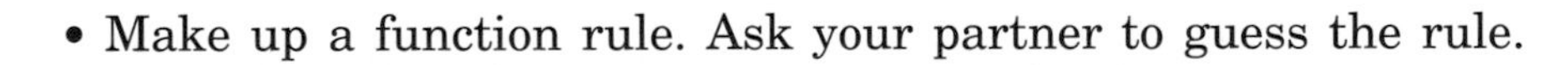

- Make up a function rule. Ask your partner to guess the rule.

You can represent a function with an equation in two variables. Let x represent the input. Let y represent the output, or $f(x)$.

Example 2 At Video Master, videos rent for \$3.50 for the first night and \$2.00 per night for each extra night.

a. Let x represent the number of extra nights. Write an equation in two variables to represent the total cost of a rental as a function of the number of extra nights.

$$y = 3.50 + 2x$$

b. Make an input/output table.
   - Substitute 0, 1, and 2 for x. The table at the right represents the function.

Input x (extra nights)	Output y (fee)
0	3.50
1	5.50
2	7.50

LOOK BACK Does $x = 0$ make sense? Explain.

TRY THESE

Does the first quantity depend on the second? Explain.

4. the number of tiles needed to tile a floor; the area of the floor

5. the cost of filling your car's gas tank; the time of day you go to the gas station

Use the function rule $f(n) = 3n^2 - 7$. Find the following.

6. $f(0)$ 7. $f(-2)$ 8. $f(2)$ 9. $f(10)$ 10. $f(5.5)$

Complete each table. Write a function rule.

11.

n	$f(n)$
1	5
5	9
10	14
15	
	24

12.

n	$f(n)$
1	−2
2	−1
3	0
4	
10	
	14

13.

n	$f(n)$
1	9
3	13
5	17
	21
9	
	14

ON YOUR OWN

Does the first quantity depend on the second? Explain.

14. the length of time it takes to type a paper; the rate at which you type

15. the value of a coupon; the time of day you shop

Complete each table. Write a function rule.

16.

n	$f(n)$
1	4.3
2	6.3
3	
	10.3
10	22.3

17.

n	$f(n)$
2	7
4	19
6	
	67
15	85

18.

n	$f(n)$
1	2
2	8
3	14
4	
	26

Mixed REVIEW

Write the next three terms of each sequence.

1. 400, −200, 100, −50, . . .
2. 9, 16, 23, 30, . . .

State the coordinates of the point after each reflection.

3. $B(-2, 6)$ reflected over the x-axis
4. $C(5, -7)$ reflected over the y-axis

Solve.

5. $-5.7 = 6.8 + n$
6. $x - 3.3 = -7.9$

Extra SKILLS PRACTICE

Find each value.
Use $f(n) = n^2 - 2n + 3$.

1. $f(0)$ 2. $f(1)$
3. $f(-1)$ 4. $f(5)$
5. $f(-2)$ 6. $f(10)$

Use $f(n) = 3n^2 + n - 1$.

7. $f(1)$ 8. $f(2)$
9. $f(-1)$ 10. $f(0)$
11. $f(6)$ 12. $f(-4)$

Use the function rule $f(n) = 5 + n - n^2$. Find the value.

19. $f(0)$ **20.** $f(-2)$ **21.** $f(2)$ **22.** $f(5)$ **23.** $f(-5)$

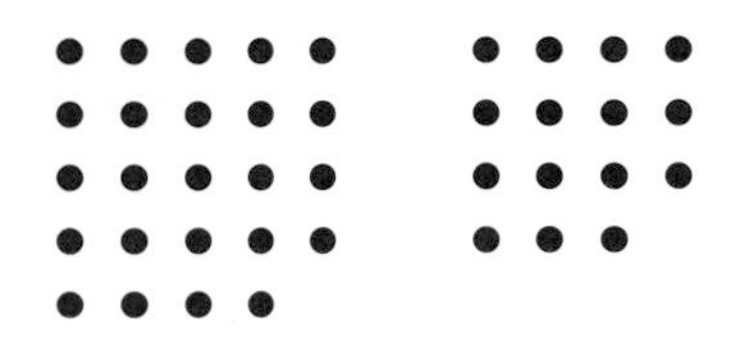

24. Consider the pattern of dots at the right.

a. Let n = the number of dots in the top row of a figure. Write a function rule that describes the total number of dots in that figure.

b. Describe how you determined the function rule.

25. Consumer Issues At Rub-a-Dub Laundry it costs $.75 per load of wash and $.75 for 30 min of dryer time. An average load takes 1 h to dry.

a. Let n = the number of loads of wash. Write a function rule to describe the total cost of washing and drying as a function of the number of loads.

b. Find the total cost of doing 3 loads of laundry.

c. Suppose it costs $.65 for soap for each load of wash. Write a new function rule to represent the total cost.

26. Energy A color television set uses about 0.23 kilowatts per hour. The Tchong family watches television an average of 4 h a day.

a. Let n = the number of days they watch TV. Make an input/output table to represent the amount of power used for two days.

b. Write the function rule using function notation.

c. Use the equation to find how many kilowatts of power the television used in the month of April.

Lake Assal, Djibouti, *is one of the lowest and hottest places in the world. At 156 ft below sea level, its summer temperatures can reach a scorching 135°F.*

Source: *National Geographic*

27. Research Is temperature a function of altitude? Make a conjecture about what happens to the temperature at higher altitudes. Test your conjecture by collecting data about the average temperature for cities at various altitudes.

28. Investigation (p. 246) In newspapers or magazines, find ads for groups of items that differ from each other only in size (tires, picture frames, lumber, carpets, construction materials, etc.). What patterns, if any, can you find in the prices that are charged for different size items?

29. Writing Explain how to determine a function rule from an input/output table.

What's Ahead

- Representing linear functions as equations and graphs

WHAT YOU'LL NEED

✓ Graph paper

6-3 Function Graphs

WORK TOGETHER

Carlos charges \$3.00 an hour for baby-sitting, plus an extra \$5.00 if he makes a meal. He has a regular baby-sitting job on Saturday that begins at 5 P.M., includes dinner, and ends at various times. If the parents stay home, they still pay him \$5 for reserving the time.

1. What does Carlos earn if the parents return at 8 P.M.?
2. Write a rule in $f(x)$ notation to represent Carlos's pay as a function where x is the time in hours.
3. Make a table of values of x and $f(x)$ for $x = 0, 1, 2, 3, 4, 5$.
4. Write the values from your table as ordered pairs. Use x as the first coordinate and $f(x)$ as the second coordinate. Graph your ordered pairs. Let the horizontal axis represent x values and the vertical axis represent $f(x)$ values.

Grandparents provide child care for 13.9% of the children under age five whose mothers are employed.

Source: *Statistical Abstract of the United States*

THINK AND DISCUSS

5. Discuss each question. Then complete your function graph.
   a. Why is it appropriate to connect the points?
   b. Should your final graph extend into other quadrants?
   c. Should your graph have a highest or a lowest point?

Graphing Functions Points of a **linear function** lie on a line.

Example 1 Graph the linear function $f(x) = 2x - 3$.

- If the horizontal axis represents x and the vertical axis represents $f(x)$ or y, you can write $y = 2x - 3$.
- Notice that the function rule is the equation of a line in slope-intercept form. The slope is 2 and the y-intercept is -3.
- Draw the graph. Start at $(0, -3)$ and move to the right 1 unit and up 2 units to $(1, -1)$.

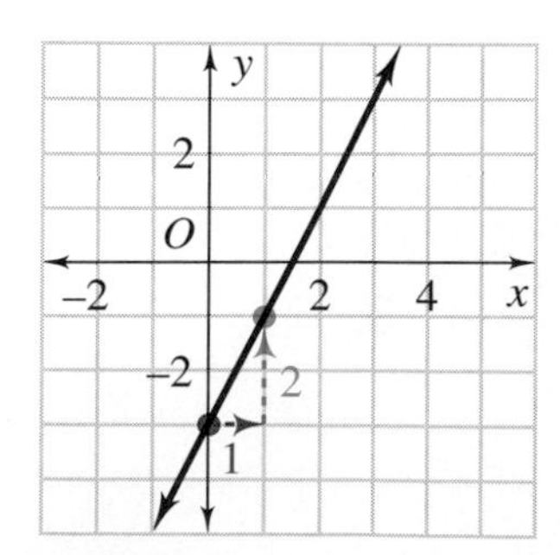

Writing Function Rules You can write a function rule for the graph of a linear function. Find the slope and the y-intercept from the graph and use them to write the rule.

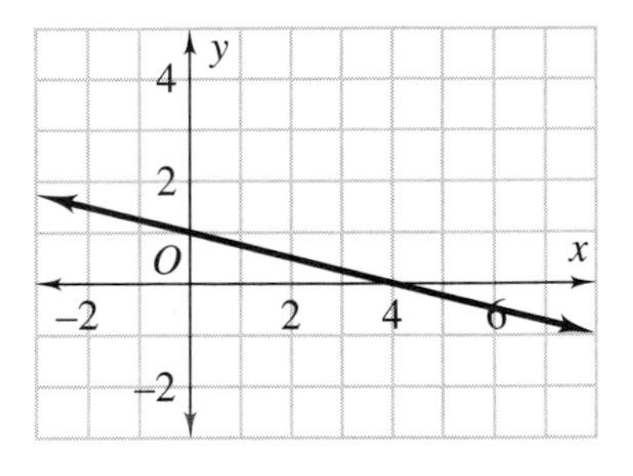

Example 2 Write a rule for the linear function graphed at the right.

- The graph crosses the y-axis at (0, 1), so the y-intercept is 1.
- Find the slope using the points (4, 0) and (0, 1).

$$\text{slope} = \frac{0-1}{4-0} = -\frac{1}{4}$$

- Substitute in the slope-intercept form.

$y = mx + b$ The equation is $y = -\frac{1}{4}x + 1$.

The function rule is $f(x) = -\frac{1}{4}x + 1$.

Should you always connect the points on a function graph?

Example 3 When you order concert tickets by mail, you pay \$24 per ticket plus a \$4 handling fee for the order. The function rule $f(x) = 4 + 24x$ gives the total cost of an order as a function of the number of tickets ordered. Graph this function.

Number of Tickets	Total Cost
1	\$28
2	\$52
3	\$76
4	\$100

- The table at the right shows the number of tickets and the total cost.
- The coordinate graph at the right shows the values from the table. The horizontal axis represents the number of tickets and the vertical axis represents the total cost. Since the function is linear, all of the points lie on a straight line.
- You don't connect the points on the function graph because the function only makes sense for whole number values.

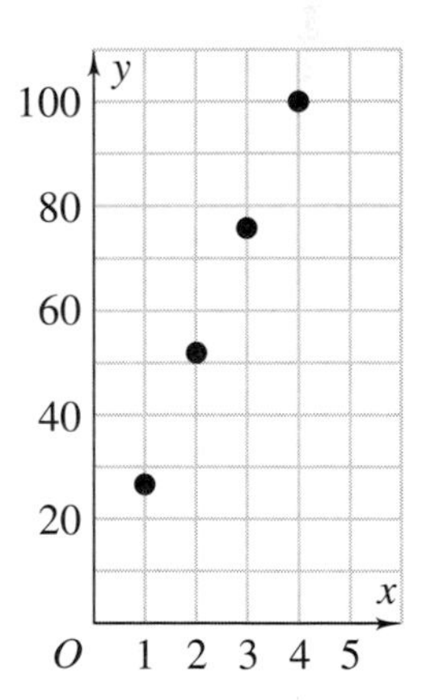

6. **Discussion** In Example 3, if you drew a line, points like (2.5, 64) would be on the function graph. What would that mean? Why wouldn't that make sense?

7. Why does the graph for Example 3 show only the first quadrant?

8. Does the function in Example 3 have a least value? a greatest value? Explain.

Mixed REVIEW

Evaluate.
$f(x) = 3x - 4$

1. $f(-2)$
2. $f(6)$

Solve and graph each solution on a number line.

3. $-y + 6 > 2$
4. $2 \leq -3 + t$
5. Six more than a number is five less than twice the number. Find the number.
6. Find the slope of a line that contains the points $A(5, 2)$ and $C(-3, 6)$.
7. Find two numbers whose difference is 42 and whose product is -405.

A German company has produced a wristwatch guaranteed to lose no more than one second in one million years. A computer chip automatically resets the watch if it loses a fraction of a second. Prices for the watch range from $200 to $6,000.

Source: *Business Week*

TRY THESE

Graph each linear function.

9. $f(x) = -2x + 5$
10. $f(x) = \frac{2}{3}x - 1$
11. $f(x) = -\frac{3}{2}x - 2$
12. $f(x) = 5x + 3$

Write the function rule for each graph.

13.

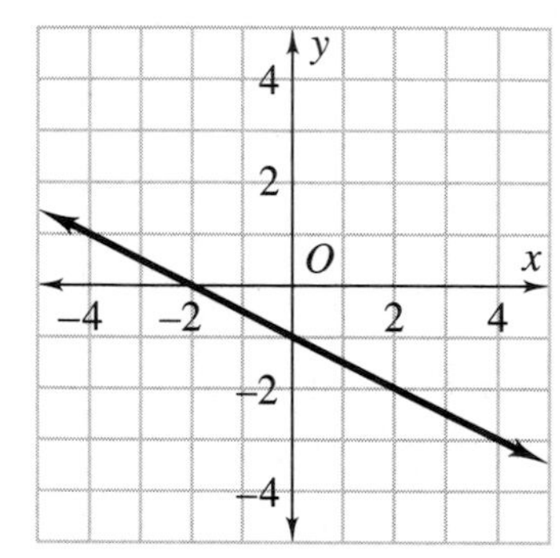

14.

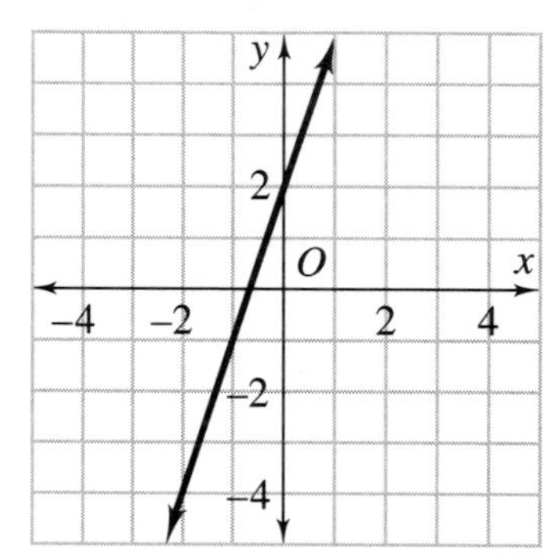

ON YOUR OWN

15. On a long-distance automobile trip, Ian averaged about 50 mi/h. Write a function rule relating his total distance to the number of hours he traveled. Graph the function.

16. **Social Studies** Cora read that people once used burning candles to measure time. She bought a box of candles and studied the rate at which they burned. She noticed that she could express the number of hours the candles burned by the function $f(x) = 7.5 - 0.5x$, where x was the height of the candle in centimeters.
    a. Graph the function.
    b. What was the original height of each candle?
    c. What was the greatest amount of time one of the candles could burn?

17. Your choral group is planning to buy music stands. The group has $198 in its treasury. Each stand costs $32. Write a function rule where x is the number of stands purchased and $f(x)$ is the amount left in the treasury. Graph your function.

Graph each function.

18. $f(x) = \frac{3}{4}x + 2$

19. $f(x) = 12 - \frac{2}{3}x$

20. Writing Give an example of a real-life situation that you could model by a linear function. Give the function rule and show its graph.

21. Oceanography The deeper a diver descends, the more pressure she experiences. The linear function $f(x) = 1 + 0.1x$, represents the pressure in kilograms per square centimeter (kg/cm^2) at x centimeters below sea level. Show the graph of this function.

WHAT? Divers can breathe pure oxygen under low pressure, but oxygen is toxic under high pressure. For this reason, divers who exceed a depth of 60 m must breathe a mixture such as oxygen with helium or nitrogen.

Source: *Encyclopedia Americana*

For each graph, find the slope and *y*-intercept. Use the values to write a function rule.

22.

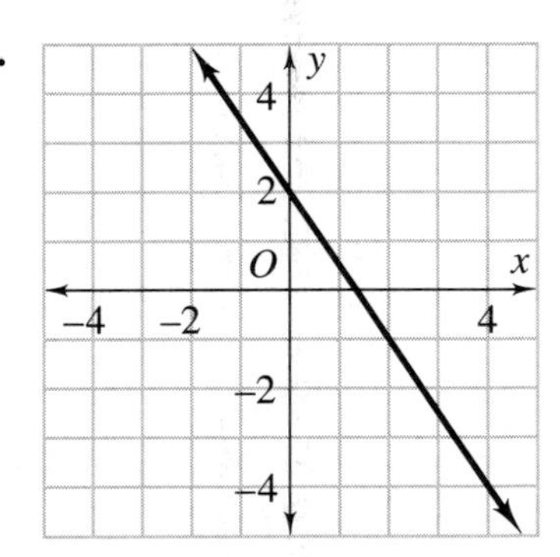

23.

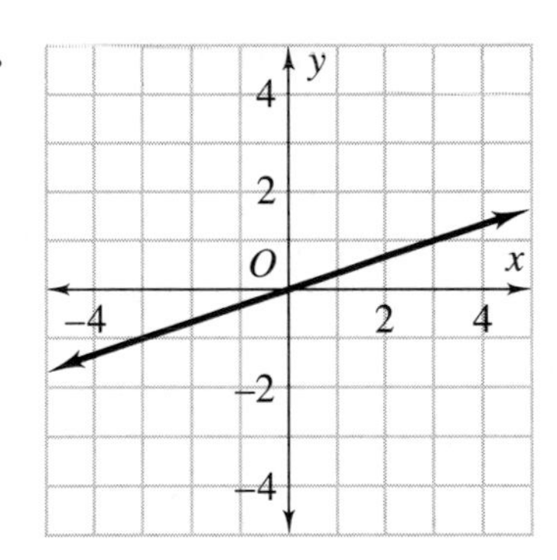

CHECKPOINT

Write the next three terms in each sequence. State whether the sequence is arithmetic, geometric, or neither.

1. 1, 4, 9, 16, . . .

2. 12, 6, 3, 1.5, . . .

3. 125, −25, 5, −1, . . .

4. 21.4, 21.1, 20.8, 20.5, . . .

5. $\frac{2}{3}, \frac{1}{2}, \frac{1}{3}, \frac{1}{6}, \ldots$

6. 12, 23, 34, 45, . . .

Use the function rule $f(x) = -3x - 2$. Find the following.

7. $f(-1)$

8. $f(5)$

9. $f(0)$

10. $f\left(-\frac{1}{2}\right)$

PROBLEM SOLVING

6-4 Solve a Simpler Problem

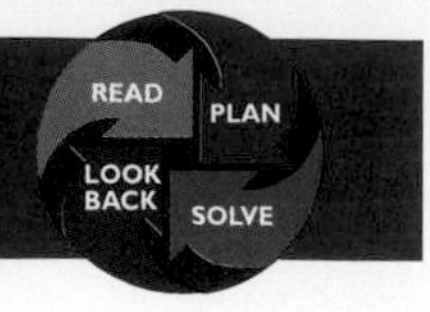

What's Ahead

- Solving problems by using a simpler problem

Sometimes when you are faced with a complicated problem situation, it helps to break the problem into simpler steps and look for a pattern.

1 unit²

> How many squares of different sizes are there on a standard checkerboard? Consider each small square as 1 square unit.

READ

Read and understand the given information. Summarize the problem.

Read the problem carefully.

1. What is the problem about?
2. What information do you need to find?

PLAN

Decide on a strategy to solve the problem.

Make up a simpler problem that is similar to the given problem. Then solve the simpler problem. Use the same reasoning to solve the given problem.

3. What different size squares do you see on the checkerboard? For example, there are squares of 1 unit by 1 unit. There are squares of 2 units by 2 units.

SOLVE

Try out the strategy.

Think of the simplest situation involving more than 1 unit² that is similar to the problem you want to solve.

1

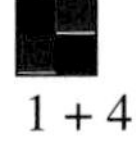

1 + 4

1 + 4 + 9

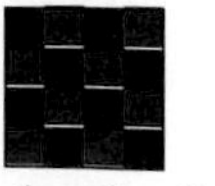

1 + 4 + 9 + 16

4. What is the simplest board on which you can count multiple squares? How many squares are on this board?
5. What is the next simplest situation? How many squares are there in this situation?
6. Describe the pattern for finding the number of squares on the next two square boards.
7. Use the pattern to find the number of squares on the checkerboard.

8. What other strategies could you use to solve the checkerboard problem?

9. **Writing** Write a rule for finding the number of squares on any $n \times n$ checkerboard. Is the number of squares a function of n? Explain.

LOOK BACK

Think about how you solved the problem.

TRY THESE

Use the strategy of solving a simpler problem.

10. Look at the figure at the right.
    a. How many small triangles are there in row 7?
    b. What is the total number of small triangles in the figure?
    c. Suppose you extend the figure to show three more rows. How many small triangles would there be in row ten?
    d. Suppose you extend the figure to ten rows. How many small triangles would there be in the complete figure?
    e. Suppose you extend the figure to show a total of n rows. What would be the total number of small triangles?
    f. Is the total number of small triangles a function of the number of rows? If so, write the rule in function notation.

Row
1
2
3
4
5
6
7

11. **Sports** In a tennis tournament each participant plays one game against each of the other players. There are 10 participants. How many games will be played?

ON YOUR OWN

Use any strategy to solve the problem. Show your work.

12. A writer just finished typing the manuscript for a book and is numbering the pages.
    a. The book is 354 pages long. How many times will the number 3 appear in the page numbers?
    b. There will be one illustration on every 30th page of the book. How many illustrations are planned?

"*Simplify does not mean to eliminate ideas, but to express the same ideas with a minimum of means.*

—Edna Hibel
(1917–)

Mixed REVIEW

Make a table of values. Graph the function.

1. $f(x) = -2x - 1$
2. $f(x) = 4 + 5x$

Solve. Graph the solution on a number line.

3. $-2a + 4 < 6$
4. $8 + 5t \geq -23$

Use a calculator to evaluate.

5. $-8 + 6(-2.5 + 5.6)$
6. $-10 - 3(-1.8 - 7)$

13. A tree in the schoolyard is now 5 ft tall. The tree grows at the rate of 1 ft 6 in. per year. In how many years will the tree reach a height of 29 ft?

14. **Consumer Issues** The Community Youth Club bought booster buttons at a wholesale price of 3 for $1. They sold the buttons for $.50 each. How much profit did the club make on the sale of 5 doz buttons?

15. **Sports** Regina scored 16 points, 22 points, and 24 points in three basketball games. What is the least number of points she must score in her next game to average 20 points per game for the four games?

16. How many different arrangements of children by age can there be in families with a total of four children? (*Hint:* boy-girl-girl-boy is different from boy-boy-girl-girl.)

17. Enrico walked at an average speed of 3.4 mi/h for 2.25 h. How far did he walk?

18. The sum of two numbers is 17. The lesser number is x. Write an expression for the greater number.

19. **Jobs** Malcolm sells magazine subscriptions. He earns $15 a week plus $3 for each subscription he sells. How many subscriptions must he sell to earn $90 in one week?

20. Paper plates come in packages of 15 or 20. Karl bought 10 packages and had a total of 170 plates. How many of each size package did he buy?

21. **Critical Thinking** The sum of two integers is -16. Their difference is 12. What are the two integers?

22. A Creole gumbo recipe calls for 1 tsp of thyme and 10 oz of okra. Suppose you use $1\frac{1}{4}$ lb of okra. How many teaspoons of thyme should you use?

23. How many more boxes would you need to package 80 magazines in boxes of 5 rather than in boxes of 8?

24. **Investigation (p. 246)** Use the data you gathered for Exercise 28, page 253. Display the sizes and prices of each group of items in a table. Then graph the function values from your table.

What's Ahead

- Interpreting graphs of real-world situations
- Drawing graphs to represent real-world situations

WHAT YOU'LL NEED

✓ Stopwatch 

✓ Graph paper

6-5 Interpreting Graphs

THINK AND DISCUSS

We use graphs to describe a variety of real-world situations. Drawing graphs helps us to visualize relationships and interpret data.

The graph below shows the speed of Mr. Klee's van as he picked up band members for a rehearsal.

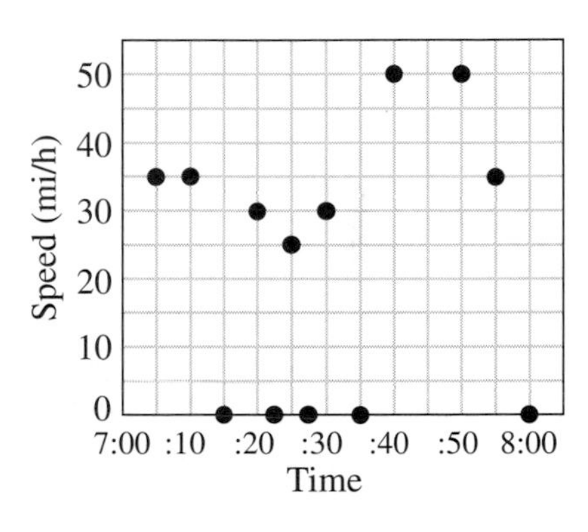

1. How long did it take Mr. Klee to drive from his home to the rehearsal hall?
2. How many stops did he make on the way?
3. What was Mr. Klee's fastest speed?
4. Between which two times did the speed of the van change the most? What was the change?
5. **Discussion** What factors determine the speed of Mr. Klee's van at a particular time?
6. **Discussion** Does either graph below show the points connected in an appropriate way? Explain your reasoning.

Graph I

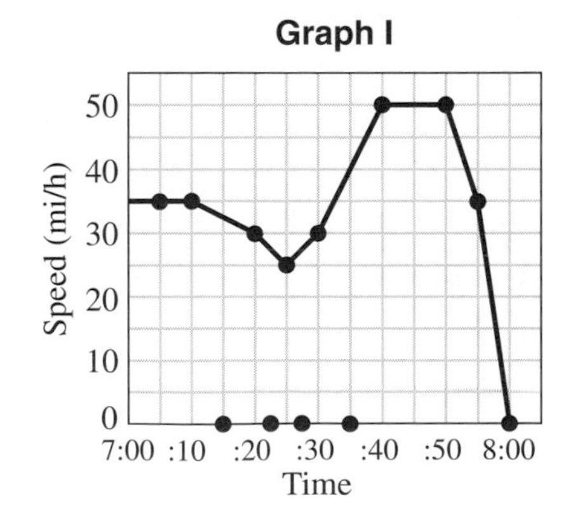

Graph II

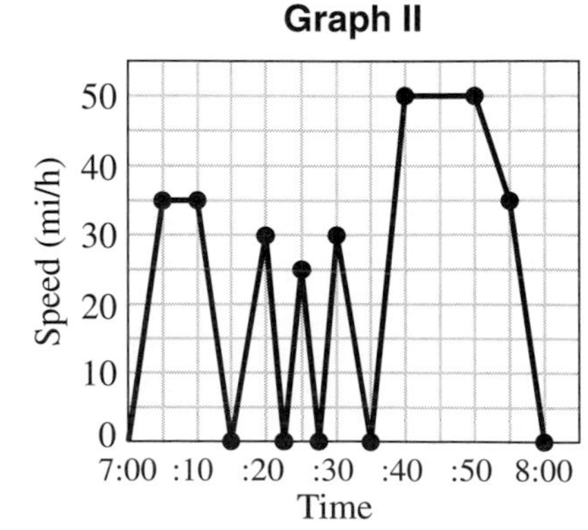

***In Western nations** an orchestra usually includes violins and other stringed instruments. Many African and Asian orchestras have only percussion instruments such as drums, gongs, and xylophones.*

Source: *World Book Encyclopedia*

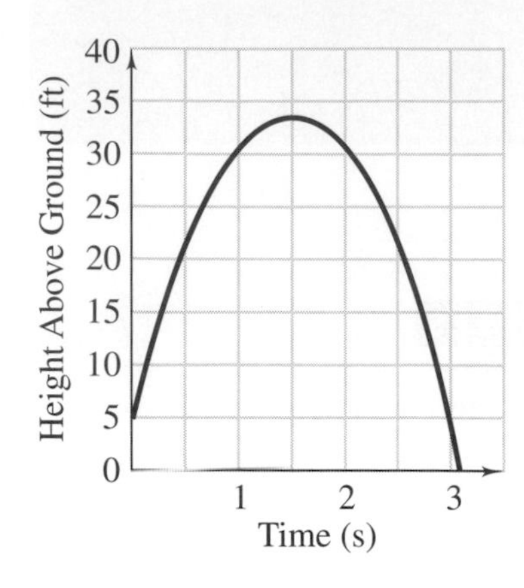

7. **Writing** Describe a situation that the graph at the left might represent.

8. Each graph represents a situation. Match a graph with the appropriate situation. Explain your choices.

I. 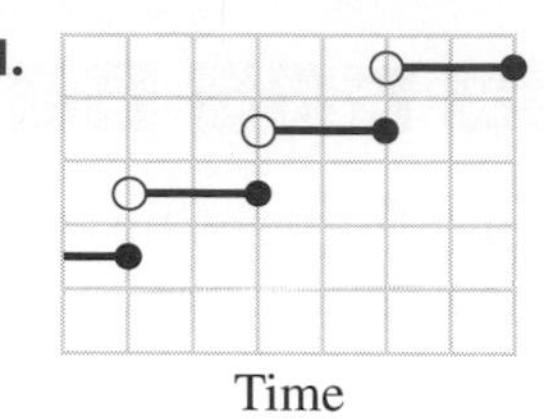

II. 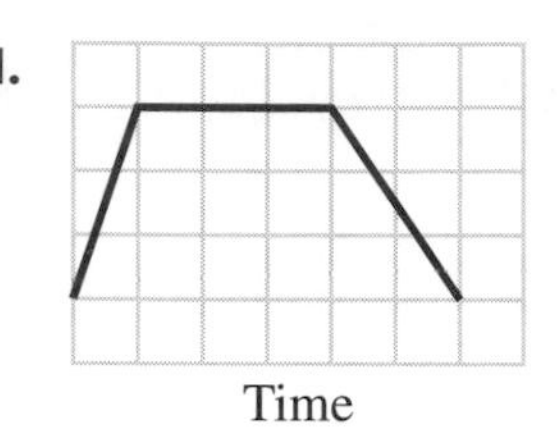

III. 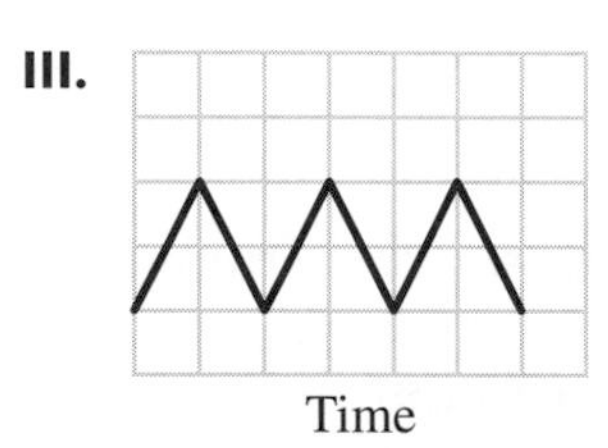

IV. 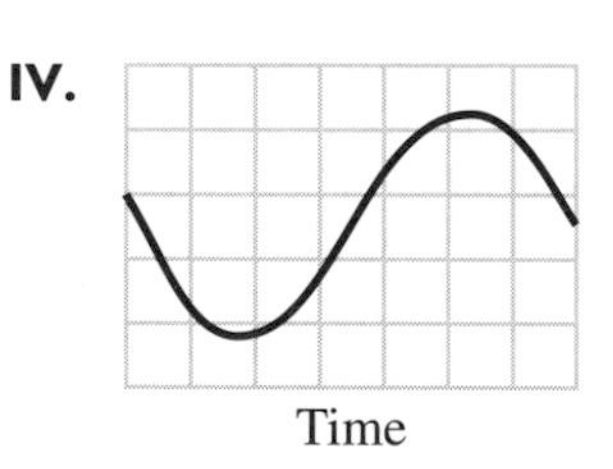

a. the height above the ground of a Ferris-wheel car during a ride of three revolutions

b. the temperature of the air during a 24-h period beginning at 9:00 P.M.

c. an athlete's pulse rate during a 50-min aerobic workout, including a warm-up period and a cool-down period

d. parking fees: $3 for the first half hour; $2 for each additional hour or portion of an hour

George W. Ferris designed the original Ferris Wheel. It was 250 ft in diameter and had 36 cars. The largest-diameter wheel operating today is the Cosmoclock 21 in Japan. It is 328 ft in diameter and has 60 gondolas with eight seats each.

Source: *The Guinness Book Records*

9. Graph I above is a special type of graph called a "step graph." Think of another situation that can be represented using a step graph.

   a. How would you label the axes?

   b. Draw a graph for the situation.

   c. **Discussion** Describe the information that is shown in your graph. Compare your graph with those of your classmates. How are the situations you chose alike? How are they different?

WORK TOGETHER

In this activity you will explore the relationship between time and the number of steps you take jogging in place. Work in pairs.

- Take turns with one partner being the jogger and the other partner being the recorder.
- The partner that is jogging should count the total number of steps taken. The other partner should record the number of steps after 15 s, 30 s, 45 s, and so on for two minutes.
- Make a table for each partner showing the data.
- Make two graphs showing the data for each table on the same coordinate plane.

10. Compare the data for each pair.

  a. Did you speed up or slow down during the activity?

  b. During which 15-s interval did you take the most steps? the fewest?

  c. **Discussion** Is it appropriate to connect the points on your graph? Explain your reasoning.

11. **Writing** Describe another situation that might have a graph shaped like the one for jogging in place.

Mixed REVIEW

Write each equation in slope-intercept form. Identify the slope and y-intercept.

1. $-2x + 6y = -12$

2. $10 = y - 5x$

$\triangle LDA \cong \triangle TWB$ Complete.

3. $\angle A \cong \angle$ ■

4. $BT =$ ■

5. Find the sum of the whole numbers from 10 through 30.

ON YOUR OWN

12. **Aviation** An airplane flew from Boston to New York in 50 min. The plane took 20 min to reach a cruising altitude of 20,000 ft. The plane took 15 min to make its descent into New York. Sketch a graph showing this information.

13. **Choose A, B, or C.** The function table at the right describes the distance in feet that a stone falls over time. Which graph best describes the information?

Time (s)	Distance (ft)
0	5
1	20
2	45
3	80
4	125

A.

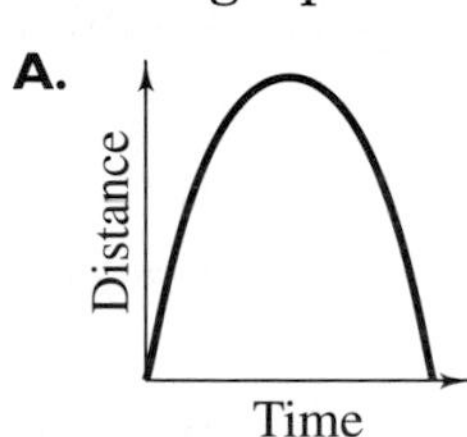

B.

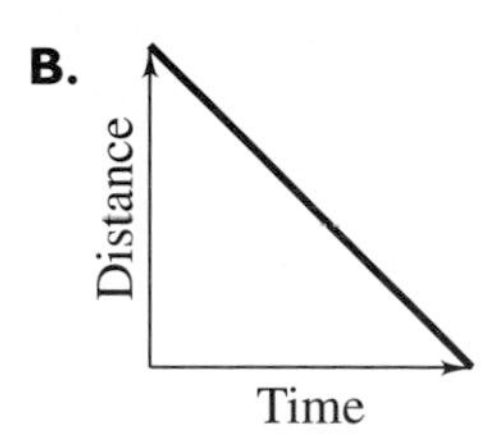

C.

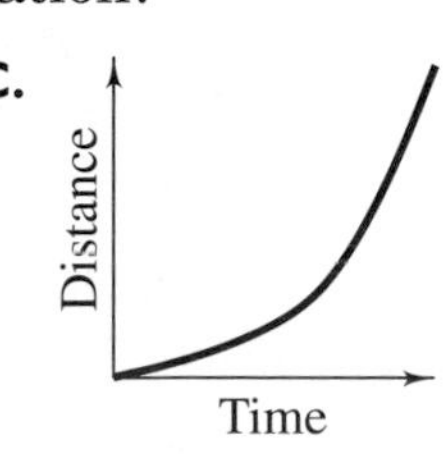

What Goes Up Must Come Down

The high tides at the Bay of Fundy are world famous. Situated between New Brunswick and Nova Scotia, the Bay of Fundy is about 180 mi long and has an average width of 35 mi. Scientists believe that the bay's long narrow shape accounts for its extreme tidal range. The difference between the water level at low tide and at high tide averages 39.4 ft, but can be as much as 70 ft.

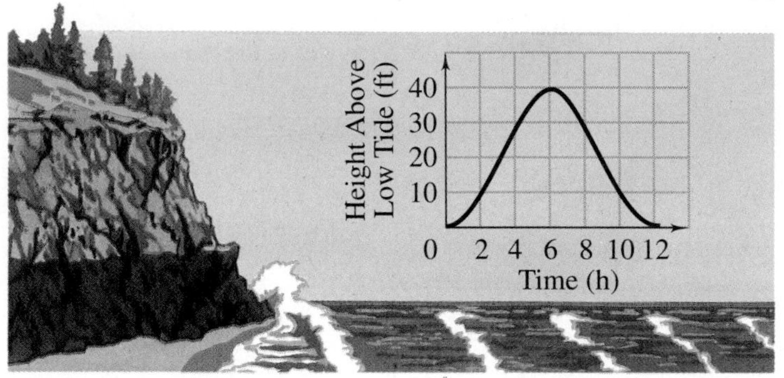

14. a. Writing Explain how the graph at the left describes the water level between low tides at the Bay of Fundy.

b. Suppose low tide occurs at 3:30 P.M. At what time will the tide have risen 30 ft?

15. Data File 5 (pp. 192–193) During Olympic training, swimmers work up to an average distance of 80 km/wk.

a. According to the graph, for how many weeks is this peak training level maintained?

b. How many weeks does it take to reach the level of peak training?

c. During which two weeks does the greatest increase in swimming distance happen? What is the increase?

d. What is the change in the average swimming distance between Weeks 24 and 25?

16. Consumer Issues A Best Buy personal computer system usually sells for a regular price of $1,200. During Back-to-School sales in August and September, the system sells for 25% less. During a winter sale in December and a spring sale in April, the system sells for 15% off its regular price.

a. How much does the system sell for during the Back-to-School sale? during the winter sale?

b. Make a graph showing the selling price of the Best Buy computer system over a 12-month period.

Practice

Write the next three terms of each sequence. State whether the sequence is arithmetic, geometric, or neither.

1. 13, 16, 19, 22, . . .
2. 0, 3, 8, 15, . . .
3. $-480, -240, -120, -60, \ldots$
4. $-12, -7, -2, 3, \ldots$
5. 8, 27, 64, 125, . . .
6. $\frac{1}{256}, \frac{1}{64}, \frac{1}{16}, \frac{1}{4}, \ldots$
7. Find the fifth term of a geometric sequence with a common ratio of -2 and first term equal to 8.

Write a function rule for each table.

8.

x	$f(x)$
3	8
-3	2
0	5
1	6

9.

x	$f(x)$
9	30
0	3
4	15
-3	-6

10.

x	$f(x)$
0	0
-1	1
-3	9
4	16

Make an input/output table for each function. Find $f(-2)$, $f(-1)$, $f(0)$, $f(1)$, and $f(2)$.

11. $f(x) = -x - 4$
12. $f(x) = 3x^2 + 1$
13. $f(x) = -\frac{1}{2}x - 2$
14. If $f(x) = x^3 - 5x + 1$, find $f(0)$, $f(1)$, $f(-1)$, and $f\left(\frac{1}{2}\right)$.
15. **Data File 6 (pp. 244–245)** Use function notation to write a rule for the number of years it will take to double your savings in an account that is growing at $x\%$ per year. Find the value of $f(x)$ for $x = 6$.
16. **Choose A, B, or C.** A student walks home from school, stopping at a friend's house on the way. Which graph could describe the total distance walked?

A.

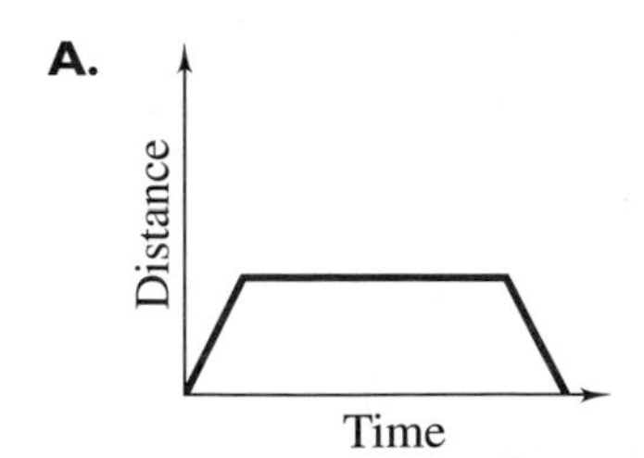

B.

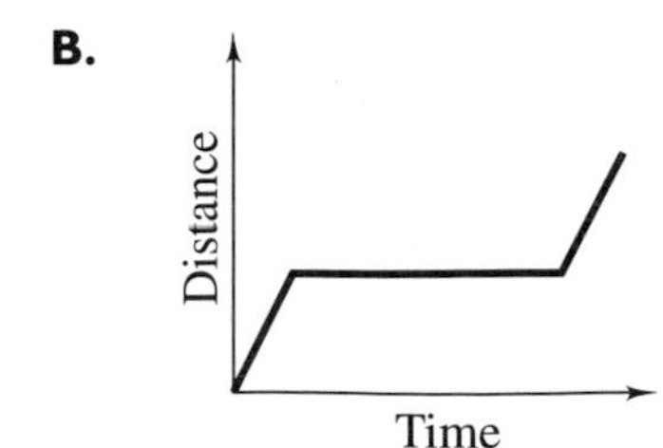

C.

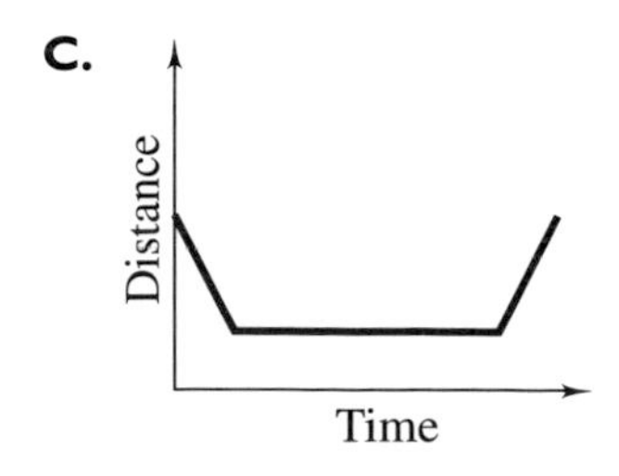

What's Ahead

- Graphing quadratic functions

6-6 Quadratic Functions

WHAT YOU'LL NEED

✓ Graph paper

THINK AND DISCUSS

Exploring Quadratic Functions A class is going to plant a rectangular garden against a wall of the school. The class has 20 ft of fencing to enclose the other three sides. How do the dimensions they choose affect the area?

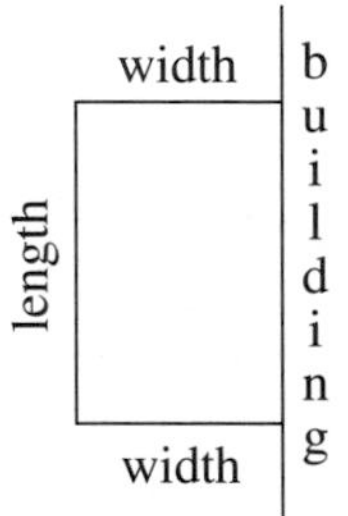

1. Let the width be 1 ft.
   a. Find the length of the garden.
   b. Find the area of the garden.
2. What is the area of the garden if the width is 2 ft? 3 ft?

Suppose the width of the rectangle is x. The length is $20 - 2x$. The area is the product $x(20 - 2x) = 20x - 2x^2$. So, you can express the area as a function. Area $= f(x) = 20x - 2x^2$

The area function is an example of a **quadratic function** because the greatest power of the variable is 2. The graph of a quadratic function is a curve.

x	$20x - 2x^2$	$(x, f(x))$
0	0	(0, 0)
1	18	(1, 18)
2	32	(2, 32)
3	42	(3, 42)
4	48	(4, 48)
5	50	(5, 50)
6	48	(6, 48)
7	42	(7, 42)
8	32	(8, 32)
9	18	(9, 18)
10	0	(10, 0)

Example 1 To see how the area changes, make a table of values. Graph the quadratic function $f(x) = 20x - 2x^2$.

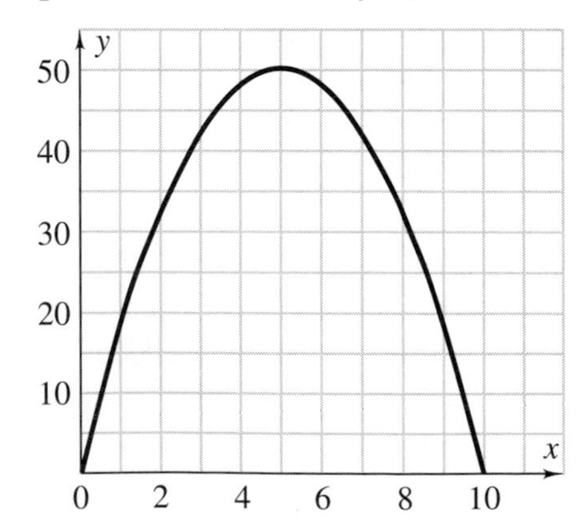

3. a. Why is it appropriate to connect the points on this graph?
   b. What value of x results in the largest garden?

Using Any Quadrant Because width and area are always positive, the graph in Example 1 included only values in the first quadrant. If a quadratic function is not restricted by a real-life situation, its graph may be in any quadrant.

Example 2 Use the integers from -3 to 3 to create a table of values for the function $f(x) = \frac{1}{2}x^2 - 1$. Use the values to draw a graph of the function.

x	$\frac{1}{2}x^2 - 1$	$(x, f(x))$
-3	$\frac{7}{2}$	$(-3, \frac{7}{2})$
-2	1	$(-2, 1)$
-1	$-\frac{1}{2}$	$(-1, -\frac{1}{2})$
0	-1	$(0, -1)$
1	$-\frac{1}{2}$	$(1, -\frac{1}{2})$
2	1	$(2, 1)$
3	$\frac{7}{2}$	$(3, \frac{7}{2})$

WORK TOGETHER

Physical Science A model rocket is launched straight up from the ground with an initial speed of 64 ft/s. The quadratic function $f(x) = 64x - 16x^2$ gives the rocket's distance above the ground in feet after x seconds.

4. **Discussion** Answer the questions with your group. Give reasons for your answers.
   a. How do you expect the graph of the function to look?
   b. What values of x are appropriate for evaluating the function?
   c. In which quadrants will the graph lie?

5. Work with a partner to create a table of values. Then graph the function. Use your table of values to help you choose a scale for the y-axis.

6. Compare your graph with those of others in your group. If the graphs differ, decide why and make any necessary corrections.

The Model Rocketry Safety Code was established in 1958 by the National Association of Rocketry. Since then more than 300 million safe launches have occurred.

Source: *Estes Flying Model Rocket Catalog*

Mixed REVIEW

The graph shows fee schedules for plumbers *A* and *B*.

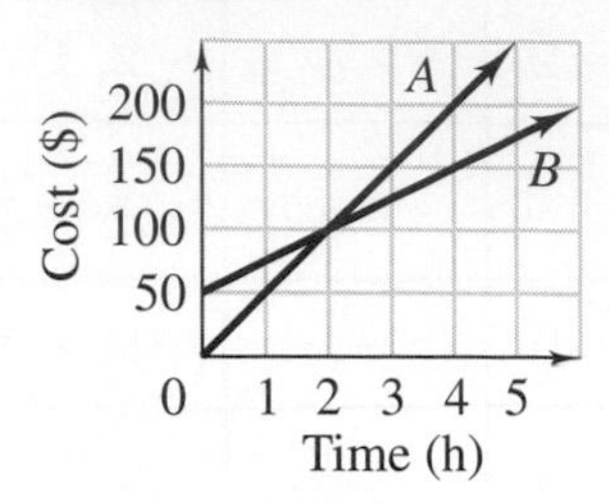

1. You call a plumber, but manage to fix the leak before the plumber arrives. What will plumber *A* charge? plumber *B*?

2. After two hours, which plumber charges a higher fee for each additional hour of work?

Graph a line passing through the origin with the given slope.

3. slope $= -2$

4. slope $= \frac{3}{2}$

TRY THESE

For each quadratic function, complete the table and then sketch the graph.

7. $f(x) = x^2 - 2$

x	$x^2 - 2$	$(x, f(x))$
-3	■	■
-2	■	■
-1	■	■
0	■	■
1	■	■
2	■	■
3	■	■

8. $f(x) = 9 - x^2$

x	$9 - x^2$	$(x, f(x))$
-1	■	■
0	■	■
1	■	■
2	■	■
3	■	■
4	■	■
5	■	■

ON YOUR OWN

9. Choose A, B, C, or D. Which is not a quadratic function?

A. $f(x) = 3x^2 + 17$ **B.** $f(x) = x^3 + x^2 + x$

C. $f(x) = 11 - 4x^2$ **D.** $f(x) = -2x^2$

Make a table of values. Graph each quadratic function.

10. $f(x) = x^2$ **11.** $f(x) = -2x^2$ **12.** $f(x) = x^2 - 4$

13. $f(x) = 5 - x^2$ **14.** $f(x) = x^2 - 2x$ **15.** $f(x) = -x - x^2$

16. Farming An agricultural department found that the number of bushels of walnuts a tree produces is a function of the number of trees planted per acre. The function rule is $f(x) = -0.01x^2 + 0.8x$.

a. Evaluate the function for 10, 20, 30, 40, 50, and 60 trees per acre. Then, graph the function.

b. Writing Write a paragraph describing how the number of trees planted per acre affects walnut production.

17. Investigation (p. 246) Write a function rule that gives the area of a pizza as a function of its diameter. Choose five diameters and make a table of values for the function. Then use the table of values to graph the function.

TECHNOLOGY

6-7 Families of Graphs

What's Ahead

- Exploring equations and their graphs
- Using computers to explore graphs

WHAT YOU'LL NEED

✓ Computer 

✓ Software 

THINK AND DISCUSS

Imagine you waited in line for hours to get concert tickets. Now you are front and center in the concert hall absorbed in every note of the performance.

The good news is that the concert will last two hours. The bad news is that with every minute that elapses, there is one less minute of music left to enjoy.

Input, x (min)	Output, $f(x)$ (min left)
0	120
10	■
20	■
60	■
90	■
100	■
120	■

1. **a.** How much time is left in the concert if the band has already played for 10 min? Explain your calculations.
   b. Copy and complete the table at the left. Why does the second column begin with 120?
   c. Write an equation that gives the function rule for the data in the table.

2. **a.** Use a graphing program or graph paper. Plot a point for each pair of values in the table.
   b. Draw a smooth curve through the points. Do the points lie on a straight line? Describe the graph.
   c. **Critical Thinking** What if you extend the graph into other quadrants? Which part of the graph would apply to the concert data?

When planning a concert, a band decides the number and title of songs to perform. In a two-hour concert, the average time allowed for each song depends on the number of songs chosen.

Input, x (number of songs)	Output, $f(x)$ (avg. length, min)
10	■
12	■
24	■
20	■
30	■
6	■
1	■

3. **a.** What would be the average time allowed for each song if the group played 10 songs during the concert? Explain your calculations.
   b. Copy and complete the table at the left.
   c. Write an equation that you could use to calculate the average time allowed for each song.

4. a. Make a conjecture about whether the points in the table will lie along a curve or a straight line.
   b. Use a graphing program or graph paper. Plot a point for each pair of values in the table.
   c. Draw a smooth curve through the points. Describe the graph. How accurate was your conjecture in part (a)?

5. a. Compare the shapes of the two graphs you drew.
   b. **Discussion** Make a conjecture about why the graphs of the equations have different shapes. Test your conjecture.

The absolute value of an integer is its distance from zero on a number line.

Different equations result in graphs of different shapes. Let's look at the graph of an equation involving absolute value.

$$y = |x - 2|$$

6. Find y for each value of x.

   a. $x = 1$ b. $x = 3$ c. $x = 0$ d. $x = -2$

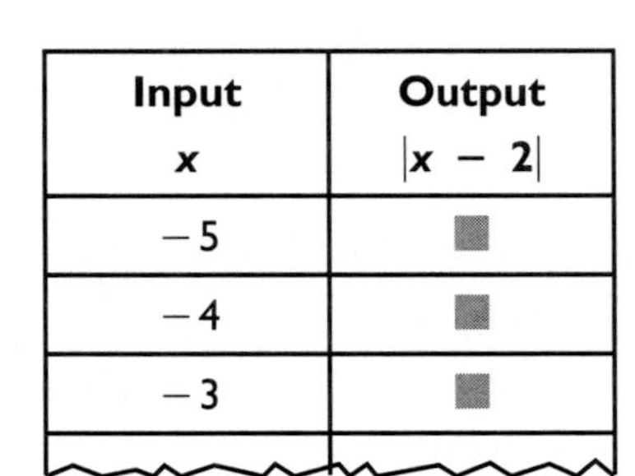

Input x	Output $\lvert x - 2\rvert$
-5	■
-4	■
-3	■

7. a. Copy and complete the table at the left for values of x from -5 through 5.
   b. Plot a point for each pair of values in the table. Connect the points.
   c. Describe the shape of the graph. How does the shape differ from the graphs of the equations you graphed earlier?
   d. Is the shape of the graph typical of other equations involving absolute value? Make tables and graph several other equations to find out.

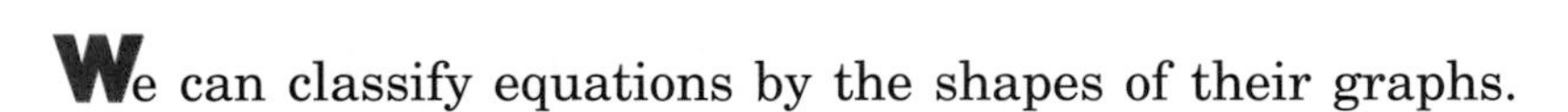

We can classify equations by the shapes of their graphs.

8. Consider the equations below.

   i. $y = \frac{3}{x}$ ii. $y = x + 3$ iii. $y = x - 3$

   iv. $y = 3 - x$ v. $y = x^2 + 3$ vi. $y = |x + 3|$

   vii. $y = -x^2$ viii. $y = |3x|$ ix. $y = \frac{3}{x} - 4$

   a. Group the equations into different "families," that is, groups of equations with similar characteristics.

b. Will all the equations in each family have similar shapes? Explain.

c. Match each family of equations with a shape at the right.

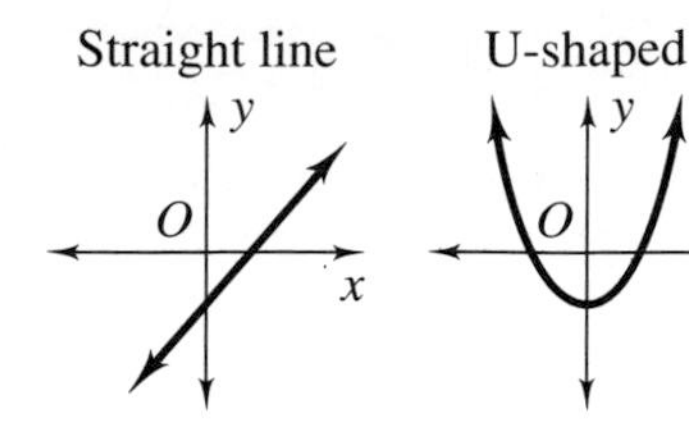

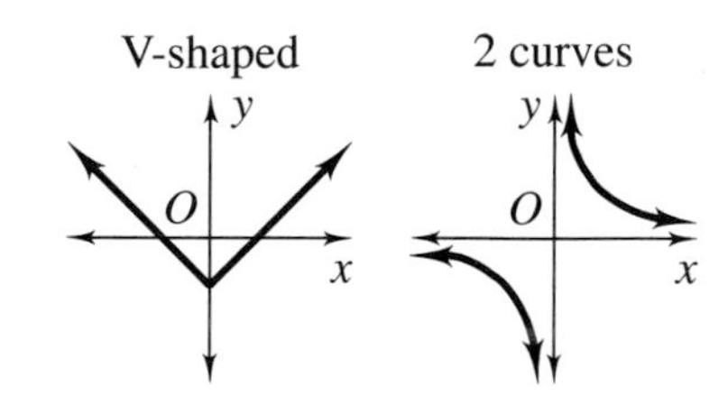

WORK TOGETHER

Choose Use a computer or graphing calculator. If you do not have access to a computer graphing program or a graphing calculator, use graph paper.

9. Work with a partner. Take turns making graphs of the equations in each family below. Keep a record of the equations and their graphs.

i. $y = \frac{1}{x}, y = \frac{1}{x} + 3, y = \frac{1}{x} - 2$

ii. $y = x, y = x + 3, y = x - 2$

iii. $y = |x|, y = |x| + 3, y = |x| - 2$

iv. $y = x^2, y = x^2 + 3, y = x^2 - 2$

a. Writing Identify the shape of each family of graphs. What characteristics affect the shape of the graph?

b. In what ways are the graphs within each family different? the same?

10. Take turns making graphs of the equations below. Keep a record of the equations and their graphs.

$$y = x^2, y = 4x^2, y = -2x^2, y = \frac{1}{3}x^2$$

a. In what ways are the graphs different? the same?

b. Describe how the graph of $y = 5x^2$ is different from the graph of $y = x^2$.

c. Describe any general relationships you find between the equations in this family and their graphs.

d. Do the relationships you found in part (c) also apply to the graphs of the equations below? Draw the graphs of these equations to find out.

$$y = |x|, y = 4|x|, y = -2|x|, y = \frac{1}{3}|x|$$

1. Choose an appropriate graph and graph the data in the table.

Favorite Sport	
soccer	9
tennis	5
hockey	6
softball	7
other	3

Graph on the same coordinate plane.

2. $y = 2x^2 - 1$
3. $y = 2x^2 + 3$

4. The sum of two positive integers is 28 and their difference is less than 6. Find all possible pairs of numbers.

ON YOUR OWN

11. An artist is creating the cover for a new CD that will feature an insert with a laser design. The insert must be a rectangle with an area of 60 mm^2.
    a. What are some possible lengths and widths of the insert?
    b. If you graphed the equation $xy = 60$, where x = length and y = width, what kind of graph do you think you would get?
    c. Find more values of x and y that fit the equation $xy = 60$. Include negative values.
    d. Plot points to see what kind of graph you get. Is it the graph you expected? Explain.
    e. **Critical Thinking** What part of the graph of $xy = 60$ does *not* have a meaning for the insert?

CHECKPOINT

Use the graph at the left below to answer Exercises 1–3.

1. In which decade was immigration as a percent of population growth the greatest? the least?
2. In which decade(s) was immigration responsible for less than 10% of the population growth in the United States?
3. Does the graph show that a greater number of immigrants came to the United States between 1981 and 1990 than between 1911 and 1920? Explain.
4. **Choose A, B, C, or D.** Which of the following is not a quadratic function?

   A. $y = 7x^2 + 5x - 2$ **B.** $y = -3 + x^2$
   C. $x^2 - 5y = 10$ **D.** $6y + 1 = x^3$

For each problem, graph the family of equations on the same coordinate plane.

5. $y = x^2; y = x^2 + 2; y = x^2 - 1$
6. $y = |x|; y = |x| + 2; y = |x| - 1$
7. $y = x; y = x + 2; y = x - 1; y = 3x$

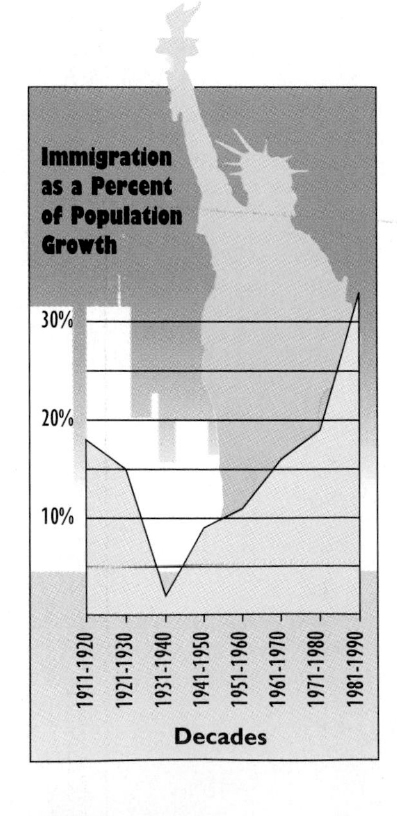

Problem Solving Practice

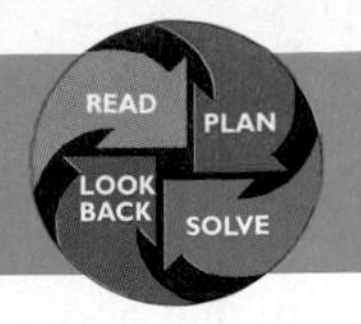

PROBLEM SOLVING STRATEGIES

Make a Table
Use Logical Reasoning
Solve a Simpler Problem
Too Much or Too Little Information
Look for a Pattern
Make a Model
Work Backward
Draw a Diagram
Guess and Test
Simulate a Problem
Use Multiple Strategies
Write an Equation
Use a Proportion

Solve. The list at the left shows some strategies you might use.

1. How many different ways can you tear three postage stamps from a sheet so that they are still attached to each other?

2. There are two types of cones, three flavors of frozen yogurt, and four kinds of toppings. How many different ways can you order a yogurt cone with topping?

3. A collection of 24 quarters and nickels is worth \$3.40. How many of the 24 coins are quarters?

4. At 60 mi/h, how far would a car travel in 2 h 40 min?

5. An eight-inch square cake serves six people. How many twelve-inch square cakes do you need to provide equivalent servings for eighteen people?

6. A rubber ball bounces exactly half as high as it did on the previous bounce. It bounces 128 in. high on the first bounce. How high does it bounce on the tenth bounce?

7. The average of a set of 4 numbers is 83. The number 92 is removed from the set. By how much will the average drop?

8. The sum of the digits of a two-digit number is 10. When the digits are reversed, the resulting number is 36 larger than the original number. Find the original number.

9. Frank and his sister Rose were each traveling from home to their aunt's house. Frank left home at noon walking at 3 mi/h. Rose left at 1:30 P.M. biking at 6 mi/h.
   a. At what time did Rose catch up with Frank?
   b. How many miles from home were they when they met?

10. A 9 ft by 12 ft floor is to be tiled using either 9-in. square tiles or 12-in. square tiles. A 9-in. square tile costs \$1.20 and a 12-in. square tile costs \$1.50. Which is the more economical choice? How much do you save by buying the more economical choice?

MATH AND PHYSICS

What's Ahead

- Graphing and applying direct and inverse variations

6-8 Direct and Inverse Variation

THINK AND DISCUSS

Two famous laws of physics describe the relationships among the volume, pressure, and temperature of gases. Charles's law states that at constant pressure, the volume of a fixed amount of gas varies directly with its temperature (in Kelvins).

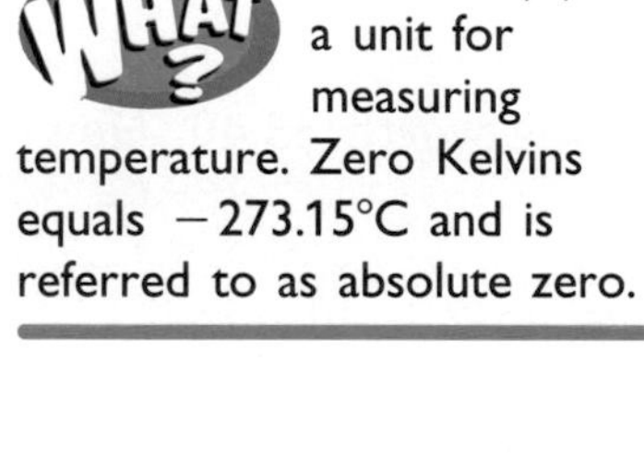

A Kelvin (K) is a unit for measuring temperature. Zero Kelvins equals $-273.15°C$ and is referred to as absolute zero.

1. How does the volume change as the temperature increases? as it decreases?
2. Draw a graph of the values. What kind of graph does this relationship represent?

Temperature (K)	Volume (cm^3)
100	50
273	136.5
300	150
500	250

Direct Variation An equation in the form $y = kx$, $k \neq 0$, is an example of **direct variation.** We call k the **constant of variation.** Direct variation means that both variables increase or both variables decrease at the same rate.

A gas has a volume of 250 mL at 300K. What is its volume if the temperature increases to 420K?

- The volume depends on the temperature.
  Let x = the temperature (in Kelvins).
  Let y = the volume.

$$y = kx \quad \text{Direct variation.}$$
$$250 = 300k \quad \text{Substitute and find } k.$$
$$\frac{250}{300} = \frac{300k}{300}$$
$$\frac{5}{6} = k$$
$$y = \frac{5}{6}x \quad \text{Rewrite the equation.}$$
$$y = \frac{5}{6}(420) \quad \text{Substitute 420 for } x.$$
$$y = 350$$

The volume of the gas at 420K is 350 mL.

When you compress the air in a tire pump, you change the volume, the pressure, and the temperature of the air in the tire.

The direct variation equation $y = kx$ is similar to the equation $y = mx + b$. The graph of a direct variation equation is a straight line with slope k that passes through the origin.

3. Draw a graph of the direct variation in Example 1.

Inverse Variation The volume of an amount of gas varies inversely with the pressure of the gas.

We represent **inverse variation** by an equation in the form $xy = k$, where $k \neq 0$. Again, we call the constant k the **constant of variation.** Inverse variation means that as one variable increases the other variable decreases.

Example 2 The volume of a gas is 50 ft^3 under 6 lb of pressure. What is its volume under 10 lb of pressure?

- The volume depends on the pressure.
  Let x = the pressure
  Let y = the volume

$$xy = k \quad \text{Inverse variation.}$$
$$6(50) = k \quad \text{Substitute and find } k.$$
$$300 = k$$
$$xy = 300 \quad \text{Rewrite the equation.}$$
$$(10)y = 300 \quad \text{Substitute 10 for } x.$$
$$\frac{10y}{10} = \frac{300}{10}$$
$$y = 30$$

The volume of the gas under 10 lb of pressure is 30 ft^3.

Other Functions We can also write the equation $xy = k$ as $y = \frac{k}{x}$, $x \neq 0$. This is a new type of function since the equation is unlike the standard linear function ($y = mx + b$) or the quadratic function where an x^2 term occurs. Its graph must have a different shape.

Example 3 Graph the inverse variation in Example 2.

- Make a table of values for the equation $y = \frac{300}{x}$.
- Graph the pairs from the table as shown at the right.

x	y
5	60
15	20
50	6
60	5

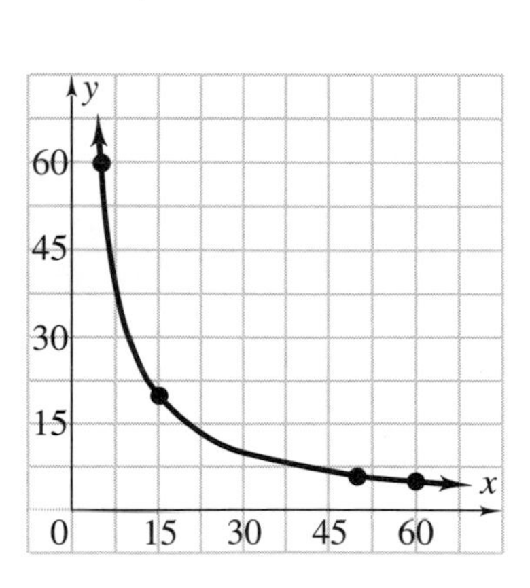

TRY THESE

State whether the data vary directly or inversely. Write an equation to describe each variation. Sketch the graph.

4.

x	y
2	5
4	10
6	15
8	20

5.

x	y
1	12
2	6
3	4
4	3

6.

x	y
-6	-3
-2	-9
-1	-18
-4	-4.5

7. A gas has a volume of 150 mL at 15°C. The temperature of the gas is increased to 20°C. What is its volume?

8. Ms. Kimura drove for 4 h at 45 mi/h. How long would it have taken to cover the same distance at 50 mi/h?

9. The circumference of a circle varies directly with the diameter. What is the constant of variation?

10. **Jobs** A job pays \$240 for 30 h. What would it pay for 40 h?

DECISION MAKING

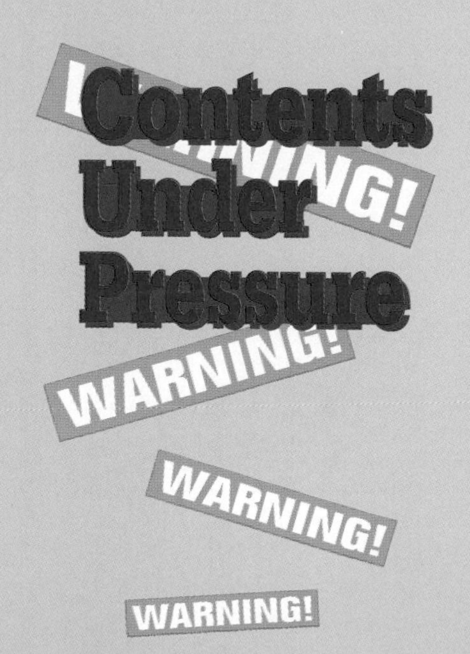

Many consumer products are packaged in pressurized cans.

COLLECT DATA

1. Find five products that are packaged under pressure. Why is it useful to have a product packaged in a pressurized can?

2. Read the warning label on each product you found. Describe in what ways the warnings are similar.

ANALYZE DATA

Use Charles's law or Boyle's law to support each answer.

3. What do you think might happen to a container that is stored above the recommended temperature?

4. When you apply pressure to a container, what happens to the contents?

ON YOUR OWN

State whether each equation is a direct or inverse variation, or neither. For each variation, state the constant of variation and sketch the graph.

11. $y = 4x$ **12.** $x + y = 6$ **13.** $xy = 6$ **14.** $\frac{y}{x} = \frac{1}{2}$

Choose Use mental math, estimation, paper and pencil, or a calculator to solve.

15. **Travel** You can make a trip in $5\frac{1}{2}$ h at 50 mi/h. How long will the trip take at 55 mi/h?

16. **Music** The frequency at which a piano string vibrates varies inversely with its length. A piano string 32 in. long vibrates at a frequency of 650 cycles/s. At what frequency does a 40-in.-long piano string vibrate?

17. **Writing** You go into an office supply store with $5.00 to buy erasers. The prices are $.10, $.20, and $.50 for erasers of different sizes. Write a problem involving direct variation and one involving inverse variation that could occur.

Mixed REVIEW

Graph each pair of equations on the same axes.

1. $y = 3x + 4$;
$y = 3x - 1$

2. $y = 4x^2 + 3$;
$y = 4x^2 - 5$

Solve each system graphically.

3. $x + 6y = -10$
$y - x = -4$

4. $2x - 5y = 13$
$x + 3y = 12$

Use the formula $d = r \cdot t$. Solve.

5. $d = 140$ km;
$r = 79$ km/h; find t.

6. $r = 50$ mi/h; $t = 3.5$ h; find d.

---

5. Why do airlines recommend that passengers not bring products in pressurized cans aboard airplanes?

6. Do you think that there is a minimum temperature under which pressurized products must be stored?

MAKE DECISIONS

Some products that are packaged under pressure contain gases that are harmful to the environment.

7. What environmental concerns arise from the use of chlorofluorocarbons in a container stored under pressure?

8. What are some alternative packaging methods that manufacturers could use?

9. What are some things you can do to promote these alternatives?

Ozone-depleting chemicals are no longer used in aerosol sprays because of their negative effect on the environment.

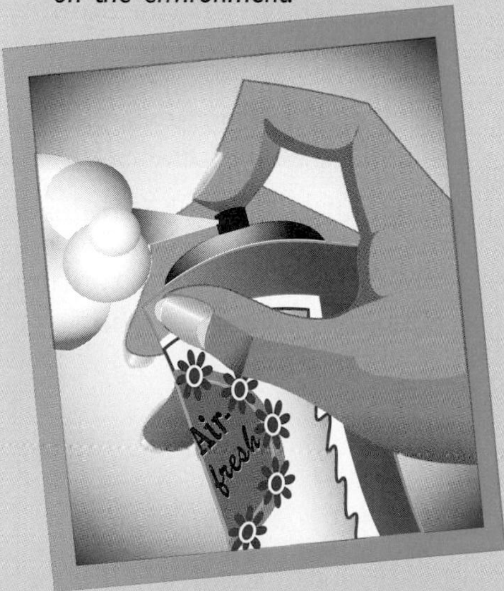

CHAPTER 6

Wrap Up

Sequences 6-1

You find each term of an ***arithmetic sequence*** by adding a fixed number, called the ***common difference,*** to the preceding term.

You find each term of a ***geometric sequence*** by multiplying the preceding term by a fixed number, called the ***common ratio.***

State whether each sequence is arithmetic, geometric, or neither. Find the next four terms.

1. 1600, 400, 100, 25, . . .
2. 14, 21, 28, 35, . . .
3. -40, -39, -37, -34, . . .

Function Rules 6-2

Function notation gives a rule $f(x)$, for expressing one variable as a function of another.

Use the function rule $f(x) = -4x^2 - 1$. Find the following.

4. $f(3)$
5. $f(0)$
6. $f(-5)$
7. $f(-1)$

Strategies and Applications 6-4

Sometimes you can solve a complicated problem by first solving a simpler problem.

8. The digits in the number 235 have a sum of 10. How many numbers between 0 and 300 have digits with a sum of 10?

Interpreting Graphs 6-5

You can use graphs to describe real-world situations.

Writing Describe a situation that could be represented by each of the following graphs.

9. 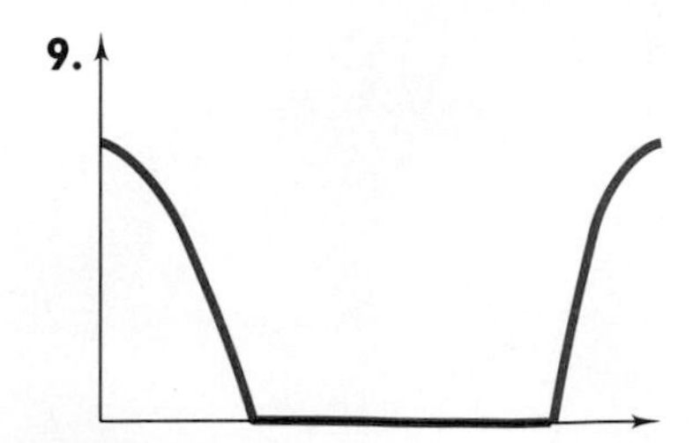

10.  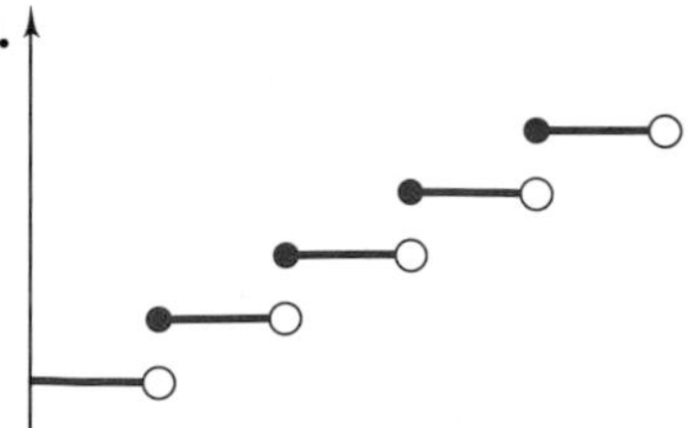

Linear Functions, Quadratic Functions 6-3, 6-6

A ***linear function*** is a function in the form $f(x) = mx + b$. Its graph lies on a straight line.

A ***quadratic function*** is a function in which the highest power of the variable is 2. Its graph is a curve.

Make a table of values. Then graph each function.

11. $f(x) = 2x - 4$ **12.** $f(x) = -\frac{1}{2}x + 1$ **13.** $f(x) = x^2 - 3$ **14.** $y = -x^2 + 2$

Families of Graphs 6-7

Functions can be classified by the shape of their graphs. Some shapes you have studied are lines, V-shaped graphs, U-shaped graphs, and graphs with two curves.

Graph each function.

15. $y = 3x + 5$ **16.** $y = x^2 - 4$ **17.** $y = |x|$ **18.** $y = \frac{1}{x}$

19. $y = |x| - 1$ **20.** $y = -|x|$ **21.** $y = \frac{2}{x}$ **22.** $y = |x + 2|$

Direct and Inverse Variation 6-8

Direct variation is a relationship described by an equation of the form $y = kx$, where $k \neq 0$. We say that y varies directly as x.

Inverse variation is a relationship described by an equation of the form $xy = k$, where $k \neq 0$. We say that y varies inversely as x.

In each case, k is called the ***constant of variation.***

23. Choose A, B, C, or D. Which of these equations does *not* describe a direct variation?

A. $y = -5x$ **B.** $xy = 8$ **C.** $\frac{x}{14} = y$ **D.** $\frac{x}{y} = 6$

24. If y varies directly as x and $y = 16$ when $x = 0.25$, find the value of y when $x = 1$.

GETTING READY FOR CHAPTER 7

Use a calculator to simplify.

1. $2 \cdot 2 \cdot 3 \cdot 3 \cdot 3 \cdot 5$ **2.** $7^2 \cdot 5^3 \cdot 6 \cdot 2^4$ **3.** $10^5 \cdot 2^3 \cdot 3^2$

4. Express the ratio 1 to 4 as a fraction, a decimal, and a percent.

PUTTING IT ALL TOGETHER

How Much For a Pizza?

At the beginning of the chapter you decided on prices for the two new pizzas on Mr. Zorella's menu. Now reconsider your decision based on your study of the chapter. Write your final report for Mr. Zorella. Explain the reasons behind your recommendation. The following are suggestions to help you support your proposal.

- ✔ Use patterns.
- ✔ Draw a graph.
- ✔ Use functions.

The problems preceded by the magnifying glass (p. 253, # 28; p. 260, # 24; and p. 268, # 17) will help you complete the investigation.

Excursion: Companies often charge less for items if you buy in large quantities. One ballpoint pen might sell for 59¢, but the price might drop to 49¢ if you buy 100 pens, and 39¢ if you buy 500. This type of pricing encourages customers to buy large quantities. Give examples of products that might cost **more** per unit if you purchase large quantities of them.

THE GAME OF SEQUENCES

Rules:

- Play with three or more people.
- One person, "the sequencer," secretly chooses a rule for generating a sequence. The rule may be as simple or complex as the sequencer desires. The sequencer writes the first two terms of the sequence for all players to see.
- Players proceed in turn to guess the next term of the sequence. The sequencer says "Yes" or "No" to indicate whether a guess is correct or not. When a correct guess is made, the new term is added to the sequence.
- A player scores a point for making a correct guess. The first player to score five points wins.
- The winner is the sequencer in the next game.

WHAT'S THE MEANING OF THIS?

"Success is a function of hard work."

This motto illustrates that the word *function* has a verbal as well as a mathematical meaning. Notice that the two uses are related. According to the motto, success depends on hard work, just as the value of $f(x)$ *depends* on the value of x.

Try this with your group.

- Make a list of words that have mathematical as well as verbal meanings.
- For each word discuss the connection between the two meanings.

CALCULATOR CONSTANT CHALLENGE

With the *constant* function of your calculator, you can generate sequences of numbers. Challenge yourself to solve a problem with the help of the constant function on your calculator. Which term in the sequence 5676, 6553, 7430,..., contains three 4's in a row?

The sequence is an arithmetic sequence with a difference of 877. To solve the problem, program your calculator to add 877 constantly, beginning with the addend 5676. Then press [=] until you reach a term with three 4's in a row.

Write other problems that can be solved by using the constant function on a calculator.

Conduct a survey to determine the average number of hours that the people in your survey sleep each night. Record the age of each person. Graph your data. Discuss the following in a presentation to your class:

- ***Is the amount of time that a person sleeps a function of the person's age?***
- ***What would you predict to be the number of hours a person of a different age would sleep?***

***Excursion:** Conduct research to find the amount of time that animals sleep. Which animals sleep about as long as humans?*

Assessment

1. Tell whether each situation produces an arithmetic or a geometric sequence. State the common difference or ratio.
   a. A car loses 15% of its original price each year.
   b. A clock loses 30 s/h.
   c. The number of bacteria in a pond triples each day.

2. Write the next four terms in the sequence with a common ratio of $\frac{4}{5}$ and the first term of 125.

3. The sixth term of a sequence is $-\frac{1}{2}$ and the common difference is $-2\frac{1}{2}$. Find the first five terms.

4. If $f(x) = -x^2 - 3x$, find each.
   a. $f(-6)$ b. $f(3.5)$ c. $f\left(-\frac{2}{3}\right)$

5. Make a table to display the taxi fare described by $f(x) = 2.40x + 3$. The dollar fare is $f(x)$ and the distance in miles is x.

6. State whether each equation represents direct or inverse variation. For each inverse variation, state the constant of variation.
   a. $xy = 26$ b. $y = 7x$
   c. $6.5x = y$ d. $x = \frac{6}{y}$

7. Graph each pair of functions on the same coordinate plane.
   a. $f(x) = x^2$, $f(x) = 3x^2$
   b. $f(x) = x^2 + 1$, $f(x) = 3x^2 - 4$

8. Twenty points are placed around a circle. How many segments are needed to join each point to every other point?

9. Match each equation with its graph.
   a. $y = -x - 1$ b. $y = x^2 + 1$
   c. $y = x - 1$ d. $y = |x - 4|$

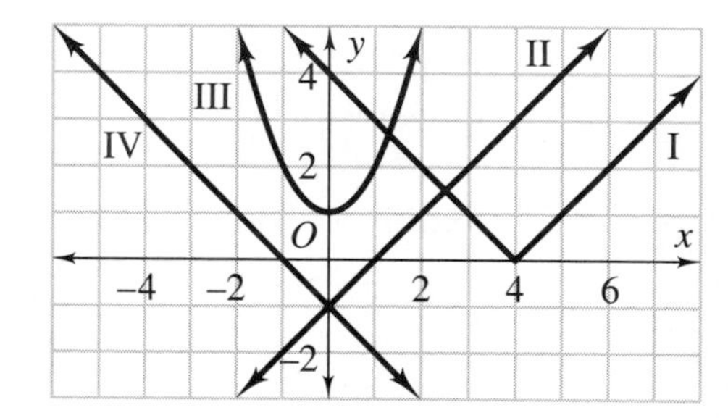

10. **Choose A, B, C, or D.** Which could *not* be a value of $f(x)$ if $f(x) = |x - 2|$?
    A. 43 B. 27 C. -2 D. 108

11. **Writing** The graph shows the afternoon route of a school bus. Write a story describing its trip.

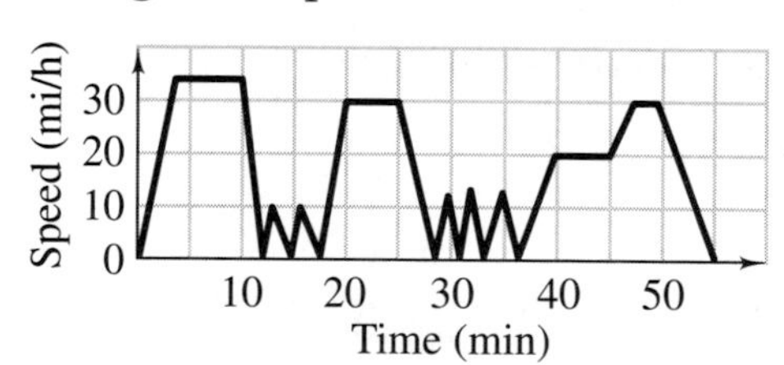

12. In a circuit, the voltage varies directly with the current. When the voltage is 60 volts, the current is 12 amps. Find the voltage when the current is 15 amps.

13. **Writing** Describe four different families of graphs. Give specific examples of each.

CHAPTER 6

Cumulative Review

Choose A, B, C, or D.

1. You have a set of data with five data items. The median is 14, the mean is 14.8, the mode is 14, and the range is 4. Which could be the correct data?

   A. 14, 14, 14, 16, 18
   B. 12, 14, 14, 15, 20
   C. 13, 14, 14, 16, 17
   D. 12, 13, 14, 16, 16

2. Which variable expression is *not* equivalent to $2(x - 3)$?

   A. $2(x) - 2(3)$ **B.** $2(-3) + 2x$
   C. $(x - 3) + (x - 3)$ **D.** $2x - 3$

3. Describe the relationship in the scatter plot at the right.

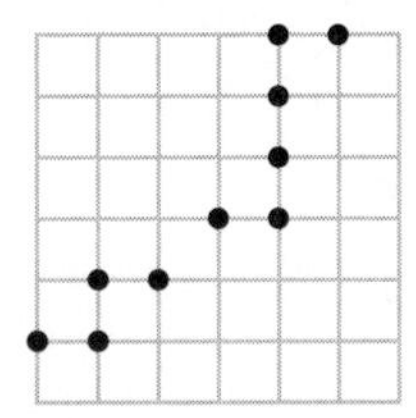

   A. no correlation
   B. positive correlation
   C. negative correlation
   D. positive and negative correlation

4. Which could *not* be a value of $f(x)$ if $f(x) = 2x^2 - 3$?

   A. 5 **B.** -3 **C.** 15 **D.** -5

5. If y varies directly as x, and $y = 15$ when $x = 3$, what is the value of y when $x = -8$?

   A. -40 **B.** 5 **C.** $\frac{1}{5}$ **D.** 3

6. Which inequality is represented by the graph below?

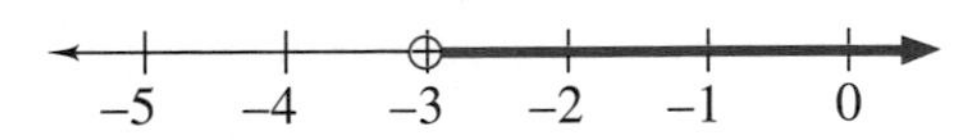

   A. $\frac{x}{-3} < 1$ **B.** $6z > 18$
   C. $2 + y \leq -1$ **D.** $5 - 2w \geq 1$

7. What is the range of the data given in the stem-and-leaf plot?

3	1 2 2 2
4	3 4 5 5 9
5	0 0 2 3 6 8

3|1 means 31

   A. 58 **B.** 49 **C.** 27 **D.** 32

8. The data given in the stem-and-leaf plot above could most likely represent

   A. record high temperatures in the desert.
   B. heights of professional basketball players.
   C. numbers of hours spent exercising in one day.
   D. numbers of minutes students spend studying for a test.

9. The perimeter of a rectangular garden is 32 ft. The width is 7 ft. What is the length?

   A. 25 ft **B.** 9 ft **C.** 13 ft **D.** 18 ft

10. What is the eighth term in the sequence 4, 12, 36, 108, . . . ?

   A. 8,748 **B.** 216 **C.** 2,916 **D.** 324

CHAPTER 7 Rational Numbers

Data File 7

In 1971, the 26th amendment of the U. S. Constitution granted every person 18 years or older the right to vote.

The 1972 election was the first presidential election in which 18, 19, and 20 year olds were allowed to vote. Nearly 50% of all 18–24 year olds voted. In the 1992 presidential election about 43% of 18-24 year olds voted.

1992 Presidential Election

Results of the Popular Vote

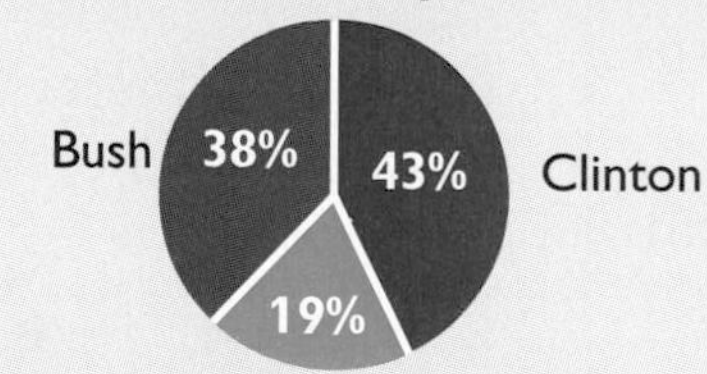

Results of the Electoral Vote

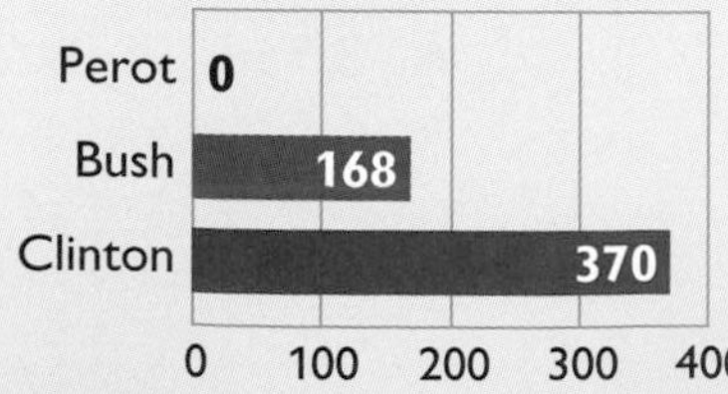

Source: *USA Today*

WHAT YOU WILL LEARN

- how to solve problems involving rational numbers
- how to use technology to explore irrational numbers
- how to solve problems by working backwards

In 1895, Australia granted women the right to vote. Switzerland did not grant women the right to vote until 1971.

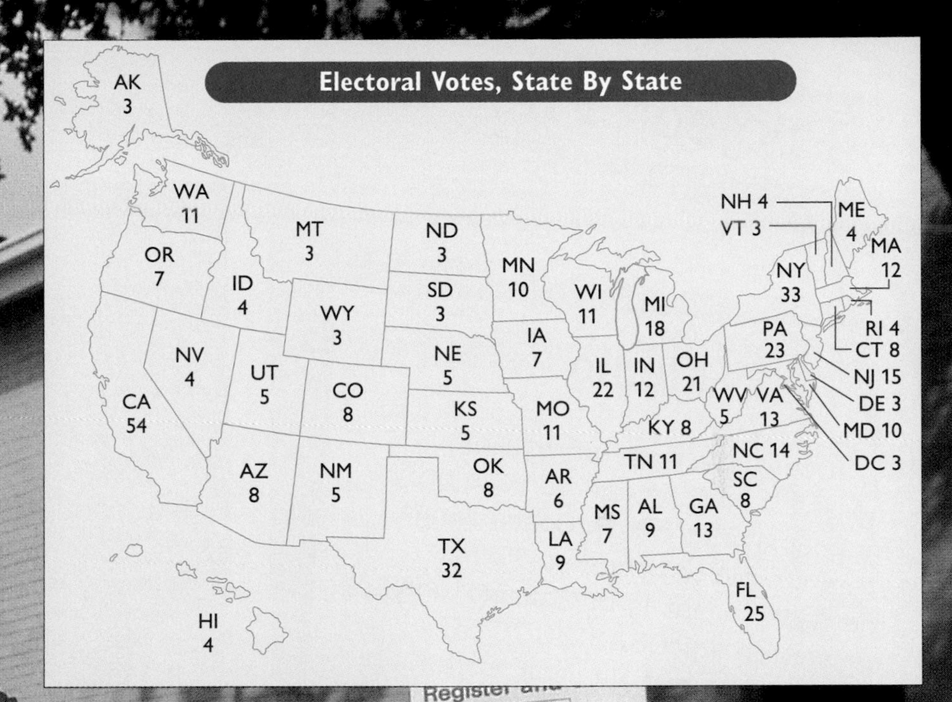

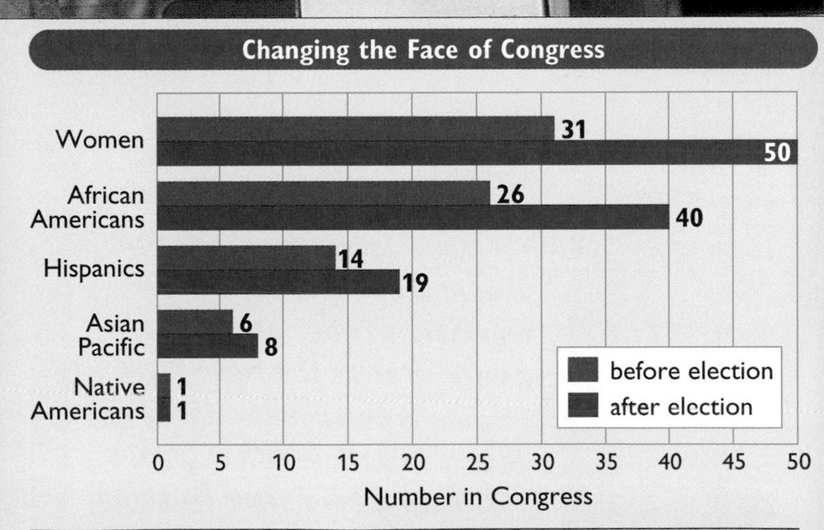

investigation

Project File

Memo

Codes are ways of writing messages so they can be read only by people with a key. Codes range from simple to complex. The message "agent is in Chicago" may be written as "OGACIHC NI SI TNEGA" in a simple code. Computer codes are very complex. Computers can handle billions of arrangements of letters. During World War II the U.S. military used the Navajo Indian language to transmit secret messages. The Japanese were never able to break the code.

Mission: Create a code for transmitting messages. Your code should be simple enough for members of your group to use easily. But at the same time, it should be complex enough that members of other groups will have a hard time breaking your code.

Leads to Follow

✓ What codes are you familiar with? How do they work?

✓ How can you determine whether your code is too easy or too hard?

✓ How can you use mathematics to create a code?

What's Ahead

- Determining the prime factorization of numbers
- Using prime factorization to determine the GCF

WHAT YOU'LL NEED

✓ Graph paper 

7-1 Prime Factorization

THINK AND DISCUSS

Factors This figure shows all the rectangles you can make with 12 squares.

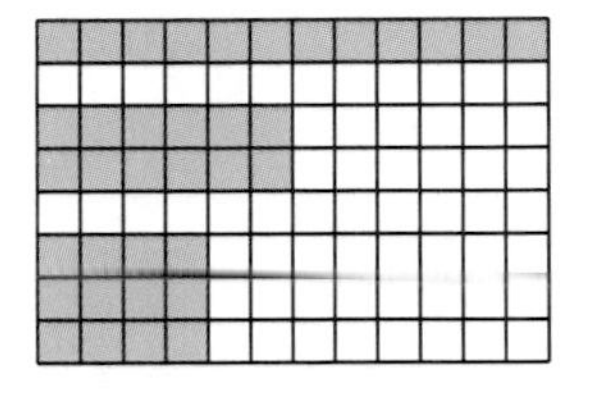

1 by 12 2 by 6 3 by 4

The figure shows that the numbers 1, 2, 3, 4, 6, and 12 are all the *factors* of 12.

One number is a **factor** of a second number if it divides that number with no remainder. You say that the second number is **divisible** by the first.

1. a. Draw all the rectangles you can make with 36 squares.
   b. List all the factors of 36.
   c. Is 36 divisible by 4? Is 36 divisible by 5? Explain.

WHAT ? New York City has a parade policy that any group, no matter how large or small, has a right to a permit to march down the city's streets. In 1990, the city hosted 765 parades, only 110 of which drew crowds of over 1,000 people.

Source: *The New York Times*

You can apply factors to many everyday situations. For instance, suppose your club is sponsoring a parade. A band with 42 members is marching behind a band with 72 members. You must arrange the bands so each marches in the same number of columns. Begin by finding the factors of 42 and 72.

factors of 42: 1, 2, 3, 6, 7, 14, 21, 42

factors of 72: 1, 2, 3, 4, 6, 8, 9, 12, 18, 24, 36, 72

The rings around 1, 2, 3, and 6 indicate that these factors are the same for both numbers. You call these the **common factors** of 42 and 72. Using the common factors, you know that you can arrange each band into 1, 2, 3, or 6 columns.

The greatest factor common to both numbers is 6. So, 6 is the **greatest common factor (GCF)** of 42 and 72. Using the GCF, you know that the greatest number of columns you can have is 6.

2. What is the greatest number of columns you can have if a band of 36 members is marching behind a band of 64?

3. **Discussion** Describe a different everyday use of factors.

Primes and Composites

Primes and Composites Here are all the rectangles you can make with 11 squares. Only one rectangle measures 1 by 11. So, the only factors of 11 are 1 and 11. Therefore, 11 is a *prime number.*

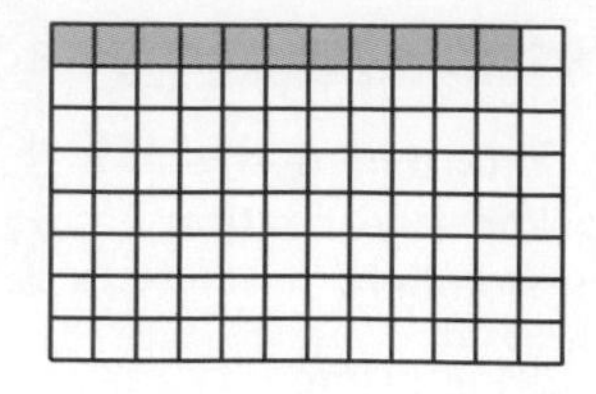

A **prime number** is a whole number greater than 1 with exactly two factors, 1 and itself. A whole number greater than 1 with more than two factors is a **composite number.**

Divisibility Rules

A number is divisible by 2 if the ones' digit is 0, 2, 4, 6, or 8.

A number is divisible by 5 if the ones' digit is 0 or 5.

A number is divisible by 10 if the ones' digit is 0.

A number is divisible by 3 if the sum of the digits is divisible by 3.

A number is divisible by 9 if the sum of the digits is divisible by 9.

Example 1 Tell whether 551 is prime or composite.

- Check the prime numbers, beginning with 2, to determine whether any is a factor of 551.

2: no   3: no   5: no   ← **Use divisibility rules or a calculator.**

7: no   11: no   13: no

17: no   19: $551 \div 19 = 29$

$551 = 19 \cdot 29$, so 551 is composite.

4. Explain why you check only prime numbers as factors.

5. a. Use the method of Example 1 to show that 179 is prime.

b. Discussion What was the greatest prime number that you had to check as a factor? Explain.

Prime Factorization

Prime Factorization Writing any composite number as a product of prime numbers is the **prime factorization** of the number. Use a **factor tree** to find the prime factorization.

Example 2 Find the prime factorization of 315.

Follow these steps.

The ones' digit is 5, so 315 is divisible by 5.

1. Write the number as the product of two factors.
2. Repeat Step 1 with any remaining composite factors.
3. Stop when all factors are prime.
4. Write the prime factorization.

$315 = 3 \cdot 3 \cdot 5 \cdot 7 = 3^2 \cdot 5 \cdot 7$

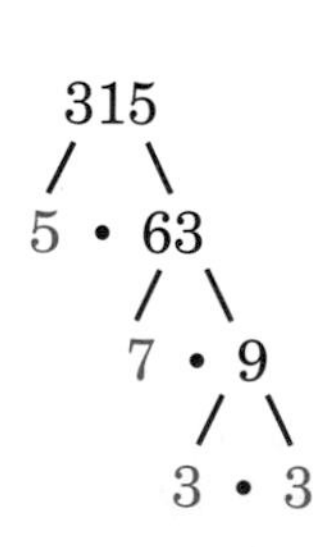

6. a. Make a different factor tree for 315.

b. Discussion Did you find a different prime factorization for 315? Explain.

You can use prime factorizations to find a GCF.

Example 3 Find the GCF of 60, 72, and 156.

- Find the prime factorization of each number. Underline the common prime factors.

$$60 = \underline{2}^2 \cdot \underline{3} \cdot 5$$
$$72 = \underline{2}^3 \cdot \underline{3}^2$$
$$156 = \underline{2}^2 \cdot \underline{3} \cdot 13$$

- Multiply the least powers of each underlined factor.

$$2^2 \cdot 3 = 12$$

The GCF is 12. You write GCF(60, 72, 156) = 12.

> *Among the integers, the prime numbers play a role that is analogous to the elements of chemistry.*
> —*The Mathematical Experience*

TRY THESE

List all the factors of each number.

7. 30 **8.** 31 **9.** 55 **10.** 64 **11.** 1

12. List all the whole numbers from 100 to 110. Identify each number in the list as *prime* or *composite.*

13. a. Write the prime factorization of 54, of 90, and of 108.

b. Use the prime factorizations to find GCF(54, 90, 108).

14. Three pieces of timber have lengths 63 ft, 84 ft, and 105 ft. A sawmill operator needs to cut the timber into logs of equal length. What is the greatest possible length of the logs?

15. Discussion What is the GCF of any set of prime numbers?

In 1992, scientists in England using a Cray-2 supercomputer discovered the greatest known prime number in only 19 h. The number has 227,832 digits. This is three times as many as the previously recorded prime. It had 65,087 digits and required a supercomputer working on and off for over a year to find.

Source: *Science News*

ON YOUR OWN

Tell whether the first number is a factor of the second.

16. 1; 65 **17.** 9; 345 **18.** 6; 2,058 **19.** 17; 1,615

20. Name a number other than 1 that has an odd number of factors.

21. Critical Thinking The numbers 4, 12, and 24 are all factors of a number n. List three other factors of n.

22. a. Copy and complete the factor tree at the right.

b. Write the prime factorization of the number.

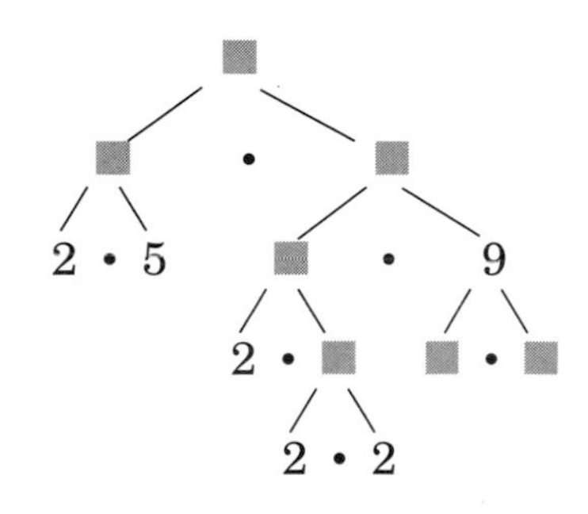

Mixed REVIEW

Use mental math to find each answer.

1. 6($4.95) + 6($2.05)
2. 4(19 • 25)

Determine whether each equation is a direct or inverse variation. State the constant of variation.

3. $n = 22m$
4. $ab = 63$

5. Sally bought a rug for $76 during a 20% off sale. What was the original price of the rug?

Tell whether each number is *prime* or *composite*.

23. 21 **24.** 23 **25.** 93 **26.** 471 **27.** 391

28. Writing Write a paragraph explaining why the numbers 0 and 1 are neither prime nor composite.

29. In 1742, the mathematician Christian Goldbach made a conjecture that every even number can be expressed as the sum of two odd prime numbers. Do you think this is true? Try to write each of the following numbers as the sum of two odd prime numbers.

a. 6 **b.** 16 **c.** 24 **d.** 32 **e.** 60

Write the prime factorization of each number.

30. 48 **31.** 150 **32.** 225 **33.** 186 **34.** 621

35. Find a number between 50 and 100 that has exactly two prime factors.

36. Mr. Sheng's eighth-grade class harvested 152 tomatoes and 114 cucumbers from their garden. The cucumbers and tomatoes were divided equally among the students. What is the greatest number of students there can be in the class?

Find the GCF of each set of numbers.

37. 20, 125 **38.** 84, 136 **39.** 28, 56, 70 **40.** 72, 126, 175

41. Choose A, B, C, or D. Which set of statements is true when $n = 98$?

A. $n > 28$ and GCF(n, 28) $= 7$
B. $n > 63$ and GCF(n, 63) $= 7$
C. $n < 70$ and GCF(n, 70) $= 7$
D. $n < 72$ and GCF(n, 72) $= 2$

42. Ms. Cabrera has the art supplies listed at the left. She wants to give the supplies to as many classes as possible. Each class must receive an equal number of each supply.

a. What is the greatest number of classes that can get supplies?
b. How many of each item will each class receive?

What's Ahead

- Studying the meaning of rational numbers
- Expressing a rational number as a fraction written in simplest form

7-2 Rational Numbers

The world's largest thermometer, *which measures 134 ft, stands outside a restaurant in Baker, California. It cost $750,000 to build in 1992 and its height is a reminder of the highest temperature ever recorded in North America at nearby Death Valley: 134°F on July 10, 1913.*

Source: *Sunset*

THINK AND DISCUSS

Identifying Rational Numbers Numbers that you use everyday, like 33, $\frac{1}{2}$, 2.73, and integers on a thermometer are examples of *rational numbers.* A **rational number** is any number you can write in the form $\frac{a}{b}$, where a is any integer and b is any nonzero integer. Below, all are rational numbers.

proper fractions:	$\frac{2}{5}, -\frac{1}{2}$
improper fractions:	$\frac{9}{4}, -\frac{24}{5}$
mixed numbers:	$3\frac{1}{2} = \frac{7}{2}, -2\frac{4}{7} = -\frac{18}{7}$
integers:	$33 = \frac{33}{1}, -450 = -\frac{450}{1}, 0 = \frac{0}{1}$
some decimals:	$0.6 = \frac{3}{5}, -3.875 = -3\frac{7}{8} = -\frac{31}{8}, 0.\overline{3} = \frac{1}{3}$

You can express any rational number as a set of equal fractions.

$$\frac{2}{5} = \frac{4}{10} = \frac{6}{15} = \cdots \quad \text{and} \quad \frac{2}{5} = \frac{-2}{-5} = \frac{-4}{-10} = \frac{-6}{-15} = \cdots$$

You can write negative rational numbers in three ways. For example,

$$-\frac{1}{2} = \frac{-1}{2} = \frac{1}{-2}.$$

1. a. Explain why -2.1 is a rational number.
   b. Write five fractions equal to -2.1.
2. In the expression $\frac{a}{b}$, why can b not equal 0?

You can graph rational numbers on a number line.

Example 1 Graph $-1\frac{3}{8}$, -0.5, $\frac{1}{4}$, and 1.125 on a number line.

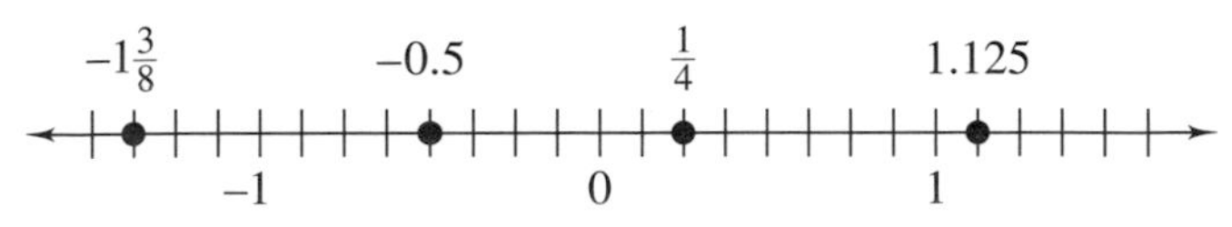

3. Where would you place $1\frac{1}{2}$ and -1.25 on the number line?

You can use a number line to find the absolute value and the opposite of a rational number.

The *absolute value* of a number is its distance from zero on a number line.

Opposites are two numbers that are the same distance from zero on a number line, but in opposite directions.

Example 2 Find the absolute value and the opposite of $-\frac{5}{6}$.

Locate $-\frac{5}{6}$ on a number line.

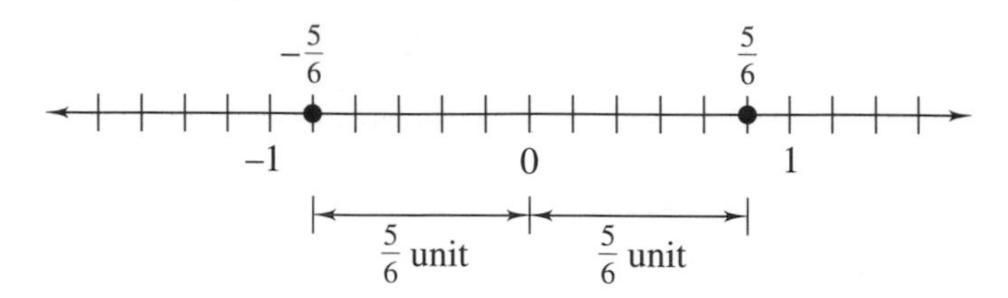

$-\frac{5}{6}$ is $\frac{5}{6}$ unit to the left of zero, so its absolute value is $\frac{5}{6}$.

The number that is $\frac{5}{6}$ unit to the *right* of zero is $\frac{5}{6}$, so the opposite of $-\frac{5}{6}$ is $\frac{5}{6}$.

The symbol for absolute value is $| \; |$.

$$\left|-\frac{5}{6}\right| = \frac{5}{6}$$

4. Find the absolute value and the opposite of $2\frac{3}{4}$.

Writing Simplest Form Usually a fraction is written in *simplest form.* A fraction is in **simplest form** when the GCF of the numerator and denominator is 1.

Example 3 Write $\frac{54}{72}$ in simplest form.

Method 1

Find the GCF of 54 and 72.

$$\begin{aligned} 54 &= 2 \cdot 3^3 \\ 72 &= 2^3 \cdot 3^2 \end{aligned} \quad \rightarrow \quad \text{GCF} = 2 \cdot 3^2 = 18$$

Divide the numerator and denominator by the GCF.

$$\frac{54}{72} = \frac{54 \div 18}{72 \div 18} = \frac{3}{4}$$

Method 2

Write the prime factorization of 54 and 72. Divide by all the common prime factors.

$$\frac{54}{72} = \frac{\overset{1}{\cancel{2}} \cdot \overset{1}{\cancel{3}} \cdot \overset{1}{\cancel{3}} \cdot 3}{\underset{1}{\cancel{2}} \cdot 2 \cdot 2 \cdot \underset{1}{\cancel{3}} \cdot \underset{1}{\cancel{3}}} = \frac{3}{2 \cdot 2} = \frac{3}{4}$$

5. a. Explain why $-\frac{27}{45}$ is not in simplest form.

b. What is the simplest form of $-\frac{27}{45}$?

TRY THESE

Write a rational number for each situation.

6. Zakiya received two fifths of the votes.
7. The divers located the shipwreck 20.5 m below sea level.
8. The temperature fell to twelve degrees Celsius below zero.
9. The price of the stock rose two and three-fourths points.

Jay Browning, a 13-year-old from Palatka, Florida, has been helping his father's company excavate the wreck of a Spanish sailing ship sunk for over 500 y in 20 ft of water off the Bahamas. Jay has made about 50 dives, spending around 4 h on each. The team has recovered over 5,000 artifacts, including the helmet of a conquistador.

Source: *National Geographic World*

Write the absolute value and the opposite of each rational number.

10. $-2\frac{1}{2}$ 11. 6.2 12. $\frac{1}{6}$ 13. $\frac{-4}{5}$ 14. 0

Write each rational number in simplest form.

15. $-\frac{45}{54}$ 16. $\frac{62}{8}$ 17. $\frac{-6}{40}$ 18. $\frac{36}{-108}$ 19. $\frac{320}{480}$

20. Graph 1.25, $\frac{5}{8}$, -2, $\frac{1}{4}$, -0.625, and $-1\frac{1}{2}$ on a number line.

ON YOUR OWN

Write each number in the form $\frac{a}{b}$, where a is any integer and b is any nonzero integer.

21. -8 22. 0.93 23. -2.7 24. $6\frac{1}{3}$ 25. 0

Write three fractions equal to each rational number.

26. $3\frac{1}{2}$ 27. -0.75 28. $-\frac{25}{2}$ 29. 1.1 30. 0

31. **Estimation** Estimate the rational number represented by each point on this number line.

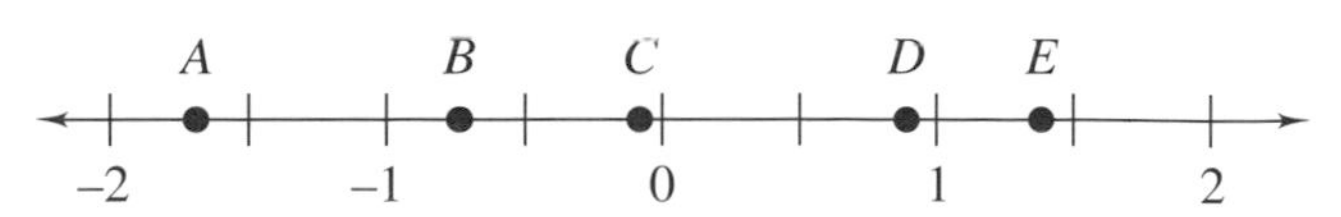

Extra SKILLS PRACTICE

Write the absolute value and opposite of each.

1. -0.57
2. $\frac{4}{5}$
3. 2.14

Write in simplest form.

4. $\frac{48}{64}$ 5. $\frac{-56}{80}$
6. $\frac{93}{9}$ 7. $\frac{-120}{252}$
8. $\frac{340}{50}$ 9. $\frac{425}{-250}$

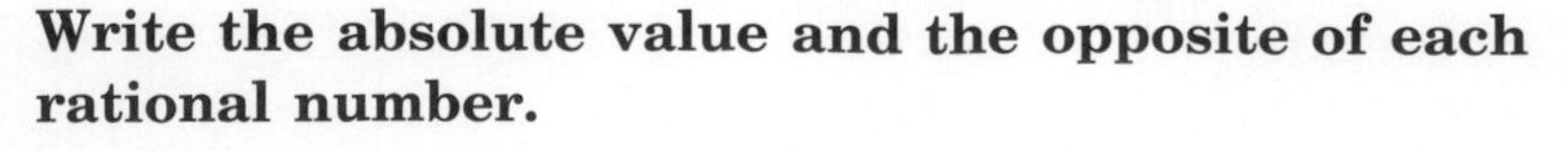

Write the absolute value and the opposite of each rational number.

32. $-\frac{2}{3}$ **33.** $1\frac{2}{3}$ **34.** $\frac{-54}{7}$ **35.** -5.07 **36.** $\frac{9}{10}$

37. Critical Thinking Each of these statements is *sometimes* true. For each statement, give an example to show when it is true and when it is false.

a. $\left|\frac{a}{b}\right| = \frac{a}{b}$ **b.** $\left|\frac{a}{b}\right| > \frac{a}{b}$

38. Writing When is the opposite of a rational number equal to its absolute value? When are they not equal? Explain.

Choose Use a calulator, paper and pencil, or mental math to write each rational number in simplest form.

39. $\frac{55}{88}$ **40.** $\frac{-72}{96}$ **41.** $-\frac{54}{12}$ **42.** $\frac{14}{98}$ **43.** $\frac{24}{-60}$

44. Choose A, B, C, D, or E. Which is *not* equal to $\frac{-15}{12}$?

A. -1.25 **B.** $-1\frac{1}{4}$ **C.** $\frac{-45}{-36}$ **D.** $\frac{60}{-48}$ **E.** $-1\frac{6}{24}$

45. a. Graph 2.8, $\frac{4}{5}$, -1, $1\frac{1}{5}$, and 0 on a number line.

b. Graph the opposite of each number on the same number line.

Identify each number using as many names as apply. Choose from *natural number, whole number, integer,* and *rational number.*

46. -24 **47.** 1.2 **48.** $\frac{-4}{7}$ **49.** 0 **50.** $5\frac{1}{2}$

Replace each ■ with *All, Some,* or *No* to make a true statement.

51. ■ integers are rational numbers.

52. ■ rational numbers are integers.

53. ■ rational numbers have an opposite that is negative.

54. ■ rational numbers have a negative absolute value.

Mixed REVIEW

Solve.

1. $2x + 13 = -5$
2. $4 = -7x - 38$

Write the prime factorization in exponential form.

3. 96 4. 130
5. 576 6. 1008

7. Construct an equilateral triangle.

FLASHBACK

The *natural numbers* are 1, 2, 3, 4, 5, . . .

The *whole numbers* are 0, 1, 2, 3, 4, 5, . . .

The *integers* are . . . , −2, −1, 0, 1, 2, . . .

What's Ahead

- Writing fractions as decimals
- Writing decimals as fractions

WHAT YOU'LL NEED

✓ Calculator 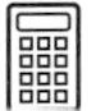

7-3 Fractions and Decimals

THINK AND DISCUSS

Writing Decimals Sometimes, you need to write a fraction as a decimal. In baseball, a batting average represents the fraction of times at bat that a player makes a hit. It is customary to give the player's batting average as a decimal.

Example 1 Celia made 3 hits in 8 times at bat, giving her a batting average of $\frac{3}{8}$. Write her average as a decimal.

Divide the numerator by the denominator.

Use paper and pencil, as shown at the right, or enter this key sequence on a calculator.

3 ÷ 8 = 0.375

$$\begin{array}{r} 0.375 \\ 8\overline{)3.000} \\ \underline{24} \\ 60 \\ \underline{56} \\ 40 \\ \underline{40} \\ 0 \end{array}$$

Celia's batting average is 0.375.

1. Write each fraction as a decimal: **a.** $\frac{1}{4}$ **b.** $-\frac{5}{16}$ **c.** $\frac{7}{2}$

Any fraction can be written as a decimal by dividing the numerator by the denominator. If the division ends with a remainder of zero, the decimal is called a **terminating decimal.** Otherwise, the division produces a repeating pattern of nonzero remainders, and the decimal is called a **repeating decimal.**

Example 2 Write $\frac{4}{11}$ as a decimal.

Use a calculator or paper and pencil to find 4 ÷ 11.

4 ÷ 11 = 0.36363636

$$\begin{array}{r} 0.3636... \\ 11\overline{)4.0000...} \\ \underline{33} \\ 70 \\ \underline{66} \\ 40 \\ \underline{33} \\ 70 \\ \underline{66} \\ 4 \end{array}$$

With either method, the quotient suggests that "36" repeats without end. Write a bar over these digits.

$$\frac{4}{11} = 0.3636363636363636\ldots$$

$$\frac{4}{11} = 0.\overline{36}$$

In 1941, Joe DiMaggio had a 56-game hitting streak in which he collected 56 singles, 16 doubles, 4 triples, 15 home runs, and had 55 RBIs for a batting average of 0.408 and a slugging average of 0.717.

Source: The Nation

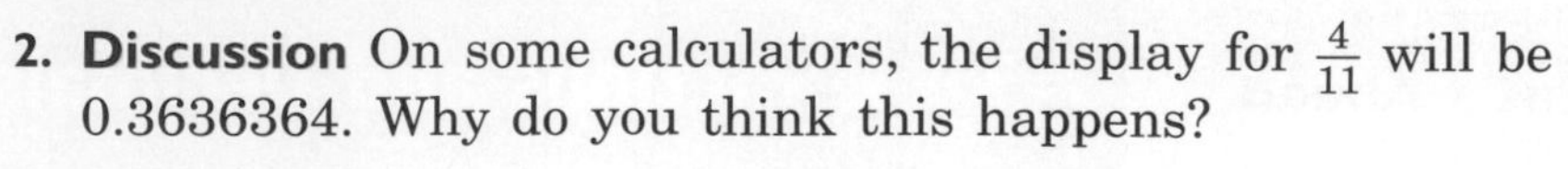

2. **Discussion** On some calculators, the display for $\frac{4}{11}$ will be 0.3636364. Why do you think this happens?

3. Write each fraction as a decimal: **a.** $\frac{2}{33}$ **b.** $-\frac{1}{12}$ **c.** $5\frac{2}{3}$

The decimal point as we know it was first used by John Napier (1550–1617), a Scottish baron and distinguished mathematician who used the point for writing decimal fractions smaller than one.

Source: *Academic American Encyclopedia*

Writing Fractions Sometimes you need to write a decimal as a fraction. When the decimal is terminating, first write it as a fraction whose denominator is a power of 10.

Example 3 Write 0.12 as a fraction in simplest form.

$$0.12 = \frac{12}{100} = \frac{12 \div 4}{100 \div 4} = \frac{3}{25} \leftarrow \text{GCF}(12, 100) = 4$$

4. When writing a terminating decimal as a fraction, how do you know which power of 10 to use as a denominator?

5. **a.** Write -0.068 as a fraction in simplest form.

   b. Write 7.4 as a mixed number in simplest form.

To write a repeating decimal as a fraction, you can use some simple algebra.

Example 4 Write $0.\overline{45}$ as a fraction in simplest form.

Let the variable n equal the given decimal.

$$n = 0.\overline{45}$$
$$100n = 45.\overline{45} \quad \leftarrow \text{Multiply each side by 100.}$$

Subtract one equation from the other.

$$100n = 45.45454545\ldots$$
$$-\ \ n = 0.45454545\ldots$$
$$99n = 45.00000000\ldots$$

Now solve the new equation.

$$99n = 45$$
$$\frac{99n}{99} = \frac{45}{99} \quad \leftarrow \text{Divide each side by 99.}$$
$$n = \frac{45}{99} = \frac{45 \div 9}{99 \div 9} = \frac{5}{11}$$

6. Why do you multiply each side of $n = 0.\overline{45}$ by 100?

7. **a.** By what number would you multiply if your original equation were $n = 0.\overline{7}$? Explain.

   b. Write $0.\overline{7}$ as a fraction in simplest form.

Extra SKILLS PRACTICE

Write as decimals.

1. $-\frac{5}{8}$
2. $1\frac{4}{15}$
3. $-2\frac{7}{12}$
4. $\frac{5}{27}$
5. $4\frac{5}{11}$

Write as fractions or mixed numbers in simplest form.

6. $-1.\overline{7}$
7. $0.2\overline{3}$
8. -0.34375
9. $2.8\overline{3}$
10. $-3.0\overline{5}$

WORK TOGETHER

8. a. Work with a partner. Write each fraction at the right as a decimal. What pattern do you see?

$\frac{1}{9}$	$\frac{2}{9}$	$\frac{3}{9}$	$\frac{4}{9}$	$\frac{5}{9}$

b. Use your pattern to predict what decimal is equal to $\frac{8}{9}$. Use a calculator to check your prediction.

9. Repeat Exercise 8 with the fractions at the right. This time, predict what decimal is equal to $\frac{8}{11}$.

$\frac{1}{11}$	$\frac{2}{11}$	$\frac{3}{11}$	$\frac{4}{11}$	$\frac{5}{11}$

Do you think there are other sets of fractions that have similar patterns? Make a conjecture. Then use a calculator to test it.

Share your patterns with the rest of the class. Make a list of all the patterns that your class finds.

TRY THESE

Rewrite each repeating decimal with a bar over the block of repeating digits.

10. 0.717171 . . . **11.** 0.3144444 . . . **12.** 0.528282828 . . .

Write each fraction or mixed number as a decimal.

13. $-\frac{3}{10}$ **14.** $-\frac{1}{3}$ **15.** $2\frac{5}{6}$ **16.** $\frac{9}{16}$ **17.** $-1\frac{7}{8}$

Write each decimal as a fraction or mixed number in simplest form.

18. 0.005 **19.** $-5.\overline{2}$ **20.** -0.56 **21.** $0.\overline{48}$ **22.** 6.09

Volcanic dust *consists of particles $\frac{1}{100}$ in. in diameter.* ***Express this fraction as a decimal.***

Source: *The World Book Encyclopedia*

23. Critical Thinking Although you cannot see the repetition in the calculator display, there is a repeating block of digits in the decimal that is equal to $\frac{1}{7}$. What is it? Explain.

24. a. Copy and complete the chart below.

b. Discussion The chart contains the equal fractions and decimals that are used most often. Many people find it helpful to memorize them. Is there a way to reorganize the chart so the numbers are easier to memorize?

Fraction	$\frac{1}{8}$	$\frac{1}{6}$	$\frac{1}{5}$	$\frac{1}{4}$	$\frac{1}{3}$	$\frac{3}{8}$	$\frac{2}{5}$	$\frac{1}{2}$	$\frac{3}{5}$	$\frac{5}{8}$	$\frac{2}{3}$	$\frac{3}{4}$	$\frac{4}{5}$	$\frac{5}{6}$	$\frac{7}{8}$
Decimal	■	■	■	■	■	■	■	■	■	■	■	■	■	■	■

Mixed REVIEW

Solve each inequality and graph the solution on a number line.

1. $12t > -6$

2. $-x \geq 5$

Write an integer for each situation.

3. Marla spent ten dollars.

4. Death Valley is 86 m below sea level.

5. A group of three children worked all day cleaning a vacant lot. A fourth child worked for only half the day. If the owner gave them $70, what is a fair way to divide the money?

ON YOUR OWN

Choose Use a calculator, paper and pencil, or mental math. Write each fraction or mixed number as a decimal.

25. $\frac{7}{12}$ **26.** $-4\frac{3}{20}$ **27.** $\frac{2}{3}$ **28.** $1\frac{3}{11}$ **29.** $-\frac{4}{5}$

30. Data File 7 (pp. 284–285) Give each answer as a fraction in simplest form and as a decimal.

a. Bush received all of North Carolina's electoral vote. What part of his total electoral vote was this?

b. Clinton received all of Minnesota's electoral vote. What part of his total electoral vote was this?

Write each decimal as a fraction or mixed number in simplest form.

31. -0.28 **32.** 1.625 **33.** $0.\overline{4}$ **34.** 12.012 **35.** $7.\overline{48}$

36. Critical Thinking Give three examples of denominators that will always produce a terminating decimal when the fraction is expressed as a decimal.

37. Writing Write about two situations when you would use fractions and two situations when you would use decimals.

American Families by Size 1991

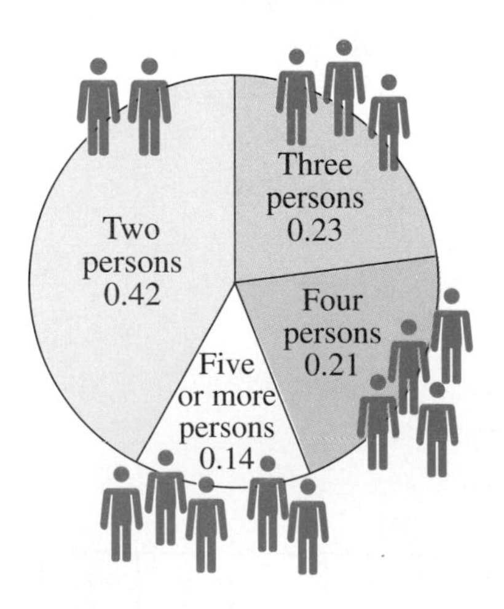

Use the graph at the left. Write a fraction in simplest form for the part of American families in each category.

38. 2 persons **39.** 3 persons **40.** 4 or more persons

CHECKPOINT

1. Find the prime factorization of 1,932.

2. Find GCF(104, 156).

3. Write $-\frac{72}{56}$ as a mixed number in simplest form. Then find its opposite and absolute value.

Write each fraction as a decimal. Write each decimal as a fraction or mixed number in simplest form.

4. $\frac{17}{16}$ **5.** 0.4 **6.** $\frac{1}{18}$ **7.** 0.16 **8.** $0.\overline{54}$

What's Ahead

- Using prime factorization to determine the LCM
- Comparing and ordering rational numbers

7-4 Comparing Rational Numbers

THINK AND DISCUSS

Multiples and LCM A **multiple** of a number is the product of that number and any nonzero whole number.

multiples of 4: 4, 8, (12,) 16, 20, (24,) 28, 32, (36,) . . .

multiples of 6: 6, (12,) 18, (24,) 30, (36,) 42, . . .

The circles around 12, 24, 36, . . . indicate multiples that are the same for both numbers. These are the **common multiples** of 4 and 6. The least multiple that is the same for both numbers is 12. So, 12 is the **least common multiple (LCM)** of 4 and 6.

1. a. List the multiples of 8 and the multiples of 10.
   b. What is the LCM of 8 and 10?

You can find an LCM using prime factorizations.

Example 1 Find the LCM of 18, 56, and 84.

- Find the prime factorization of each number.
  $18 = 2 \cdot 3^2$
  $56 = 2^3 \cdot 7$
  $84 = 2^2 \cdot 3 \cdot 7$
- Multiply the greatest powers of the prime factors that occur in *any* of the numbers. $2^3 \cdot 3^2 \cdot 7 = 504$

So, the LCM is 504. You write LCM(18, 56, 84) = 504.

2. What is the LCM of 18 and 56? of 56 and 84? of 18 and 84?

To compare integers like -5 and -1, think of a number line. The integer farther to the right is the greater integer.

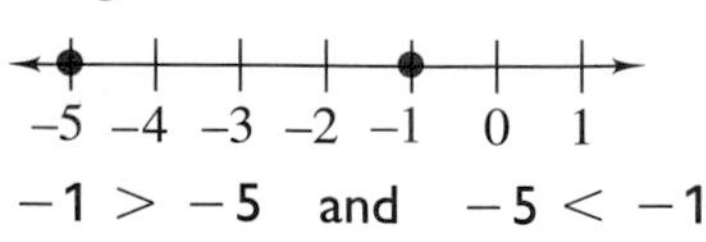

$-1 > -5$ and $-5 < -1$

Many times you need to compare rational numbers that are expressed as fractions. When the fractions have the same denominator, like $-\frac{5}{12}$ and $-\frac{1}{12}$, just compare their numerators.

$$-\frac{5}{12} = \frac{-5}{12} \text{ and } -\frac{1}{12} = \frac{-1}{12} \qquad -5 < -1, \text{ so } -\frac{5}{12} < -\frac{1}{12}.$$

When the fractions have different denominators, you need to find a *common denominator*. The **least common denominator (LCD)** is the LCM of the denominators.

Example 2 Compare $-\frac{5}{12}$ and $-\frac{4}{9}$.

- LCM(12, 9) = 36, so the LCD is 36.

$$-\frac{5}{12} = \frac{-5}{12} = \frac{-5 \cdot 3}{12 \cdot 3} = \frac{-15}{36} \qquad -\frac{4}{9} = \frac{-4}{9} = \frac{-4 \cdot 4}{9 \cdot 4} = \frac{-16}{36}$$

Since $-15 > -16$, $\frac{-15}{36} > \frac{-16}{36}$, and $-\frac{5}{12} > -\frac{4}{9}$.

3. How would Example 2 be different if the fractions were

a. $\frac{5}{12}$ and $\frac{4}{9}$? **b.** $-\frac{5}{12}$ and $\frac{4}{9}$? **c.** $\frac{5}{12}$ and $-\frac{4}{9}$?

4. Tell how to order $-\frac{5}{12}$, $-\frac{4}{9}$ and $-\frac{7}{18}$ from least to greatest.

5. Write $-1\frac{5}{12}$ and $-1\frac{4}{9}$ as improper fractions. Which is greater?

FLASHBACK

To compare decimals like 0.32 and 0.3125, line up the decimal points and compare the digits from left to right.

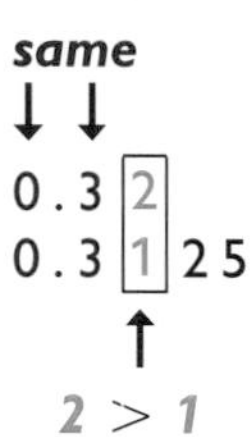

Comparing and Ordering Rational Numbers

First, write each number in the same form.

Example 3 Compare 0.32 and $\frac{5}{16}$.

- Use a calculator to find the decimal equal to $\frac{5}{16}$.

Since $0.32 > 0.3125$, $0.32 > \frac{5}{16}$.

6. Discussion Describe how to compare 0.32 and $\frac{5}{16}$ by writing 0.32 as a fraction. Which method do you prefer? Explain.

To order a set of rational numbers, you can use a number line.

Example 4 Order $\frac{5}{8}$, -0.37, 1.12, $-\frac{29}{40}$, and 0.3 from least to greatest.

- First write each fraction as a decimal.

$$\frac{5}{8} = 0.625 \qquad -\frac{29}{40} = -0.725$$

Then graph each decimal on a number line.

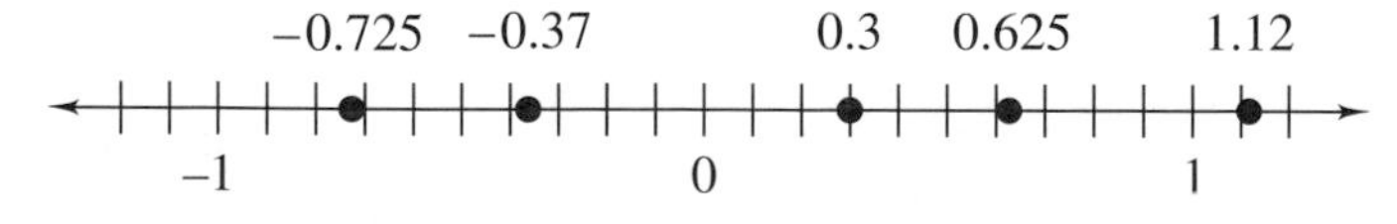

The order of the points, left to right, gives the order of the numbers, least to greatest.

$-0.725 < -0.37 < 0.3 < 0.625 < 1.12$, so

$-\frac{29}{40} < -0.37 < 0.3 < \frac{5}{8} < 1.12$.

WORK TOGETHER

- Work in a group. Draw a number line on a sheet of paper. Label a point at the far left *0* and a point at the far right *1*.
- The first person in the group graphs a *decimal* between 0 and 1. The second person graphs a *fraction* between the decimal and 1. The third person graphs a *decimal* between the last two numbers. Continue taking turns, alternating between fractions and decimals, until each person graphs three numbers.
- **Discussion** Is it possible for each person to have five more turns? Why or why not?

SKILLS PRACTICE

Compare. Use >, < or =.

1. $\frac{7}{9}$ ■ $\frac{5}{6}$
2. -0.35 ■ $-\frac{4}{15}$
3. $\frac{15}{24}$ ■ $\frac{10}{16}$
4. $-\frac{2}{3}$ ■ -0.65
5. $\frac{2}{5}$ ■ $\frac{5}{12}$
6. -0.375 ■ $-\frac{3}{8}$
7. $\frac{10}{27}$ ■ $\frac{1}{3}$
8. $\frac{5}{9}$ ■ $\frac{16}{25}$
9. $-\frac{9}{11}$ ■ -0.95
10. 0.45 ■ $\frac{3}{13}$

TRY THESE

7. **a.** List the first ten multiples of 9 and the first ten multiples of 15. Give two common multiples. What is the LCM?
   b. Show how to find LCM(9, 15) using prime factorization.

Compare. Use >, <, or =.

8. $-\frac{3}{8}$ ■ $-\frac{4}{9}$ **9.** $\frac{2}{3}$ ■ $\frac{12}{18}$ **10.** $\frac{6}{7}$ ■ 0.78 **11.** -0.83 ■ $-\frac{5}{6}$

12. **a.** To order $-\frac{5}{8}$, $\frac{9}{14}$, and $-\frac{7}{12}$ from least to greatest, do you need to find LCM(8, 14, 12)? Explain.
    b. Order the fractions from least to greatest.

13. **Discussion** Explain how this problem relates to multiples. Karen exercises at the gym every 3 days. Her friend Mai exercises at the same gym every 5 days. They met at the gym June 1. When will they next meet there?

Only 36% of students in grades 1–12 participate in daily exercise programs. The National Association for Sport and Physical Education recommends that elementary school children exercise for 30 min each day and high school students exercise for a minimum of 50 min a day.

Source: *Journal of the American Medical Association*

ON YOUR OWN

Find the LCM of each set of numbers.

14. 2, 15 **15.** 18, 45 **16.** 3, 5, 9 **17.** 14, 35, 50

18. **Critical Thinking** How can you find the LCM of any set of prime numbers? Give some examples to support your answer.

Mixed REVIEW

Solve each inequality and graph the solution on a number line.

1. $3a - 9 \leq -6$
2. $12 < -2y + 8$

Write each fraction as a decimal.

3. $8\frac{3}{20}$ 4. $-\frac{5}{11}$

5. Sound travels about 1,100 ft/s. How far away is lightning if you timed 8.5 s between seeing the flash and hearing the thunder?

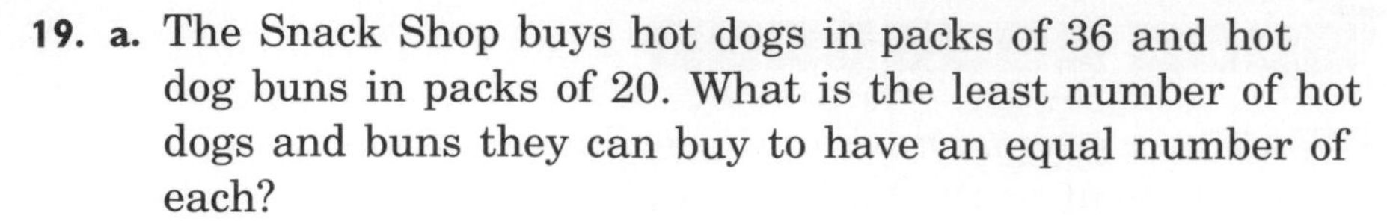

19. a. The Snack Shop buys hot dogs in packs of 36 and hot dog buns in packs of 20. What is the least number of hot dogs and buns they can buy to have an equal number of each?

b. How many *packs* of hot dogs and buns will this be?

20. Writing Explain how finding an LCM is different from finding a GCF. Be sure to give examples.

Mental Math Explain how to use mental math to compare each pair of rational numbers.

21. $-\frac{1}{11}$ ■ $-\frac{1}{9}$ **22.** $\frac{5}{7}$ ■ $\frac{5}{8}$ **23.** $\frac{1}{4}$ ■ 0.3 **24.** -0.6 ■ $-\frac{3}{7}$

25. Jake scored 9 out of 12 field goals in the third quarter of the basketball game. His opponent, Reggie, scored 3 out of 5. Who has the better average for the third quarter? Explain.

Choose Use a calculator, pencil and paper, or mental math to compare. Use >, <, or =.

26. 0.735 ■ $\frac{3}{4}$ **27.** $\frac{9}{10}$ ■ -0.91 **28.** $-2\frac{4}{5}$ ■ $-2\frac{7}{9}$

29. $-\frac{7}{8}$ ■ -0.87 **30.** $-\frac{7}{12}$ ■ -0.7 **31.** $1\frac{11}{16}$ ■ 1.67

32. Choose A, B, C, or D. Which set of rational numbers is ordered from greatest to least?

A. $0.76, \frac{3}{4}, \frac{5}{8}, 0.65$ **B.** $-0.9, -\frac{7}{8}, -0.52, -\frac{1}{2}$

C. $\frac{12}{15}, \frac{2}{3}, 0.4, \frac{5}{16}$ **D.** $\frac{2}{3}, -0.61, -\frac{3}{8}, -0.01$

33. Estimation Match each rational number below with a point on the number line.

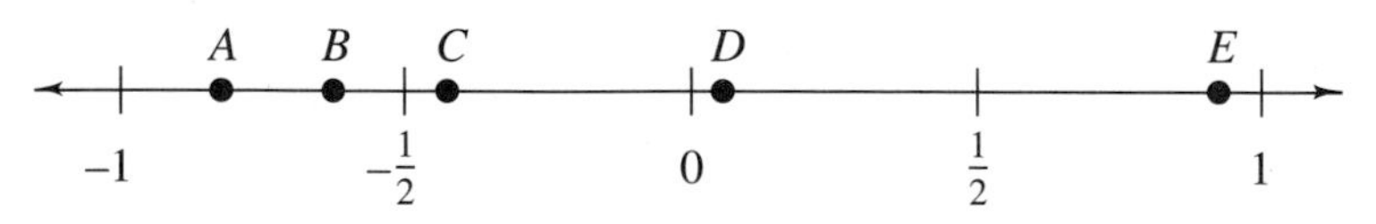

I. $-\frac{5}{8}$ **II.** 0.055 **III.** $\frac{15}{16}$ **IV.** $-\frac{5}{12}$ **V.** -0.8125

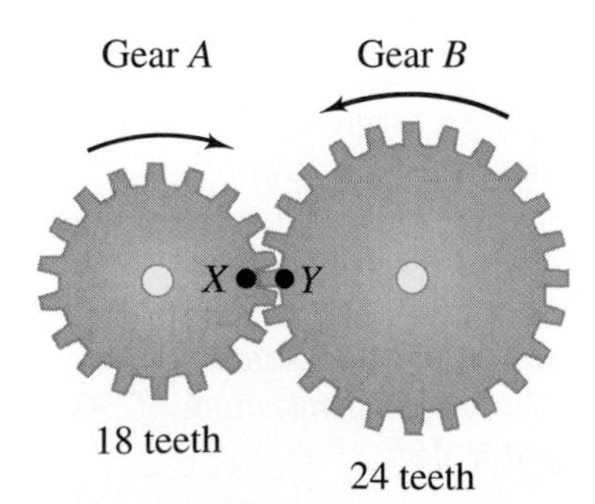

34. Gear *A* turns clockwise and gear *B* turns counterclockwise. In the figure at the left, point *X* is aligned with point *Y*. How many complete turns of gears *A* and *B* must occur before points *X* and *Y* are aligned again?

Problem Solving Practice

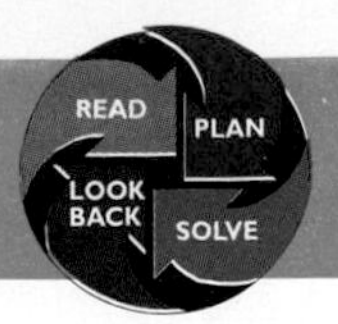

PROBLEM SOLVING STRATEGIES

Make a Table
Use Logical Reasoning
Solve a Simpler Problem
Too Much or Too Little Information
Look for a Pattern
Make a Model
Work Backward
Draw a Diagram
Guess and Test
Simulate a Problem
Use Multiple Strategies
Write an Equation
Use a Proportion

I see nothing in space as promising as the view from a Ferris wheel.

—E. B. White (1899-1985)

Solve. The list at the left shows some possible strategies you can use.

1. Jamal bought $3\frac{1}{4}$ lb of cheese. He used half of the cheese for a casserole. He then used $1\frac{1}{4}$ lb for sandwiches. How much cheese was left?

2. Will a circular peg with a 3 in. circumference go through a square hole with a 4 in. perimeter? Explain.

3. Drama club has 28 students. Of these, 8 paint scenery and 17 perform. If 3 students do both, how many do neither?

4. A painter can paint an 8 ft by 50 ft wall in one hour. How long will it take to paint a wall 10 ft by 60 ft?

5. What is a four-digit number in which the first digit is half the second, the third digit is the product of the first two, and the last digit is the sum of the first three?

6. Find the next two numbers in each pattern.
   a. 2, 5, 10, 17, 26, ■, ■
   b. 7, 8, 6, 7, 5, 6, 4, 5, 3, ■, ■

7. A Ferris wheel has 12 seats each holding 3 people. It takes 9 min for the ride to run and for all of the seats to empty and reload. You get in line for the ride at 12:48 P.M. just as a ride is starting. At what time will your ride start if there are 120 people in front of you in line?

8. A famous author published a new book every five years. When the fourth book was published, the sum of the books' publication years was 7,938. When was the first book published?

9. There are two patterns determining the numbers in the boxes. Copy the diagram and find the missing numbers.

						3						
					3							
						−2		2				
					9				9			
		12		2				4				
	44				30		23		19		14	
29		15		17		13		10				5

What's Ahead

- Adding and subtracting rational numbers

7-5 Addition and Subtraction

WHAT YOU'LL NEED

✓ Fraction bars 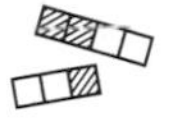

WORK TOGETHER

Using Models

- Work in pairs. Without looking, choose six bars from a set of fraction bars.
- Make as many combinations as you can whose sum is 1. Use the bars to help.

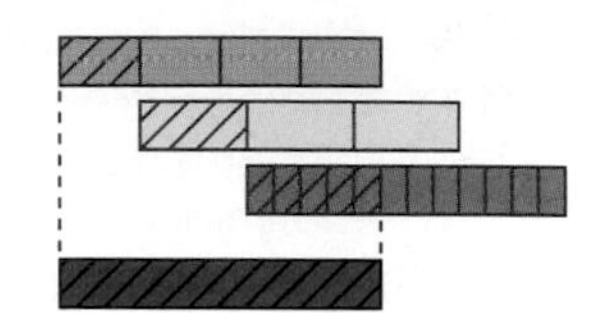

$\frac{1}{4} + \frac{1}{3} + \frac{5}{12} = 1$

THINK AND DISCUSS

Using Fractions Often you need to add or subtract rational numbers that are fractions. If the fractions have a common denominator, first add or subtract the numerators. Then write the sum or difference over the common denominator.

Example 1 Find the sum: $-\frac{6}{7} + \frac{2}{7}$

$$-\frac{6}{7} + \frac{2}{7} = \frac{-6}{7} + \frac{2}{7}$$

$$= \frac{-6 + 2}{7} = \frac{-4}{7}$$

$$= -\frac{4}{7}$$

To add or subtract fractions with different denominators, you can use their LCD.

Example 2 Find the difference: $\frac{1}{4} - \frac{3}{7}$

$$\frac{1}{4} - \frac{3}{7} = \frac{1 \cdot 7}{4 \cdot 7} - \frac{3 \cdot 4}{7 \cdot 4}$$ ← **The LCD is 28.**

$$= \frac{7}{28} - \frac{12}{28}$$

$$= \frac{7 - 12}{28}$$

$$= \frac{-5}{28} = -\frac{5}{28}$$

Using Mixed Numbers

Using Mixed Numbers Many problems involve adding or subtracting rational numbers that are mixed numbers. If the numbers are positive, you can add or subtract the whole number and fraction parts separately.

Example 3 Find the difference: $5\frac{1}{8} - 1\frac{13}{16}$

Estimate: $5\frac{1}{8} - 1\frac{13}{16} \approx 5 - 2 = 3$

$$5\frac{1}{8} - 1\frac{13}{16} = 5\frac{2}{16} - 1\frac{13}{16} \quad \leftarrow \text{The LCD is 16.}$$

$$= 4\frac{18}{16} - 1\frac{13}{16} \quad \leftarrow 5\frac{2}{16} = 4 + 1\frac{2}{16} = 4\frac{18}{16}$$

$$= (4 - 1) + \left(\frac{18}{16} - \frac{13}{16}\right)$$

$$= 3\frac{5}{16}$$

1. Find the sum: $6\frac{5}{12} + 10\frac{3}{4}$

When an addition or subtraction involves both positive and negative mixed numbers, rewrite them as improper fractions.

Example 4 Find the sum: $-4\frac{2}{3} + 6\frac{1}{2}$

Estimate: $-4\frac{2}{3} + 6\frac{1}{2} \approx -5 + 7 = 2$

$$-4\frac{2}{3} + 6\frac{1}{2} = \frac{-14}{3} + \frac{13}{2} \quad \leftarrow \text{Write improper fractions.}$$

$$= \frac{-14 \cdot 2}{3 \cdot 2} + \frac{13 \cdot 3}{2 \cdot 3} \quad \text{The LCD is 6.}$$

$$= \frac{-28}{6} + \frac{39}{6}$$

$$= \frac{11}{6} = 1\frac{5}{6}$$

2. **Discussion** Describe a different method for adding the mixed numbers in Example 4.

You can perform a rational-number addition or subtraction on your calculator using the change-sign key and the fraction key. Here is one way to find the sum in Example 4.

4 [a b/c] 2 [a b/c] 3 [a b/c] [+/-] [+] 6 [a b/c] 1 [a b/c] 2 [a b/c] [=] 1_ 5⌋6

The calculator fraction 1_ 5⌋6 means $1\frac{5}{6}$.

The piece of wood that a carpenter calls a 2 by 4 is actually only $1\frac{1}{2}$ in. wide by $3\frac{1}{2}$ in. thick. ***If two 2 by 4's are hammered together, what is the maximum thickness of the resulting block of wood?***

Source: *Old Farmer's Almanac*

TRY THESE

Use the model to complete each number sentence.

3.

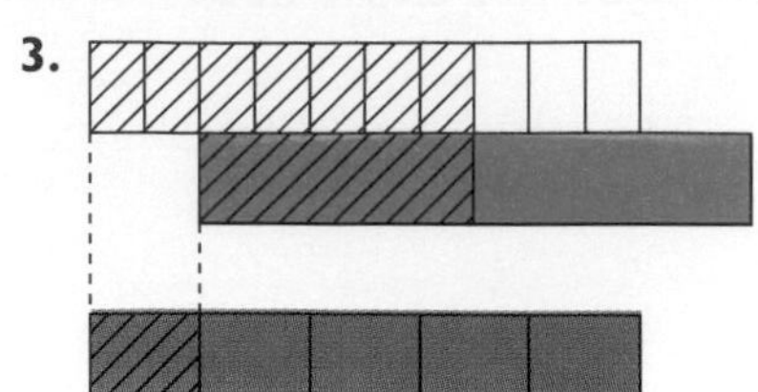

a. ■ − ■ = $\frac{1}{5}$

b. ■ + ■ = $\frac{1}{5}$

4.

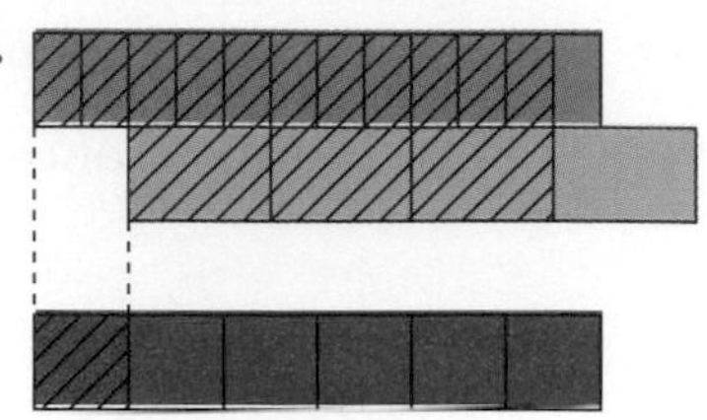

a. ■ − ■ = $\frac{1}{6}$

b. ■ + ■ = $\frac{1}{6}$

Write each sum or difference in simplest form.

5. $\frac{5}{6} - \frac{1}{4}$
6. $-\frac{3}{8} + \left(-\frac{7}{8}\right)$
7. $\frac{1}{2} - 3\frac{4}{7}$
8. $-3\frac{1}{12} + 5\frac{3}{4}$
9. a. For a craft project, Sheila needs three pieces of wire with lengths $7\frac{1}{2}$ in., $5\frac{3}{4}$ in., and $6\frac{3}{8}$ in. What is the total length of wire that she needs?

   b. Sheila bought a 24-in. length of wire for $.99. What length will remain after she cuts the three pieces from it?

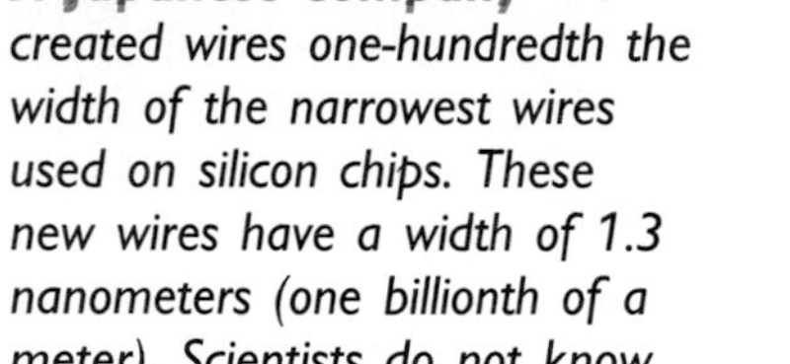

***A Japanese company** has created wires one-hundredth the width of the narrowest wires used on silicon chips. These new wires have a width of 1.3 nanometers (one billionth of a meter). Scientists do not know whether the wires will conduct electricity because there are no electrodes small enough to attach to them.*

Source: *The New York Times*

Mental Math **Add or subtract mentally. Write each sum or difference as a fraction or mixed number in simplest form and as a decimal.**

10. $\frac{3}{10} - \frac{1}{5}$
11. $-\frac{1}{2} + \frac{3}{8}$
12. $-0.5 + \left(-\frac{1}{2}\right)$
13. $1\frac{3}{5} + (-0.1)$

ON YOUR OWN

Sketch a model to find each sum or difference.

14. $\frac{3}{4} + \frac{1}{8}$
15. $\frac{7}{10} - \frac{3}{5}$
16. $\frac{5}{8} + \left(-\frac{1}{2}\right)$
17. $1\frac{1}{2} - \frac{1}{5}$

Calculator **Use the fraction key on your calculator to find each sum or difference.**

18. $4\frac{1}{3} - 6\frac{1}{4}$
19. $-7\frac{2}{5} + \left(-2\frac{3}{4}\right)$
20. $-5\frac{1}{2} + 8\frac{2}{3}$
21. $7\frac{4}{5} + \left(-11\frac{1}{3}\right)$

Choose Use a calculator, paper and pencil, or mental math. Write each answer in simplest form.

22. $\frac{5}{8} + \frac{7}{12}$
23. $4\frac{2}{3} + \left(-\frac{7}{8}\right)$
24. $-5\frac{1}{5} - \left(-3\frac{7}{10}\right)$
25. $-\frac{3}{4} - \frac{1}{8}$
26. $\frac{2}{7} + \frac{2}{3} - \frac{4}{7}$
27. $-2\frac{1}{24} + \left(-1\frac{29}{60}\right)$

28. a. **Data File I (pp. 2–3)** Suppose you made a model for a new racing car. The length of the axle is $34\frac{5}{8}$ in. Is this more or less than the maximum allowed? By how much?
    b. Your model has a $64\frac{3}{4}$-in. wheelbase. Is this over or under the minimum allowed? By how much?
    c. Will you have to adjust your model in order to meet the regulations? Explain.

29. **Writing** Explain how the rules for adding and subtracting integers are used in adding and subtracting fractions. Be sure to give examples.

Estimate each answer.

30. $13.59 + \left(-1\frac{2}{3}\right)$
31. $-6\frac{4}{7} - 2.05$
32. $4.9 + \left(-1\frac{5}{8}\right) + (-2.6)$
33. $1\frac{5}{6} - 0.925 - 4\frac{3}{11}$

34. Darryl is applying glaze to 16 ceramic bowls of equal size. He started with $2\frac{1}{2}$ c of glaze. After glazing four bowls, he has $1\frac{3}{4}$ c of glaze left. Do you think he will have enough for the remaining bowls? Explain.

35. **Critical Thinking** Do the commutative and associative properties apply to addition of rational numbers? What about subtraction? Explain.

Write each answer as a fraction or mixed number in simplest form and as a decimal.

36. $\frac{1}{3} + \left(-\frac{4}{9}\right) - \frac{2}{3}$
37. $-\frac{3}{8} + \frac{1}{16} - \frac{1}{4} + \left(-\frac{3}{16}\right)$
38. $-0.125 - \frac{1}{4} + 0.75 - \frac{3}{8}$
39. $-1.25 + \frac{5}{6} - 1.75 + 1\frac{1}{3}$

40. **Investigation (p. 286)** Find out how Morse Code is used. Exchange Morse Code messages with a classmate.

Mixed REVIEW

Find the square root of each number.

1. 529
2. 6.25
3. 0.81
4. 1.96

Compare using <, >, or =.

5. $0.44 \;\blacksquare\; \frac{5}{11}$
6. $-\frac{7}{13} \;\blacksquare\; -0.5$
7. What is the greatest 5-digit number you can write if each digit must be odd and no numbers are repeated?

Extra SKILLS PRACTICE

Find each sum or difference.

1. $\frac{2}{3} + \frac{7}{8}$
2. $\frac{5}{6} - \frac{3}{10}$
3. $-\frac{4}{5} + \frac{3}{8}$
4. $\frac{5}{12} - \left(-\frac{3}{4}\right)$
5. $\frac{1}{8} - \frac{2}{3} + \frac{5}{6}$
6. $\frac{2}{9} + \frac{5}{6} - \frac{1}{4}$
7. $5\frac{1}{6} - 1\frac{3}{4}$
8. $1\frac{2}{3} - \left(-6\frac{4}{5}\right)$
9. $-3\frac{7}{8} + 1\frac{1}{6}$
10. $-2\frac{1}{12} - 5\frac{7}{10}$

What's Ahead

- Multiplying and dividing rational numbers

7-6 Multiplication and Division

THINK AND DISCUSS

Using Models About $\frac{3}{4}$ of the world's fresh water is in glaciers. Antarctica has $\frac{9}{10}$ of the world's glaciers. To find the fraction of the fresh water that is in Antarctica's glaciers, you can use a model or you can multiply $\frac{3}{4}$ by $\frac{9}{10}$.

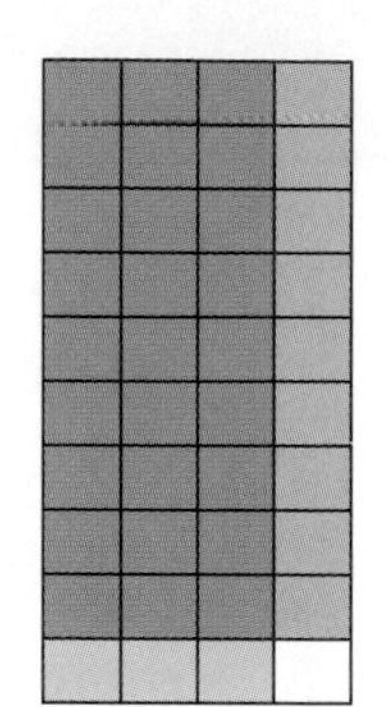

$$\frac{3}{4} \cdot \frac{9}{10} = \frac{3 \cdot 9}{4 \cdot 10} = \frac{27}{40}$$

With either method, you find that about $\frac{27}{40}$ of the world's fresh water is in Antarctica's glaciers.

***Scientists in Antarctica** have drilled 8,694 ft into the Antarctic ice sheet. They have obtained samples of ice formed from snow that fell between 270,000 and 280,000 years ago.*

Source: *The New York Times*

Multiplying Rational Numbers Multiply their numerators and multiply their denominators.

Example 1 Find the product: $\frac{5}{8} \cdot \left(-\frac{7}{15}\right)$

$$\frac{5}{8} \cdot \left(-\frac{7}{15}\right) = \frac{5}{8} \cdot \left(\frac{-7}{15}\right)$$

$$= \frac{5 \cdot (-7)}{8 \cdot 15}$$

$$= \frac{-35}{120} = -\frac{7}{24}$$

Write the product in simplest form.

1. **Discussion** In Example 1, how can you use the common factors of the numerators and denominators to simplify before multiplying?

To multiply rational numbers expressed as mixed numbers, write each mixed number as an improper fraction.

Example 2 Find the product: $-2\frac{1}{4} \cdot \left(-3\frac{3}{5}\right)$

Estimate: $-2\frac{1}{4} \cdot \left(-3\frac{3}{5}\right) \approx -2(-4) =$ about 8

$$-2\frac{1}{4} \cdot \left(-3\frac{3}{5}\right) = -\frac{9}{4} \cdot \left(-\frac{18}{5}\right)$$

Write improper fractions.

$$= \frac{-9 \cdot (-18)}{4 \cdot 5}$$

$$= \frac{162}{20} = 8\frac{1}{10}$$

Two numbers whose product is 1 are called **reciprocals.**

$\frac{3}{4} \cdot \frac{4}{3} = 1 \qquad -\frac{7}{2} \cdot \left(-\frac{2}{7}\right) = 1 \qquad -5 \cdot \left(-\frac{1}{5}\right) = 1$

↖ ↗ reciprocals ↖ ↗ reciprocals ↖ ↗ reciprocals

2. What is the reciprocal of **a.** $\frac{1}{7}$? **b.** $-2\frac{3}{4}$? **c.** 1 **d.** -1?

The symbol for the reciprocal of a nonzero number a is $\frac{1}{a}$. The reciprocal of a number also is called its **multiplicative inverse.**

Dividing Rational Numbers Multiply by the reciprocal of the divisor.

Example 3 Find the quotient: $-\frac{2}{5} \div \left(-\frac{3}{7}\right)$

$$-\frac{2}{5} \div \left(-\frac{3}{7}\right) = -\frac{2}{5} \cdot \left(-\frac{7}{3}\right) = \frac{-2 \cdot (-7)}{5 \cdot 3} = \frac{14}{15}$$

← **The reciprocal of $-\frac{3}{7}$ is $-\frac{7}{3}$.**

When division involves mixed numbers or integers, begin by rewriting the numbers as improper fractions. Then multiply by the reciprocal of the divisor.

Example 4 Find the quotient: $10\frac{2}{3} \div (-3)$

Estimate: $10\frac{2}{3} \div (-3) \approx 12 \div (-3) = -4$

$$10\frac{2}{3} \div (-3) = \frac{32}{3} \div \left(-\frac{3}{1}\right) = \frac{32}{3} \cdot \left(-\frac{1}{3}\right) = \frac{32 \cdot (-1)}{3 \cdot 3} = \frac{-32}{9} = -3\frac{5}{9}$$

← **The reciprocal of $-\frac{3}{1}$ is $-\frac{1}{3}$.**

3. a. Estimate the quotient: $7\frac{7}{8} \div \left(-1\frac{3}{4}\right)$

b. Which number is the divisor? What is its reciprocal?

c. Find the quotient.

TRY THESE

4. Write a multiplication sentence for this model.

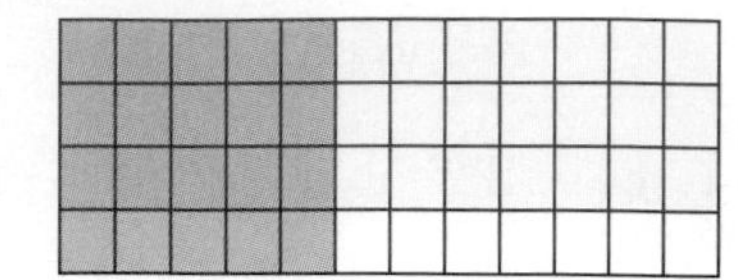

5. Write a division sentence for this model.

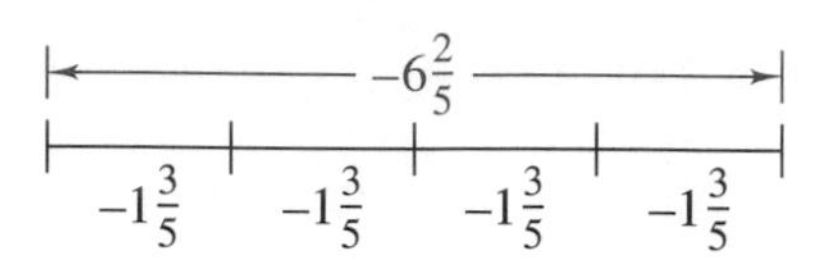

Write each product or quotient in simplest form.

6. $\frac{2}{5} \cdot \frac{6}{7}$
7. $-15 \cdot \frac{4}{5}$
8. $-\frac{8}{9} \div \left(-\frac{1}{6}\right)$
9. $-3\frac{2}{3} \div 1\frac{1}{4}$

10. **Calculator** You can use the following key sequence to find the product $-\frac{3}{4} \cdot \frac{2}{9}$.

3 [a b/c] 4 [+/-] [×] 2 [a b/c] 9 [=] -1⌋6

Remember that the calculator fraction -1⌋6 means $-\frac{1}{6}$. Adjust the key sequence to find each of these products.

a. $-\frac{3}{4} \cdot \left(-\frac{2}{9}\right)$
b. $-3\frac{3}{4} \cdot \frac{2}{9}$
c. $-3\frac{3}{4} \cdot \left(-2\frac{2}{9}\right)$

Mental Math Multiply or divide mentally.

11. $-\frac{1}{4} \cdot (-36)$
12. $12 \div \left(-\frac{1}{2}\right)$
13. $\frac{9}{10} \cdot \frac{5}{7}$
14. $-\frac{1}{4} \div \frac{1}{5}$

15. Paulo needs $1\frac{3}{4}$ yd of fabric to make one banner. How many banners can he make from a 20-yd length of fabric?

Mixed REVIEW

Write a variable expression for each.

1. Bill's age next year if he was x years old last year
2. the amount of money in your pocket if you have n quarters and three less dimes

Find each difference.

3. $\frac{4}{9} - \frac{1}{4}$
4. $\frac{2}{3} - \frac{3}{4}$

5. Find two numbers whose sum is 46 and whose difference is 12.

ON YOUR OWN

Sketch a model to find each product or quotient.

16. $\frac{1}{3} \cdot \frac{1}{4}$
17. $\frac{3}{10} \cdot \frac{2}{5}$
18. $\frac{1}{2} \div 4$
19. $-1\frac{1}{2} \div 6$

20. **Choose A, B, C, or D.** Which product is *not* equal to 1?

A. $\frac{2}{5} \cdot 2\frac{1}{2}$ B. $-4 \cdot \left(-\frac{1}{4}\right)$ C. $-\frac{3}{8} \cdot \frac{24}{9}$ D. $-1 \cdot (-1)$

21. **Writing** Explain why the number zero has no reciprocal.

22. a. How many quarters are in $30?
b. How many half-dollars are in $75?

Extra SKILLS PRACTICE

Find each answer.

1. $-\frac{4}{5} \cdot \frac{3}{8}$
2. $-\frac{5}{6} \div \left(-\frac{2}{3}\right)$
3. $-15 \div \frac{3}{8}$
4. $\frac{7}{9} \cdot 45$
5. $-2\frac{3}{4} \div \frac{7}{12}$
6. $4\frac{1}{8} \cdot \left(-5\frac{1}{3}\right)$

Choose Use a calculator, paper and pencil, or mental math to find each product or quotient.

23. $-4\frac{5}{6} \cdot 2\frac{1}{4}$

24. $\frac{1}{2} \div \left(-\frac{3}{4}\right)$

25. $-\frac{34}{35} \cdot (-7)$

26. $-8\frac{9}{10} \div \frac{1}{10}$

27. $-5 \div \frac{1}{8}$

28. $-5\frac{5}{6} \div \left(-2\frac{1}{3}\right)$

29. The perimeter of a square is $4\frac{1}{2}$ in. What is its area?

30. **Critical Thinking** Do $\frac{1}{\frac{1}{2}}$ and $\frac{\frac{1}{1}}{2}$ have the same value? Explain.

Write each answer as a fraction or mixed number in simplest form and as a decimal.

31. $-0.8 \cdot \frac{5}{8}$

32. $-4.3 \div \left(-\frac{1}{2}\right)$

33. $-\frac{3}{4} \cdot (-1.6)$

Twins Win First Prize at Fair

On August 25, local twins Janet and Kevin Washington won first prize in the annual Springfield County Fair bake-off. Their molasses-bran muffins were the unanimous favorite of the five judges. Their recipe for one dozen muffins appears at the right.

Janet and Kevin, eighth-graders at Springfield Regional Middle School, say that the muffins are easy to make. Whether they are making one dozen or ten dozen, it takes them only about fifteen minutes to measure and mix the ingredients. Their parents think the muffins taste great, but they also like that the cost for ingredients for each molasses-bran muffin is only about 11¢. Each muffin has 180 calories.

Janet and Kevin plan to put their $100 prize into their college fund.

3/4 c milk
1 1/2 c wheat bran cereal
1 egg
1/2 c vegetable oil
1/3 c molasses
1 1/4 c whole wheat flour
3 tsp baking powder
1 tsp salt

Heat oven to 400°F. Grease bottoms only of 12 medium muffin cups. Pour milk on cereal and let stand 1 min. Beat in egg, oil, and molasses. Stir in remaining ingredients all at once. Mix just until flour is moistened. Pour into muffin cups. Bake about 20 min. Remove from muffin cups immediately.

To make *date-nut muffins,* add 1/2 c chopped dates and 1/3 c chopped walnuts.

34. One pound of flour contains about four cups. About how many muffins can you make from a 5-lb bag of flour?

35. The information panel on a 16-oz box of cereal indicates that it contains sixteen $\frac{2}{3}$-c servings. Is there enough cereal in the box to make four dozen muffins? Explain.

36. **a.** How much of each ingredient would you need to make $2\frac{1}{2}$ dozen molasses-bran muffins?
    b. What would be the total cost of the ingredients?

PROBLEM SOLVING

7-7 Work Backward

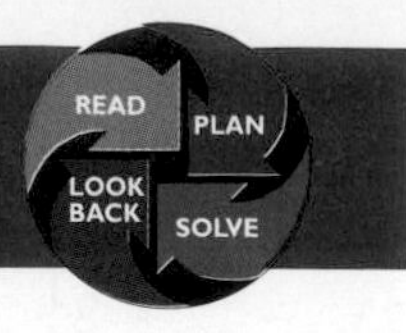

What's Ahead

- Solving problems by working backward

To solve some problems, you may need to work backward.

> International spies Cara Brimhat and Rex Coattails accidentally left clues to their whereabouts when they deposited money in several banks using a false name. At the start of their mission, they deposited two thirds of their money in Paris. Then they deposited \$5,000 in Cairo. Their mission took them to Tokyo, where they deposited half their remaining money. Now they have \$7,500 left, but investigators have almost caught up to them. What amount did they have at the start of their mission?

"*In solving a problem of this sort, the grand thing is to be able to reason backward. That is a very useful accomplishment, and a very easy one, but people do not practise it much.*"
—Sir Arthur Conan Doyle (1859–1930)

READ

Read and understand the given information. Summarize the problem.

1. Think about the information you are given.
   - **a.** What amount do Cara and Rex have now?
   - **b.** In which cities did Cara and Rex make deposits?
   - **c.** Describe their deposit in each city.
   - **d.** Summarize the goal of the problem in your own words.

PLAN

Decide on a strategy to solve the problem.

In this problem, you know a *final* amount of money. To find the *starting* amount, it makes sense to work backward. Begin with \$7,500 and "undo" the deposits.

SOLVE

Try out the strategy.

2. Complete.
   - **a.** \$7,500 is $\frac{1}{2}$ the amount they had when they got to Tokyo. So, when they got to Tokyo they had 2 • \$7,500, or ■.
   - **b.** The amount they took to Tokyo was \$5,000 less than what they had when they got to Cairo. So, when they got to Cairo they had \$5,000 more, or ■.
   - **c.** The amount they took to Cairo was only $\frac{1}{3}$ the amount they had when they began in Paris. So, when they began in Paris they had 3 times as much, or ■.

3. What is the solution of the problem?

When you work backward to solve a problem, you can check your solution by working *forward*.

4. a. What is your solution of the problem?

b. Take $\frac{1}{3}$ of that amount. What is the result?

c. Subtract $5,000. What is the result?

d. Take $\frac{1}{2}$ of that amount. Is the result $7,500?

LOOK BACK

Think about how you solved the problem.

TRY THESE

Work backward to solve each problem.

5. Look back at the problem about Cara and Rex.

a. Suppose that the final amount was $8,500. What would be the starting amount?

b. Suppose that the final amount was $7,500, but Cara and Rex deposited only one third of their money in Paris. What would be the starting amount?

6. a. If you start with a number, subtract 8, multiply by $\frac{1}{2}$, add 5, then divide by 11, the result is 5. Find the number.

b. Discussion What operations did you use to solve this problem? How are they related to the operations mentioned in the problem?

7. Ray returned home from mowing lawns at 3:00 P.M. on Saturday. It took $1\frac{1}{2}$ h to mow the first lawn. It took twice as long to mow the next lawn. After a half-hour break, it took $1\frac{1}{4}$ h to mow one more lawn. At what time did he start?

ON YOUR OWN

Use any strategy to solve each problem. Show all your work.

8. You can buy balloons in packs of 25 or packs of 75. Jill bought eight packs and had 450 balloons in all. How many packs of each size did she buy?

9. Find the next three numbers in this pattern.

$$\frac{1}{32}, \frac{1}{8}, \frac{1}{16}, \frac{1}{4}, \frac{1}{8}, \frac{1}{2}, \frac{1}{4}, \ldots$$

Mixed REVIEW

Describe each translation.

1. $P(3,2) \rightarrow P'(-1,-2)$

2. $P(1,10) \rightarrow P'(-4,2)$

Find each product or quotient.

3. $15 \cdot \frac{4}{7}$

4. $\frac{5}{12} \div 2\frac{1}{4}$

5. In the first exercise class, students do 6 push-ups. The teacher tells the class that the number of push-ups will increase by two each time they come to class. How many push-ups will the class have to do on the ninth day?

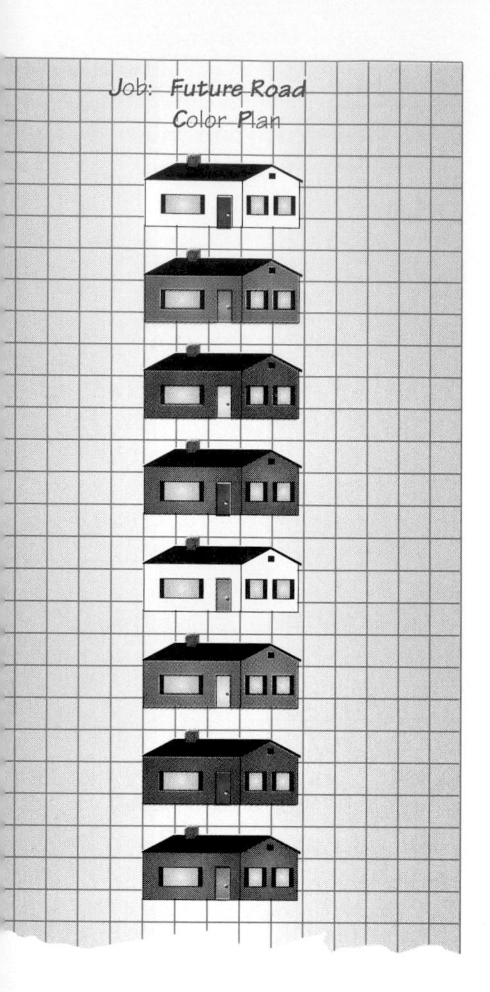

10. Red Apple Farm has 32 rows of apple trees in its orchard. Each row contains 28 trees. This year's harvest is 17,920 bushels of apples. What is the average number of bushels of apples that each tree produces?

11. The vending machine in the school cafeteria takes quarters, dimes, and nickels only. Right now, a small light indicates that you must use exact change.
    a. Suppose you want to buy crackers that cost 65¢. How many different combinations of coins could you use?
    b. If you use exactly six coins, what coins do you use?

12. Bert bought a case of pens. On Monday he sold half the pens. On Tuesday he sold 30 more. On Wednesday he sold half the pens that were left. On Thursday he sold the remaining 40 pens. How many pens were in the case?

13. Each house on Future Road is painted white, blue, brown, or gray. The front door can be red, green, or yellow. Suppose that the builder used the pattern shown at the left. Describe the next house in the pattern.

14. Buses leave a local terminal for Chicago every 35 min starting at 5:15 A.M. If you arrive at the terminal at 8:40 A.M., what time does the next bus leave for Chicago?

15. **Investigation (p. 286)** Explain how a cryptographer might use the strategy *work backward* to break a code.

CHECKPOINT

1. Find LCM(8, 12, 28).

2. Order 0.72, $-1\frac{2}{3}$, -0.58, $\frac{3}{4}$, and $-\frac{5}{8}$ from least to greatest.

Write each answer as a fraction or mixed number in simplest form.

3. $-\frac{1}{4} + \frac{5}{6}$ 4. $-\frac{3}{8} \cdot \left(-\frac{14}{15}\right)$ 5. $6\frac{3}{4} \div (-8)$ 6. $-5\frac{1}{3} - \frac{3}{4}$

7. Gina spent three fourths of her money on books. Then she spent $2.95 for lunch. When she got home, she had $1.50 remaining. How much did she have to begin with?

What's Ahead

- Simplifying expressions with positive, negative, and zero exponents

7-8 Rational Numbers with Exponents

THINK AND DISCUSS

Positive Exponents You might read in a biology textbook that the diameter of a cell is 6×10^{-4} mm. What does the negative exponent mean? To find out, first explore the connection between rational number division and exponents.

Let's find the quotient $7^5 \div 7^3$. We'll write the division as a fraction and write all the factors of each number.

$$7^5 \div 7^3 = \frac{7^5}{7^3} = \frac{\overset{1}{\cancel{7}} \cdot \overset{1}{\cancel{7}} \cdot \overset{1}{\cancel{7}} \cdot 7 \cdot 7}{\underset{1}{\cancel{7}} \cdot \underset{1}{\cancel{7}} \cdot \underset{1}{\cancel{7}}} = \frac{7 \cdot 7}{1} = 7^2 = 49$$

FLASHBACK

In the expression 7^5, 7 is the *base* and 5 is the *exponent.* An exponent indicates the number of times the base is used as a factor.

$$7^5 = \underbrace{7 \cdot 7 \cdot 7 \cdot 7 \cdot 7}_{5 \text{ times}}$$

You read 7^5 as *seven to the fifth power.*

1. Use the method shown above to find each quotient.

a. $\frac{3^7}{3^3}$ **b.** $\frac{4^7}{4^5}$ **c.** $2^7 \div 2^6$ **d.** $5^4 \div 5$

The examples above suggest the following rule.

Rule of Exponents for Division

To divide numbers with the same base, subtract the exponents.

Arithmetic	Algebra
$\frac{7^5}{7^3} = 7^{5-3} = 7^2$	$\frac{a^m}{a^n} = a^{m-n} \quad a \neq 0$

FLASHBACK

Any number to the first power is equal to that number.

$5^1 = 5$

2. Use the rule above to find each quotient.

a. $\frac{2^{12}}{2^7}$ **b.** $\frac{11^9}{11^8}$ **c.** $6^4 \div 6$ **d.** $\frac{r^9}{r^6}$, $r \neq 0$

Zero as an Exponent Let's look at the quotient $7^5 \div 7^5$.

$$\frac{7^5}{7^5} = 7^{5-5} = 7^0 \quad \text{and} \quad \frac{7^5}{7^5} = \frac{\overset{1}{\cancel{7}} \cdot \overset{1}{\cancel{7}} \cdot \overset{1}{\cancel{7}} \cdot \overset{1}{\cancel{7}} \cdot \overset{1}{\cancel{7}}}{\underset{1}{\cancel{7}} \cdot \underset{1}{\cancel{7}} \cdot \underset{1}{\cancel{7}} \cdot \underset{1}{\cancel{7}} \cdot \underset{1}{\cancel{7}}} = \frac{1}{1} = 1$$

Since $7^5 \div 7^5 = 7^0$, and $7^5 \div 7^5 = 1$, you know that $7^0 = 1$. This suggests the following definition of zero as an exponent.

$$a^0 = 1 \text{ for all } a \neq 0$$

Negative Exponents Sometimes the exponent in the denominator is greater than the exponent in the numerator.

$$\frac{7^3}{7^5} = 7^{3-5} = 7^{-2} \quad \text{and}$$

$$\frac{7^3}{7^5} = \frac{\overset{1}{\cancel{7}} \cdot \overset{1}{\cancel{7}} \cdot \overset{1}{\cancel{7}}}{\underset{1}{\cancel{7}} \cdot \underset{1}{\cancel{7}} \cdot \underset{1}{\cancel{7}} \cdot 7 \cdot 7} = \frac{1}{7 \cdot 7} = \frac{1}{7^2}$$

Since $7^3 \div 7^5 = 7^{-2}$, and $7^3 \div 7^5 = \frac{1}{7^2}$, you know that $7^{-2} = \frac{1}{7^2}$. This suggests the following fact about negative exponents.

For any nonzero integers a and n, $a^{-n} = \frac{1}{a^n}$.

There are over 40,000 species of spiders. The common house spider, known scientifically as Tegenaria, has an average weight of 10^{-4} kg.

Sources: *Comparisons and The Encyclopedia Americana*

Simplify each of the following.

3. 5^0 **4.** $(-8)^0$ **5.** 3^{-1} **6.** 2^{-3} **7.** $(-2)^{-3}$

8. Write two equal expressions for each quotient. One should have a positive exponent and one a negative exponent.
a. $\frac{7^4}{7^6}$ **b.** $\frac{3^4}{3^5}$ **c.** $\frac{2}{2^8}$ **d.** $\frac{w^4}{w^8}$, $w \neq 0$

WORK TOGETHER

9. a. Find the missing terms. 16, 8, 4, 2, 1, ■, ■, ■

b. Each term can be rewritten as a power of 2. Complete.
$2^4, 2^3, 2^2, 2^1, 2^0$, ■, ■, ■

10. Write each term as a power of 5 and complete the sequence.
3125, 125, 5, ■, ■, ■

11. Work with your partner to create a sequence where each term is expressed as a power of 3.

Extra SKILLS PRACTICE

Simplify.

1. 7^0 **2.** 5^{-3}

3. $\frac{6^{10}}{6^8}$ **4.** $\frac{(-1)^5}{(-1)^6}$

5. $\frac{-2^9}{(-2)^5}$ **6.** $(-1)^{-9}$

7. $\frac{-3^5}{-3^8}$ **8.** -8^{-2}

9. 2^{-7} **10.** $(-3)^{-4}$

11. $\frac{(-4)^3}{4^6}$ **12.** $(-20)^{-1}$

ON YOUR OWN

Simplify each expression.

12. 9^{-2} **13.** $(-6)^0$ **14.** 4^{-1} **15.** $(-5)^{-3}$ **16.** 12^0 **17.** 3^{-4}

Rewrite each expression using a negative exponent.

18. $\frac{1}{6^5}$ **19.** $\frac{1}{(-4)^8}$ **20.** $\frac{1}{c^7}$, $c \neq 0$ **21.** $\frac{1}{9}$ **22.** $\frac{1}{-8}$ **23.** $\frac{1}{100}$

24. Calculator You can use this key sequence to simplify 2^{-3}.

2 [y^x] 3 [+/-] [=] 0.125 ← **Recall that 0.125 = $\frac{1}{8}$.**

Use a calculator to simplify. Give the answer as a decimal.

a. 2^{-5} **b.** 3^{-3} **c.** $(-6)^{-2}$ **d.** $(-4)^{-2}$ **e.** 4^{-3}

Simplify each quotient, using a positive exponent when appropriate. Assume each variable does not equal zero.

25. $\frac{c^9}{c^7}$ **26.** $\frac{s^6}{s^{10}}$ **27.** $g^{12} \div g^{12}$ **28.** $m \div m^8$

29. Writing In Chapter 3, you learned the rule of exponents for multiplication. Compare it to the rule for division. How are the rules different? How are they alike?

30. Critical Thinking When does the expression a^{-3} represent a negative number? a positive number? zero?

Choose Use a calculator, paper and pencil, or mental math to simplify each expression. Give the answer as a fraction or whole number.

31. $\frac{5^4}{5}$ **32.** $9^5 \div 9^7$ **33.** $\frac{(-4)^6}{(-4)^9}$ **34.** $\frac{7^3}{7^0}$

35. $1^{10} \div 1^{20}$ **36.** $\frac{6}{6^5}$ **37.** $(-3)^7 \div (-3)^4$ **38.** $\frac{10^8}{10^{12}}$

Tell whether each statement is *true* or *false*. Explain your reasoning.

39. $4^0 = 4^1$ **40.** $8^0 = (-8)^0$ **41.** $1^{-5} = (-1)^5$ **42.** $2^1 \div 2^{-1} = 2^0$

Write each number as a power of 10.

Sample: $0.01 = \frac{1}{100} = \frac{1}{10^2} = 10^{-2}$

43. 0.001 **44.** 0.1 **45.** 0.0001 **46.** 0.000001 **47.** 10

48. Choose A, B, C, or D. Which number is equal to 6×10^{-4}?

A. $-60{,}000$ **B.** 10^2 **C.** $\frac{6}{10{,}000}$ **D.** -0.0006

49. Write $4^7 \div 4^3$ in three other ways.

Mixed REVIEW

1. What is the sum of the measures of the angles of a nonagon?

2. What is the measure of one angle of a regular hexagon?

Simplify.

3. $3^9 \div 3^4$

4. $\frac{5^7}{5^{10}}$

5. $5 + 3 \cdot 2 - 20$

6. Ali is thinking of a number. If you divide it by 2, square the result, subtract 4, and then divide by 6, the result is 10. What is the number?

MATH AND SCIENCE

7-9 Scientific Notation

What's Ahead

- Writing numbers using scientific notation

WHAT YOU'LL NEED

✓ Calculator

WORK TOGETHER

1. a. Work in pairs. Copy and complete each statement.

$6.71 \times 10^3 = 6.71 \times 1{,}000 = \blacksquare$
$6.71 \times 10^2 = 6.71 \times \blacksquare = \blacksquare$
$6.71 \times 10^1 = 6.71 \times \blacksquare = \blacksquare$
$6.71 \times 10^0 = 6.71 \times \blacksquare = \blacksquare$
$6.71 \times 10^{-1} = 6.71 \times \frac{1}{10} = 6.71 \times 0.1 = \blacksquare$
$6.71 \times 10^{-2} = 6.71 \times \blacksquare = 6.71 \times \blacksquare = \blacksquare$
$6.71 \times 10^{-3} = 6.71 \times \blacksquare = 6.71 \times \blacksquare = \blacksquare$

b. **Discussion** What patterns do you see in your answers?

The diameter of the moon,** 2,160 mi, is about one quarter of the diameter of the earth. However, the volume of the moon, 5,280,000 mi³, is only about one fiftieth of the volume of the earth.* ***Express the volume of the moon in scientific notation.

Source: *Comparisons*

THINK AND DISCUSS

Our planet Earth is roughly spherical in shape. Like any sphere, it has a volume. But, unlike other spheres you may have studied, its volume is very, very large—about 259,000,000,000 mi³!

Using Scientific Notation Scientists often write very large numbers in **scientific notation,** which consists of two factors. The first factor is a number greater than or equal to 1 and less than 10. The second factor is a power of 10.

Example 1 Write 259,000,000,000 in scientific notation.

- Move the decimal point to obtain a factor greater than or equal to 1 but less than 10. — 259,000,000,000. (11 places)

  The decimal point was moved 11 places to the left. Use this number as the exponent of 10. — 2.59×10^{11}

2. What is the volume of Earth, written in scientific notation?

3. a. Is the volume of Earth equal to 25.9×10^{10} mi³?

   b. Explain why the expression 25.9×10^{10} is *not* written in scientific notation.

You also can write very small numbers in scientific notation.

Example 2 Write 0.00000005 in scientific notation.

- Move the decimal point to obtain a factor greater than or equal to 1 but less than 10.

  0.00000005 (8 places)

  The decimal point was moved 8 places to the right. The exponent of 10 is -8.

  So, $0.00000005 = 5 \times 10^{-8}$.

Using Standard Form You can change numbers from scientific notation to **standard form** by working backward.

Example 3 Write 1.9×10^5 in standard form.

- Move the decimal point *to the right* the same number of places as the exponent of ten.

  1.9×10^5
  1.90000 (5 places)

So, $1.9 \times 10^5 = 190{,}000$

Example 4 Write 4.519×10^{-7} in standard form.

- The exponent of 10 is -7. Move the decimal point 7 places *to the left.*

  4.519×10^{-7}
  0000004.519 (7 places)

So, $4.519 \times 10^{-7} = 0.0000004519$.

To compare and order numbers written in scientific notation, look at their exponents first.

Example 5 Order the animals in the chart, slowest to fastest.

- First order the exponents: $-6 < -2 < -1$

  Next compare numbers with the same exponent.

  $$2.4 \times 10^{-1} < 2.7 \times 10^{-1}$$

  Now order all the speeds from least to greatest.

2.7×10^{-6}	4.8×10^{-2}	2.4×10^{-1}	2.7×10^{-1}
sea horse	snail	sloth	giant tortoise

On a calculator, you can enter a number in scientific notation, like 3.9×10^{-14}, using the *exponent* key.

key sequence	*display*
3.9 EXP 14 +/-	3.9 -14

On some calculators, the exponent key is labeled *EE*.

Mixed REVIEW

Write each equation in slope-intercept form. Name the slope and the y-intercept.

1. $x + 5y = -15$
2. $3x - 2y = 4$

Write each number in standard form.

3. 2.03×10^6
4. 4.29×10^{-5}

5. Write the next three terms of the sequence: 2, 1, -1, -4, . . .

Approximate Speeds of Selected Animals (km/h)

Animal	Speed
giant tortoise	2.7×10^{-1}
snail	4.8×10^{-2}
sloth	2.4×10^{-1}
sea horse	2.7×10^{-6}

Extra SKILLS PRACTICE

Write each number in scientific notation.

1. 23,000
2. 0.0101
3. 8,100
4. 6,250,000
5. 0.003

Write each number in standard form.

6. 9.5×10^{-1}
7. 1.32×10^{5}
8. 5×10^{-4}
9. 7×10^{7}
10. 3.6×10^{-3}

TRY THESE

4. Explain why each is *not* scientific notation for 0.000072.
   a. 72×10^{-6} **b.** 7.2×10^{5} **c.** 7.2×0.00001

Write each number in scientific notation.

5. 45,600 6. 0.000000013 7. 80,000,000 8. 0.2

Write each number in standard form.

9. 7×10^{-9} 10. 1.362×10^{8} 11. 4.02×10^{-5} 12. 4×10^{3}

13. Order 2.15×10^{-7}, 3.1×10^{-5}, 4.2×10^{-8}, and 5.678×10^{-5} from least to greatest.

Write each number in scientific notation.

14. The temperature inside the sun is greater than 16,000,000°C.

15. The smallest flowering and fruiting flower is the duckweed, which weighs 0.00001 oz.

GREAT EXPECTATIONS

Meteorologist

I am interested in a career as a meteorologist. This career appeals to me because I have always been fascinated by the different kinds of weather. I think it would be fun to use the satellites and computers to help people be prepared for the upcoming weather. I've always been the family weatherman. I always watch the weather forecasts on television. I also have watched the temperature since I was old enough to read a thermometer.

Anthony Beale

ON YOUR OWN

Write the number on each calculator display first in scientific notation, then in standard form.

16. 7.892 -10 **17.** 6. 13 **18.** 4.9 -12

19. Order the substances in the chart at the right starting with the substance through which sound travels the fastest.

Speed of Sound in Selected Substances (km/h)	
air	1.246×10^3
aluminum	1.8×10^4
cork	1.8×10^3
glass	1.63×10^4
water	5.39×10^3

Change to scientific notation or to standard form.

20. 7.01×10^{12} **21.** 3.904×10^{-9} **22.** 0.00000001

23. 4×10^6 **24.** 900,000,000,000 **25.** 0.00000003008

26. **Writing** A number written in scientific notation is doubled. Explain why the exponent of 10 may or may not change.

27. One liter (L) equals one million cubic millimeters (mm^3). Use scientific notation to write the number of red blood cells in 1 L of human blood if there are 5,000,000 red blood cells in 1 mm^3 of blood.

Dear Anthony,

I am pleased that you are interested in a career in meteorology in order to help people cope with the weather. The science of modern meteorology has benefited from advances in computers, satellites, and electronics. Computers in particular have greatly improved the accuracy of weather forecasts. The laws of physics as expressed in mathematical equations are used to describe how atmospheric circulation patterns change with time. Supercomputers help to solve these equations and predict what the future weather will be.

I encourage you to take as many mathematics and science courses as you can. This will help prepare you to enter the exciting field of meteorology.

Kenneth E. Kunkel, Meteorologist

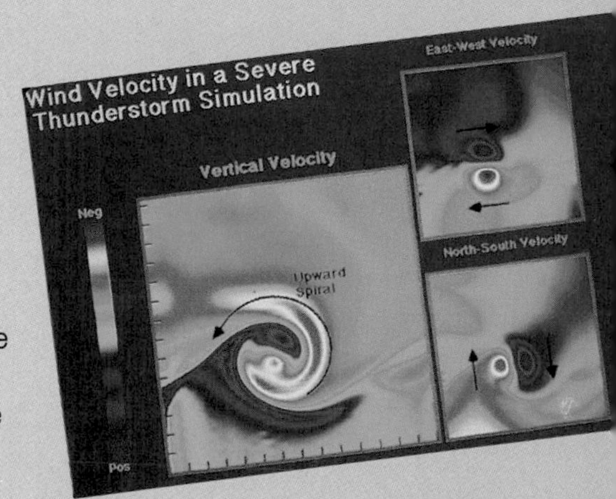

What's Ahead

- Solving one-step and two-step equations involving rational numbers

7-10 Rational Number Equations

THINK AND DISCUSS

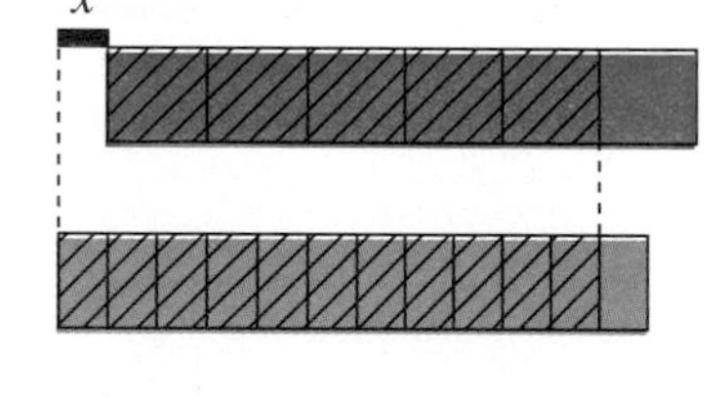

1. Which equation is modeled at the left? Explain.

   A. $x - \frac{5}{6} = \frac{11}{12}$ **B.** $x + \frac{5}{6} = \frac{11}{12}$ **C.** $x + \frac{11}{12} = \frac{5}{6}$

2. What is the solution of the equation? Tell how you know.

Solving One-step Equations You can solve equations using rational numbers with many of the methods you used to solve equations using integers. For example, you can use addition or subtraction to solve many rational number equations.

FLASHBACK

Addition and subtraction are inverse operations. Subtraction "undoes" addition, and addition "undoes" subtraction.

Example 1 Solve $m + \frac{7}{10} = \frac{4}{15}$.

$$m + \frac{7}{10} = \frac{4}{15}$$

$$m + \frac{7}{10} - \frac{7}{10} = \frac{4}{15} - \frac{7}{10}$$ ← **Subtract $\frac{7}{10}$ from each side.**

$$m = \frac{8}{30} - \frac{21}{30} = -\frac{13}{30}$$ ← **The LCD is 30.**

3. Why do you subtract $\frac{7}{10}$ from each side in Example 1?

To solve rational number equations involving multiplication, you can use reciprocals.

Example 2 Solve $\left(-\frac{1}{2}\right)t = 2\frac{1}{3}$.

$$\left(-\frac{1}{2}\right)t = 2\frac{1}{3}$$

$$\left(-\frac{2}{1}\right)\left(-\frac{1}{2}\right)t = \left(-\frac{2}{1}\right)\left(2\frac{1}{3}\right)$$ ← **Multiply each side by $-\frac{2}{1}$.**

$$1 \cdot t = \left(-\frac{2}{1}\right)\left(\frac{7}{3}\right)$$ ← **Write $2\frac{1}{3}$ as an improper fraction.**

$$t = \frac{-14}{3}$$

$$t = -4\frac{2}{3}$$

Two-step Equations Some equations require two steps.

Example 3 Solve $\frac{2}{3}y - \frac{2}{5} = -\frac{1}{2}$.

$$\frac{2}{3}y - \frac{2}{5} = -\frac{1}{2}$$

$$\frac{2}{3}y - \frac{2}{5} + \frac{2}{5} = -\frac{1}{2} + \frac{2}{5} \quad \leftarrow \text{Add } \tfrac{2}{5} \text{ to each side.}$$

$$\frac{2}{3}y = -\frac{5}{10} + \frac{4}{10}$$

$$\frac{2}{3}y = -\frac{1}{10}$$

$$\frac{3}{2} \cdot \frac{2}{3}y = \frac{3}{2} \cdot \left(-\frac{1}{10}\right) \quad \leftarrow \text{Multiply each side by } \tfrac{3}{2}.$$

$$y = -\frac{3}{20}$$

Extra SKILLS PRACTICE

Solve each equation.

1. $\frac{-2}{3}g = 18$
2. $0.78 - w = -3.4$
3. $-0.2b + 0.8 = -0.4$
4. $\frac{1}{8}m = 2\frac{3}{4}$
5. $-\frac{5}{6} + d = 1\frac{1}{3}$
6. $\frac{1}{4}k - 4 = -1$
7. $\frac{1}{5} + \frac{3}{10}a = 2$
8. $1.8 - 0.2p = -0.5$

TRY THESE

Write and solve an equation that each model represents.

4. 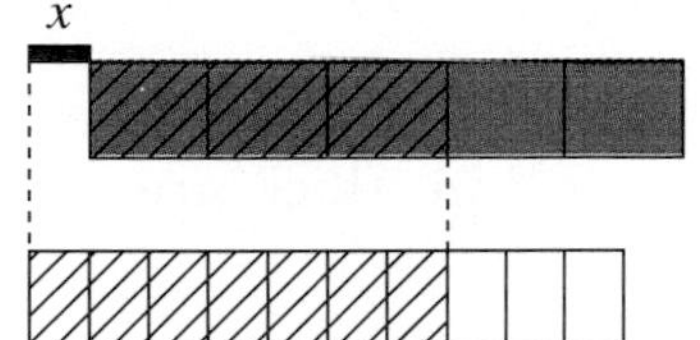

5. 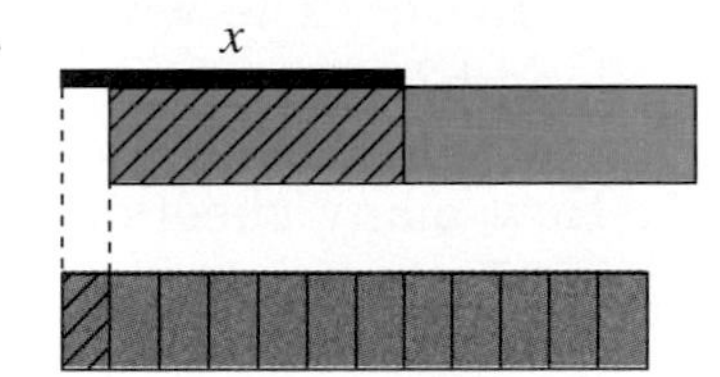

Solve each equation.

6. $\frac{2}{3}k + 3 = 2$
7. $n + 8\frac{1}{6} = 3\frac{4}{9}$
8. $c - 2.3 = 1\frac{1}{5}$

9. **a.** Write an equation to represent this problem.
   A plant that is 5 ft tall is growing at the rate of $1\frac{2}{3}$ in. per day. After how many days will the plant be 9 ft tall?
   b. Solve the equation in part (a) and answer the question.
   c. Suppose the plant is 4.5 ft tall and grows $1\frac{2}{3}$ in. per day. After how many days will the plant be 9 ft tall?
   d. Suppose the plant is 5 ft tall and grows $1\frac{1}{4}$ in. per day. After how many days will the plant be 9 ft tall?

Mental Math Solve each equation mentally.

10. $q + \frac{1}{4} = -\frac{1}{2}$
11. $-\frac{1}{4}w = \frac{1}{12}$
12. $g + 1.5 = -2.1$

Kudzu, a vine that is grown for cattle fodder, can grow as much as 60 ft in one season. When kudzu escapes to the wild, it quickly becomes an agricultural pest.

Source: *The Encyclopedia Americana*

ON YOUR OWN

Sketch a model for each equation. Show how to use the model to solve the equation.

13. $x - \frac{3}{5} = \frac{3}{10}$ **14.** $x + \frac{1}{3} = \frac{11}{12}$

Choose Use a calculator, paper and pencil, or mental math to solve each equation.

15. $b + \frac{2}{3} = \frac{1}{4}$ **16.** $\frac{1}{3}p = -4$ **17.** $2s - \frac{1}{4} = 1\frac{1}{3}$

18. $-\frac{3}{5}v = -12$ **19.** $t + \left(-\frac{3}{5}\right) = 2.3$ **20.** $-\frac{4}{5}n + 1\frac{3}{5} = 3.2$

Solve each problem by writing and solving an equation.

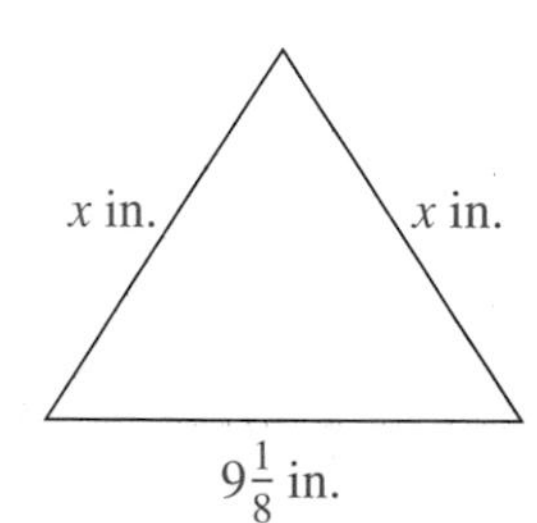

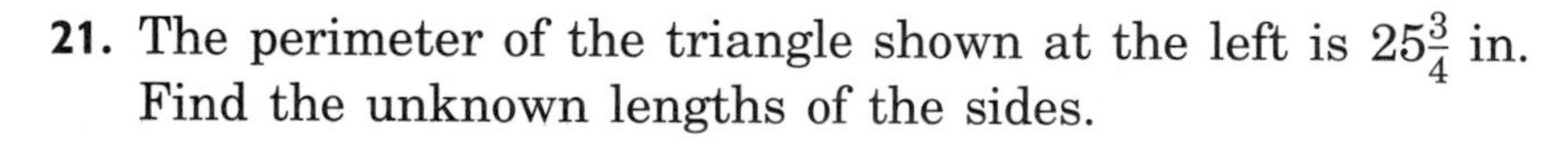

21. The perimeter of the triangle shown at the left is $25\frac{3}{4}$ in. Find the unknown lengths of the sides.

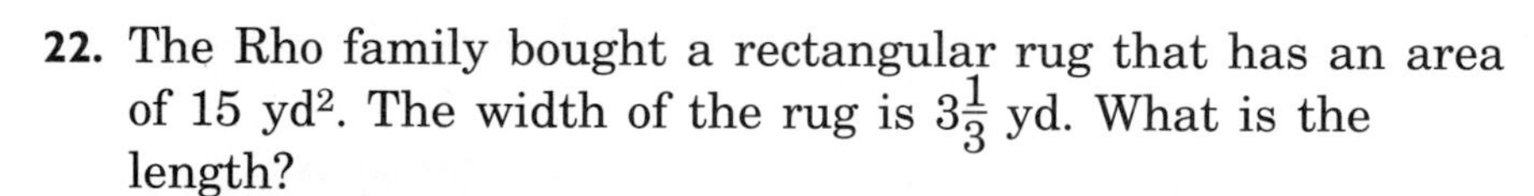

22. The Rho family bought a rectangular rug that has an area of 15 yd^2. The width of the rug is $3\frac{1}{3}$ yd. What is the length?

23. How many sheets of plywood that are $\frac{3}{4}$ in. thick are in a stack that is 9 in. high?

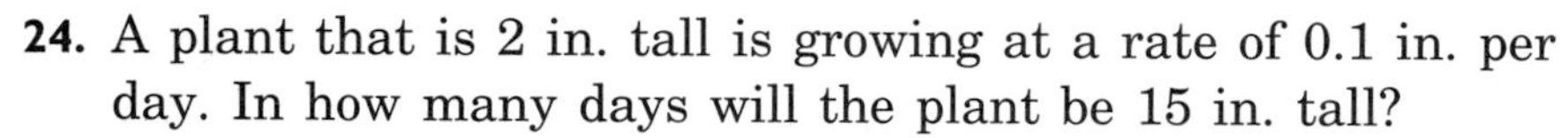

24. A plant that is 2 in. tall is growing at a rate of 0.1 in. per day. In how many days will the plant be 15 in. tall?

Mixed REVIEW

Classify each angle as obtuse, acute, or right.

1. 89° **2.** 112° **3.** 54°

Solve each proportion.

4. $\frac{a}{2} = \frac{3}{10}$

5. $\frac{3}{5} = \frac{y}{9}$

6. A sum of money is divided into four piles. Half the money is in the first pile, one-fourth is in the second pile, one-fifth is in the third pile, and \$30 is in the fourth pile. How much money is there?

Choose from -2, $-1\frac{1}{2}$, -1, $-\frac{1}{2}$, 0, $\frac{1}{2}$, 1, $1\frac{1}{2}$ and 2. Find *all* the numbers that are solutions of each equation.

25. $|n| = \frac{1}{2}$ **26.** $|n| = -\frac{1}{2}$ **27.** $|n| + \frac{1}{2} = 2$

28. $|n + \frac{1}{2}| = 2$ **29.** $2|n| = 1$ **30.** $2|n - 1| = 1$

31. Writing How is solving an equation that involves rational numbers similar to solving an equation that involves integers? How is it different? Be sure to give examples.

Write an equation for each diagram. Then solve the equation.

32.

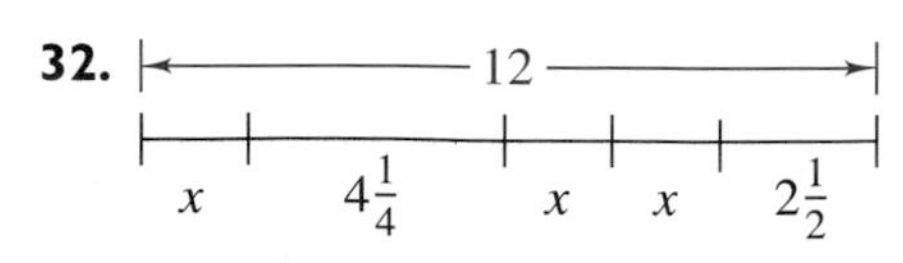

33.

34. Choose A, B, or C. Which has a negative solution?

A. $n - \frac{1}{5} = -\frac{1}{7}$ **B.** $p + \frac{1}{6} = -\frac{7}{8}$ **C.** $\frac{3}{11}a - 6 = 2$

35. Investigation (p. 286) An archeologist deciphered the following.

$$\Delta\Delta\Delta\Omega\Omega\Omega = 33$$
$$\Sigma\Sigma\Sigma\Sigma\delta\delta\Omega\Omega\Omega = 400{,}203$$
$$\Sigma\Sigma\beta = 210{,}000$$

How would 120,120 be written in this ancient system?

WHO? Archeologists use radiocarbon dating to determine the age of a specimen that was once living. By measuring the amount of carbon-14 present, a range of dates, such as A.D. 800, plus or minus 30 y, can be found.

Source: *The Encyclopedia Americana*

Active Day for Local Stocks

Yesterday was a day of dramatic financial activity for local companies. Chairperson Anna Zites of DeQuentin Corporation commented, "The day's activity was gratifying, to say the least." President Aloysius Zameo of Zameo Company was "ecstatic."

Although there was a slight decrease in the stock of the Hicks-Porter Group, a company spokesperson was quick to point out that yesterday's closing price was $4\frac{4}{8}$ points above the closing price exactly one year ago.

36. a. Use the chart at the right. For each company, write and solve an equation to find the amount of change between the opening and closing prices.

b. Write and solve an equation to find the closing price of HPG stock one year ago.

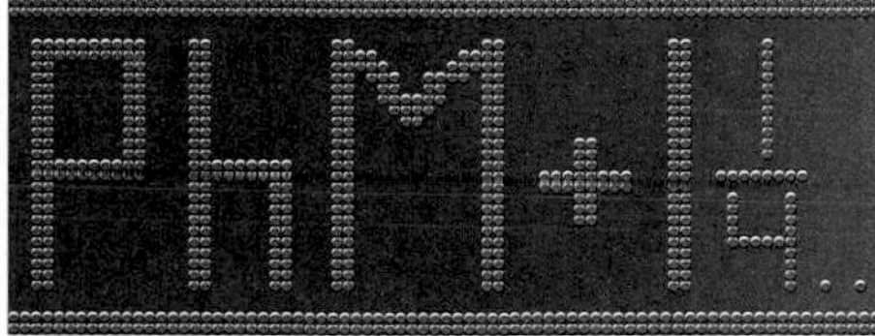

Company	Opening Price	Closing Price
DeQ	$22\frac{1}{2}$	$26\frac{1}{8}$
HPG	$33\frac{3}{4}$	$29\frac{5}{8}$
MJC	$25\frac{1}{4}$	19
ZaC	$47\frac{3}{4}$	$54\frac{3}{4}$

CHECKPOINT

Simplify each expression.

1. 3^{-3} **2.** $(-5)^{-2}$ **3.** 64^0 **4.** $\frac{r^{10}}{r^2}, r \neq 0$ **5.** $\frac{d}{d^6}, d \neq 0$

Write in scientific notation or in standard form.

6. 4.66×10^{-3} **7.** 223,000,000 **8.** 7.99×10^5 **9.** 0.00049

Solve each equation.

10. $\frac{3}{4}j = -\frac{4}{5}$ **11.** $h - \left(-\frac{3}{10}\right) = -\frac{2}{3}$ **12.** $3r - 2\frac{1}{3} = 2$

Practice

Write the prime factorization of each number.

1. 360 **2.** 2,025 **3.** 504 **4.** 1,200 **5.** 1,125

Find the GCF and LCM of each set of numbers.

6. 16, 36 **7.** 30, 12, 15 **8.** 6, 8, 12 **9.** 15, 18, 45

Write each fraction as a decimal.

10. $\frac{8}{9}$ **11.** $\frac{5}{3}$ **12.** $\frac{11}{4}$ **13.** $\frac{5}{8}$

Write each decimal as a fraction or mixed number in simplest form.

14. 18.4 **15.** $0.\overline{83}$ **16.** 6.125 **17.** 24.36

Compare. Use >, <, or =.

18. $\frac{13}{50}$ ■ 0.259 **19.** 3.5 ■ $\frac{14}{4}$ **20.** $-\frac{2}{3}$ ■ $\frac{16}{25}$ **21.** -9.8 ■ -9.81

Simplify.

22. $-\frac{3}{8} + \frac{5}{12}$ **23.** $8\frac{1}{2} - 5\frac{1}{3}$ **24.** $-0.875 \cdot \left(-\frac{4}{7}\right)$ **25.** $-\frac{4}{9} \div 5\frac{1}{3}$

Rewrite each expression using a negative exponent.

26. $\frac{1}{5^3}$ **27.** $\frac{1}{(-2)^4}$ **28.** $\frac{1}{y^5}$ **29.** $\frac{1}{-27}$ **30.** $\frac{1}{8^2}$

Rewrite in scientific notation or in standard form.

31. 0.000659 **32.** 8.06×10^4 **33.** 17,500,000 **34.** 4×10^{-5}

Solve.

35. $\frac{7}{8}x = -35$ **36.** $z + \frac{2}{3} = -\frac{1}{2}$ **37.** $\frac{2}{5} = \frac{3}{10}y - 4$ **38.** $-2d - \frac{1}{4} = \frac{5}{12}$

39. A number is divided by -6, multiplied by $\frac{3}{4}$ and added to $6\frac{1}{2}$. The result is 18.5. What is the number?

40. Lea rode her bike for 45 min to Lilly's house. They studied for 1.5 h, and then walked 20 min to the gym. What time did Lea leave home, if they arrived at the gym at 7:10 P.M.?

TECHNOLOGY

7-11 Exploring Irrational Numbers

What's Ahead

- Using calculators to explore irrational numbers
- Using Venn diagrams to classify real numbers

WHAT YOU'LL NEED

✓ Calculator 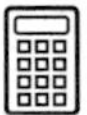

THINK AND DISCUSS

Exploring Irrational Numbers You can write any rational number as a terminating or a repeating decimal.

1. Write as a decimal: **a.** $\frac{1}{10}$ **b.** $\frac{1}{9}$ **c.** $\frac{7}{16}$ **d.** $\frac{7}{33}$

You also saw that any terminating or repeating decimal is a rational number. This means that you can write any terminating or repeating decimal as a fraction whose numerator is an integer and whose denominator is a nonzero integer.

2. Write as a fraction: **a.** 0.3 **b.** $0.\overline{3}$ **c.** 0.12 **d.** $0.\overline{12}$

There are many, many decimals, however, that have a pattern in their digits that neither terminates nor repeats. One such *nonrepeating, nonterminating* decimal is shown below.

$$0.02022022202222\ldots$$

3. **a. Discussion** Describe the pattern of 0's and 2's in the decimal above.
   b. Write a decimal similar to the one above that involves the digits 5 and 9.
   c. Write a nonrepeating, nonterminating decimal involving the digits 0, 1, and 2.

A number that is represented by a nonrepeating, nonterminating decimal is called an **irrational number.**

The German mathematician Johann Heinrich Lambert (1728–1777) was the first to prove that the number π is irrational.

Source: *The History of Mathematics*

4. Tell whether each number is *rational* or *irrational.* Explain your reasoning.
   a. 0.818118111 **b.** 0.818118111. . . **c.** $0.\overline{81}$ **d.** $\frac{9}{11}$

The decimals for many other irrational numbers have no pattern at all. Two familiar examples are the numbers π and $\sqrt{2}$.

$$\pi = 3.141592653\ldots \qquad \sqrt{2} = 1.414213562\ldots$$

WORK TOGETHER

x	x^2
2.2	■
2.23	■
2.236	■
2.2360	■
2.23606	■
2.236067	■
2.2360679	■
2.23606797	■
2.236067977	■

5. a. Work in pairs. Using a calculator, copy and complete the table at the left.

b. What is happening to the numbers in the second column of the table?

c. Use the square root key on your calculator to find $\sqrt{5}$. How do the numbers in the table compare to the display?

d. Discussion Suppose that you could add more digits to the number in the first column. Would the number in the second column ever be an integer? Explain.

You may not have realized it at the time, but many of the square roots that you worked with in Chapter 2 were irrational numbers. In fact, the square root of any positive integer that is not a perfect square is an irrational number.

FLASHBACK

If $\sqrt{n}$ is an integer, then n is a *perfect square.*

6. Identify each number as *rational* or *irrational.*

a. $\sqrt{7}$ **b.** $\sqrt{9}$ **c.** $\sqrt{144}$ **d.** $\sqrt{145}$ **e.** $\sqrt{899}$

Classifying Real Numbers Rational and irrational numbers together form the set of **real numbers.** A **Venn diagram** like the one below shows the relationships among these and other sets of numbers that you have studied.

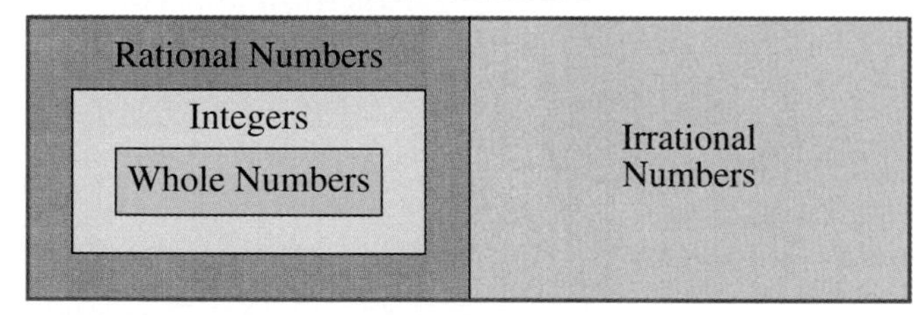

7. Use the Venn diagram to answer each question.

a. If a number is irrational, can it also be rational?

b. If a number is an integer, can it also be a real number?

8. Name two numbers that fit each description.

a. a real number that is not a rational number

b. a rational number that is not an integer

c. an integer that is not a whole number

Extra SKILLS PRACTICE

Identify each number as rational or irrational.

1. $\sqrt{12}$
2. $\sqrt{90}$
3. $\sqrt{324}$
4. $\sqrt{225}$
5. $\sqrt{250}$

Find each product to the nearest hundredth.

6. $\sqrt{2} \cdot \sqrt{10}$
7. $\sqrt{5} \cdot \sqrt{6}$
8. $\sqrt{3} \cdot \sqrt{8}$
9. $\sqrt{7} \cdot \sqrt{2}$
10. $\sqrt{12} \cdot \sqrt{5}$

ON YOUR OWN

For each number, write all the categories to which it belongs. Choose from *real number, rational number, irrational number, integer,* and *whole number.*

9. $-\frac{3}{5}$ **10.** $0.1\overline{53}$ **11.** π **12.** 3.14

13. 3 **14.** 5.121231234 . . . **15.** $-\sqrt{36}$ **16.** $\sqrt{104}$

FLASHBACK

In any right triangle with legs a and b and hypotenuse c, $a^2 + b^2 = c^2$.

17. In the triangle at the right, is AB a rational number or an irrational number? Explain.

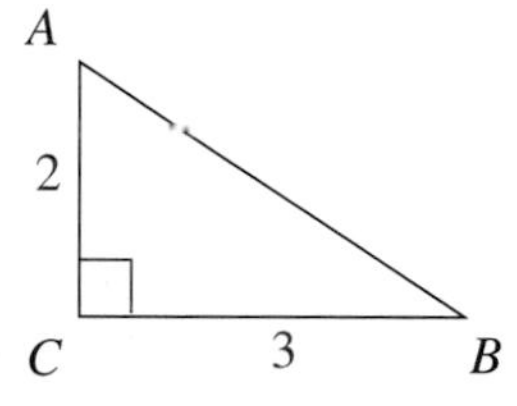

18. Writing Another commonly used set of numbers is the set of *natural numbers*:

{1, 2, 3, 4, 5, 6, . . .}

Where would you place the set of natural numbers in the Venn diagram of the real number system? Explain.

Tell whether each statement is *true* or *false*. If the statement is false, give an example to explain why.

19. All integers are real numbers.

20. Some irrational numbers are integers.

21. No integers are irrational numbers.

22. All square roots are irrational numbers.

23. a. Critical Thinking An addition of two irrational numbers is shown below. Find the sum.

$$\begin{array}{r} 0.01001000100001\ldots \\ +\ 0.10110111011110\ldots \\ \hline \end{array}$$

b. Is the sum a rational or an irrational number? Explain.

24. a. Calculator Find each product.

i. $\sqrt{2} \cdot \sqrt{5}$ **ii.** $\sqrt{3} \cdot \sqrt{6}$ **iii.** $\sqrt{2} \cdot \sqrt{8}$

iv. $\sqrt{3} \cdot \sqrt{12}$ **v.** $\sqrt{5} \cdot \sqrt{15}$ **vi.** $\sqrt{5} \cdot \sqrt{20}$

b. Which products in part (a) are rational numbers?

c. Find two different square roots that are irrational numbers, but whose product is a rational number.

Mixed REVIEW

Evaluate.
$a = -3,\ b = -5,\ c = -1$

1. $b^2 - a$ **2.** $a + bc$

3. $c^9 \div a^2$ **4.** $(b - a)^4$

State whether each number is rational or irrational.

5. 4.1010010001 . . .

6. 3.1212 . . .

7. Determine the ones digit of 3^{5438}.

CHAPTER 7

Wrap Up

Prime Factorization 7-1

To find all the ***prime factors*** of a composite number, divide by prime numbers until the quotient is 1, or use a factor tree.

Write the prime factorization using division or a factor tree.

1. 360 **2.** 700 **3.** 1440 **4.** 378 **5.** 7020

Rational Numbers, Fractions, Decimals, Irrational Numbers 7-2, 7-3, 7-11

A ***rational number*** is a number that can be written in the form $\frac{a}{b}$, where a is any integer and b is any nonzero integer.
A nonrepeating, nonterminating decimal is called an ***irrational number.***

Determine whether each number is rational or irrational.

6. 0.75 **7.** -3.5 **8.** 0.333 . . . **9.** 3.5656 . . . **10.** 1.232895 . . .

Ordering Rational Numbers 7-4

To order rational numbers, write as fractions with a common denominator and compare the numerators, or write the fractions as decimals and compare.

Compare. Use >, <, or =.

11. $\frac{3}{5}$ ■ $\frac{7}{9}$ **12.** 0.625 ■ $\frac{5}{8}$ **13.** -4.66 ■ $-\frac{14}{3}$ **14.** $\frac{5}{6}$ ■ $\frac{8}{9}$

Addition and Subtraction of Rational Numbers 7-5

To add or subtract rational numbers that are fractions, write equivalent fractions with a common denominator and add or subtract the numerators.

To add or subtract mixed numbers, combine the integers and fractions separately.

Find each sum or difference.

15. $\frac{7}{8} + \frac{3}{4}$ **16.** $3\frac{1}{6} + 2\frac{1}{2}$ **17.** $-2\frac{4}{5} - \left(-1\frac{3}{10}\right)$ **18.** $-\frac{5}{9} + \frac{2}{3}$

Multiplication and Division of Rational Numbers 7-6

To multiply rational numbers expressed as fractions, multiply the numerators and multiply the denominators. To divide, multiply by the reciprocal of the divisor.

To multiply or divide rational numbers expressed as mixed numbers, change the mixed numbers to improper fractions, then multiply or divide.

Find the product or quotient.

19. $\frac{4}{5} \cdot \frac{5}{8}$ **20.** $-4\frac{2}{3} \div 2\frac{2}{9}$ **21.** $-\frac{1}{6} \cdot \left(-\frac{3}{8}\right)$ **22.** $2\frac{1}{2} \div \frac{10}{13}$

Rational Numbers with Exponents 7-8

To divide numbers with the same base, subtract the exponents.

Simplify.

23. 6^{-2} **24.** $(-15)^0$ **25.** $\frac{t^7}{t^9}$ $(t \neq 0)$ **26.** $\frac{4}{4^{-2}}$ **27.** $\frac{-2^4}{-2^6}$

Scientific Notation 7-9

Scientific notation is a form of writing numbers using powers of 10.

Write each number in a scientific notation.

28. 295.6 **29.** 0.0083 **30.** 90,560 **31.** 0.03 **32.** 0.5987

Rational Number Equations 7-10

To solve ***rational number equations,*** use the properties of equality.

Solve.

33. $\frac{1}{2}y - 3 = \frac{3}{4}$ **34.** $-6t + 2\frac{2}{3} = 9$ **35.** $\frac{1}{4} = 2x - \frac{5}{12}$ **36.** $-\frac{1}{2}w + \frac{1}{3} = 1$

Problem Solving 7-7

Many problems can be solved by working backward.

37. It will take the Guptas 9.25 h to drive to Albany. If they want to arrive at 4:30 P.M., what time should they leave?

GETTING READY FOR CHAPTER 8

Write three equivalent fractions for each.

1. $\frac{3}{4}$ **2.** $\frac{2}{3}$ **3.** $\frac{4}{5}$ **4.** $\frac{1}{6}$ **5.** $\frac{7}{10}$

PUTTING IT ALL TOGETHER

Writing in Code

At the beginning of the chapter you created a code. Revise your code now based on your study of the chapter. The problems preceded by the magnifying glass (p. 307, # 40; p. 314, # 15; and p. 325, # 35) may give you some ideas. Divide your group into encoders and decoders. Your teacher will give a written message to the encoders. They will use the code to rewrite the message. Then they will give it to the decoders in your group and to the encoders in another group. Decoders will decode the message. Encoders will try to break the other group's code. Discuss your results as a class.

Excursion: Create a secret code: Take the letter you wish to encode and assign it a number based on the key A = 1, B = 2, . . . , Z = 26. Divide this number by 2. If there is a remainder, drop it. Now go back to the key and find the letter that is assigned to this new number. Using this code, the letter Q would be encoded as H. What problem does this code present to the decoder?

Prime numbers have always intrigued number theorists because primes refuse to appear with predictable regularity. Nevertheless, it is possible to find patterns in lists of prime numbers.

Try this with a partner.

- List all primes less than 100.
- Look for patterns in the list. Describe your findings.

Excursion: Suppose you add two prime numbers, neither of which is 2. Would the sum be prime or composite? Why?

Back to the Suspect

One evening Detective Brainy was called to Haughty Manor to investigate a robbery. Brainy went over the grounds carefully, turning up several important clues. It was the thief's bad luck that Brainy was an expert in the use of the problem solving strategy, work backward. Brainy followed the clues backward one by one. Sure enough, they led him directly to the thief.

Write the story of the crime. What happened? What clues did the thief leave behind? How did Brainy use the clues to capture the thief?

Repeating Decimals

Every repeating decimal is a rational number. But which rational number is it? You can use your calculator to find out easily.

Write as decimals:

1. $\frac{2}{9}$ $\frac{7}{9}$ $\frac{8}{9}$
2. $\frac{13}{99}$ $\frac{46}{99}$ $\frac{75}{99}$
3. $\frac{248}{999}$ $\frac{710}{999}$
4. $\frac{8551}{9999}$

Study your results. Describe a method you could use to write any given repeating decimal as a rational number. Give examples.

Millions and Billions

Scientific notation makes it easy to write large numbers. But understanding the *meaning* of large numbers is another matter. One way this can be done is to represent a large number as a series of small and understandable steps or ideas. For example, the number 1 million is a little easier to grasp when you know that a football field, including end zones, is just about the right size to hold 1 million baseball cards laid out side by side.

- Create other comparisons to explain 1 million.
- Create ways that explain the concept of 1 billion.

Assessment

1. Write a rational number for each point on the number line.

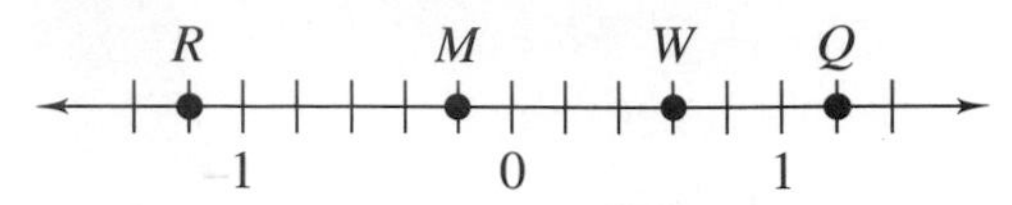

   a. R b. W
   c. M d. Q

2. **Estimation** Tell whether each number is closer to 0, $\frac{1}{2}$, or 1.

   a. $\frac{1}{5}$ b. $\frac{11}{20}$
   c. $\frac{21}{25}$ d. $0.\overline{6}$

3. Compare. Use >, <, or =.

   a. $\frac{3}{8}$ ■ 0.4 b. $-\frac{1}{2}$ ■ $-\frac{5}{12}$
   c. -0.9 ■ $-\frac{9}{10}$ d. $\frac{4}{9}$ ■ $0.\overline{4}$

4. Find the GCF and LCM of each set.

   a. 12, 16
   b. 6, 25
   c. 9, 24
   d. 32, 48, 60

5. Write each answer in simplified form.

   a. $3\frac{1}{4} + \left(-2\frac{2}{3}\right)$ b. $\frac{11}{12} - \frac{3}{4}$
   c. $-3\frac{1}{5} \cdot 1\frac{7}{8}$ d. $4.5 \div \left(-\frac{1}{2}\right)$

6. Solve.

   a. $x + \frac{5}{6} = -\frac{1}{2}$ b. $\frac{9}{10}y - 1 = \frac{3}{4}$
   c. $-2 = 1\frac{2}{3} + d$ d. $-5c + \frac{1}{4} = -\frac{3}{8}$

7. **Choose A, B, C, or D.** In which set are all three values equal?

   A. $\frac{5}{11}$, 0.45, $\frac{45}{99}$ B. $\frac{3}{4}$, 0.72, $\frac{75}{100}$
   C. $\frac{2}{9}$, 0.022, $0.\overline{2}$ D. $\frac{1}{8}$, 0.125, 0.1250

8. **Writing** Describe the differences between rational and irrational numbers.

9. Evaluate.

   a. -5^3 b. $\frac{4^5}{4^2}$
   c. $2^0 \cdot 6^{-1}$ d. $2^{-3} - \left(\frac{1}{2}\right)^3$

10. Write in scientific notation.

    a. 0.00459 b. 18 million
    c. 7,590 d. 0.03

11. Write in standard form.

    a. 9.35×10^3 b. 1.53×10^{-4}
    c. 6.125×10^{-1} d. 918×10^0

12. After each bounce of a ball, it goes $\frac{2}{3}$ as high as on the previous bounce. After the second bounce, the ball is 12 in. off the floor. How high was the ball before the first bounce?

13. A number increased by $3\frac{1}{2}$ is $2\frac{5}{6}$. Find the number.

14. **Writing** Describe a problem that can be solved using the equation $\frac{1}{2}t + 5 = 15$. Give the solution.

Cumulative Review

Choose A, B, C, or D.

1. Estimate the measure of $\angle WXZ$.

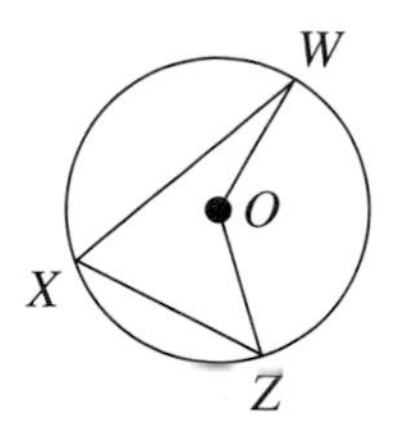

   A. 30° **B.** 50° **C.** 70° **D.** 100°

2. Which statement is *true*?

   A. $\frac{2}{7} + \frac{2}{5} = \frac{2}{7 + 5}$

   B. $\frac{5}{6} \div \frac{3}{4} = \left(\frac{5}{6} \div 3\right) \div 4$

   C. $\frac{2}{3} \cdot \frac{8}{3} = \frac{2 \cdot 8}{3}$

   D. $\frac{11}{8} - \frac{7}{8} = \frac{11 - 7}{8}$

3. How many different paths are there from A to B if you must move either right or up and you must travel along the grid lines?

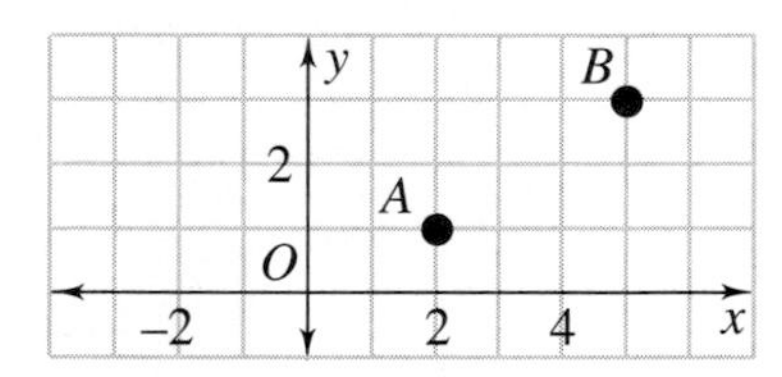

   A. 6 **B.** 7 **C.** 8 **D.** 10

4. If $m\angle A = m\angle B$, what measure is impossible for $\angle A$?

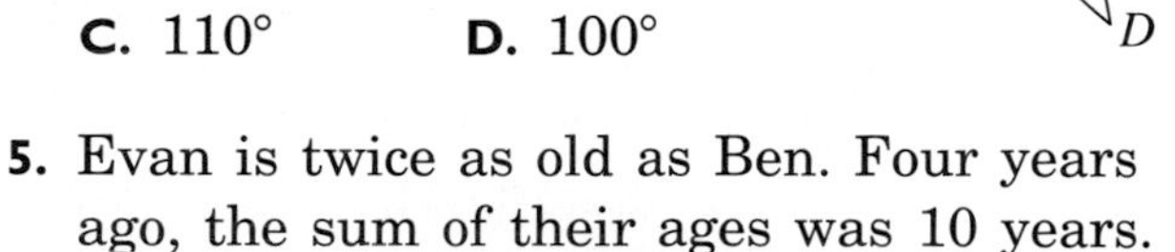

   A. 140° **B.** 120° **C.** 110° **D.** 100°

5. Evan is twice as old as Ben. Four years ago, the sum of their ages was 10 years. How old is Evan now?

   A. 10 y **B.** 12 y **C.** 14 y **D.** 16 y

6. A point P is reflected over the y-axis and then this image is reflected over the x-axis. This image is (2, 1). What are the coordinates of P?

   A. $(-1, -2)$ **B.** $(-2, 1)$ **C.** $(-2, -1)$ **D.** $(2, -1)$

7. Which statement is *false*?

   A. $6^0 = 1^0$ **B.** $(-1)^2 = 1^{-2}$ **C.** $2^{-4} = 4^{-2}$ **D.** $(-3)^3 = 3^{-3}$

8. How many different prime factors does the number 504 have?

   A. 3 **B.** 5 **C.** 7 **D.** 9

9. Which statement will allow you to conclude that $m \parallel n$?

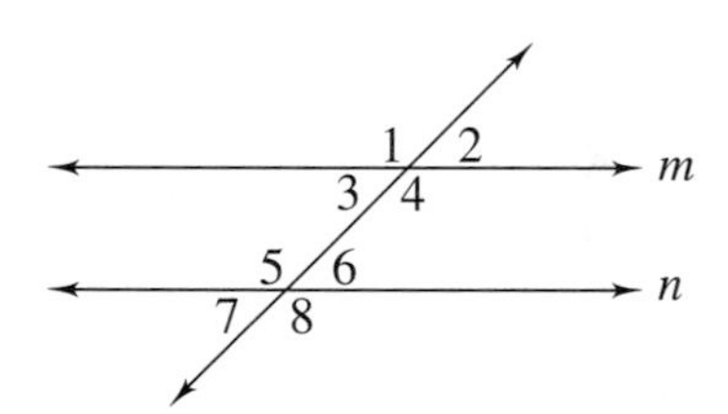

   A. $m\angle 1 = m\angle 2$ **B.** $m\angle 1 = m\angle 4$ **C.** $m\angle 4 = m\angle 8$ **D.** $m\angle 3 = m\angle 5$

10. Which pair of numbers have GCF 21?

    A. 14 and 21 **B.** 84 and 105 **C.** 630 and 126 **D.** 42 and 84

11. Which equation has a graph containing the points $(-3, 3)$, $(0, 1)$, and $(6, -3)$?

    A. $y = -x + 1$ **B.** $y = -3x + 1$ **C.** $2x + 3y = 3$ **D.** $y = -\frac{2}{3}x$

CHAPTER 8 Applications of Proportions

Data File 8

To launch a rocket safely, find a large field with no power lines, tall trees, or low-flying aircraft. Make sure the area has no dry weeds or other materials that might catch fire. Never launch a rocket without adult supervision.

Dr. Mae Jemison was the first African-American woman to be part of a space shuttle crew. She spent 190 h 30 min 23 s in space.

MODEL ROCKET ALTITUDE TRACKING

Rocketeers use triangulation and an altiscope to figure out how high their rockets fly.

- First, a tracker measures the distance to the launch pad.
- Next, the tracker uses an altiscope to measure the angle of the rocket's highest altitude.
- Finally, the tracker looks up the tangent of the angle and uses a proportion to estimate the height of the rocket.

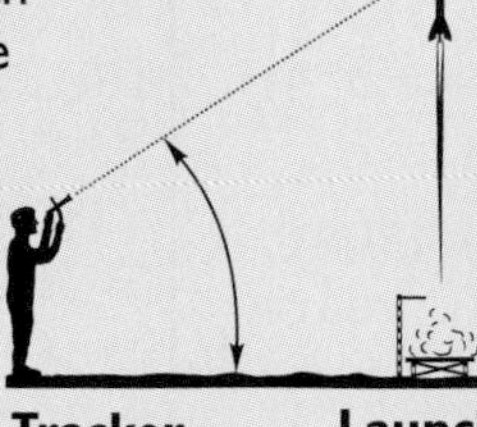

Source: *Estes Flying Model Rocket Catalog*

Aboard the Space Shuttle Endeavour
Left to right, front: N. Jan Davis, Mark Lee, Mamoru Mohri; *rear*: Curtis Brown, Jr., Jay Apt, Robert Gibson, Mae Jemison

WHAT YOU WILL LEARN

- how to apply proportional thinking
- how to use technology to explore the tangent ratio
- how to solve problems by using proportions

Recommended Launch Area

Engine Type*	Maximum Altitude (ft)	Site Diameter** (ft)
$\frac{1}{2}$ A	200	50
A	400	100
B	800	200
C	1,600	400
D	1,800	500

*These refer to standard engine types. Each has twice the power of the engine listed directly above it.
**Minimum launch site dimension for circular area is diameter in feet.

Source: *Estes Flying Model Rocket Catalog*

investigation

Project File

Memo

There are many ways to estimate distances that cannot be measured directly. Planes are sometimes prohibited from landing if the cloud cover, known as the "ceiling," is too low. The height of the ceiling can be estimated by shining a powerful light straight upward. A known distance away, an observer measures the angle from the runway to the spot on the cloud. The height is found by using the tangent of the angle.

Mission: Estimate a distance without measuring it directly. Some possibilities are the height or width of your classroom; the height of your school, a tree, or a nearby building. Explain the method you used to calculate your estimate.

Leads to Follow

- ✓ Practice your estimating method by using a distance that has already been measured accurately. How close can you come to the actual distance using your method?
- ✓ What other quantities besides distance can you measure that might help you find the distance you are looking for?

What's Ahead

- Exploring ratios, rates, and equal ratios

8-1 Exploring Ratios and Rates

THINK AND DISCUSS

Exploring Ratios Statistics show that 2 out of every 5 people in the United States have brown eyes. In this statement, 2 and 5 form a *ratio.*

Ratio

A **ratio** is a comparison of two quantities by division. The quantities are called the **terms** of the ratio.

Arithmetic			Algebra			
2 to 5	2 : 5	$\frac{2}{5}$	a to b	$a:b$	$\frac{a}{b}$	$(b \neq 0)$

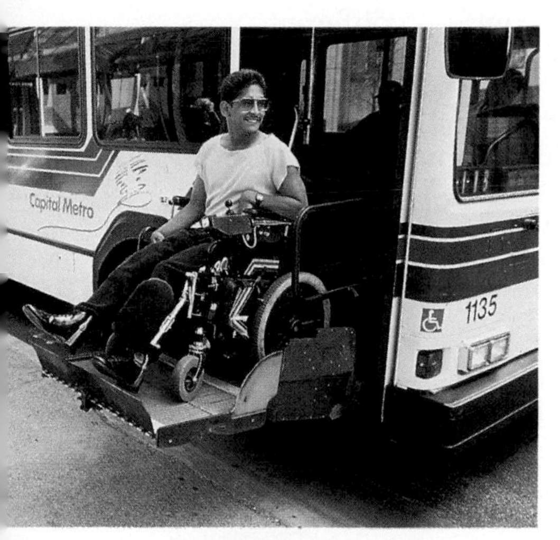

In 1992, the federal government spent approximately $32 billion to improve transportation in the U.S. They spent $19 billion on ground transportation, $9 billion on air transportation, and $4 billion on water transportation. **Write three ratios for these expenditures.**

Source: *Magruder's American Government*

1. Give two other examples of ratios in everyday situations.

You can use a ratio to compare a *part* to another *part*, a *part* to the *whole*, or the *whole* to a *part*.

Example 1 Write three ratios for the jar of marbles.

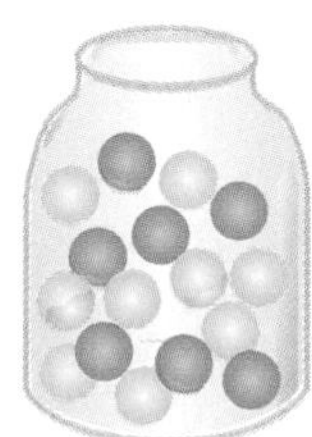

$\frac{\text{part}}{\text{part}} \rightarrow \frac{\text{blue}}{\text{yellow}} = \frac{7}{9}$

$\frac{\text{part}}{\text{whole}} \rightarrow \frac{\text{blue}}{\text{total}} = \frac{7}{16}$

$\frac{\text{whole}}{\text{part}} \rightarrow \frac{\text{total}}{\text{yellow}} = \frac{16}{9}$

2. Write three other ratios for the jar of marbles in Example 1.

You also can use a ratio to compare three quantities.

Example 2 The win : loss : tie record for the Raiders is 11 : 7 : 4. What is their ratio of losses to games played?

- The ratio represents 11 wins, 7 losses, and 4 ties. The number of games played is $11 + 7 + 4 = 22$.

So, the ratio of losses to games played is 7 : 22.

3. Use the data in Example 2 to write three other ratios that compare two quantities.

Finding Equal Ratios You find *equal ratios* by multiplying or dividing each term of a ratio by the same nonzero number.

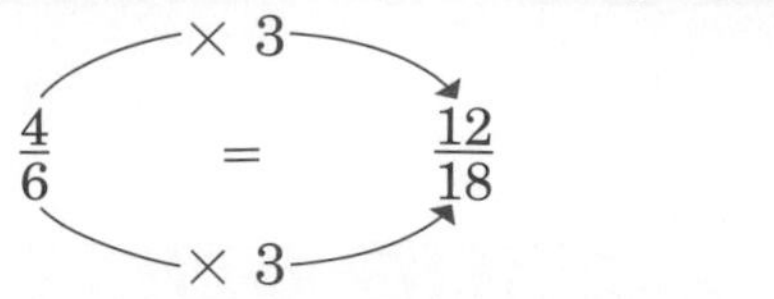

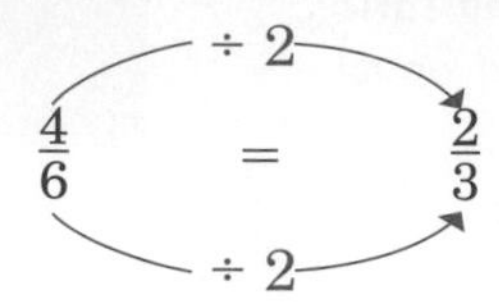

***Robert C. Maynard** (1937–1993) was the first person to move from editor to owner/publisher of a major daily newspaper. He purchased* The Oakland Tribune *in 1983.*

To write a ratio in *simplest form,* you write it as a fraction and find the simplest form of the fraction.

Example 3 Write the ratio 20 to 24 in simplest form.

$$20 \text{ to } 24 \rightarrow \frac{20}{24} \overset{\div 4}{=} \frac{5}{6} \rightarrow 5 \text{ to } 6$$

Finding Rates A **rate** is a ratio comparing two different types of quantities. A **unit rate** is one unit of a given quantity.

Example 4 It costs $9 to place six lines of copy in the classified section of a newspaper. Find the unit rate.

$$\frac{\text{cost in dollars}}{\text{number of lines}} \rightarrow \frac{9}{6} \overset{\div 6}{=} \frac{1.5}{1}$$

Divide each term by 6.

The unit rate is $1.50 per line, or $1.50/line.

4. It costs $8 to place five lines of copy. What is the unit rate?

WORK TOGETHER

5. **Calculator** Find the cereal that has the lowest unit price.

FLASHBACK

The *unit price* of an item is the price per unit. At a grocery store, the unit is usually a measure of weight or liquid capacity, such as ounce, kilogram, fluid ounce, or milliliter.

6. **Discussion** Is the product with the lowest unit price always the "best buy"? Explain your reasoning.

TRY THESE

Write three ratios that each model can represent.

7. 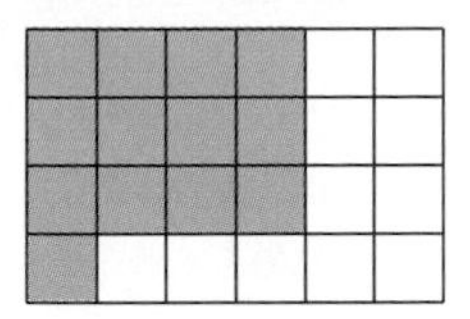

8. 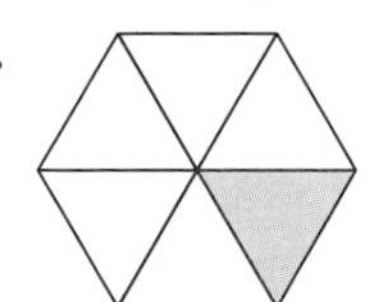

9. 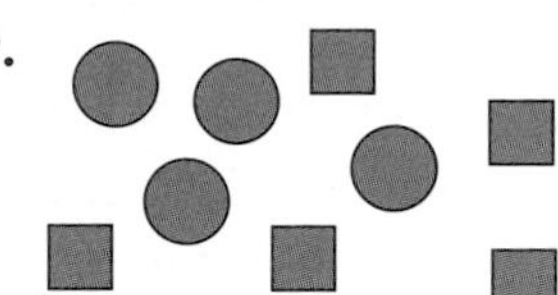

10. Write four ratios that are equal to the ratio 6 : 9.

Write each ratio in simplest form.

11. 4 : 28   12. $\frac{27}{9}$ 13. 10 out of 16   14. $\frac{30}{45}$ 15. 12 to 8

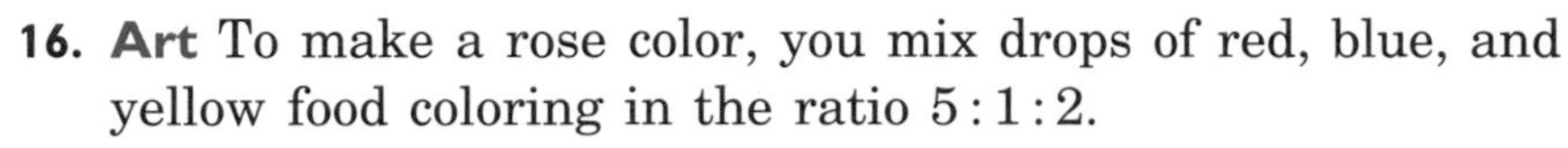

16. **Art** To make a rose color, you mix drops of red, blue, and yellow food coloring in the ratio 5 : 1 : 2.
    a. What is the ratio of yellow drops to the total number of drops, written in simplest form?
    b. What would be the ratio of red to blue to yellow drops if you were to use 24 drops of food coloring in all?

Write the unit rate.

17. 20 gal in 4 min   18. $21 for 12 roses   19. 200 m in 22 s

20. a. Today, Gretchen is 16 years old and Josh is 12 years old. What is the ratio of Gretchen's age to Josh's age?
    b. Will the ratio be the same two years from now? Explain.
    c. **Discussion** What happens to the ratio as they get older?

State-of-the-art *color monitors using 16-bit video boards, can produce 256,000 colors. Computers using 24-bit video boards can produce 16 million colors.*

Extra SKILLS PRACTICE

Write in simplest form.

1. $\frac{24}{36}$ 2. 40 to 15
3. 18 : 8   4. $\frac{64}{36}$
5. $\frac{15}{50}$ 6. 10 out of 55
7. $\frac{33}{15}$ 8. 4 : 16
9. 27 : 12   10. 96 to 8

ON YOUR OWN

21. a. Sketch a model for the ratio 3 : 8.
    b. Write three other ratios that your model represents.

The table at the right shows the results of a survey. Write each ratio as a fraction in simplest form and as a decimal rounded to the nearest hundredth.

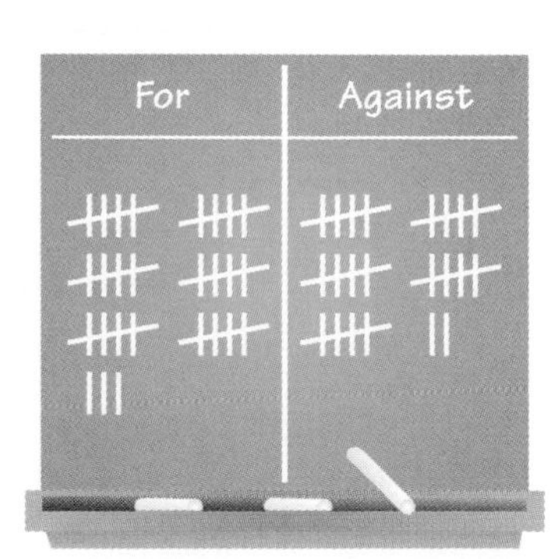

22. *For* to *Against*   23. *Against* to *For*

24. *For* to the total   25. *Against* to the total

FLASHBACK

The sum of the measures of the angles of a triangle is 180°.

26. **a.** In $\triangle ABC$, the ratio $m\angle A : m\angle B : m\angle C$ is $2:1:1$. What is the measure of each angle?

b. Classify $\triangle ABC$ by its angles and by its sides.

27. **Consumer Issues** A carton of twelve cans of juice costs \$3.99, while a carton of six cans costs \$2.79. How much do you save per can if you buy the carton of twelve?

Write the unit rate.

28. 676 mi in 13 h **29.** 412 words in 10 min **30.** \$66 for 8 h

31. **Writing** Describe the difference between a ratio and a rate.

32. **Cars** A midsize car can travel 200 mi on 7 gal of gasoline. A minivan can travel 350 mi on 12 gal. Which has the greater fuel efficiency? Explain.

33. **Critical Thinking** A bag contains 7 red marbles and 5 black marbles. You must add 60 marbles to the bag, but the ratio of red to black marbles must remain the same. How many of each color should you add?

A Sappy Story

Vermont is one of the country's major producers of maple syrup. There are close to 2,500 maple growers in Vermont, each of whom taps an average of 1,000 trees. About 500,000 gallons of maple syrup are produced each year.

When the sap is running, growers collect it from their trees daily and boil it down to make the syrup. Traditionally, the season for "sugaring," as this process is called, begins on the first Tuesday in March. In reality, though, the sap runs only when temperatures rise to 40°F–50°F during the day and fall to 20°F–30°F at night.

A grower can tap 7,000 gallons of sap from 1,000 trees per season, yielding 200 gallons of syrup, which is then sold at \$4.50 per half-pint.

34. On average, how many trees are there per grower?

35. How many gallons of sap are tapped per tree?

36. What is the ratio of the gallons of sap a grower taps to the gallons of syrup made from it, in simplest form?

Mixed REVIEW

Is the number rational or irrational?

1. -2.5 **2.** $\frac{7}{8}$

3. $\sqrt{5}$ **4.** $\sqrt{16}$

Use $f(x) = 4x - 3$.

5. Find $f(-3)$ and $f(2.5)$.

6. Graph the function using 0, 2, 4, 6, 8 for the input values.

7. Suppose you divide a number by -6, add 2, multiply by 10, subtract 5 and the result is 10. Find the number.

What's Ahead

- Converting units of measure by using dimensional analysis

8-2 Using Dimensional Analysis

THINK AND DISCUSS

Converting Measures The method of converting units of measure using ratios is called **dimensional analysis.** This is how you use dimensional analysis to convert 1.2 mi to ft.

$$1.2 \text{ mi} = \frac{1.2 \cancel{\text{mi}}}{1} \cdot \frac{5{,}280 \text{ ft}}{1 \cancel{\text{mi}}} = \frac{(1.2)(5{,}280) \text{ ft}}{1} = 6{,}336 \text{ ft}$$

In this example, the ratio $\frac{5{,}280 \text{ ft}}{1 \text{ mi}}$ is called the *conversion factor.* Since 5,280 ft = 1 mi, it is a 1 to 1 ratio. If you were converting a number of feet to miles, you would use the reciprocal ratio.

The reciprocal of $\frac{a}{b}$ is $\frac{b}{a}$.

$$7{,}345 \text{ ft} = \frac{7{,}345 \cancel{\text{ft}}}{1} \cdot \frac{1 \text{ mi}}{5{,}280 \cancel{\text{ft}}} = \frac{7{,}345 \text{ mi}}{5{,}280} \approx 1.4 \text{ mi}$$

1. **Discussion** Suppose that you need to convert a number of ounces to pounds. How do you decide whether to use $\frac{16 \text{ oz}}{1 \text{ lb}}$ or $\frac{1 \text{ lb}}{16 \text{ oz}}$ as a conversion factor?

HOW? Describe a method you could use to determine how many times you blink your eyes in a day, in a week, and in a year.

2. Show how to use dimensional analysis to convert.
   a. 75 min to seconds **b.** 75 s to minutes

Sometimes you need to use two or more conversion factors. For instance, here is one way to convert 1.5 years to hours.

$$1.5 \text{ y} = \frac{1.5 \cancel{\text{y}}}{1} \cdot \frac{365 \cancel{\text{da}}}{1 \cancel{\text{y}}} \cdot \frac{24 \text{ h}}{1 \cancel{\text{da}}} = \frac{(1.5)(365)(24)\text{h}}{1} = 13{,}140 \text{ h}$$

1c = 8 fl oz
1 pt = 2 c
1 qt = 2 pt

3. Change $5\frac{1}{2}$ qt to fluid ounces using dimensional analysis.

Estimating Measurements You can use dimensional analysis to *estimate* the number of hours in 123 min. Begin by rounding 123 min to 120 min.

$$120 \text{ min} = \frac{120 \cancel{\text{min}}}{1} \cdot \frac{1 \text{ h}}{60 \cancel{\text{min}}} = \frac{120 \text{ h}}{60} = 2 \text{ h}$$

So, 123 min is about 2 h.

4. Estimate the number of cups in 50 fl oz.

On February 20, 1990, a garden snail named "Verne" completed a 12.2-in. course at West Middle School in Plymouth, MI, in a record 2 min 13 s. **What was the snail's average speed in in./s? ft/s?**

Source: *The Guinness Book of Records*

Rules for Converting Measures	
larger unit to smaller unit	multiply
smaller unit to larger unit	divide

Converting Rates The cheetah, the fastest land animal, has been clocked at a speed at 92.4 ft/s. How many feet does the cheetah travel in one minute? Convert 92 ft/s to an equal rate in ft/min by using dimensional analysis.

$$92.4 \text{ ft/s} = \frac{92.4 \text{ ft}}{1 \cancel{\text{s}}} \cdot \frac{60 \cancel{\text{s}}}{1 \text{ min}} = \frac{(92.4)(60) \text{ ft}}{1 \text{ min}} = 5{,}544 \text{ ft/min}$$

5. a. Convert the cheetah's speed to mi/h.

b. Discussion Do you think a cheetah actually can cover this distance in one hour? Explain.

ON YOUR OWN

Use dimensional analysis to convert each measure.

6. 32 in. = ▪ ft **7.** 325 da = ▪ h **8.** 9 gal = ▪ c

9. Writing Compare the rules shown at the left to dimensional analysis. Which method do you prefer? Write a paragraph to explain.

GREAT EXPECTATIONS

Broadcast Journalist

For my career, I am planning on being a broadcast journalist for a local or even a national network. Being a broadcast journalist would give me a chance to meet new and exciting people. I could go places I have never been before. I have always had a love for television, and hope to someday make my career plans come true.

April Lott

Use dimensional analysis to find an equal rate.

10. 90 in./min = ■ ft/min

11. \$27/h = \$■ /min

12. 14 cm/s = ■ m/h

13. 64 yd/h = ■ in./s

14. **Sports** Some pitchers can throw a baseball as fast as 95 mi/h. How many feet per second is this?

15. A cockroach can travel at a speed of 29 cm/s. A centipede can travel at 30 m/min. Which can travel faster? Explain.

16. **Data File 2 (pages 48–49)** Follow the given instructions to find your pulse rate in beats/min. Then use dimensional analysis to find your pulse rate in beats/year.

Use dimensional analysis to find a reasonable estimate.

17. 3.04 mi → about ■ ft

18. 354 s → about ■ min

19. In 1990, there were approximately 141,542,000 live births in the world. About how many births was this per day? per hour? per minute? per second?

Mixed REVIEW

Express as a unit rate.

1. \$16.80 for 14 gal

2. 5 lb of meat for \$17.45

3. 292.5 mi in 6.5 h

4. The land area of Washington, D.C., is 61.4 sq. mi. The population is 607,000. Find the population per sq. mi.

Weights in lb: 105, 90, 112, 83, 97, 98, 94, 139, 127, 100, 134, 125, 95, 87, 99

5. Make a stem-and-leaf plot.

6. In which interval do most of the weights occur?

7. Find the range of weights.

Dear April,

Broadcast journalism is indeed a most exciting career. Satellite dishes and cable systems allow us to send pictures and words around the world instantaneously. I am still amazed by that!

I use math every day in many aspects of my business. I time my stories and shows, and make sure the satellite signal is placed in exactly the correct coordinates so broadcasts are received on the other end.

The most amazing thing about broadcast journalism is that we are only at the beginning of the communication technology timeline. There are simply no limits to how we will be able to communicate in the next 20 years. Good luck. Reach for the stars.

Liz Walker
TV News Anchor

What's Ahead

- Solving proportions
- Using proportions to solve problems

8-3 Solving Proportions

THINK AND DISCUSS

Solving Proportions Write a **proportion** for 2 equal ratios.

Proportion

A proportion is a statement that two ratios are equal.

Arithmetic	Algebra
6 is to 9 as 8 is to 12.	a is to b as c is to d.
6:9 = 8:12	$a:b = c:d$
$\frac{6}{9} = \frac{8}{12}$	$\frac{a}{b} = \frac{c}{d}$ $b \neq 0, d \neq 0$

The numbers 10-10-5 on a container of fertilizer or plant food represent the percentage by weight of nitrogen, phosphorus, and potassium. A 5-5-5 fertilizer has the same proportion of chemicals as a 30-30-30 fertilizer, but in different strengths (or concentrations).

In a proportion, the **cross products** of the terms are equal.

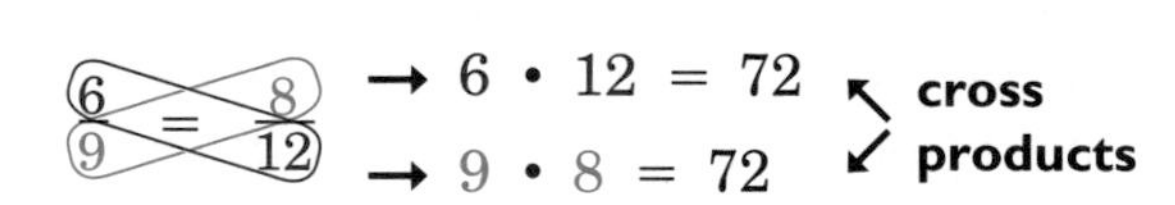

1. Use cross products. Do $\frac{1.3}{6}$ and $\frac{3.6}{18}$ form a proportion?

Often a proportion involves a variable. To *solve the proportion,* you find a value of the variable that makes the statement true.

Example 1 Solve $\frac{7}{12} = \frac{z}{51}$.

$7 \cdot 51 = 12z$ ← Write the cross products.

$357 = 12z$

$\frac{357}{12} = \frac{12z}{12}$ ← Divide each side by 12.

$29.75 = z$

Estimating Solutions You can use mental math to *estimate* the solution of a proportion.

Example 2 Estimate the solution of $\frac{9}{16} = \frac{70}{n}$.

- The ratio $\frac{9}{16}$ is a little more than $\frac{1}{2}$.

The value of n is a little less than $2 \cdot 70$, or 140.

2. Estimate the solution of $\frac{4}{15} = \frac{3}{c}$. Then solve.

Solving Problems

Proportions can help solve problems.

Example 3 The table at the right shows some *exchange rates* for foreign currencies on a recent day. On this day, how many Canadian dollars would you receive in exchange for 250 United States dollars?

- Let c represent the number of Canadian dollars.

$$\frac{\text{United States dollars}}{\text{Canadian dollars}} \begin{matrix}\rightarrow \\ \rightarrow\end{matrix} \frac{0.7615}{1} = \frac{250}{c}$$

$0.7615 \cdot c = 1 \cdot 250$ ← **Write the cross products.**

$0.7615c = 250$

$\frac{0.7615c}{0.7615} = \frac{250}{0.7615}$ ← **Divide each side by 0.7615.**

250 [÷] 0.7615 [=] 328.29941 ← **Use a calculator.**

$328.30 = c$ ← **Round to the nearest cent.**

You would receive $328.30 in Canadian dollars.

LOOK BACK Does it make sense for you to receive more Canadian dollars for your United States dollar? Explain.

Exchange Rates

Unit of Foreign Currency	U.S. Dollars per Foreign Unit
Australian dollar	0.6493
British pound	1.5570
Canadian dollar	0.7615
French franc	0.1792
Spanish peseta	0.007890

TRY THESE

Mental Math Solve each proportion mentally.

3. $\frac{2}{9} = \frac{10}{a}$ **4.** $\frac{k}{4} = \frac{21}{12}$ **5.** $\frac{45}{15} = \frac{y}{1}$ **6.** $\frac{12}{t} = \frac{8}{6}$

Write a proportion for each situation. Then solve.

7. Twelve oranges cost $2.99. What do 30 oranges cost?

8. Karl runs 12 yd in $2\frac{1}{2}$ s. How long will it take him to run 100 yd?

9. Choose A, B, C, or D. Which proportion does *not* have the same solution as the others?

A. $\frac{3.9}{4.7} = \frac{n}{5}$ **B.** $\frac{3.9}{n} = \frac{4.7}{5}$ **C.** $\frac{n}{4.7} = \frac{5}{3.9}$ **D.** $\frac{4.7}{3.9} = \frac{5}{n}$

10. a. Use the exchange rates above. How many Spanish pesetas would you receive for 400 United States dollars?

b. How many United States dollars would you receive for 400 Spanish pesetas?

WHAT? United States dollars are now available only in denominations of $1, $2, $5, $10, $20, $50, and $100. In 1945, the government stopped printing $500, $1,000, $5,000, and $10,000 notes.

Mixed REVIEW

Use dimensional analysis to find an equal rate.

1. 0.25 m/s = ■ m/min
2. 168 yd/h = ■ ft/da

Graph the following on the same coordinate plane.

3. $A(3,8)$, $B(6,4)$, $C(2,2)$, $D(1,5)$; connect the points.
4. a reflection of $ABCD$ over the x-axis
5. a 180° rotation of $ABCD$ about the origin
6. a translation of $ABCD$ 8 units to the left and up 2 units

7. Find two numbers whose difference is 13 and whose product is 300.

Extra SKILLS PRACTICE

Solve each proportion.

1. $\frac{x}{8} = \frac{3}{10}$
2. $4:9 = 15:n$
3. $5:g = 8:25$
4. $\frac{16}{7} = \frac{4}{a}$
5. $\frac{h}{12} = \frac{18}{45}$
6. $6:25 = c:30$

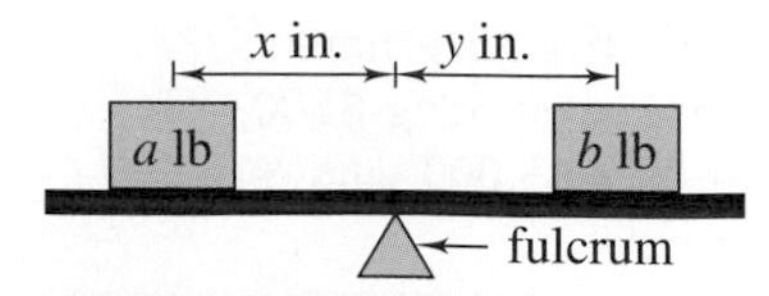

ON YOUR OWN

11. a. Write two proportions that the model at the right represents.
    b. Draw a model to represent *6 is to 16 as 3 is to 8.*

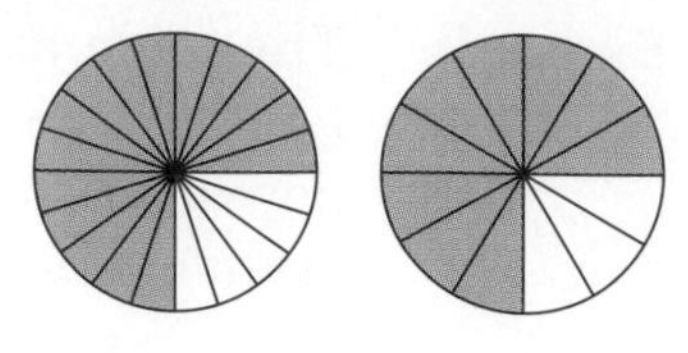

Estimation Estimate the solution of each proportion.

12. $\frac{k}{20} = \frac{12}{47}$ 13. $\frac{5}{2} = \frac{31}{b}$ 14. $\frac{18}{5.9} = \frac{w}{7}$ 15. $\frac{1.5}{r} = \frac{2.5}{4.97}$

16. Write three different proportions whose terms are 0.4, 1.2, 1.6, and 4.8.

17. **Critical Thinking** What do you think is the solution of the proportion $6:n = n:1.5$? Explain your reasoning.

Choose Use a calculator, paper and pencil, or mental math. Solve each proportion.

18. $\frac{2}{5} = \frac{m}{45}$ 19. $4:k = 64:264$ 20. 8.1 is to 3 as y is to 1

21. $\frac{18}{11} = \frac{49.5}{s}$ 22. $6:3 = d:7$ 23. 3 is to 8 as 50 is to g

24. **Writing** In 3 h, Jim can walk 14 mi. To find the time it would take to walk 25 mi, he wrote the proportion $\frac{3}{14} = \frac{25}{h}$. What is his mistake?

Write a proportion to describe each situation. Then solve.

25. Li Su paid $1.08 to make 18 copies at the Copy Shoppe. At that rate, how much would she pay for 40 copies?

26. According to the label, there are 50 calories in 4 fl oz of orange juice. How many calories are in 14 fl oz of the juice?

27. **Data File I (pp. 2-3)** In 1990, the population of Japan was about 123,778,000. About how many automobiles were on the road in Japan in that year?

28. The seesaw shown at the left is balanced when $a:y = b:x$. Suppose that a 50-lb weight rests 29 in. from the fulcrum. You must place a 30-lb weight on the other side. How far from the fulcrum must you place it to balance the seesaw?

Problem Solving Practice

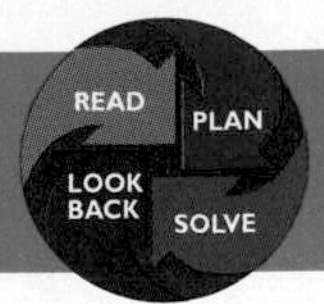

PROBLEM SOLVING STRATEGIES

Make a Table
Use Logical Reasoning
Solve a Simpler Problem
Too Much or Too Little Information
Look for a Pattern
Make a Model
Work Backward
Draw a Diagram
Guess and Test
Simulate a Problem
Use Multiple Strategies
Write an Equation
Use a Proportion

Solve if possible. If not, tell what information is needed. The list at the left shows some possible strategies you can use.

1. You lend half of your money to Nadine. You give Catherine one third of what was left. Then Jerry asks to borrow money for lunch. So, you give him half of what is left. Now you have \$5.00. How much money did you start with?

2. Mr. Carlos Ojeda, a mathematician, was always forgetting his bank password. However, he has an excellent memory for anything numerical. So, he created a new password in the form *ABCDE*, where *A, B, C, D,* and *E* are digits. Use the clues below to figure out Mr. Ojeda's new password.
   - The five digits are positive, unique, and none are prime.
   - Even and odd digits alternate.
   - *B, C,* and *D* are square numbers.
   - $A + D = B$

Steffi Graff was a teenager when she won the tennis "Grand Slam" in 1988, the same year that she won the women's singles Olympic gold medal.

3. During a delivery of 100 cans of racquetballs and tennis balls, an accident occurred and all 255 balls landed in the pool. Tennis balls are packaged three to a can and racquetballs are packaged two to a can. How many cans of each type of ball were in the delivery?

4. Imagine writing the whole numbers from 1 through 100. In what percent of the numbers do you write at least one 5?

5. At Martin Luther King School, students take 5 academic subjects. Each student also takes 1 health class, 1 music class, 1 computer class, and 1 art class each week. Once a week, students take a "special course" in cooking, sewing, metal work, or wood work. Half the students take wood work, 30 take cooking, and an equal number take sewing and metal work. How many students take sewing?

6. The Manchester field hockey team played 18 games during the season. They won 8 more games than they lost. Give the ratio of wins to losses for the team.

What's Ahead

- Identifying similar and congruent polygons
- Using proportional reasoning to find parts of similar polygons

WHAT YOU'LL NEED

✓ Graph paper

8-4 Similar Figures

THINK AND DISCUSS

Exploring Similarity Figures that have the same shape but not necessarily the same size are called **similar figures.** For example, when you project a slide onto a screen, the image on the screen is similar to the image on the slide.

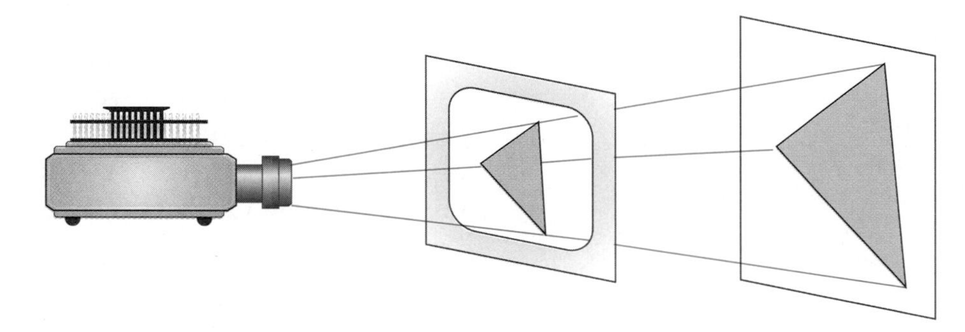

1. Name some other everyday examples of *similarity.*

> *Similarity is not the same thing as identity.*
> —Ibo proverb

When two *polygons* are similar, you can pair their vertices in such a way that

- corresponding angles are congruent, and
- corresponding sides are in proportion.

The symbol ~ means *is similar to.* So, if you take the triangles from above and label them as shown, you can write $\triangle ABC \sim \triangle XYZ$. Then you can identify the relationships among corresponding parts.

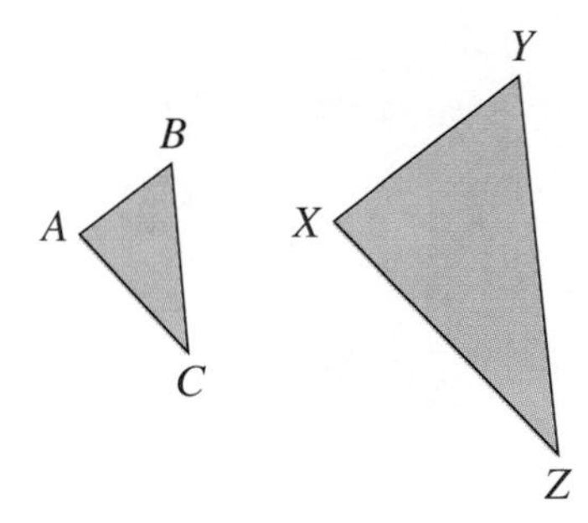

$\angle A \cong \angle X$
$\angle B \cong \angle Y$ $\quad \frac{AB}{XY} = \frac{BC}{YZ} = \frac{AC}{XZ}$
$\angle C \cong \angle Z$

FLASHBACK

The ≅ symbol means *is congruent to.* Two angles that are congruent have the same measure.

2. a. Given that quadrilateral *RSTU* ~ quadrilateral *FGHJ*, name all the pairs of congruent corresponding angles.
   b. Write a proportion to express the relationships among all the pairs of corresponding sides.

Finding Unknown Lengths You can use the fact that in similar polygons corresponding sides are in proportion.

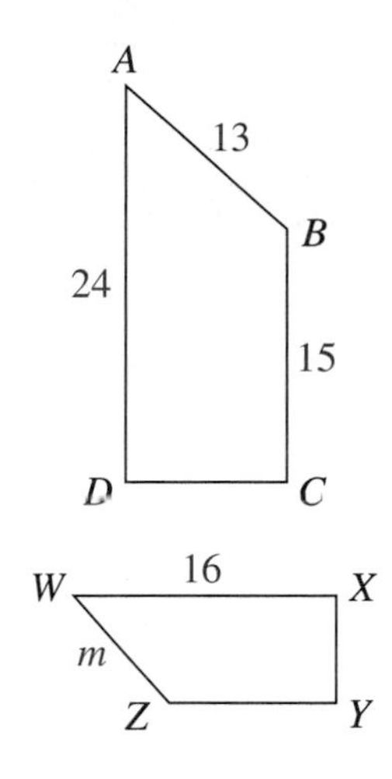

Example 1 Trapezoid $ABCD \sim$ trapezoid $WZYX$. Find m.

Write a proportion.

$\frac{AD}{WX} = \frac{AB}{WZ}$	$\overline{AD}$ corresponds to $\overline{WX}$. $\overline{AB}$ corresponds to $\overline{WZ}$.
$\frac{24}{16} = \frac{13}{m}$	Substitute.
$24 \cdot m = 16 \cdot 13$ $\frac{24m}{24} = \frac{208}{24}$	Write the cross products and solve.
$m = 8\frac{2}{3}$	

3. Refer to the trapezoids at the right. Find the length of $\overline{YZ}$.

In similar polygons, the ratio of the lengths of corresponding sides is the **scale factor** of the similarity. So, in Example 1, the scale factor of trapezoid $ABCD$ to trapezoid $WZYX$ is $\frac{24}{16}$, or $\frac{3}{2}$.

4. What is the scale factor of trapezoid $WZYX$ to trapezoid $ABCD$?

Often similar polygons overlap each other.

Example 2 $\triangle JKL \sim \triangle GKH$. Find the value of t.

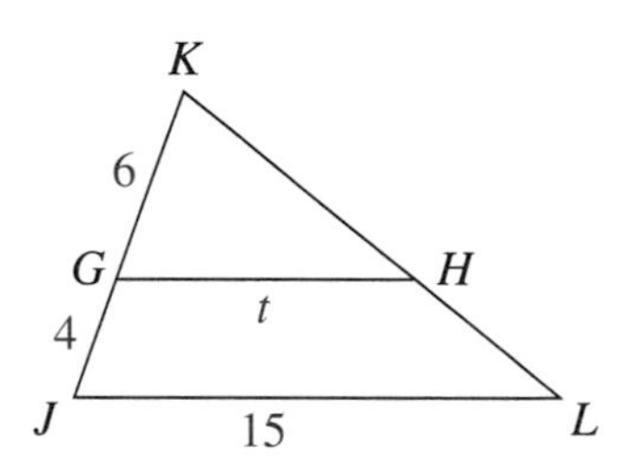

Write a proportion.

$\frac{KG}{KJ} = \frac{GH}{JL}$	$\overline{KG}$ corresponds to $\overline{KJ}$. $\overline{GH}$ corresponds to $\overline{JL}$.
$\frac{6}{10} = \frac{t}{15}$	Substitute. Notice that $KJ = 6 + 4 = 10$.
$6 \cdot 15 = 10 \cdot t$ $\frac{90}{10} = \frac{10t}{10}$	Write the cross products and solve.
$9 = t$	

5. Suppose $KL = 15$. What is the length of $\overline{KH}$? of $\overline{HL}$?

6. a. What is the scale factor of $\triangle JKL$ to $\triangle GKH$?

b. What is the scale factor of $\triangle GKH$ to $\triangle JKL$?

c. Explain how your answers to parts (a) and (b) are related.

WORK TOGETHER

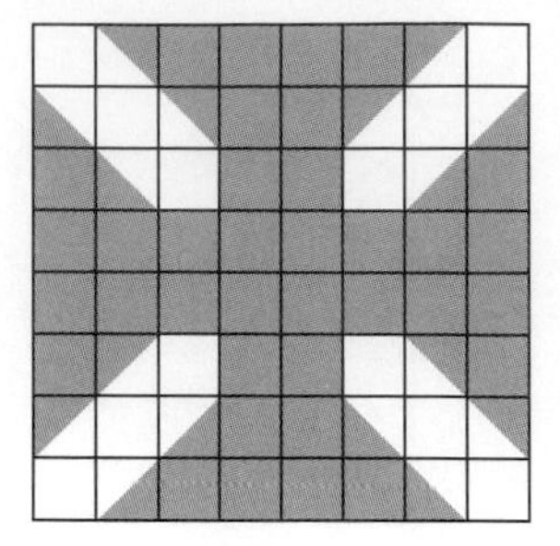

Work with a partner. Copy the figure at the left onto graph paper.

7. Draw two figures similar to your original. For the first figure, the scale factor of the new figure to the original should be $\frac{1}{2}$. For the second, the scale factor should be $\frac{3}{2}$.

8. a. **Discussion** Would a scale factor of $\frac{5}{4}$ give you an *enlargement* or a *reduction* of your original? What about a scale factor of $\frac{1}{4}$? Explain your reasoning.
   b. What would happen if you used a scale factor of 1?

TRY THESE

Tell whether each figure contains a pair of similar polygons. If so, state the similarity. Then give the scale factor of the smaller polygon to the larger.

9.

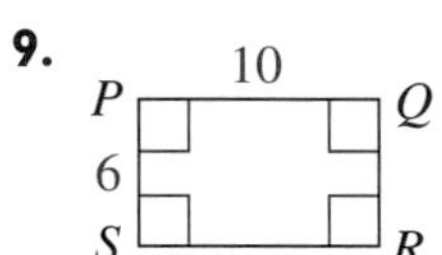

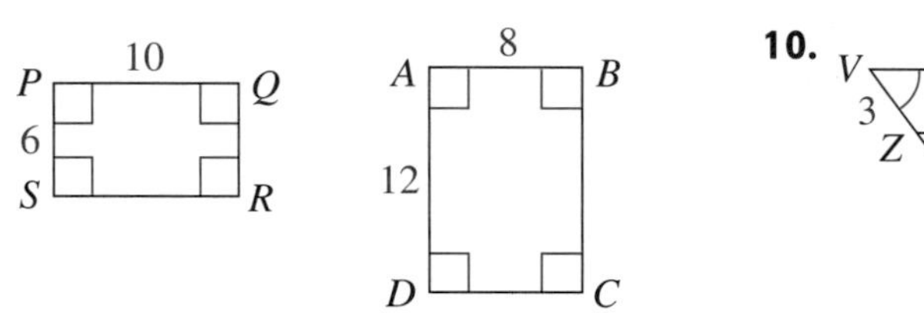

10.

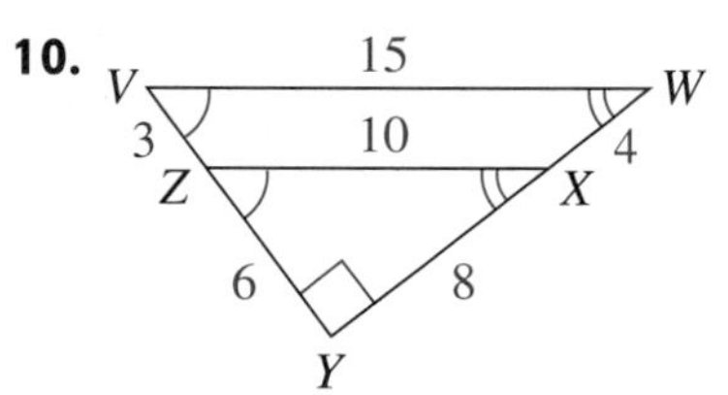

Each figure shows a pair of similar polygons. Find all the unknown lengths.

11.

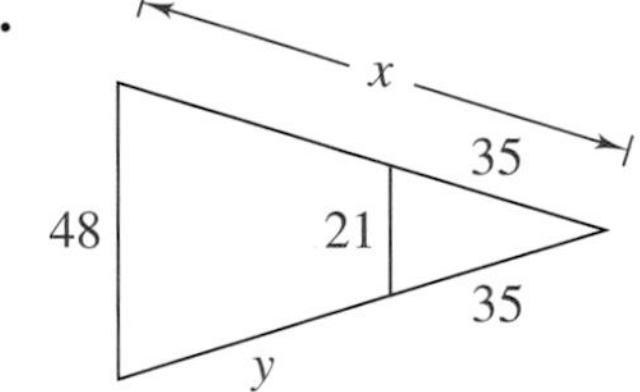

12.

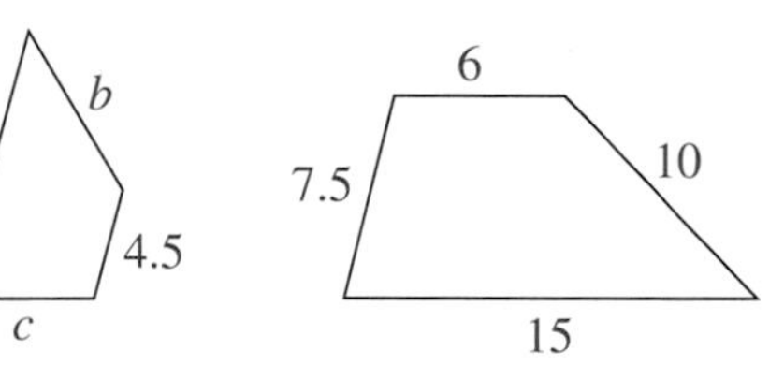

ON YOUR OWN

13. **Choose A, B, C, or D.** Which statement is false?
   A. All regular pentagons are similar.
   B. Triangles that are congruent are similar.
   C. Not all circles are similar.
   D. Not all rectangles are similar.

Mixed REVIEW

Solve.

1. $\frac{d}{5} = \frac{3}{8}$
2. $\frac{9}{10} = \frac{15}{y}$

Evaluate for $x = 4$.

3. $\frac{3}{4}x^3 + \frac{x}{8}$

Use a calculator to evaluate.

4. $15 - 9^2 \cdot 4 \div (-12)$
5. $(7 + (-2) \cdot 8)^3 - 16$

6. Draw a tessellation on a $8\frac{1}{2}$ in. × 11 in. piece of paper using only equilateral triangles and regular hexagons. Cover the paper with the pattern.

Each figure shows a pair of similar polygons. Find all the unknown lengths.

14.

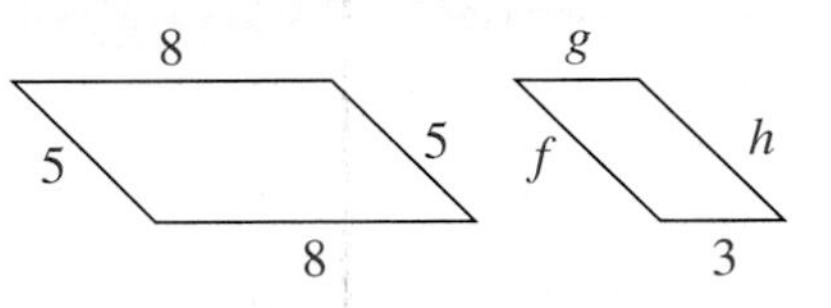

15. m, 1.6, 3.4, 10.2, 3, n

For a square:
- perimeter $P = 4s$
- area $A = s^2 = s \cdot s$

For a rectangle:
- perimeter $P = 2l + 2w$
- area $A = lw$

16. Writing Explain why these statements are true.

a. Congruent figures are always similar.

b. Similar figures *may* be congruent, but are not necessarily congruent.

17. Computer Generate data for perimeters and areas of squares by making a spreadsheet like the one at the right. In Column A, enter lengths of sides from 1 through 24.

a. When the length of each side is doubled, what happens to the perimeter? What happens to the area?

b. What happens to the perimeter and area when the length of each side is tripled?

c. What happens to the perimeter and area when the figure is enlarged by a scale factor of n?

d. Adjust the spreadsheet to generate data for perimeters and areas of rectangles. Then repeat parts (a) through (c).

	A	B	C
1	S	4*S	S*S
2	1	■	■
3	2	■	■
4	3	■	■
5	4	■	■
6	5	■	■
7	6	■	■
8	7	■	■
9	8	■	■

CHECKPOINT

1. Write the ratio "12 out of 30" in simplest form.

2. It costs $58 to have eight pages typed. What is the unit rate?

3. Aviation An airplane is flying at 455 miles per hour. What is its speed in feet per minute?

Solve each proportion.

4. $\frac{2}{5} = \frac{n}{15}$ **5.** $3:20 = t:10$ **6.** $\frac{16}{15} = \frac{4}{m}$ **7.** $\frac{0.7}{k} = \frac{7}{28}$

8. In the figure at the right, the triangles are similar.

a. Complete: $\triangle PQT \sim \triangle$■.

b. Find each unknown length.

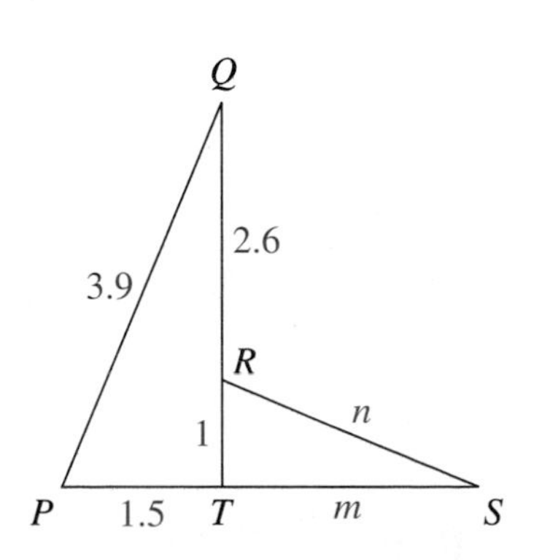

PROBLEM SOLVING

What's Ahead

- Using proportions to solve problems

8-5 Use a Proportion

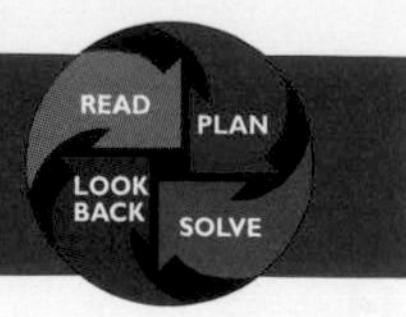

A *scale model* represents an actual object. Many people think of scale models as being smaller than the objects they represent, such as models of trains and doll houses. In the sciences, however, people often make large scale models of very tiny objects, such as insects and microorganisms. In either case, the ratio of the length of the model to the actual length is called the **scale** of the model.

> An architect wants to make a scale model of a proposed farm silo. The actual height of the silo will be 75 ft. The scale of the model is 1 in. : $2\frac{1}{2}$ ft. What will be the height of the model?

READ

Read and understand the given information. Summarize the problem.

Read the problem carefully.

1. What is a scale model?
2. What does the expression *1 in. : $2\frac{1}{2}$ ft* represent?
3. Summarize the goal of the problem in your own words.

PLAN

Decide on a strategy to solve the problem.

The scale of a model is a ratio. To find an unknown length, a good strategy is to use this ratio to write a proportion. Use a variable like h to represent the height of the silo in the model.

SOLVE

Try out the strategy.

Write a proportion and use cross products to solve.

$$\frac{\text{model height (in.)}}{\text{actual height (ft)}} \rightarrow \frac{1}{2\frac{1}{2}} = \frac{h}{75}$$

$$2\tfrac{1}{2}h = 75 \quad \text{Write the cross products.}$$

$$\tfrac{5}{2}h = 75 \quad \text{Write the mixed number as an improper fraction.}$$

$$\tfrac{2}{5} \cdot \tfrac{5}{2}h = \tfrac{2}{5} \cdot 75 \quad \text{Multiply each side by } \tfrac{2}{5}.$$

$$h = 30$$

The height of the model will be 30 in.

4. How can you check the solution of the problem?

5. Is it possible to use a different proportion to solve the problem? Explain.

LOOK BACK
Think about how you solved this problem.

TRY THESE

6. Look back at the problem about the silo.
   a. Suppose that the diameter of the proposed silo is 15 ft. What will be the diameter of the model?
   b. Suppose that the scale of the model is to be 1 in. : 6 ft. What will be the height and diameter of the model?
   c. A competing architect made a model of the silo that is 20 in. high. What is the scale of this model? (Give your answer in the form 1 in. : ■ ft.)

Use a proportion to solve each problem. Show all your work.

7. **Map Making** The scale of the map of Texas at the right is 1 cm : 160 km.
   a. Use a metric ruler to find the map distance between Abilene and Houston.
   b. What is the actual distance in km?

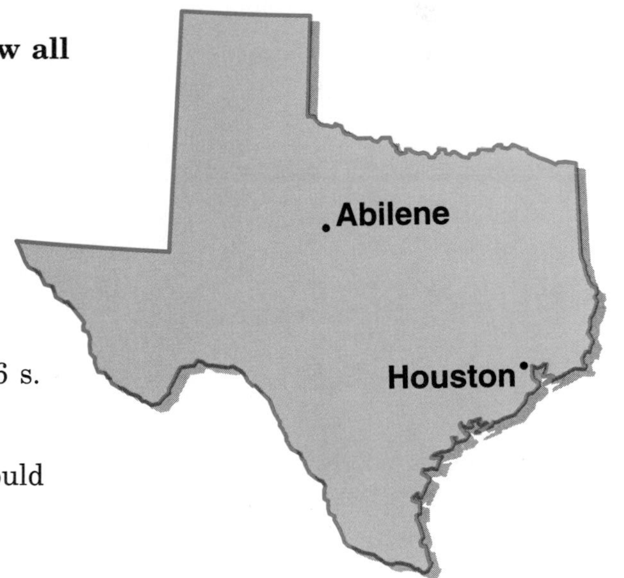

8. An average adult's heart beats 8 times every 6 s. How many times does the heart beat in 90 s?

9. Six ounces of cheese cost $1.85. How much would $1\frac{1}{2}$ lb of this cheese cost?

ON YOUR OWN

Use any strategy to solve each problem. Show all your work.

10. The total of all the scores on an eighth grade mathematics test was 2,145 points. The mean score was 82.5 points. If there are 14 girls in the class, how many boys are there?

11. Pierre was born in the 20th century and will be x years old in the year x^2. In what year was Pierre born?

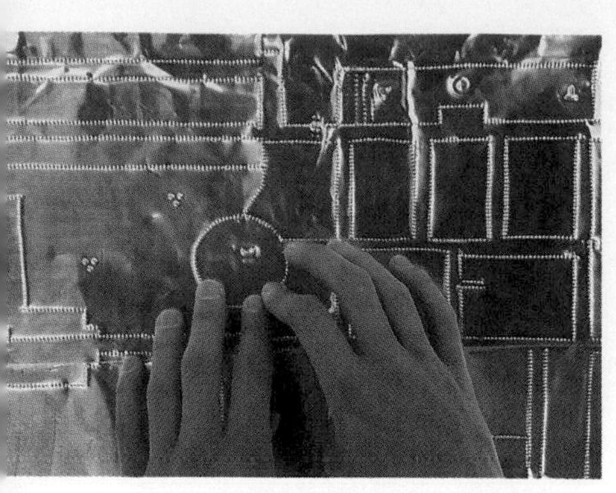

***Two students** from Linton High School in Schenectady, New York, turned the school's floor plan into a wall map for blind students and won first prize in a contest for their efforts.*

Source: *National Geographic World*

12. The figure at the right is a scale drawing of a regulation tennis court. The scale of the drawing is $\frac{1}{4}$ inch : 6 feet. What are the length and width of a regulation tennis court?

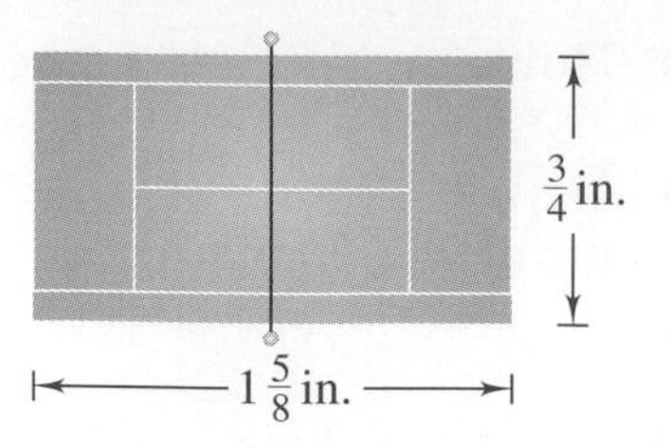

13. A carpenter has exactly 36 m of fencing to make a rectangular pen for a pig. Assume that both the length and the width must be a whole number of meters. What size rectangle will give the pig the most room?

14. The punch for a class party is to be a mixture of two parts ginger ale to three parts fruit juice. The fruit juice will be donated by a parent, but the students must buy the ginger ale. Suppose that 60 cups of punch are needed. How many quarts of ginger ale should the students buy?

15. The bleacher seats of Central Stadium are arranged as shown in the table below. Suppose that the pattern in the table continues for all the rows in the stadium. In which row would you find seat 100?

Seat Numbers						
row 1	1					
row 2	2	3				
row 3	4	5	6			
row 4	7	8	9	10		
row 5	11	12	13	14	15	
row 6	16	17	18	19	20	21

16. Renting an office in Tokyo, Japan, is very expensive. It can cost $192.24 to rent just one square foot of space. At this rate, what is the cost per square yard?

17. Suppose you are in charge of special effects for a school play. You must make an actor 5 ft tall appear to be shrunk to the height of a tissue box. A regular tissue box is $9\frac{1}{2}$ in. long, $4\frac{3}{4}$ in. wide, and 4 in. tall. What must be the dimensions of your stage model of the box in order to produce the special effect?

18. **Investigation (p. 338)** Explain how you could use a proportion to find the distance you estimated.

Mixed REVIEW

$\triangle KGT \sim \triangle MBY$

1. $MY = 12$ cm, $BY = 9$ cm, and $GT = 10$ cm. Find KT.
2. $m\angle G = 55°$, $m\angle Y = 70°$. Find $m\angle K$.

Solve.

3. $9a - \frac{2}{3} = \frac{5}{6}$
4. $\frac{1}{4} - 2k = \frac{1}{2}$
5. $\frac{7}{8} = \frac{3}{z}$

Find the measure of each angle of the regular polygon.

6. nonagon 7. heptagon

What's Ahead

- Measuring distances indirectly using similar triangles

8-6 Indirect Measurement

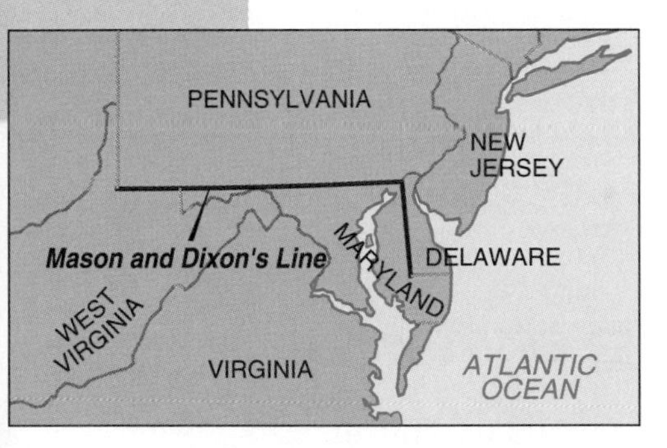

Between 1763 and 1767, two English surveyors, Charles Mason and Jeremiah Dixon, determined the boundary known as Mason and Dixon's Line to settle a dispute between the colonies of Pennsylvania and Maryland.

Source: *World Book Encyclopedia*

THINK AND DISCUSS

Finding Unknown Heights When a length or distance is relatively small, you measure it *directly* with a ruler or tape measure. Sometimes you can find the length or distance only by means of an **indirect measurement.** One common method of indirect measurement involves the use of similar triangles.

Example 1 Jerome is 6 ft tall and casts a shadow 17 ft long. At the same time, a nearby tree casts a shadow 102 ft long. What is the height of the tree?

- The rays of the sun, the shadows, and the heights form a pair of similar triangles, as shown below.

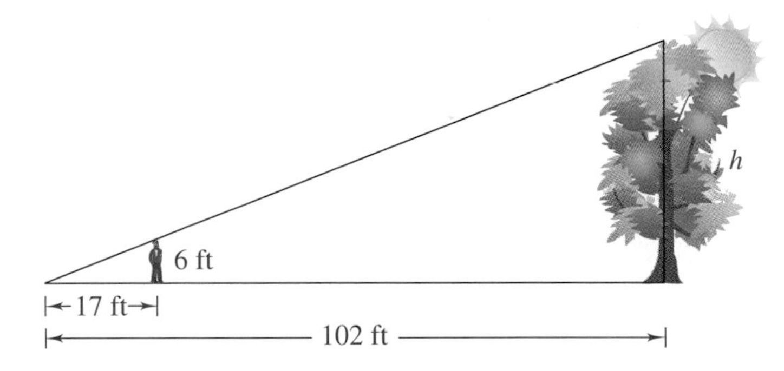

Use the similar triangles to set up a proportion.

$$\frac{\text{tree's height}}{\text{length of tree's shadow}} = \frac{\text{Jerome's height}}{\text{length of Jerome's shadow}}$$

$$\frac{h}{102} = \frac{6}{17} \quad \textbf{Substitute.}$$

$$17h = 612 \quad \textbf{Write the cross products and solve.}$$

$$\frac{17h}{17} = \frac{612}{17}$$

$$h = 36$$

The height of the tree is 36 ft.

1. Write a different proportion for the problem in Example 1.
2. What proportion would you use to solve the problem if Jerome were 5 ft 9 in. tall?

Finding Unknown Distances

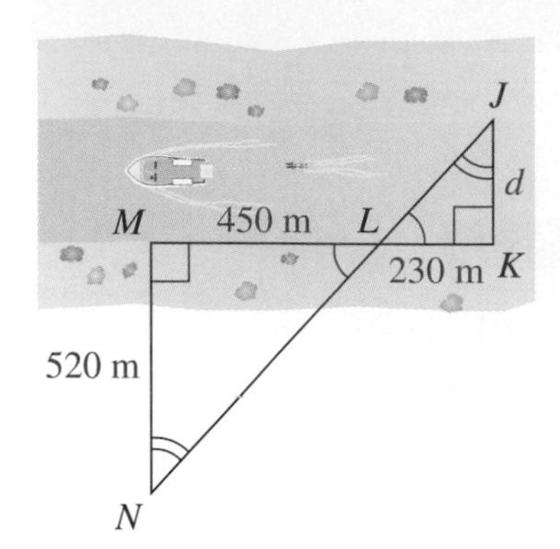

Example 2 A surveyor took the measurements shown in the figure at the left. Find d, the distance across the river.

- In the figure $\triangle JKL \sim \triangle NML$.
  Use the similar triangles to set up a proportion.

$$\frac{JK}{NM} = \frac{KL}{ML}$$ $\overline{JK}$ corresponds to $\overline{NM}$. $\overline{KL}$ corresponds to $\overline{ML}$.

$$\frac{d}{520} = \frac{230}{450}$$ Substitute.

$$450d = 119{,}600$$
$$\frac{450d}{450} = \frac{119{,}600}{450}$$ Write the cross products and solve.

119,600 ÷ 450 = 265.77778

The distance across the river is about 266 m.

TRY THESE

3. Draw a figure to show this situation.
   A 15-ft flagpole casts a shadow 10 ft long. At the same time, a building that is 45 ft tall casts a shadow 30 ft long.

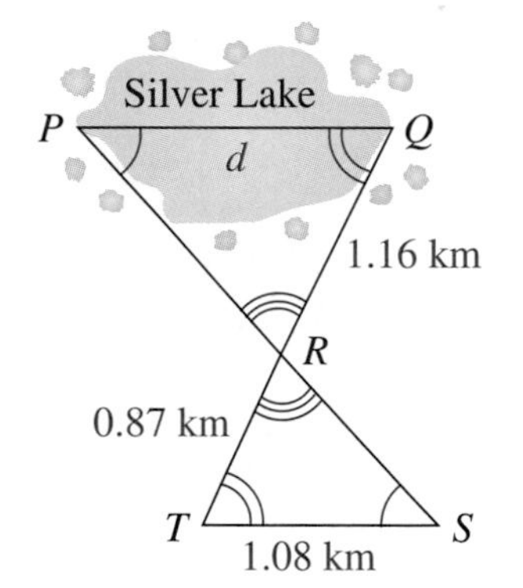

4. a. **Discussion** Describe the situation shown at the left.
   b. Write a proportion that relates PQ, QR, TR, and ST.
   c. Find d.

5. A girl 5 ft tall casts a shadow 7.5 ft long. She stands next to a cactus whose shadow is 18 ft long. How tall is the cactus?

ON YOUR OWN

Use the similar triangles to find each unknown height.

6. 7.

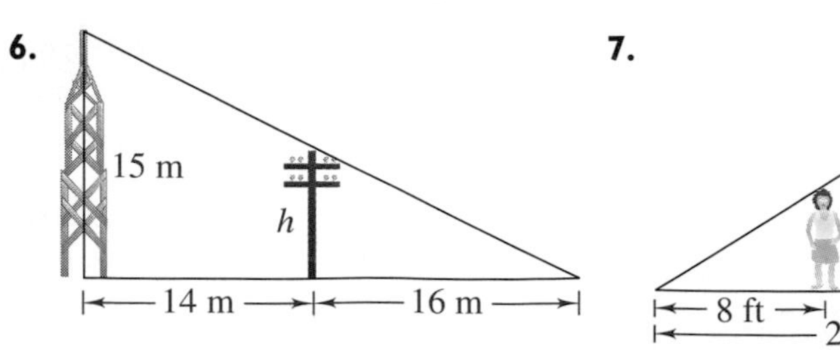

8. The Bunker Hill Monument in Charlestown, Massachusetts, is 221 ft tall. It casts a shadow 189 ft long at the same time that a nearby tree casts a shadow 29 ft long. To the nearest foot, how tall is the tree?

9. The tallest unsupported flagpole in the world is located in Vancouver, British Columbia. It casts a shadow 376 ft long at the same time that a man who is 6 ft tall casts a shadow 8 ft long. How tall is the flagpole?

Use the similar triangles to find each unknown distance.

10.

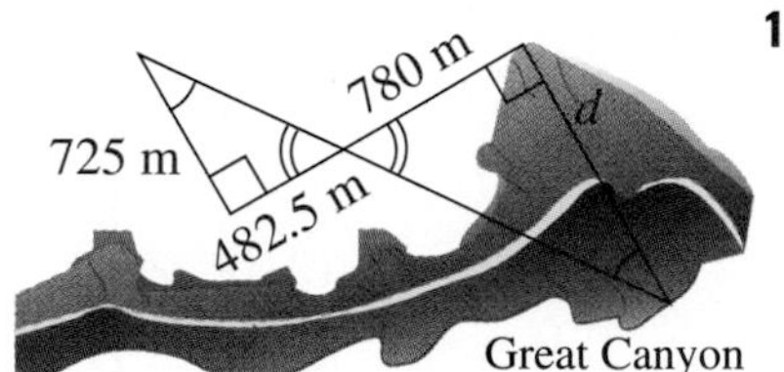

11.

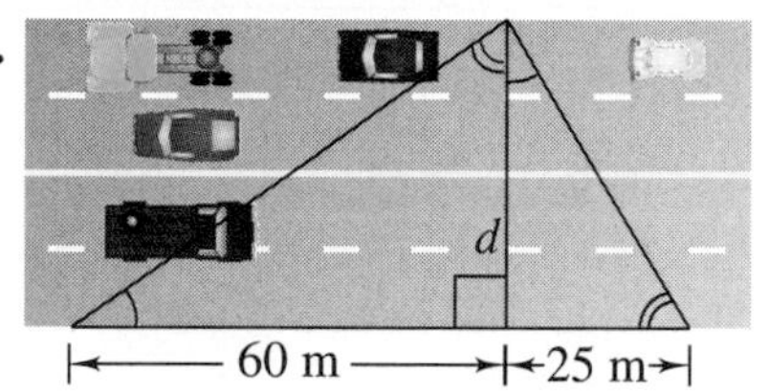

12. **Writing** Describe an everyday situation in which you might measure a distance indirectly.

13. Surveyors took the measurements below on the shores of Lake Mandelbrot. Find the unknown distances *x, y,* and *z.* (*Hint:* Use similar triangles *and* the Pythagorean Theorem.)

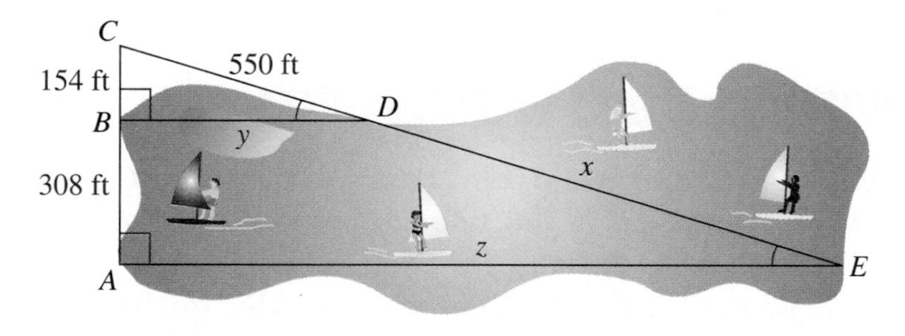

14. **Critical Thinking** The figure at the right shows a method of indirect measurement that involves the use of a mirror.

a. How do you determine the position of the mirror?

b. State the similarity between the triangles.

c. Write a proportion that represents the relationships among *XY, XZ, WV,* and *WZ.*

d. Explain how you use the proportion to find *h.*

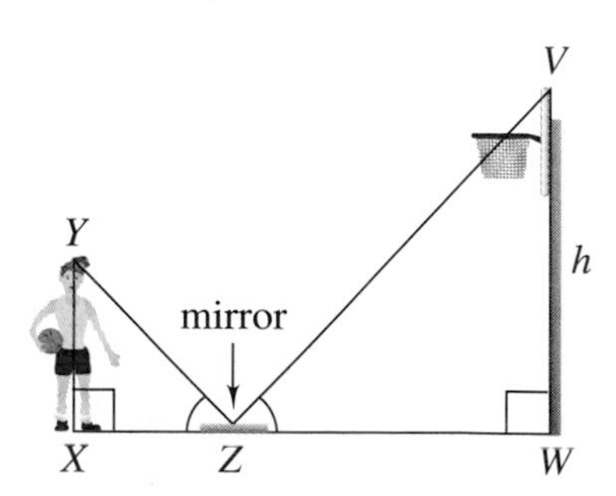

15. **Investigation (p. 338)** Explain how you could use similar triangles to find the distance you estimated.

Mixed REVIEW

Write a proportion.

1. On a map, the distance between Grapeland and Peachland is 16 cm. If the scale is 2 cm : 25 km, what is the actual distance?

Write an equation for each line.

2. slope $= -3$
   y-intercept $= 2$

3. slope $= \frac{2}{5}$
   y-intercept $= -2$

4. slope $= 0$
   y-intercept $= 5$

5. Find the smallest number divisible by 3, 5, 6, and 8.

The Pythagorean Theorem: In any right triangle with legs a and b and hypotenuse c, $a^2 + b^2 = c^2$.

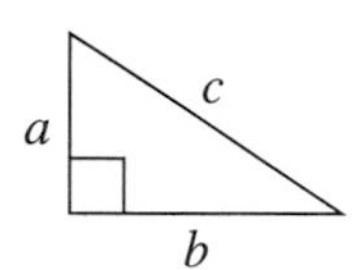

TECHNOLOGY

8-7 The Tangent Ratio

What's Ahead

- Using technology to explore the tangent ratio
- Solving problems using the tangent ratio

WHAT YOU'LL NEED

✓ Computer

✓ Geometry software

✓ Calculator

WORK TOGETHER

1. Work with a partner. Use geometry software to construct a figure like the one below at the right.

a. Copy and complete this table.

$BC = ■$	$AB = ■$	$\frac{BC}{AB} = ■$
$DF = ■$	$AD = ■$	$\frac{DF}{AD} = ■$
$GH = ■$	$AG = ■$	$\frac{GH}{AG} = ■$

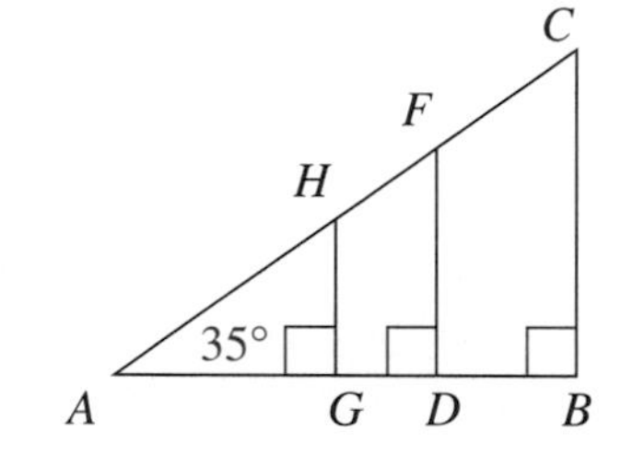

b. Discussion What pattern(s) do you notice in the table?

2. Repeat Exercise 1. This time construct the figure so that $m\angle A = 62°$.

3. Discussion Make a conjecture. What do you think happens if $m\angle A = 45°$? Adjust the figure and test your conjecture.

THINK AND DISCUSS

Exploring Tangent Ratio In $\triangle ABC$, at the left, $\overline{BC}$ is the side **opposite** $\angle A$, and $\overline{AC}$ is the side **adjacent** to $\angle A$. For any given measure of $\angle A$, the ratio of BC to AC is always the same number, no matter how large or small $\triangle ABC$ might become. This ratio has a special name, the **tangent** ratio, abbreviated *tan.*

B
hypotenuse
opposite
A
adjacent
C

$$\tan A = \frac{\text{length of side opposite } \angle A}{\text{length of side adjacent to } \angle A}$$

Example 1 In $\triangle RST$ at the right, find tan T.

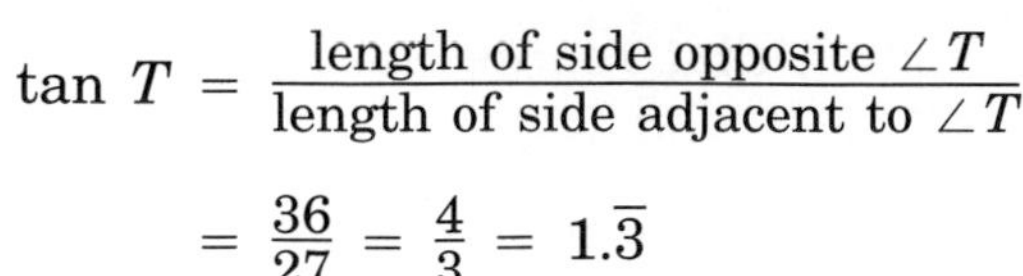

$$\tan T = \frac{\text{length of side opposite } \angle T}{\text{length of side adjacent to } \angle T}$$

$$= \frac{36}{27} = \frac{4}{3} = 1.\overline{3}$$

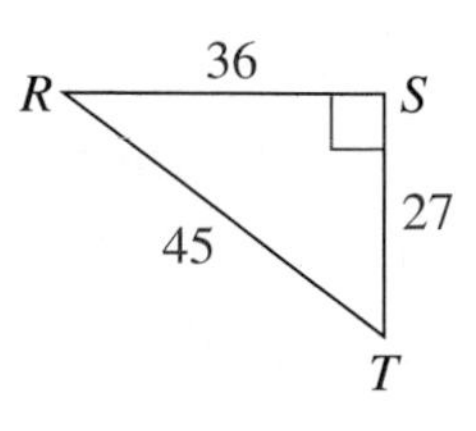

4. Write tan R as a fraction in simplest form and as a decimal.

If you know the measure of an acute angle of a right triangle, you can use a calculator to find its tangent.

Example 2 Find $\tan K$ as a decimal rounded to the nearest ten-thousandth.

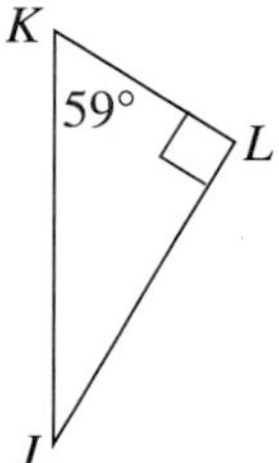

- Use a calculator to find tan 59°.

59 TAN 1.6642794

$\tan K \approx 1.6643$

An acute angle has a measure less than 90°.

The symbol $\approx$ means is approximately equal to.

Two angles are **complementary** if the sum of their measures is 90°. In any right triangle, the acute angles are complementary. So, you can make the following statements about $\triangle JKL$ above.

$\angle J$ and $\angle K$ are complementary $\rightarrow$ $m\angle J + m\angle K = 90°$

5. a. In $\triangle JKL$, what is the measure of $\angle J$?
   b. Find $\tan J$, rounded to the nearest ten-thousandth.

Solving Problems The tangent ratio helps solve problems.

Example 3 The planners of a light show aim a laser at a screen 200 ft away. The laser beam makes an angle of 25° with the ground. How high above ground will the beam hit the screen and show a red dot?

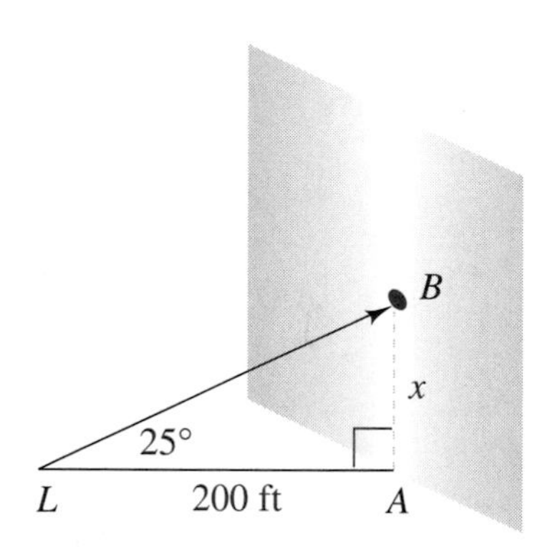

- Draw a diagram like the one at the right.

$$\tan L = \frac{AB}{LA}$$

$$\tan 25° = \frac{x}{200}$$ **Substitute.**

$$0.4663 \approx \frac{x}{200}$$ **Find tan 25° using a calculator.**

$$200 \cdot 0.4663 \approx 200 \cdot \frac{x}{200}$$ **Multiply each side by 200.**

$$93.26 \approx x$$

The beam will hit the screen about 93 ft above the ground.

6. How high above the ground will the beam hit the screen if the beam makes an angle of 37° with the ground?

7. The planners want the red dot to hit the screen 400 ft above ground when the beam makes an angle of 50° with the ground. How far from the screen should the laser be?

On May 9, 1962, a beam of light was reflected from the moon by a laser attached to a 48-in. telescope at the Massachusetts Institute of Technology. The spot was estimated to be 4 mi in diameter on the moon.

Source: *The Guinness Book of Records*

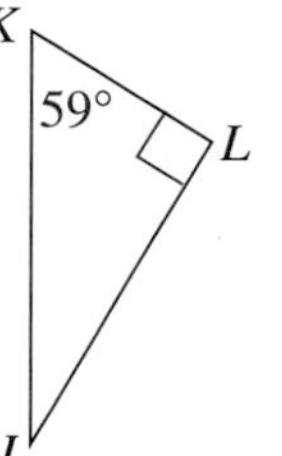

Mixed REVIEW

1. Aishah is planning a mural for the school cafeteria. Her scale drawing of the mural is 40 cm long and 24 cm high. If the mural will be 6 m long, how high will it be?

Solve each system of equations by graphing.

2. $2x + 5y = -8$
   $x - y = -4$
3. $-x + y = 3$
   $4x - 2y = 10$

Write the prime factorization.

4. 320   5. 288

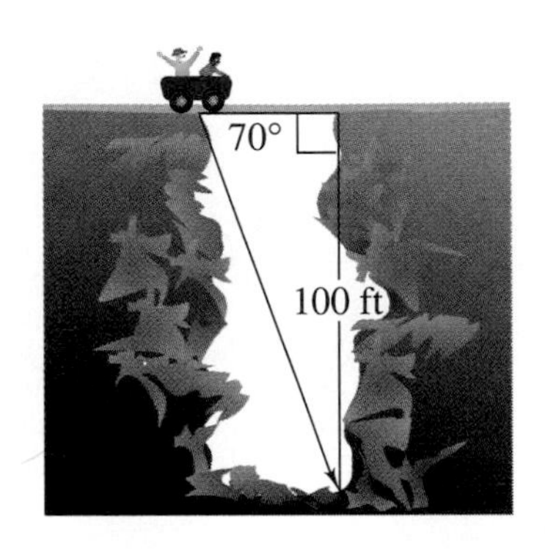

FLASHBACK

The longest side of a right triangle is the hypotenuse.

TRY THESE

8. Refer to $\triangle XYZ$, at the right.
   a. Which side is opposite $\angle X$? $\angle Z$?
   b. Which side is adjacent to $\angle X$? $\angle Z$?
   c. Find tan X as a fraction in simplest form and as a decimal. Then find tan Z.
   d. What is the relationship between tan X and tan Z?

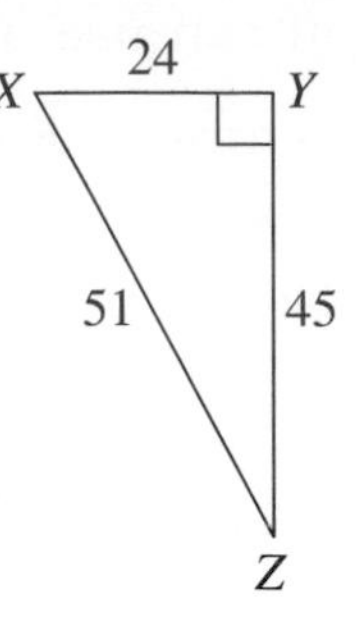

Use a calculator to find each tangent. Round to the nearest ten-thousandth.

9. tan 13°   10. tan 85°   11. tan 22°   12. tan 45°

13. Refer to $\triangle RST$, at the right.
    a. Find m by writing and solving an equation that involves tan R.
    b. Find m by writing and solving an equation that involves tan S.
    c. **Discussion** How do the solution methods in parts (a) and (b) compare?

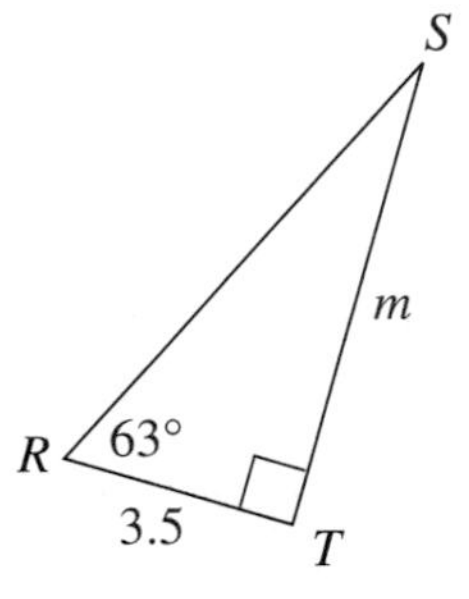

14. The Bridge of Doom adventure ride crosses a canyon that is 100 ft deep, as shown at the left. From one end of the bridge, you can see the bottom of the canyon on the opposite side by looking down at an angle of 70°. To the nearest foot, what is the length of the Bridge of Doom?

ON YOUR OWN

For each figure, use a calculator to find tan A and tan B. Round to the nearest ten-thousandth.

15.
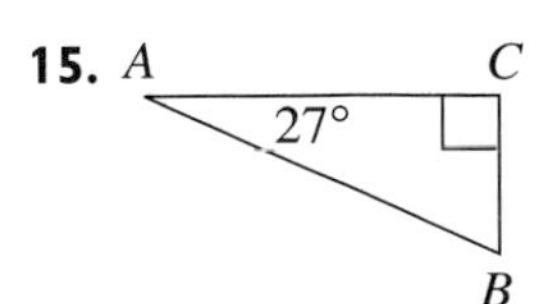

16.
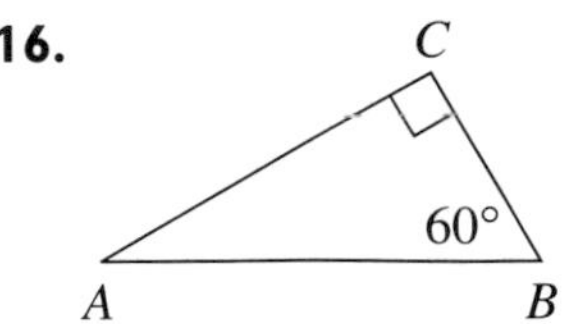

17.
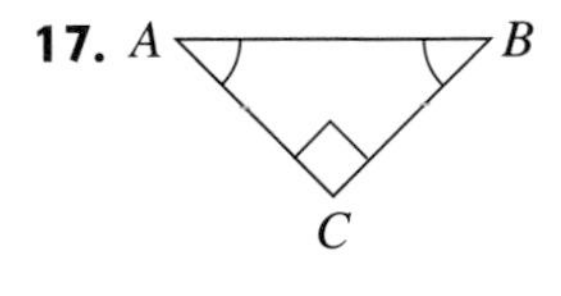

18. In $\triangle PQR$, $PQ = 25$, $PR = 60$, and $QR = 65$. Find tan Q as a fraction in simplest form and as a decimal.

In each figure, find n. Round to the nearest tenth.

19.

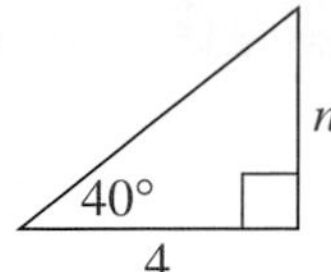

20.

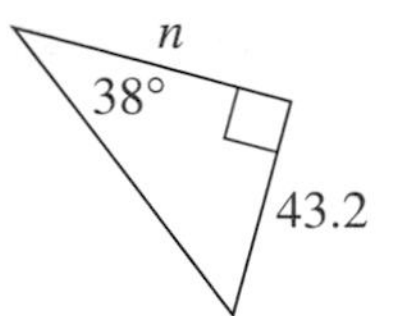

21.

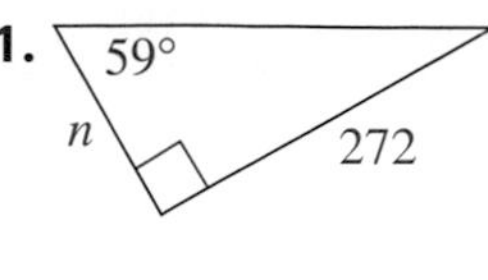

22. **a.** **Critical Thinking** If $\tan A = 1$, find $m\angle A$.

b. Is $\tan 74°$ greater than 1 or less than 1? Explain.

c. If $\tan A < 1$, what generalization can you make about $\angle A$?

23. In the T-Rex Scrambler ride, cars spin at the ends of a bar as shown in the figure at the right. What is the distance between car A and car B?

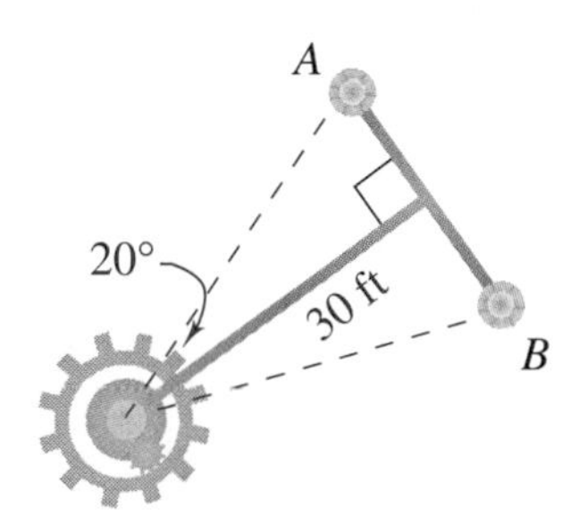

24. **Writing** Make up a problem that you can solve using the tangent ratio. Write a solution for your problem.

25. **Data File 8 (pp. 336–337)** Estimate the altitude of a rocket if the tracker is 100 m from the location of the launch and sights the rocket at an angle of 50°.

Extra SKILLS PRACTICE

Find the tangent of each angle to the nearest hundredth.

1. $\angle D = 20°$
2. $\angle X = 85°$
3. $\angle P = 72°$
4. $\angle K = 15°$
5. $\angle H = 63°$

In $\triangle ABC$, $\angle C = 90°$ and $\angle A = 35°$. Find each of the following.

6. $m\angle B$
7. $\tan A$
8. $\tan B$
9. AC if $BC = 24$
10. AC if $BC = 50$
11. BC if $AC = 8.5$
12. BC if $AC = 34.6$

Students Become Surveyors

At Carver Middle School, students became surveyors by making an inexpensive version of a surveying instrument called a *transit.* "It's easy," said one student. "All you need is a protractor taped to a board and a straw pinned to the protractor."

The students used their transit to measure the distance across the river to Memorial Tower. When they later compared their result to city records, it was only one hundredth of a mile greater than the distance in the records.

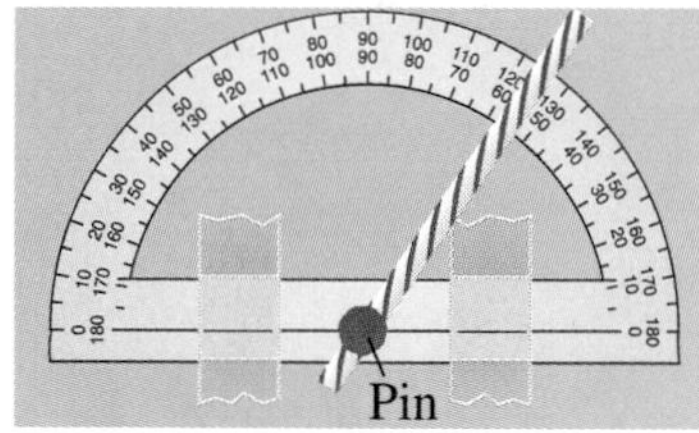

The Carver Students' Simple Homemade Transit

26. **a.** According to the students' calculations at the right, what is the distance in feet from the school to the tower?

b. According to the city records, what is the distance in miles from the school to the tower?

27. **Project** Make a transit as shown in the article. Use it to measure the distance across a large playground or field.

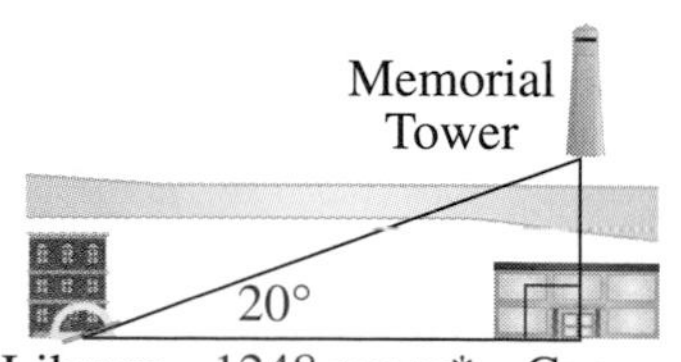

Their Calculations to Find the Distance to Memorial Tower

8-8 The Sine and Cosine Ratios

What's Ahead

- Defining the sine and cosine of an acute angle of a right triangle
- Using the sine and cosine ratios to solve problems

WHAT YOU'LL NEED

✓ Computer 

✓ Geometry software 

✓ Calculator 

Never be afraid to sit awhile and think.

—Lorraine Hansberry (1930–1965)

WORK TOGETHER

1. Work with a partner. Use geometry software to construct a figure like the one at the right.

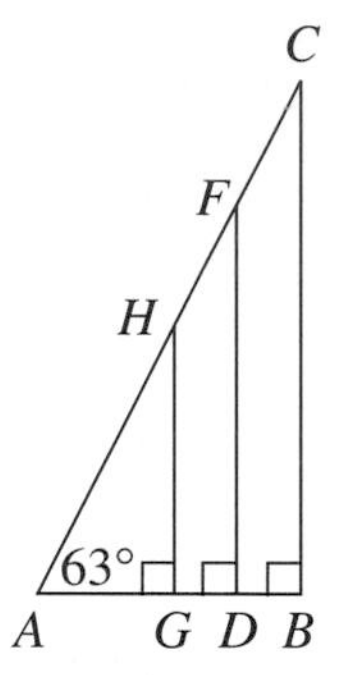

   a. Copy and complete this table.

$BC = ■$	$AB = ■$	$AC = ■$	$\frac{BC}{AC} = ■$	$\frac{AB}{AC} = ■$
$DF = ■$	$AD = ■$	$AF = ■$	$\frac{DF}{AF} = ■$	$\frac{AD}{AF} = ■$
$GH = ■$	$AG = ■$	$AH = ■$	$\frac{GH}{AH} = ■$	$\frac{AG}{AH} = ■$

   b. Discussion What pattern(s) do you notice in the table?

2. Repeat Exercise 1. This time, use $m\angle A = 23°$.

3. Make a conjecture. For what measure of $\angle A$ will the two ratios be equal? Adjust the figure and test your conjecture.

THINK AND DISCUSS

Exploring Sine and Cosine The tangent ratio involves the lengths of the legs of a right triangle. The *sine* and *cosine* ratios involve the lengths of the hypotenuse and one of the legs. These three ratios are called **trigonometric ratios.**

B
hypotenuse
opposite
A
adjacent
C

Trigonometric Ratios

tangent of $\angle A$: $\tan A = \frac{\text{length of side opposite } \angle A}{\text{length of side adjacent to } \angle A}$

sine of $\angle A$: $\sin A = \frac{\text{length of side opposite } \angle A}{\text{length of hypotenuse}}$

cosine of $\angle A$: $\cos A = \frac{\text{length of side adjacent to } \angle A}{\text{length of hypotenuse}}$

You may prefer to use the definitions in these shortened forms.

$$\tan = \frac{\text{opposite}}{\text{adjacent}} \qquad \sin = \frac{\text{opposite}}{\text{hypotenuse}} \qquad \cos = \frac{\text{adjacent}}{\text{hypotenuse}}$$

Example 1 Find sin G and cos G.

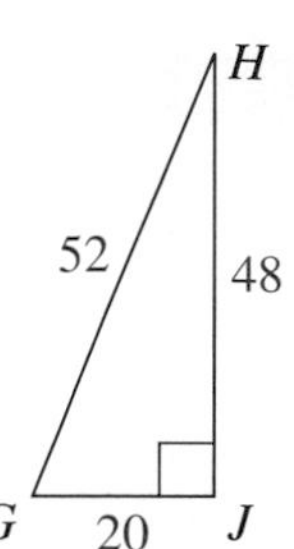

$$\sin G = \frac{\text{opposite}}{\text{hypotenuse}} = \frac{48}{52} = \frac{12}{13}$$

$$\cos G = \frac{\text{adjacent}}{\text{hypotenuse}} = \frac{20}{52} = \frac{5}{13}$$

4. Write sin H and cos H as fractions in simplest form.

If you know the measure of an acute angle of a right triangle, you can approximate its sine and cosine using a calculator.

Surveying *is the technique of measuring to determine the position of points on, beneath, or above the earth. A surveyor maps boundaries with a transit. A laser transit uses a concentrated beam of light to measure angles and determine distances.*

Source: *World Book Encyclopedia*

Example 2 Find sin P and cos P.

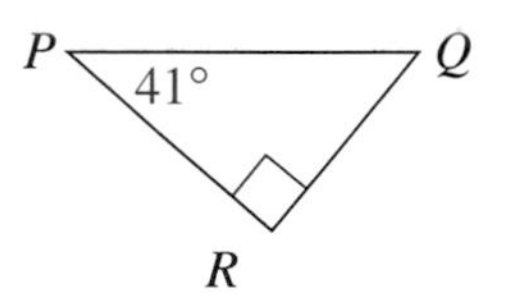

Use a calculator to find sin 41° and cos 41°. Round to the nearest ten-thousandth.

41 SIN 0.656059 → $\sin P \approx 0.6561$

41 COS 0.7547096 → $\cos P \approx 0.7547$

5. Use a calculator to find sin Q and cos Q.

Solving Problems

The tangent ratio helps solve problems.

Example 3 Find x in $\triangle LMN$.

$\overline{LN}$ is the side adjacent to $\angle L$.
$\overline{LM}$ is the *hypotenuse.*

You can use $\cos = \frac{\text{adjacent}}{\text{hypotenuse}}$.

$$\cos L = \frac{LN}{LM}$$

$$\cos 37° = \frac{200}{x}$$ **Substitute.**

$$0.7986 \approx \frac{200}{x}$$ **Find cos 37° using a calculator.**

$$0.7986 \cdot x \approx \frac{200}{x} \cdot x$$ **Multiply each side by x.**

$$0.7986x \approx 200$$

$$\frac{0.7986x}{0.7986} \approx \frac{200}{0.7986}$$ **Divide each side by 0.7986.**

$$x \approx 250.43$$ **Round to hundredth.**

6. Show how to find x using the sine ratio.

Write each trigonometric ratio as a fraction in simplest form.

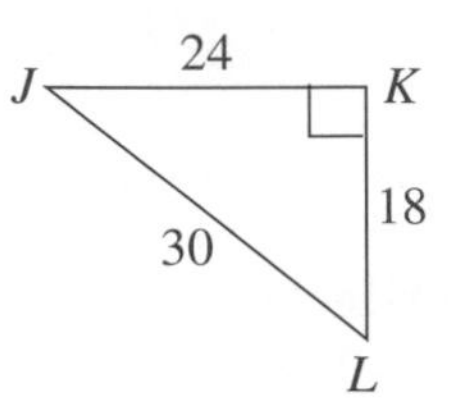

7. sin J 8. cos J 9. sin L

10. cos L 11. tan J 12. tan L

Use a calculator to find each sine or cosine. Round to the nearest ten-thousandth.

13. sin 80° 14. cos 4° 15. sin 71° 16. cos 19°

17. Refer to $\triangle ABC$ at the right.

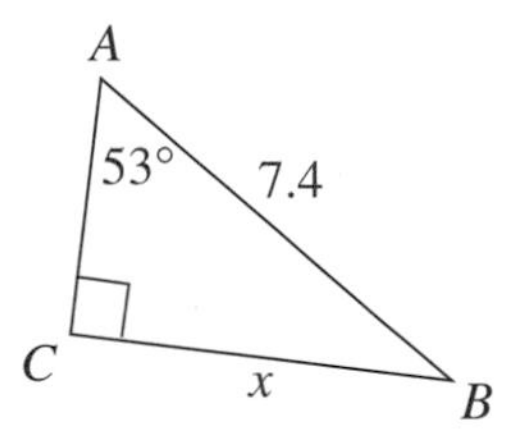

   a. Find x by writing and solving an equation that involves the sine ratio.

   b. Find x by writing and solving an equation that involves the cosine ratio.

18. a. A 16-ft ladder rests against a building so that it forms a 75° angle with the ground. To the nearest tenth of a foot, what is the distance from the top of the ladder to the base of the building?

   b. To the nearest tenth of a foot, what is the distance from the bottom of the ladder to the base of the building?

In the pueblos of Arizona and New Mexico, the lowest levels originally had no doors. The only access to all levels was by way of a ladder up to the roof and then down a ladder through a smoke hole. The ladders could easily be removed for defense.

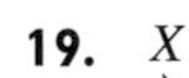

Use the Pythagorean Theorem to find *n*. Then write sin *X*, cos *X*, and tan *X* as fractions in simplest form.

19.

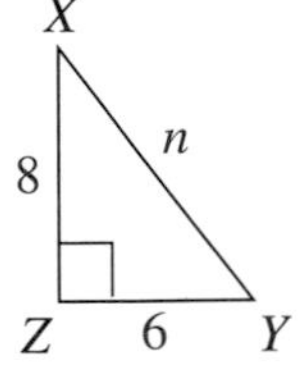

20.

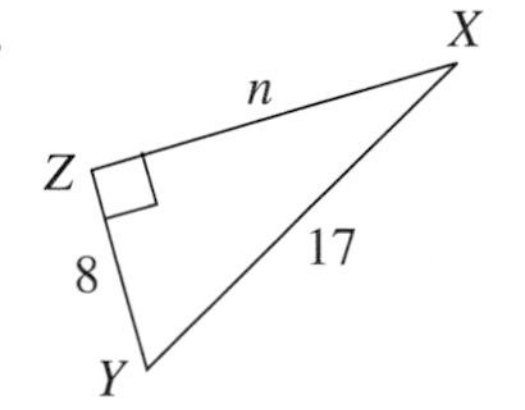

21.

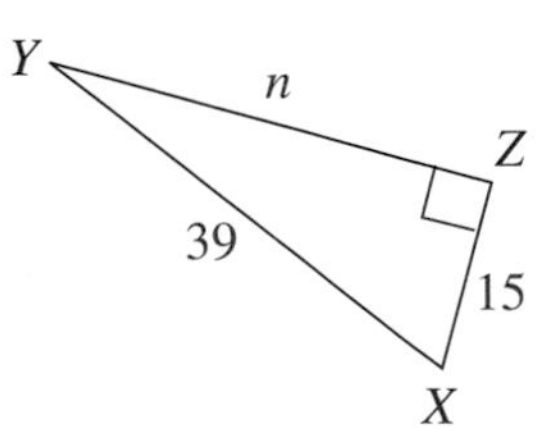

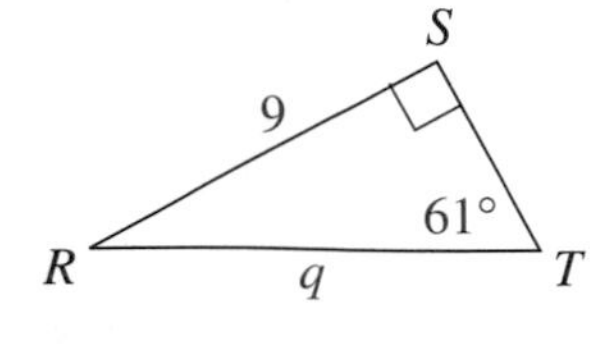

22. **Choose A, B, C, or D.** In $\triangle RST$, at the left, which equation can you use to find q?

   I. $\sin 61° = \frac{9}{q}$ II. $\cos 29° = \frac{q}{9}$ III. $\tan 29° = \frac{9}{q}$

   A. I only **B.** I or II only **C.** II or III only **D.** I, II, or III

In each figure, find *t*. Round to the nearest tenth.

23. 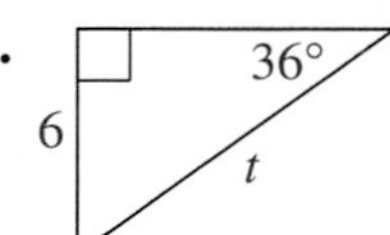

24. 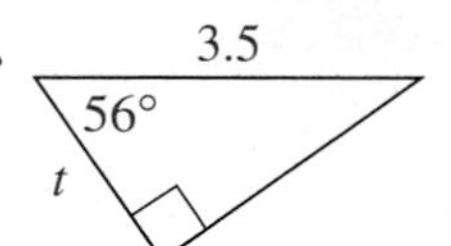

25. 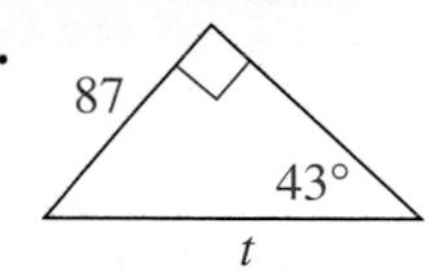

26. Writing Your best friend, who has moved to another state, is having some trouble figuring out whether to use the sine, cosine, or tangent ratio to solve a problem. Write a letter to your friend explaining how to choose an appropriate ratio.

27. The Leaning Tower of Pisa makes an angle of 85° with the ground. If you drop an object from the top, it will land 16 ft from the base!

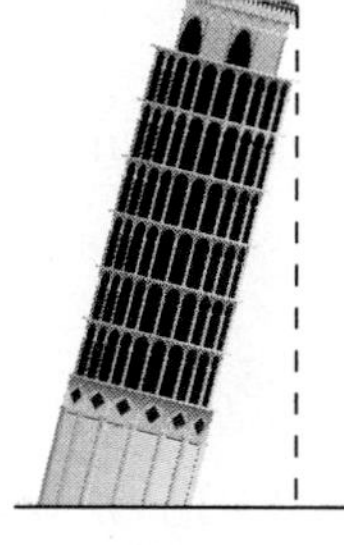

a. Make a sketch like the one at the right. Label it with the given information.

b. Write and solve an equation to find how far the object fell.

28. A slide at the Watermania Resort in Orlando, Florida, is called the "Rainforest." It starts at a height of 20 ft and descends in a straight line that makes an angle of about 30° with the ground. About how long is the slide?

29. Investigation (p. 338) Explain how to use a trigonometric ratio to find the distance you estimated in the investigation.

Complete each equation.

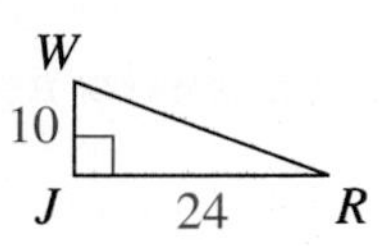

1. tan R = $\frac{■}{■}$

2. tan W = $\frac{■}{■}$

3. Find the length of the hypotenuse in $\triangle RJW$.

Draw ⊙*P* with diameter $\overline{BY}$ and chord $\overline{BD}$ intersecting chord $\overline{DY}$ at point *D* on the circle.

4. Find $m\angle D$.

5. If $m\angle Y$ = 30°, find $m\angle B$.

CHECKPOINT

1. The scale of a model airplane is to be 1 in. : $3\frac{1}{2}$ ft. The actual wingspan is 35 ft. What will be the wingspan of the model?

2. a. Describe the situation shown in the figure at the right.

b. Find h.

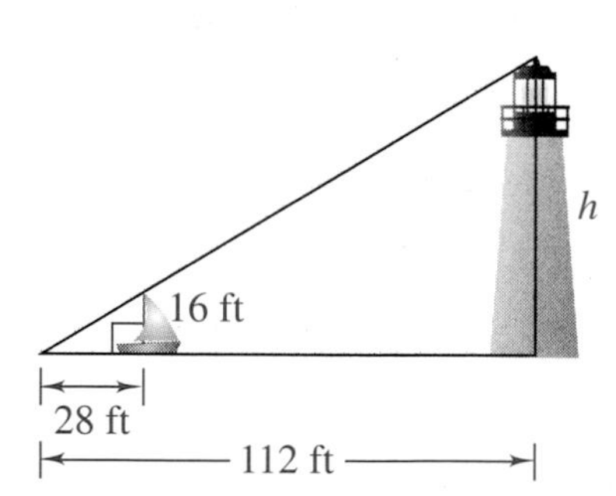

3. Write sin S, cos S, and tan S as fractions in simplest form and as decimals.

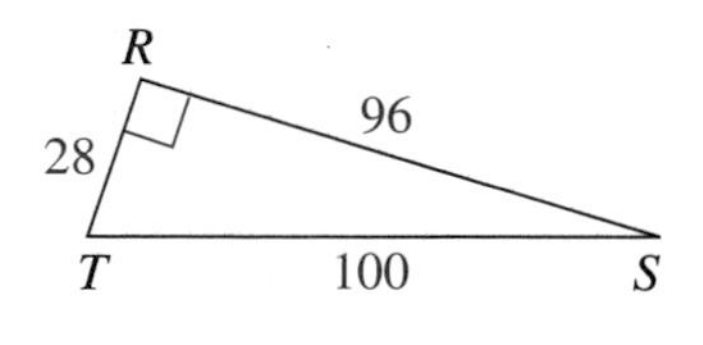

4. Find m and n. Round to the nearest tenth.

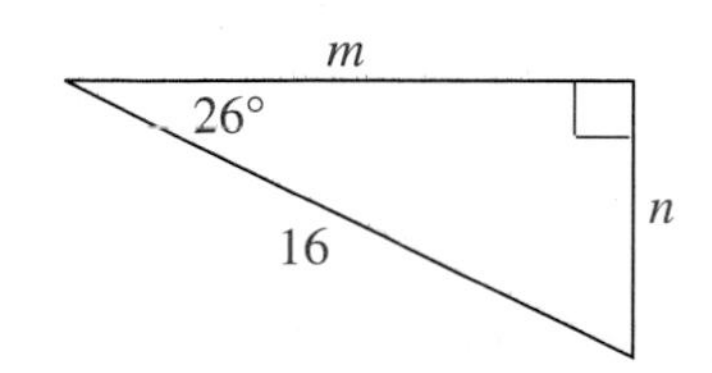

Practice

Write each ratio as a fraction in lowest terms.

1. 13 to 52
2. 28 : 84
3. 45 min per h
4. 130 pupils in 5 classrooms
5. 8 hits out of 20 times at bat
6. 2 ft : 8 yd

Compare. Write = or ≠.

7. $\frac{12}{15} \blacksquare \frac{4}{9}$
8. $\frac{19}{20} \blacksquare \frac{76}{80}$
9. $\frac{18}{5} \blacksquare \frac{108}{30}$

Express as a unit rate.

10. 18 laps in 12 min
11. \$3.78 for $\frac{7}{8}$ lb
12. 195 km in 1.3 h
13. 240 cal for 8 oz
14. 40 lb of lawn food per 10,000 ft^2
15. 25,000 people live in 1,000 mi^2

Use dimensional analysis to find an equal rate.

16. 84 m/min = $\blacksquare$ m/s
17. 0.075 km/s = $\blacksquare$ m/min

Solve each proportion. Round to the nearest tenth.

18. $\frac{27}{n} = \frac{6}{7}$
19. $\frac{n}{8} = \frac{9.5}{10}$
20. $\frac{6}{25} = \frac{4.5}{n}$

The polygons shown are similar. Find each unknown length to the nearest tenth of a centimeter.

21.

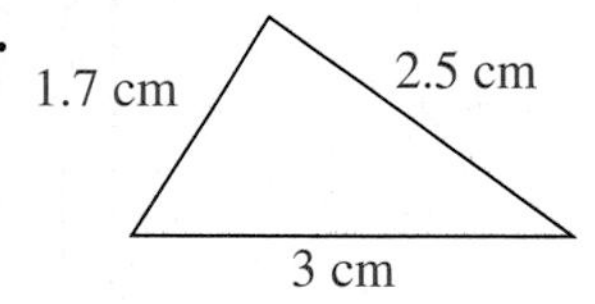

22.

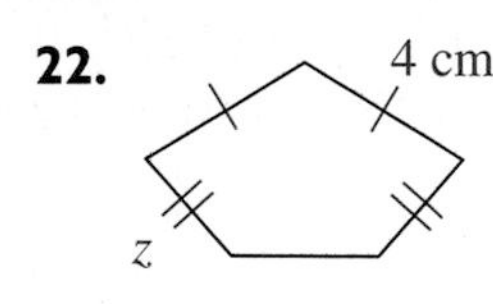

Write a proportion to describe each situation. Solve.

23. The scale on a map is 2 in. : 150 mi. Find the actual distance between Greenfield and Longview if the distance on the map is $7\frac{1}{2}$ in.

24. The most densely populated country in the world is Bangladesh. If 116,601,000 people live in an area of 55,598 mi^2, how many people live in an area of 5 mi^2?

What's Ahead

- Exploring self-similarity and fractals

8-9 Exploring Self-Similarity and Fractals

WORK TOGETHER

WHAT YOU'LL NEED

✓ Compass 

✓ Straightedge

In 1975, Benoit B. Mandelbrot coined the word "fractal" to describe irregular and self-similar shapes.

Source: *The Mathematical Tourist*

- Work with a partner. With compass and straightedge, construct a large equilateral triangle. Use a pencil to shade the entire triangle lightly, as shown in *Stage 0* below.
- Locate the midpoint of each side of the triangle. Connect the midpoints to form four new triangles. Erase the shading inside the middle triangle, as shown in *Stage 1* below.
- Repeat the preceding step on each of the three "corner" triangles. The result should look like *Stage 2* below.

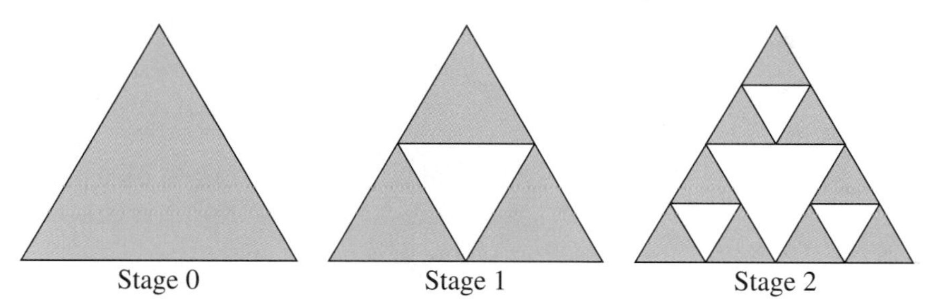

Stage 0 Stage 1 Stage 2

The triangles above are **self-similar.** This means that at each stage each part of the figure is similar to the whole figure. If the pattern continued infinitely, each stage would be self-similar. A figure with this property is a **fractal.** Stages 3 and 4 of this pattern, known as the *Sierpinski triangle,* are shown at the left.

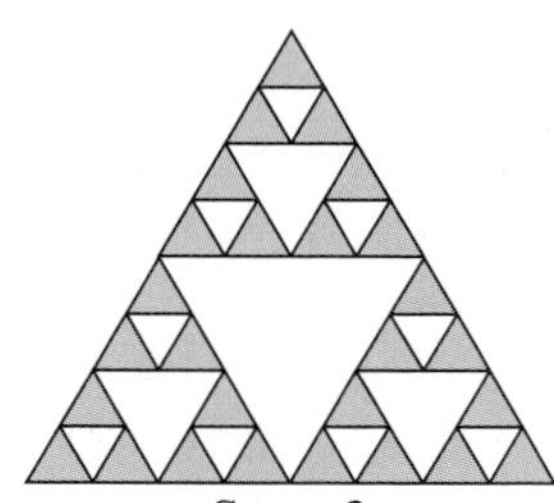

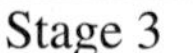

Stage 3

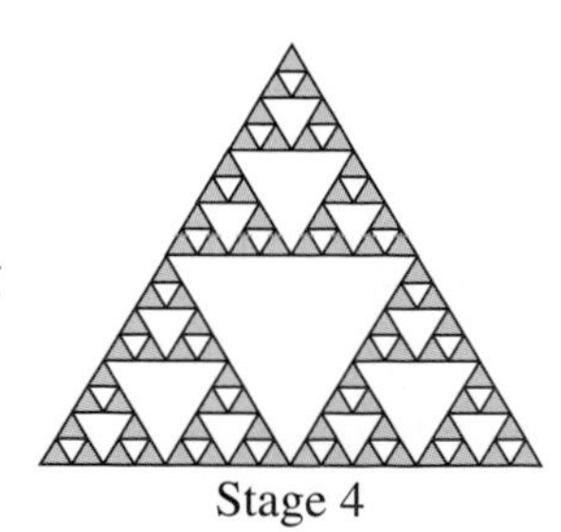

Stage 4

1. a. Copy and complete this table for the Sierpinski triangle.

Stage	0	1	2	3	4
Number of shaded triangles	■	■	■	■	■

b. What pattern(s) do you see in the table?

c. How many shaded triangles will there be at Stage 6?

d. Let n represent the number of the stage. Write an expression for the number of shaded triangles at Stage n.

ON YOUR OWN

2. The first three stages of a pattern are shown below.

Stage 0

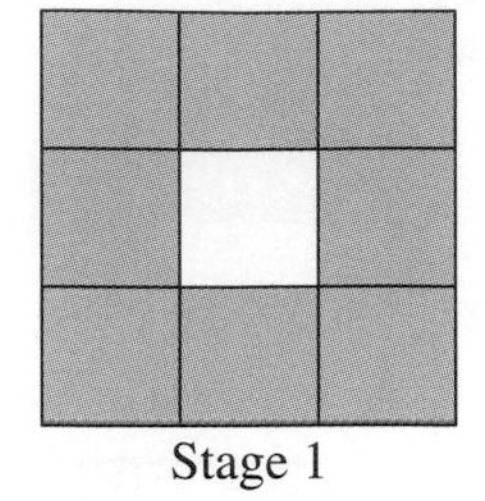
Stage 1

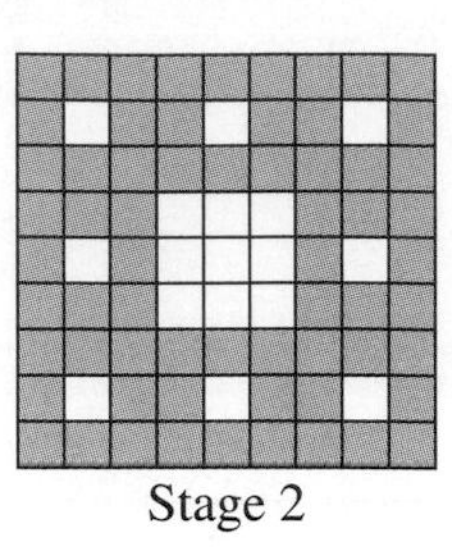
Stage 2

a. Copy and complete this table.

Stage	0	1	2
Number of shaded squares	■	■	■

b. How many shaded squares will there be at Stage 3?

c. Let n represent the number of the stage. Write an expression for the number of shaded squares at Stage n.

3. The first three stages of a pattern are shown below. At each stage, you remove the middle third of each segment in the preceding stage.

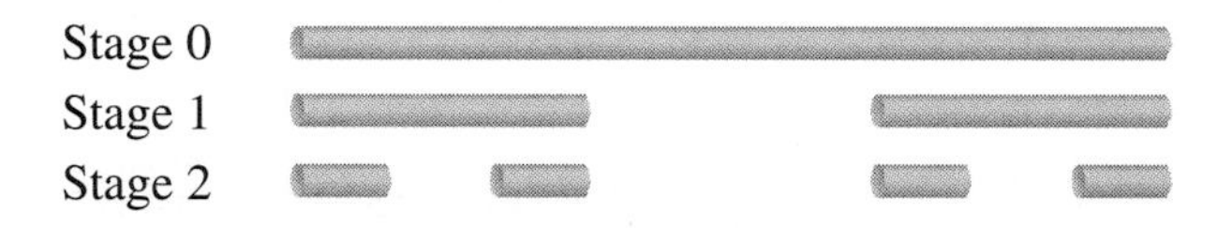

a. How many segments will there be in Stage 9?

b. Let n represent the number of the stage. Write an expression for the number of segments at Stage n.

4. **Writing** The first three stages of a pattern called the *Koch snowflake* are shown below. Describe the steps that you use to obtain each stage.

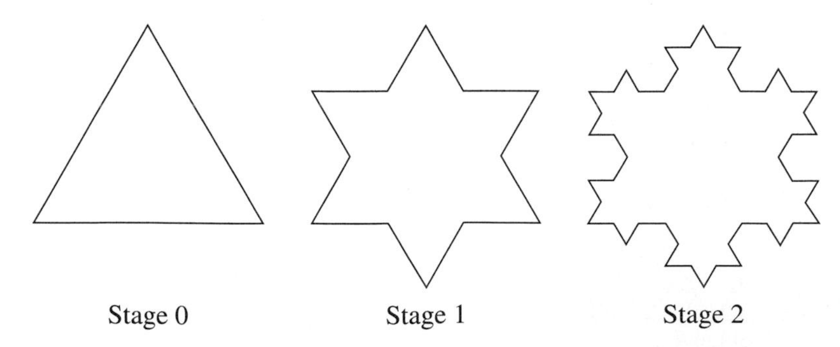

Complete.

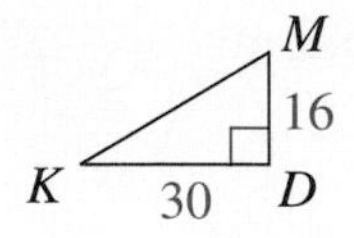

1. KM = ■

2. $\sin K = \frac{■}{■}$

3. $\cos M = \frac{■}{■}$

4. Draw $\overline{LN}$ with a length of 2.4 cm. Construct its perpendicular bisector.

Write an inequality for each sentence. Solve and graph the solution on a number line.

5. 5 less than a number is greater than -9.

6. Two more than twice a number is less than 14.

5. a. Start with Stage 0 of the Sierpinski triangle and let the length of one side be 1 unit. This means that in Stage 1, the length of one side of each shaded triangle is $\frac{1}{2}$, as shown at the right. Copy and complete this table.

Stage	0	1	2	3	4
Length of one side of each shaded triangle	1	$\frac{1}{2}$	■	■	■
Perimeter of one shaded triangle	3	■	■	■	■
Total perimeter of all shaded triangles	3	$\frac{9}{2}$	■	■	■

b. What pattern(s) do you see in the table?

c. What happens to the total perimeter as the number of the stage becomes larger and larger?

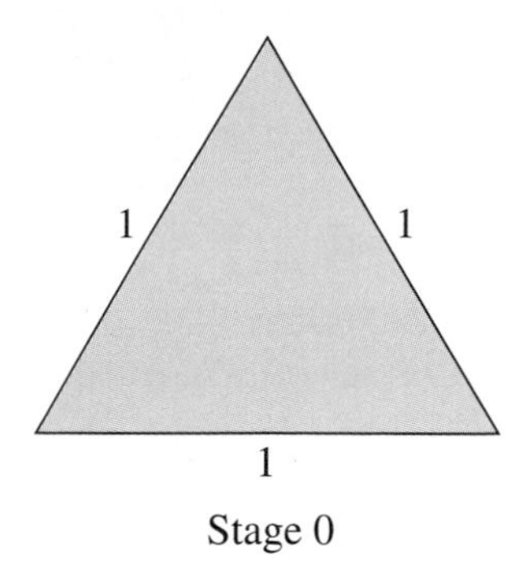

Stage 0

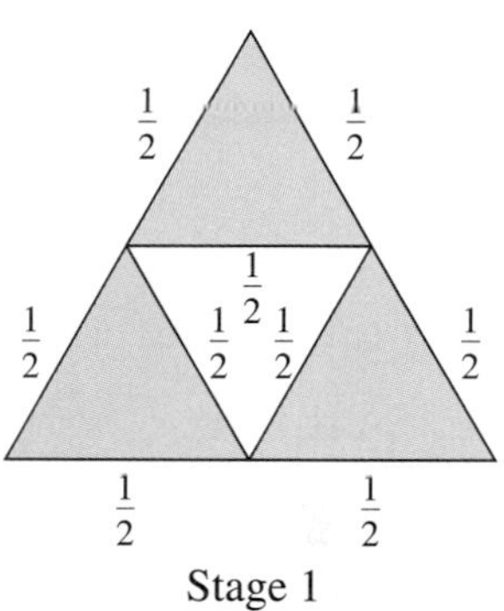

Stage 1

6. **Critical Thinking** Start with Stage 0 of the Sierpinski triangle and let its area be 1 square unit.

a. What is the total area of the shaded triangles at Stage 1?

b. What happens to the total shaded area as the number of the stage becomes larger and larger?

The perimeter of a figure is the sum of the lengths of all its sides.

The area of a figure is the amount of space that it encloses.

Draw Stage 2 of each fractal pattern.

7.

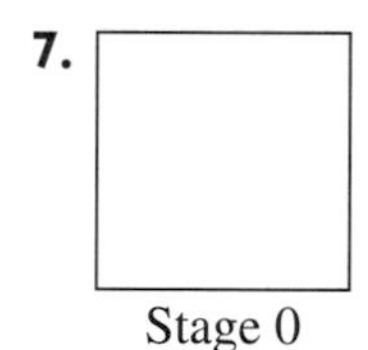
Stage 0

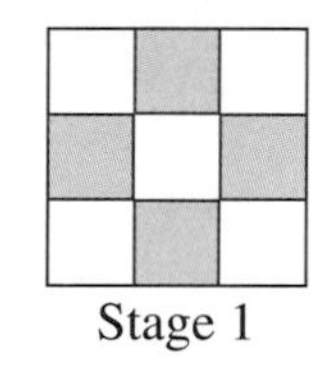
Stage 1

8.

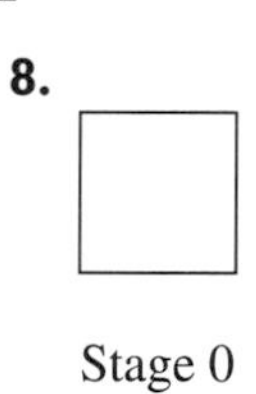
Stage 0

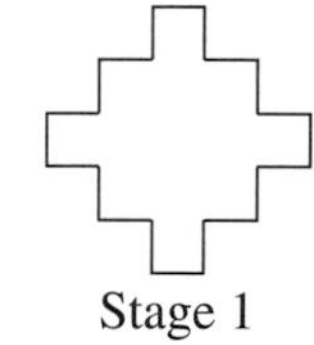
Stage 1

Draw Stage 0 of each fractal pattern. What is the number of the stage that is shown?

9.

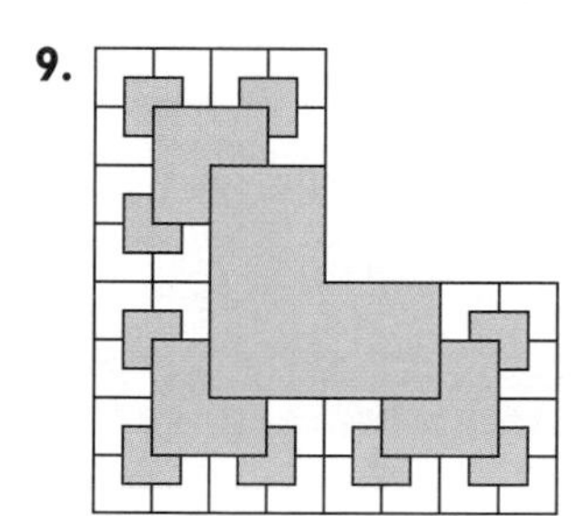

10.

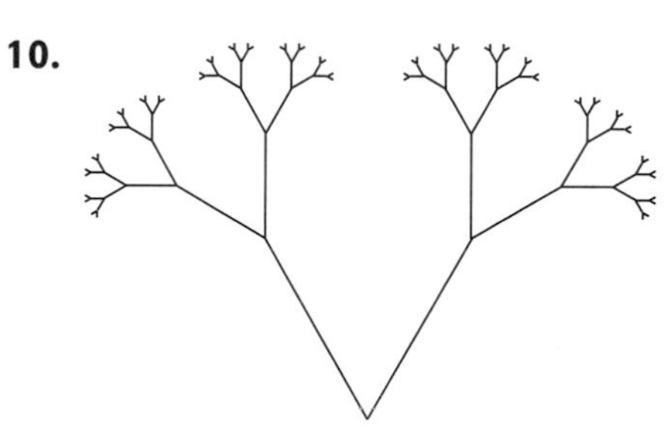

11. Create an original figure that is self-similar.

CHAPTER 8

Wrap Up

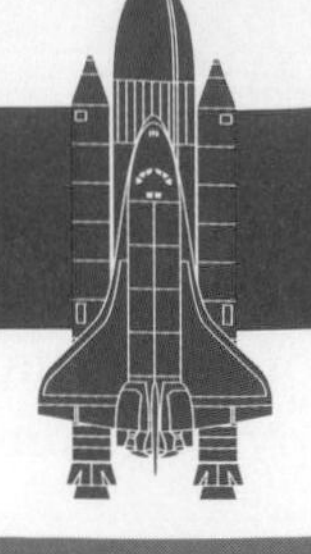

Ratios and Rates 8-1

A ***ratio*** is a comparison of two quantities by division. A ***rate*** is a ratio that compares two different types of quantities. A ***unit rate*** is the rate for one unit of a given quantity.

Write each ratio in simplest form.

1. 16 : 48 **2.** $\frac{32}{8}$ **3.** 12 out of 45 **4.** 15 to 9

Write the unit rate.

5. $42 for 1.5 h **6.** 826 mi in 14 h **7.** 150 km per 24 L **8.** 3 cans for $1.98

Using Dimensional Analysis 8-2

Dimensional analysis is used to convert units of measure.

Use dimensional analysis to convert each measure.

9. 75 min = ■ h **10.** 36.8 ft/s = ■ ft/min **11.** 7900 km/h = ■ m/s

Solving Proportions, Using Proportions to Solve Problems 8-3, 8-5

To solve a proportion, write the cross products, then solve.

Solve.

12. $\frac{4}{5} = \frac{y}{3.9}$ **13.** $\frac{x}{8} = \frac{3}{10}$ **14.** $\frac{9}{20} = \frac{2}{w}$ **15.** $\frac{8}{z} = \frac{5}{9}$

Use a proportion to solve.

16. Lin had 325 copies made for $19.50 at Dynamo Copiers. How much will it cost to have 400 copies made at the same rate?

Similar Figures, Indirect Measurement 8-4, 8-6

Similar figures are figures that have the same shape but not necessarily the same size. The corresponding angles of ***similar polygons*** are congruent and the corresponding sides are in proportion. The ***scale factor of similarity*** is the ratio of the lengths of the corresponding sides.

$\triangle ACE \sim \triangle BCD$. **Find each measure.**

17. AE **18.** CE **19.** DE

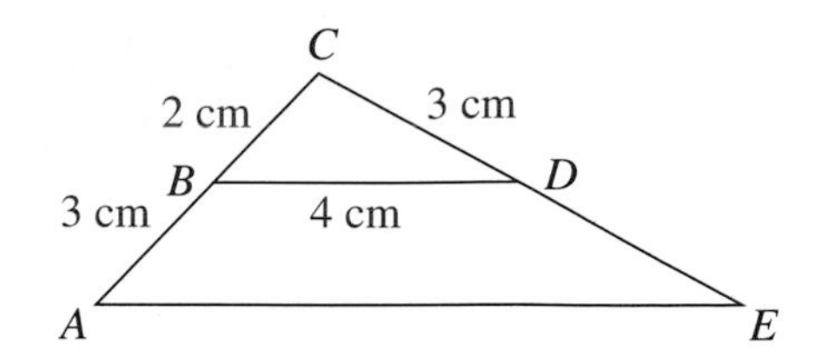

20. Tai is 5 ft 6 in. and casts a 21 ft shadow. A building casts a 45 ft shadow at the same time. How high is the building?

21. Writing Explain what a scale factor means and give at least two examples of its use.

Tangent, Sine, and Cosine Ratios 8-7, 8-8

To find measures in a right triangle, use a ***trigonometric ratio.***

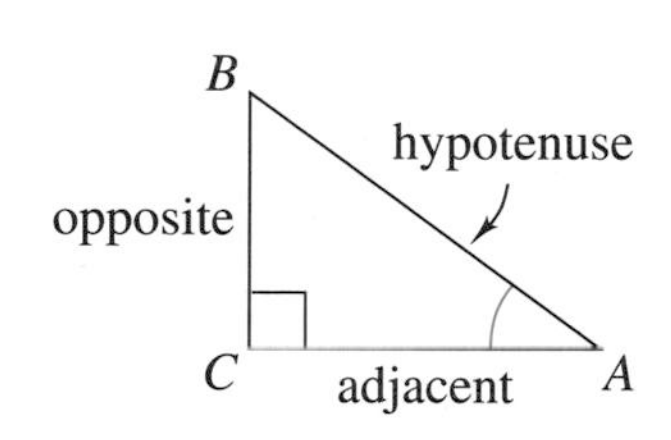

$\sin A = \frac{\text{opposite}}{\text{hypotenuse}}$ $\cos A = \frac{\text{adjacent}}{\text{hypotenuse}}$ $\tan A = \frac{\text{opposite}}{\text{adjacent}}$

22. Choose A, B, C, or D. In $\triangle LMC$, at the right, $LM = 8$. Which equation can you use to find x?

I. $\sin 53° = \frac{8}{x}$ **II.** $\cos 37° = \frac{x}{8}$ **III.** $\tan 53° = \frac{8}{x}$

A. I only **B.** I or II only **C.** II or III only **D.** I, II, or III

Self-Similarity and Fractals 8-9

A ***fractal*** is a geometric pattern that is ***self-similar.*** Each stage of the figure is similar to the whole figure.

23. Draw Stage 0 of the fractal pattern shown at the right. What is the number of the stage that is shown?

GETTING READY FOR CHAPTER 9

Draw a diagram or picture for each situation. Solve.

1. Three friends line up for a picture, side by side. How many different ways can they arrange themselves in this way?

2. Evan has 2 ties, 3 shirts, and 4 pairs of pants. How many different outfits does he have?

PUTTING IT ALL TOGETHER

Estimating Distances

In this chapter you have learned several methods you can use to find distances that you cannot measure directly. Look again at the distance you estimated. Make a new estimate of the distance based on your study of this chapter. The following are suggestions to help you revise your estimate.

✓ Use proportions.
✓ Use indirect measurement.
✓ Use trigonometry.

The problems preceded by the magnifying glass (p. 356, # 18; p. 359, # 15; and p. 367, # 29) will help you revise your estimate.

Your estimate may be different from that of another student estimating the same distance. This does not mean that either of you is wrong. If both of you use sound methods and apply them accurately, then both estimates are reasonable. Far more important than the "right" distance is a sensible, carefully applied method for estimating the distance.

Excursion: About 225 B.C. the Greek mathematician Eratosthenes estimated Earth's circumference to be 24,000 miles. That is remarkably close to today's accepted figure of 24,901.55 miles. How did Eratosthenes arrive at his estimate?

Pollsters tell us how the public feels about a wide variety of issues. To do this, they interview a small number of people on a certain subject. With the aid of proportional reasoning, the pollster *projects* the results of the small sample to apply to an entire population. Try this polling activity to see how it works. You may wish to work with a group.

- Choose an interesting topic relevant to your school or class.
- Prepare a list of questions about your topic.
- Take a poll of your class by asking each class member to answer the questions. Be sure to record their answers.
- Use proportional reasoning to *project* the results of your poll to reflect the attitudes of the entire school population.
- Prepare a statement announcing the results of your poll.

Photo Opportunity

Try this activity to show how the images in a photograph are similar to the real objects in the picture.

- Find a photograph of an object that you own or can borrow.
- Take measurements of the object.
- Measure the image of the object in the photo.
- Compare the measurements to show how the image and object are similar.

A Critic's Eye

A *golden rectangle's* length and width are in the *golden ratio*, approximately $\frac{13}{8}$. For hundreds of years, artists and architects have believed that paintings, sculptures, and buildings with designs based on the golden rectangle are most pleasing to the viewer's eye.

- Create a piece of artwork (for example, a drawing or a clay vase) with proportions based on the golden rectangle.
- Create a similar work based on slightly different proportions.
- Conduct a survey to find out which work viewers find more pleasing to look at.

Excursion Research the golden rectangle. Make a list of artwork and architecture that shows examples of the golden rectangle.

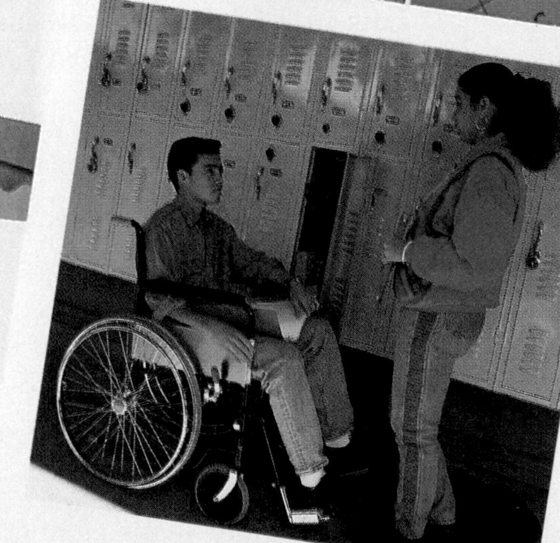

Imagine That!

You can use proportional reasoning to estimate. For example, to estimate the number of words in a three-page report, you could count the number of words on one page, then multiply by 3.

Choose one of the following. Estimate the amount by using proportional reasoning. Explain to a friend how you made your estimate.

1. Number of leaves on a nearby tree
2. Number of bricks used to construct a local building
3. Number of tennis balls you could stuff into your classroom

CHAPTER 8

Assessment

1. Write each ratio in simplest form.

   a. 6 : 36 b. $\frac{54}{6}$

   c. 24 to 18 d. 23 out of 92

2. Use dimensional analysis to convert each measure.

   a. 4 h = ■ sec b. 448 in. = ■ ft

   c. 23 qt = ■ gal d. 22 wk = ■ h

3. Use dimensional analysis to find an equal rate.

   a. \$33/h = \$ ■ /min

   b. 186 ft/sec = ■ ft/min

4. **Estimation** During a recent power outage, the police station logged in 343 calls in 3.5 h. About how many calls did the police station receive per hour?

5. **Choose A, B, C, or D.** Which of these ratios form a true proportion?

   A. $\frac{3}{7} = \frac{6}{15}$ B. $\frac{2}{8} = \frac{9}{36}$

   C. $\frac{25}{4} = \frac{80}{14}$ D. $\frac{12}{5} = \frac{30}{13}$

6. A stock investment of 160 shares paid a dividend of \$584. At this rate, what dividend would be paid on 270 shares of stock?

7. A 20-ft ladder leans against a tree and makes an angle of 40° with the ground. To the nearest tenth of a foot, what is the distance from the top of the ladder to the base of the tree?

8. $\triangle ABC \sim \triangle DEF$. The length of $\overline{BC}$ is 90 m, the length of $\overline{EF}$ is 72 m, and the length of $\overline{DE}$ is 40 m. Find the length of $\overline{AB}$.

9. The scale drawing of a new office building uses a scale of 0.75 in. to 3 ft. How long is a room that measures 4.75 in. on the drawing?

10. Write the proportion relating the lengths of the corresponding sides of the similar triangles.

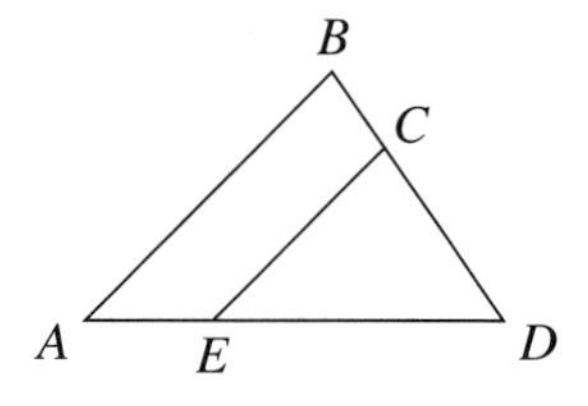

11. In $\triangle XYZ$ write each as a fraction in simplest form and as a decimal.

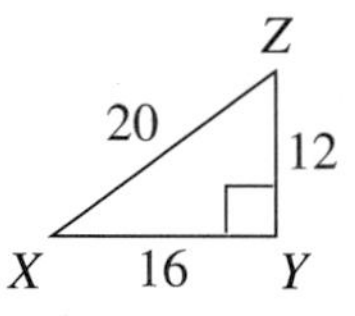

   a. $\tan X$ b. $\sin X$ c. $\cos X$

12. Use the Pythagorean Theorem to find n. Then write each as a fraction in simplest form.

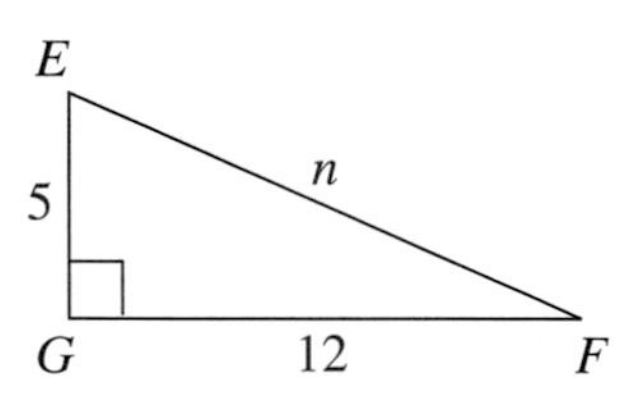

   a. $\sin E$ b. $\cos E$ c. $\tan E$

13. Jimica is 5 ft 3 in. tall and casts a shadow 16 ft long. At the same time of day, a telephone pole casts a shadow 90 ft long. What is the height of the pole?

14. **Writing** What does it mean for a figure to be self-similar? Give an example.

CHAPTER 8

Cumulative Review

Choose A, B, C, or D.

1. Which phrase cannot be written as $2n + 9$?
   - **A.** nine more than twice n
   - **B.** two times n, increased by nine
   - **C.** double the sum of n and nine
   - **D.** nine greater than twice n

2. What is the scale factor of the similar triangles $\triangle ABC$ and $\triangle XYC$?
   - **A.** 2 : 1
   - **B.** 12 : 5
   - **C.** 8 : 5
   - **D.** 3 : 2

3. Using the diagram above, which equation is correct?
   - **A.** $\tan A = \frac{12}{5}$
   - **B.** $\cos A = \frac{5}{12}$
   - **C.** $\tan A = \frac{4}{5}$
   - **D.** $\sin A = \frac{4}{5}$

4. Use the chart to determine the relationship between p and q.
   - **A.** p and q vary directly.
   - **B.** p and q vary inversely.
   - **C.** q is a linear function of p.
   - **D.** q is a quadratic function of p.

p	q
-4	6
3	-8
16	$-\frac{3}{2}$

5. The LCD of $\frac{13}{21}$, $\frac{25}{12}$, and a third fraction is 84. Which cannot be the third fraction?
   - **A.** $\frac{1}{6}$
   - **B.** $\frac{25}{28}$
   - **C.** $\frac{40}{49}$
   - **D.** $\frac{29}{14}$

6. What is the value of $-3 + x - y$ if $x = -8$ and $y = -4$?
   - **A.** -7
   - **B.** 7
   - **C.** -15
   - **D.** -9

7. What are the next three numbers in the pattern $-162, 54, -18, 6, \ldots$?
   - **A.** $-3, 0, -\frac{1}{2}$
   - **B.** $-2, \frac{2}{3}, -\frac{2}{9}$
   - **C.** $0, -6, -18$
   - **D.** $-2, 0, 2$

8. Alicia can read four pages in 12 min. Which proportion can be used to figure out how long it will take her to read an 18-page chapter?
   - **A.** $\frac{4}{12} = \frac{x}{18}$
   - **B.** $\frac{4}{18} = \frac{12}{x}$
   - **C.** $\frac{12}{18} = \frac{4}{x}$
   - **D.** $\frac{4}{x} = \frac{18}{12}$

9. Which is *not* equivalent to $\frac{9}{16}$?
   - **A.** $3^2 \cdot 4^{-2}$
   - **B.** $\left(\frac{3}{4}\right)^2$
   - **C.** $9 \cdot 2^{-4}$
   - **D.** $3 \cdot 4^{-2}$

10. Which is the graph of the linear function $y = f(x)$ if $f(0) = -2$ and $f(-1) = 1$.

A.

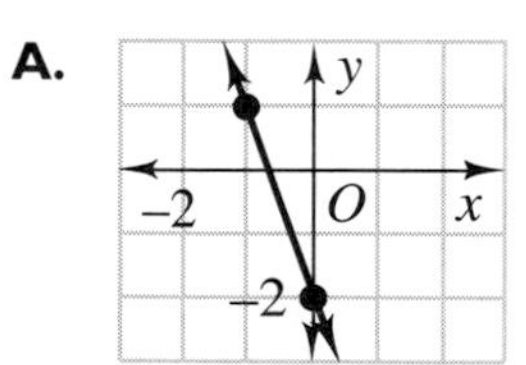

B.

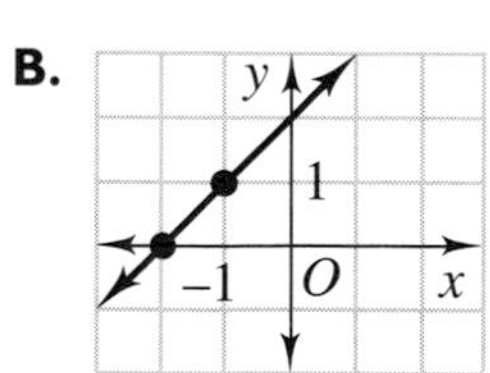

C.

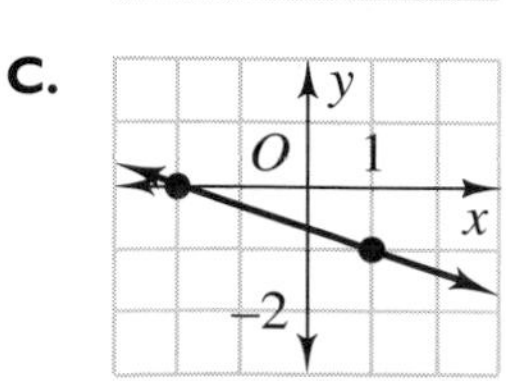

D.

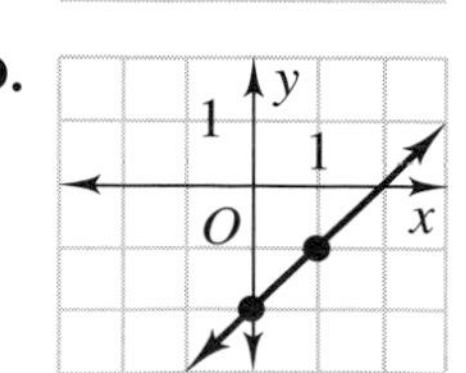

CHAPTER 9 Probability

Data File 9

When 9,965 United States teens were asked if they had smoked during the previous week, here is how they responded.

Who's Smoking?

	White	Black	Hispanic
Male	13.4%	4.2%	9.3%
Female	12.8%	2.7%	9.3%
All	13.1%	3.5%	9.3%

Source: *Centers for Disease Control*

The table below shows the annual premium male smokers and non-smokers would pay for the same $500,000 life insurance policy.

Life Insurance Costs

Age	Non-Smokers	Smokers
35	$ 355	$ 560
40	460	720
45	580	960
50	775	1,295
55	1,110	1,995
60	1,940	3,235
65	2,945	4,330

Source: *Go Figure*

Estimated Risks of Activities

Activity or Event	Annual Fatalities Per 1 Million Exposed Persons
Active smoking	7,000 (a)
Alcohol related	
Accident	275
Disease	266
Motor vehicle accident	
Alcohol-involved	95
Non-alcohol-involved	92
Accidents at work	113
Swimming	22
Football	6
Electrocution	2
Lightning	0.5

Note: Activities are not mutually exclusive; there are overlaps between categories.

(a) Number of deaths per 1,000,000 smokers who started smoking before 1965

Source: *Report of the Surgeon General*

WHAT YOU WILL LEARN

- how to understand and apply probability concepts
- how to use samples to make predictions
- how to use technology to model experimental probability
- how to use simulation to solve problems

Investigation

Project File

Memo

Many of our planet's animal and plant species are in danger of becoming extinct. Habitat destruction, poaching, and poisons in the environment are just three of many causes contributing to this crisis. Some animals, including elephants, pandas, and gorillas, may disappear from the wild. One of the challenges facing wildlife biologists is estimating the numbers of animals in threatened populations so that appropriate action can be taken. There is disturbing evidence that the woolly woozle may be in trouble. Unfortunately, no one knows exactly how many woozles remain.

Mission: Estimate the number of remaining woozles. Use a bag full of beans, paper clips, or other small items to represent the woozles. The woozles are scattered throughout the forest so you may not perform any operation, such as weighing, on the entire population. You may capture woozles, tag them, then release the tagged woozles into the forest, or do anything else wildlife biologists do.

Leads to Follow

- ✓ What methods do you know for estimating numbers of objects too large to count?
- ✓ How could you use a small number of captured woozles to help you find the size of the entire population?

What's Ahead

- Using the counting principle to find the number of possible outcomes
- Using tree diagrams

9-1 Counting and Displaying Outcomes

WORK TOGETHER

Work in small groups to design a new license plate for motor vehicles in your state.

1. List all the information you will display on each plate.
2. Seven identification characters fit on each plate. Decide on a plan for the characters. Will you use digits and/or letters?
3. Make a scale drawing of the license plate you design. The dimensions of the plate are 12 in. wide by 6 in. high. Each identification character is 2.5 in. high.

THINK AND DISCUSS

FLASHBACK

The set of all possible outcomes of an event is the *sample space.*

Using the Counting Principle License plates for Massachusetts display three digits followed by three letters.

4. How many choices are there for each letter?
5. How many choices are there for each digit?

To find out how many different license plates are possible, you can use the *counting principle.*

The Counting Principle

The number of outcomes of an event is the product of the number of outcomes for each stage of the event.

The product below gives the number of different plates possible.

digit		digit		digit		letter		letter		letter		
10	•	10	•	10	•	26	•	26	•	26	=	17,576,000

6. Which of these license plate systems provides more possible outcomes, one with five letters or one with seven digits? Explain your answer.

FLASHBACK

A *tree diagram* uses a branch for each choice. The tree diagram below shows all six possible outcomes for a T-shirt available in three sizes and two colors.

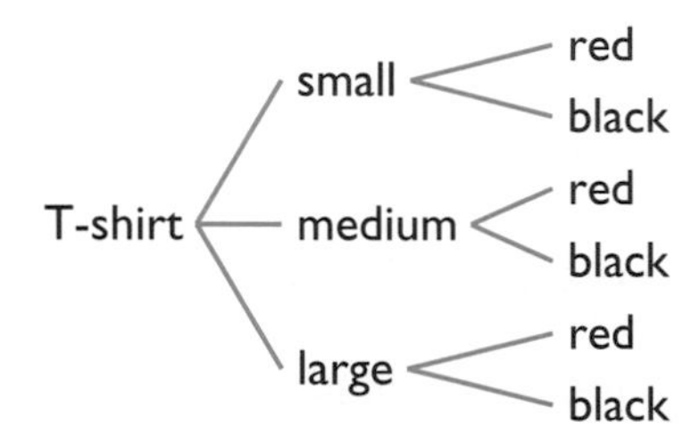

Using a Tree Diagram You can display all possible outcomes.

7. A sporting goods store sells jeans in 5 sizes (28, 30, 32, 34, and 36) in regular fit, slim fit, and relaxed fit. The jeans come in 2 different colors: black and blue. The manager stocks at least one pair in each category.
   a. Use the counting principle to find the number of possible outcomes for one pair of jeans in each category. Consider each size, type, and color of jeans.
   b. Draw a tree diagram to display all possible outcomes for the jeans. How do you know you have displayed *all* outcomes?

8. **Computer** A small spreadsheet consists of rows labeled 1–9 and columns labeled A–Z. Each cell in the spreadsheet is identified by a letter and a number, such as D3. Use the counting principle to find the total number of cells in the spreadsheet.

9. **Discussion** When is it better to use the counting principle? a tree diagram? both? Give some examples.

Mixed REVIEW

1. Find the value of x by using the sine or cosine ratio.

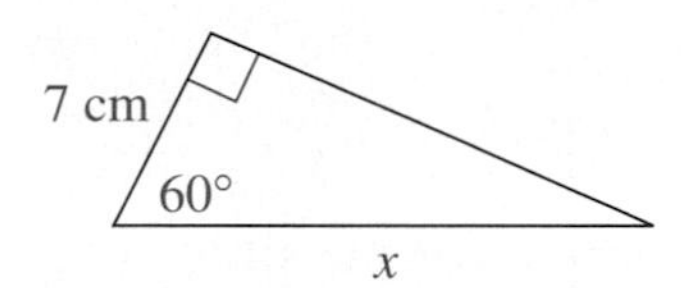

2. Give three examples of fractal patterns in nature.

$\triangle MCT \cong \triangle RZY$.

3. If $m\angle Z = 75°$ and $m\angle T = 35°$, $m\angle M =$ ■

4. If $MC = 58$ cm, $RY = 42$ cm, and $CT = 40$ cm, find the perimeter of $\triangle RZY$.

Solve.

5. $\frac{2}{3}n + \frac{1}{2} = -8$

6. $\frac{3}{5} = 2\frac{7}{10}y - 48$

ON YOUR OWN

Choose Use a calculator, paper and pencil, or mental math.

10. In Texas, license plates for passenger cars display three letters, two digits, and one letter. Are there more possible plates in Texas or Massachusetts? Explain.

11. In New York, each character on a license plate can be either a letter or a digit. How many different license plates made of 6 characters are possible?

12. **Research** Find out the system your state or county uses for license plates. How many different plates are possible with the system? About how many motor vehicles are registered?

13. **Cars** A car dealership offers three styles of car: sedan, hatchback, and wagon. Each style comes with either standard or automatic transmission, and is available in 8 different colors. How many different kinds of car does a potential buyer have to consider?

14. **Photography** You need to buy a roll of film for your 35-mm camera. Choices are given at the right.

    a. How many different decisions do you need to make?

    b. Draw a tree diagram to display all possible choices for a roll of film. How many different kinds of film can you buy?

    c. The store is sold out of slide film in 12 exposures. How many choices does this eliminate? Explain.

Color Film Available	
Speed	100, 200, or 400
Exposures	12, 24, or 36
Type	Print or Slide

15. ZIP codes were first introduced on July 1, 1963 to help simplify the distribution of mail by the U.S. Postal Service. ZIP stands for Zone Improvement Program.

    a. The first ZIP codes consisted of 5 digits. How many possible 5-digit codes are there?

    b. How many 5-digit codes end in an even number?

    c. Current ZIP codes consist of 9 digits: a 5-digit number followed by a 4-digit number, such as 12345-6789. How many more codes are there with a 9-digit code than with a 5-digit code?

16. **Fashion** Serina has 3 necklaces, 5 pairs of earrings, and 6 bracelets in her jewelry box. How many different combinations of a necklace, a pair of earrings, and a bracelet can she wear?

17. A dinner special at a restaurant consists of soup or salad, a main dish, dessert, and coffee or tea.

    a. If there are 8 different main dishes and 5 different desserts to choose from, how many different dinner specials can be ordered?

    b. How many choices do you have if you just order a main dish and dessert?

18. Radio station call letters begin with either the letter K or W and are either 3 or 4 letters long.

    a. How many different 3-letter stations can there be?

    b. How many more stations are there that can have 4 call letters than have 3?

19. **Writing** When you construct a tree diagram to find the total number of possible outcomes, does it make a difference which stage of an event you list first? Explain.

In the game of chess, *there are 20 possible ways a player can make the first move. Each of the 8 pawns has 2 possible places it can be moved and each of the 2 knights has 2 possible places it can be moved.* ***How many different first moves can a player make in a game of checkers?***

What's Ahead

- Finding the number of permutations
- Using factorial notation

9-2 Permutations

THINK AND DISCUSS

Exploring Permutations For a school-wide game show, each mathematics class selects one contestant and one alternate. Use your own class data for Questions 1–3.

1. How many ways can you choose a contestant from your class?
2. Once a contestant is selected, how many choices are there for an alternate from your class?
3. Use the counting principle to find the number of different contestant-alternate pairs possible for your class.
4. A class selected Raquel as the contestant and Matt as the alternate. To represent this, write (Raquel, Matt). What does (Matt, Raquel) represent? Is it different from (Raquel, Matt)?

A **permutation** is an arrangement of a set of objects in a particular order. The pairs (Matt, Raquel) and (Raquel, Matt) are two different permutations of the two names.

5. Write all the different permutations of the names Matt, Raquel, and Jordan. Use a tree diagram if it will help.
6. Use the counting principle to find the number of different permutations of the three names Matt, Raquel, and Jordan.

"*Since we cannot know all there is to be known of everything, we ought to know a little about everything.*"

—Blaise Pascal (1623–1662)

Using Factorials What is the number of permutations of 7 different names? Using the counting principle, it would be

$$7 \cdot 6 \cdot 5 \cdot 4 \cdot 3 \cdot 2 \cdot 1 = 5{,}040.$$

When there are a lot of possibilities to choose from, you can use a shorthand notation called *factorial*. The symbol for factorial is an exclamation point. 7! is read "7 factorial" and means the product of all whole numbers from 7 to 1.

$$7! = 7 \cdot 6 \cdot 5 \cdot 4 \cdot 3 \cdot 2 \cdot 1$$

7. Many CD players have a randomize feature that randomly selects the order in which the songs are played. Your favorite CD has 9 songs on it.
   a. In how many different orders can the songs be played? Write your answer in factorial notation.
   b. **Calculator** Find the value of your answer to part (a). If your calculator has a factorial key, use it to find the value.

Using Permutation Notation Fifteen students select a contestant-alternate pair. There are 15 possible choices for the contestant. Once a contestant is chosen there are 14 possible choices for the alternate. Therefore are $15 \cdot 14 = 210$ possible ways to choose 2 people. You can write this as

$$_{15}P_2 = 15 \cdot 14$$

which means 15 things taken 2 at a time.

8. Complete: $_{20}P_5 = \blacksquare \cdot \blacksquare \cdot \blacksquare \cdot \blacksquare \cdot \blacksquare = \blacksquare$.

9. The eighth-grade class of 144 students selects a president, vice-president, and treasurer. Explain why you would use $_{144}P_3$ to find the number of possible outcomes.

You can use permutations to solve many problems.

Example At a Denver horse show, ribbons are given for first, second, third, and fourth place. There are 20 horses in the show. How many different arrangements of four winning horses are possible?

- Find the number of permutations of 4 horses selected from a total of 20 horses.

$$_{20}P_4 = 20 \cdot 19 \cdot 18 \cdot 17 = 116{,}280$$

There are 116,280 different arrangements.

TRY THESE

10. In how many different ways can all the letters of your first name be arranged? Write the value in factorial notation.

11. How does having repeated letters in your name affect the number of possible arrangements?

Extra SKILLS PRACTICE

Find the value of each factorial.

1. 4!
2. 7!
3. 3!
4. 5!
5. 8!

Use a calculator to find the value of each expression.

6. $_{25}P_3$
7. $_{18}P_2$
8. $_{32}P_3$
9. $_{8}P_4$
10. $_{400}P_2$
11. $_{12}P_5$
12. $_{52}P_3$
13. $_{6}P_6$
14. $_{10}P_4$

If a school has 18,000 students, it is certain that at least 424 students will have the same 3 initials as another student. **Can you figure out why?**

Source: *Beyond Numeracy*

An *anagram* is a word formed by rearranging the letters of another word. The letters of some words can be rearranged to form very interesting word pairs as seen in the chart below.

ADMIRER	MARRIED
BRUSH	SHRUB
CANOE	OCEAN
DETOUR	ROUTED
RECIPES	PRECISE

Do you agree or disagree with each statement? Explain.

12. 6! is the product of all the whole numbers from 1 to 6.

13. The two arrangements ABCDEF and ABCDFE count as the same permutation because they use the same letters.

14. The number of permutations of six different letters in a word is 6! or ${}_6P_6$.

15. ${}_4P_3$ is not the same as ${}_4P_4$.

ON YOUR OWN

Use a calculator to find the value.

16. 10! **17.** ${}_7P_5$ **18.** ${}_{14}P_3$ **19.** $\frac{5!}{3!}$

20. Writing Describe two different ways you can use a calculator to compute 8!

21. Theater The New London Barn Players are producing the musical "Annie" this summer. They advertise for the parts of Annie and five orphans. If 50 children audition, in how many ways can the six parts be assigned?

22. Each spring the Fay Middle School holds a speech contest. Each finalist prepares and presents a speech to the whole school. There are seven finalists this year. In how many different orders can the speeches be given?

23. Make a list of all permutations of the numbers 1, 2, 3, and 4.

24. Use the digits 1, 3, 5, 7, and 9 to list as many 2-digit numbers as possible. Do not repeat a digit.

25. How many different ways can you arrange 6 friends in a row at a rectangular table? around a circular table?

Write *true* or *false*. Show your work.

26. $1! + 2! + 3! = 6!$ **27.** $6! \div 4! = 6 \cdot 5$

28. $3! \cdot 3! = 9!$ **29.** $7! - 3! = 7 \cdot 6 \cdot 5 \cdot 4$

30. ${}_{19}P_{19} = 19!$ **31.** ${}_5P_2 = 5 \cdot 4 \cdot 3 \cdot 2$

Mixed REVIEW

Simplify.

1. $\left(\frac{1}{2}\right)^3$ **2.** $\left(\frac{9}{10}\right)^2$

3. $(10)^{-2}$ **4.** $(10)^{-3}$

Draw a tree diagram for each situation.

5. A number cube is rolled and a coin is tossed.

6. A spinner with colors black, blue, and red is spun twice.

7. Lucy has 35 coins and a few $1 bills in her wallet. She has twice as many nickels as bills, 4 more dimes than nickels, and 3 more quarters than dimes. If the amount of money in her wallet is $9.35, how many dimes does she have?

What's Ahead

- Finding the number of combinations
- Solving problems that require distinguishing between permutations and combinations

9-3 Combinations

THINK AND DISCUSS

1. In Lesson 9-2, you found the number of different possible contestant-alternate pairs you could choose from your class. How many of the pairs consisted of the same two people?

Exploring Combinations Suppose two people from your class need to be selected as members of the student council. Use your own class data for Question 2.

2. How many choices are there for the two student council members?

3. A class selected Amber and Dimitri as student council members. Is this the same as selecting Dimitri and Amber as members? Explain.

A **combination** is a group of items in which the *order* of the items is *not* important. The combination (Amber and Dimitri) is the same as the combination (Dimitri and Amber). Together, they form the same group.

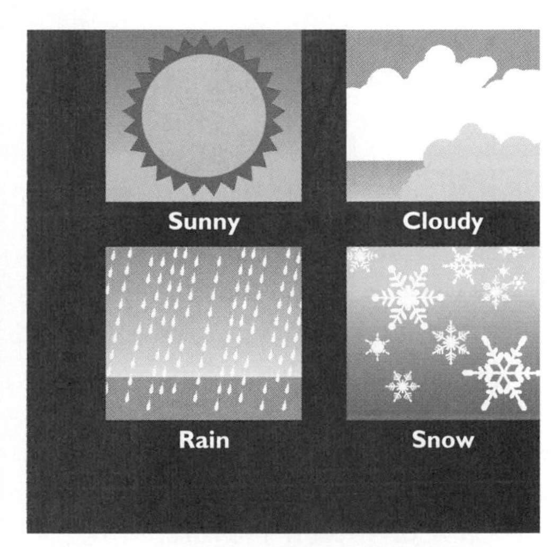

Meteorologists *commonly speak about probabilities when giving weather predictions.*

4. Write all the different pairs of the names Amber, Dimitri, and Carlos. How many combinations of two names are there?

5. Write all the different permutations of pairs of the names Amber, Dimitri, and Carlos. Can you use this list to find the number of combinations?

You can use permutations to find the number of combinations. The number of combinations of 5 things taken 2 at a time is written ${}_5C_2$. You can find this number by taking the number of permutations of 5 things taken 2 at a time, ${}_5P_2$, and dividing by the number of ways 2 things can be arranged, or 2!.

$${}_5C_2 = \frac{{}_5P_2}{2!} = \frac{5 \cdot 4}{2 \cdot 1} = 10$$

6. Which is larger, the number of combinations of a set of objects or the number of permutations? Explain.

7. Complete: $_6C_3 = \frac{■}{■} = ■$.

8. From a group of six students, your teacher selects three tutors. How many outcomes are possible?

WHAT? A great white shark was the largest fish ever caught on a rod. It weighed 2,664 lb. The shark measured 16 ft 10 in. and was caught by Alf Dean off South Australia in 1959. **How many tons did this shark weigh?**

Solving Problems

Combinations can help solve problems.

Example In deep sea fishing, you put several fishing lines off the back of the boat at one time. The boat Lady Jane uses 5 lines. Each holds one lure, and there are 12 different lures. How many different combinations of lures can be used at one time?

- Find the number of ways 5 lures can be selected from a total of 12 lures.

$$_{12}C_5 = \frac{_{12}P_5}{5!} = \frac{12 \cdot 11 \cdot 10 \cdot 9 \cdot 8}{5 \cdot 4 \cdot 3 \cdot 2 \cdot 1} = 792$$

There are 792 different combinations of 5 lures.

9. **Discussion** Explain why the number of permutations of 5 lures from a total of 12 lures is divided by 5!.

10. If the Lady Jane uses 7 lines rather than 5 lines, are more combinations possible? First estimate, then calculate.

WORK TOGETHER

Work in pairs. Decide if each situation describes a permutation or a combination. Find the number of possible outcomes.

11. Arrange four children in a line for a family picture.

12. Select three items from a choice of ten items at a salad bar.

13. Start five basketball players from a team of fifteen players.

14. Deal six cards from a deck of 52 cards.

15. Form a line of ten people at a customer service window.

16. **Writing** Explain how to decide if a situation describes a permutation or a combination.

TRY THESE

Find the number of combinations.

17. 2 pencils from 14

18. 3 letters from HARMONY

19. ${}_8C_5$

20. ${}_6C_2$

21. Four friends, Juan, Ester, Ken, and Corey, want to know how many pairs they can make among themselves. "We want to make sure that everyone plays a game of tennis with everyone else," stated Ken. Make a list of all possible pairs.

22. Are there more combinations or permutations of 2 people from a total of 4? Explain.

23. A president and a vice-president are to be elected from 52 members of a club. How many outcomes are possible?

Mixed REVIEW

Use a calculator to compute.

1. 5!
2. ${}_3P_2$
3. 9!
4. $\frac{100!}{99!}$

Find a rule for each sequence.

5. 5, 12, 19, 26, . . .
6. 1, 0, −1, −2, . . .
7. For the function $f(x) = 4x^2 - 3$, make a table that includes the following values for x: −3, −2, −1, 0, 1, 2, 3. Sketch the graph.

ON YOUR OWN

Compute each number of combinations.

24. ${}_7C_4$

25. ${}_3C_1$

26. ${}_9C_6$

27. **Travel** A group of six tourists arrive at the airport 15 min before flight time. At the gate they learn there are only two seats left on the airplane. How many different groups of two could get on the airplane? How many different groups of four would not get on the airplane?

28. Is each expression equivalent to ${}_8C_4$? Write yes or no.

   a. $\frac{{}_8P_4}{{}_4C_4}$ b. $\frac{{}_8P_4}{{}_4P_4}$ c. $\frac{{}_8C_4}{{}_4P_4}$ d. $\frac{8 \cdot 7 \cdot 6 \cdot 5 \cdot 4!}{4!}$

29. On many lakes, boats must be licensed. License numbers are five digits, which cannot be repeated. How many license numbers are possible?

30. **Music** Sixteen listeners called a radio station to request that a song be played. No song was requested by more than one listener. The disc jockey has time to play only ten more songs. How many different sets of six songs will the disc jockey *not* play?

Extra SKILLS PRACTICE

Compute each number of combinations.

1. ${}_{10}C_3$
2. ${}_6C_2$
3. ${}_{13}C_5$
4. ${}_9C_2$
5. ${}_7C_3$
6. ${}_{16}C_3$
7. ${}_{10}C_2$
8. ${}_{12}C_5$
9. ${}_5C_3$
10. ${}_9C_4$
11. ${}_{20}C_4$
12. ${}_{16}C_2$

Known as the "Rhino Man," *Michael Werikhe of Mombasa, Kenya, won the Goldman Environmental Prize for his work raising awareness about the plight of the black rhinoceros. Their population has decreased by 95% and they are dangerously close to becoming extinct.*

Source: *National Geographic Magazine*

31. Twenty people enter a chess tournament. Each person plays every other person once. How many matches are necessary?

32. Sports From a track team of twelve students, a coach selects four students for the relay race. How many different groups of four can the coach select?

33. Sports From a girls' softball team of eighteen students, a coach selects one girl as the pitcher and one as the catcher. How many different pairs can the coach select?

34. Writing Describe a situation that involves combinations. Then change the situation so that it involves permutations.

35. Choose A, B, C, or D. Which situation described has ${}_{10}C_2$ possible outcomes?

A. Select two digits from 0 to 9 for a secret code number.

B. Form pairs among ten friends for a tournament.

C. Choose a winner and a runner-up from ten finalists.

D. Arrange ten books on two shelves.

36. Investigation (p. 380) Research an endangered species. What is the current population? Why has the species become endangered? What is being done to protect the species?

CHECKPOINT

Compute.

1. ${}_{12}P_5$ **2.** ${}_{12}C_5$ **3.** $5!$

4. Choose A, B, C, or D. Which expression gives the number of ways you can choose 3 birthday cards from a group of 10?

A. ${}_{10}P_3$ **B.** $3!$ **C.** ${}_{10}C_3$ **D.** ${}_{3}P_{10}$

5. There are 240 students at Jackson Middle School. One third of the students play in the orchestra and are divided equally among the brass, string, percussion, and woodwind sections.

a. How many possible string quartets can be formed?

b. A student jazz group needs a new drummer and two horn players. In how many ways can they be chosen?

Problem Solving Practice

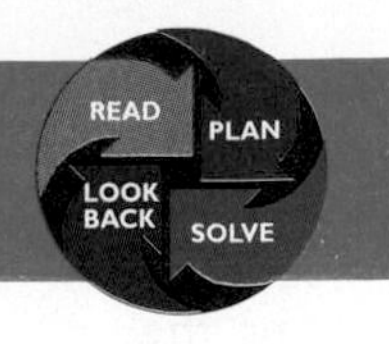

PROBLEM SOLVING STRATEGIES

Make a Table
Use Logical Reasoning
Solve a Simpler Problem
Too Much or Too Little Information
Look for a Pattern
Make a Model
Work Backward
Draw a Diagram
Guess and Test
Simulate a Problem
Use Multiple Strategies
Write an Equation
Use a Proportion

Use any strategy to solve each problem. Show all your work.

1. In a school election Sandra beat Sam by 46 votes to become class president. If there were a total of 308 votes for either Sandra or Sam, how many votes did each candidate receive?

2. A beehive houses about 40,000 worker bees, 250 drones, and one queen. What percent of the colony does each represent?

3. In the game of "Library Jeopardy" there are five questions in each of five categories all about books. In how many ways can you arrange the five questions in each category?

4. You are asked to paint a flagpole according to the directions below. Find the length of the flagpole.
   - $\frac{1}{3}$ will be painted yellow.
   - $\frac{1}{2}$ of what remains will be painted blue.
   - $\frac{1}{4}$ of what remains will be painted green.
   - $\frac{2}{3}$ of what remains will be painted red.
   - The last 9 inches will be left unpainted.

5. At the Sandwich Shop you build a sandwich by choosing one meat, one cheese, and as many extras as you want. There are 6 meats, 3 cheeses, and the following extras: lettuce, tomato, pickle, mayonnaise, and mustard. How many different sandwiches are possible at the Sandwich Shop?

6. The county fair has a race where 20 eggs are placed 1 ft apart in a straight line. You start on a piece of tape, run 1 ft to pick up the first egg and return it to the tape. Then you run to pick up the second egg and return it to the tape. Continue this pattern until you pick up and return the 20th egg. Find the distance you run to complete the race.

7. **Data File 6 (pp. 244–245)** You put $1,000 into a savings account that earns 6% interest per year. You make no deposits or withdrawals. When will the balance be $3,000?

What's Ahead

- Finding the probability and odds of an event and its complement
- Finding experimental and theoretical probabilities

9-4 Probability and Odds

THINK AND DISCUSS

Exploring Probability The **probability** of an *event* is a number describing the chance that the event will happen.

An event that is certain to happen has a probability of 1. An event that cannot possibly happen has a probability of zero. If there is a chance that an event will happen, then its probability is between zero and 1.

1. Give several examples of events with probability equal to 1. Give several examples with probability equal to zero.

When you toss a coin, there are two possible *outcomes,* "heads" or "tails." It is slightly possible that a coin could land on its side, but it is not very probable!

The two outcomes of tossing a coin are **equally likely,** which means that each has the same chance of happening. When all outcomes of an event are equally likely, the probability that the event will happen is given by the ratio below.

FLASHBACK

You can write a probability as a fraction, a decimal, or a percent.

$$\text{Probability of an event} = P(E) = \frac{\text{number of favorable outcomes}}{\text{number of possible outcomes}}$$

When you roll a number cube, each number is equally likely to be on top. To find P(rolling an odd number) you first find the number of *favorable outcomes.* There are 3 ways to roll an odd number and 6 possible ways of rolling the number cube. So, P(rolling an odd number) $= \frac{3}{6} = \frac{1}{2}$.

2. Find P(rolling a number > 2). What is the probability of *not* rolling a number greater than 2?

You can use the symbol E' to show that an event E *does not* happen. Events E and E' are **complementary.** Their probabilities are related by this equation.

$$P(E') = 1 - P(E)$$

3. Give an example of a pair of complementary events.

Using Odds Another ratio you can use when outcomes are equally likely is **odds.**

$$\text{Odds in favor of an event} = \frac{\text{number of favorable outcomes}}{\text{number of unfavorable outcomes}}$$

4. How are the odds in favor of an event related to the probability of that event?

Example 1 The names of 15 girls and 12 boys are placed in a box. One name is drawn at random.

a. What is the probability that a girl's name is drawn?

$$P(\text{girl}) = \frac{\text{number of favorable outcomes}}{\text{number of possible outcomes}} = \frac{15}{27} = \frac{5}{9}$$

b. What is the probability that a girl's name is not drawn?

$$P(\text{not a girl}) = 1 - P(\text{girl}) = 1 - \frac{5}{9} = \frac{4}{9}$$

c. What are the odds that a boy's name is drawn?

$$\text{odds} = \frac{\text{number of favorable outcomes}}{\text{number of unfavorable outcomes}} = \frac{12}{15} = \frac{4}{5}$$

Using Experiments Gregor Mendel (1822–1884) is famous for his work in developing the laws of heredity. In one experiment, he crossbred a pure pea plant that had yellow seeds with a pure pea plant that had green seeds. He found that the resulting offspring always had yellow seeds.

Mendel then crossbred these offspring and found that of the second generation of pea plants, 6,022 had yellow seeds and 2,001 had green seeds. Mendel used the results of his experiments with plants to estimate the probability of second-generation seeds being either yellow or green.

When probability is based on data it is called **experimental probability.** When probability is based on theory, by examining all possible outcomes, it is called **theoretical probability.** Theoretical probability indicates what will happen over the long run or with a large number of trials.

5. Estimation Use Mendel's data to estimate the experimental probabilities $P(\text{green})$ and $P(\text{yellow})$.

Mixed REVIEW

Compute.

1. ${}_6C_5$ **2.** ${}_4C_2$

3. ${}_7P_3$ **4.** $\frac{12!}{3!}$

Write a proportion and solve.

5. 36% of what number is 72?

6. 105 is what percent of 30?

7. Find the sale price of a \$48 jacket that is reduced by $33\frac{1}{3}\%$.

Sometimes you can think of probability as the area of a region.

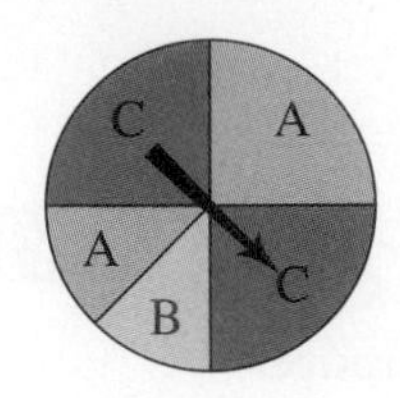

Example 2 Find the probability of each outcome for the spinner shown at the left.

- Let the circle represent 1 or 100%. Divide the circle into eight equal sections.

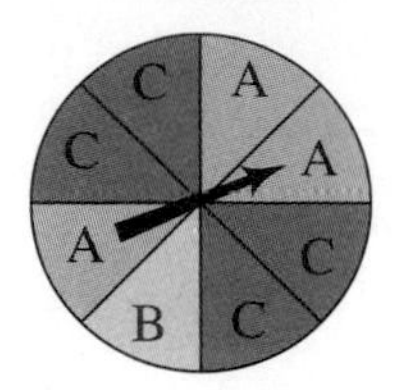

$P(A) = \frac{3}{8} = 37.5\%$

$P(B) = \frac{1}{8} = 12.5\%$

$P(C) = \frac{4}{8} = \frac{1}{2} = 50\%$

Check $37.5\% + 12.5\% + 50\% = 100\%$ ✓

WORK TOGETHER

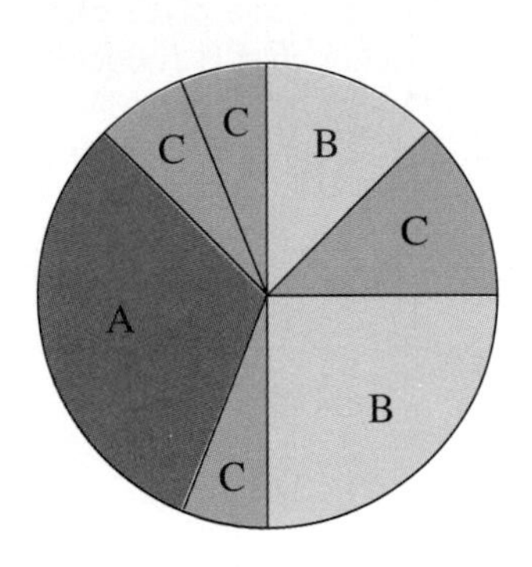

Work with a partner.

6. A dart is thrown randomly at the game board shown at the left. Are all outcomes equally likely? Find $P(A)$, $P(B)$, and $P(C)$.

7. Design a game board so that the odds in favor of your winning are 7 : 5.

TRY THESE

8. Use class data to find the experimental probability that someone in your class has exactly one brother and one sister.

9. If E and E' are complementary events, find $P(E) + P(E')$.

10. The odds in favor of winning a contest are 1 to 3.

a. Find the probability of winning the contest.

b. Find the probability of *not* winning the contest.

11. Draw a spinner so that $P(A) = 0.25$, $P(B) = 0.4$, $P(C) = 0.1$, and $P(D) = 0.25$.

12. What is the greatest number a probability can be? Explain your answer.

ON YOUR OWN

13. **Gardening** A package of wildflower seeds contains 50 daisy seeds, 80 sunflower seeds, 100 black-eyed Susan seeds, and 20 lupine seeds. What is the probability that a seed selected randomly will be a daisy seed?

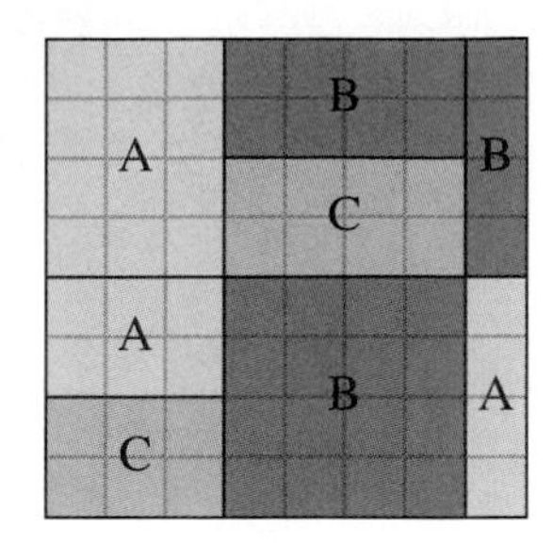

14. A dart is thrown randomly at the game board shown at the right. Find the probability of each possible outcome.

15. a. You buy a raffle ticket to win a bicycle. One of 500 tickets will be drawn from a box to determine the winner. Find the probability and odds that you will win.

    b. How do the probability and odds of your winning change if you buy two tickets?

16. **Chemistry** Use the information at the right. Paul noticed that most of the first twelve elements in the periodic table end with the letter "m" or "n." If he randomly selects one element, what is the probability that it ends with "m" or "n"?

Jons Jakob Berzelius prepared the first comprehensive list of elements in 1828. Currently, there are 109 elements in the periodic table. The first twelve elements are: hydrogen, helium, lithium, beryllium, boron, carbon, nitrogen, oxygen, fluorine, neon, sodium, and magnesium.

17. **Data File 9 (pp. 378–379)** Estimate the probability that in 1995 an adult male chosen at random will be a smoker. Is this probability experimental or theoretical? Why?

Each figure represents 100%. Estimate the area shaded, and describe an event that has this probability.

18. 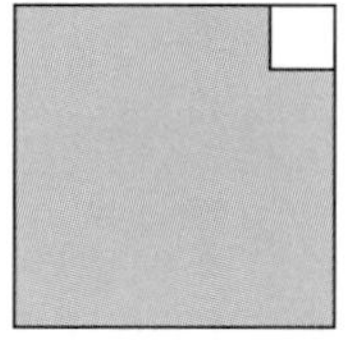

19. 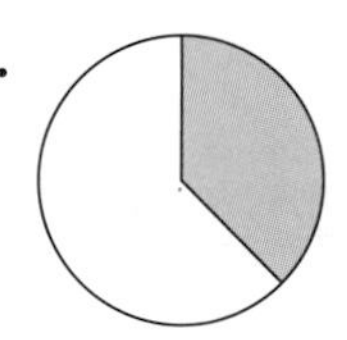

20. 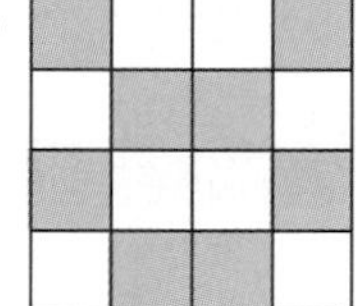

21. A relish tray contains green olives and black olives. If you randomly select one olive, $P(\text{green}) = 0.4$. Find $P(\text{black})$. How many olives are possibly on the tray?

22. **Activity** Toss a coin 50 times. Record your results in a table.

    a. Use your data to find $P(\text{heads})$ and $P(\text{tails})$.

    b. Are "heads" and "tails" equally likely outcomes? Explain.

    c. **Writing** Why might the experimental probability of an event not equal the theoretical probability of the event?

23. Draw a spinner with five equally likely outcomes.

What's Ahead

- Finding probability of independent and dependent events

9-5 Independent and Dependent Events

WHAT YOU'LL NEED

✓ Square tiles

WORK TOGETHER

Use three square tiles. Mark one tile with an X on both sides. Mark the second tile with an O on both sides. Mark the third tile with an X on one side and an O on the other. Put the tiles in a bag. If you pick a tile at random, and the side facing you is X, do you think the probability that the other side is X is greater than, less than, or equal to 0.5? Carry out the following experiment to check your prediction.

Select a tile at random. Look at the side facing you. If it is O, put the tile back. If it is X, turn the tile over and record what is on the other side. Put the tile back, and repeat until you have drawn 30 X-tiles. Keep a tally of the results.

Twins are born about once in every 89 births. These six sets of twins are all freshman athletes at the same college.

1. Was your prediction correct? If not, use the results of this experiment to revise your prediction. Estimate the probability that there is an X on the reverse side given that there is an X on the side facing you.
2. **Discussion** Does an X on the facing side affect the probability of an X on the reverse side?

THINK AND DISCUSS

When the outcome of one event does not affect the outcome of a second event, the events are **independent.** When the outcome of one event does affect the outcome of the second event, the events are **dependent.**

3. Is each pair of events dependent or independent?
   a. Toss a coin. Then roll a number cube.
   b. Choose a bracelet and put it on. Choose another bracelet.
   c. Select a card. Do not replace it. Then select another card.
   d. Select a card. Replace it. Select another card.
   e. Pick one flower from a garden, then pick another.

Independent Events Multiply to find the probability.

Probability of Two Independent Events

If A and B are independent events, $P(A \text{ and } B) = P(A) \times P(B)$.

Example 1 A bag contains 4 red marbles and 6 blue marbles. You draw a marble at random, replace it, and draw another marble. Find the probability that both marbles you draw are blue.

- These are independent events.

$$P(\text{blue and blue}) = P(\text{blue}) \times P(\text{blue})$$
$$= \frac{6}{10} \times \frac{6}{10}$$
$$= \frac{36}{100} = 36\%$$

4. a. Find P(two red marbles).

b. Find P(two different colors).

Dependent Events

Probability of Two Dependent Events

If A and B are dependent events, then $P(A, \text{ then } B) = P(A) \times P(B/A)$, where $P(B/A)$ is the probability of B given that A has happened.

Example 2 Two girls and three boys enter a drawing. Two names are selected randomly as winners. Find the probability that both winners are girls.

- The two events are dependent.
- Since there are 5 names, the probability that the first name drawn is a girl's is $\frac{2}{5}$.
- If the first name drawn is a girl's, there is only 1 girl's name left out of the total of 4 names, so $P(\text{girl/girl}) = \frac{1}{4}$.

$$P(\text{girl, then girl}) = P(\text{girl}) \times P(\text{girl/girl})$$
$$= \frac{2}{5} \times \frac{1}{4}$$
$$= \frac{1}{10} = 10\%$$

Mixed REVIEW

1. Find the probability of winning a contest if the odds in favor of winning are 1 to 999.

2. Draw a spinner so that $P(\text{red}) = 0.2$, $P(\text{green}) = 0.4$, $P(\text{blue}) = 0.3$, and $P(\text{black}) = 0.1$.

Rewrite each number as a decimal and a percent.

3. $\frac{3}{8}$ **4.** $6\frac{3}{4}$

5. A firefighter wants the top of a 50 ft ladder to reach a window 40 ft above the ground. How far away from the base of the building should the bottom of the ladder be?

Name 1 Name 2

$\frac{2}{5}$ G — $\frac{1}{4}$ G
■ B
■ B — ■ G
■ B

5. The tree diagram at the left displays the outcomes for Example 2. The probability is written along each branch that leads to the outcome GG. You multiply along the branches to find the probability of each outcome. Copy and complete the tree diagram. Find each probability.

   a. P(GB) **b.** P(BG) **c.** P(BB)

Probability and Area

Sometimes you can use area models.

Example 3

A mouse is placed in the maze at the left. Find the probability that the mouse will find the cheese.

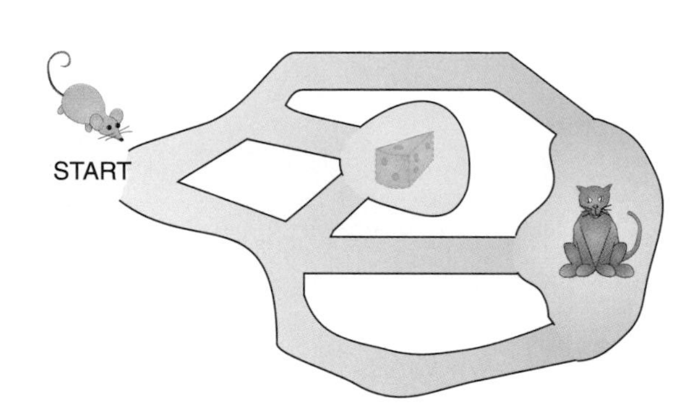

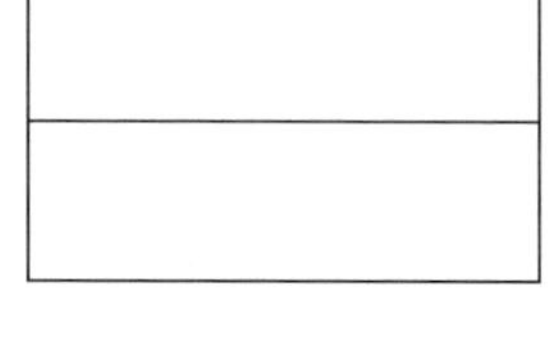

Draw a rectangle to represent the sample space. The mouse must first make a choice between two paths. Divide the rectangle into two congruent pieces.

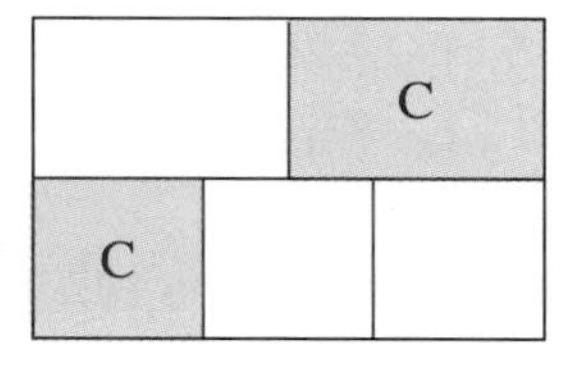

The upper path splits into two paths. Divide the upper rectangle into two congruent pieces. The lower path splits into three paths.

The areas labeled C represent the probability that the mouse finds the cheese. Find the sum of the areas.

$$\frac{1}{4} + \frac{1}{6} = \frac{5}{12} \approx 0.42 = 42\%$$

The mouse has a 42% chance of finding the cheese.

6. Explain why the choices in the maze are dependent events.

TRY THESE

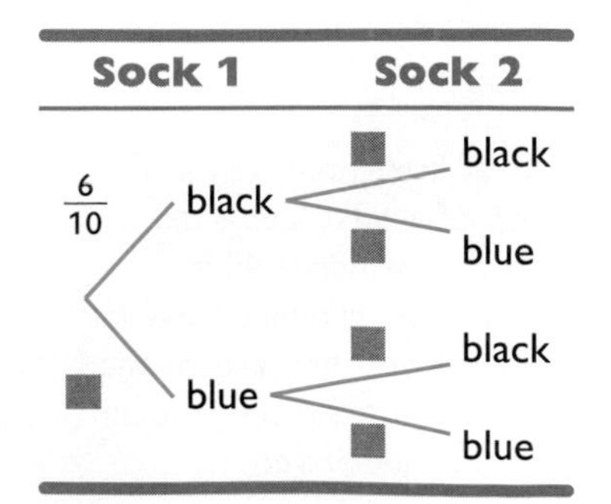

7. A variety pack of juice boxes contains 4 apple, 4 cherry, 4 orange, and 4 grape. If you and a friend each take a juice box, what is the probability that you will both get grape?

8. There are six black socks and four blue socks in a drawer.

   a. Copy and complete the tree diagram at the left.

   b. If you take two socks from the drawer, find P(two blue).

9. Suppose you toss a coin four times with these results: head, head, head, head. Find *P*(tail) on the fifth toss.

ON YOUR OWN

10. Two letters of the alphabet are chosen randomly without replacement. Find each probability.

    a. *P*(I, then a vowel) b. *P*(Z, then a consonant)

11. One manufacturer packages 6 mini-boxes of sweetened cereal and 8 mini-boxes of unsweetened cereal together. Two boxes are selected. Draw a tree diagram that shows the probability of each possible outcome.

Biology **Use the data at the right for colorblindness.**

Colorblind (CB) Data		
	Male	Female
CB	40	2
Not CB	460	498
Total	500	500

12. Find *P*(colorblind/male) and *P*(colorblind/female).

13. Are colorblindness and gender independent or dependent events? Explain your answer.

14. Of 100 people, how many would you expect to be colorblind?

15. Use an area model to find the probability of a mouse finding the cheese on its first attempt in the maze at the right.

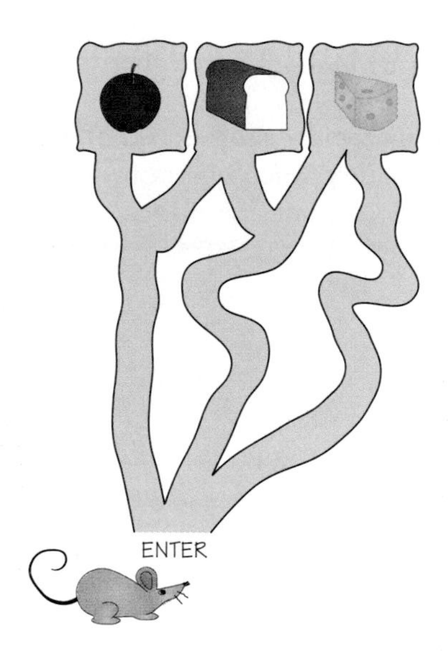

16. **Calculator** A jigsaw puzzle has 200 pieces.

    a. You take four puzzle pieces from the box. What is the probability that all four are corner pieces?

    b. The first 100 pieces you take are not corner pieces. What is the probability that the next piece is a corner piece?

17. **Critical Thinking** Suppose you like to put together edge and corner pieces first. You take one piece at a time from the box. If it is a corner or edge piece, you place it in a pile. Would you then continue with Method A or B? Explain why.

    Method A If it is not a corner or edge piece, you put it back in the box.

    Method B If it is not a corner or edge piece, you place it in a pile separate from the corner and edge pieces.

18. **Writing** Use your own words to explain the difference between dependent and independent events. Give examples.

What's Ahead

- Using Pascal's triangle to find probabilities and the number of combinations

9-6 Pascal's Triangle

THINK AND DISCUSS

Finding Probabilities The arithmetic triangle, known as Pascal's triangle, has fascinated many people. Blaise Pascal (1623–1662) didn't discover this triangle, but he developed ways to apply it to solutions of probability problems.

Pascal's Triangle

Row														Sum
0							1							1
1						1		1						■
2					1		2		1					■
3				1		3		3		1				■
4			1		4		6		4		1			■
5		1		5		10		10		5		1		■
6	1		6		15		20		15		6		1	■

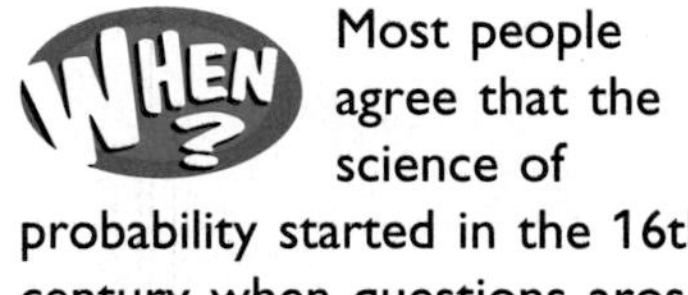

Most people agree that the science of probability started in the 16th century when questions arose about games of chance.

1. What patterns do you notice in Pascal's triangle? Look along rows and diagonals.

2. a. Make a copy of the triangle. Then find the groups below in the triangle. What relationship do you see among the numbers in each group?

   1 2   10 10   10 5   3 1

    3   20   15   4

   b. How can you use this relationship to extend the triangle?

   c. Complete two more rows.

3. a. Find the sum of the numbers in each row of the triangle.

   b. Write each sum using exponents.

   c. **Discussion** Devise a rule for finding the sum of the *nth* row in Pascal's triangle.

You can use Pascal's triangle to find probabilities when there are two equally likely outcomes for each event.

WORK TOGETHER

Consider the probability that three traffic lights in a row are green. Assume that traffic lights are either red or green, not yellow, and that red and green are equally likely events.

4. What is the probability that any traffic light will be green?

5. **Discussion** Assume the traffic lights work independently of each other, rather than being timed to work together. How does this affect the probability of three green lights in a row?

6. Draw a tree diagram to show all possible outcomes for the three traffic lights. What is the total number of possible outcomes? How does this sum relate to Pascal's triangle?

7. Suppose you let R represent a red light and G represent a green light. You can sort all the possible outcomes as follows.

0 green	1 green	2 green	3 green
RRR	RRG	RGG	GGG
	RGR	GRG	
	GRR	GGR	
1	3	3	1

How does the table relate to Pascal's triangle?

8. Find each probability for the three traffic lights using Pascal's triangle.

   a. P(no green lights)
   b. P(one green light)
   c. P(two green lights)
   d. P(three green lights)

9. **Discussion** Explain how you used Pascal's triangle to find the probability of three green lights in a row.

10. Look at Row 6 of Pascal's triangle. It gives you information about six traffic lights in a row. Describe what each number in Row 6 tells you in terms of the six traffic lights.

11. Suppose you toss four coins in a row. Use Pascal's triangle to find the probability of getting:

    a. two heads and two tails
    b. one head and three tails

The longest traffic jam ever reported was on February 16, 1980. Cars were stretched northwards from Lyons to Paris, France, for 109.3 mi!

Source: *The Guinness Book of Records*

A bag contains 7 red tiles and 3 green tiles. You draw two tiles from the bag. Find each probability.

1. P(red, then red)
2. P(green, then green)
3. P(the tiles are different colors)

Copy this design. Draw each rotation.

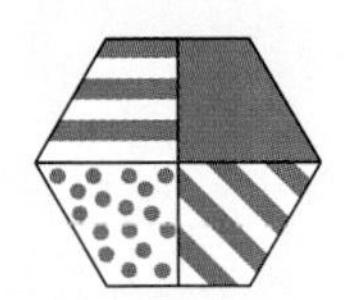

4. 270° rotation
5. 180° rotation

The number of combinations $_nC_r$ is the number of ways r objects can be selected from a set of n distinct objects.

$$_nC_r = \frac{_nP_r}{r!}$$

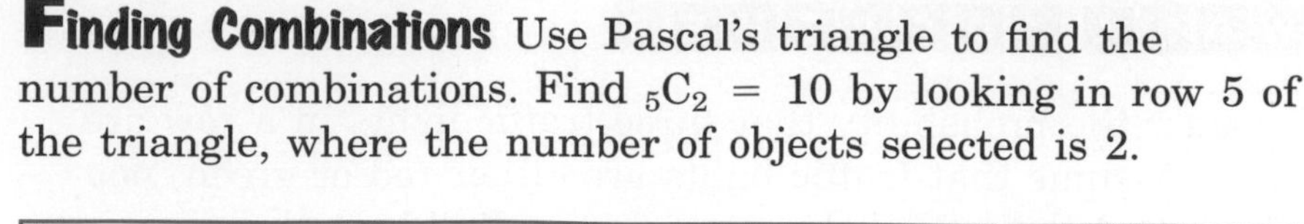

Finding Combinations Use Pascal's triangle to find the number of combinations. Find $_5C_2 = 10$ by looking in row 5 of the triangle, where the number of objects selected is 2.

Row 5 of Pascal's triangle	1	5	10	10	5	1
Number of objects selected	0	1	2	3	4	5

12. Find $_5C_0$ and $_5C_5$. Explain what each expression means.

13. Use Pascal's triangle to find the number of ways 3 people can be selected from a set of 7 distinct people. Use the combination formula to check your result.

ON YOUR OWN

Use Pascal's triangle to solve each problem.

14. Suppose you flip a penny, a dime, a nickel, and a quarter. What is the probability of getting one head and three tails?

15. The Mattapan police department has six police officers. On Friday night three officers will be on duty. How many different sets of three officers are possible for Friday night?

16. A family plans to have six children. Find the probability of three girls and three boys in any order.

17. A couple plans to have two children. Find the probability of having one boy and one girl in any order. Compare this with the probability of having one boy and then one girl.

18. A family has eight girls. Compare P(ninth child is a girl) with P(nine girls in a row). Why are they different?

19. Look for symmetry in Pascal's triangle. Why is $_3C_1$ the same as $_3C_2$? Are all the rows symmetric? Explain.

20. **Writing** How are situations that involve tossing a coin and getting heads and tails, the birth in a family of boys or girls, or true or false questions similar in terms of probability?

21. Suppose you guess on all 10 questions of true-false test. What are the odds in favor of answering all 10 questions correctly?

Mrs. Emory Landon Harrison of Johnson City, Tennessee, was named the 1955 "Honor Mother of the Year." She had 13 sons in a row! **What's the probability of this?**

22. Use the diagram at the right. Start at F and trace a path to each E by connecting F-I-V-E. Letters must be diagonal to each other in order to be connected.

  a. How many paths are there to the first E? the second E? the third E? the fourth E?

  b. How are the number of paths in the FIVE triangle related to Pascal's triangle?

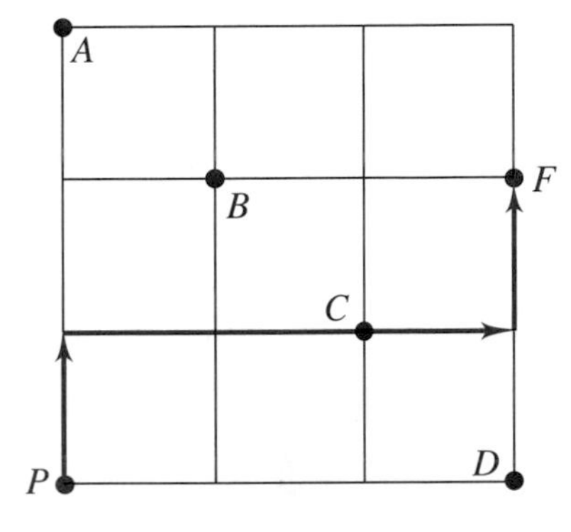

23. Use the street map at the right. Pascal lives at point P and wants to visit Fermat at point F. How many different routes are there for Pascal to travel from P to F if he only travels "up" and "right"? One route is marked on the map. How do routes to A, B, C, and D relate to Pascal's triangle?

24. To find ${}_{24}C_8$ would you use Pascal's triangle or the combination formula? Why?

25. **Investigation (p. 380)** Count the number of students in your class with a 4-letter first name. Estimate the number of students in your school with a 4-letter first name. Explain your method.

CHECKPOINT

1. a. You toss 3 coins. Find $P(3 \text{ heads})$.

  b. Find $P(E')$ if $P(E) = 0.75$.

2. Draw a spinner modeling the chances of getting 0, 1, 2, 3, or 4 heads with 4 flips of a coin.

3. Suppose that a dart is thrown randomly at the game board shown at the right. Find P(A) and P(B).

<table>
<tr><td rowspan="3">B</td><td rowspan="2">A</td><td rowspan="6">A</td></tr>
<tr></tr>
<tr><td rowspan="2">B</td></tr>
<tr><td rowspan="3">A</td></tr>
<tr><td rowspan="2">A</td></tr>
<tr></tr>
</table>

4. **Choose A, B, C, or D.** Which of the following *cannot* be computed using Pascal's triangle?

  A. the number of ways to get 3 heads flipping a coin 5 times

  B. P(3 girls in a family of 3 children)

  C. P(a number is divisible by 3)

  D. ${}_{7}C_{4}$

PROBLEM SOLVING

9-7 Simulate the Problem

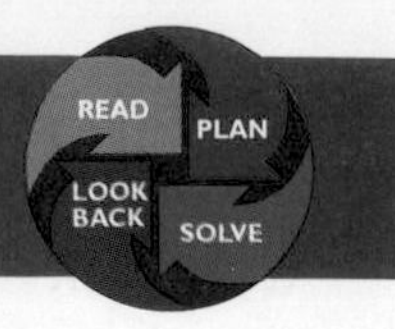

What's Ahead

- Solving problems by simulation

WHAT YOU'LL NEED

✓ Paper cups 

✓ Spinners 

You can solve many probability problems by simulating the problem. You develop an appropriate model, complete a number of trials to generate data, then use the data to solve the problem.

> At a street fair, a clown is playing a game with three paper cups turned upside down. The clown puts a small red ball under one cup and tells you that if you can guess where it is, you win a prize. The clown moves the cups around so fast that you lose track of the ball. So you make a guess. The clown then lifts up one of the other cups that turns out to be empty and asks if you want to stay with your first choice or switch to the remaining cup. **What should you do, stay or switch?**

READ

Read and understand the given information. Summarize the problem.

Think about the characteristics of this problem and its solution.

1. Read the problem carefully. Is it asking you to decide which is the better strategy—to stay or to switch? Is it asking you to find and compare two probabilities?
2. Does the clown know where the ball is hidden? Is this information important to the problem? Why or why not?
3. If you were playing the game and did not have much time to think about it, would you stay or switch? Why?

PLAN

Decide on a strategy to solve the problem.

Try this game to see what happens. Play the game with paper cups and a small object or simulate the game by using other materials such as marked index cards or spinners.

4. Gather materials to play the game with a partner. One of you will simulate the actions of the clown and the other will simulate the actions of the player. What must the clown do? What must the player do? Try the game once to practice.

5. Design a table you can use to record the results. Each time you play the game, or simulate the problem, you complete one trial. The player must "stay" for a number of trials and "switch" for a number of trials in order to make comparisons.

6. **Discussion** Decide how many trials each pair in your class will complete. Why might you want to combine class data to increase the number of trials?

SOLVE

Try out the strategy.

Now play or simulate the game to generate some data. You can then use the data to solve the problem.

7. Simulate the problem. Present your data in a table.

8. Use your data to find the experimental probability of winning if the player stays with the original choice.

9. Use your data to find the experimental probability of winning if the player switches to the other choice.

10. What should you do when you play this game, stay or switch? Why?

LOOK BACK

Think about how you solved this problem.

11. Does the answer surprise you? Does it seem reasonable? Are you convinced that your solution to this problem is valid?

12. Think back to your answer in Question 3. Explain what was right or wrong about your reasoning at that point.

13. **Discussion** Besides giving you an answer to the problem, did the simulation give you any insight on the problem and its solution? Can you solve this problem without simulating it?

TRY THESE

Solve by simulating the problem. Show all your work.

14. You and a partner play a game in which you each toss a coin. You score a point for each head and your partner scores a point for each tail. The first person to score ten points wins. The score is 9 to 8 in favor of your partner when the bell rings and you must stop. If you continue the game the next day, what is the probability that your partner will win?

Problem Solving Hint

Use a spinner divided into fourths to simulate the problem. Let some sections stand for sunny weather.

15. A weather forecaster reports that the probability of sunny weather is 75%. You begin a three-day camping trip. Simulate this situation to find the probability of three sunny days in a row.

ON YOUR OWN

Use any strategy to solve each problem. Show your work.

16. A piglet born on May 1 weighs 10 lb. It gains 1.5 lb per day. How much will the piglet weigh on June 1? Find the percent of weight increase from May 1 to June 1.

17. The numbers 1, 2, and 3 are placed at the vertices of the triangle at the right. Use the numbers 4, 5, 6, 7, 8, and 9 only once. Find at least one way to place two numbers on each side of the triangle so that the sum of all four numbers on each side is equal to 17.

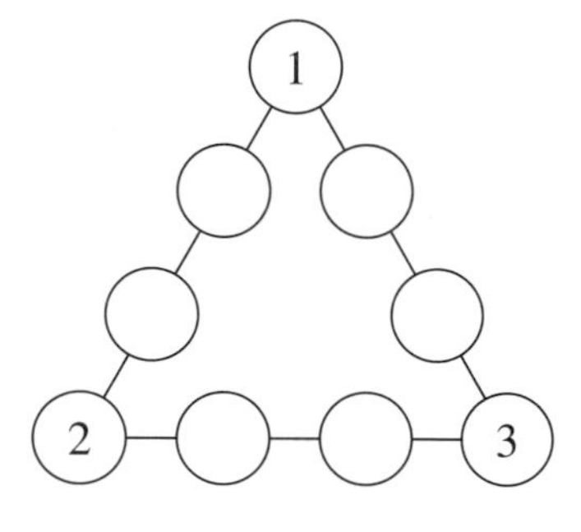

18. A teacher at a day-care center looks out a window and counts 15 children riding tricycles or bicycles. "There are 42 wheels in action," she comments. How many children are riding bicycles and how many children are riding tricycles?

19. A multiple-choice test has 6 questions. Each question has 4 possible answers. Find the probability of answering all the questions correctly if you guess on all six of them.

20. A TV game show, *The Choice Is Yours,* offers contestants the chance to win a prize hidden behind one of 4 doors. After a contestant chooses a door, the host opens one of the doors without prizes. The contestant can then switch to one of the remaining closed doors or stay with the original choice. Which method—to switch or to stay—gives the contestant a better chance of winning? Explain your reasoning.

21. Writing Write a paragraph explaining what it means to "simulate the problem."

Mixed REVIEW

Use Pascal's Triangle to find each value.

1. ${}_6C_2$ **2.** ${}_9C_7$

Determine which is the better buy, A or B.

3. A: 4 bars of soap for $1.98
B: 6 bars of soap for $2.98

4. A: 6 muffins for $3.29
B: 12 muffins for $6.49

5. Graph the step function.

Shipping & Handling	
Orders ($)	**Cost**
to $20.00	$2.00
$20.01 to $30.00	$2.50
$30.01 to $40.00	$3.00
$40.01 to $50.00	$3.50
over $50.00	$4.00

Practice

Find the value of each factorial.

1. 3!
2. 7!
3. $\frac{9!}{8!}$
4. $\frac{4!}{5!}$
5. $\frac{8!7!}{10!}$
6. $\frac{75!}{73!}$

A spinner numbered 1 to 16 is spun randomly. Find the probability that the spinner lands on each.

7. an even number
8. a number divisible by 4
9. 20
10. a square number
11. a number less than 10
12. 3 or 13

Compute.

13. ${}_{11}C_9$
14. ${}_5P_2$
15. ${}_6C_6$
16. ${}_8P_8$

Use Pascal's Triangle to find each value.

17. ${}_5C_3$
18. ${}_7C_4$
19. ${}_4C_3$
20. ${}_7C_3$

The spinner at the right is spun and a number cube is rolled. Make a tree diagram to find the sample space. Find each probability.

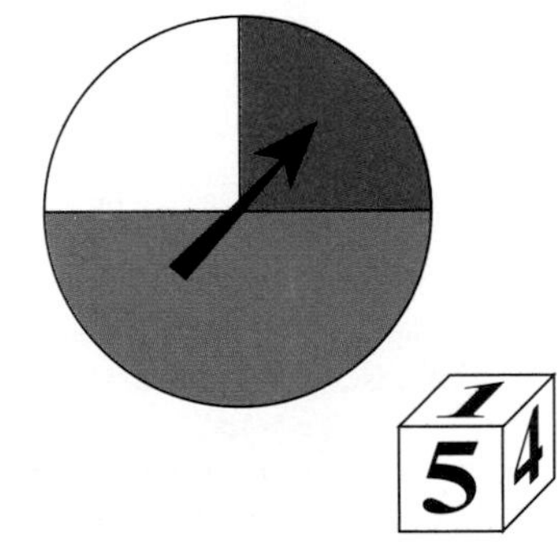

21. P(red, 4)
22. P(not red, prime)
23. P(not blue, odd)

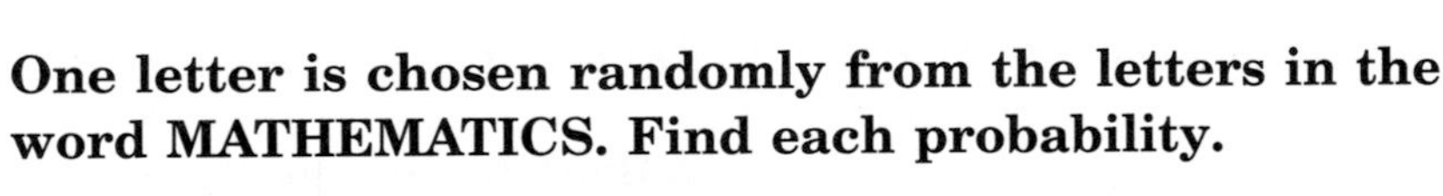

One letter is chosen randomly from the letters in the word MATHEMATICS. Find each probability.

24. P(a vowel)
25. P(S)
26. P(N)

Solve.

27. Karen and Steve are playing a game with number cubes. Karen wins if both cubes are even or both are odd. Steve wins if one cube is even and the other is odd. What is the probability that Karen wins? that Steve wins?

28. Liam has 4 blue and 4 brown socks in his drawer. On a dark morning he reaches in and pulls out a blue sock. What is the probability that the next sock he pulls out is a match? What are the odds against pulling a match?

29. Channel 52 reported that 3 out of 5 people polled were voting for the seat belt referendum. If 28,500 people voted, how many do you think voted "yes"?

30. **Data File 10 (pp. 420–421)** What are the odds that a high school dropout is employed?

TECHNOLOGY

What's Ahead

- Using technology and random digits to determine the fairness of games

9-8 Fair Games and Random Digits

WHAT YOU'LL NEED

✓ Dice  

✓ Computer 

✓ Software 

WORK TOGETHER

A game is **fair** if the players are equally likely to win. Play the game *Doubles or Nothing* with a partner.

1. Read the directions below for *Doubles or Nothing.* Do you think this game is fair or unfair? Explain your reasoning.

Doubles or Nothing

- Decide who is Player A and who is Player B.
- Each player rolls two dice. If the four dice show exactly one pair of doubles, Player A scores one point. Otherwise, Player B scores one point.
- The player with the most points after 30 rounds wins.

2. Play the game. Now do you think this game is fair? Explain.
3. Design and play one game that is fair and one that is unfair.

THINK AND DISCUSS

You can use random digits to simulate a problem or a game.

Random Number Table

23948	71477	12573	05954
65628	22310	09311	94864
41261	09943	34078	70481
34831	94515	41490	93312
09802	09770	11258	41139
66068	74522	15522	49227
00458	48800	33785	67694
45713	06400	87143	19586
57648	49551	40424	72908
21397	31604	84615	40513

4. A list of random digits is given at the left. To simulate *Doubles or Nothing,* let each digit in the list represent the result of one roll of a die. Which digits in the list will you use and which will you ignore?
5. How many digits in the list will you group together to represent one *round* of *Doubles or Nothing?*
6. Use the list to simulate *Doubles or Nothing.* Record the result of each round. Which player won the game?
7. **Computer** Generate enough random digits to simulate 100 rounds of *Doubles or Nothing.* Which player won the game?
8. Combine your results from Exercises 1, 2, 6, and 7 to make a conclusion. Is the game fair or unfair?

ON YOUR OWN

Read the directions given for the two games.

Rolling Thunder

- Decide who is Player A and who is Player B.
- Each player rolls two dice. Player A finds the product of the numbers rolled. Player B finds the sum of all four numbers rolled. The player with the higher result scores one point.
- The player with more points after 30 rounds wins.

Three's a Crowd

- Decide who is Player A and who is Player B.
- Each player tosses two coins. If there are exactly three heads or three tails, Player A scores one point. Otherwise, Player B scores one point.
- The player with more points after 30 rounds wins.

9. Decide if each game seems fair or unfair. If it seems unfair, which player is more likely to win?

10. **Writing** Describe how you can use the given list of random digits to simulate *Rolling Thunder.*

11. Suppose you want to use a list of random digits to simulate *Three's a Crowd.* You will use all the digits 0–9. Decide which digits represent "heads" and which represent "tails."

12. Suppose you want to use a computer to simulate *Three's a Crowd.* You can program the computer to generate any number of digits. You will not use all of the digits 0–9 because there are not ten possible outcomes. Decide which digit represents "heads" and which represents "tails."

13. a. Simulate *Rolling Thunder* and *Three's a Crowd.* Is each game fair or unfair?
    b. **Critical Thinking** If either of the games is unfair, how can you change the game to make it fair?

14. Greta created a game for two players, A and B. The game is fair. What do you know about $P(\text{A wins})$ and $P(\text{B wins})$?

15. Andy played a game 10 times and decided it was unfair. Sam used random digits to simulate the same game 100 times and decided that it was fair. With whom do you agree? Why?

Mixed REVIEW

Describe an appropriate simulation to estimate each probability.

1. the probability that in a list of 15 phone numbers, 9 end with an odd digit
2. the probability of answering 10 true and false questions correctly, without reading the questions

$\angle ARB$ is a 40° central angle. $\overline{AC}$ is a diameter.

3. $m\angle BRC = $ ■
4. $m\angle ACB = $ ■

Use a calculator to evaluate each.

5. $(-4)^2 - 7 \cdot 2^3$
6. $15 \div (-3) + 6^2 - 1$

MATH AND BUSINESS

What's Ahead

- Using samples for product inspection

9-9 Using Samples for Quality Control

THINK AND DISCUSS

The Flyer Company makes plastic saucer-shaped disks. They want the disks to sail smoothly through the air. They sample using a method of quality control called **product inspection.**

1. The Flyer Company inspects a sample of 500 disks and finds that ten are defective. Based on this data, what is the probability that a disk is defective?

2. The Flyer Company adjusts their manufacturing process. They inspect a sample of 800 disks and find two defective ones. Did quality improve?

3. The Flyer Company produces about 10,000 disks each week. Use the results of Question 2. Predict the number of defective disks each week.

Another important method of quality control is **process control.** The quality of a *product* can improve during the manufacturing *process.* The **simplified flow chart** below shows a method to check the process of making a pizza.

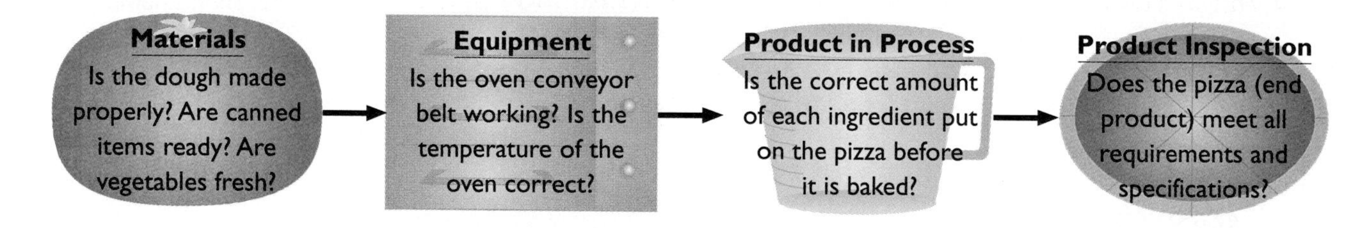

4. What data might you collect at each stage of the flow chart?

5. **Discussion** Do you think it makes more sense to improve quality during the process or after the product is completed?

You can use a **process control chart** to graph data collected during a manufacturing process. The chart at the top of the next page shows sample data for the mass of the material used to make a frisbee. The target value is the ideal measure. Control limits give the range of acceptable values for the mass.

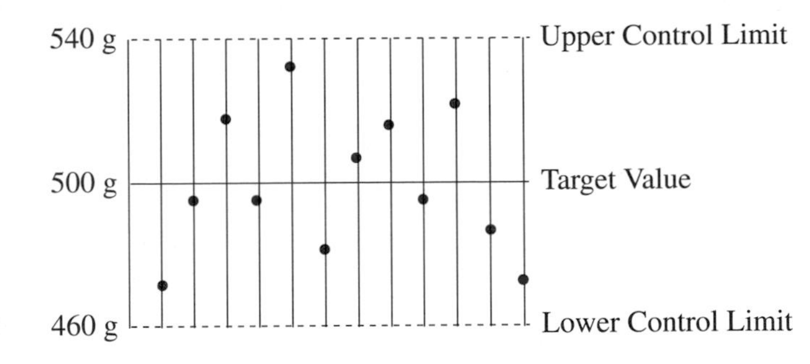

6. What is the target value for the mass? How is this value related to the mean of the data points graphed on the chart?

7. Identify the control limits on the chart. What is the range of acceptable values? What does this tell you?

8. From each lot of 50 computer chips, six chips are measured before they are accepted. The measurement taken on the sample is the width of a metal line on a chip. The mean values of 25 samples are given at the right. The target value is 1.06 μm. The control limits are 0.94 μm and 1.18 μm. Make a process control chart for the data.

Width in microns (μm)				
1.00	0.95	0.98	1.01	1.03
1.06	1.10	1.11	1.12	1.04
0.98	0.96	1.01	1.06	1.06
0.99	0.92	1.00	1.01	1.04
1.11	1.06	1.03	0.98	1.00

1 micron = 1×10^{-6} meters

You can use a process control chart to see when quality does not meet specifications. You then stop the process, find out what the problem is, and solve it. If a process is working perfectly, data points on the chart fall randomly above and below the target value within the control limits. Stop the process if a data point falls outside the range of acceptable values. Or, stop the process if data points show a distinct upward or downward trend over time, an abrupt shift, or a recurring pattern.

9. Use the process control chart you made for Exercise 8. Are there any points where the process should be stopped?

10. Sketch a process control chart that shows a trend, a shift, or a pattern. Include lines for target value and control limits.

WORK TOGETHER

Work in small groups. Suppose you are managers of a small company. Choose a product that your company manufactures. Describe methods of quality control your company uses. How do they measure quality? Draw a flow chart to show steps in the process where quality is checked.

ON YOUR OWN

W. Edwards Deming, an American expert on quality control, taught Japanese industrialists about statistical process control in the 1950s. His efforts were so successful that Japan's annual award for excellence in quality control is named after him.

11. Air conditioners are quite reliable. An average of 2.5% of all Cool air conditioners need repairs in the first five years of service. A Cool store sells 120 air conditioners one week. Predict how many will need repairs in the next five years.

12. **Writing** Each Thursday from 10:00 A.M. to 11:00 A.M. a mail-order company inspects all packages before they are sealed. They rarely find an error, yet they keep receiving complaints. What is wrong with their method of quality control? Give several suggestions for improving the process.

13. Draw a simplified flow chart that shows how the process of making a wooden desk might be checked.

14. For each process control chart, identify any points where you would stop the process and explain why.

a. 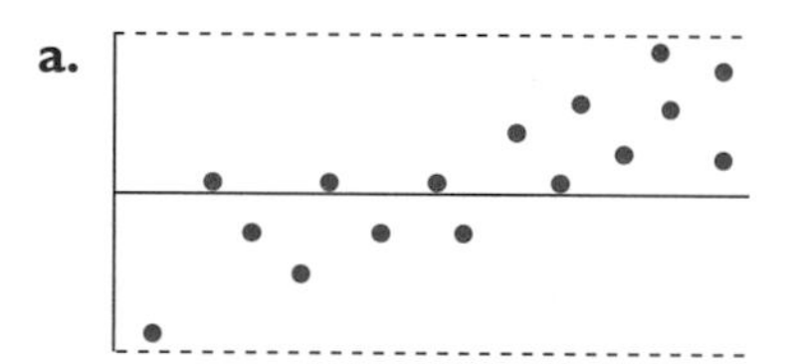

b. 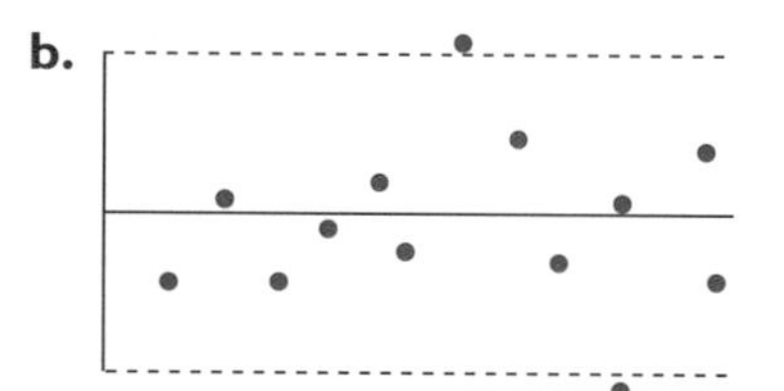

GREAT EXPECTATIONS

Musician

A profession I may choose when I grow older might be a musician. It sounds like an exciting job where I would meet a lot of people. I would like to write my own music. If I am able to write my own music, it would be original. Right now I am learning many things in school that would help me. Musicians use math for many things. I would need to count the number of beats a certain note contains. Math would help me to figure out how many beats there are in each measure. I know this from my music classes and singing I do in a choir. Are there any other ways I might use math as a musician?

Moneet Kohli

Quality On the Rise

Quality control efforts have improved many products. Competition, especially from Japan, has driven American companies to produce high-quality products efficiently.

Using statistical process control (SPC) has become widespread among American companies. The range of acceptable values, determined by control limits, is becoming smaller. For example a semiconductor company requires that the output electrical voltage of a computer chip fall within 0.1% of the mean. As a result, instruments used to measure materials and give readings must be extremely precise.

15. The target value for the output electrical voltage of a computer chip is 3.5 eV. What would the control limits be?

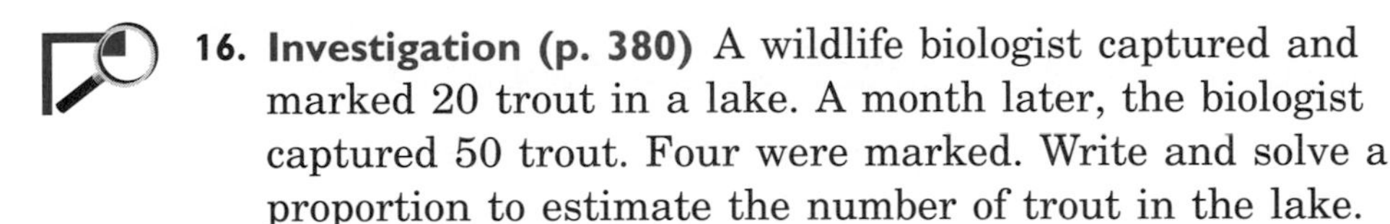

16. **Investigation (p. 380)** A wildlife biologist captured and marked 20 trout in a lake. A month later, the biologist captured 50 trout. Four were marked. Write and solve a proportion to estimate the number of trout in the lake.

Two number cubes are rolled.

1. Player A wins if the sum is less than 8 and Player B wins if the sum is greater than or equal to 8. Is this a fair game?

Solve and graph the solution set on a number line.

2. $3n - 5 > -8$

3. $\frac{1}{2} \leq -6n + \frac{3}{4}$

Find the slope of the line containing each pair of points.

4. $A(-4, 7)$; $B(3, 11)$

5. $C(10, -6)$; $D(1, 6)$

Dear Moneet,

You are correct in your ideas about math and music. I help my music students to understand and feel the beat and rhythm of the music they are playing. Sometimes we work together to write our own music.

Music is written in a certain time signature that is chosen by the composer. Next time you see sheet music, look for the time signature expressed as a fraction at the beginning of the first line. Time signature of 4/4 means there are four beats per measure, and the quarter note gets one beat. When you compose your own music, you will need to choose a time signature.

Sydonia M. Brooks, Piano and Organ Teacher

CHAPTER 9

Wrap Up

Counting and Displaying Outcomes 9-1

Use the ***Counting Principle*** to find the number of outcomes for two or more events. Multiply the number of outcomes for each event. Use a factorial when the outcomes are an ordered arrangement.

Find the value of each factorial.

1. $4!$ **2.** $7!$ **3.** $\frac{5!}{3!}$ **4.** $\frac{12!}{9!}$

5. Max has 3 hats, 4 ties, 2 shirts, and 5 pairs of pants. How many different outfits does Max have?

Permutations, Combinations, Pascal's Triangle 9-2, 9-3, 9-6

A ***permutation*** is an arrangement of a set of objects in a particular order. The number of permutations of nine things taken four at a time can be written ${}_9P_4$.

$${}_9P_4 = 9 \cdot 8 \cdot 7 \cdot 6$$

A ***combination*** is a group of items in which the order of the items is not important. The number of combinations of nine things taken four at a time, ${}_9C_4$, is ${}_9P_4$ divided by 4!

$${}_9C_4 = \frac{{}_9P_4}{4!}$$

6. Choose A, B, C, or D. Which has the largest value?

A. ${}_6P_6$ **B.** ${}_5P_3$ **C.** ${}_7C_2$ **D.** ${}_{10}C_9$

7. How many different 3-digit numbers can you write using the whole numbers 1 to 5 without repeating a digit?

8. How many different ways can you choose 2 magazines from a shelf of 10 magazines in a convenience store?

9. How many games will be played if twelve people are playing in a checker tournament and each person plays every other person?

10. How many different ways can you randomly choose 6 baseball cards to trade from a set of 25 cards?

Pascal's triangle can be used to find combinations.

Use Pascal's triangle to find each value.

11. ${}_6C_4$ **12.** ${}_9C_9$ **13.** ${}_5C_2$ **14.** ${}_8C_5$

Probability and Odds 9-4

The ***probability*** of an event is the number describing the chance that the event will happen. The ***odds*** in favor of an event is the ratio of the number of favorable outcomes to the number of unfavorable outcomes.

Find the probability and odds in favor of each.

15. a head when a coin is tossed

16. two tails when two coins are tossed

17. a sum of 9 when two number cubes are rolled

Independent and Dependent Events 9-5

When the outcome of one event does not affect the outcome of a second event, the events are ***independent.*** When it does affect the outcome of a second event, the events are ***dependent.***

18. Writing Give an example of two independent and two dependent events.

Simulate the Problem, Using Samples for Quality Control 9-7, 9-9

Many probability problems can be solved by ***simulating the problem.*** Companies use ***samples*** and ***product inspection*** for quality control.

19. How can you simulate the problem of finding the probability of guessing correctly 3 out of 5 true-false questions?

20. A toy company sampled 10 toys and found 3 defective. Predict how many toys out of 250 will not be defective.

Fair Games and Random Digits 9-8

A game is ***fair*** if the players have an equal chance of winning.

21. Two players are tossing three coins. Player A gets 1 point for each head that is tossed. Player B gets 3 points for tossing 3 heads or 3 tails. The player with the most points after 10 turns wins. Is this a fair game? Explain why or why not.

GETTING READY FOR CHAPTER 10

Express each fraction as a fraction with a denominator of 10, 100, or 1,000 and then write each as a decimal.

1. $\frac{3}{4}$

2. $\frac{4}{5}$

3. $\frac{1}{2}$

4. $\frac{3}{8}$

5. $\frac{2}{5}$

6. $\frac{7}{8}$

Follow Up

How Many Woozles?

The World Woozle Watch is mounting a gigantic campaign to publicize the plight of the woozle. The WWW has contacted you for help. The organization wants you to give your estimate of the number of remaining woozles and to explain how you reached your estimate. Go back to the estimate you made at the beginning of the chapter. Revise it if necessary based on your study of the chapter. Then do one of the following for the WWW.

- ✓ Prepare a brochure.
- ✓ Give an oral presentation.
- ✓ Present a radio or television report.

The problems preceded by the magnifying glass (p. 390, # 36, p. 403, # 25 and p. 413, # 16) will help you complete the investigation.

Some environmentalists estimate that more than 100 plant and animal species are becoming extinct daily. The greatest cause of the extinctions is the ongoing destruction of the tropical rain forest.

Excursion: Explain a method you could have used to estimate the size of the woozle population if you had been permitted to weigh the entire population.

Forecasting the Future

Businesses that spot a trend early and are the first to develop that trend are sure to be successful. How good are you at predicting the future? Try this to find out.

- Work with a partner to choose a business that interests you.
- Describe what is happening today in that field.
- Predict major developments in the field over the next two years.
- Describe a product that you believe a company should develop in order to be a leader in the field two years from now.

Pennies Tell Pi!

How can you use probability to approximate the value of π? Work with a partner to find out.

- Use $\frac{3}{4}$-inch grid paper.
- Toss a penny 100 times onto the grid. If any part of the penny covers an intersecting point of two grid lines, record the toss as a "hit." Otherwise record it as a "miss."
- Calculate the experimental probability of tossing a hit. Multiply the probability by 4. Compare with the value of π. What do you know?

Could You Win A Million?

The number of lotteries and sweepstakes in the United States is skyrocketing. How likely is it that you will win a lottery? Let's see.

- Choose a lottery or sweepstakes. Your state may have a lottery. Or, check your mail for sweepstake offerings.
- Obtain information on the chances of winning each of the prizes in the contest by writing to the address given.
- Do your chances of winning the contest justify the cost of entering it?
- Prepare a presentation. Support your assessment of the lottery or sweepstakes with examples.

THAT'S NOT FAIR!

The Wicked Brothers Carnival is having a contest for a new game to entertain its customers while they wait in line for tickets. They require:

- ***A fun game***
- ***Handmade materials***
- ***Unfair game for the participants (The owners want to win!)***

Work with your group to design an unfair game for the Wicked Brothers Carnival. Demonstrate it to your classmates.

Assessment

1. A stationery store sells paper and envelopes separately. Both come in cream, purple, and peach colors, and in two styles. How many different paper and envelope combinations are there?

2. Which license plate system provides more possible outcomes, two digits and three letters or seven digits?

3. **Choose A, B, C, or D.** A basketball team is choosing a forward, a center, and a guard. There are 20 people on the team. Which expression best describes the number of possible outcomes?

   A. ${}_{20}P_2$ **B.** ${}_{20}P_3$
   C. 20! **D.** 3!

4. Find each value.

   a. 8! **b.** ${}_4P_3$ **c.** ${}_{18}C_2$
   d. $\frac{6!}{2!}$ **e.** $P(E')$ if $P(E) = 0.53$

5. Is each expression equivalent to ${}_{12}C_3$? Write *yes* or *no*.

   a. ${}_{12}C_9$ **b.** $\frac{12!}{9!}$
   c. $\frac{12 \cdot 11 \cdot 10}{3!}$ **d.** ${}_{12}P_4$

6. **a.** You buy a raffle ticket to win a dinner for four at a local restaurant. One of 400 tickets is drawn to determine the winner. Find the probability and odds that you win.

   b. How do the probability and odds change if you buy 5 tickets?

7. Each number from 1 to 50 is placed in a hat. One number is drawn at random. Find each probability.

   a. $P(\text{even})$

   b. $P(\text{multiple of } 3)$

   c. $P(57)$

8. Use Pascal's triangle to find the probability of tossing 2 heads and 2 tails in four tosses of a coin.

9. Simulate the problem to find the probability of guessing correctly on all 5 questions of a true-false quiz.

10. Caitlin used 10 trials to simulate a game between two players, A and B. She found that $P(\text{A wins}) = 0.55$. Can she conclude that this game is fair or unfair? Why?

11. **Writing** For each process control chart, identify the points, if any, where you would stop the process. Explain why.

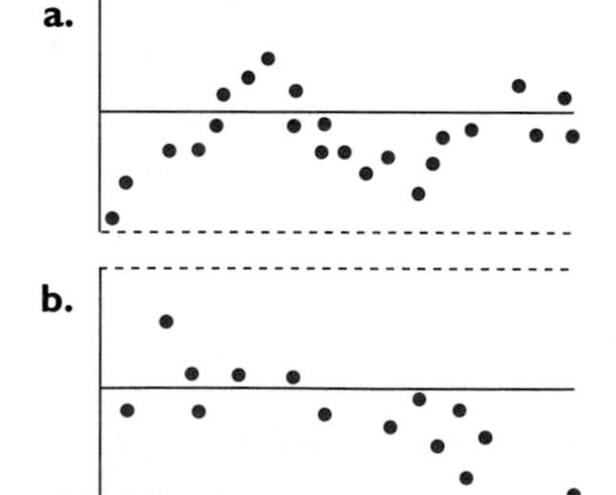

12. Jasper's Welding Shop found that out of 126 fenders welded, 7 had cracks. Predict the number of fenders with cracks out of a total of 198 fenders.

Cumulative Review

Choose A, B, C, or D.

1. If $a < b$, which of these statements is always true?

I. $b > a$ **II.** $\frac{a}{c} < \frac{b}{c}$

III. $a - c < b - c$

A. I only **B.** II only

C. I and III only **D.** I, II, and III

2. Which set of rational numbers is ordered from least to greatest?

A. $0.38, \frac{3}{8}, \frac{1}{2}, 0.65$

B. $\frac{12}{27}, 0.58, \frac{3}{7}, 0.89$

C. $-0.1, -0.74, \frac{-2}{3}, \frac{-9}{11}$

D. $0.16, \frac{2}{5}, 0.86, \frac{19}{20}$

3. In the figure below, the triangles are similar. Find the unknown length h.

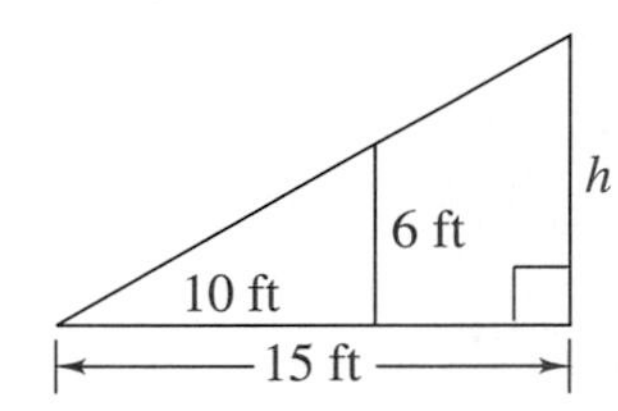

A. 6 ft **B.** 9 ft **C.** 3 ft **D.** 30 ft

4. Which expression is *not* equivalent to $\frac{6^3}{6^7}$?

A. $6^3 \times 6^{-7}$ **B.** $6^3 \div 6^7$

C. 6^{-4} **D.** 6^{10}

5. Which expression gives the number of different ways a group of 5 paintings can be selected from 12 paintings?

A. 5! **B.** ${}_{12}P_5$ **C.** ${}_{12}C_5$ **D.** ${}_5P_{12}$

6. If you start with a number, multiply by $\frac{3}{4}$, subtract 3, then divide by 12, the result is 2. What is the number?

A. 36 **B.** 108 **C.** 6 **D.** 27

7. Which proportion could *not* be represented by the model below?

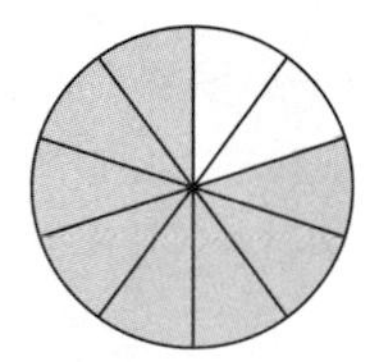

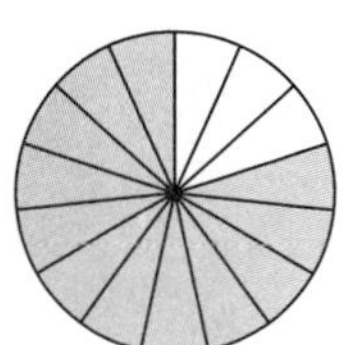

A. $\frac{12}{15} = \frac{8}{10}$ **B.** $\frac{2}{8} = \frac{3}{12}$

C. $\frac{3}{10} = \frac{2}{15}$ **D.** $\frac{4}{5} = \frac{8}{10}$

8. In how many different ways can 5 out of 8 people be seated in a row of 5 chairs?

A. 6,720 **B.** 56

C. 40,320 **D.** 120

9. In a class of 24 students, 8 are members of the honor society. What is the probability that a randomly selected student is *not* a member of the society?

A. $\frac{1}{3}$ **B.** $\frac{2}{3}$ **C.** 1 **D.** $\frac{1}{2}$

10. Find the area of the figure at the right.

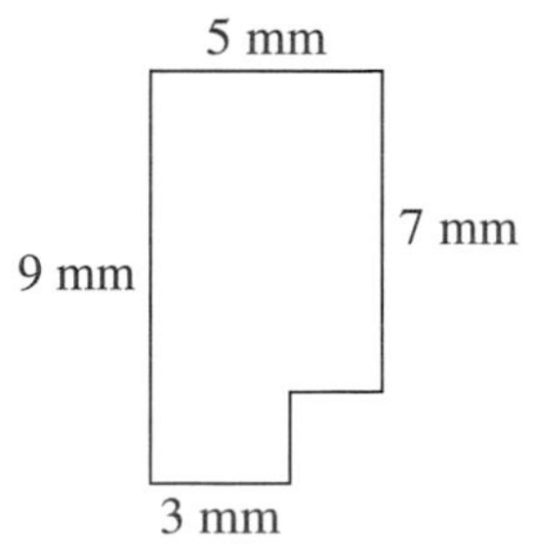

A. 26 mm^2

B. 41 mm^2

C. 45 mm^2

D. 20 mm^2

CHAPTER 10 Applications of Percent

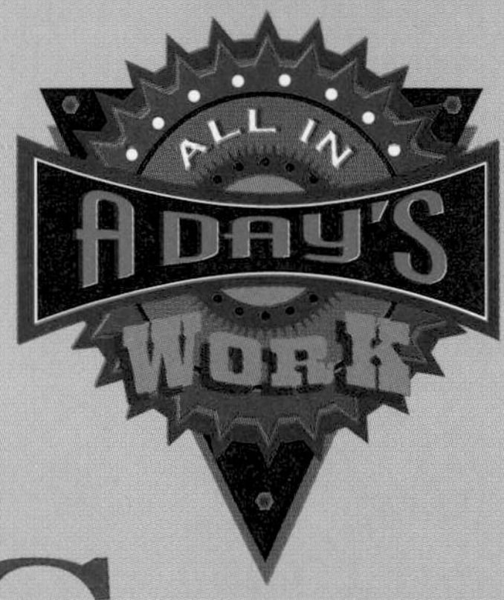

Computers have become an essential tool for almost every job or career. To become computer literate, a person needs to learn basic application programs. Higher levels of computer literacy require mathematics and technical knowledge of electronics. However all computer literacy involves problem solving.

Employment Outlook, 1990–2005

Growth Occupations	Percent Change
computer programmer	56.1
registered nurse	44.4
child care worker	48.8
cook	33.0
teacher	28.4
truck driver	26.1
Declining Occupations	
electronic assembler	−45.1
statistical clerk	−36.1
meter reader	−24.8
switchboard operator	−23.2
farmer	−20.9
service station attendant	−7.1

Source: CQ Researcher

Data File 10

WHAT YOU WILL LEARN

- how to estimate and work with percent
- how to solve problems involving percent of change
- how to use technology to compute interest
- how to solve problems by making a table

investigation

Project File

Memo

Today it is estimated that there are several hundred thousand millionaires in the United States. The average annual salary in the National Basketball Association is more than a million dollars. If that makes it seem as though a million dollars is no longer a lot of money, keep in mind that more than 99.9% of Americans are not millionaires. Now, however, you have a chance to become a millionare. An anonymous donor has decided to give you an opportunity to make a million dollars!

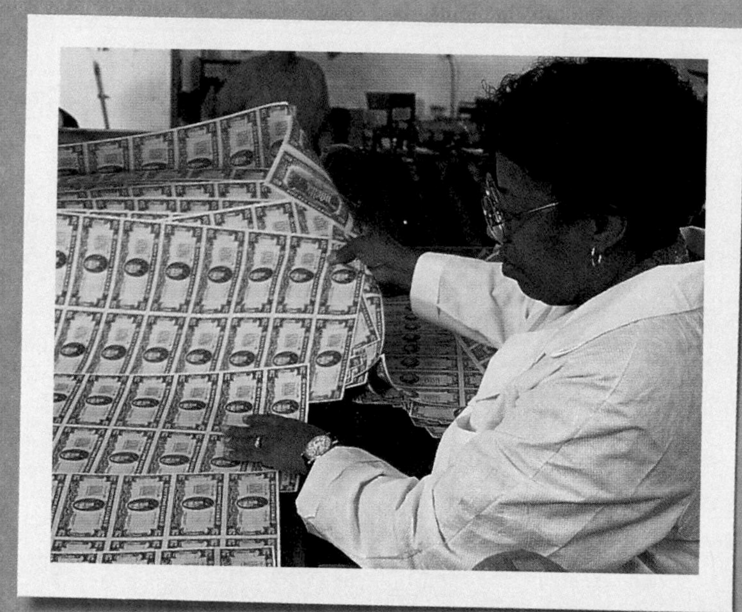

Mission: The donor presents you with $50,000 in cash. You must submit a plan for turning the money into $1 million within 50 years. Tell why you think your plan is a sound one and estimate how much you will have in 50 years. If in 50 years the amount exceeds $1 million, you may keep all of the money. Otherwise you must return everything to the donor.

Leads to Follow

- ✓ What are some good investments that you know of? What are some poor ones?
- ✓ Which is better, a rigid plan completely determined from the beginning or a plan that allows for change as time passes? Explain.

What's Ahead

- Relating fractions, decimals, and percents

10-1 Fractions, Decimals, and Percents

WHAT YOU'LL NEED

✓ Calculator 

THINK AND DISCUSS

Writing Fractions as Percents *Entertainment Weekly* found that $\frac{2}{5}$ of the people who answered a survey said that cable television was not worth the money people pay for it.

Another way to express the fraction $\frac{2}{5}$ is to write it as a *percent*. A **percent** is a ratio that compares a number to 100. To express $\frac{2}{5}$ as a percent, first write it as an equivalent fraction with denominator 100. Then express the fraction as a percent.

$$\frac{2}{5} = \frac{2 \cdot 20}{5 \cdot 20} = \frac{40}{100} = 40\%$$

1. Will this method for changing a fraction to a percent work well for all fractions? Explain.

2. If you were writing an article about this survey, would you prefer to use fractions or percents? Explain.

FLASHBACK

You can use a decimal model to show 40%.

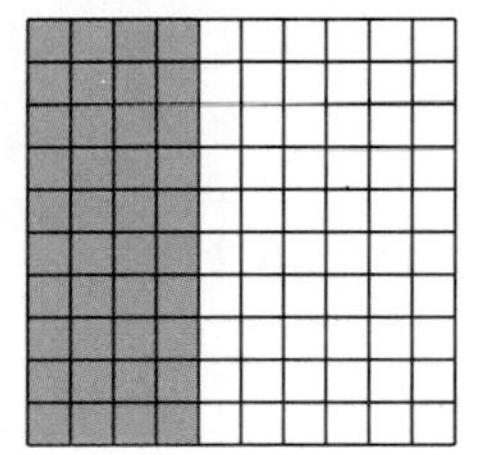

It may not always be easy to write a fraction as an equivalent fraction with denominator 100. You can rewrite any fraction as a percent by using a proportion.

Example 1 In the United States, the average weight of a one-year-old female baby is $\frac{22}{135}$ of the average weight of a female adult. Express this fraction as a percent.

$\frac{22}{135} = \frac{x}{100}$ Write a proportion.

$22 \cdot 100 = 135x$ Write the cross products.

$x = 16.\overline{296}$

$\frac{22}{135} \approx \frac{16.3}{100} = 16.3\%$

The average weight of a one-year-old female baby is about 16.3% of the average weight of a female adult.

Writing Decimals as Percents First write the decimal as a fraction with a denominator 100.

Example 2 According to the 1990 census, the population of the United States was 0.12 African American and 0.008 Native American. The total population in 1990 was 1.1 times the 1980 population. Express each decimal as a percent.

- $0.12 = \frac{12}{100}$

  $0.12 = 12\%$

- $0.008 = \frac{8}{1,000}$

  $= \frac{8 \div 10}{1,000 \div 10}$

  $= \frac{0.8}{100}$

  $0.008 = 0.8\%$

- $1.1 = \frac{11}{10}$

  $= \frac{11 \cdot 10}{10 \cdot 10}$

  $= \frac{110}{100}$

  $1.1 = 110\%$

Multiply or divide the numerator and denominator by the same power of ten to change the denominator to 100.

The 1990 population was 12% African American, 0.8% Native American, and 110% of the 1980 population.

WHEN? In 1993, the population of the United States was 258.7 million. The Census Bureau predicts that the population will rise to 300 million in 2010 and 392 million in 2050.

Source: *The Boston Globe*

Example 2 suggests the following rule for writing decimals as percents.

To write a decimal as a percent, move the decimal point two places to the right and write the percent sign.

Relating Fractions, Decimals, and Percents

A calculator can make it easy to convert fractions to decimals.

FLASHBACK

$\frac{2}{3}$ means "2 divided by 3."

Example 3 Write each fraction as a percent.

a. $\frac{1}{8}$ 1 ÷ 8 = 0.125 $\frac{1}{8} = 12.5\%$

b. $\frac{3}{500}$ 3 ÷ 500 = 0.006 $\frac{3}{500} = 0.6\%$

c. $2\frac{2}{3}$ 8 ÷ 3 = 2.6666667 $2\frac{2}{3} \approx 267\%$

d. $1\frac{3}{4}$ 7 ÷ 4 = 1.75 $1\frac{3}{4} = 175\%$

To change a percent to a fraction, write the percent as a fraction with denominator 100, then simplify the fraction.

Dividing by a number is the same as multiplying by its reciprocal.

Example 4 Eighteen karat gold is 75% pure gold and 14 karat gold is $58\frac{1}{3}\%$ pure gold. Express each of these percents as a fraction in simplest form.

- $75\% = \frac{75}{100} = \frac{3}{4}$
- $58\frac{1}{3}\% = \frac{58\frac{1}{3}}{100} = 58\frac{1}{3} \div 100 = \frac{175}{3} \times \frac{1}{100} = \frac{175}{300}, \text{ or } \frac{7}{12}$

Eighteen karat gold is $\frac{3}{4}$ pure gold and 14 karat gold is $\frac{7}{12}$ pure gold.

3. Ten karat gold is $41\frac{2}{3}\%$ pure gold. What fraction of 10 karat gold is pure gold?

Most of the gold reserve of the United States is stored in guarded vaults at Fort Knox, Kentucky. These vaults hold gold bullion bars valued at more than 6 billion dollars. Each bar is 99.99% pure gold. ***What percent of each bar is not pure gold?***

Source: *The World Book Encyclopedia*

TRY THESE

Mental Math Write each decimal as a percent.

4. 0.36 5. 0.04 6. 0.003 7. 5.2

Use a calculator, paper and pencil, or mental math. Write each fraction as a percent. Round to the nearest tenth.

8. $\frac{3}{5}$ 9. $\frac{17}{20}$ 10. $\frac{1}{6}$ 11. $3\frac{1}{8}$

Write each percent as a fraction in simplest form.

12. 70% 13. 93% 14. $4\frac{3}{4}\%$ 15. 782%

ON YOUR OWN

16. **Choose A, B, C, or D.** In which set are all three values equal?

A. 52%, 0.052, $\frac{52}{100}$ B. 0.52%, 0.52, $\frac{52}{100}$

C. 52%, 0.52, $\frac{52}{100}$ D. 0.52%, 0.0052, $\frac{52}{100}$

Mixed REVIEW

1. How many rainy days would you expect in April if the probability of a rainy day is $\frac{1}{3}$?

2. What is the probability of choosing a red marble from a bag containing 3 red, 6 blue, and 5 green marbles?

Compare. Replace each ■ with <, >, or =.

3. 0.75 ■ $\frac{2}{3}$

4. $\frac{3}{8}$ ■ 0.38

Solve.

5. $\frac{4}{5} = \frac{n}{8}$ 6. $\frac{9}{n} = \frac{3}{7}$

Extra SKILLS PRACTICE

Write each percent as a fraction in simplest form and as a decimal.

1. 6%
2. 37.5%
3. 180%
4. 43.75%

Write each as a percent to the nearest tenth.

5. 0.03 6. 2.40

7. 0.075 8. 0.8

9. $\frac{12}{7}$ 10. $\frac{7}{15}$

11. $\frac{6}{25}$ 12. $\frac{3}{20}$

13. $\frac{7}{9}$ 14. $2\frac{2}{3}$

Express each percent as a fraction in simplest form.

17. 60% 18. 5% 19. 120% 20. $2\frac{1}{5}$%

Use a calculator, paper and pencil, or mental math. Write each fraction as a percent. Round to the nearest tenth.

21. $\frac{7}{10}$ 22. $\frac{8}{5}$ 23. $\frac{5}{12}$ 24. $4\frac{3}{7}$

25. Did you know that in the 10 to 18 year-old age group, 1 in 7 teenagers is without health insurance? Express this fraction as a percent rounded to the nearest tenth.

26. **Writing** Explain why 0.05 is different from 0.05%.

27. There are 864 schools in the National Collegiate Athletic Association (NCAA). Only 99 of them have a female athletic director. What percent of the NCAA schools have a female athletic director? Round to the nearest tenth.

28. At Chicago's Albany Park Multicultural Academy, 39% of the students are Hispanic, 27% are Asian, 12% are African American, and the rest are Caucasian. For the four groups, write the percent each of them represents as a fraction in simplest form.

29. **Nutrition** Emilio took a vitamin that supplied 835% of his minimum daily requirement of vitamin C. How many times his minimum daily requirement of vitamin C did he receive?

30. **Research** Look in newspapers or magazines for examples of percents greater than 100 or less than 1.

31. There are 31 million adolescents between 10 and 18 years of age in the United States. Unfortunately, 1.5 million of these teens are homeless. What percent of the adolescents in the U.S. are homeless? Round to the nearest tenth.

32. **Chemistry** BHA is a preservative that is added to foods to preserve freshness. A can of shelled walnuts, for example, contains 0.02% BHA. Express this percent as a fraction in simplest form.

33. **Investigation (p. 422)** Survey adults you know to find out what percent of them think that real estate is a good investment.

What's Ahead

- Estimating using fractions, decimals, and percents

10-2 Estimating with Percents

THINK AND DISCUSS

Using Compatible Numbers Inez wants to buy a jacket that costs \$64.95. Her parents will pay 25% of the cost. Her grandfather will pay 20% of the cost. To see if she can afford the jacket, she needs to estimate how much her parents and grandparents will contribute.

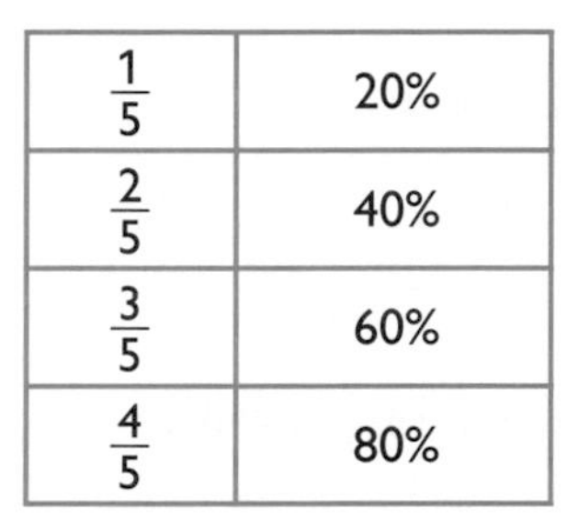

$\frac{1}{5}$	20%
$\frac{2}{5}$	40%
$\frac{3}{5}$	60%
$\frac{4}{5}$	80%

$\frac{1}{6}$	$16\frac{2}{3}\%$
$\frac{1}{3}$	$33\frac{1}{3}\%$
$\frac{2}{3}$	$66\frac{2}{3}\%$
$\frac{5}{6}$	$83\frac{1}{3}\%$

$\frac{1}{8}$	$12\frac{1}{2}\%$
$\frac{1}{4}$	25%
$\frac{3}{8}$	$37\frac{1}{2}\%$
$\frac{1}{2}$	50%
$\frac{5}{8}$	$62\frac{1}{2}\%$
$\frac{3}{4}$	75%
$\frac{7}{8}$	$87\frac{1}{2}\%$

When using percents to estimate, it is helpful to know the percent equivalents of common fractions. The tables at the left show several common equivalents.

To estimate her parents' contribution, Inez uses $\frac{1}{4}$, the fractional equivalent of 25%. She then replaces \$64.95 with an integer close to it in value. She chooses \$64 so that she will have **compatible numbers** that are easy to multiply or divide.

1. What is Inez's estimate of her parents' contribution?
2. a. What fraction would you use to estimate her grandfather's contribution?
   b. **Critical Thinking** What number would you use to replace \$64.95 to make the estimate easier?
   c. Estimate her grandfather's contribution.

Another way to mentally compute a percent of a number is to replace the percent with a common fraction close to it in value.

3. **Music** A band director claims that 38.6% of his 88 students are "stars," those who practice for an hour or more a day.
   a. Estimate the number of "stars" by replacing 38.6% with a common fraction that is compatible with 88. Then multiply.
   b. Estimate by replacing 38.6% with a different common fraction than you used in part (a). Replace 88 with a number compatible with that fraction. Then multiply.
   c. Compare your estimate in parts (a) and (b).

Using Benchmarks You can use percents that are easy to work with such as 1% and 10%.

4. Of the 56,246 pilots in the United States military, only 1.8% are women. To estimate the number of women pilots, first round 1.8% to 2%.
   a. Estimate 1% of the pilots.
   b. Use your answer from part (a) to estimate the number of women pilots.

5. **Money** Your family goes out to dinner and the bill is $29.70. You want to estimate a 15% tip.
   a. Estimate a 10% tip.
   b. Use your answer to part (a) to estimate a 5% tip.
   c. Use your answers to parts (a) and (b) to estimate a 15% tip.

You can use the same methods to estimate percents smaller than 1 and greater than 100.

6. Estimate 0.6% of 590 by estimating 1% of 590 and taking half of your result.

7. Estimate 165% of 87 by replacing with a common fraction.

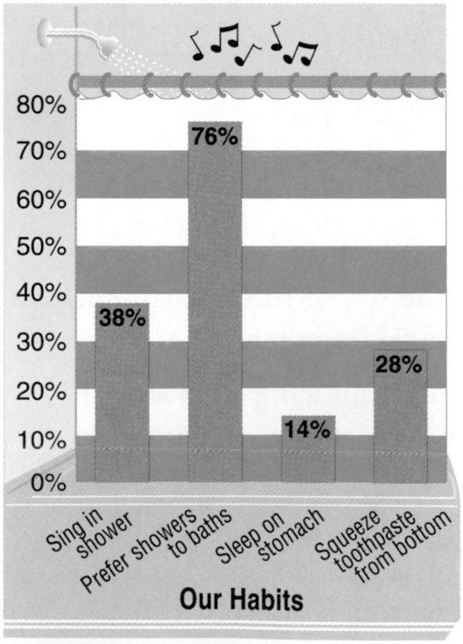

Our Habits
80%
70%
60%
50%
40%
30%
20%
10%
0%
38% Sing in shower
76% Prefer showers to baths
14% Sleep on stomach
28% Squeeze toothpaste from bottom

WORK TOGETHER

The First Really Important Survey of American Habits reports on how people respond to a national survey. Some of the results are shown at the left.

8. a. Count the number of students in your class.
   b. Use each of the percents in the survey results to estimate the number of students in your class who would respond in the same way.

9. **Discussion** Compare estimates with members of your group.

10. Choose one of the survey statements. Find the number of students in your class who agree with it. Compare this number with your group's estimates.

ON YOUR OWN

Estimate the percent of the number using any method.

11. 33% of 88
12. 65% of 242
13. 16.9% of 31
14. 0.4% of 175
15. 39% of 75
16. 270% of 109
17. **Music** The sizes of the four sections of a school orchestra are given. Estimate how many of the 68 members are in each section.
    a. string, 48.5%
    b. woodwind, 17.6%
    c. brass, 23.5%
    d. percussion, 10.3%

Compare. Use >, <, or =.

18. 85% ■ $\frac{5}{6}$
19. 65% ■ $\frac{2}{3}$
20. 12.5% ■ $\frac{1}{8}$
21. **Money** Estimate a 15% tip on a dinner that costs $34.50.
22. **Choose A, B, or C.** Estimate 20% of 304.
    A. 6 B. 60 C. 600
23. **Choose A, B, or C.** Estimate 0.5% of 195.
    A. 1 B. 10 C. 100
24. **Writing** Explain why it is important to estimate with percents even when you are using a calculator to find the exact answer.
25. **Environment** In 1992, of the 92.4 billion cans made in the United States 67.9% were recycled. Estimate the number of cans recycled.
26. **Data File 6 (pp. 244–245)** A survey conducted by *Seventeen Magazine* asked teens how they feel about money.
    a. Using the data given, estimate how many students in your school might worry that they won't have enough money when they are adults.
    b. Estimate the number of teens in a class of 30 who are likely to agree with the statement, "It's important to save money for the future."

Mixed REVIEW

Rewrite each percent as a decimal and a fraction.

1. 15%
2. 120%
3. $\frac{1}{2}$%
4. $87\frac{1}{2}$%

Write each number in scientific notation.

5. 78.5
6. 0.0475
7. Yolanda's garden is shaped like a rhombus. How many feet of fencing does she need if each side is 12 ft long?

Extra SKILLS PRACTICE

Estimate.

1. 79% of 29
2. 4.9% of 81
3. 52% of 57.8
4. 9.8% of 139
5. 23% of 39
6. 1.9% of 413
7. 58% of 99
8. 21.8% of 48
9. 38% of 198
10. 11% of 649
11. 24.9% of 15.8
12. 52.8% of 8.89

What's Ahead

- Using proportions to solve problems involving percent

10-3 Percents and Proportions

WHAT YOU'LL NEED

✓ Calculator 

THINK AND DISCUSS

Finding the Part or the Percent Some of you may pay sales tax whenever you make a purchase. Like many other taxes, sales taxes are based on percents.

In the state of Virginia, the sales tax is 4.5%. If you want to buy a \$195 bicycle in Virginia, how much tax will you pay?

1. Estimate the tax you will pay.

To solve this problem, you can write a proportion that compares the "part" represented by the tax to the "whole" represented by the cost of the bicycle.

$$\frac{\text{part} \rightarrow}{\text{whole} \rightarrow} \quad \frac{n}{195} = \frac{4.5}{100} \leftarrow 4.5\% = \frac{4.5}{100}$$

2. a. Using a calculator, cross multiply and divide to find the tax. Round your answer to the nearest hundredth.
   b. Compare your answer to your estimate. Is your answer reasonable?

California has the highest sales tax at 8.75% while some states such as New Hampshire have none. Sales tax can add up on high-priced items. **How much sales tax would a resident of California pay on a new \$14,000 automobile?**

Example 1 **Social Studies** Of the 435 members in the House of Representatives, 52 are from California. What percent of the members are from California?

Estimate 52 out of 435 is about 1 out of 10 or 10%.

$$\frac{\text{part} \rightarrow}{\text{whole} \rightarrow} \quad \frac{52}{435} = \frac{n}{100}$$ **Write a proportion.**

$$435n = 52 \cdot 100$$ **Cross multiply and solve.**

$n = 5200$ ÷ 435 = 11.954023

Rounded to the nearest tenth, representatives from California make up about 12.0% of the House of Representatives.

LOOK BACK Is your answer reasonable? Look at your estimate.

Finding the Whole Sometimes you know the percent that a "part" represents, but you do not know the "whole."

Example 2 **Education** Many students pay for their college educations by working full-time and going to school part-time. In a recent year, there were 114,162 part-time college students in Massachusetts. Part-time students represented 34% of the state's college students. How many college students were there?

Estimate: 34% is approximately $\frac{1}{3}$ and 114,162 is about 100,000. Since $\frac{1}{3}$ of 300,000 is 100,000, use 300,000 as an estimate.

$$\frac{\text{part} \rightarrow}{\text{whole} \rightarrow} \quad \frac{114{,}162}{n} = \frac{34}{100}$$

$$34n = 114{,}162 \cdot 100$$

$$n = 11{,}416{,}200 \; \boxed{\div} \; 34 \; \boxed{=} \; 335770.59$$

There were 335,771 college students.

LOOK BACK Is your answer reasonable? Look at your estimate.

Percents Greater than 100% You can use proportions when the "part" is bigger than the "whole." This situation occurs when the percent involved is greater than 100%.

Example 3 **Sports** In 1992, Terry Pendleton of the Atlanta Braves had 199 hits. This was 106.4% of the number of hits that he had in 1991. How many hits did he have in 1991?

Estimate: The number of 1991 hits should be less than, but close to, 199.

$$\frac{\text{part} \rightarrow}{\text{whole} \rightarrow} \quad \frac{199}{n} = \frac{106.4}{100}$$

$$106.4n = 199 \cdot 100$$

$$n = 19{,}900 \; \boxed{\div} \; 106.4 \; \boxed{=} \; 187.03008$$

Terry Pendleton had 187 hits in 1991.

LOOK BACK Is your answer reasonable? Look at your estimate.

The 1993 American League Baseball Batting Champion was John Olerud of the Toronto Blue Jays with a 0.363 batting average. ***What percent of the times up at bat did Olerud not get a hit?***

Source: *The Boston Globe*

Mixed REVIEW

Graph the numbers on a number line.

1. $\frac{1}{2}, \frac{3}{4}, \frac{3}{2}, 3$
2. 4.0, −3.25, −1.5, 0, 0.5

Estimate.

3. 5% of 815
4. 33% of 24
5. If $f(x) = 2x - 3$, find $f\left(\frac{1}{2}\right)$.
6. If $f(x) = 10x + 8$, find $f(0.9)$.
7. If a 6% sales tax is charged on a $45 purchase, what is the final cost?

WORK TOGETHER

Calculator Count the number of students in your class, then work with a partner to answer each of the following questions. One partner should estimate each answer. The other partner should write a proportion and use a calculator to find the answer. Compare your answers.

3. Find the percent of students in your class who are wearing each of the following.
   a. a watch **b.** sneakers
4. Find the percent of your class that each of the following numbers represents.
   a. 17 **b.** 38
5. How many students would represent each percent of your class?
   a. 28% **b.** 130%

TRY THESE

Choose A, B, C, or D. For each of the following choose the proportion that will help you answer the question.

6. What percent is 17 of 42?
   A. $\frac{17}{42} = \frac{n}{100}$ **B.** $\frac{n}{42} = \frac{17}{100}$ **C.** $\frac{17}{n} = \frac{100}{42}$ **D.** $\frac{n}{17} = \frac{42}{100}$
7. What is 35% of 90?
   A. $\frac{35}{90} = \frac{n}{100}$ **B.** $\frac{n}{90} = \frac{35}{100}$ **C.** $\frac{35}{n} = \frac{90}{100}$ **D.** $\frac{n}{35} = \frac{100}{90}$
8. 92 is 80% of what number?
   A. $\frac{n}{92} = \frac{80}{100}$ **B.** $\frac{80}{n} = \frac{92}{100}$ **C.** $\frac{80}{92} = \frac{n}{100}$ **D.** $\frac{92}{n} = \frac{80}{100}$

> *You miss 100% of the shots you never take.*
>
> —Wayne Gretzky (1961–)

Choose Use a calculator, paper and pencil, or mental math to solve each of the following.

9. 80% of 72 is ■.
10. 33 is 15% of ■.
11. 78 is ■% of 50.
12. 70 is 20% of ■.
13. 63 is 29% of ■.
14. 345% of ■ is 224.

ON YOUR OWN

Choose **Use a calculator, paper and pencil, or mental math.**

15. What percent of 30 is 18?

16. 29 is 20% of what number?

17. What is 125% of 65?

18. 160 is what percent of 80?

19. **Geography** Rhode Island is the smallest state in the United States, with an area of 1,212 square miles. It accounts for only 0.03% of the country's area. Use this information to find the area of the United States in square miles.

20. **Writing** Explain why you frequently use proportions where one of the ratios has a denominator of 100.

21. Ivana bought a set of wrenches for $89. Her total bill including sales tax was $94.34. Find the percent of the sales tax.

22. A teacher spent $129.60 on classroom supplies. This was 72% of his classroom budget. How much was his budget?

Teeth Are Big Business

People in the United States visit dentists almost 500 million times a year. Children ages 5 to 17 are among the most frequent visitors, averaging 2.4 visits per year.

Even with such a big market for their products, toothbrush manufacturers conduct market research.

For example, in a recent survey of 500 people, the leading choice of toothbrush color was blue at 23%. Red brushes came in second at 20%, and yellow third at 16%.

More than half of those surveyed, 55%, admitted they leave the water running while brushing their teeth.

23. **a.** How many of the people surveyed chose blue toothbrushes?

b. **Activity** Ask the people in your household if they leave the water running while brushing their teeth. Find the percent of your household that says "yes."

Extra SKILLS PRACTICE

Solve.

1. 15% of ■ is 18.
2. 30% of 48 is ■.
3. 2.4 is ■% of 60.
4. 110 is 55% of ■.
5. 10.8 is ■% of 180.
6. 2% of ■ is 1.4.
7. 85% of 400 is ■.
8. 13.5 is ■% of 75.
9. 105% of ■ is 630.
10. 210 is ■% of 84.
11. 60% of 355 is ■.
12. 4.5 is ■% of 300.

What's Ahead

- Using equations to solve problems involving percent

10-4 Percents and Equations

WHAT YOU'LL NEED

✓ Calculator 

THINK AND DISCUSS

You have learned to solve percent problems using a proportion.

$$\frac{\text{part}}{\text{whole}} = \frac{n}{100}$$

If you replace $\frac{n}{100}$ with P, the percent expressed as a decimal, you have the following equation.

$$\frac{\text{part}}{\text{whole}} = P$$

Multiplying each side by the "whole" results in the equation

$$\text{part} = P \cdot \text{whole}.$$

You can use this percent equation to solve different problems involving percent. Remember that the "part" will be greater than the "whole" when you are working with percents that are greater than 100%.

In 1981, the median selling price for a home in the United States was $66,400. By 1992 the median price had risen to $100,900.

Source: *The World Almanac*

Finding the Part Some sales jobs pay an amount based on how much you sell. This is called **commission.** To solve problems involving commission use: part = P • whole.

1. Hui sells real estate and receives a 3% commission on property she sells. She wants to know how much money she will receive if she sells a house for $118,000.
   - **a.** To find the value of P, express 3% as a decimal.
   - **b.** Does the $118,000 price of the house represent the "part" or the "whole"?
   - **c.** Substitute in the equation and solve to find how much money Hui will receive.

2. Leon sells shoes. He receives a salary of $115 each week plus a 12.5% commission on all sales. During one week, he sells $2,300 worth of shoes. What are Leon's total earnings for the week?

Finding the Percent A percent equation can be used to find P, the percent expressed as a decimal.

Example 1 **Entertainment** Of the 8,945 commercial radio stations in the United States, 2,314 have a country format. What percent of the stations have a country format?

Estimate: 2,314 out of 8,945 is about 2,000 out of 10,000 or 20%.

$\text{part} = P \cdot \text{whole}$

$2{,}314 = P \cdot 8{,}945$ — The "part" is 2,314 and the "whole" is 8,945.

$P = \frac{2{,}314}{8{,}945}$ — Solve for P.

2,314 [÷] 8,945 [=] 0.2586920

$0.259 \approx P$ — P is the percent expressed as a decimal.

About 25.9% of the commercial radio stations in the United States have a country format.

Finding the Whole You can find the "whole" when you know the percent that the "part" represents.

Example 2 **Environment** Over the past 200 years, the state of Florida has lost more acres of wetland than any other state. According to the U.S. Department of the Interior, Florida lost 9,286,713 acres, or about 46% of its wetland. About how many acres of wetland did Florida have 200 years ago?

Not long ago, *wetlands were considered useless. Now we know the importance of wetlands as an ecosystem. In the United States, about 45% of the endangered animals and 26% of the endangered plants can survive only in wetlands.*

Source: *The Information Please Environmental Almanac*

Estimate: 46% is approximately $\frac{1}{2}$ and 9,286,713 is about 10,000,000. 10,000,000 is $\frac{1}{2}$ of 20,000,000.

$\text{part} = P \cdot \text{whole}$

$9{,}286{,}713 = 0.46 \cdot \text{whole}$ — The "part" is 9,286,713 and P is 0.46.

9,286,713 [÷] 0.46 [=] 20188507

Two hundred years ago, Florida had about 20,188,507 acres of wetland.

Example 3 **Environment** Your class collected returnable bottles to raise money for the library. Your goal was to collect 80 bottles. You succeeded in collecting 100 bottles. What percent of your goal did you reach?

In states with beverage container deposit laws, roadside litter has been reduced by up to 50%.

Source: *The Information Please Environmental Almanac*

Estimate: Since you collected more than your goal, your answer will be a percent greater than 100%.

part $= P \cdot$ whole

$100 = P \cdot 80$ **The "part" is 100 and the "whole" is 80.**

$\frac{100}{80} = P$

$1.25 = P$

You reached 125% of your goal.

TRY THESE

Use an equation to solve each of the following. Round to the nearest tenth.

3. What percent of 75 is 30?
4. 16.4 is what percent of 5?
5. 92% of what number is 68?
6. Find 31% of 82,150.
7. 25% of what number is 300?
8. What percent of 360 is 2?
9. **Education** In a survey reported in *USA TODAY,* students were asked to choose what they would do if they were principal for a day. Of those surveyed, 935 students, or 18.7% chose "Raise money for the homeless." How many students were surveyed?

Extra SKILLS PRACTICE

Solve. Round to the nearest tenth.

1. 50 is ■% of 118.
2. 23% of 67 is ■.
3. 65 is 112% of ■.
4. 12% of ■ is 3.5.
5. 13% of 250 is ■.
6. ■ is 73% of 28.
7. 430 is 95% of ■.
8. ■% of 370 is 20.
9. 25 is 35% of ■.
10. ■% of 175 is 120.
11. 10 is ■% of 18.
12. 2.3% of ■ is 0.04.

ON YOUR OWN

Choose Use a calculator, paper and pencil, or mental math.

10. 16 is what percent of 80?
11. 7.3 is 2% of what number?
12. What is 165% of 40?
13. 50 is what percent of 42?

14. **Health** In the United States, tobacco use causes 434,000 deaths each year. Presently, about 2,162,000 people die in the United States each year. What percent of these deaths is caused by tobacco use?

15. **Entertainment** In a recent survey, 438 people, or 73% of the sample, chose popcorn as their favorite movie theater snack. How many people were in the sample?

16. **Health** Calcium is important for bones and teeth. The RDA (recommended daily allowance) of calcium is set at 800 mg. If you consume 1500 mg of calcium, what percent of the RDA are you satisfying?

17. **Business** Augustina sold $3735 worth of building materials. What percent commission did she receive if she earned $672.30?

18. **Writing** You can solve percent problems with the equation part = P • whole. Write a problem where the "part" is bigger than the "whole." Show the solution to your problem.

19. **Sports** According to the United States Fish and Wildlife Service, anglers spend $24 billion a year fishing. If 39% of this amount is spent on equipment, what is the annual amount spent on fishing equipment?

Each kernel of popcorn is about 13.5% water. When a kernel is heated, the water inside expands, causing the kernel to explode or pop.

Source: *When Do Fish Sleep?*

CHECK POINT

Express each of the following as a decimal, a percent, and a fraction in simplest form.

1. 30%
2. 0.12
3. 210%
4. $\frac{5}{8}$

Estimate each of the following.

5. 15% of 198
6. 78% of 95
7. 32% of 145

8. **Jobs** In 1991, 29% of the civilian labor force was 25 to 34 years old. If there were 125 million workers, how many of them were 25 to 34 years old?

Use any method to solve. Round when appropriate.

9. What percent of 84 is 63?
10. What is 23% of 17?

Mixed REVIEW

True or false?

1. Some isosceles triangles are obtuse.
2. 5 − (−8) = 8 + 5

Solve using a proportion.

3. 80% of what number is 24?
4. 18 is what percent of 12?
5. Find $66\frac{2}{3}$% of 15.
6. The soccer team made $64.40 selling mixed nuts. They made $.35 on each bag of nuts. How many bags did they sell?

What's Ahead

- Constructing circle graphs

10-5 Constructing Circle Graphs

WHAT YOU'LL NEED

✓ Calculator 

✓ Compass 

✓ Protractor 

THINK AND DISCUSS

Some of us do not have enough to eat. Many people receive meals and groceries from food banks. The circle graph below shows the ages of people in the United States who use food banks.

Ages of People Using Food Banks

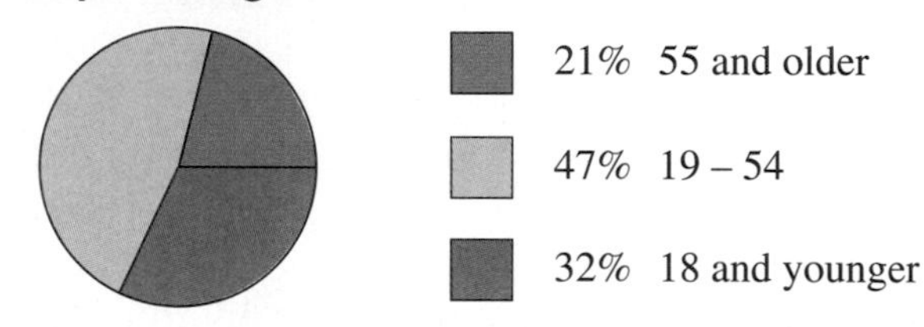

Source: *USA TODAY*

1. a. Find the sum of the percents in the circle graph.
   b. **Critical Thinking** Could you make a circle graph where the sum of the percents was a different number? Explain.

2. a. Use a protractor to measure each central angle.
   b. **Critical Thinking** Find the sum of the measures of the central angles. Explain why the sum should be about 360°.

FLASHBACK

A central angle is an angle whose vertex is at the center of a circle.

You can use a circle graph to display data that represent parts of a whole.

Serious Boating Accidents in 1992

Cause	Number of Accidents
Colliding with another boat	2,203
Colliding with a fixed object	839
Capsizing	458
Other	772

Source: *U.S. Coast Guard*

Example The table at the left gives data on the causes of boating accidents. Display the data in a circle graph.

- Find the total number of accidents.

2,203 [+] 839 [+] 458 [+] 772 [=] 4272

- Express each category as a percent of the total.

2,203 [÷] 4,272 [=] 0.5156835 ≈ 51.6%

839 [÷] 4,272 [=] 0.1963951 ≈ 19.6%

458 [÷] 4,272 [=] 0.1072097 ≈ 10.7%

772 [÷] 4,272 [=] 0.1807116 ≈ 18.1%

- Since there are 360° in a circle, multiply each decimal by 360 to find the measure of the central angle for each category.

360 ⊠ 0.516 ⊟ *185.76* 185.76 ≈ 186°

360 ⊠ 0.196 ⊟ *70.56* 70.56 ≈ 71°

360 ⊠ 0.107 ⊟ *38.52* 38.52 ≈ 39°

360 ⊠ 0.181 ⊟ *65.16* 65.16 ≈ 65°

The sum of these angle measures is 361°. Since there are only 360° in a circle, the approximations need to be adjusted. Three of the approximations were rounded up. Only one was rounded down. To adjust for this, round 38.52 down to 38°.

- Use a compass to draw a circle with any radius. Draw the central angles with a protractor.
- To complete the graph, label each section and add a title as shown in the sketch below.

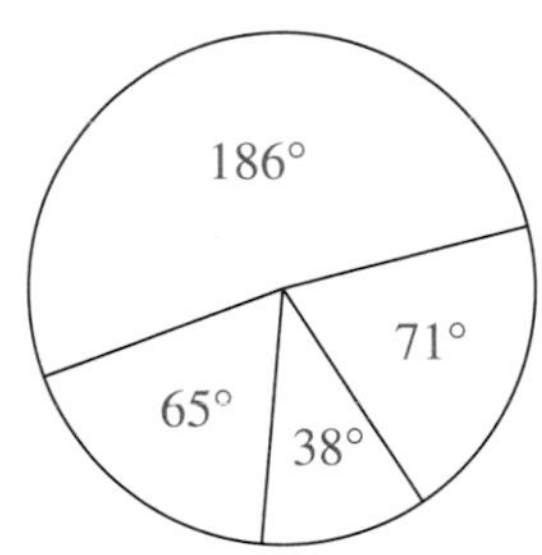

Causes of Serious Boating Accidents

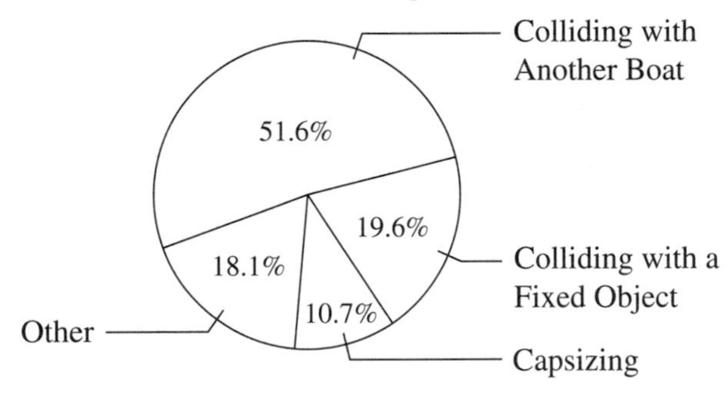

WORK TOGETHER

Work in a group to create a survey about how students got to school today. Categories might include school bus, walking, biking, in-line skating, skateboarding, public transportation, and car. Decide on three categories that are appropriate for your school. Use "other" as a fourth category to include all options not listed. Survey your class and display the results in a circle graph.

***With over 3.6 million** people participating, in-line skating is one of the fastest growing sports in the United States. An experienced skater uses up an average of 650 calories per hour.*

Sources: *U.S. News and World Report* and *Current Health*

Mixed REVIEW

Evaluate each expression for $x = 0.3$ and $y = 0.21$.

1. $3x + 4y$

2. $\frac{1}{7}y - x^3$

Write an equation and solve.

3. What number is 7.5% of 280?

4. Twenty-five percent of what number is 10?

5. What percent of $500 is $25?

6. Give an example of dependent events.

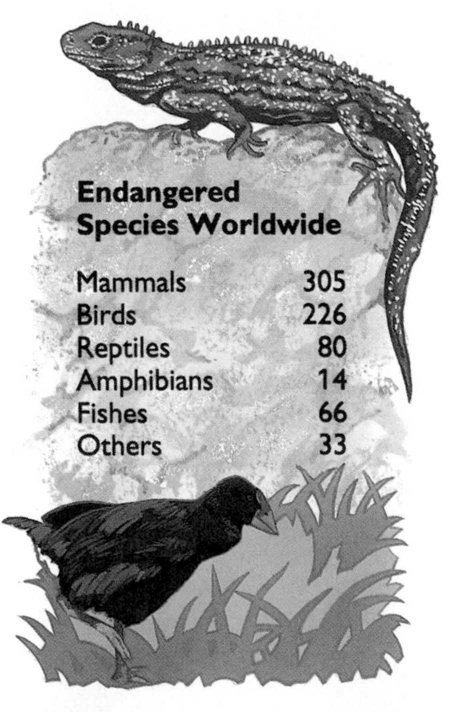

TRY THESE

3. *Self* magazine asked readers to respond to the question, "Do you think technological advances or changes are happening too rapidly, or not?" Here is how they responded.

too rapidly: 27.9% not too rapidly: 68.0% don't know: 4.1%

Display the responses in a circle graph.

4. Your class has a budget for a museum field trip. Complete the table below and use the results to construct a circle graph.

Category	Amount Budgeted	Percent of Total	Degrees in Central Angle
Bus	$72	■	■
Admission	$60	■	■
Lunch	$48	■	■
Tolls	$10	■	■

ON YOUR OWN

5. Health *Women's Sports and Fitness* conducted a survey on women's exercise habits. They found that 27.7% exercise frequently, 37.4% exercise occasionally, and 34.9% never exercise. Display the results in a circle graph.

6. Nutrition Health Focus Inc. surveyed consumers on whether they were buying more vegetables than they bought two years ago. Here is how they responded.

more: 56.3%, the same: 40.1%, fewer: 1.9%, no response: 1.7%

Display the responses in a circle graph.

7. Writing Explain why it is easier to make a circle graph for a budget if categories are given as percents rather than as dollar amounts.

8. Ella surveyed 81 students in the cafeteria about their favorite school lunch. Here is what they chose.

pizza: 35 spaghetti: 20 hamburger: 18 grilled cheese: 8

Display the survey results in a circle graph.

9. Environment The table at the left gives information about endangered species. Display this information in a circle graph.

Problem Solving Practice

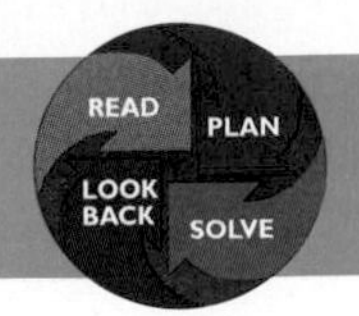

PROBLEM SOLVING STRATEGIES

Make a Table
Use Logical Reasoning
Solve a Simpler Problem
Too Much or Too Little Information
Look for a Pattern
Make a Model
Work Backward
Draw a Diagram
Guess and Test
Simulate a Problem
Use Multiple Strategies
Write an Equation
Use a Proportion

Solve. The list at the left shows some possible strategies you can use.

1. To make an orange dye, 3 parts of red dye are mixed with 2 parts of yellow dye. To make a purple dye, 2 parts of blue dye are mixed with 1 part of red dye. Suppose equal amounts of orange and purple are mixed. What percent of the mixture is red dye?

2. **Money** Baptista's family plans to buy a television. She offers to do some comparison shopping for her parents. She finds the same television on sale at two different stores. Which one is the better buy?
   - $279.98 on sale at 15% off
   - $299.99 on sale at 20% off

3. Franklin, a camp counselor, has a unique way to choose partners for the camp's three-legged race. He puts three red and three black chips in a bag. One camper reaches into the bag and picks a chip. The next camper reaches in and picks a chip. If the chips are the same color, these campers are partners; if not, other campers are allowed to choose a chip until there is a pair of campers with matching chips.
   a. If the chips are replaced after each draw, what is the probability that the first two campers will be partners?
   b. If the chips are not replaced after each draw, what is the probability that the first two campers will be partners?
   c. If the chips are not replaced after each draw, what is the greatest number of students who would have to draw before two will be partners?

4. At Jackson Middle School, 60% of the students are girls. Of these girls, 75% sing in the school chorus. What percent of all students are girls who do not sing in the school chorus?

5. A backgammon club holds a tournament. Each of the 10 players in the tournament plays just one game with each of the other players. Altogether how many backgammon games are played in the tournament?

In 1982, Alan M. Beckerson played the shortest backgammon game on record, using just 16 throws.

Source: *The Guinness Book of Records*

What's Ahead

- Solving problems that involve percent of increase or decrease

10-6 Percent of Change

WHAT YOU'LL NEED

✓ Calculator 

THINK AND DISCUSS

Finding the Percent of Decrease The elephant population in Kenya is endangered. In 1973, there were 167,000 elephants. By 1993, there were only 26,000. This is a significant decrease in the number of elephants.

The percent something increases or decreases from its original amount is the **percent of change.** Finding percent of change requires two steps.

- Subtract to find the amount of change.
- Use the equation $P = \frac{\text{amount of change}}{\text{original amount}}$ where P is the percent of change expressed in decimal form.

1. **a.** Find the amount of change in the number of elephants from 1973 to 1993.
   b. Decide which value is the original amount.
   c. Use the equation above to find the percent of change.

Daphne Sheldrick lives in Nairobi National Park in Kenya and raises baby elephants who have been orphaned by poachers. She found that elephants less than a year old need a special milk formula and must be fed every three hours, day and night!

Finding the Percent of Increase You can use the same approach to find the percent of increase.

Example 1 In 1980, there were 27.7 million public school students in kindergarten through eighth grade. In 1990, there were 29.5 million. Find the percent of increase.

$29.5 - 27.7 = 1.8$ — Find the amount of change.

$P = \frac{1.8}{27.7}$ ← amount of change / ← original amount

1.8 [÷] 27.7 [=] 0.0649819

$P \approx 0.065$

The percent of increase is about 6.5%.

When working with measures, be sure to express all measures in the same units.

Example 2 From birth to age two, the average baby boy grows from 1 ft 8 in. to 2 ft 11 in. Find the percent of increase.

1 ft 8 in. = 20 in. **Write measures in the same units.**
2 ft 11 in. = 35 in.

35 − 20 = 15 **Find the amount of change.**

$$P = \frac{15}{20} \begin{matrix} \leftarrow \text{amount of change} \\ \leftarrow \text{original amount} \end{matrix}$$

$$P = 0.75$$

The percent of increase is 75%.

2. Explain how to use mental math to convert $\frac{15}{20}$ to 75%.

TRY THESE

3. Discussion Explain why it is important to know which amount is the original amount when solving a percent of change problem.

Mental Math Find each percent of change. Label your answer as increase or decrease.

4. 20 to 25 **5.** 40 to 30 **6.** 50 to 55 **7.** 80 to 70

Find each percent of change. Label your answer as increase or decrease. Round to the nearest tenth.

8. 83 to 105 **9.** 21 to 11.5 **10.** 15 to 95

11. 7 to 8.5 **12.** 190 to 52 **13.** 1.35 to 4.9

14. Environment The city of Seattle is saving money by switching from rubbish collection and disposal at a cost of $105 a ton to recycling and processing at a cost of $50 a ton. Find the percent of decrease in the city's cost.

15. Money In 1950, the minimum wage for nonfarm workers was $.75 per hour. In 1993, it was $4.25 per hour. Find the percent of increase.

Mixed REVIEW

For Exercises 1 and 2, use the survey results displayed below.

Favorite Color	
blue	7
black	6
green	1
red	2
purple	4

1. Find the percent of those surveyed who chose each color.

2. Draw a circle graph to display the data.

3. Draw a 15 mm segment and construct a line perpendicular to it.

4. The lockers in a corridor are numbered 175 to 398. How many lockers are there?

Extra SKILLS PRACTICE

Find each percent of change.

1. 25 to 15
2. 65 to 80
3. 45 to 30
4. 120 to 95
5. 75 to 110
6. 4 to 7.5
7. 12.3 to 8.2
8. 34 to 21.7
9. 55.2 to 63

From 1980 to 1992, the percent of young Canadians who smoked fell dramatically. In the 15- to 19-year-old age group, the percent of those smoking decreased from about 45% to approximately 15%.

Source: *The Boston Globe*

ON YOUR OWN

16. **Health** To discourage smoking, Canada raised the tax on a pack of cigarettes from \$.38 in 1980 to \$3.25 in 1992. Find the percent of increase.

17. **Sports** In the 1948 Olympics, Olga Gyarmati of Hungary won the women's long jump with a jump of 18 ft $8\frac{1}{4}$ in. In 1992, Heike Drechsler of Germany won with a jump of 23 ft $5\frac{1}{4}$ in. Find the percent of increase in the length of the jump.

18. **Writing** If you increase 100 by 20% and then decrease the result by 20%, do you get an answer of 100? Explain why or why not.

19. **Data File 10 (pp. 420–421)** In 1990, there were 565,000 computer programmers. If forecasts are correct, how many computer programmers will there be in 2005?

Typical Cost of a Ticket to a First-run Movie

City	1983	1993
Albuquerque	\$3.50	\$6.00
Boise, ID	\$4.00	\$5.50
Louisville, KY	\$4.00	\$6.50
New York, NY	\$5.00	\$7.50
Sioux City, IA	\$3.00	\$5.25

Source: *Self*

Is Hollywood Nervous?

Although there are long lines for hit movies, people aren't going to the movies as much as they used to. There has been a steady decline in the number of tickets sold from a high of 1.2 billion in 1984, to 964 million in 1992.

Young people have traditionally made up the largest movie audience, but today this group looks to home videos for their week-end entertainment.

In the past two years, admissions for people ages 12 to 29 have dropped 12% while the average cost of a movie ticket has soared to well over \$5.00.

20. For each city in the table at the left, determine the percent of increase in the price of a movie ticket.

21. Find the percent of decrease in movie ticket sales from 1984 to 1992.

22. **Investigation (p. 422)** Choose a collectible object such as a baseball card, a stamp, or an antique toy. Gather data and find the percent of change in its value over a period of time. Decide whether or not the collectible is a good thing to invest in.

10-7 Markup and Discount

What's Ahead

- Solving problems involving markup and discount

WHAT YOU'LL NEED

✓ Calculator 

THINK AND DISCUSS

To cover expenses and make a profit, stores charge more for merchandise than they pay for it. The amount the price is increased is called the **markup.**

1. The school store sells stationery supplies such as paper, pencils, and notebooks. Each notebook costs the store $.79. The store wants to mark up the price by 65%.
   a. To find the markup, calculate 65% of $.79. Round your answer to the nearest cent.
   b. Add the markup to the store's cost to find the selling price.
   c. **Critical Thinking** Describe a way to find the selling price by just multiplying instead of multiplying and then adding.

When an item goes on sale, a store reduces its regular price to a sale price. The amount the price is reduced is called the **discount.**

Manufacturers in the United States give out 392 million coupons a day, worth more than 70 million dollars. It is reported that less than 4% of these coupons are used. ***Estimate the total value of coupons that are not redeemed each day.***

Source: *In One Day*

Example Save-More regularly sells a CD player for $159.98. It advertises a discount of 20% off the regular prices. Find the sale price of the CD player.

There are two ways to find the sale price.

Method 1 0.2 ⊠ 159.98 ⊟ 31.996 — **Find the amount of discount.**

discount = $32.00

159.98 − 32.00 = 127.98 — **Subtract the discount to find the sale price.**

The sale price is $127.98.

Method 2 The sale price is 100% − 20%, or 80% of the regular price.

0.8 ⊠ 159.98 ⊟ 127.984 — **Multiply the regular price by 0.8 to find the sale price.**

The sale price is $127.98.

Mixed REVIEW

Find each percent of change.

1. 24 to 54

2. 41.4 to 55.2

3. 3.5 to 0.8

Use the diagram below. Write each ratio as a fraction and as a decimal.

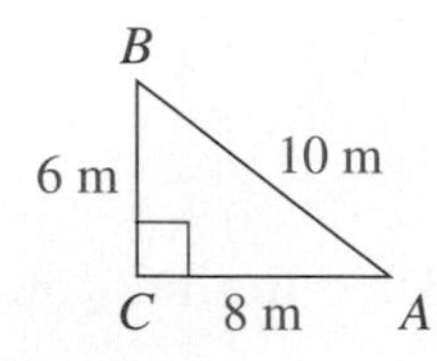

4. $\sin A$ **5.** $\cos A$

TRY THESE

Find the selling price. Round to the nearest cent.

2. cost: $89
markup rate: 60%

3. cost: $134.98
markup rate: 55%

Find the sale price. Round to the nearest cent.

4. regular price: $180
discount rate: 40%

5. regular price: $35.50
discount rate: 25%

ON YOUR OWN

Choose **Use a calculator, paper and pencil, estimation, or mental math.**

6. Cassette tapes are on sale for 40% off the list price of $8.99. Thelma has $35 to spend on cassettes. How many cassettes can she buy at the reduced price?

GREAT EXPECTATIONS

Athletic Trainer

Hello. As you know, I am an eighth grade student and will be attending high school very soon. I have many interests, but I think there are only two careers that would support me, yet I will enjoy doing at the same time. They would be a sports trainer and a recording technician.

I would love to be in the Major Leagues or the NBA, but I know there is a very slight chance of making it. Therefore, being a sports trainer would be a more realistic career.

I am also very interested in many types of music. I like rap, á cappella, and rock. As a recording technician, I could listen to all of them while also helping to record them.

Ben Combetta

7. A merchant donated $175 worth of T-shirts to Lewis Middle School. The school plans to mark them up 80% and sell them. If all the T-shirts sell, will the school have enough money to buy $320 worth of band uniforms? Explain.

8. Zina buys book bags for $3.75 and sells them for $6.00. What is her percent of markup?

9. Greg McSweeney bought a canoe for a sale price of $335.75. If he received a 20% discount off the regular price, what was the regular selling price?

10. **Writing** A store manager buys shirts and marks them up 50%. When the shirts don't sell, she discounts them by 50% and they sell out. Explain whether the store makes money, loses money, or comes out even on the sale of the shirts. Include sample prices to help explain your answer.

11. **Estimation** Ben has $16. Does he have enough money to buy a $37.99 sweater after it is marked down 60%? Explain.

Extra SKILLS PRACTICE

Find the selling price or the sale price.

1. cost: $9.50
   markup: 35%
2. cost: $45.70
   markup: 70%
3. cost: $176.80
   markup: 45%
4. cost: $55.89
   discount: 30%
5. cost: $76.29
   discount: 15%
6. cost: $163.19
   discount: 45%

Dear Ben,

As an athletic trainer, I work with athletic teams to treat and help prevent sports injuries. There are many applications of mathematics in my job. For example, there is a need to understand degrees of an angle when evaluating an athlete's range of motion in her shoulder. This is vital in planning an exercise or rehabilitation program for an injury. Also, when testing an individual's muscle strength, I use various kinds of equipment that print results as a graph. Statistics play an important role in my end-of-the-season injury summary reports. They are a good tool to use for seeing where the most injuries occur, so we can try to prevent them from happening.

Darlene F. Moore
Head Athletic Trainer, Simmons College

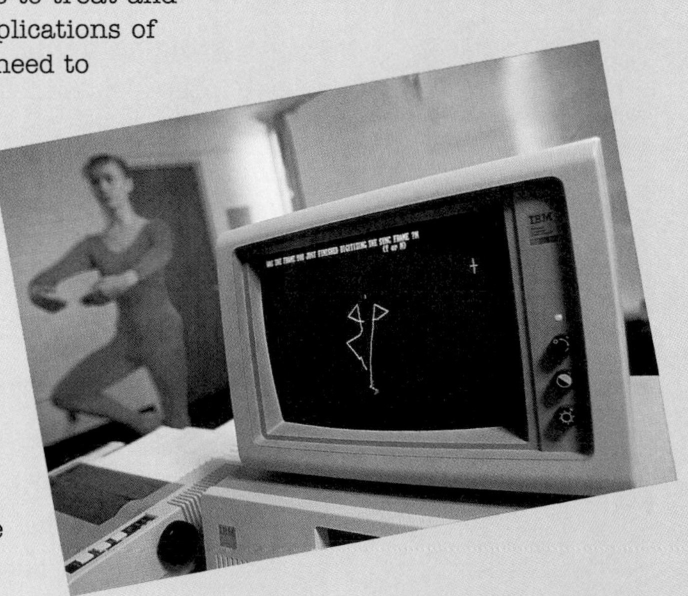

What's Ahead

- Using spreadsheets and calculators to find simple and compound interest

WHAT YOU'LL NEED

✓ Calculator  

✓ Computer 

✓ Spreadsheet software 

FLASHBACK

The amount of money that you start with in a bank or other investment is called the *principal.*

TECHNOLOGY

10-8 Simple and Compound Interest

THINK AND DISCUSS

At the beginning of eighth grade, you put $100 in the bank to save for your education. Your money is collecting interest at an annual rate of 6% compounded yearly for five years. You want to know how much money you will have in five years.

Finding Simple Interest One way to estimate how much money you will have is to use the formula for simple interest.

$I = p \cdot r \cdot t$ where I is the interest,
p is the principal,
r is the interest rate per year,
t is the time in years.

1. a. Use the formula to find the simple interest on $100 invested at 6% annual interest for five years.
   b. The **balance** in an account is the principal plus the interest earned. Add the $100 principal to your answer in part (a) to find the balance at the end of five years.

Finding Compound Interest Interest is **compounded** when interest is added to the balance at certain intervals. The interest for the next interval is then calculated based on the new balance. This spreadsheet shows the balance at the end of the first two years of annual compounding.

	A	B	C	D	E
1	Year	Start of Year	Rate	Interest	End of Year
2	1st	$100	0.06	$6.00	$106.00
3	2nd	$106	0.06	$6.36	$112.36

2. a. **Calculator or Computer** Use a calculator or computer to complete the spreadsheet and find the balance at the end of five years.
   b. How much more money will you earn with compound interest than with simple interest?

3. **Critical Thinking** In each row of the spreadsheet, you multiplied the beginning balance by 0.06 and added the result to the beginning balance. Explain why this is the same as multiplying the beginning balance by 1.06.

Each year's beginning balance is 1.06 times the previous year's beginning balance. Thus, another way to find the balance after five years is to multiply the beginning balance by 1.06 five times.

4. a. **Calculator** Evaluate.
   $100 \cdot 1.06 \cdot 1.06 \cdot 1.06 \cdot 1.06 \cdot 1.06$
   b. Does your answer to part (a) agree with your answer to Question 2(a)?
   c. **Calculator** How can you use the y^x key to make your calculations in part (a) easier?

***President Clinton** established the National Service Trust Program in 1993. The program gives people the opportunity to borrow money for college and either repay a percent of their earnings or perform community service. Students receive $4,725 per year for up to two years.*

Source: *The Boston Globe*

The following formula summarizes the method for finding the final amount when interest is being compounded.

$A = p(1 + r)^n$ where A is the final amount,
p is the principal,
r is the interest rate for one time period,
n is the number of time periods.

Suppose you invest $200 for two years at an annual interest rate of 5% compounded quarterly (four times a year). The spreadsheet below shows the balance at the end of the first two quarters.

	A	B	C	D	E
1	Quarter	Start of Quarter	Rate	Interest	End of Quarter
2	1st	$200	0.0125	$2.50	$202.50
3	2nd	$202.50	0.0125	$2.53	$205.03

5. Why is the rate in the spreadsheet 0.0125 instead of 0.05?

6. How many rows need to be added to the spreadsheet in order to find the balance at the end of two years?

7. **Calculator or Computer** Use a calculator or computer to complete the spreadsheet and find the final balance.

***The graph above** shows the average interest rates on one-year certificates of deposit from 1984 to 1991.*

Source: *Statistical Abstract of the United States*

8. **Calculator** Another way to find the final balance for $200 invested at 5% compounded quarterly for two years is to use the formula $A = p(1 + r)^n$.
   a. What values will you use for p, n, and r?
   b. Evaluate the formula.
   c. Compare the amount found using the formula to the amount found using the spreadsheet in Question 7.

WORK TOGETHER

Calculator or Computer Work with a partner and use either a spreadsheet or the formula $A = p(1 + r)^n$. You have $10,000 to invest for two years at 4% annual interest. One partner should find the final balances for interest compounded annually and monthly. The other partner should find the final balances for interest compounded quarterly and semiannually (twice a year). Compare your answers. Which is the best investment?

Mixed REVIEW

Find the selling price of each of the following.

1. regular price: $65
   discount: 20%
2. cost: $239
   markup: 45%

$\triangle ABC \sim \triangle TSW$. Complete.

3. $\frac{AC}{TW} = \frac{\blacksquare}{TS}$
4. If $AC = 6$, $AB = 8$, and $TS = 12$, find TW.

Solve.

5. $18 = -6 - d$
6. $12 + c = -17$

ON YOUR OWN

Calculator or Computer Use a calculator or a computer. Round amounts to the nearest cent.

Banking **For Exercises 9–16, find the final balance in each account.**

9. $900 at 3% simple interest for 2 years
10. $500 at 5% simple interest for 6 years
11. $1200 at 7.5% simple interest for 4 years
12. $1700 at 7% compounded annually for 2 years
13. $14,000 at 3% compounded annually for 3 years
14. $115 at 4% compounded semiannually for 2 years
15. $10,300 at 8% compounded quarterly for 1 year
16. $1,000 at 6% compounded monthly for 6 months

17. **Consumer Issues** Bank accounts pay interest, but credit card companies charge interest. Erin charges a $350 set of encyclopedias. She must pay 18% annual interest compounded monthly on any unpaid balance.

   a. At the end of the first month, she makes a $50 payment. After her payment is deducted, the interest is computed. How much interest is Erin charged?

   b. When the interest is added to the unpaid balance, how much does Erin owe on her credit card?

   c. **Writing** Erin bought the encyclopedias because they were on sale. Explain why she may not save any money in the long run.

18. You have $500 in a checking account that pays interest at an annual rate of 3.65%. The interest in this account is compounded daily for each of the 365 days of the year. What is the balance in this account at the end of five days?

19. **Investigation (p. 422)** A principal invested at 3% annual interest compounded annually will more than quadruple in 50 years. Use the formula $A = p(1 + r)^n$ to prepare a chart showing the value of $100 after 50 years of annual compounding at rates of 6%, 9%, and 12% annual interest.

Extra SKILLS PRACTICE

Find the final balance to the nearest dollar.

1. $600: 4% simple interest, 2 years
2. $1,500: 8% simple interest, 4 years
3. $850: 5% simple interest, 3 years
4. $3,000: 6.2% simple interest, 6 months
5. $700: 4% compounded annually, 2 years
6. $1,600: 7% compounded annually, 4 years
7. $800: 5% compounded annually, 3 years
8. $2,500: 6% compounded quarterly, 1 year
9. $3,200: 4% compounded quarterly, 6 months

CHECKPOINT

1. The table at the right gives the results of a 1993 poll on interest rates. Display this data in a circle graph.

Interest Rates Paid by Mortgage Holders

Interest Rate of Mortgage (%)	Percent of Mortgage Holders
0–7.9	29%
8.0–10.9	49%
11.0+	7%
not sure	15%

Source: *Fannie Mae*

Find each percent of change.

2. 52 to 65   3. 24 to 21.48   4. 30,859 to 82,226

5. **Choose A, B, C, or D.** How many different ways can you combine coins to total $.29?

   A. 13   B. 10   C. 9   D. 12

6. Roller blades regularly sell for $36.95 in Elsa's store. Find the sale price if Elsa offers a discount of 20%.

7. **Calculator or Computer** Find the final balance if $570 is invested at an annual interest rate of 8% compounded semiannually for two years.

Practice

Choose **Use a calculator, pencil and paper, or mental math.**

Express each of the following as a fraction, a decimal, and a percent.

1. 0.47 **2.** 2.06 **3.** 0.4% **4.** 872% **5.** $\frac{7}{9}$

6. $\frac{5}{8}$ **7.** 0.0034 **8.** 0.1203 **9.** $3\frac{1}{2}$ **10.** $5\frac{3}{4}\%$

Estimate the percent of the number using any method.

11. 55% of 151 **12.** 0.7% of 504 **13.** 17.8% of 42 **14.** 280% of 209

Complete using proportions.

15. 20% of ■ = 225 **16.** 61 is ■ % of 40 **17.** 36 is 82% of ■

18. 2.3% of 37 = ■ **19.** 125% of 6 = ■ **20.** 35 is ■ % of 89

Use an equation to complete. Round when appropriate.

21. 17% of 125 is ■ **22.** 15 is ■ % of 54 **23.** 35.7 is ■ % of 71

24. 29% of ■ is 96 **25.** 25% of ■ is 30 **26.** 21% of 627 is ■

27. Tony sleeps for 9 h, goes to school for 6 h, studies for 3 h, and does chores for 1 h. Construct a circle graph to show how Tony spends his day. Include a category for other activities.

Find each percent of change.

28. 80 to 96 **29.** 32 to 13 **30.** 63 to 98 **31.** 125 to 375

32. 15.2 to 3.5 **33.** 154 to 300 **34.** 0.5 to 25.5 **35.** 6.7 to 3

Find the selling price. Round to the nearest cent.

36. cost: $98
markup rate: 60%

37. cost: $143.89
markup rate: 45%

38. cost: $267.55
markup rate: 20%

39. regular price: $20
discount rate: 15%

40. regular price: $155.75
discount rate: 35%

41. regular price: $345.50
discount rate: 30%

PROBLEM SOLVING

10-9 Make a Table

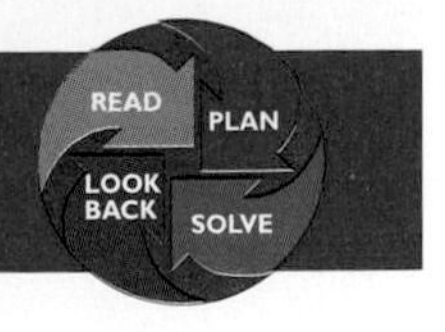

What's Ahead

- Solving problems by making a table

African American students in the Chicago area can compete in a TV game show called "Know Your Heritage." By answering questions about their history and culture, students can win scholarship prizes.

Source: *Chicago*

When you need to look at many possibilities in order to solve a problem, you can organize the information in a table.

> In Jefferson County, a local cable station produces a show called "Academic Challenge." Each week a different middle school sends a team to try to win money for its school. Each team is asked ten questions. The team is awarded $50 for each correct answer, but has $25 subtracted from its winnings for each incorrect answer. If the team from Madison Middle School received $275, how many questions did the team answer correctly?

READ

Read and understand the given information. Summarize the problem.

Read the problem carefully.

1. What information are you asked to find?
2. What information will you need to use to solve the problem?

PLAN

Decide on a strategy to solve the problem.

Make a table that shows the amount of money won for each possible combination of correct and incorrect answers. Making a table will allow you to account for all possibilities and help you avoid using the same combination more than once.

SOLVE

Try out the strategy.

3. **a.** Copy and complete the table below.

Number Correct	0	1	2	3	4	5	6
Number Incorrect	10	9	8	7	6	■	■
Money Won	$0	$0	$0	$0	$50	■	■

b. How many questions did the team answer correctly?

LOOK BACK

Think about how you solved the problem.

4. What other strategies could you use to solve this problem?
5. **Writing** This problem has one solution. Use the information about "Academic Challenge" to write a problem with more than one solution.

TRY THESE

Use the Make a Table strategy to solve each problem.

6. How many ways are there to make change for a half dollar, using only nickels, dimes, and quarters?

7. **Sports** In Erica Machut's first college basketball game, she scored nine points. How many different combinations of one-, two-, and three-point shots could she have scored?

8. **Consumer Issues** You have four 29-cent stamps and three 19-cent stamps. How many different amounts of postage can you have?

9. A palindrome is a number that reads the same forward and backward, such as 11 or 82,128. Single-digit numbers are not considered palindromes. How many palindromes are there between the numbers 0 and 300?

10. **Sports** In the final round of the Middle School Tennis Championship, the winner is the first person to win three out of five matches. In how many different ways can a player win the championship?

WHAT? Since the beginning of this millennium, there has only been one palindrome per century. The palindromes: 1001, 1111, 1221, 1331, and so on, have occurred at 110-year intervals. Within 11 years, we will have two palindromes: 1991 and 2002.

Source: *Innumeracy*

ON YOUR OWN

Use any strategy to solve each problem. If there is not enough information, state what information you need. Show all your work.

11. **Sports** In the 1992 Summer Olympics, the United States won 26 more medals than Germany. Thirty-three of Germany's medals were gold medals. How many medals did Germany win?

12. Mr. Romero asks his math class to open their books so that the product of the page numbers on the two facing pages is 2,756. What are the page numbers?

13. Alex and his grandfather have the same birthday, which they celebrate with a party every year. Alex's age was a divisor of his grandfather's age for six birthdays in a row. What were their ages at each of those birthdays?

Mixed REVIEW

Find the simple interest to the nearest cent.

1. $985 at 7.5% for 2 y
2. $1,500 at 8% for 5 y

$\triangle JBD \cong \triangle YFA$. Complete.

3. $\angle A \cong$ ■
4. $\overline{DJ} \cong$ ■
5. Find three consecutive even numbers whose sum is 678.
6. Ana's age now is four times Sofia's age last year. If Ana is 16 years old, how old will Sofia be next year?

14. The sum of two numbers is 38. If the larger number is divided by the smaller number, the remainder is 5. What are the numbers?

15. **Architecture** The Great Pyramid was erected at Giza by Pharaoh Khufu around 2500 B.C. The ratio of the perimeter of the base of the pyramid to its height is about 6 to 1. The height of the Great Pyramid is 485 ft.

   a. Find an approximation for the perimeter of the base of the Great Pyramid.

   b. Approximately how many years ago was the Great Pyramid built?

The Pyramid Arena Facility *in Memphis, Tennessee, was built in the shape of the Great Pyramid of Khufu in Egypt. The arena, which is 290 ft tall and can seat up to 23,300 people, was built at a cost of $70 million.*

Source: *Building Design and Construction*

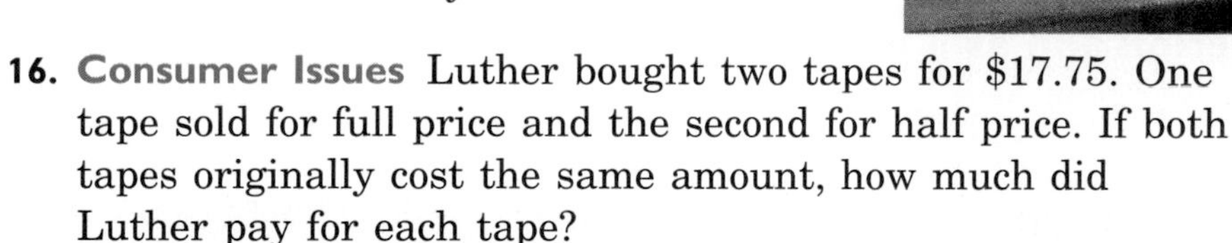

16. **Consumer Issues** Luther bought two tapes for $17.75. One tape sold for full price and the second for half price. If both tapes originally cost the same amount, how much did Luther pay for each tape?

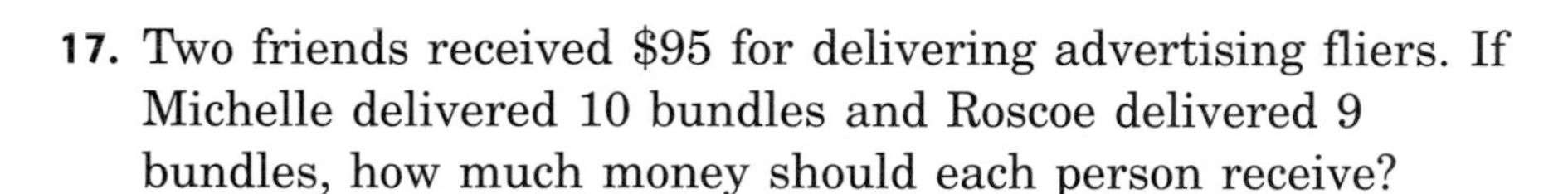

17. Two friends received $95 for delivering advertising fliers. If Michelle delivered 10 bundles and Roscoe delivered 9 bundles, how much money should each person receive?

18. Sarah is digging postholes on her farm. She is fencing a triangular plot that is 100 yd by 200 yd by 150 yd. She starts at a corner and digs a hole every 10 yd. How many holes must she dig?

19. **Consumer Issues** Lio rented a car for five days. The rate was $27.50 per day. He was allowed 100 free miles for each rental day. For any miles above this amount, the rate was $.34/mi. If Lio drove 600 mi, how much was he charged?

20. A wooden cube measuring 4 cm along each edge is painted yellow. The painted cube is then cut into centimeter cubes. How many of the small cubes are painted on two sides?

21. I am thinking of a number. The number is a multiple of 6. One of the digits is 6. The sum of the digits is an odd number. The difference between the digits is a prime number. What is the smallest number that I could be thinking of?

CHAPTER 10

Wrap Up

Fractions, Decimals, and Percents 10-1

A ***percent*** is a ***ratio*** of a number to 100.

To write a fraction as a percent, use a proportion to find an equivalent fraction with a denominator of 100.

To write a decimal as a percent, write the decimal as a fraction with a denominator of 100.

Write each percent as a fraction in simplest form.

1. 25% **2.** 6.2% **3.** 15% **4.** 0.03% **5.** 130%

Write each decimal as a fraction and as a percent.

6. 0.35 **7.** 1.25 **8.** 0.7 **9.** 0.05 **10.** 2.35

Estimating with Percent 10-2

When working with percents, it is helpful to estimate.

Estimate the percent of the number using any method.

11. 24% of 97 **12.** 7% of 61 **13.** 150% of 211 **14.** 68% of 85

Percents and Proportions, Percents and Equations 10-3, 10-4

A percent problem can be solved using a ***proportion*** or an ***equation***.

$$\frac{\text{part}}{\text{whole}} = \frac{n}{100}$$

$$\text{part} = P \cdot \text{whole}$$

Solve each of the following. Round to the nearest tenth.

15. What percent of 50 is 40?

16. 30% of what number is 24?

17. 15 is $87\frac{1}{2}$% of what number?

18. What percent of 35 is 50?

Constructing Circle Graphs 10-5

A ***circle graph*** displays data that are parts of a whole.

19. Nell spent \$4 for lunch, \$2 for bus fare, \$4.50 for a movie, and \$1.50 for post cards. Display this data in a circle graph.

Percent of Change, Markup, and Discount 10-6, 10-7

The ***percent of change*** expressed as a decimal is $P = \frac{\text{amount of change}}{\text{original amount}}$.

The amount a price is increased is the ***markup***. The amount a price is decreased is the ***discount***.

20. Choose A, B, C, or D. Which of the following changes represents a 25% increase?

A. 75 to 100 **B.** 100 to 75 **C.** 30 to 40 **D.** 12 to 15

Find the final price.

21. regular price: \$450, discount: 30%

22. cost: \$60, markup: 75%

Simple and Compound Interest 10-8

To find ***simple interest,*** use the formula $I = p \cdot r \cdot t$.

To find the final balance when interest is ***compounded,*** use the formula $A = p(1 + r)^n$.

Find the final balance for \$1000 invested in each of the following ways.

23. 5% simple interest for 5 years

24. 7% compounded annually for 3 years

25. Writing Explain why quarterly compounding of interest produces a greater final amount than simple interest.

Problem Solving 10-9

You can solve some problems by making a table.

26. Uli bought shirts for \$18 each and socks for \$1.75 a pair. If he spent \$97, how many of each did he buy?

GETTING READY FOR CHAPTER 11

Find the area of each shaded region.
□ represents 1 square unit of area.

1. 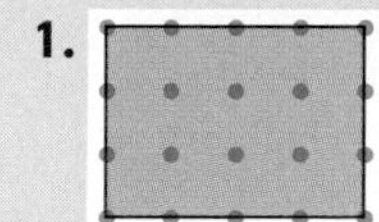

2. 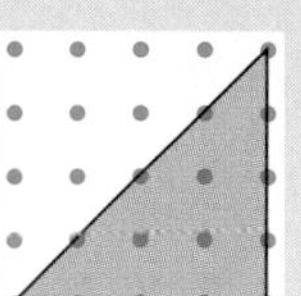

3. 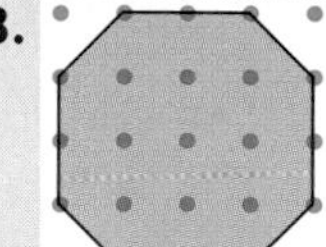

4.

PUTTING IT ALL TOGETHER

Make a Million

Today is the day you must present your million-dollar plan to the $50,000 donor. If your plan is a sound one, the donor will issue you a check at once. Look back at the plan you came up with at the beginning of the chapter. Revise it if you wish, based on your study of the chapter. Then present your plan to the donor. Explain why you believe your ideas make good financial sense. The following are suggestions to help you support your proposal.

- ✓ Make a spreadsheet.
- ✓ Make a graph or chart.
- ✓ Make a display.

The problems preceded by the magnifying glass (p. 426, # 33; p. 444, # 22; and p. 451, # 19) will help you complete the investigation.

While a million dollars may no longer seem quite as unattainable a sum as it once did, a billion dollars remains a lot of money. Placed end to end, one billion dollar bills would extend about four times around the world. At $1 per minute it would take you about 2,000 years to spend $1 billion.

Excursion: Ounce-for-ounce, an 1856 British Guiana stamp may be the most valuable item on earth. Originally sold for 1 cent, the stamp recently sold for $850,000. Estimate the stamp's value in dollars per pound.

Each month, the Bureau of Labor Statistics publishes the Consumer Price Index (CPI). This statistic tells us the change in cost of hundreds of products and services.

- Research the CPI.
- Choose one product or service.
- Find the percent increase or decrease in the cost of your product or service each year for the past 10 years.
- Draw a graph showing the price changes .

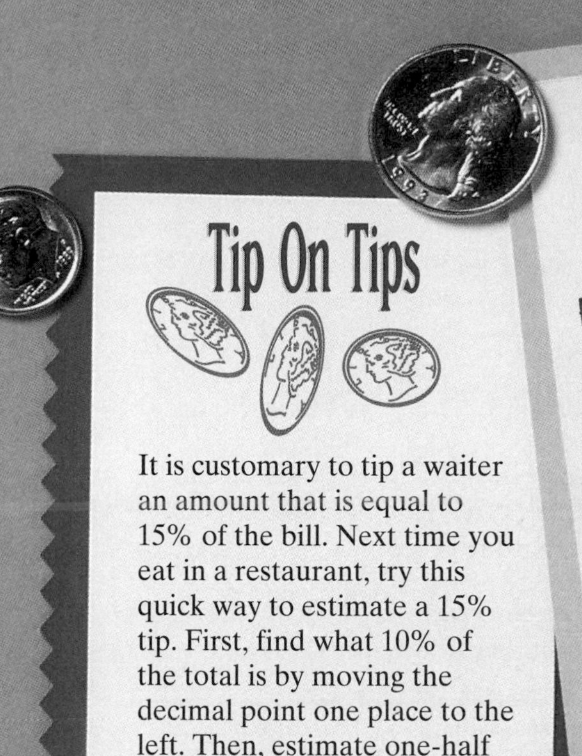

Tip On Tips

It is customary to tip a waiter an amount that is equal to 15% of the bill. Next time you eat in a restaurant, try this quick way to estimate a 15% tip. First, find what 10% of the total is by moving the decimal point one place to the left. Then, estimate one-half of this amount. Finally, add both these numbers together. The sum is the amount of your tip. For example, if a check is $23.76, the 15% tip would be $3.60. Explain why this is so.

How Does It Rate?

Have you heard of 4-star restaurants, 5-star hotels, or 1-star movies? If so, then you know that stars are used as symbols to rate the quality of a restaurant, hotel, or movie. Create a rating system for something familiar to you. You may wish to rate parks, malls, video stores, or brands of cereal. Choose a creative symbol to show your rating. Rate as many of the items in your category as you can. Describe how your rating system works. Use your rating system to make recommendations to your friends and family.

Sports Stats

Highest lifetime batting average: Ty Cobb, .367
Lowest seasonal ERA: Ferdinand Schupp, 0.90
Highest seasonal base-stealing percent: Max Carey, 96.2%

Part of the fun of sports is compiling and interpreting statistics. Create a sports statistic. Show it as a percent. Describe it to a friend.

CHAPTER 10

Assessment

1. Replace each ■ with >, <, or =.

   a. 0.8% ■ 0.8 b. $\frac{5}{6}$ ■ 85%

   c. 450% ■ 4.5 d. 0.625 ■ $\frac{5}{8}$

2. Find each percent of change.

   a. 180 to 120 b. 25 to 75

   c. 87.5 to 62.5 d. $33\frac{1}{3}$ to $66\frac{2}{3}$

3. Estimate each of the following.

   a. 76% of 48 b. 250% of 29

   c. 21% of 36 d. 0.5% of 498

4. Solve using a proportion.

   a. What percent of 32 is 20?

   b. 18 is 30% of what number?

   c. Find 95% of 350.

5. Find the new price to the nearest cent after each markup or discount.

	Price	Markup/Discount
a.	$64.00	25% discount
b.	$19.99	15% markup
c.	$850.00	10% markup
d.	$90.00	33% discount

6. **Calculator** Find the final balance.

   a. $250 at 4% simple interest for 3 years

   b. $4,500 at 7% compounded annually for 2 years

   c. $8,000 at 8% compounded quarterly for 1 year

7. **Choose A, B, C, or D.** In which set are all three values equal?

   A. $\frac{3}{5}$, 0.3, 30% B. $\frac{3}{5}$, 0.6, 6%

   C. $\frac{3}{5}$, 0.06, 6% D. $\frac{3}{5}$, 0.6, 60%

8. Wendy purchased a pair of shoes for $40.80 during a "15% off" sale. What was the regular price?

9. Make a circle graph to display the grading system shown in the table.

Type of Assessment	Percent of Grade
Tests	40%
Quizzes	25%
Classwork	20%
Homework	15%

10. **Writing** The Drama Club bought canned nuts for $4 and sold them for $5. Ellen claims that the markup rate is 20% because $1 is 20% of $5. Explain what is wrong with Ellen's reasoning and give the correct markup rate.

11. Ms. Marcus bought 24 boxes of markers for her art class. A box of 24 permanent markers costs $15. A box of 18 washable markers costs $13. If she spent $332 for 492 markers, how many boxes of each type did she buy?

12. Last year, Brett earned $3.00 per hour baby sitting. This year he earns $3.50 per hour. What is the percent of increase?

CHAPTER 10

Cumulative Review

Choose A, B, C, or D.

1. Write $3\frac{1}{2}\%$ as a fraction in simplest form.

   A. $\frac{7}{2}$ B. $\frac{7}{20}$ C. $\frac{7}{200}$ D. $\frac{3.5}{100}$

2. An HO scale model railroad is $\frac{1}{87}$ scale, which means that 1 inch of an HO train is equal to 87 inches of a real train. What is the size of an HO boxcar if a real boxcar measures 50 *feet*?

   A. About 3.5 in. B. About 7 in.
   C. About 7 ft D. About 15 in.

3. Which graph could be $y = -3x + 2$?

   A.
   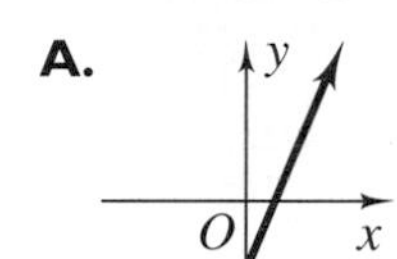

   B.
   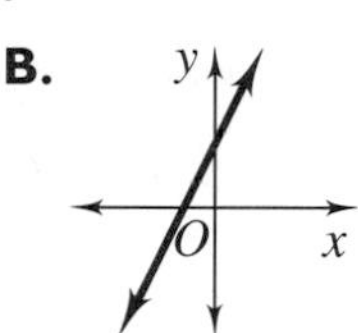

   C.
   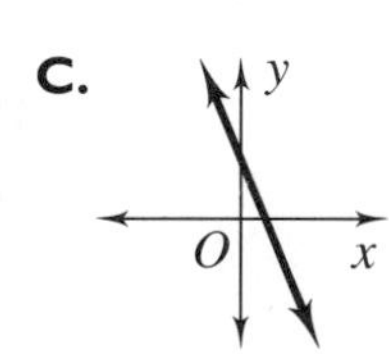

   D.
   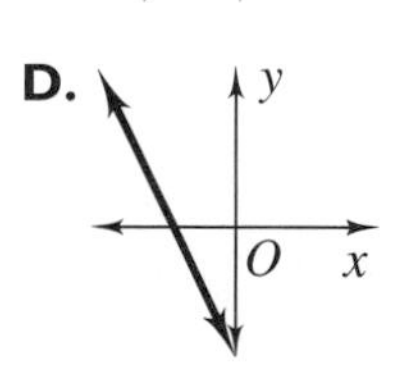

4. A radio disc jockey wants to play five different top ten songs in a row. How many different ways can she do this?

   A. 5 B. 5!
   C. 5 • 5 D. 10 • 9 • 8 • 7 • 6

5. A jacket whose regular price was $79.99 is on sale for 35% off. Estimate the sale price of the jacket.

   A. About $53.00 B. About $60.00
   C. About $45.00 D. About $40.00

6. Which value is greatest?

   A. sin X
   B. cos Y
   C. tan X
   D. tan Y

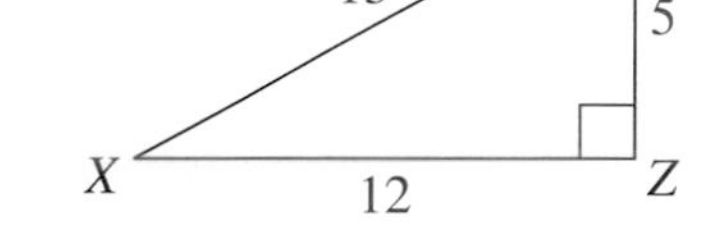

7. In which quadrant are the x-coordinates of all ordered pairs positive and the y-coordinates all negative?

   A. I B. II C. III D. IV

8. Which does not equal the others?

   A. 60% of 80 B. 80% of 60
   C. 80 decreased by 40% D. 40 increased by 80%

9. Which events are *not* independent?

   A. Rolling a number cube twice
   B. Tossing two pennies at the same time
   C. Drawing a card from a deck of cards and then drawing a second card
   D. Selecting a ball from a bag of colored balls, putting the ball back in the bag and selecting a second ball

10. Which investment of $100 will give you the most money at the end of one year?

    A. 4.5% compounded yearly
    B. 4.5% compounded semiannually
    C. 4% compounded quarterly
    D. 4% compounded monthly

CHAPTER 11 Geometry and Measurement

Data File 11

Most synthetic plastics do not break down over time and therefore are considered an environmental problem. Recycling is the most practical way to deal with plastics. The process of recycling plastic bottles is relatively straightforward and many communities now ask that plastic bottles be separated before the trash is picked up. Some plastics can be recycled and made into warm jackets and blankets.

JUST SOME OF THE FACTS...

- Americans use 2.5 million bottles every hour.
- Americans use 35 million paper clips each year.
- Plastic waste in the oceans kills 30,000 seals each year.
- Australians toss an estimated $8 million worth of reusable aluminum and glass each year.
- Battery manufacturing uses 50% more energy than the batteries store.

Source: *Counting on a Small Planet*

What Happens To Our Garbage?

Millions of Tons

200
180
160
140
120
100
80
60
40
20
0

1960: 56, 5.9, 27
1980: 120, 14.5, 11, 2.7
1990: 130, 33.4, 2.2, 29.7

Waste-to-Energy
Recycling
Incineration
Landfills

Source: *National Solid Wastes Management Association*

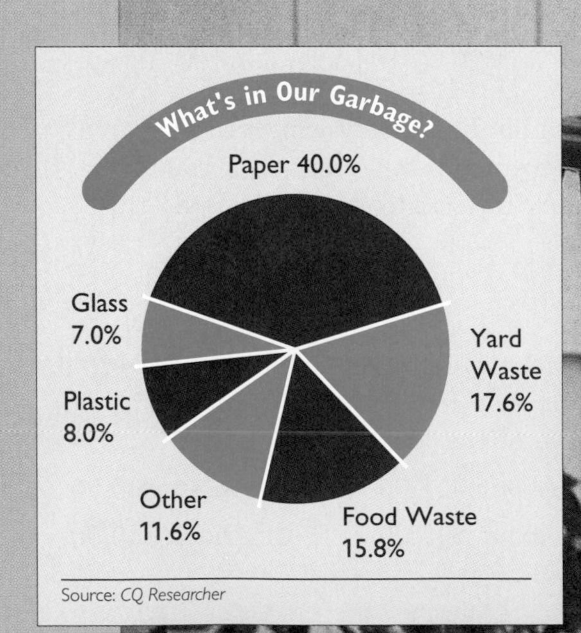

Source: *CQ Researcher*

WHAT YOU WILL LEARN

- how to visualize spatial relationships
- how to develop and apply formulas
- how to use technology to explore surface area and volume similar figures

THE ANNUAL GARBAGE HEAP

All the garbage collected in the United States in one year could form a block weighing 196 million tons. The block would be as tall as a 246 story building.

Source: *National Solid Wastes Management Association*

WORLD VIEW

There are 14 million copies of the Japanese newspaper, *Asahi Shimbun,* sold every day. The paper used accounts for about 34,000 trees.

investigation

Project File

Memo

It is estimated that by 1995, 1.7 million passengers will board U.S. airlines each day. Every year about 70 million flight operations will take place at U.S. airports. At any given moment half a dozen planes, each traveling several hundred miles an hour, may be circling over a typical airport. Air traffic controllers keep track of these planes and help them to land safely. One of the most important skills an air traffic controller must possess is the ability to visualize objects in space and to understand their spatial relationships with one another.

Mission: Draw up a set of simple safety guidelines for pilots and air traffic controllers at a mid-size airport. Your guidelines should establish distances that will separate planes in the air and on the ground and altitudes and speeds at which planes can fly.

Leads to Follow

- ✓ Imagine that you are an airline passenger. What safety precautions are most important to you?
- ✓ What are the greatest dangers to planes on takeoff and landing? What can be done to reduce these dangers?

What's Ahead

- Identifying three-dimensional figures

11-1 Three-Dimensional Figures

THINK AND DISCUSS

Figures that do not lie in a plane are *space figures,* or *three-dimensional figures.* Some space figures are shown below.

FLASHBACK

The flat surfaces of these three-dimensional figures are called *faces.*

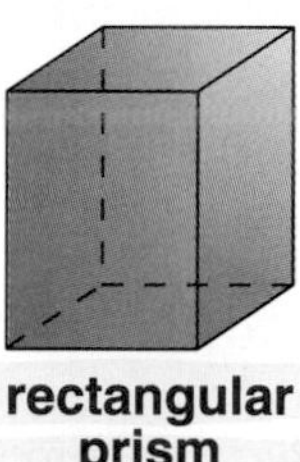

rectangular prism

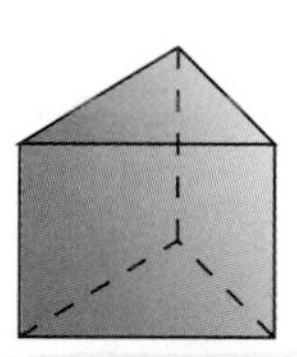

triangular prism

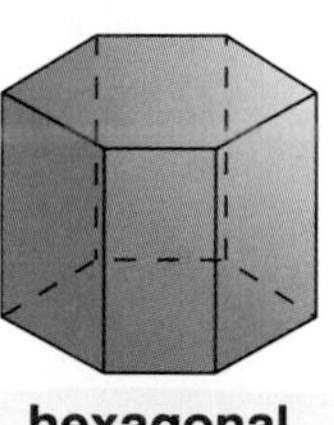

hexagonal prism

1. **a.** How are these three figures alike?
   b. How are the three *prisms* different?

2. What do you think is the name of this figure?

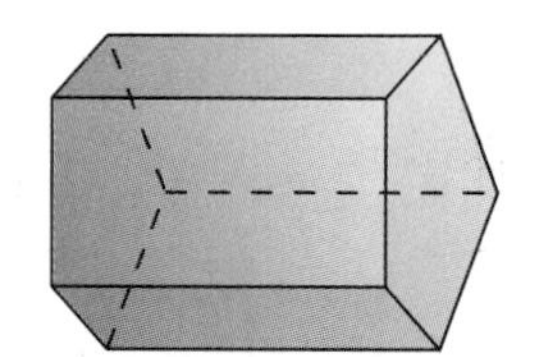

3. Prisms have two parallel and congruent polygonal faces, called *bases.* What kind of prism has more than one pair of parallel and congruent faces?

4. **a.** Describe a cube.
   b. Is a cube a prism? Explain.

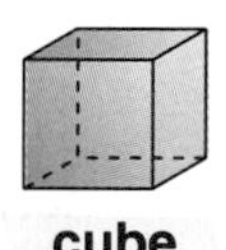

cube

***Prisms produce rainbows** of color when light passing through the prism is refracted, or bent. The glass in the prism slows some colors more than others thereby producing a band of colors.*

Source: *Exploring Physical Science*

5. Two *pyramids* are shown below. What names would you give them? Why?

a.

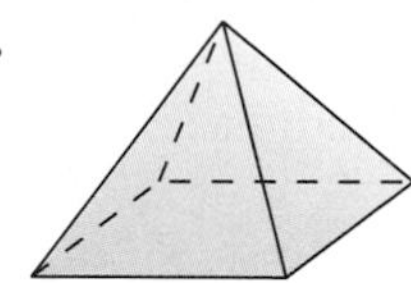

b.

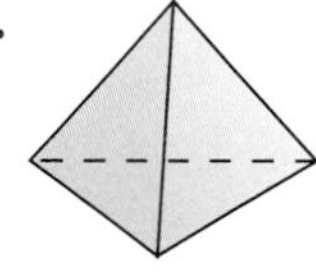

6. **a.** How are pyramids and prisms alike?
   b. How are they different?

7. What shape is a face of a pyramid that is not a base?

Three more space figures are shown below.

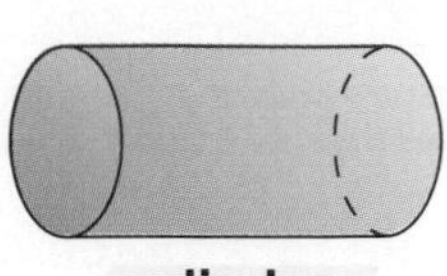

sphere

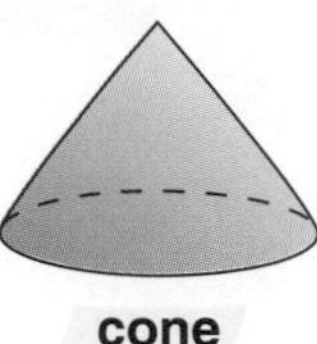

8. a. How are cylinders, spheres, and cones alike?
   b. How are they different?

9. a. How are cylinders and prisms alike?
   b. How are they different?

10. a. How are cones and pyramids alike?
    b. How are they different?

Each segment formed by the intersection of two faces is an *edge*. A point where edges meet is a *vertex*.

WORK TOGETHER

The mathematician Euler discovered a relationship between the number of faces, vertices, and edges of a prism. Work with your group to complete a table like the one below. Then look for a pattern.

Prism	Number of Faces (F)	Number of Vertices (V)	Number of Edges (E)
Triangular	■	■	■
Rectangular	■	■	■
Pentagonal	■	■	■
Hexagonal	■	■	■

11. What relationship did you find among the number of faces, vertices, and edges?

12. Count the number of faces, vertices, and edges of several different pyramids. Is the same relationship true for pyramids?

ON YOUR OWN

Match each description with the correct name below.

a. sphere	*b. rectangular pyramid*
c. triangular prism	*d. cylinder*
e. cone	*f. triangular pyramid*
g. rectangular prism	*h. cube*

This East German stamp, *issued in 1983, commemorates the bicentennial of the death of the famous Swiss mathematician, Leonhard Euler.*

13. a space figure with faces that are rectangles and with two parallel bases that are congruent

14. a space figure with two circular, parallel, and congruent bases

15. a space figure with one circular base and one vertex

16. a space figure with triangular faces

17. a space figure that is the set of all points that are the same distance from a given point called the *center*

18. a space figure with faces that are congruent squares

19. a space figure with a rectangular base and triangular faces that meet at a vertex

20. a space figure with two parallel bases that are congruent triangles and other faces that are rectangles

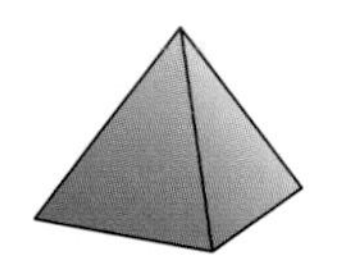

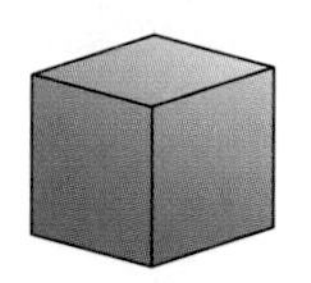

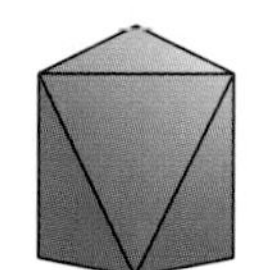

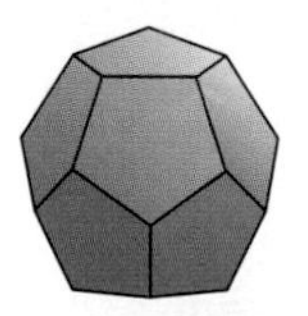

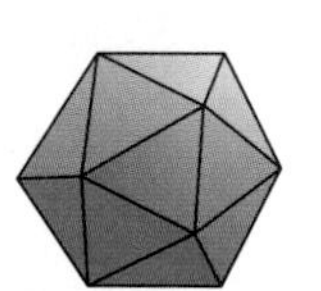

A *polyhedron* is a solid figure bounded by polygons. There are only five different *regular* polyhedra: the tetrahedron, the hexahedron or cube, the octahedron, the dodecahedron, and the icosahedron. These are often referred to as the Platonic solids, named after Plato.

Source: *An Introduction to the History of Mathematics*

Copy each figure on graph paper. Write the name of the figure.

21.

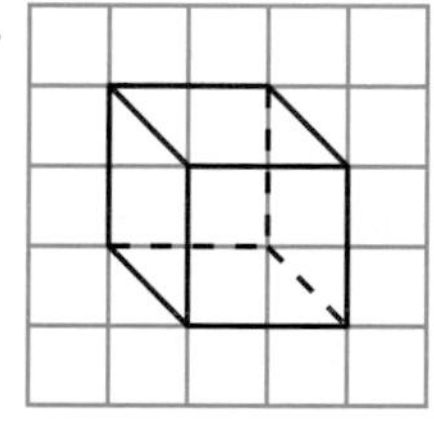

22.

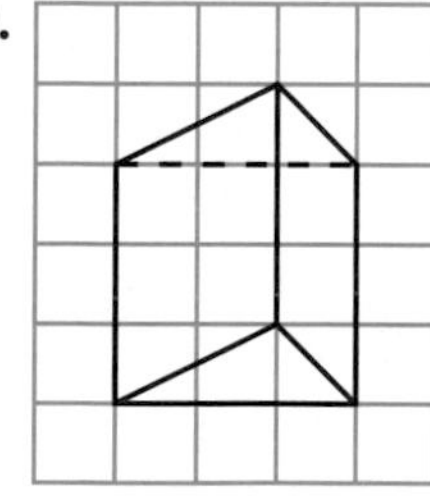

23.

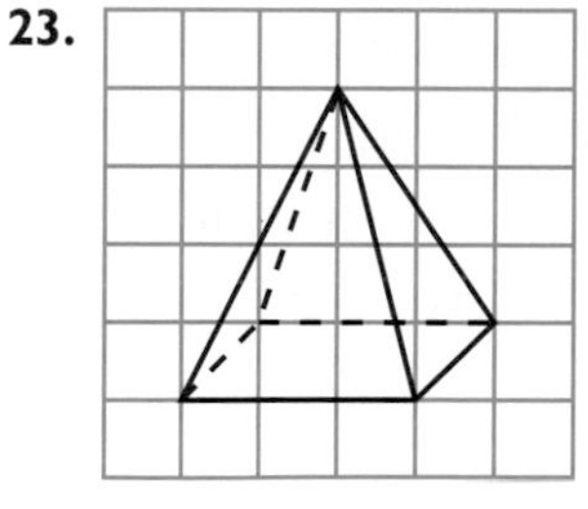

24. Sketch a cylinder.

The Pentagon is the largest office building in the world. Its perimeter of 4,600 ft could easily accommodate the Great Pyramid of Cheops with a couple of hundred feet to spare. Within its 3.8 million ft^2 of office space are 17 mi of corridors.

Source: *American Heritage*

Name each three-dimensional figure.

25. a cereal box

26. a tennis ball

27. a teepee

28. the Pentagon building

29. Critical Thinking How are a sphere and a circle alike? How are they different?

30. What do dashed lines represent in drawings of three-dimensional figures?

31. Writing Two views of the same rectangular prism are shown below. Explain how the points of view are different.

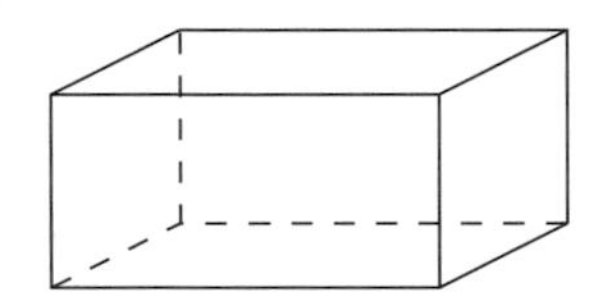

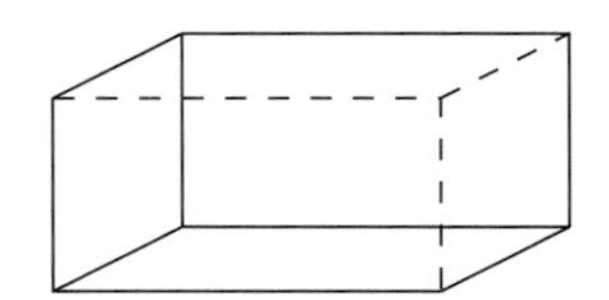

Complete.

32. A ■ has exactly one circular base.

33. A pentagonal prism has ■ faces.

34. A hexagonal prism has ■ edges.

35. A square pyramid has four faces that are shaped like ■.

36. A prism whose faces are all congruent squares is a ■.

37. Choose A, B, C, or D. If a sphere and a plane intersect, what shape is the intersection?

A. a point

B. a circle

C. a point or a circle

D. a point, circle, or line

38. Choose A, B, C, or D. If a cube and a plane intersect, which of the following can be the shape of the intersection?

I. a square

II. an equilateral triangle

III. an isosceles triangle

IV. a trapezoid

A. I only

B. I and II

C. I, II, and III

D. I, II, III, and IV

Mixed REVIEW

Solve using two methods.

1. Find 85% of 120.

2. What % of 60 is 20?

3. 24 is 25% of what number?

Write each percent as a decimal and a simplified fraction.

4. 65%

5. 150%

6. $37\frac{1}{2}\%$

7. $83\frac{1}{3}\%$

8. Cora has quarters, dimes, and nickels in her pocket. The ten coins are worth $1.65. What coins does she have?

Problem Solving Practice

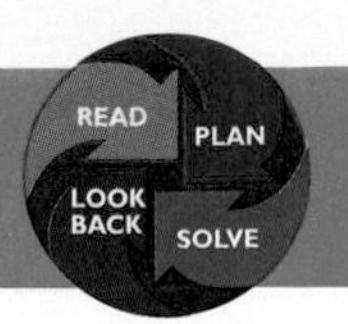

PROBLEM SOLVING STRATEGIES

Make a Table
Use Logical Reasoning
Solve a Simpler Problem
Too Much or Too Little Information
Look for a Pattern
Make a Model
Work Backward
Draw a Diagram
Guess and Test
Simulate a Problem
Use Multiple Strategies
Write an Equation
Use a Proportion

Solve. The list at the left shows some possible strategies you can use.

1. Jana counted 13 bugs, with a total of 88 legs, in the science lab. There were beetles with 6 legs and spiders with 8 legs. How many beetles and how many spiders were there?

2. Tomas has 2 straws that together are as long as 5 pencils. The 5 pencils are as long as 16 paper clips. How many paper clips are as long as 1 straw?

3. **Choose A, B, C, or D.** Which pair of numbers continues the pattern?

   1, 4, 5, 11, 12, 13, 22, 23, 24, 25, ■, ■

   A. 26, 27 **B.** 34, 35 **C.** 35, 36 **D.** 37, 38

4. Derrick is 68 in. tall. Marcus is 66 in. tall. Derrick is standing in a hole 15 in. deep. Marcus is standing on a stool 24 in. high. What is the vertical distance from the top of Derrick's head to the top of Marcus's head?

5. $m\angle 1 = m\angle 2 = m\angle 3 = m\angle 4 = 35°$.
   How many angles are shown?
   How many of the angles are obtuse?

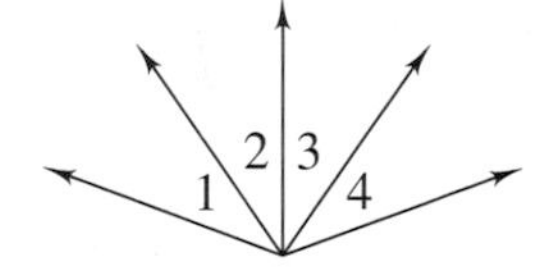

6. a. **Calculator** Make a table that shows 7^1, 7^2, 7^3, 7^4, 7^5, 7^6, 7^7, and 7^8.

   b. Use your table to find the units digit of 7^{55}.

7. This diagram shows Aaron's house in relation to Ryan's house. Walking on the grid shown, Aaron can walk directly to Ryan's house six different ways. Each route is four blocks long. Draw diagrams showing each route.

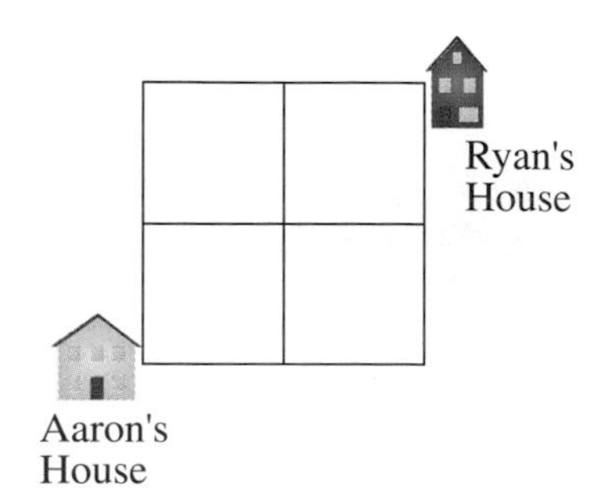

What's Ahead

- Identifying patterns that fold into three-dimensional figures
- Finding the area of composite two-dimensional figures

11-2 Composite Figures

WHAT YOU'LL NEED

✓ Centimeter graph paper

✓ Compass

✓ Scissors

✓ Calculator

WORK TOGETHER

The figures below are two-dimensional patterns that you could fold to form three-dimensional figures.

- Copy each pattern onto centimeter graph paper.
- Cut the patterns out.
- Fold the patterns to form three-dimensional figures.

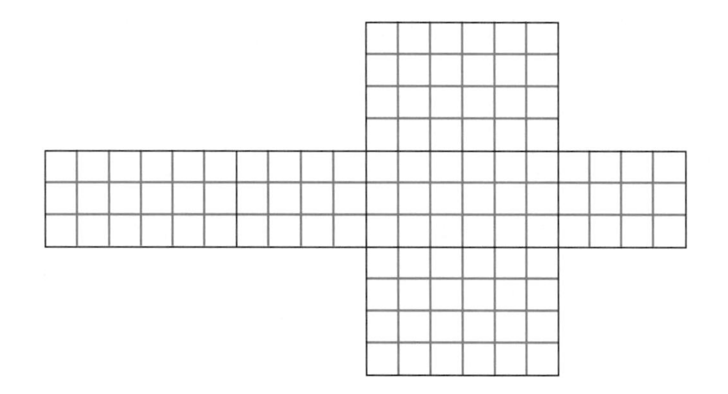

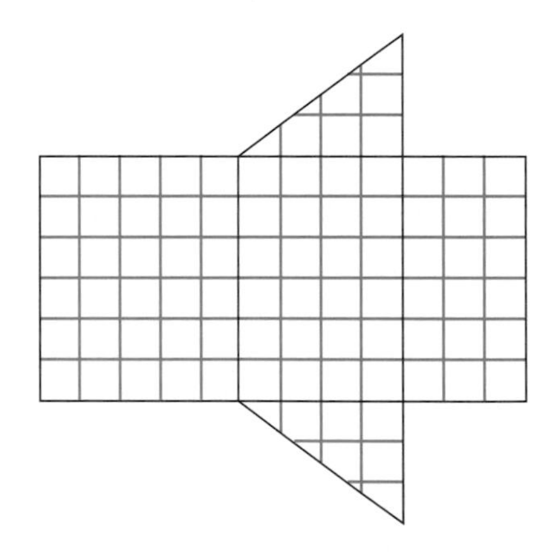

Hector Rojas, from La Paz, Bolivia, folded plain paper to make these kangaroos. Then he colored them. The art of paper-folding, known as origami, originated in Japan.

1. What three-dimensional figures did you form?
2. Draw a different pattern that you could fold to form the rectangular prism.

THINK AND DISCUSS

Each of the patterns in the Work Together activity is made up of geometric figures.

3. Describe the polygons in the pattern for the rectangular prism. Include the dimensions and whether any of the polygons are congruent.
4. What is the area of the pattern for the rectangular prism?
5. Why is it possible to have different patterns that fold to form the same prism?
6. **Critical Thinking** What are the essential features of a pattern that will fold to form the rectangular prism?
7. a. Describe the polygons in the pattern for the triangular prism.
   b. Find the area of the pattern for the triangular prism.
   c. Explain how you found the area of the pattern.
8. a. Describe the geometric figures in the pattern for the cylinder.
   b. **Critical Thinking** How can you find the area of the pattern for the cylinder?
   c. Find the area of the pattern.

Scott Bruce of Cambridge, MA, has collected over 1,000 vintage cereal boxes. He started his collection with the first two boxes of Shredded Wheat, which he obtained from the original printer. Pre-1975 cereal boxes in mint condition are so rare that they can cost $1,000.

Source: *House and Garden*

ON YOUR OWN

Choose Use mental math, pencil and paper, or a calculator to find the area of each figure.

9.
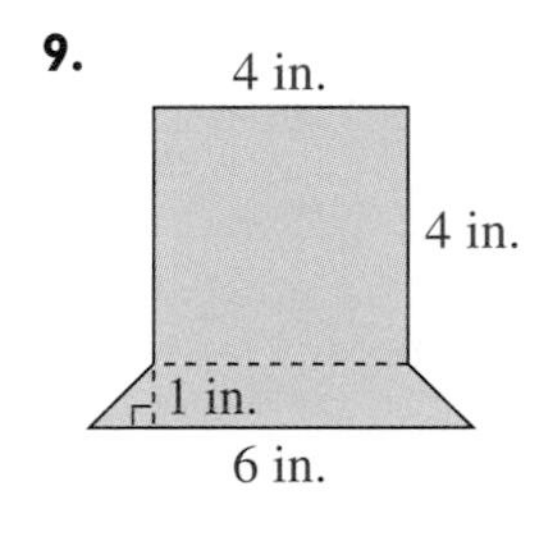

10.
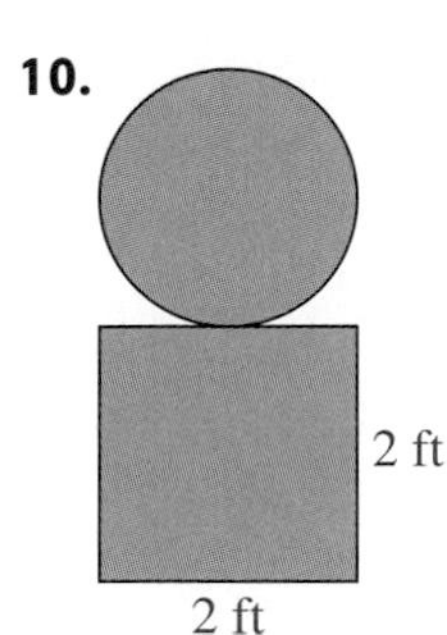

11.
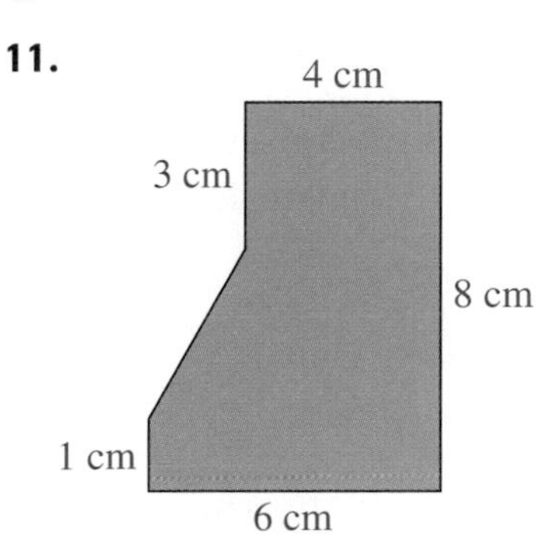

Calculator Find the area of each shaded region to the nearest square unit.

12.

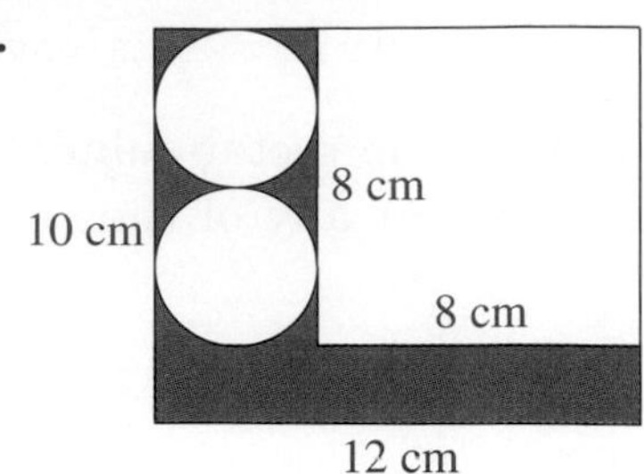

13.

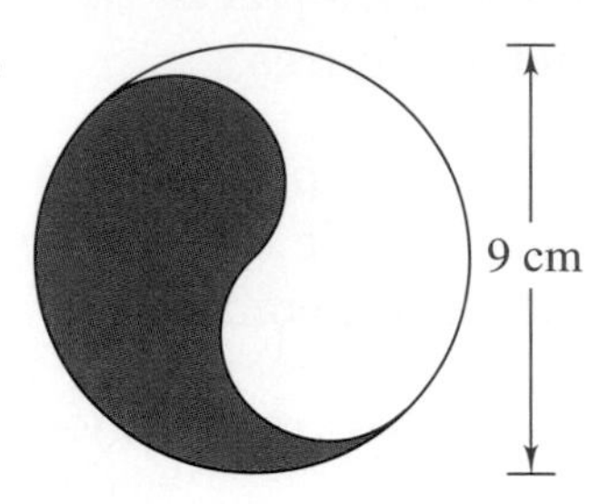

14.

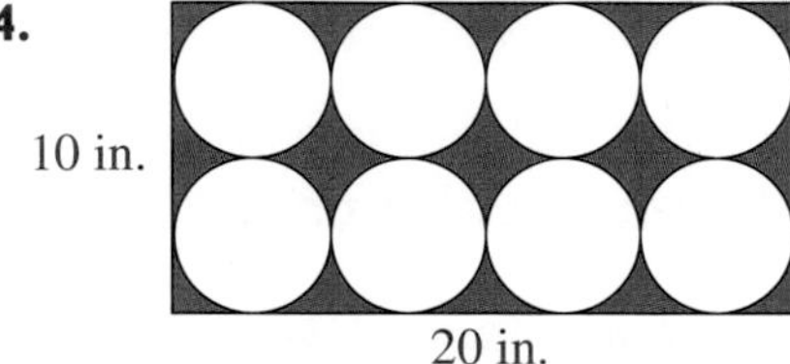

15.

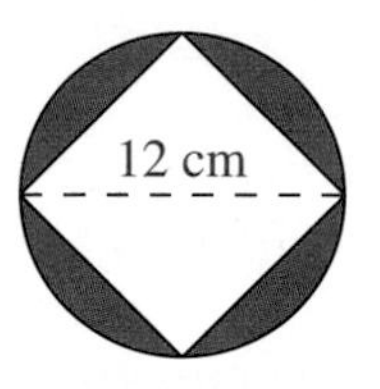

16. a. Find the area of the shaded region. (*Hint:* Look for the simplest solution.)

b. Writing Explain how you found the area.

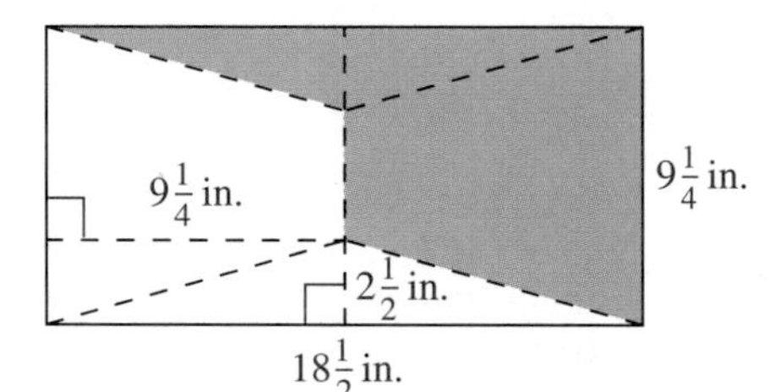

Name the three-dimensional figure that can be formed by folding each pattern.

17.

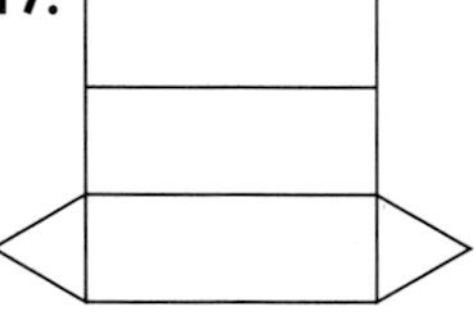

18.

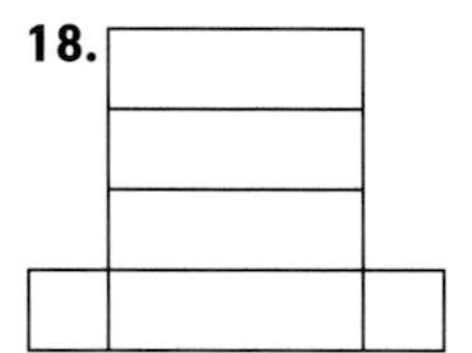

19.

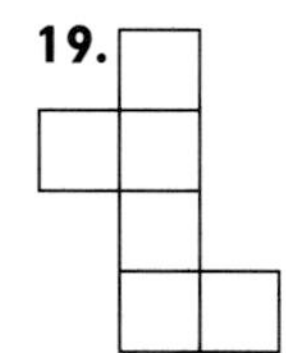

20. a. Find the area of the pattern.

b. Name the three-dimensional figure for which this is a pattern.

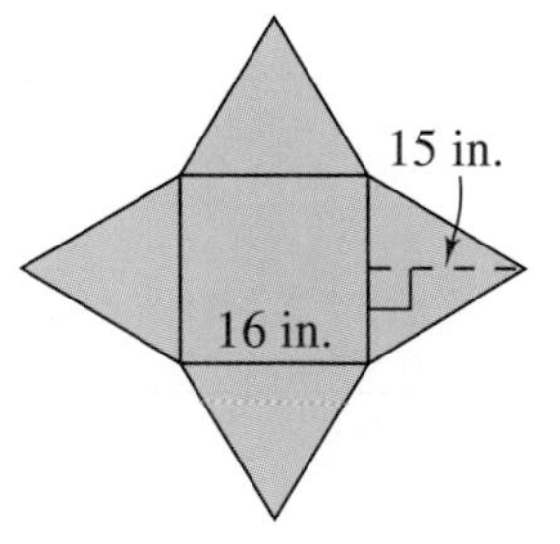

Mixed REVIEW

Solve.

1. $\frac{7}{8} = \frac{t}{12}$ 2. $\frac{t}{5} = \frac{2}{3}$

The following are test scores: 70, 98, 85, 95, 100, 79, 85, 83, 90, 85.

3. Find the mean, mode and median.

4. Draw a box and whisker plot for the data.

Draw and label each figure.

5. a rectangular prism with a base 2 cm by 1.5 cm and a height of 2.5 cm

6. a prism with a height of 1.5 cm and a right triangle base with legs 6 mm and 8 mm

Draw a pattern for each three-dimensional figure. Choose the dimensions for the figure.

21. cylinder

22. triangular prism

23. cube

24. rectangular prism

25. a. Describe the size and shape of the faces of this prism.

b. Imagine that you unfold the prism and look at the two-dimensional pattern. Find the area of the pattern.

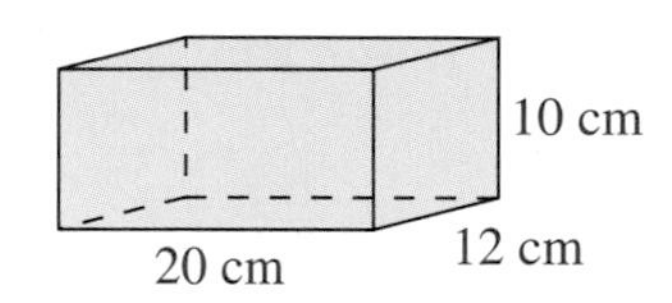

26. Each square below is 1 cm by 1 cm. Estimate the area of the figure.

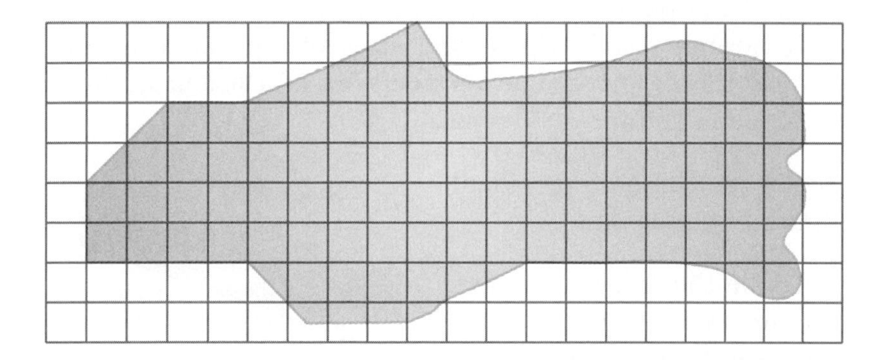

27. Each square below is 0.5 cm by 0.5 cm. Estimate the area of the figure.

Estimate each partially filled square as 0, $\frac{1}{2}$, or 1 square unit.

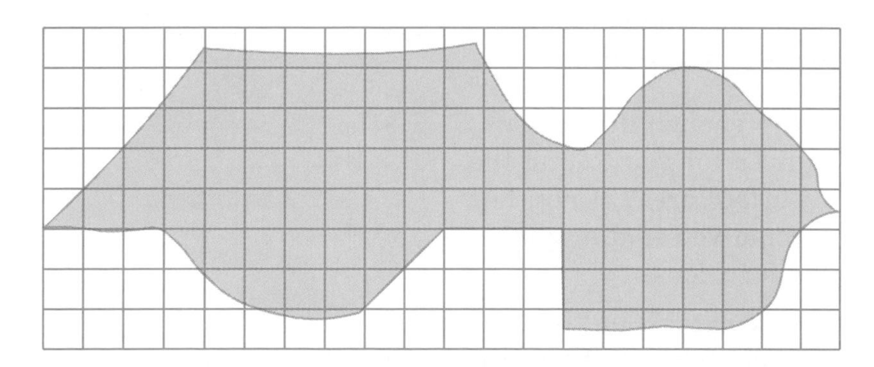

28. Investigation (p. 464) Contact your local airport. What safety rules govern flights into and out of the airport?

What's Ahead

- Finding the surface area of rectangular and triangular prisms

11-3 Surface Area of Prisms

WHAT YOU'LL NEED

✓ Calculator 

THINK AND DISCUSS

Many items that you buy at the store are packaged in prisms.

The cost of the package is part of the price of the item. Manufacturers consider the *surface area* of a package when they calculate the price. The **surface area** of a prism is the sum of the areas of the faces.

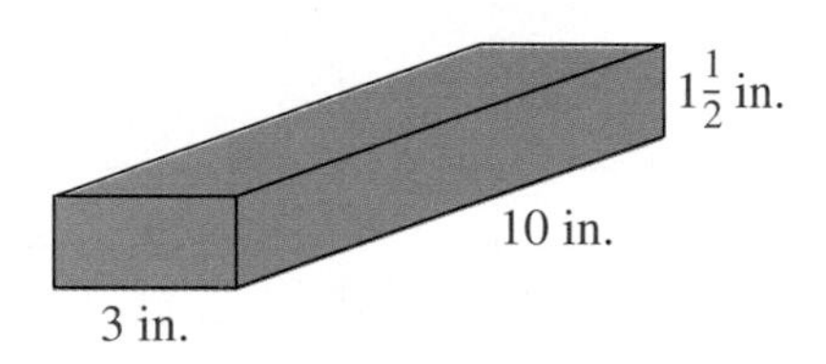

1. Name the three-dimensional figure at the right.
2. Describe the faces. Include the dimensions and whether any faces are congruent.
3. Find the surface area.

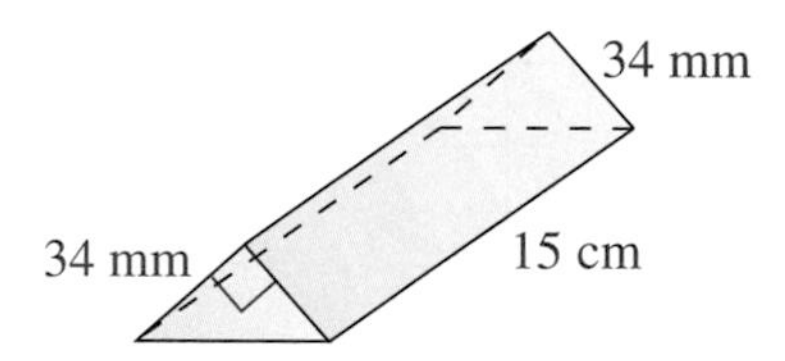

4. Name the three-dimensional figure at the right.
5. **a.** Are enough dimensions given for you to find the surface area? If not, how could you find any missing dimensions?
   b. **Calculator** Find the missing dimensions to the nearest millimeter.
   c. Describe the faces.
6. Find the surface area in square millimeters.
7. Find the surface area in square centimeters.

Crystals that are longer than they are tall or wide are called "prismatic" crystals. This crystal has six long rectangular faces and two hexagonal faces on either end.

Source: *Crystal & Gem*

WORK TOGETHER

Work with your group to solve this problem.

One base of a rectangular prism is 3 in. by 10 in. The surface area is 242 in.^{2}. What is the height of the prism?

ON YOUR OWN

Choose Use mental math, pencil and paper, or a calculator to find the surface area of each prism.

8.

3 in.
20 in.
5 in.

9.

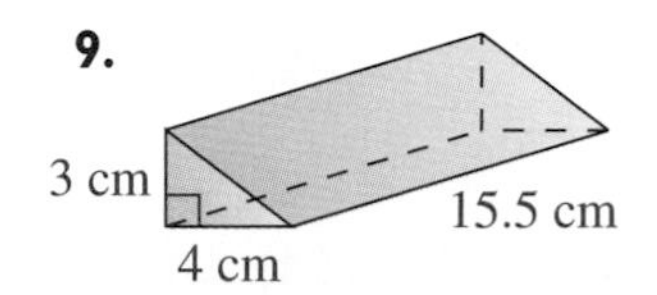

10.

6 m
6 m
8 m

11.

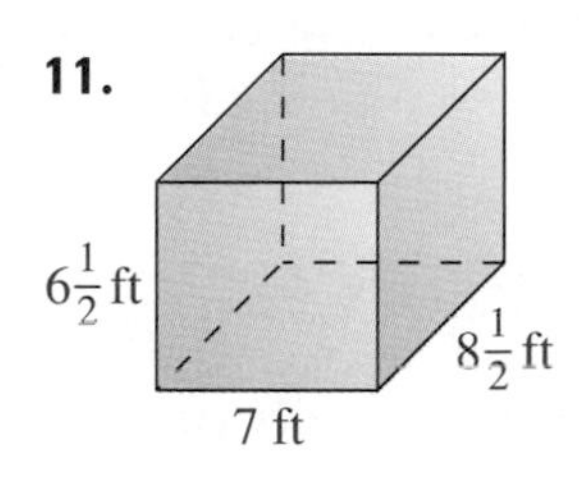

12. Find the surface area of a cube with each edge 4 cm long.

13. Find the surface area of a rectangular prism that is 35 cm by 7 cm by 9 cm.

14. The surface area of a cube is 486 cm^2. What is the length of each edge?

15. Choose A, B, C, or D. The surface area of the prism on the left below is ▇ the surface area of the prism on the right.

A. equal to
B. half
C. less than half
D. greater than half

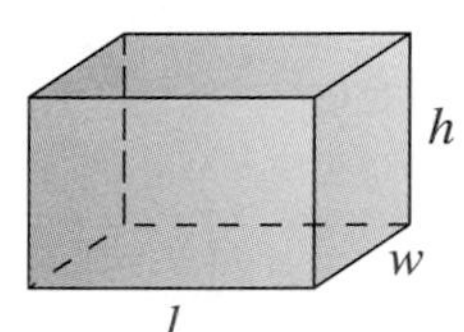

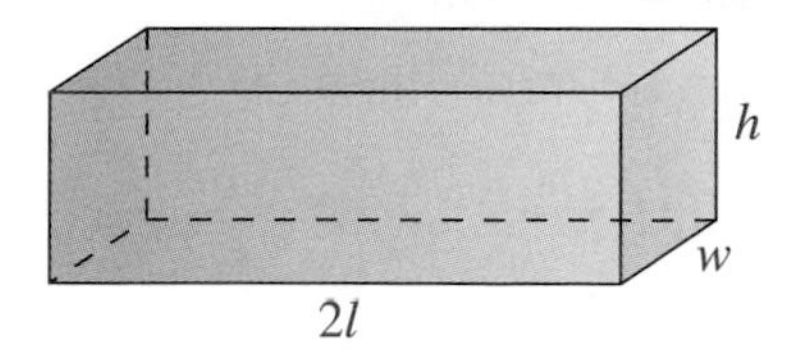

Mixed REVIEW

Solve.

1. $-6(m + 1) - 2m = 4$
2. $8 - 7m = -2m + 3$

Estimate.

3. 32% of 18
4. 96% of 15

Name the three-dimensional figure that can be formed by folding each pattern.

5.

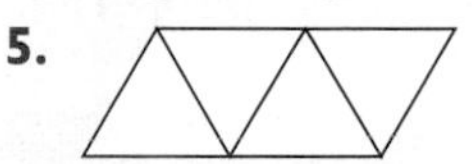

6.

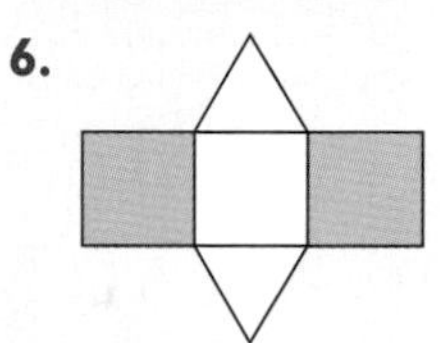

Extra SKILLS PRACTICE

Find the surface area of each rectangular prism.

1. 5 in. by 4 in. by 8 in.
2. 12 cm by 9 cm by 15 cm
3. 24 ft by 20 ft by 6 ft
4. 50 m by 45 m by 60 m
5. 32 ft by 28 ft by 10 ft
6. 70 in. by 70 in. by 85 in.
7. 8.2 m by 6.5 m by 10 m
8. 12.4 m by 10 m by 10 m

16. Which box will require more cardboard to make: a box 9 in. by 5.5 in. by 11.75 in. or a box 8 in. by 6.25 in. by 10.5 in.? Explain.

17. **Writing** Explain why opposite faces of a rectangular prism have equal areas but the faces of a triangular prism do not necessarily have equal areas.

18. Which of the following have right triangles for bases? If you can find the surface area, do so. If you can't, explain why.

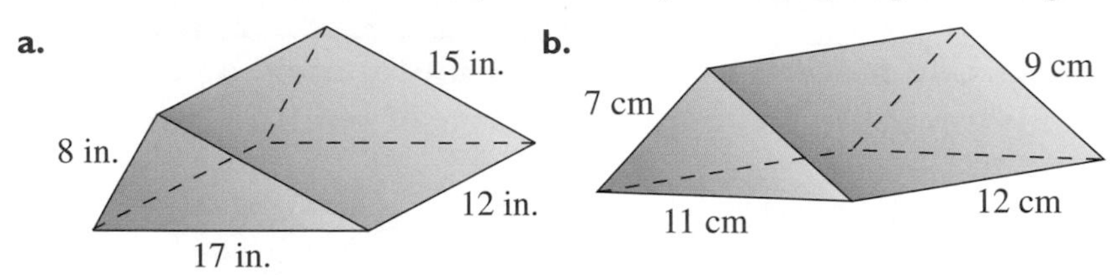

19. **Investigation (p. 464)** Describe the airspace over your local airport. What is the shape of the space? What is inside it? Where are the objects in relation to one another?

Use a ruler and graph paper to draw an example of each.

1. a cone
2. a cylinder
3. a hexagonal prism

Draw a pattern for each.

4. a triangular pyramid
5. a cube with an edge of 3 cm

Find the area of each shaded region. Use 3.14 for π.

6.

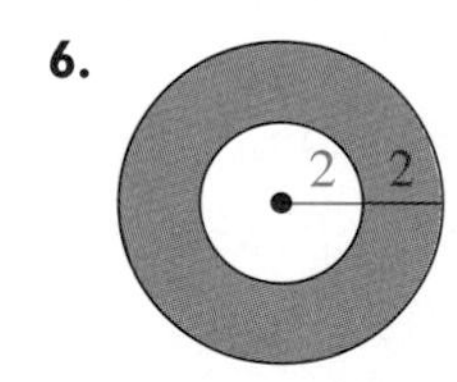

7.

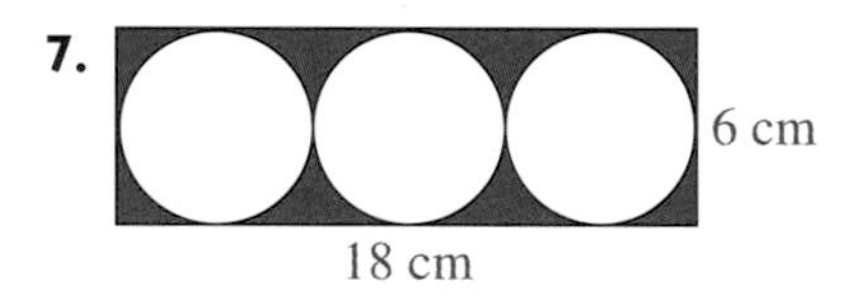

Draw a diagram and find the surface area of each.

8. a cube with an edge of 8 cm

9. a rectangular prism with a height of 5.5 cm and whose base is 8.5 cm by 6 cm.

10. a triangular prism with a height of 12 cm whose base is a right triangle with legs of 7 cm and 24 cm.

Although they look like hexagonal crystals, the steps of the Giant's Causeway in Northern Ireland were actually formed from lava as it cooled.

Source: *Crystal & Gem*

What's Ahead

- Finding the surface area of a cylinder

11-4 Surface Area of Cylinders

WHAT YOU'LL NEED

✓ $8\frac{1}{2}$ in. × 11 in. paper 

✓ Tape 

✓ Calculator  

✓ Ruler

✓ Compass  

✓ Scissors 

WORK TOGETHER

You have seen that a pattern for a cylinder involves a rectangle and two circular regions. Suppose you use a $8\frac{1}{2}$ in. by 11 in. sheet of paper for the rectangle. What size will the circles be? Does it matter which way you roll the sheet of paper?

- Work with a partner. Roll two $8\frac{1}{2}$ in. by 11 in. sheets of paper different ways. Tape the edges together to form the curved sides of two cylinders.
- Determine the circumference of each circular base. Use a calculator to determine each radius.
- Use a compass to draw the circular bases. Cut the bases out and tape them to the curved sides.

THINK AND DISCUSS

Using Patterns The **surface area** of a cylinder is the sum of the areas of the bases and the area of the curved surface.

1. **Calculator** What are the surface areas of the two cylinders you made in the Work Together activity? Give your answers to the nearest tenth of a square inch.

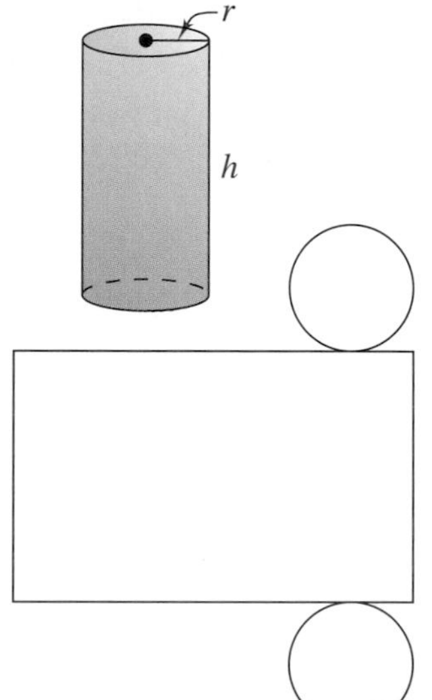

The dimensions of a cylinder usually are given in terms of the radius r of a base and the height h of the cylinder.

As you saw in the Work Together activity, the size of each circular base of a cylinder is related to one of the dimensions of the rectangle in the pattern for the cylinder.

2. In terms of r and/or h, what is the area of one base of the cylinder? What is the area of both bases?

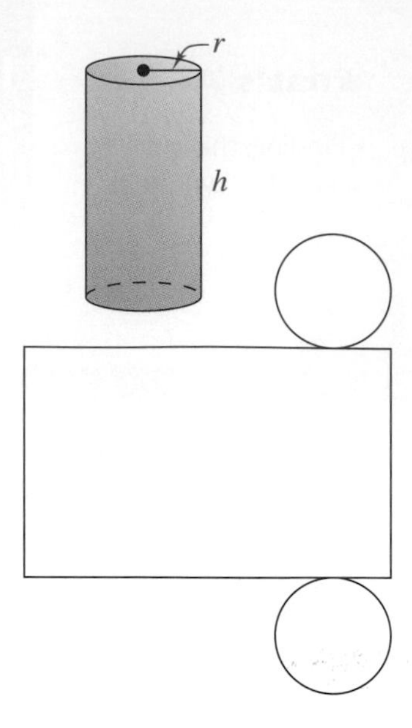

3. a. In terms of r and/or h, what are the dimensions of the rectangle in the pattern for the cylinder?

   b. In terms of r and/or h, what is a formula for the area of the rectangle?

Using Formulas Adding the formulas for the areas in the pattern for a cylinder gives the formula for the surface area.

Surface Area of a Cylinder
Surface area of a cylinder $= 2\pi r^2 + 2\pi rh$

In 1962, Andy Warhol did a series of 32 nearly identical canvases of 200 Campbell's soup cans. Warhol painted with the aid of 32 handcut stencils, one for each variety of soup.

Source: *Pop Art*

4. a. The area of each base of a cylinder is expressed in square units. Why?

   b. The area of the cylinder's curved side is expressed in square units. Why?

   c. In what type of unit is the surface area of a cylinder expressed? Explain.

Example Find the surface area of the cylinder to the nearest square centimeter.

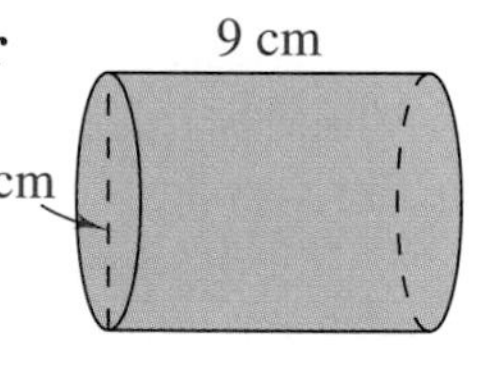

- First find r.

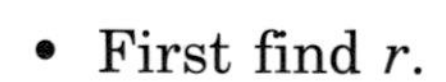

- Surface area $= 2\pi r^2 + 2\pi rh$

  $= 2\pi \cdot 3.5^2 + 2\pi \cdot 3.5 \cdot 9$

2 × π × 3.5 x^2 = 76.96902

The surface area of the cylinder is about 275 cm^2.

5. a. Find the surface area of the cylinder to the nearest square inch.
   b. How many square inches are there in a square foot?
   c. What is the surface area of the cylinder to the nearest square foot?

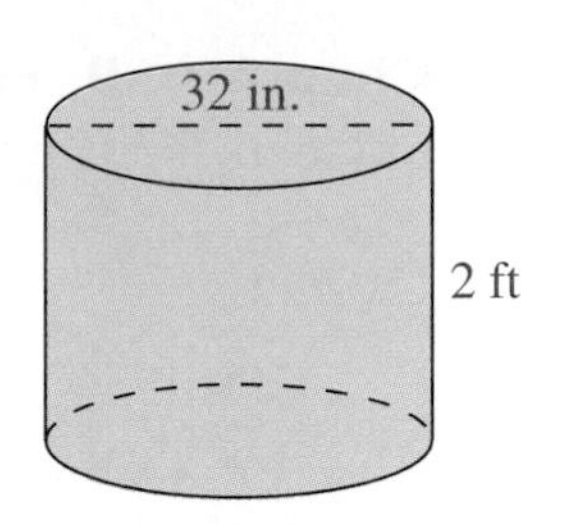

TRY THESE

Calculator **Find the surface area of each cylinder to the nearest square unit.**

6. 

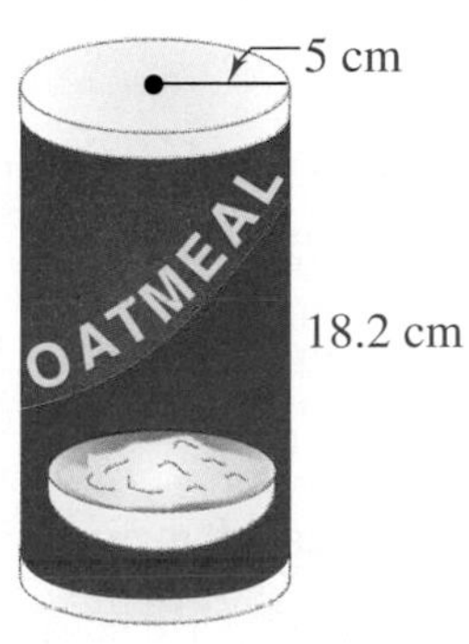

7. 

ON YOUR OWN

Calculator **Find the surface area of each three-dimensional figure to the nearest square unit.**

8. 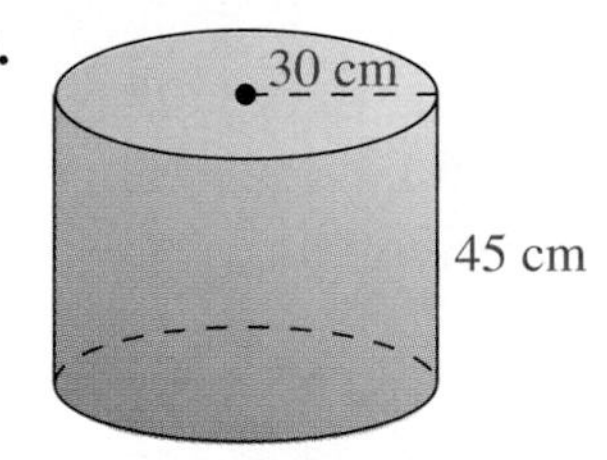

9. 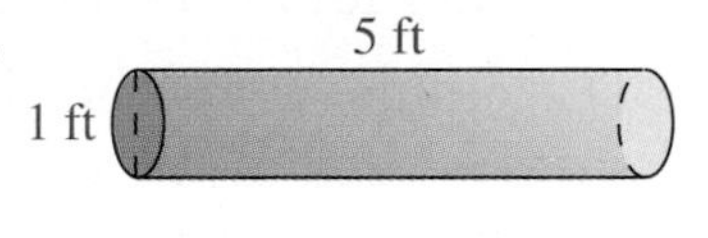

10. 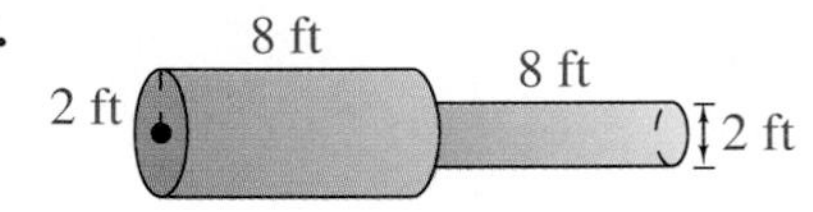

11. 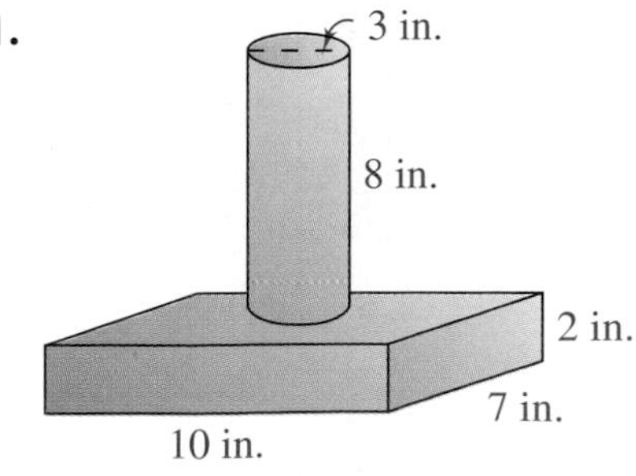

Mixed REVIEW

Solve each inequality and graph the solution on a number line.

1. $4b - 2 \geq 8$
2. $-3 < -2y + 1$

Write each fraction as a decimal and a percent.

3. $\frac{5}{8}$ 4. $\frac{1}{9}$

Draw a diagram and find the surface area.

5. a cube with an edge 3 cm long
6. a rectangular prism with a height of 5 cm and a base 4 cm by 6 cm
7. a triangular prism with a height of 10 cm and a right triangle base with legs of 3 cm and 4 cm

The world's largest oil tanks are located in Ju'ayman, Saudi Arabia. The five cylindrical tanks are each 72 ft tall and have a diameter of 386 ft. **If the outside of one of these tanks was being painted, how much surface area would the paint cover?**

Source: *The Guinness Book of Records*

Extra SKILLS PRACTICE

Find the surface area of each cylinder to the nearest square unit.

1. $r = 12$ ft, $h = 15$ ft
2. $r = 6$ cm, $h = 10$ cm
3. $r = 2$ yd, $h = 14$ yd
4. $r = 5$ mm, $h = 9$ mm
5. $r = 2.5$ m, $h = 6.5$ m
6. $d = 8$ ft, $h = 12$ ft
7. $d = 20$ in., $h = 15$ in.
8. $d = 6$ ft, $h = 8$ ft
9. $d = 3$ cm, $h = 6$ cm
10. $d = 4.2$ m, $h = 5.3$ m

12. **Choose A, B, or C.** Which of the following could be a pattern for a cylinder?

A. 

B. 
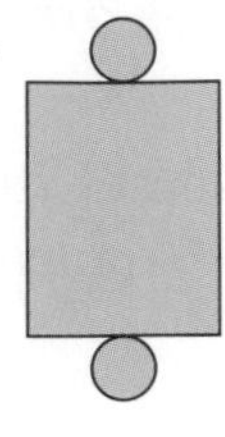

C. 

13. All exterior surfaces of a cylindrical storage tank need painting. The diameter of the tank is 20 ft. Its height is 12.5 ft. Each gallon of paint will cover 325 ft^2. How many gallons of paint are needed? Explain.

14. The surface area of a cylinder is about 814 in.^2. The radius of each base is $6\frac{1}{4}$ in. Find the height of the cylinder.

15. a. **Writing** Explain how you can find the area of a circle if you know its circumference.

    b. Explain how you can find the circumference of a circle if you know its area.

16. a. Suppose the base radius and height of a cylinder are equal. What is an expression for the surface area of the cylinder in terms of the radius r?

    b. The radius and height of a cylinder are equal. The surface area of the cylinder is about 1963.5 cm^2. What are the radius and height of the cylinder?

    c. The diameter and height of a cylinder are equal. The surface area of the cylinder is about 1963.5 cm^2. What are the diameter and height of the cylinder?

Mental Math Estimate each surface area.

17. 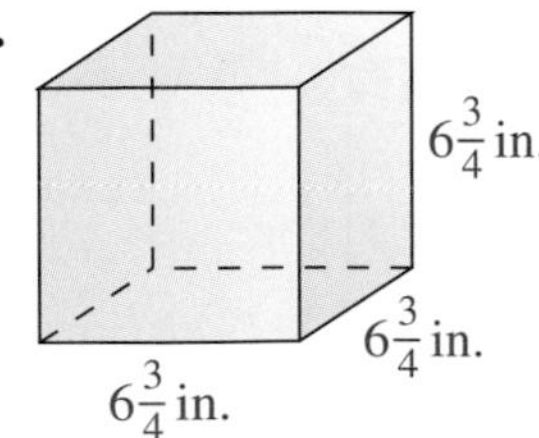

18. 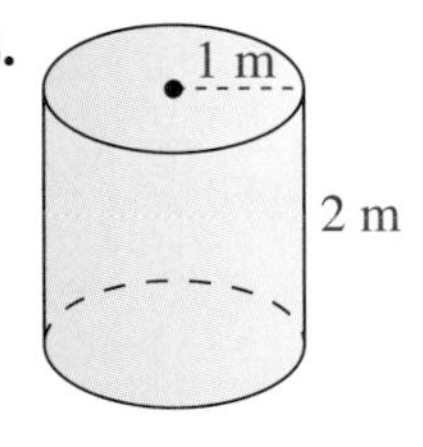

What's Ahead

- Finding the volume of rectangular and triangular prisms

11-5 Volume

THINK AND DISCUSS

Using Formulas The **volume** of a 3-dimensional figure is the number of cubic units needed to fill the space inside it.

1. Each edge of the cube on the left below is 1 cm long.
   a. **Estimation** Estimate the number of these cubes it would take to fill the rectangular prism shown.
   b. How did you estimate your answer to part (a)?

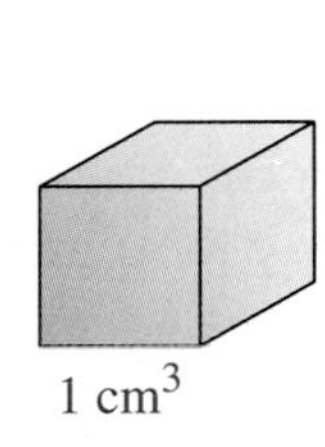

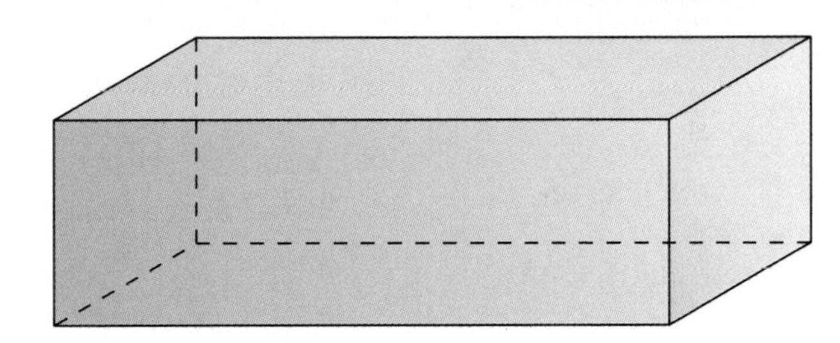

You can express the volume V of a rectangular prism as the product of the length l, width w, and height h.

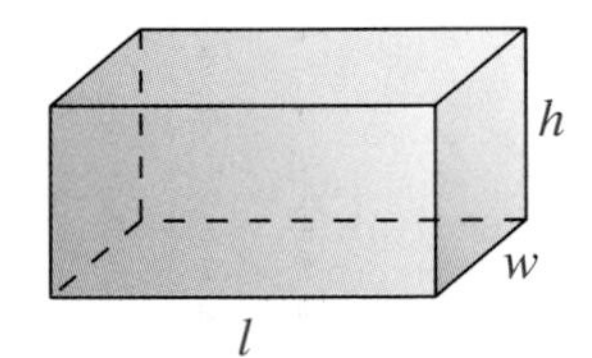

Volume of a Rectangular Prism

$$V = lwh$$

2. Suppose B represents the area of a base of a rectangular prism. What is the formula for the volume in terms of B? Why?

3. a. **Critical Thinking** How would you find the volume of this triangular prism?
   b. Find the volume.
   c. Did you need to use all the given dimensions? Explain.

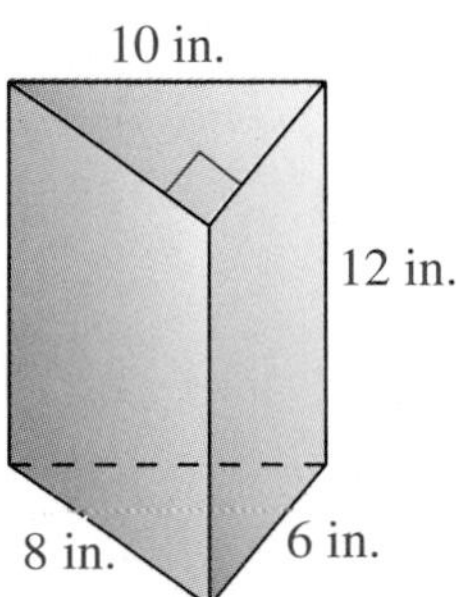

Solving Problems Landscape gardeners improve land by planting flowers, shrubs, and trees. Landscaping often involves area and volume. For example, suppose your class is helping to landscape part of a park near your school.

4. You need to add 4 in. of topsoil to a garden area 12 ft by 3 ft. How many cubic feet of topsoil do you need?

Your class is going to plant bulbs in an area shaped like a right triangle with legs 6 ft long.

5. First your class decides to improve the soil by adding peat moss to it. You will use a 3 in. layer of peat moss and mix it with the soil to a depth of about 8 in. How many cubic feet of peat moss do you need?

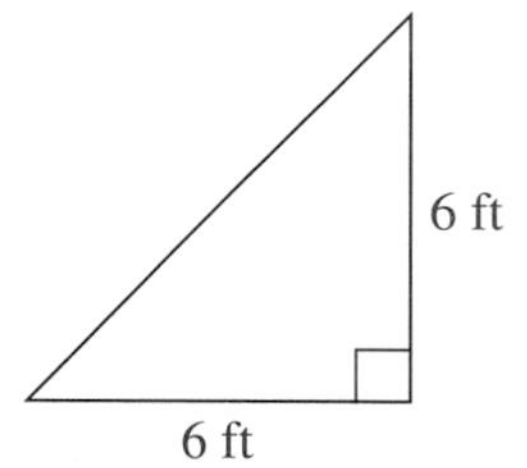

6. You are going to plant the bulbs about 6 in. apart. About how many bulbs can you plant in the triangular garden?

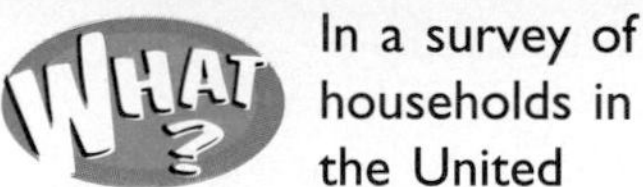

In a survey of households in the United States, the Gallup organization found that 48% were engaged in flower gardening and 37% in vegetable gardening.

Source: *Statistical Abstract of the United States*

WORK TOGETHER

Discuss with your group which of the following situations involve only area and which of the following situations involve volume. Explain your reasoning.

7. determining how large a region you can fence with a certain amount of fencing

8. determining how much water you need in order to fill a small cement pond

9. determining how many bricks you need in order to build a walkway

10. determining how much cement you need in order to build a sidewalk

11. Do the situations that involve volume also involve area? Explain.

ON YOUR OWN

Choose Use a calculator, paper and pencil, or mental math to find the volume of each figure to the nearest cubic unit.

12.

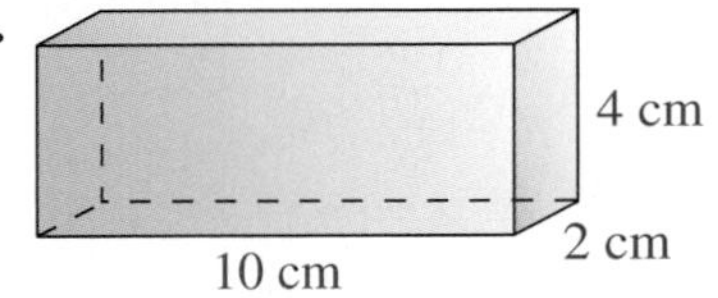

13.

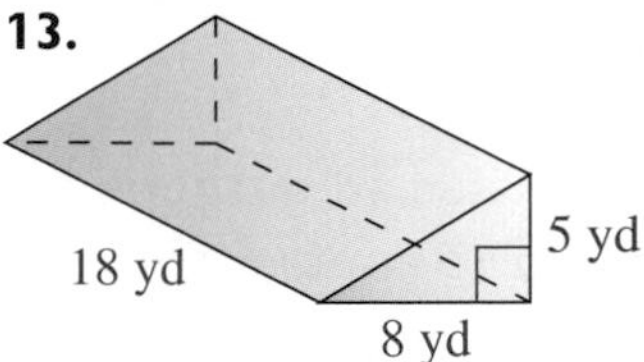

14.

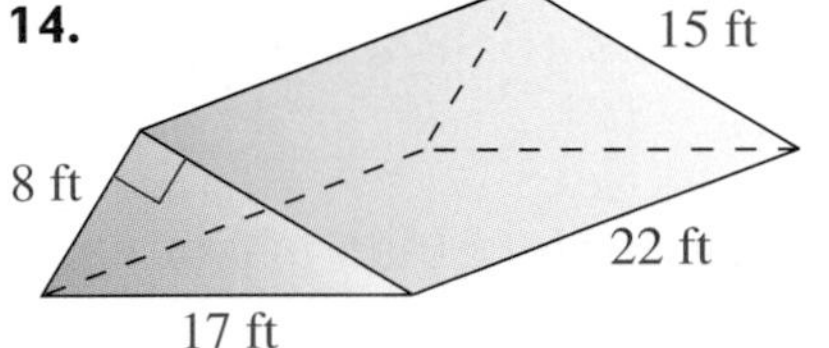

15.

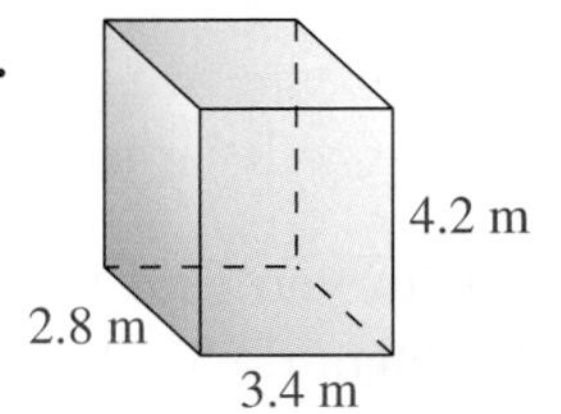

16. If you have a wood-burning stove and do not have your own wood to cut, you probably buy wood by the *cord.* A *cord* of wood is equal to a stack of wood 8 ft by 4 ft by 4 ft.

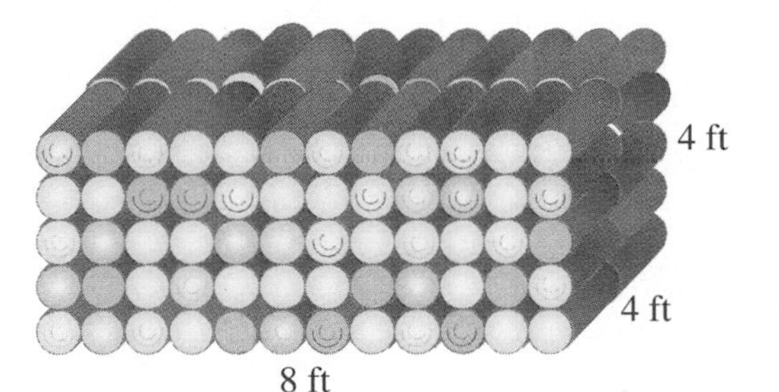

a. How many cubic feet is a cord?

b. A stack of wood is 10 ft by 8 ft by 4 ft. How many cords does it represent?

17. When you purchase concrete, you buy it by the cubic yard. Suppose you want to buy concrete for a patio 27 ft by 16 ft by 6 in.

a. How many *cubic feet* of concrete will you need? How many *cubic yards*?

b. Concrete costs $55/yd^3. How much will the concrete for the patio cost?

18. Suppose you are planning a rectangular garden 20 ft by 4 ft 6 in. You want to buy enough topsoil to add 4 in. to your garden.

a. How many cubic feet of topsoil do you need?

b. **Calculator** If topsoil is $1.79/ft^3, how much will the topsoil cost?

Extra SKILLS PRACTICE

Find the volume of each rectangular prism.

1. 16 in. by 12 in. by 20 in.
2. 8 ft by 7 ft by 10 ft
3. 10 cm by 8 cm by 15 cm
4. 12 yd by 12 yd by 20 yd
5. 4 mm by 3 mm by 10 mm
6. 20 ft by 15 ft by 8 ft
7. 5 in. by 2 in. by 17 in.
8. 3.5 cm by 3 cm by 8 cm
9. 6.1 m by 5.5 m by 3.3 m
10. 0.2 m by 0.1 m by 3.5 m

Mixed REVIEW

Estimate each square root.

1. $\sqrt{150}$
2. $\sqrt{75}$
3. $\sqrt{110}$
4. $\sqrt{200}$

Find the surface area of each cylinder with the given height and radius. Use 3.14 for π.

5. $h = 15$ in., $r = 6$ in.
6. $h = 5.6$ cm, $r = 2.8$ cm

7. Find the surface area of the largest cylinder which can fit into a cube with a side of 10 cm.

19. You plan to incorporate 3 in. of peat moss in a rectangular garden area that is 9 ft 6 in. by 4 ft.
   a. How much peat moss do you need?
   b. How much will the peat moss cost? Explain.

20. Mulch is used in gardens to conserve water and to control weeds.
   a. You plan to use 4 in. of mulch on a garden area 18 ft by 6 ft. How much mulch do you need?
   b. The mulch you are going to use costs $6.99 for a 3 ft^3 bag. What will be the total cost?

21. **Writing** Can you find the volume of a triangular prism by using the formula $V = \frac{1}{2}bh^2$? Explain.

GREAT EXPECTATIONS

Pastry Chef

One of the jobs that I would like to do when I grow up is be a pastry chef. In the pastry business, there are many math problems that I would have to solve. If I were baking apple puffs for a party, I would need to figure out how many apples I would need to make enough slices to fill the dough. If I had to bake something for a large group of people, I would have to determine how much each person would get so I'd be sure to have enough.

Where did you get your education and training? Should I enroll in a vocational high school program? Do all of the best pastry chefs go to fancy schools?

Shateel Alam

22. If e is the length of each edge of a cube, what is the formula for the volume of the cube?

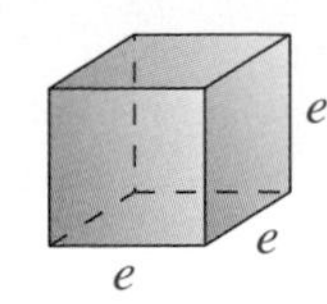

23. **Hobbies** An aquarium is 22 in. long, 15 in. wide, and 14 in. high.

    a. **Calculator** What is the volume of the aquarium?

    b. A gallon of water occupies 231 $in.^3$ of space. If the aquarium is filled to the top, how many gallons does it hold?

24. One base of a triangular prism is shown. The volume of the prism is 315 ft^3. What is the height of the prism?

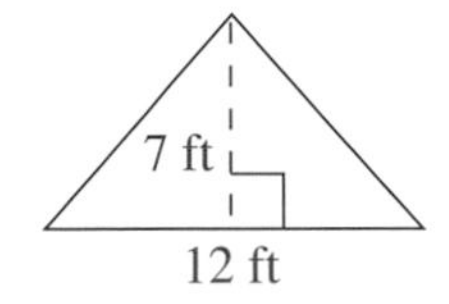

Dear Shateel,

Congratulations on your interest in pursuing one of the most stable, creative, and enjoyable careers. Math is extremely important in pastry production. Measurements must be accurate to make consistent products. Knowing how much to buy, when to buy it, and how much you need to charge to sell your item is critical. Setting your prices requires you to calculate cost, plus overhead, plus profit. You need to compare your price with others in your area. You must know metrics when making European pastries.

Education in the pastry field is very important because bakery/pastry is classified as a science. A vocational school can prepare you with the science and math you need to be able to choose the right bowls, utensils, ingredients, and temperatures needed to create pastry that will give you a leading edge.

John Fitzpatrick,
Director of Food Service,
Minuteman Vocational School

TECHNOLOGY

What's Ahead

- Exploring volume and surface area of rectangular prisms

11-6 Changing Dimensions

WHAT YOU'LL NEED

✓ Calculator

THINK AND DISCUSS

Exploring Volume The tropical fish at the Bay City Aquarium have outgrown their tank. The manager has ordered a new, larger tank that is twice as long, twice as wide, and twice as high as the old tank. Will the new tank hold twice as much water?

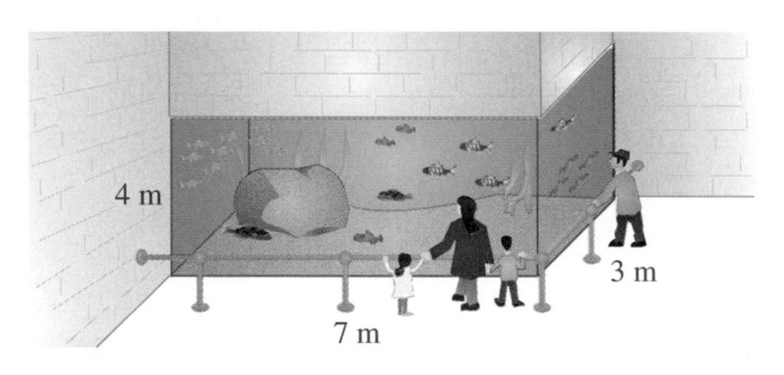

The Tennessee Aquarium has the largest freshwater tank in the world. It holds 137,000 gal.

Source: *Popular Science*

1. a. What is the volume of the old tank?
   b. What are the dimensions of the new tank?
   c. What is the volume of the new tank?
   d. How many times greater is the volume of the new tank than the volume of the old tank?

2. a. **Calculator** The aquarium manager is surprised by this result. She wants to see if the result will be the same for other tanks. Copy and complete the table below. Make up your own dimensions for the original size of a third tank.

Original Size		Doubled Dimensions		New Vol.
Dimensions (ft)	Vol. (ft^3)	Dimensions (ft)	Vol. (ft^3)	÷ Old Vol.
$1 \times 1 \times 1$	■	■	■	■
$3 \times 3 \times 8$	■	■	■	■
■	■	■	■	■

   b. **Critical Thinking** What happens to the volume of a rectangular prism when you double all the dimensions?

3. a. **Calculator** Make a new table showing what happens when you triple the dimensions of a rectangular prism. Include a 1 ft by 1 ft by 1 ft prism and a 3 ft by 3 ft by 8 ft prism. Make up your own dimensions for a third prism.

   b. **Critical Thinking** How does the volume change when you *triple* all the dimensions?

4. a. **Calculator** Make a table that shows what happens when you quadruple the dimensions of a rectangular prism. Include a 1 ft by 1 ft by 1 ft prism and a 3 ft by 3 ft by 8 ft prism. Make up your own dimensions for a third prism.

   b. **Critical Thinking** What happens to the volume when you *quadruple* all the dimensions?

5. **Critical Thinking** Suppose you multiply all the dimensions of a rectangular prism by n. What do you think would happen to the volume?

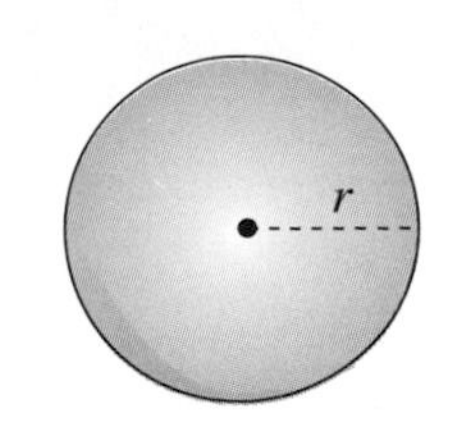

WHAT? To find the volume of a sphere with radius r, use the formula $V = \frac{4}{3}\pi r^3$. **A sphere has radius 3 cm. If the radius is doubled, how is the volume affected?**

WORK TOGETHER

Exploring Surface Area Work with your group. Double each dimension of the rectangular prisms. What happens?

6. **Calculator** Copy and complete the table. Make up your own dimensions for the original size of a fourth prism.

Original Size		Doubled Dimensions		New S.A.
Dimensions (ft)	S.A. (ft^2)	Dimensions (ft)	S.A. (ft^2)	÷ Old S.A.
1 × 1 × 1	■	■	■	■
3 × 3 × 8	■	■	■	■
6.5 × 6.5 × 6.5	■	■	■	■
■	■	■	■	■

7. **Critical Thinking** What happens to the surface area of a rectangular prism when you double all the dimensions?

8. When you double every dimension of a prism, which increases by a greater factor—the volume or the surface area?

ON YOUR OWN

9. a. What happens to the surface area of a rectangular prism when you triple each dimension? Give reasons for your answer.

   b. What happens to the surface area of a rectangular prism when you quadruple each dimension? Give reasons for your answer.

   c. **Critical Thinking** Suppose you multiply all the dimensions of a rectangular prism by n. What do you think would happen to the surface area?

WHAT? The smallest optical (triangular) prism was created by researchers at the National Institute of Standards and Technology. Each side measures just 0.001 in. It will be used for fiber optics and instrumentation research.

Source: *Guinness Book of Records*

10. A rectangular prism is 5 cm by 8 cm by 3 cm.

    a. What are the volume and surface area of the prism?

    b. If you triple each dimension of the prism, what are the new volume and surface area?

11. a. Find the volume and surface area of the triangular prism.

    b. If you double each dimension of the prism, what are the new volume and surface area?

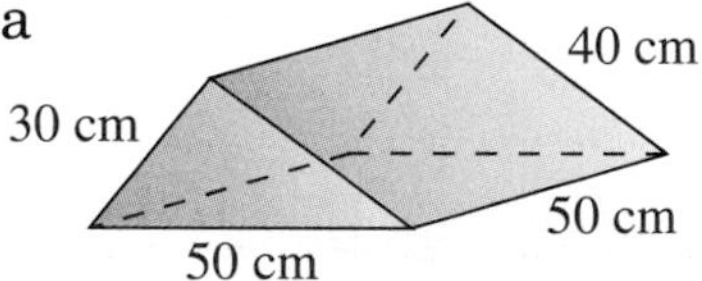

12. a. If you double only one dimension of a rectangular prism, how does the volume change?

    b. If you double exactly two dimensions of a rectangular prism, how does the volume change?

13. **Choose A, B, C, or D.** Which prisms contain about half as much water as the prism at the left?

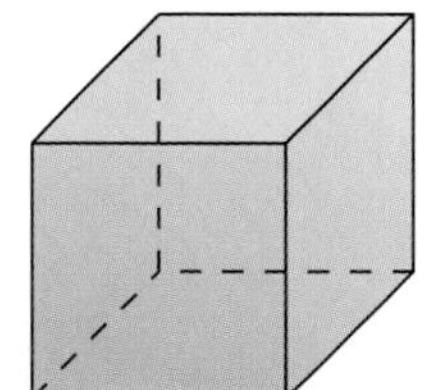

I.

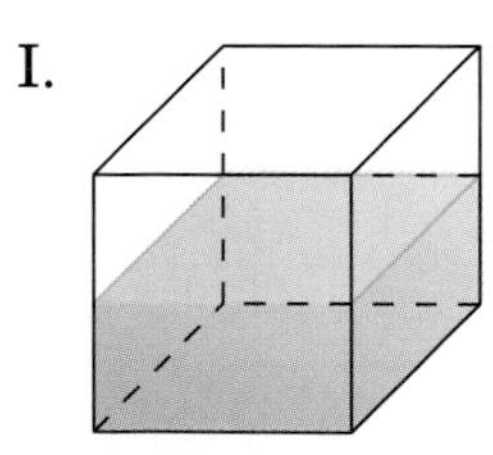

II.

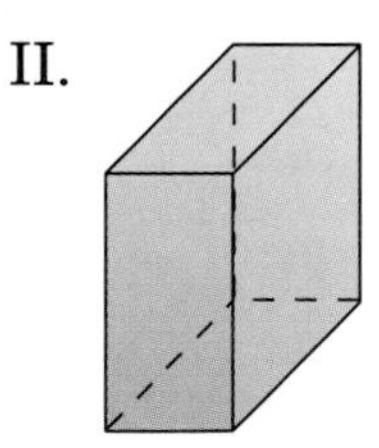

III.

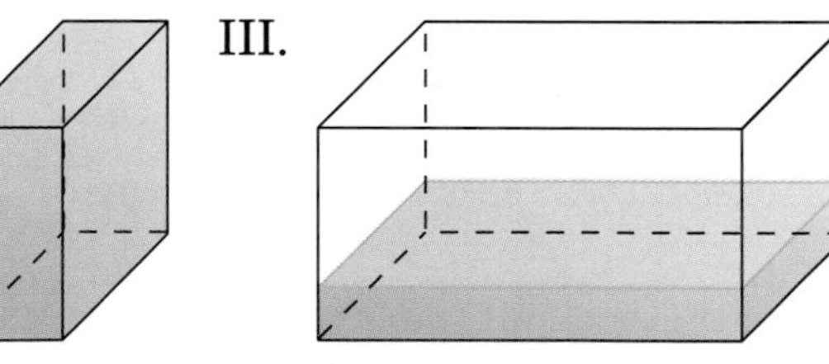

A. I only

B. I and II

C. I and III

D. I, II, and III

14. Find the length of each edge of a cube that has volume twice that of the cube shown. Give your answer to the nearest tenth of a centimeter.

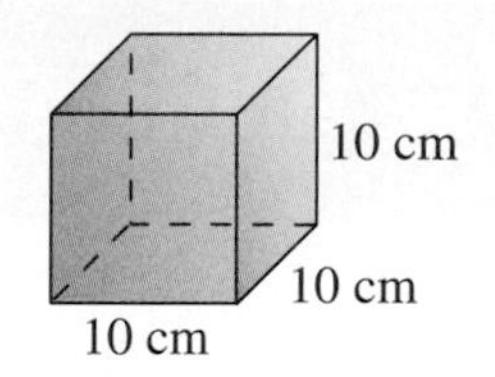

Problem Solving Hint

Use Guess and Test and a calculator.

15. The surface area of this rectangular prism is 222 in.^{2}. The volume is 189 in.^{3}.

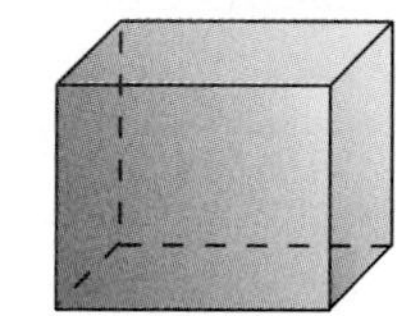

a. If all dimensions are doubled, what will be the new surface area and volume?

b. If all dimensions are tripled, what will be the new surface area and volume?

16. **Data File II (pp. 462–463)** If each dimension of the annual garbage heap doubles, what would be the new weight?

17. The surface area of a rectangular prism is 54 m^2. The volume is 40 m^3. If each dimension is multiplied by 5, what will be the new surface area and volume?

18. If the dimensions of a rectangular prism are halved, what will happen to the volume? to the surface area?

19. **Writing** Do you think that this advertisement is accurate or misleading? Explain.

Channel 5 has twice as many viewers as channel 4

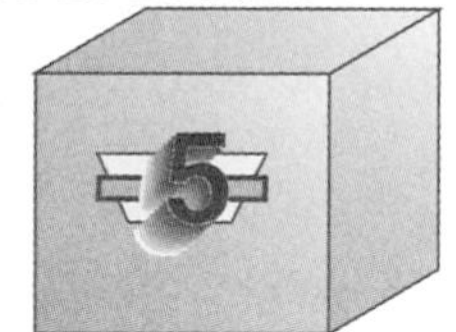

20. The box at the right holds 14 oz of rice.

a. Design a box to hold 28 oz of rice. Be sure to give the dimensions of the box.

b. **Research** Check the prices of different-sized containers of the same item at a local store. Does the store generally charge twice as much for a box that holds twice as much? Why do you think this is so?

Mixed REVIEW

1. The odds in favor of winning a prize are 1 to 99,999. What is the probability of winning?

2. Find the probability of getting all heads when three coins are tossed.

Simplify.

3. $\frac{4}{9} + \frac{1}{4}$

4. $\frac{2}{3} \cdot \frac{3}{4}$

5. $\frac{4}{5} \div \frac{9}{10}$

6. $\frac{8}{9} - \frac{11}{12}$

7. Find the number of cubic feet of potting soil needed to fill 4 rectangular flower boxes that are 3 ft by 5 in. by 6 in.

What's Ahead

- Solving a problem by using more than one strategy

WHAT YOU'LL NEED

✓ Calculator 

PROBLEM SOLVING

11-7 Use Multiple Strategies

Often you need to use more than one problem solving strategy to solve a problem. Consider the following problem.

> You can cut square corners off a 9 in. by 12 in. piece of cardboard to get a pattern that you could use to form an open box, without a top. What dimensions, to the nearest half inch, will give the greatest volume?

READ

Read and understand the given information. Summarize the problem.

1. Think about the information you are given and what you are asked to find.
   a. What is the original size of the rectangle?
   b. What kind of figure are you going to cut off the corners?
   c. What kind of three-dimensional figure is to be formed? What dimensions will you need to know in order to find its volume?

PLAN

Decide on a strategy to solve the problem.

It is appropriate here to *use multiple strategies. Draw a diagram* to help you plan your solution. *Make a table* to organize the results. Then *test* all possible solutions. However, if you *look for a pattern* you may be able to find a way to shorten your work.

SOLVE

Try out the strategy.

2. Draw a diagram. Let x be the length of each side of each square cut off a corner.
   a. In terms of x, what will be the length, width, and height of the box?
   b. What is the maximum value of x? Why?
   c. What are the values of x you need to consider to solve the problem?

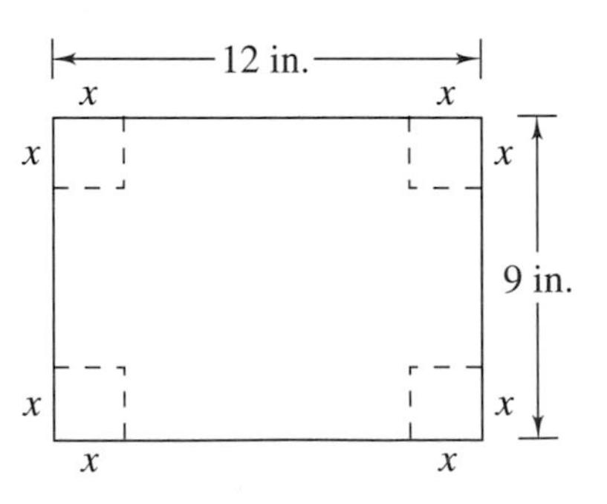

3. Find the volumes for different values of x. (A calculator may be helpful.) Make a table to organize your results. Look for a pattern.

x	length	width	height	volume
$\frac{1}{2}$ in.	■	■	■	■

4. a. What value of x, to the nearest half inch, will give the greatest volume?
   b. What would be the three dimensions of the box?
   c. What would be the greatest volume?

5. What patterns helped you to complete the table?

6. Find the value of x, to the nearest *quarter* inch, that will give the greatest volume.

LOOK BACK

Think about how you solved the problem.

TRY THESE

Use any strategy or combination of strategies to solve each problem.

7. Suppose you cut square corners off a 16 in. by 20 in. piece of cardboard to get a pattern for an open box. To the nearest half inch, what lengths for the sides of the squares will give the greatest volume?

8. A dog owner wants to use 200 ft of fencing to fence the greatest possible area for her dog. She wants the fenced area to be rectangular. What dimensions should she use?

U.S. sales of corrugated and paperboard boxes should reach $33 billion by 1996. The greatest percentage of boxes is used for packaging food and beverages.

Source: *Paperboard Packaging*

ON YOUR OWN

Use any strategy or combination of strategies to solve each problem. Show all your work.

9. How many non-straight angles can you find in this figure?

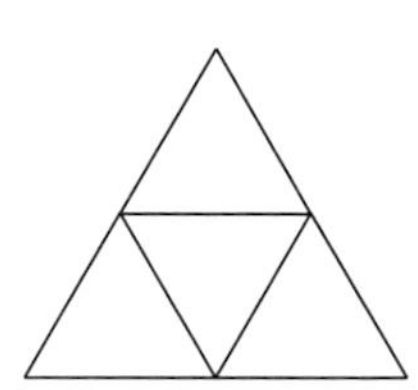

10. A customer gives you a $100 bill for a $64 purchase. In what ways can you give change if the customer will accept no more than six $1 bills?

A well-known computer game** uses arrangements of four squares in which each square shares a side with at least one other square. **How many ways can you arrange four cubes so that each cube shares a face with at least one other cube?

1. What is the sum of the measures of the angles of a 12-sided polygon?

2. What is the measure of each angle of a regular polygon with 10 sides?

Simplify.

3. $(-1)^9 \div 3^2 - 5$

4. $\sqrt{196} - (-2)^3$

The volume of a cube is n^3 cm^3. Write a variable expression for each.

5. the volume of the cube after the dimensions are tripled

6. the surface area of the cube after the dimensions are doubled

11. The largest room at the Civic Center is 150 ft long and 95 ft wide. The height of the room is 10 ft. If the occupancy guidelines recommend at least 200 ft^3 per person, what is the maximum number of people allowed in the room?

12. At a cafeteria, there are 3 choices of entrees, 4 choices of vegetables, 2 choices of salads, 3 choices of bread, and 2 choices of dessert. How many possible choices do you have if you choose one of each entree, vegetable, salad, bread, and dessert?

13. The figure shows a $3 \times 3 \times 3$ cube.

a. How many $1 \times 1 \times 1$ cubes are there?

b. How many $2 \times 2 \times 2$ cubes are there?

c. How many $3 \times 3 \times 3$ cubes are there?

d. How many cubes are there in all?

e. How many cubes are there in a $4 \times 4 \times 4$ cube?

14. Calculator A circle and a square each have area 144 cm^2. Is the circumference of the circle less than, greater than, or equal to the perimeter of the square?

15. The consecutive odd integers from 1 to n are 1, 3, 5, . . . , n. The square root of the sum of the integers is 10. What is the value of n?

16. Draw diagrams to show all the ways you can cut along the grid lines of a 4×4 square to form two congruent halves.

17. A hiker has 60 mi to walk in order to finish his trip. One day he walks 50% of the distance. The next day he walks 25% of the remaining distance. How much farther does he have to walk?

18. Four darts are thrown at this target. If each dart lands on the target, how many different point totals are possible?

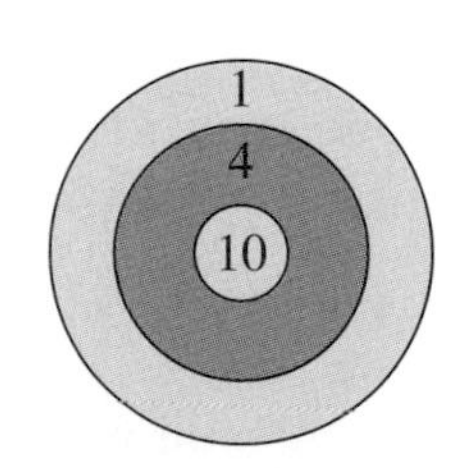

19. Each face of a cube can be painted either blue or yellow. How many different-looking cubes are possible?

What's Ahead

- Finding the volume of a cylinder

11-8 Volume of Cylinders

WHAT YOU'LL NEED

✓ Calculator 

Wedding cakes are often made using cylindrical baking pans. ***What is the volume of the cake above if each layer is 6 in. high, the diameter of the bottom layer is 12 in., and the layers decrease in diameter by 2 in.?***

FLASHBACK

One gallon of water occupies 231 $in.^3$ of space.

THINK AND DISCUSS

You can use the following formula to find the volume of a cylinder.

Volume of a Cylinder

$$V = \pi r^2 h$$

1. How is the formula for the volume of a cylinder related to the formula for the volume of a prism?

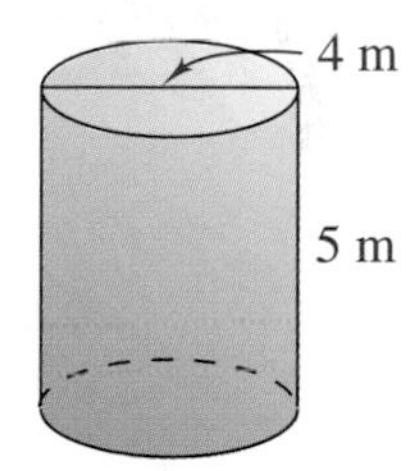

2. **Mental Math** Estimate the volume of the cylinder. Use 3 to estimate π.
3. **Calculator** Find the volume of the cylinder to the nearest cubic meter.

The amount of liquid a container can hold is measured in units such as quarts, gallons, liters (L), and milliliters (mL).

Example The diameter of a circular swimming pool is 20 ft. How many gallons of water will it take to fill the pool to a depth of 4 ft?

- $V = \pi r^2 h$

  $V = \pi \cdot 10^2 \cdot 4$ because $r = \frac{20}{2} = 10$.

  [π] [×] 10 [x^2] [×] 4 [=] 1256.6371

- Use dimensional analysis.

  $1256.6371 \text{ ft}^3 \cdot \frac{(12 \cdot 12 \cdot 12) \text{ in.}^3}{\text{ft}^3} \cdot \frac{1 \text{ gal}}{231 \text{ in.}^3}$

  1256.6371 [×] 12 [×] 12 [×] 12 [÷] 231 [=] 9400.2983

It will take about 9,400 gal.

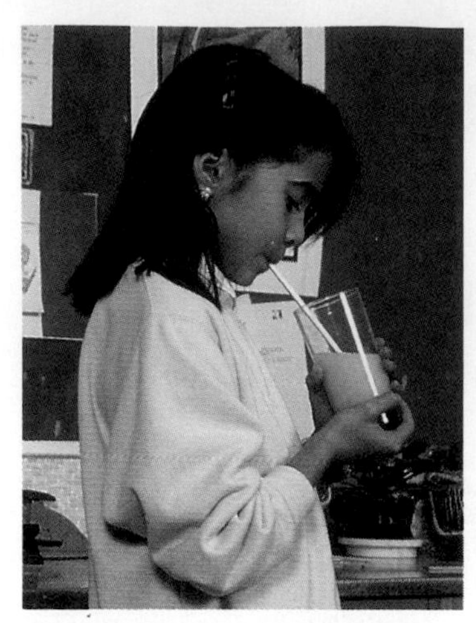

A typical straw is 19.4 cm high with a diameter of 0.6 cm. ***If 1 mL of water occupies 1 cm^3 of space, how much water can be contained in a straw?***

4. 1 mL of water occupies 1 cm^3 of space.

a. What is the volume in cubic centimeters of 1 L of water?

b. The *mass* of 1 cm^3 of water is 1 g. What is the mass of 1 L of water?

TRY THESE

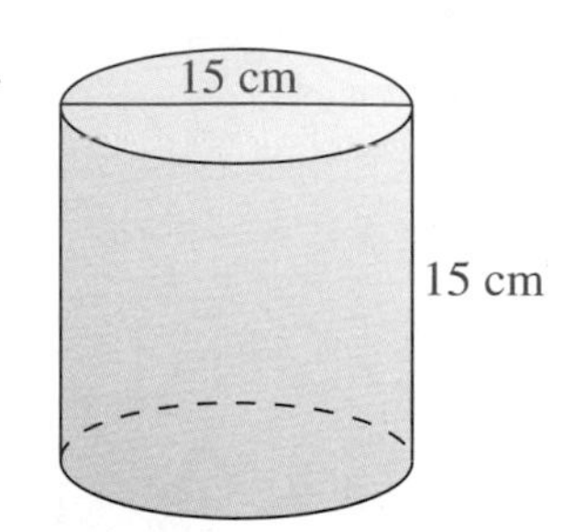

5. a. Estimate the volume of the cylinder.

b. Calculator What is the volume of the cylinder?

c. How much water can the cylinder hold?

d. If the cylinder is filled with water, what is the mass of the water?

6. The inside diameter of a cylindrical container is 8 cm. If 30 mL of a liquid is poured into the container, how much will the level rise?

ON YOUR OWN

Calculator Find the volume of each cylinder to the nearest cubic unit.

7. 4 in. 5.5 in.

8.

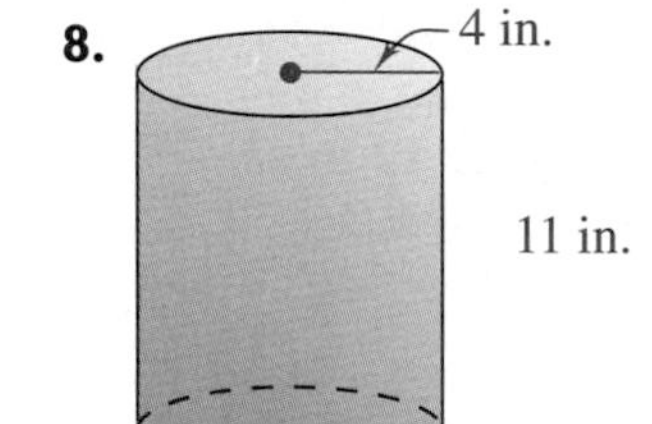

9.

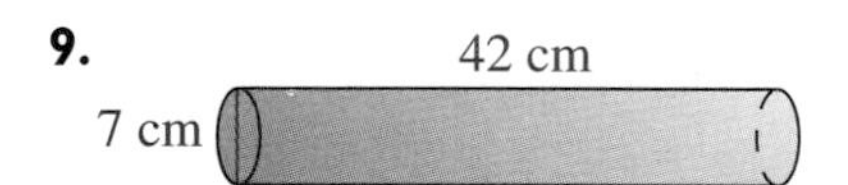

10.

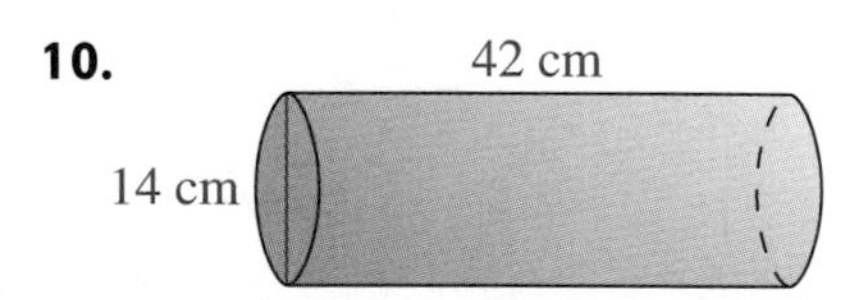

11. a. What is the ratio of the volumes of the cylinders in Exercises 7 and 8?

b. How does doubling the height affect the volume?

Find the volume of each cylinder to the nearest cubic unit.

1. $r = 3$ yd, $h = 9$ yd
2. $r = 20$ cm, $h = 10$ cm
3. $r = 5$ ft, $h = 8$ ft
4. $r = 4$ in., $h = 12$ in.
5. $r = 10$ m, $h = 15$ m
6. $d = 16$ ft, $h = 6$ ft
7. $d = 5$ mm, $h = 4$ mm
8. $d = 70$ in., $h = 40$ in.
9. $d = 9$ m, $h = 8.5$ m
10. $d = 7.6$ m, $h = 7.1$ m

12. **a.** What is the ratio of the volumes of the cylinders in Exercises 9 and 10?

    b. How does doubling the radius affect the volume?

13. **Choose A, B, C, or D.** How many times greater will the volume of a cylinder be if you triple the radius and the height?

    A. 3 times greater **B.** 9 times greater

    C. 27 times greater **D.** 81 times greater

14. The radius of the base of a cylindrical container is 7 in. The height is 15 in. About how many gallons of liquid can it hold?

15. **Data File 8 (pp. 336–337)** When launching a model rocket, a cylinder-shaped air space must be free of obstructions.

    a. Draw the cylinder of unobstructed air space necessary to launch a rocket with a type A engine. Then, find its volume in ft^3.

    b. Repeat part (a) for a type B engine.

    c. **Critical Thinking** How could you have found the answer to part (b) by using your answer to part (a)?

Rectangular designs** are the typical building blocks of American architecture. Other cultures, though, make use of a variety of geometric shapes as seen in these West African cylindrical houses. **What are some other examples of cylinders in architecture?

Salt of the Earth

Salt always comes in cylinders—or does it? The cylindrical cartons for salt were first used before World War I because boxes weren't very strong. In comparison, a salt container could support a person standing on it.

The Leslie Salt Co. decided to put its salt into 9 cm by 15 cm by 15 cm boxes to save space on grocery store shelves. Unfortunately, old habits die hard. The cylinders of salt sold out, while the boxes sat on the shelves.

16. **a.** What was the volume of the box of salt?

    b. If each cylinder of salt has a radius of 4 cm and a height of 13.5 cm, what is its volume?

    c. What is the most space-efficient way to place these cylindrical containers in a space that is 30 cm wide, 1 m long, and 14 cm high?

    d. Which shape would you buy? Explain.

Salt is a major source of sodium. Since processed foods often contain sodium, most people consume far more sodium than they actually need. A diet high in sodium can contribute to high blood pressure.

Source: *Health: Skills for Wellness*

17. **Science** To determine the volume of a bracelet, Jan drops it in a cylinder partially filled with water. The level of the water rises 8 cm when the bracelet is totally submerged. The diameter of the base of the cylinder is 12 cm.

   a. Find the volume of the bracelet.

   b. Jan weighs the bracelet and finds that it weighs 72.4 g. How many grams is that per cubic centimeter?

18. The volume of this cylinder is about 3,534 cm^3. Find the height.

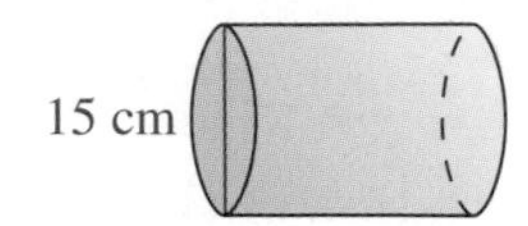

19. The volume of a cylinder is about 402 ft^3. The height is 8 ft.

   a. Calculator Find the radius of the cylinder.

   b. Writing Describe how you found the radius.

20. **Investigation (p. 464)** An air traffic control center may monitor an area covering 100,000 mi^2 of the earth's surface. If most air traffic is at or below an altitude of 8 mi, draw a cylinder with dimensions that approximate this air space.

CHECKPOINT

Find the surface area of each cylinder. Use 3.14 for π. Round each answer to the nearest tenth.

1. radius of base = 5 cm
   height = 9 cm

2. diameter of base = 8 cm
   height = 6 cm

Find the volume of each.

3.

4 cm
1.5 cm
6.5 cm

4.

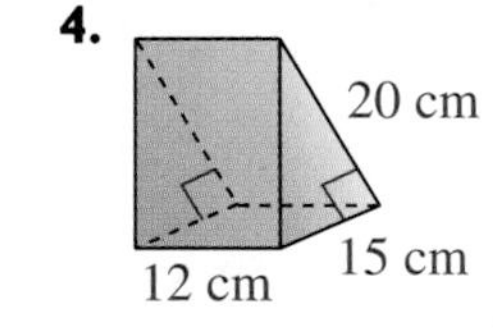

5.

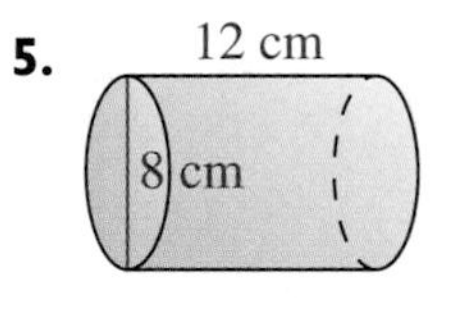

6. **Choose A, B, C, or D.** What happens to the volume of a cube if the length of each side is doubled?

   A. doubled
   B. tripled
   C. quadrupled
   D. multiplied by 8

7. A wading pool is 35 ft by 50 ft and is 2.5 ft deep. How much does it cost to fill the pool if water costs $1.78 per 100 ft^3?

Mixed REVIEW

Find each % of change. Label your answer as increase or decrease.

1. 45 to 60
2. 25 to 15
3. 16 to 12
4. 10 to 50

Solve using any strategy.

5. Find the dimensions of a cube whose surface area is the same number of cm^2 as the number of cm^3 in its volume.

6. Tyra has an average of 87 after taking 4 tests. Is it possible for Tyra to raise her average to a 90 by getting a high grade on the next test?

What's Ahead

- Finding the volume of a cone or pyramid

11-9 Volume of Cones and Pyramids

WHAT YOU'LL NEED

✓ Calculator 

THINK AND DISCUSS

Measuring Pyramids The volume of a given pyramid is related to the volume of a prism with a congruent base and the same height. Look at the cube at the right.

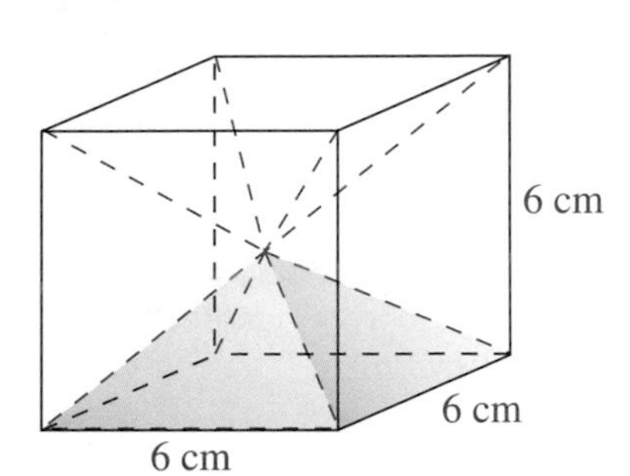

1. What is the volume of the cube?

Suppose the point in the center of the cube is connected to each vertex of the cube as shown. The cube would be divided into six congruent square pyramids.

2. Use the results of Question 1 to find the volume of each of the six congruent square pyramids.

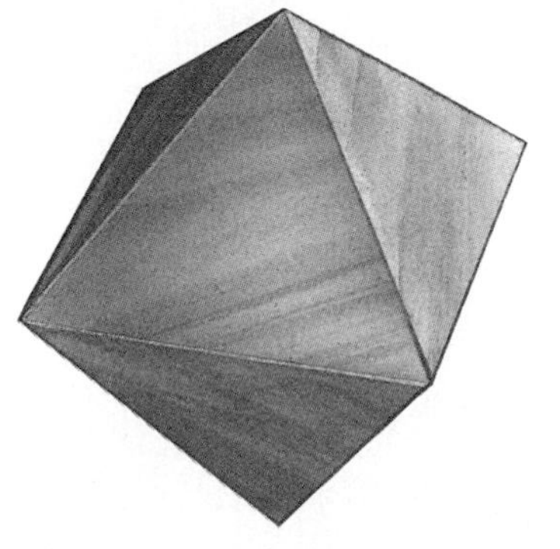

A common crystal** shape is the octahedron, which has eight equilateral triangular faces. **Describe this shape in terms of pyramids.

The perpendicular distance from the vertex of a pyramid to the base is the height h of the pyramid.

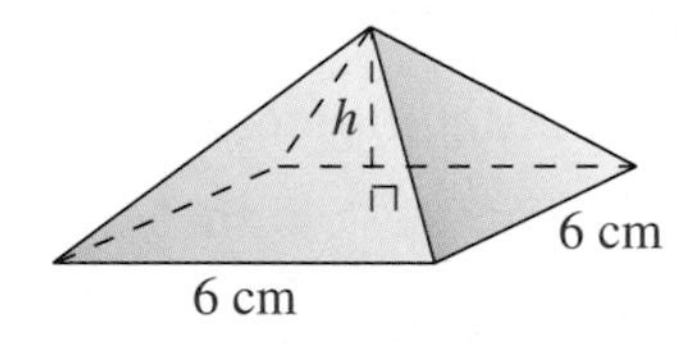

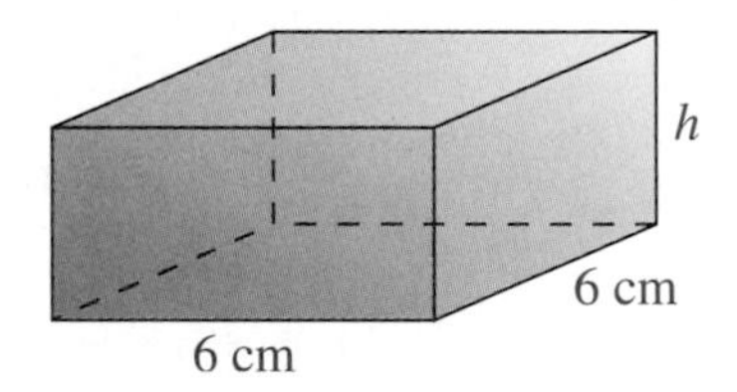

3. What is the height h of each of the six congruent square pyramids?

4. a. What is the volume of a rectangular prism whose bases are 6 cm by 6 cm and whose height h is the same as the height of the six congruent square pyramids?

   b. How do the volumes of the square pyramid and the rectangular prism compare?

***Pyramids** aren't just in Africa. The Temple of the Warriors at Chichen Itza in the Yucatan, Mexico, is one of hundreds of ancient pyramids.*

Source: *Collier's Encyclopedia*

This same relationship exists for *any* pyramid and prism with congruent bases and the same height. If B is the area of the base of a pyramid, you can use the following formula to find the volume.

Volume of a Pyramid

$$V = \frac{1}{3}Bh$$

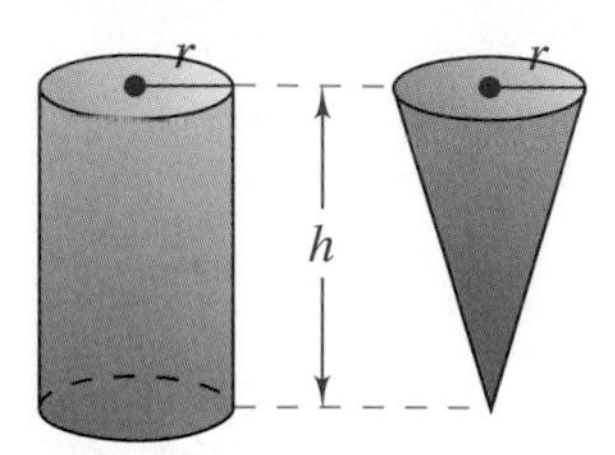

Measuring Cones A similar relationship exists for a cone and cylinder with congruent bases and the same height. If you filled a cone three times with sand and poured it into the cylinder, the cylinder would be filled.

Volume of a Cone

$$V = \frac{1}{3}Bh \qquad V = \frac{1}{3}\pi r^2 h$$

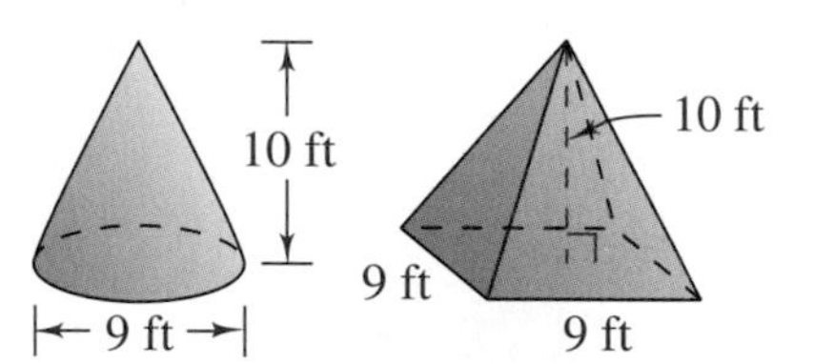

5. **a.** Find the volume of the cone.
   b. Find the volume of the pyramid.
   c. Critical Thinking What accounts for the difference in the volumes, even though the dimensions are the same?

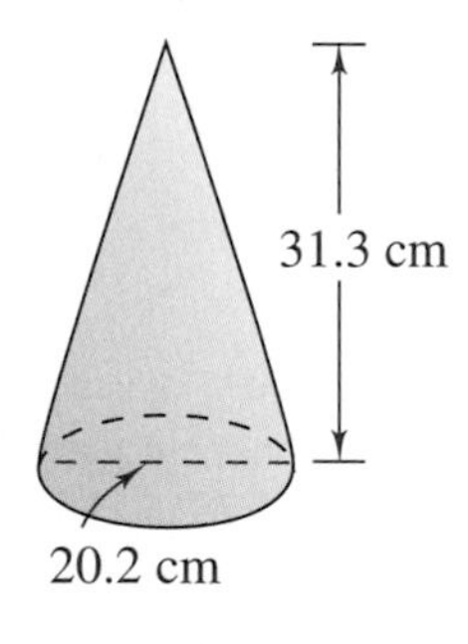

Example Estimate the volume of the cone.

- Estimate π and each dimension.
  $\pi \approx 3$, $r \approx 10$ cm, $h \approx 30$ cm
- Use $V = \frac{1}{3}\pi r^2 h$.
  $$V \approx \frac{1}{3} \cdot 3 \cdot 10^2 \cdot 30$$
  $$= 3{,}000$$

The volume of the cone is about 3,000 cm^3.

6. **Critical Thinking** Is the estimate in the Example higher or lower than the actual volume? Why?

7. The base of this pyramid is a right triangle with legs 175 cm and 90 cm long. The height is 400 cm.
   a. **Calculator** Find the volume of the pyramid.
   b. **Critical Thinking** What are two different ways to find the volume in cubic meters?
   c. Find the volume in cubic meters two different ways. Do your answers agree?

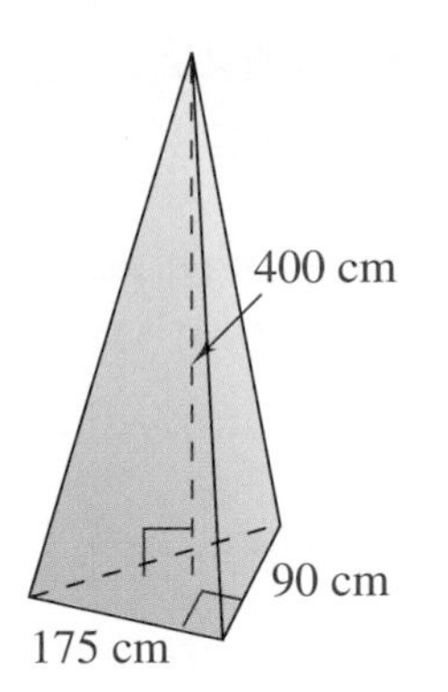

The Washington Monument is an obelisk, a tall thin pyramid topped by a small pyramid, called a pyramidion. At its base, the Monument is 55 ft 1.5 in. wide. It tapers to 34 ft 5.5 in. at the top of the 500 ft shaft. The pyramidion adds another 55 ft 1.5 in. to the height of the Monument. **Estimate the volume of the pyramidion.**

TRY THESE

Estimation Estimate the volume of each figure. Then use a calculator to find the volume to the nearest cubic unit.

8. $10\frac{1}{2}$ in. $3\frac{1}{4}$ in. 4 in.

9.

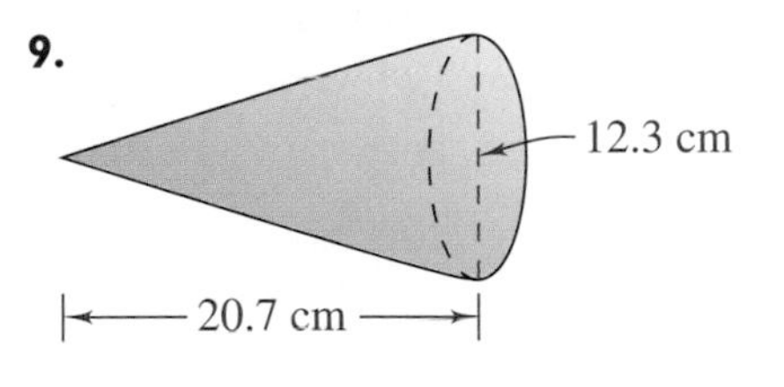

ON YOUR OWN

Choose Use mental math, paper and pencil, or a calculator to find each volume to the nearest cubic unit.

10.

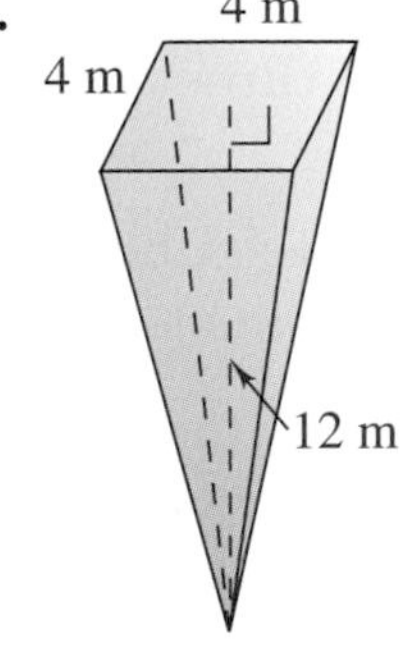

11.

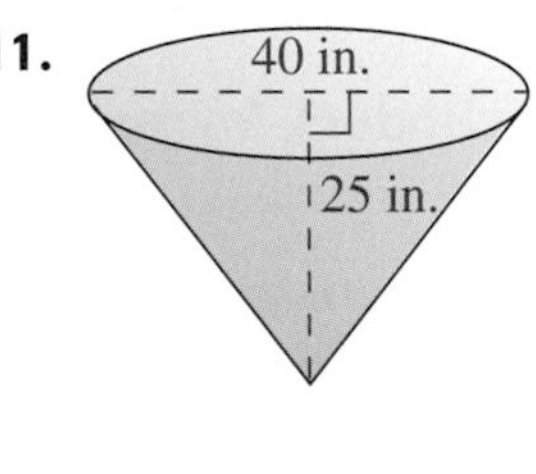

12. a triangular pyramid whose base is a right triangle with legs 3 cm and 4 cm long, and whose height is 6 cm

13. a cone with base radius 15 in. and height 35 in.

Extra SKILLS PRACTICE

Find the volume of each pyramid or cone.

1. $B = 20\text{ ft}^2$, $h = 12$ ft
2. $B = 9\text{ in.}^2$, $h = 4.5$ in.
3. $B = 16.25\text{ m}^2$, $h = 6$ m
4. $B = 50\text{ cm}^2$, $h = 6.5$ cm
5. $r = 3$ in., $h = 7$ in.
6. $r = 5$ ft, $h = 12$ ft
7. $d = 4$ m, $h = 4.5$ m

14. **Writing** Explain why you have to divide by 1,000,000 to change from cubic centimeters to cubic meters.

Find the missing dimension for each three-dimensional figure, given the volume and other dimensions.

15. rectangular pyramid, $l = 6$ m, $w = 3.5$ m, $V = 77$ m^3

16. cone, $r = 7$ in., $V \approx 626$ in.^{3}

17. square pyramid, $s = 9$ ft, $V = 324$ ft^3

18. square pyramid, $h = 7.5$ cm, $V = 40$ cm^3

19. cone, $h = 9$ in., $V \approx 681$ in.^{3}

$18\frac{3}{4}$ in.

$5\frac{1}{3}$ in.

20. Estimate the volume of the cone.

21. **Choose A, B, C, or D.** The volume of a cylinder with base radius x and height y is 600 cm^3. The radius and height of the cones below are given in terms of the same x and y. Which statements about their volumes must be correct?

I. vol. = 200 cm^3 II. vol. = 100 cm^3 III. vol. = 140 cm^3

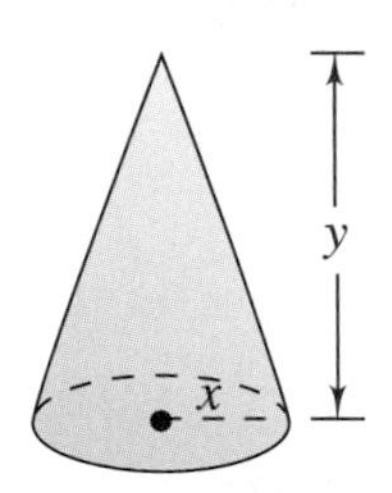

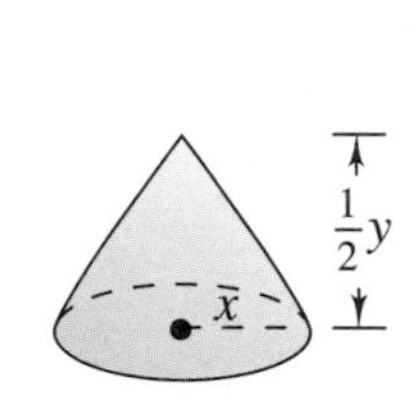

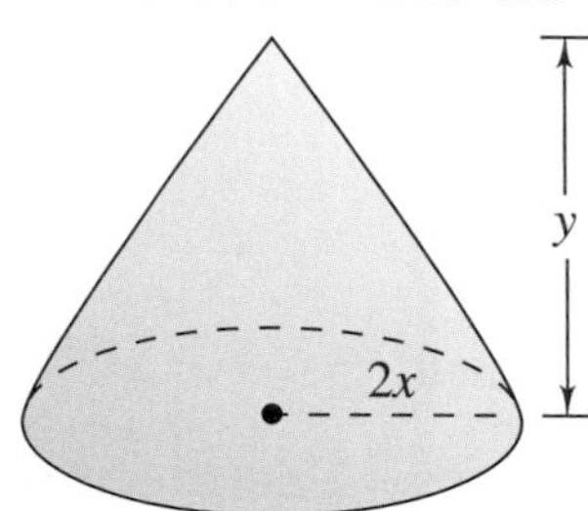

A. I only **B.** I and II **C.** I and III **D.** I, II, and III

22. Prisms, cylinders, pyramids, and cones are all three-dimensional figures.

  a. What happens to the volume of a cube if you double only one dimension? if you double exactly two dimensions? if you double all three dimensions?

  b. If you double the height, what happens to the volume of a cone?

  c. If you double the base radius, what happens to the volume of a cone?

  d. If you double both the height and base radius, what happens to the volume of a cone?

Mixed REVIEW

1. Find the area of the shaded region of circle A. Use 3.14 for π.

6 cm 8 cm

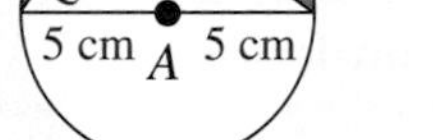

Simplify.

2. $5^{-3} \div 5^{-9}$ 3. $(-1)^{201}$

Find the volume of each. Use 3.14 for π.

4. a cylinder with a height of 4 in. and a base radius of 2 in.

5. the largest cylinder that can fit inside a rectangular prism with height 10 cm and a base 6 cm by 6 cm

Practice

Use centimeter graph paper to draw a pattern that can be folded to make each figure described below.

1. a cube with a side of 2 cm
2. a 3 cm by 4 cm by 5 cm rectangular prism
3. a triangular prism with a height of 6 cm and a base that is a right triangle with legs of 3 cm and 4 cm

Find the area of each shaded region. Use 3.14 for π.

4.

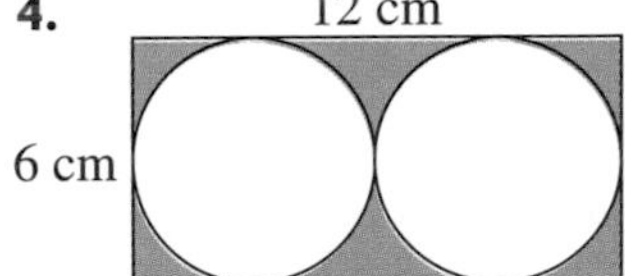

5.

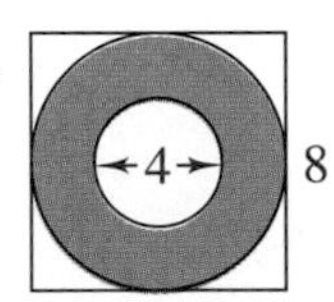

Find the volume and surface area of each figure. Use 3.14 for π.

6.

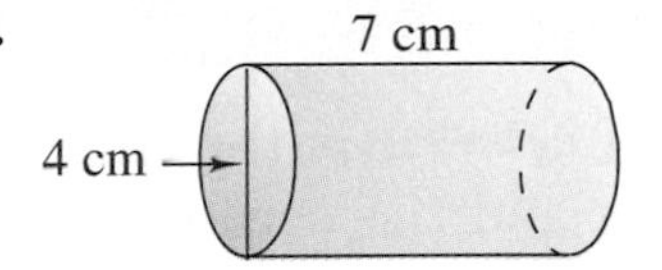

7.

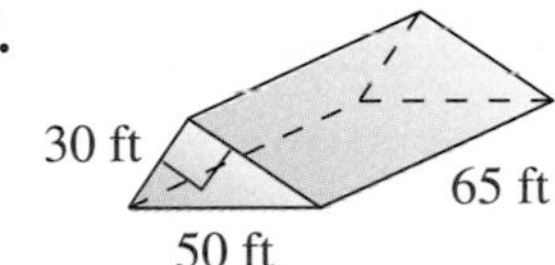

8.

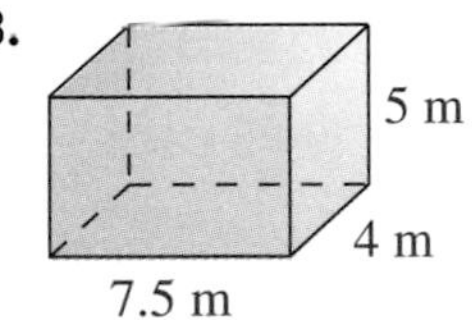

Find the volume of each figure. Use 3.14 for π.

9. A hexagonal prism is 3 cm tall. The area of its base is 34 cm^2.
10. A square pyramid is 7 in. tall. The length of its base is 10 in.
11. A cone has a height of 8 in. and a base with radius 4 in.

Find the volume and surface area of each figure after all its dimensions are doubled. Use 3.14 for π.

12. a cube with a volume of 216 cm^3
13. a cylinder 6 in. tall whose base has a radius of 2 in.
14. A recipe calls for a 9 in. by 13 in. rectangular baking pan. You only have an 11 in. by 11 in. square pan and a round pan with a diameter of 11 in. If all the pans have the same height, which of your pans could you use?

CHAPTER 11

Wrap Up

Three-Dimensional Figures, Composite Figures 11-1, 11-2

Figures that do not lie in a plane are ***space figures,*** or ***three-dimensional figures.*** Some common space figures are ***prisms, cylinders, cones,*** and ***pyramids.***

1. **Choose A, B, C, or D.** Which of the following patterns will not fold to form a space figure.

A. 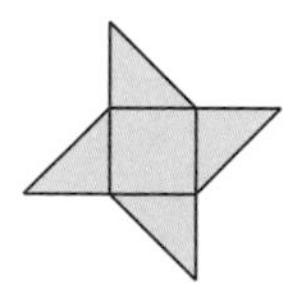

B. 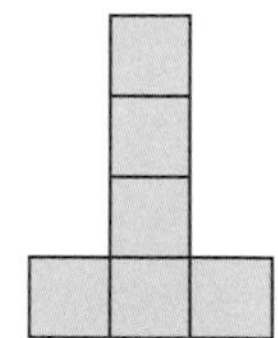

C. 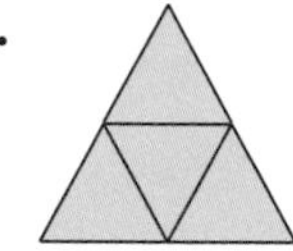

D. 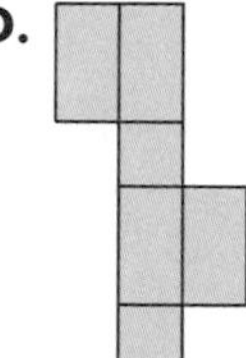

2. **Writing** Explain how you can find the area of a shaded region. Draw an example and find the shaded area.

Surface Areas of Prisms and Cylinders 11-3, 11-4

The ***surface area*** of a ***prism*** is the sum of the area of all the faces.

The ***surface area*** of a ***cylinder*** is the sum of the area of the bases and the area of the curved surface.

Find the surface area. Use 3.14 for π.

3. 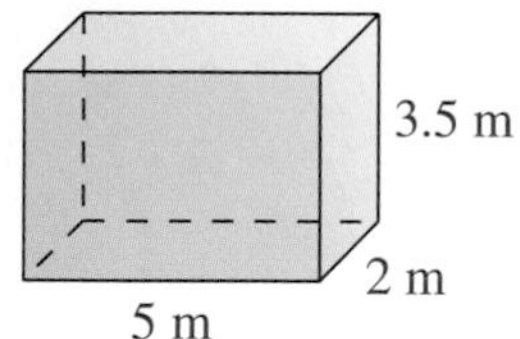

4. 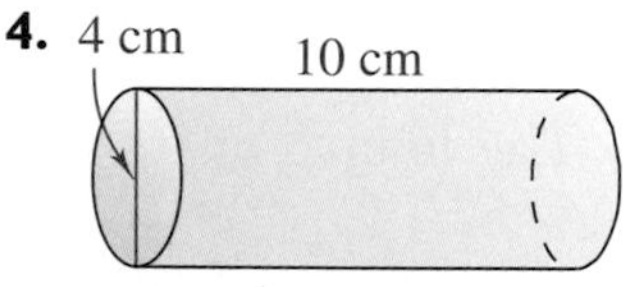

5. 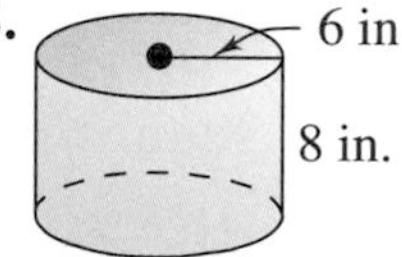

Volume 11-5

The ***volume*** of a ***three-dimensional figure*** is the number of cubic units needed to fill the space inside the figure.

The ***volume*** of a ***prism*** is the area of the base times the height.

6. How much potting soil is needed to fill a flower box that is $2\frac{3}{4}$ ft long, 6 in. wide, and 8 in. high?

Changing Dimensions 11-6

If all the dimensions of a three-dimensional figure are multiplied by n, the volume is multiplied by n^3 and the surface area is multiplied by n^2.

Find the new volume and surface area of each figure if all dimensions are doubled.

7. a rectangular prism with a volume of 24 cm³ and a surface area of 52 cm²

8. a cylinder with a volume of 785 in.³ and a surface area of 219.8 in.²

Using Multiple Strategies 11-7

To solve a problem, you may need to use more than one problem solving strategy.

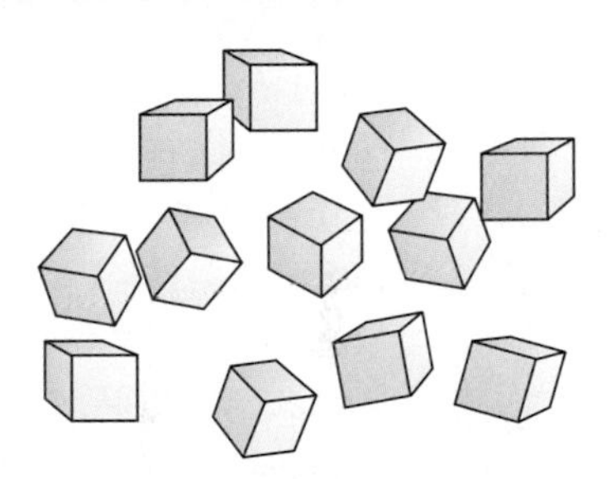

9. How many different rectangular prisms can be built using 12 cubes with each edge 1 cm long? What are the dimensions of the rectangular prism with the largest surface area? the smallest surface area?

Volumes of Cylinders, Cones, and Pyramids 11-8, 11-9

The ***volume*** of a ***cylinder*** is the area of a base times the height of the cylinder.

The ***volume*** of a ***cone*** or a ***pyramid*** is $\frac{1}{3}$ the area of the base times the height.

Find the volume. Use 3.14 for π.

10.

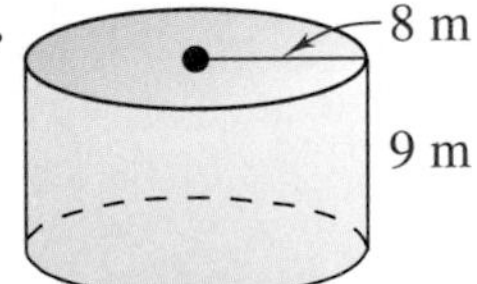

11.

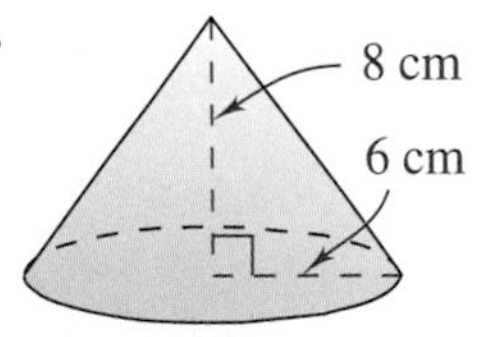

12.

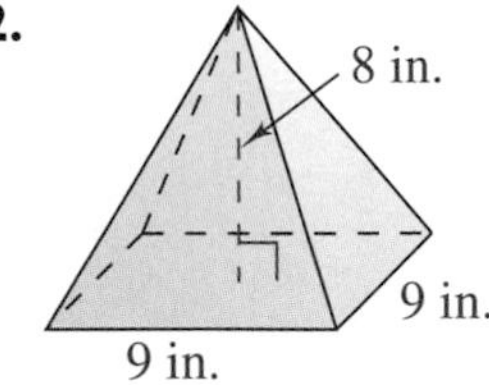

13. Find the height of a cylinder with a volume of 376.8 cm³, if the diameter of the base is 8 cm.

14. The length of a side of the square base of a pyramid is 9 m. Find the height of the pyramid if its volume is 270 m³.

15. A grocer is planning to stack cans of vegetables on a 2 m long shelf. Each can is 10 cm high and has a volume of 785 cm³. If there is only room for two layers of cans and the shelf is 22 cm deep, how many cans will fit on the shelf?

Airline Safety

At the beginning of the chapter you drew up a set of guidelines to govern air traffic safety. The Federal Aviation Administration (FAA) is considering adopting your guidelines for all airports. Review your guidelines and revise them based on your study of the chapter. Then prepare a final draft for the FAA. The following are suggestions to help you support your proposal.

- ✓ Make a graph or chart.
- ✓ Conduct a survey.
- ✓ Make a drawing.

The problems preceded by the magnifying glass (p. 473, # 28; p. 476, # 19; and p. 496, # 20) will help you complete the investigation.

Airline accidents usually take a great many lives. That together with fears over terrorism contribute to greatly exaggerated fears about airline safety. Fatality figures from 1985 to 1990 show that there was about a 1 in 38,000 chance of dying in an airline accident. During the same period the chance of dying in a car accident was about 1 in 5,000.

Excursion: Comparing airline accidents with auto accidents helps to show the relative safety of airline travel. Choose two sports or two other activities of interest to you. Gather data on accidents related to these activities and compare the relative safety of the activities.

The shape of the building you live in influences your understanding of the geometric world. For example, most people grow up in living spaces with lots of angles. Fewer people in this country grow up in round houses. Perhaps that explains why most people have a deeper understanding of squares and rectangular prisms than they have of circles and spheres.

- ***Describe the shape of the living space you are used to.***
- ***Make a list of ways that such a space may affect how you see the world.***
- ***Discuss what it would be like to live in a village of round houses.***

Marathon Mapping

A marathon is a running race that measures 26 miles 385 yards. You have just been appointed the official town race course designer for the upcoming marathon.

- Obtain a map of your town.
- Plan the route of the race. Besides measuring 26 miles 385 yards, your route should be an interesting one for runners to run. You may wish to include hills on the route, or have it take in some of your town's most interesting or pleasurable attractions.
- Explain how you calculated the length of the route.

How Much Do I Use?

The average American uses 60% more energy today than in 1950. To provide our highest standard of living, an average of 40 lb of petroleum and coal, 26 lb of agricultural products, and 19 lb of forest products must be expended for *each* American *each* day. Water is an especially critical and endangered resource. Because of high water consumption, some parts of the United States are already experiencing water shortages.

- Make a list of the many ways you use water.
- Estimate the amount of water in each category that you use in one day.
- Calculate the approximate total amount of water you use in one year.

Artistic Attributes

An artist may look at a sculpture and notice its color. A mathematician may look at the same sculpture and notice its size. Twenty other people viewing the same sculpture may notice twenty different attributes. An attribute is a quality or characteristic that something has that distinguishes it from other objects. Some attributes, like size, can be measured. Others, like color, cannot.

Work with a partner.

- Choose an object you can see.
- List as many different attributes of the object as you can.
- If an attribute can be measured, estimate the measure.
- Record your observations and compare them with observations of other objects.

CHAPTER 11

Assessment

1. Draw an example of each.
   a. a triangular prism
   b. a rectangular pyramid
   c. a cone
2. Use a triangular pyramid for each of the following.
   a. Draw a pattern that can be folded to create the figure.
   b. Find the number of edges.
3. Find the area of each shaded region to the nearest tenth of a square unit. Use 3.14 for π.

a.

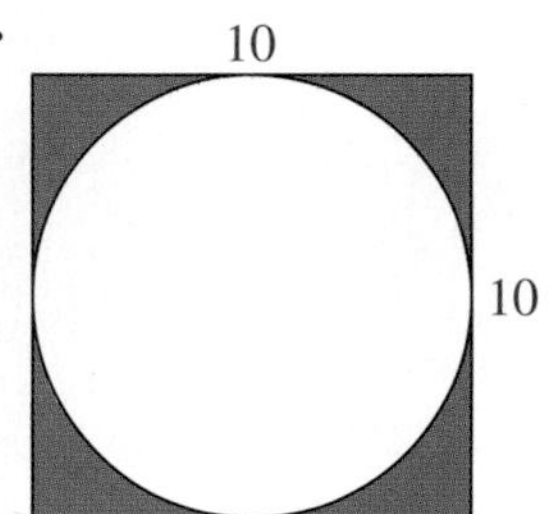

b.

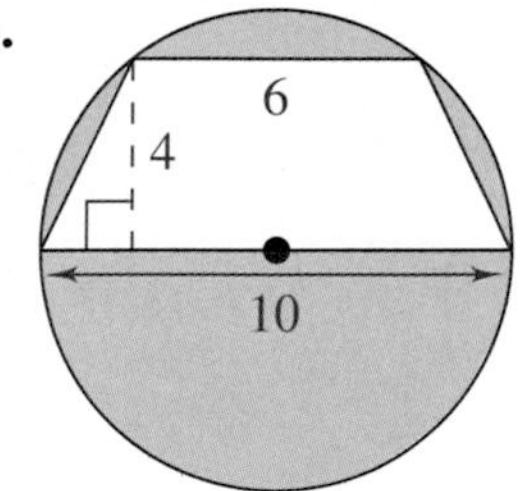

4. Find the surface area of each of the following.
   a. a cube with edge 10 cm
   b. a rectangular prism with height 9 cm and whose base is 6 cm by 8.5 cm
   c. a prism 7 in. tall whose base is a right triangle with legs 5 in. and 12 in.
5. Find the surface area of a cylinder with radius 5 cm and height 9 cm. Give your answer to the nearest square unit.
6. Find the volume of each of the following.
   a. a prism with height 7 ft and rectangular base 5.2 ft by 3 ft
   b. a pyramid with a 6 cm by 6 cm square base and height 11 cm
7. **Choose A, B, C, or D.** The length of each edge of a prism is tripled. How many times larger is the volume of the new prism than the volume of the original prism?

   A. 3 times **B.** 6 times
   C. 9 times **D.** 27 times
8. **Writing** Explain how the volume formulas for pyramids and cones relate to the volume formulas for prisms and cylinders.
9. **Calculator** Find the volume of each of the following to the nearest cubic unit.
   a. a cylinder with radius 9.2 cm and height 8 cm
   b. a cone with radius 4 m and height 5.8 m
10. Elaine is painting the walls of a room that is 18 ft long by 12 ft wide by 8 ft high. There are two rectangular windows, 3 ft by 4 ft, and one door, 3 ft by 7 ft. If Elaine paints at a rate of 100 ft^2 per hour, to the nearest half hour, how long will the job take?

Cumulative Review

Choose A, B, C, or D.

1. In 1937, it cost \$1.5 million to make the film "Snow White and the Seven Dwarfs." In 1992, it cost \$85 million to make "Aladdin." Which expression would you use to find the percent of increase in the cost of making an animated film?

   A. $\frac{1.5 + 85}{85}$ **B.** $\frac{1.5 + 85}{1.5}$
   C. $\frac{85 - 1.5}{1.5}$ **D.** $\frac{85 - 1.5}{85}$

2. A CD player can randomly play 3 recordings from a CD. If you use this feature on a CD with 12 recordings, how many different programs can be played?

   A. $12 \cdot 11 \cdot 10$ **B.** ${}_{12}C_3$
   C. 12^3 **D.** 12!

3. What is the probability that today is a day of the week that begins with the letter "T"?

   A. $\frac{1}{26}$ **B.** $\frac{1}{7}$ **C.** $\frac{7}{26}$ **D.** $\frac{2}{7}$

4. Estimate the shaded area.

   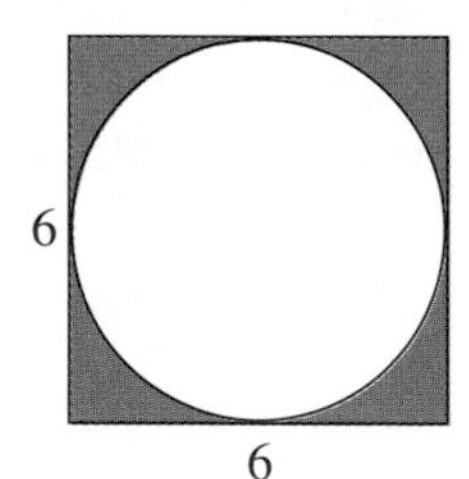

   A. about 7 units^2
   B. about 17 units^2
   C. about 27 units^2
   D. about 0.7 units^2

5. Which equation describes inverse variation of x and y?

   A. $x = 12y$ **B.** $\frac{x}{12} = y$
   C. $\frac{x}{y} = 12$ **D.** $x = \frac{12}{y}$

6. In which set are all three values equal?

   A. 0.5, 5%, $\frac{50}{100}$ **B.** $\frac{3}{8}$, 38%, 0.38
   C. 35%, 0.35, $\frac{35}{100}$ **D.** 3, 300%, $\frac{3}{100}$

7. Katia wants to buy the bread-making machine that makes the largest loaf by volume. Which model should she buy?

   A. Model I makes a cylindrical loaf with diameter 8 in. and height 10 in.
   B. Model II makes a square loaf 6 in. by 6 in. by 11 in.
   C. Model III makes a rectangular loaf 6 in. by 8 in. by 11 in.
   D. Model IV makes a square loaf 7 in. by 7 in. by 10 in.

8. Which object is *not* an example of a prism?

   A. a shoe box **B.** a domino
   C. a file cabinet
   D. a soup can

9. Of the first 50 customers to visit Daily Bagels, 11 ordered a bagel. If Daily Bagels normally has about 880 customers per day, how many bagels should they expect to sell?

   A. about 16 dozen **B.** about 80
   C. about 8 dozen **D.** about 110

10. A job pays \$160 for 25 h. What would it pay for 40 h?

    A. \$216 **B.** \$256 **C.** \$640 **D.** \$1000

Chapter 1

Extra Practice

Make a box-and-whisker plot for each set of data.

1. 33, 42, 45, 37, 54, 61, 55, 60, 27, 31, 45, 59, 45

2. 2.3, 4.2, 7.5, 6.0, 3.2, 5.1, 6.7, 4.6, 3.5, 2.9, 4.8, 3.4, 5.3

Find the mean, median, mode, and range of the data.

3. 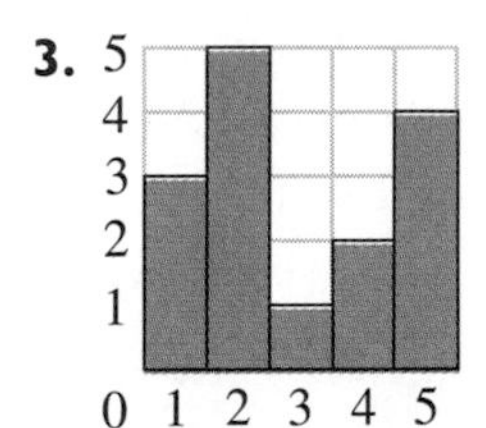

4.

```
                ×
×   ×           ×
×   ×           ×
×   ×   ×   ×   ×   ×
5   6   7   8   9
```

5.

Stem	Leaf
7	0 3 4
8	2 5
9	3 6 7 8

7 | 2 means 7.2

6. 0 2 4 6 8 10

Choose the type of graph that would best display each kind of data.

7. parts of a monthly budget

8. change in temperature in one week

9. the number of girls and boys in three kindergartens

10. a comparison of years in school and literacy rates

Solve if possible. If not, tell what information is needed.

11. In homeroom 7D, 12 students are on the soccer team, 13 work on the school paper, and 5 do neither. How many students are in the class?

12. If you have your choice of three different sandwiches, four kinds of fruit, and milk or apple juice to drink, how many different lunches could you have?

Exercises 13–16 are based on the following information.

300 carpenters are asked "Do you prefer using widgets, gidgets, or flims in your work?" 30% preferred widgets, 10% preferred gidgets, 50% preferred flims, and 10% had no preference.

13. What is the sample size?

14. Is the question open-option or closed-option?

15. Which of the three was most popular?

16. How many carpenters had no preference?

Chapter 2

Extra Practice

Exercises 1–8 use the figure at right.

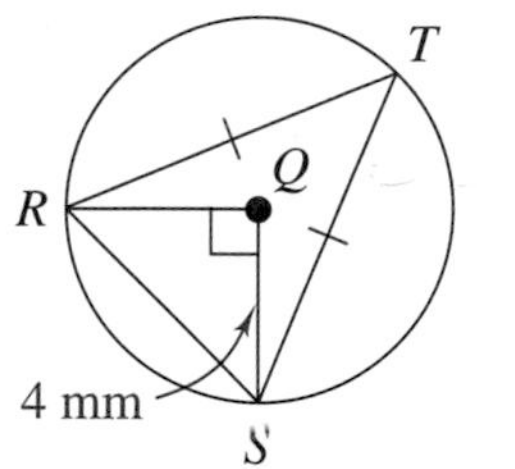

1. How long is $\overline{QR}$?
2. What is $m\angle RTS$?
3. What kind of triangle is $\triangle RQS$?
4. How long is $\overline{RS}$?
5. What kind of triangle is $\triangle RTS$?
6. What is $m\angle TRS$?
7. What is the area of circle Q?
8. How long is $\widehat{RS}$?

Name the following figures.

9. 

10. 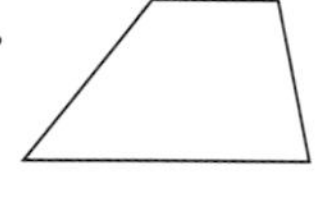

11. 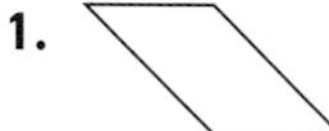

12. 

Are the following triangles congruent? If so, state the congruence and the reason why.

13. 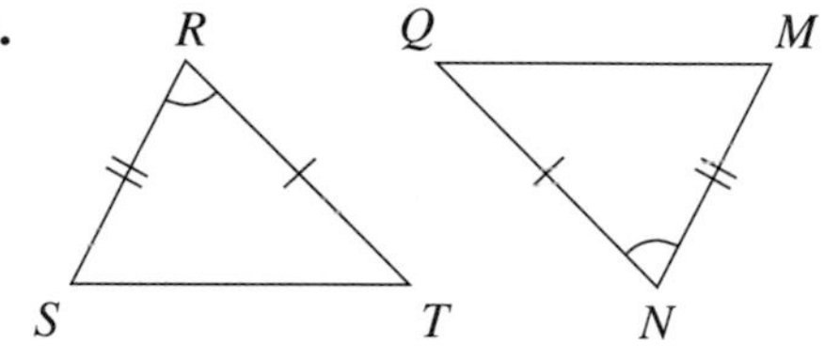

14. 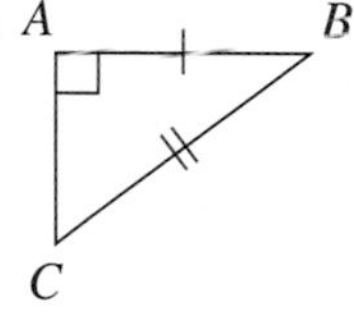

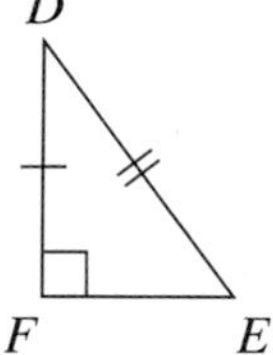

15. 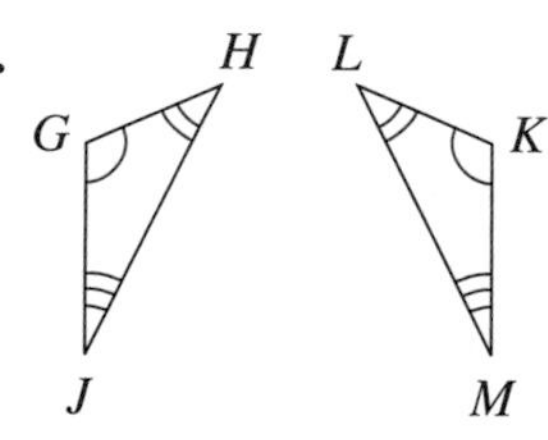

16. 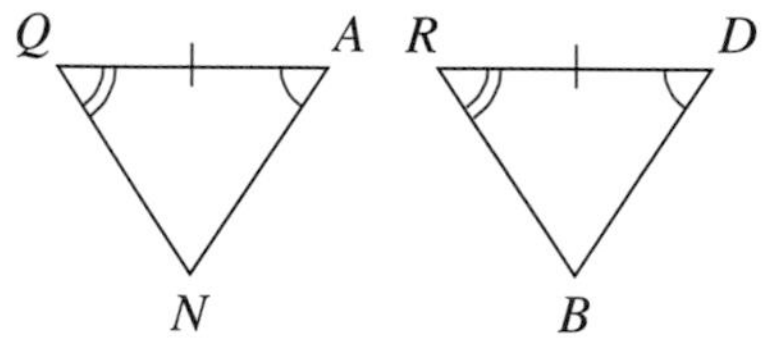

17. Can you make a tessellation using circles only? Why or why not?

18. You ordered a six slice pizza. What is the measure of the central angle of each piece?

19. How high can you build your treehouse if you have a 12-ft ladder that must be placed 3 ft from the tree for stability?

20. Find the next three numbers in the pattern: 2, 3, 5, 9, 17, ■, ■, ■.

Chapter 3

Extra Practice

Compare. Write <, >, or =.

1. $5 \blacksquare |-3 - 2|$ 2. $7 + (-3) \blacksquare 7 - (-3)$ 3. $|20 - (-6)| \blacksquare |52 - 25|$

Find each product or quotient.

4. $-45 \div 5$ 5. $(-3) \cdot 4$ 6. $|-36| \div 9$ 7. $5 \cdot (-45 \div 15)$ 8. $(-3 - 8) \div 4$

Evaluate each expression for $n = -2$, $m = 3$, and $t = 5$.

9. $3m - 4t$ 10. $|3 - m| + n$ 11. $-t + n$ 12. $2tm$ 13. $|t| - |m| + |n|$

Explain which property is illustrated by each sentence.

14. $(-3 + 4) + 5 = -3 + (4 + 5)$ 15. $1 \cdot m = m$ 16. $2(11) + 2(4) = 2(11 + 4)$

17. $2 + 0 = 2$ 18. $n \cdot p = p \cdot n$ 19. $f + g = g + f$

Write each expression using a single exponent.

20. $3^2 \cdot 3^3$ 21. $(-5)^0 \cdot (-5)^{10}$ 22. $m^6 \cdot m^7$ 23. $-4^3 \cdot 4^{10}$ 24. $(-2)^{10} \cdot (-2)^3$

Evaluate.

25. $(-2)^3 + (4 \div 2) - (-3)$ 26. $3 + 4^2 - 15$ 27. $(3 - 4)^2 - (17 + 1)^0$

28. $-3^2 - (-8)$ 29. $6n - (3 - 1)^2$ for $n = 2$ 30. $2^m + (-5)$ for $m = 3$

31. $-3a + 4b$ for $a = 3.7$ and $b = -2.8$ 32. $2r^2 + 6r + 3$ for $r = -0.8$

33. $-c^3 + 2c^2 - c + 8$ for $c = 1.2$ 34. $|c| + (-c)^2$ for $c = -3.7$

35. Julia went to the Strangeways Golf Club, where all the holes are par 4. She had 5 strokes at the first hole, 6 strokes at the second, and 3 at the third. How many strokes above or below par is she? If she wants to be at par after the next hole, how many strokes can she use for the fourth hole?

36. Dromedaries have one hump, while camels have two. Two herdsmen decided to count their herd. They counted 316 feet and 121 humps.
    a. How many of each do they have?
    b. If they are offered $1,200 for each dromedary and $1,500 for each camel, how much money can they make?

Chapter 4

Extra Practice

Simplify each expression.

1. $6x + 4 - 3x$

2. $2(x + 1) + 3(2x - 4)$

3. $-5 + p - 3(p + 2)$

4. $6b + 4d + (-3)d + 2 - 3b$

Solve each equation.

5. $6n + 3 = 21$

6. $10 - 7 = \frac{m}{5} + 2$

7. $-b + 2 = -\frac{1}{2}$

8. $9g + (-4g) = 10$

Solve each inequality. Graph each solution on a number line.

9. $4n - 3 > 2$

10. $-\frac{n}{3} - 4 \leq 5$

11. $4m + 3(6 - m) < -2.1$

12. $6c + (-3) \geq 2c + 7$

Find the area of each figure.

13.

3.2 in.

14.

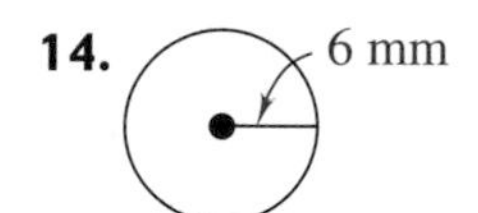

15.

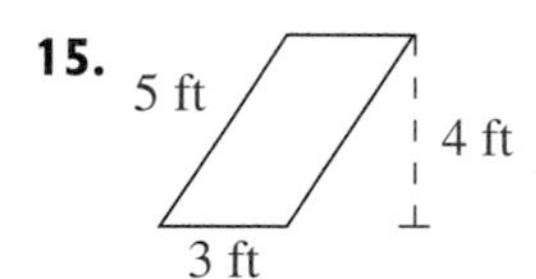

16.

8 m 7 m 8 m
7 m 7 m
8 m 7 m 8 m

17. What number is a solution to $2x + 3 \geq 4$ that is *not* a solution to $2x + 3 > 4$?

Write an equation for each problem. Solve the equation. Then give the solution of the problem.

18. In a right triangle, the length of the two legs are 12 m and 9 m. Find the length of the hypotenuse.

19. Find the length of the side of a square field that has an area of 529 yd^2.

20. In the International System, cholesterol is measured in millimoles per liter of blood (mmol/L). In the United States, it is generally measured in milligrams per deciliter (mg/dL). To find an international result (I) when given an American result (A), use $0.0259A = I$.

a. Write a formula to convert an international result to an American result.

b. If your cholesterol is 7 mmol/L, what is your cholesterol in mg/dL?

Chapter 5

Extra Practice

Find the slope and the x- and y-intercepts of each line.

1. $y = 3x + 4$
2. $3y = -2x + 6$
3. $x + 4y = 8$
4. $2x = -y - 5$

Solve each system of equations by graphing.

5. $y = -x - 2$
   $y = 2x + 4$
6. $x + 2y = -4$
   $3x - 2y = 12$
7. $-2x - 4y = 5$
   $y = 3$
8. $3x + 6 = 4y$
   $y + x = 4$
   $x = -2$

Find the slope of the line that contains the given points.

9. $C(2, 4), D(-7, 1)$
10. $B(5, 3), H(3, 9)$
11. $T(6, 4), S(-2, 4)$
12. $J(-3, -7), K(-3, -2)$

Exercises 13–16 use the figure at right.

13. If the figure were translated five right and seven down, in what quadrant(s) would it be?
14. If it were rotated 270° counter-clockwise about the origin, in what quadrant(s) would it be?
15. If it were reflected over the line $y = 1$, in what quadrant(s) would it be?
16. How many lines of symmetry does the figure have?

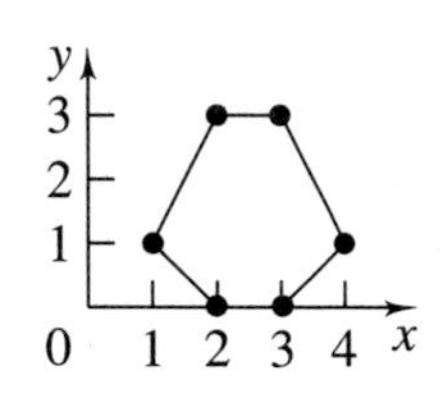

Exercises 17–20 use the following information.

Your school is having a fund raiser selling calendars. The calendar company charges the school an initial fee of $30 and $2 for each calendar. The school sells the calendars for $5 each.

17. What is the equation for expenses? for income? Graph them.
18. What are the coordinates of the break-even point?
19. How many calendars must the school sell to make a profit?
20. If the school sells 100 calendars, can they afford two new $150 slides? Explain.

Chapter 6

Extra Practice

Write the next three terms of each sequence. Identify each as arithmetic, geometric, or neither. For each arithmetic or geometric sequence, find the common difference or ratio.

1. $4, 16, 64, \ldots$

2. $-5, -3, -1, 1, \ldots$

3. $1, \frac{5}{6}, \frac{2}{3}, \frac{1}{2}, \ldots$

4. $12, 6, 3, \ldots$

5. $0, 2, 6, 12, \ldots$

6. $1, 2, 4, 8, \ldots$

Make an input/output table for each function. Find $f(-2)$, $f(-1)$, $f(0)$, $f(1)$, and $f(2)$. Then graph each function.

7. $f(x) = 3x - 2$

8. $f(x) = -\frac{1}{2}x^2 + 5$

9. $f(x) = -2x - (-6)$

Match each situation with the appropriate graph.

10. the altitude of an airplane during one flight

11. the fee for an overdue book

12. distance traveled when driving to the library

13. the speed of a school bus during its morning route

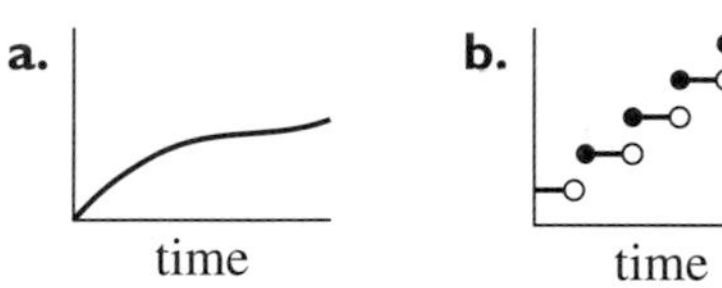

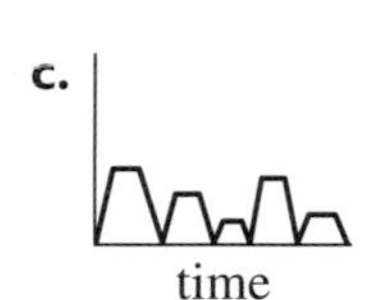

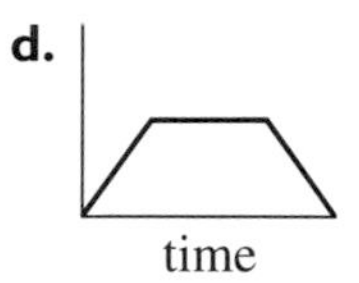

Make a table of values. Then graph each function.

14. $f(x) = -x^2 + 2$

15. $f(x) = x^2 - 4$

16. $f(x) = x^2 - 2x + 3$

State whether each function is linear or quadratic.

17. $y = 4x$

18. $y = 2x^2 + 3$

19. $x^2 = y - 2$

20. $x + y = 10$

State whether each equation is a direct or inverse variation, and state the constant of variation.

21. $y = \frac{3}{x}$

22. $y = 7x$

23. $x = 2y$

24. $xy = 5$

25. The volume of a gas is 20 ft^3 under 8 lb of pressure. What is its volume under 10 lb of pressure?

26. The volume of a gas is 175 mL at 350K. The temperature of the gas is reduced to 250K. What is its volume?

Chapter 7

Extra Practice

State whether each number is prime or composite. If it is composite, write the prime factorization.

1. 171 **2.** 2,000 **3.** 3,729 **4.** 640 **5.** 59

Find the GCF and LCM of each set of numbers.

6. 9, 33 **7.** 7, 15 **8.** 6, 15, 24 **9.** 21, 9, 30 **10.** 4, 10, 18

Write each fraction as a decimal and each decimal as a fraction in simplest form.

11. $\frac{3}{16}$ **12.** $\frac{14}{15}$ **13.** 3.54 **14.** $\frac{7}{3}$ **15.** $0.\overline{8}$

Compare. Use >, <, or =.

16. $\frac{25}{36}$ ■ $0.69\overline{4}$ **17.** 2.7 ■ $\frac{10}{3}$ **18.** -4.3 ■ -4.2 **19.** $-\frac{17}{3}$ ■ -15.9

Simplify each expression.

20. $\frac{5}{8} + \frac{7}{12}$ **21.** $-\frac{6}{7} \div \frac{8}{14}$ **22.** $7\frac{1}{3} - 6\frac{2}{5}$ **23.** $\frac{3}{4} \bullet \frac{16}{27}$

24. $\frac{2^{10}}{2^7}$ **25.** $\frac{3^5}{3^6}$ **26.** $\frac{a^6}{a^4}, a \neq 0$ **27.** $\frac{8^9}{8^8}$

Rewrite in scientific notation or in standard form.

28. 3.04×10^{-2} **29.** 1,274,000 **30.** 6×10^{-6} **31.** 5.63×10^4

State whether each number is rational or irrational.

32. 1.0203. . . **33.** 2.4444. . . **34.** $5.63\overline{663}$ **35.** 0.9090099. . .

Solve.

36. $x + \frac{2}{3} = \frac{5}{6}$ **37.** $\frac{d}{5} = 7$ **38.** $2p + \frac{4}{7} = \frac{3}{5}$ **39.** $\frac{7}{10}s - \frac{3}{4} = 6.75$

40. After school Timma spent $2\frac{1}{2}$ h at soccer practice, then walked 10 min home. What time does her school get out if she had time for $\frac{7}{12}$ h of homework before her 6 P.M. dinner?

41. A number is multiplied by 2, added to $-7\frac{3}{10}$ and divided by 5. The result is 1.34. What is the number?

Chapter 8

Extra Practice

Which ratio is not equal to the others?

1. $\frac{4}{16}, \frac{6}{24}, \frac{7}{26}$ **2.** $\frac{3}{2}, \frac{21}{15}, \frac{7}{5}$ **3.** $\frac{1}{3}, \frac{4}{9}, \frac{6}{18}$ **4.** $\frac{20}{50}, \frac{8}{20}, \frac{10}{30}$

Solve each proportion.

5. $\frac{4}{7} = \frac{x}{21}$ **6.** $\frac{3}{x} = \frac{18}{9}$ **7.** $\frac{x}{10} = \frac{8}{15}$ **8.** $\frac{3}{5} = \frac{2}{x}$

Are the polygons similar? If so, write a similarity statement.

9.

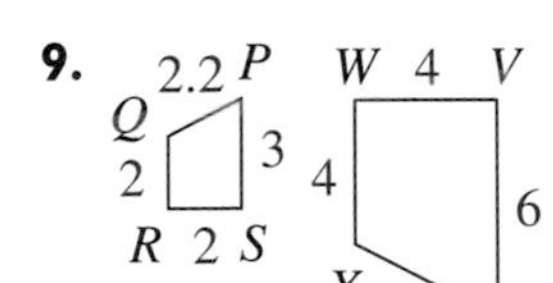

10.

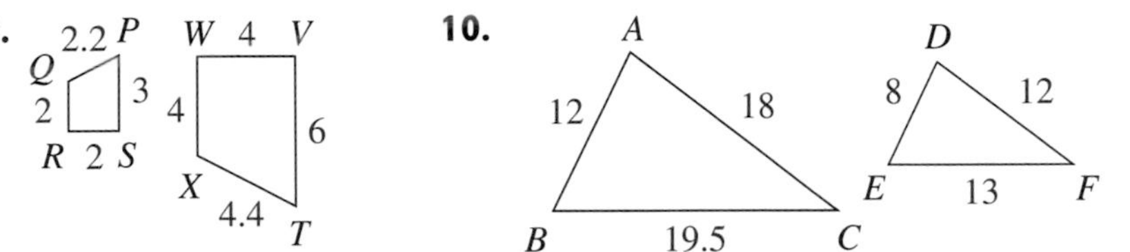

11.

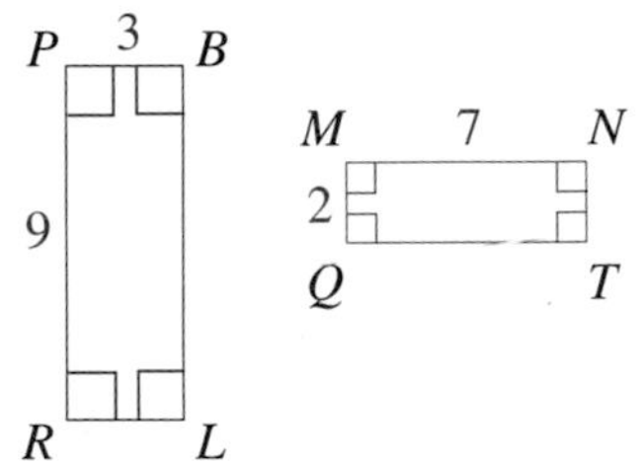

Each pair of polygons is similar. Find each unknown length, and the scale factor of the smaller to the larger.

12.

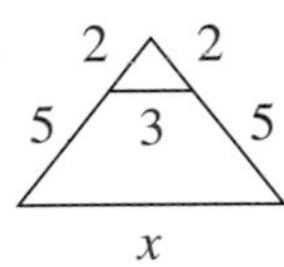

13.

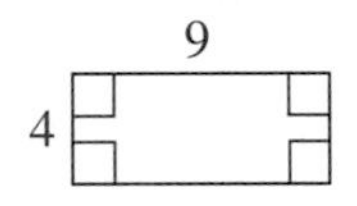

14.

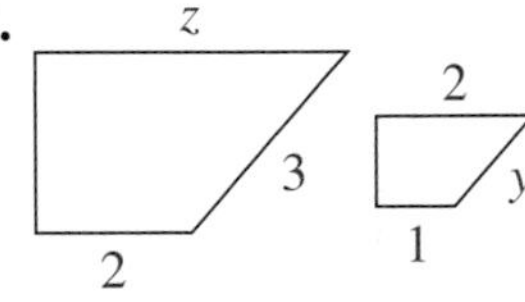

Exercises 15–17 use the figure at right.

15. What is tan B? tan C?

16. What is cos B? cos C?

17. What is sin C? sin B?

18. What is sin 68°? cos 34°? tan 17°?

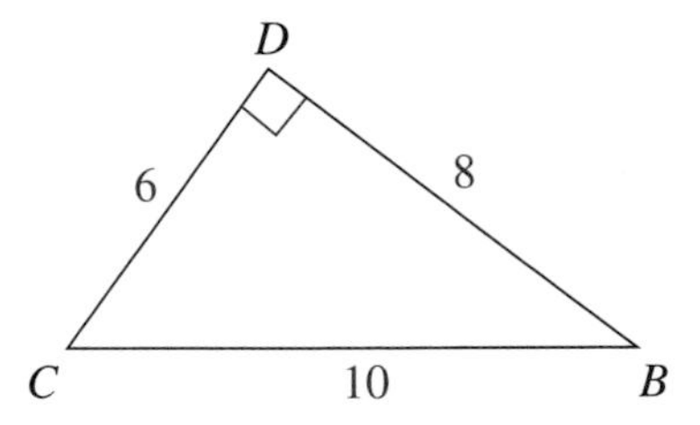

19. A telephone pole has a sign attached to it 6 ft above the ground. The pole casts a shadow 26 ft long. The shadow of the portion up to the sign is 8 ft long. What is the distance from the sign to the top of the pole?

20. When a photograph is enlarged from 3 in. by 5 in. to 4 in. by 6 in., is it enlarged proportionally?

Chapter 9

Extra Practice

Compute.

1. $6!$
2. ${}_6P_3$
3. ${}_{15}C_{12}$
4. ${}_7P_2$
5. $\frac{9!}{7!3!}$

Use Pascal's Triangle to find each value.

6. ${}_8C_7$
7. ${}_9C_4$
8. ${}_5C_2$
9. ${}_6C_1$
10. ${}_5C_3$

State whether the events are dependent or independent.

11. height of the sun; time of day
12. number of students in a school; length of the school day
13. cost of postage; distance a letter travels inside the U.S.
14. number of trees in a park; time spent raking the park

Two spinners are spun. One has the letters of the alphabet; the other has the digits 0 through 9. Find each value.

15. the number of possible outcomes
16. *P*(M and 2)
17. *P*(C and prime)
18. *P*(F and 5)
19. *P*(vowel and even)
20. *P*(consonant and 4)
21. the odds in favor of J and odd digit
22. *P*(*not* vowel and even)

State whether each probability is theoretical or experimental.

23. the chance that a person chooses banana as their favorite fruit
24. the chance of getting a 4 when rolling a number cube
25. the chance that someone has a car, according to the census
26. Use the process control chart at right.
    a. What is the target value?
    b. What are the control limits?
    c. What is the range of acceptable values?
    d. Identify any points where you would stop the process and explain why.

Chapter 10

Extra Practice

Express each of the following as a decimal, a fraction, and a percent.

1. $\frac{1}{3}$ **2.** 21% **3.** 3.47 **4.** 0.00042 **5.** $\frac{3}{20}$ **6.** 215.4%

Solve.

7. 18% of 36 is ■. **8.** 44 is ■% of 32. **9.** 145 is 15% of ■.

10. 0.4 is ■% of 5. **11.** 0.09% of 1024 is ■. **12.** 215% of 20 is ■.

Exercises 13–17 use the data at right.

Monthly Budget	
Rent	$450
Utilities	$40
Telephone	$40
Food	$200
Insurance	$70
Transportation	$50
Other	$150

13. Make a table showing the percent of the budget each item represents.

14. Add a column to the table to show what each central angle would be in a circle graph.

15. Which item is more than a third of the budget?

16. Which item is 7% of the budget?

17. Which item would have a 72° central angle?

Find each percent of change.

18. 16 to 20 **19.** 320 to 542 **20.** 1 to 0.4 **21.** 80 to 55 **22.** 0.002 to 0.003

23. a. Daniel ordered $18 sunglasses for his store. When they arrived, he decided to mark them up 50%. What is the selling price?

b. Unfortunately they weren't selling, so he marked them down to $22.95. What was the discount rate?

c. In his state, there's a 5% sales tax. How much would a customer pay for the sunglasses at the discount rate, including tax?

d. The salesperson gets a commission of 8% of the before-tax selling price. How much did she earn on this sale?

e. If her paycheck had $94.40 in commission, how much did she sell?

Chapter 11

Extra Practice

Calculator Find the area of each shaded region to the nearest square unit.

1. 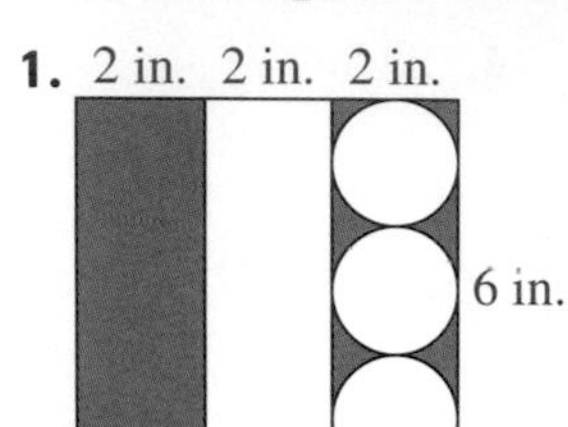

2. 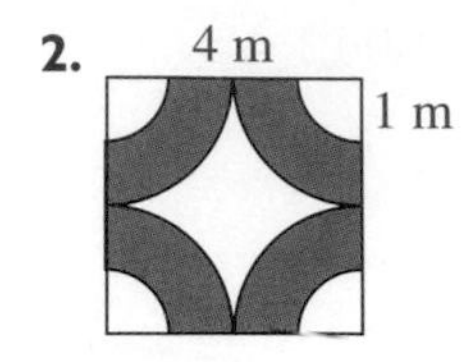

3. 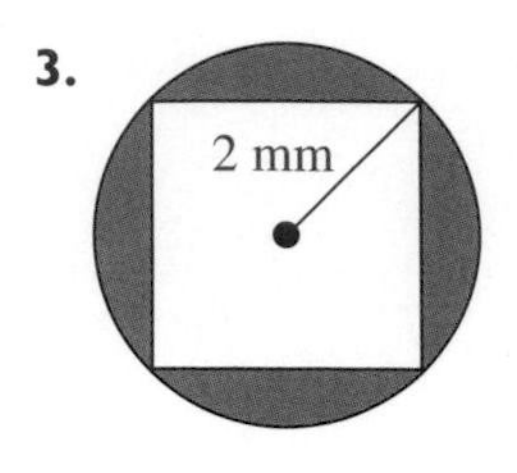

Find the volume and surface area of each figure.

4. a. a cube with a 1.2 m edge
   b. the cube of part (a) with all dimensions doubled

5. a. an 8 ft tall cylinder with a 1 ft radius
   b. the cylinder of part (a) with quadrupled dimensions

6. a. a 10 cm by 15 cm by 18 cm rectangular prism
   b. the rectangular prism of part (a) with halved dimensions

7. a. What is the volume of a 4 in. tall square pyramid with a 36 in.^{2} base?
   b. What is the volume of the square pyramid of part (a) with the height doubled?

8. How many faces, vertices, and edges does an octagonal prism have?

9. Maayan is making a concrete path to his house that is 4 ft wide, 16 ft long, and $\frac{1}{4}$ ft deep.
   a. How many cubic feet of concrete will he need?
   b. The minimum purchase is 1 yd^3. If concrete costs \$50/yd^3, how much will he spend?

10. A cord is 128 ft^3. Sivan has an 8 ft by 8 ft by 12 ft woodshed. How many cords of wood can she store?

11. Zillah has 2 bookcases each 6 ft tall, 4 ft wide, and 1 ft deep. Will they fit side by side in a 9 ft by 11 ft room? How much wall space do they cover?

Tables

Table 1 Measures

Metric

Length
10 millimeters (mm) = 1 centimeter (cm)
100 cm = 1 meter (m)
1,000 m = 1 kilometer (km)

Area
100 square millimeters (mm^2) = 1 square centimeter (cm^2)
10,000 cm^2 = 1 square meter (m^2)

Volume
1,000 cubic millimeters (mm^3) = 1 cubic centimeter (cm^3)
1,000,000 cm^3 = 1 cubic meter (m^3)

Mass
1,000 milligrams (mg) = 1 gram (g)
1,000 g = 1 kilogram (kg)

Liquid Capacity
1,000 milliliters (mL) = 1 liter (L)

United States Customary

Length
12 inches (in.) = 1 foot (ft)
3 feet = 1 yard (yd)
36 in. = 1 yd
5,280 ft = 1 mile (mi)
1,760 yd = 1 mi

Area
144 square inches (in.^{2}) = 1 square foot (ft^2)
9 ft^2 = 1 square yard (yd^2)
4,840 yd^2 = 1 acre

Volume
1,728 cubic inches (in.^{3}) = 1 cubic foot (ft^3)
27 ft^3 = 1 cubic yard (yd^3)

Weight
16 ounces (oz) = 1 pound (lb)
2,000 lb = 1 ton (T)

Liquid Capacity
8 fluid ounces (fl oz) = 1 cup (c)
2 c = 1 pint (pt)
2 pt = 1 quart (qt)
4 qt = 1 gallon (gal)

Time
1 minute (min) = 60 seconds (s)
1 hour (h) = 60 min
1 day (da) = 24 h
1 year (y) = 365 da

Table 2 Formulas

Circumference of a circle

$C = \pi d$ or $C = 2\pi r$

Area		
	parallelogram:	$A = bh$
	rectangle:	$A = bh$
	trapezoid:	$A = \frac{1}{2}h(b_1 + b_2)$
	triangle:	$A = \frac{1}{2}bh$
	circle:	$A = \pi r^2$

Volume		
	cylinder:	$V = \pi r^2 h$
	cone:	$V = \frac{1}{3}\pi r^2 h$
	rectangular prism:	$V = lwh$
	pyramid:	$V = \frac{1}{3}Bh$
	sphere:	$V = \frac{4}{3}\pi r^3$

Table 3 Symbols

Symbol	Meaning
$>$	is greater than
$<$	is less than
$\geq$	is greater than or equal to
$\leq$	is less than or equal to
$=$	is equal to
$\neq$	is not equal to
$^\circ$	degrees
%	percent
$f(n)$	function, f of n
$a : b$	ratio of a to b, $\frac{a}{b}$
$\lvert a \rvert$	absolute value of a
$P(E)$	probability of an event E
π	pi
$\perp$	is perpendicular to
$\parallel$	is parallel to
$\cong$	is congruent to
$\sim$	is similar to
$\approx$	is approximately equal to
$\odot O$	circle O
$\overline{AB}$	segment AB
$\overrightarrow{AB}$	ray AB
$\overleftrightarrow{AB}$	line AB
$\triangle ABC$	triangle ABC
$\angle ABC$	angle ABC
$m\angle ABC$	measure of angle ABC
AB	length of segment AB
$\overset{\frown}{AB}$	arc AB
$\sin A$	sine of $\angle A$
$\cos A$	cosine of $\angle A$
$\tan A$	tangent of $\angle A$
!	factorial
${}_nP_r$	permutations of n things taken r at a time
${}_nC_r$	combinations of n things taken r at a time

Table 4 Squares and Square Roots

N	N^2	$\sqrt{N}$	N	N^2	$\sqrt{N}$
1	1	1	51	2,601	7.141
2	4	1.414	52	2,704	7.211
3	9	1.732	53	2,809	7.280
4	16	2	54	2,916	7.348
5	25	2.236	55	3,025	7.416
6	36	2.449	56	3,136	7.483
7	49	2.646	57	3,249	7.550
8	64	2.828	58	3,364	7.616
9	81	3	59	3,481	7.681
10	100	3.162	60	3,600	7.746
11	121	3.317	61	3,721	7.810
12	144	3.464	62	3,844	7.874
13	169	3.606	63	3,969	7.937
14	196	3.742	64	4,096	8
15	225	3.873	65	4,225	8.062
16	256	4	66	4,356	8.124
17	289	4.123	67	4,489	8.185
18	324	4.243	68	4,624	8.246
19	361	4.359	69	4,761	8.307
20	400	4.472	70	4,900	8.367
21	441	4.583	71	5,041	8.426
22	484	4.690	72	5,184	8.485
23	529	4.796	73	5,329	8.544
24	576	4.899	74	5,476	8.602
25	625	5	75	5,625	8.660
26	676	5.099	76	5,776	8.718
27	729	5.196	77	5,929	8.775
28	784	5.292	78	6,084	8.832
29	841	5.385	79	6,241	8.888
30	900	5.477	80	6,400	8.944
31	961	5.568	81	6,561	9
32	1,024	5.657	82	6,724	9.055
33	1,089	5.745	83	6,889	9.110
34	1,156	5.831	84	7,056	9.165
35	1,225	5.916	85	7,225	9.220
36	1,296	6	86	7,396	9.274
37	1,369	6.083	87	7,569	9.327
38	1,444	6.164	88	7,744	9.381
39	1,521	6.245	89	7,921	9.434
40	1,600	6.325	90	8,100	9.487
41	1,681	6.403	91	8,281	9.539
42	1,764	6.481	92	8,464	9.592
43	1,849	6.557	93	8,649	9.644
44	1,936	6.633	94	8,836	9.695
45	2,025	6.708	95	9,025	9.747
46	2,116	6.782	96	9,216	9.798
47	2,209	6.856	97	9,409	9.849
48	2,304	6.928	98	9,604	9.899
49	2,401	7	99	9,801	9.950
50	2,500	7.071	100	10,000	10

Table 5 Trigonometric Ratios

Angle	Sine	Cosine	Tangent	Angle	Sine	Cosine	Tangent
1°	0.0175	0.9998	0.0175	46°	0.7193	0.6947	1.0355
2°	0.0349	0.9994	0.0349	47°	0.7314	0.6820	1.0724
3°	0.0523	0.9986	0.0524	48°	0.7431	0.6691	1.1106
4°	0.0698	0.9976	0.0699	49°	0.7547	0.6561	1.1504
5°	0.0872	0.9962	0.0875	50°	0.7660	0.6428	1.1918
6°	0.1045	0.9945	0.1051	51°	0.7771	0.6293	1.2349
7°	0.1219	0.9925	0.1228	52°	0.7880	0.6157	1.2799
8°	0.1392	0.9903	0.1405	53°	0.7986	0.6018	1.3270
9°	0.1564	0.9877	0.1584	54°	0.8090	0.5878	1.3764
10°	0.1736	0.9848	0.1763	55°	0.8192	0.5736	1.4281
11°	0.1908	0.9816	0.1944	56°	0.8290	0.5592	1.4826
12°	0.2079	0.9781	0.2126	57°	0.8387	0.5446	1.5399
13°	0.2250	0.9744	0.2309	58°	0.8480	0.5299	1.6003
14°	0.2419	0.9703	0.2493	59°	0.8572	0.5150	1.6643
15°	0.2588	0.9659	0.2679	60°	0.8660	0.5000	1.7321
16°	0.2756	0.9613	0.2867	61°	0.8746	0.4848	1.8040
17°	0.2924	0.9563	0.3057	62°	0.8829	0.4695	1.8807
18°	0.3090	0.9511	0.3249	63°	0.8910	0.4540	1.9626
19°	0.3256	0.9455	0.3443	64°	0.8988	0.4384	2.0503
20°	0.3420	0.9397	0.3640	65°	0.9063	0.4226	2.1445
21°	0.3584	0.9336	0.3839	66°	0.9135	0.4067	2.2460
22°	0.3746	0.9272	0.4040	67°	0.9205	0.3907	2.3559
23°	0.3907	0.9205	0.4245	68°	0.9272	0.3746	2.4751
24°	0.4067	0.9135	0.4452	69°	0.9336	0.3584	2.6051
25°	0.4226	0.9063	0.4663	70°	0.9397	0.3420	2.7475
26°	0.4384	0.8988	0.4877	71°	0.9455	0.3256	2.9042
27°	0.4540	0.8910	0.5095	72°	0.9511	0.3090	3.0777
28°	0.4695	0.8829	0.5317	73°	0.9563	0.2924	3.2709
29°	0.4848	0.8746	0.5543	74°	0.9613	0.2756	3.4874
30°	0.5000	0.8660	0.5774	75°	0.9659	0.2588	3.7321
31°	0.5150	0.8572	0.6009	76°	0.9703	0.2419	4.0108
32°	0.5299	0.8480	0.6249	77°	0.9744	0.2250	4.3315
33°	0.5446	0.8387	0.6494	78°	0.9781	0.2079	4.7046
34°	0.5592	0.8290	0.6745	79°	0.9816	0.1908	5.1446
35°	0.5736	0.8192	0.7002	80°	0.9848	0.1736	5.6713
36°	0.5878	0.8090	0.7265	81°	0.9877	0.1564	6.3138
37°	0.6018	0.7986	0.7536	82°	0.9903	0.1392	7.1154
38°	0.6157	0.7880	0.7813	83°	0.9925	0.1219	8.1443
39°	0.6293	0.7771	0.8098	84°	0.9945	0.1045	9.5144
40°	0.6428	0.7660	0.8391	85°	0.9962	0.0872	11.4301
41°	0.6561	0.7547	0.8693	86°	0.9976	0.0698	14.3007
42°	0.6691	0.7431	0.9004	87°	0.9986	0.0523	19.0811
43°	0.6820	0.7314	0.9325	88°	0.9994	0.0349	28.6363
44°	0.6947	0.7193	0.9657	89°	0.9998	0.0175	57.2900
45°	0.7071	0.7071	1.0000				

Student Study Guide and Glossary

A

Absolute value (p. 104) A number's distance from zero on the number line is called its absolute value.

Example: The absolute value of -3 is 3 because -3 is 3 units from zero on the number line.

Acute triangle (p. 66) An acute triangle is a triangle with three acute angles.

Example: $m\angle 1, m\angle 2, m\angle 3 < 90°$

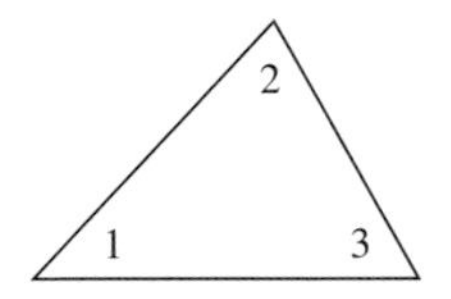

Addition properties for inequalities (p. 178) If the same number is added to both sides of an inequality, the order of the inequality will remain the same.

Example: $10 > 7$, so $10 + 3 > 7 + 3$; if $a > b$, then $a + c > b + c$.
$2 < 7$, so $2 + 3 < 7 + 3$; if $a < b$, then $a + c < b + c$.

Addition property of equality (p. 150) If the same number is added to each side of an equation, the results are equal.

Example: If $a = b$, then $a + c = b + c$.

Additive inverses (p. 111) Two numbers whose sum equals zero are called additive inverses.

Example: 23 is the additive inverse of -23 because $-23 + 23 = 0$.

Alternate interior angles (p. 80) Pairs of nonadjacent angles, both interior, on opposite sides of the transversal, are called alternate interior angles.

Example: $\angle 2$ and $\angle 3$ are alternate interior angles.

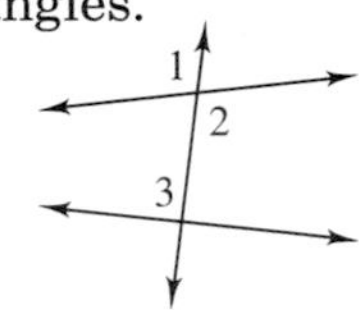

Area (p. 168) Area is the number of square units needed to cover a surface.

Example: $l = 6$ ft, and $w = 4$ ft, so the area is 24 ft^2.

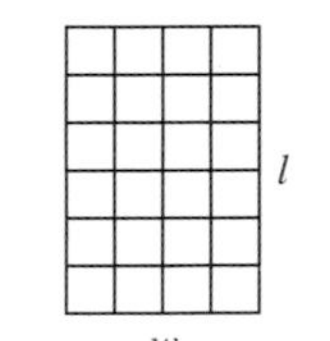

Each square equals 1 ft^2.

Arithmetic sequence (p. 247) A sequence of numbers in which each term is the result of adding the same number to the preceding term is called an arithmetic sequence.

Example The sequence 4, 10, 16, 22, 28, 34, . . . is an arithmetic sequence.

Associative property of addition (p. 121) Changing the grouping of the addends does not change the sum.

Example $(a + b) + c = a + (b + c)$

Associative property of multiplication (p. 121) Changing the grouping of the factors does not change the product.

Example $(a \cdot b) \cdot c = a \cdot (b \cdot c)$

B

Back-to-back stem-and-leaf plot (p. 29) A stem-and-leaf plot that displays two sets of data side-by-side is a back-to-back stem-and-leaf plot.

Example This back-to-back stem-and-leaf plot displays recorded times for two teams in a race. The stem records the whole number of seconds. The leaves represent tenths of a second. So 30 | 8 represents 30.8.

leaves	stem	leaves
6	27	7
954	28	568
8	29	69
53	30	8

Base (p. 127) When a number is written in exponential form, the number that is used as a factor is the base.

Example $5^4 = 5 \times 5 \times 5 \times 5$

Biased question (p. 21) A biased question is an unfair question worded so that one answer seems better than another.

Example "Do you like healthy food or junk food?"

Box-and-whisker plot (p. 32) A box-and-whisker plot shows the distribution of data in each quartile, that is, in each 25% of the data.

Example 16 19 20 26 27 29 30 30 31 34 35 36 37 39 40

16 20 24 28 32 36 40

The data above are displayed in the box-and-whisker plot. The first quartile is 26, the median is 30, and the third quartile is 36.

C

Central angle (p. 51) A central angle is an angle with its vertex at the center of the circle.

Example In circle O, $\angle AOB$ is a central angle.

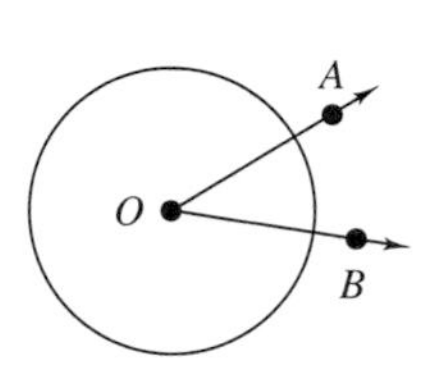

Circle graph (p. 5) A circle graph shows the parts of a whole.

Example This circle graph represents the different types of plays William Shakespeare wrote.

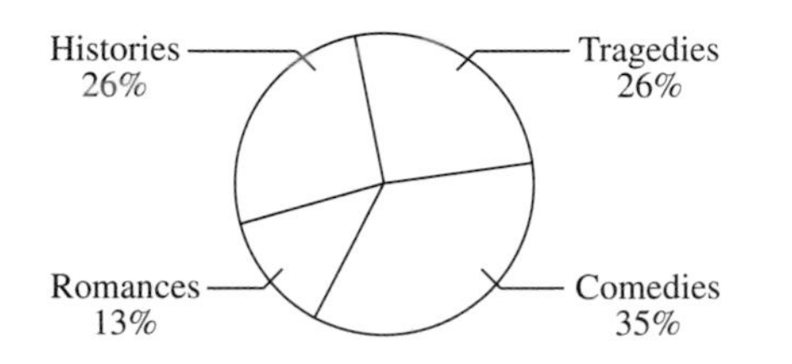

Circumference (p. 54) Circumference is the distance around a circle. You calculate the circumference of a circle by multiplying the diameter by π. $\pi \approx 3.14$

Example The circumference of a circle with a diameter of 10 cm is approximately 31.4 cm.

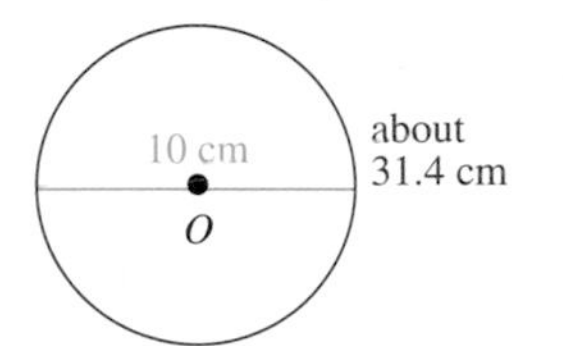

Combination (p. 387) A combination is a group of items in which the order of the items is *not* important.

Example The combination (pots and pans) is the same as the combination (pans and pots).

Commutative property of addition (p. 121) Changing the order of the addends does not change the sum.

Example $a + b = b + a$

Commutative property of multiplication (p. 121) Changing the order of the factors does not change the product.

Example $ab = ba$

Complementary angles (p. 361) Two angles are complementary if the sum of their measures is 90°.

Example $\angle BCA$ and $\angle CAB$ are complementary angles.

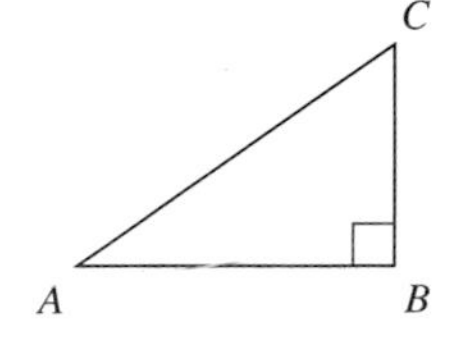

Student Study Guide

Composite numbers (p. 288) A whole number greater than 1 that has more than two factors is called a composite number.

Example 24 is a composite number that has 1, 2, 3, 4, 6, 8, 12, and 24 as factors.

Compound interest (p. 448) Compound interest is interest that is added to the balance at certain intervals and the interest for the next interval is then calculated on the new balance.

Example If $1,000 is invested for 2 years at 5% interest compounded annually, the final balance is $1,102.50.

Cone (p. 466) A cone is a space figure with one circular base and one vertex.

Example

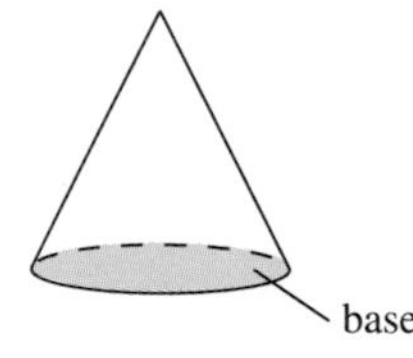

Congruent figures (p. 61) Figures that have the same size and shape are congruent.

Example $AB = QS$, $CB = RS$, and $AC = QR$. $m\angle A = m\angle Q$, $m\angle C = m\angle R$, and $m\angle B = m\angle S$. Triangles ABC and QSR are congruent.

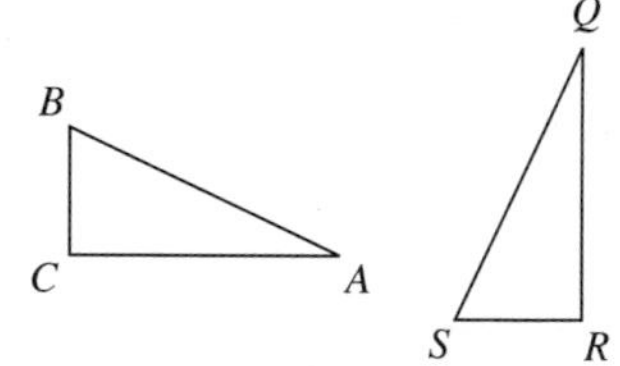

Converse of the Pythagorean theorem (p. 90) If $a^2 + b^2 = c^2$, then the triangle with sides a, b, and c is a right triangle.

Example A triangle with sides of 13 cm, 12 cm, and 5 cm is a right triangle because $5^2 + 12^2 = 13^2$.

Coordinate plane (p. 196) A coordinate plane is formed by the intersection of a horizontal number line called the x-axis and a vertical number line called the y-axis.

Example

Correlation (p. 26)

Two paired variables have a positive correlation if, in general, as the values of one variable increase, the values of the other increase also. Two paired variables have a negative correlation if, in general, as the values of one variable increase, the values of the other decrease. Two paired variables have little or no correlation if the corresponding points do not show a consistently increasing or decreasing trend.

Example

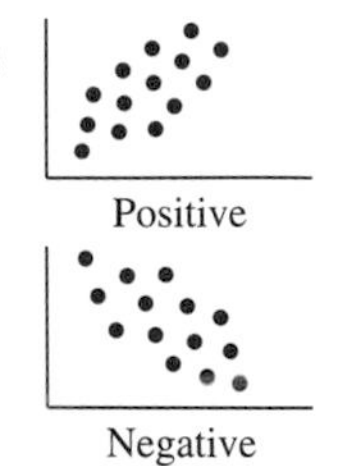

Positive

Negative

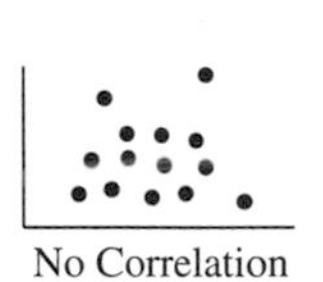

No Correlation

Corresponding angles (p. 80)

Pairs of nonadjacent angles, one interior angle and one exterior angle, both on the same side of the transversal are called corresponding angles.

Example $\angle 1$ and $\angle 3$ are corresponding angles.

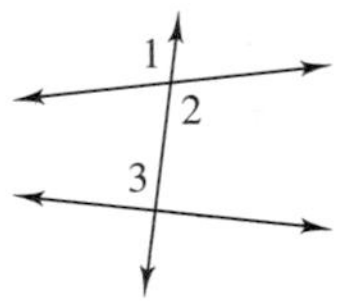

Cosine (p. 364)

In $\triangle ABC$ with right $\angle C$, $\cos A = \frac{\text{length of side adjacent to } \angle A}{\text{hypotenuse}}$.

Example $\cos A = \frac{AC}{AB} = \frac{3}{5} = 0.6$

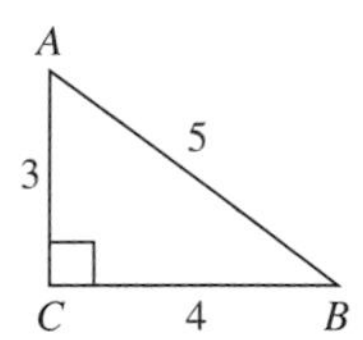

Counting principle (p. 381)

The number of outcomes for an event is the product of the number of outcomes for each stage of the event.

Example Flip a coin and roll a number cube. The total number of possible outcomes $= 2 \times 6 = 12$.

Cylinder (p. 466)

A cylinder is a space figure with two circular, parallel, and congruent bases.

Example

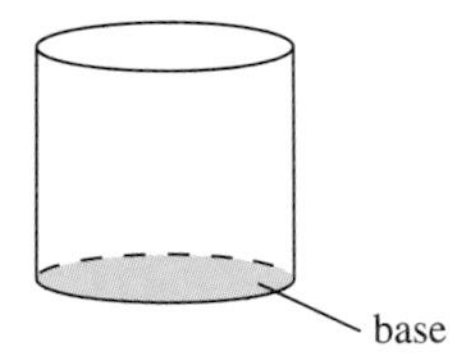

Student Study Guide

D

Decagon (p. 68) A polygon that has ten sides is a decagon.

Example

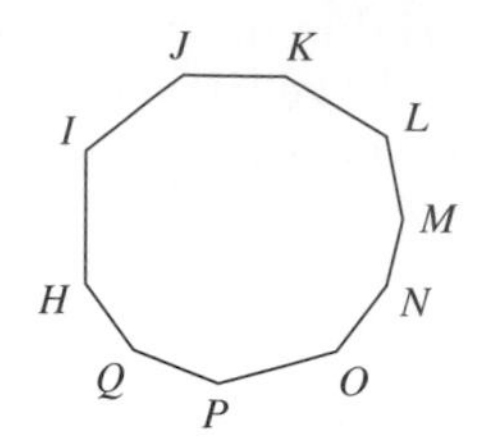

Dependent events (p. 396) Events are dependent if the outcome of the first event affects the outcome of a second event.

Example When a marble is drawn from a bag containing red and blue marbles, and not returned, the events (red, then blue) are dependent.

Dimensional analysis (p. 343) Dimensional analysis is the conversion of units of measure by using ratios.

Example $0.5 \text{ mi} = \frac{0.5 \text{ mi}}{1} \times \frac{5{,}280 \text{ ft}}{1 \text{ mi}} = 2{,}640 \text{ ft}$

Direct variation (p. 274) Direct variation is a relationship described by an equation of the form $y = kx$, where $k \neq 0$ and k is the constant of variation. We say that y varies directly as x or that y is directly proportional to x.

Example The amount of simple interest earned is directly proportional to the amount of money in the account.

Distributive property (p. 122) Each term inside a set of parentheses can be multiplied by a factor outside the parentheses.

Example $2(3 + 5) = 2 \cdot 3 + 2 \cdot 5$; $a(b + c) = ab + ac$

Division properties for inequalities (p. 179) When dividing each side of an inequality by the same positive number, the direction of the inequality stays the same. When dividing each side by the same negative number, change the direction of the inequality symbol.

Example If $a < b$ and $c > 0$, then $\frac{a}{c} < \frac{b}{c}$. If $a < b$ and $c < 0$, then $\frac{a}{c} > \frac{b}{c}$.

Division property of equality (p. 154) If both sides of an equation are divided by the same nonzero number, the results are equal.

Example If $a = b$ and $c \neq 0$, then $\frac{a}{c} = \frac{b}{c}$.

E

Equilateral triangle (p. 66) An equilateral triangle is a triangle with three congruent sides.

Example $\overline{SL} \cong \overline{LW} \cong \overline{WS}$

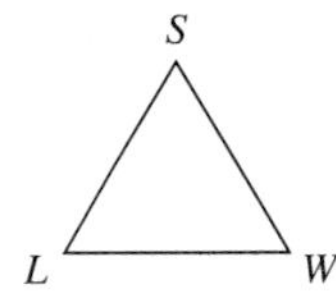

Exponent (p. 127) An exponent expresses how many times a base is used as a factor.

Example $3^4 = 3 \times 3 \times 3 \times 3$

F

Factor (p. 287) One number is a factor of a second number if it divides that number with no remainder.

Example 1, 2, 3, 4, 6, 9, 12, and 36 are factors of 36.

Factor tree (p. 288) A factor tree is used to find a number's prime factors.

Example

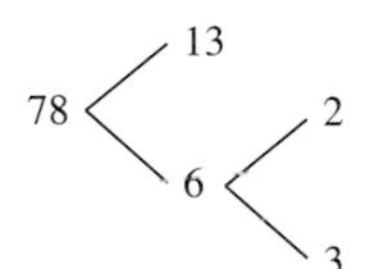

Fitted line (p. 25) A straight line that closely fits the data points on a scatter plot is called a fitted line.

Example This scatter plot displays a fitted line for an amount spent on advertising (in dollars) versus product sales (in thousands of dollars). The fitted line shows a positive correlation between the amount spent on advertising and product sales.

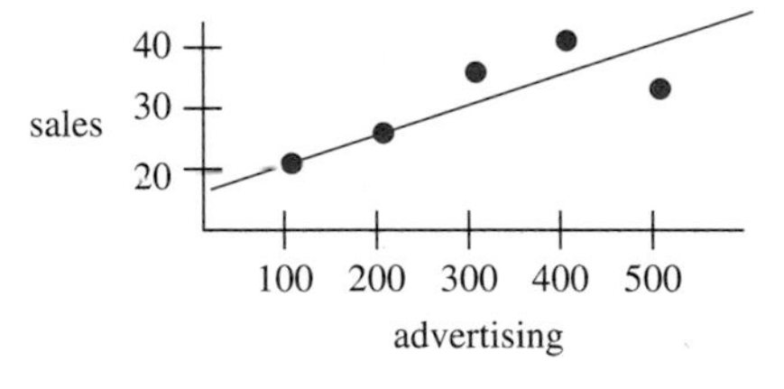

Fractal (p. 369) A fractal is a geometric pattern that is self-similar. Each stage of the figure is similar to the whole figure.

Example Snowflake and fern patterns are examples of fractals found in nature.

Frequency (p. 12) The frequency of an item is the number of times it occurs.

Example In the set 7, 7, 8, 9, 6, 8, 6, 8, 5, 8, the frequency of 8 is 4.

Student Study Guide

Frequency table (p. 12) A frequency table lists each data item with the number of times it occurs.

Example The frequency table shows the number of household telephones for a class of students.

Phones	Tally	Frequency
1	𝍸 |||	8
2	𝍸		6
3						4

Function (p. 250) A function is a relationship in which each member of one set is paired with exactly one member of a second set.

Example Earned income is a function of the number of hours worked (h). If you earn $5/h, then your income is expressed by the function $f(h) = 5h$.

G

Geometric sequence (p. 247) A sequence of numbers in which each term is the result of multiplying the preceding term by the same number is called a geometric sequence.

Example The sequence 1, 3, 9, 27, 81, . . . is a geometric sequence.

Greatest common factor (p. 287) The number that is the greatest factor of two or more numbers is the greatest common factor (GCF).

Example 12 and 30 have a GCF of 6.

H

Heptagon (p. 68) A polygon that has seven sides is a heptagon.

Example

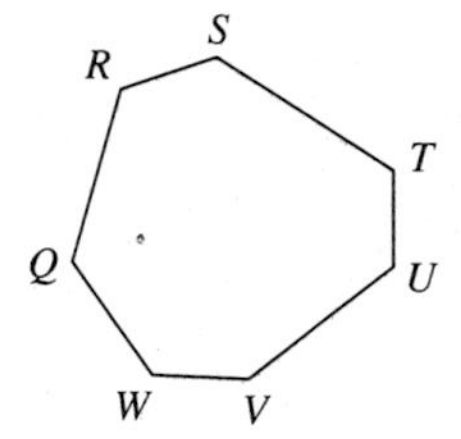

Hexagon (p. 68) A polygon that has six sides is a hexagon.

Example

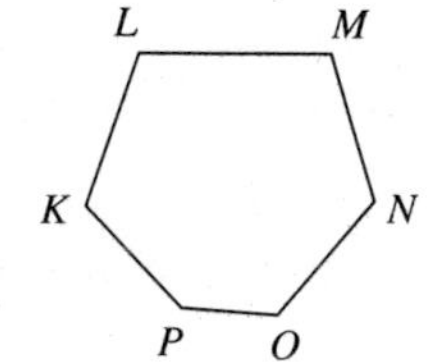

Histogram (p. 13)

A histogram is a bar graph used to show the frequency of data. There are no spaces between bars and the height of each bar gives the frequency of the data.

Example This histogram gives the frequency of watch brand names within a given price range.

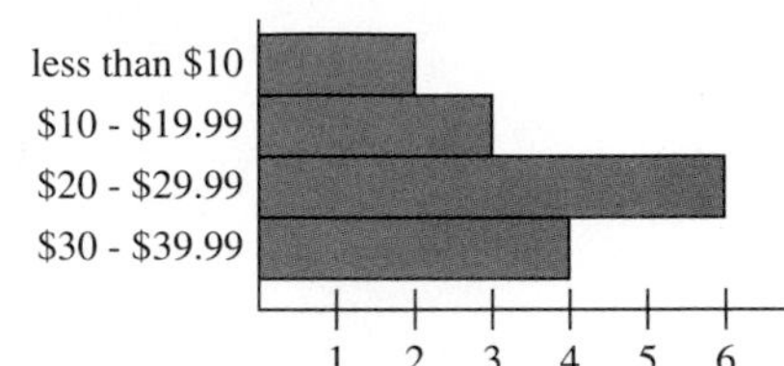

I

Identity property of addition (p. 121)

The sum of any number and 0 is that number.

Example $a + 0 = a$

Identity property of multiplication (p. 121)

The product of 1 and any number is that number.

Example $a(1) = a$

Image (p. 225)

A point, line, or figure that has been transformed to a new set of coordinates is the image of the original point, line, or figure.

Example $A'B'C'D'$ is the image of $ABCD$.

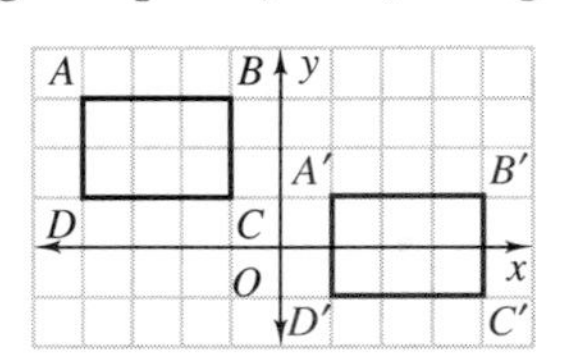

Independent events (p. 396)

Events are independent if the outcome of one event does not affect the outcome of a second event.

Example When a number cube is rolled twice, the events (6, then 3) are independent.

Indirect measurement (p. 357)

Indirect measurement is a method of determining length or distance when direct measurement is impossible.

Example $\triangle ABC$ and $\triangle RTS$ are similar with $RT = 4$, $RS = 5$, and $AB = 8$.

Then $\frac{8}{AC} = \frac{4}{5}$ and $AC = 10$.

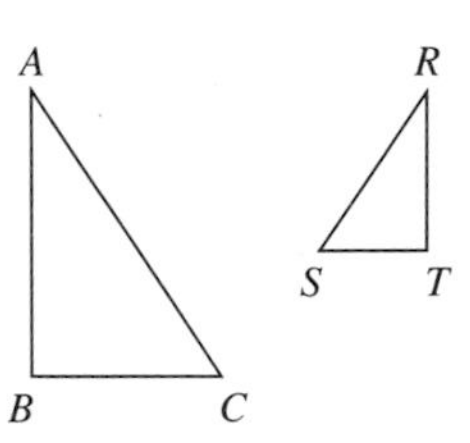

Inequalities (p. 175)

Inequalities are statements that compare two expressions.

Example $9 > y$

Student Study Guide

Inscribed angle (p. 51)

An angle that has its vertex on a circle and whose sides contain chords of the circle is an inscribed angle.

Example $\angle RPS$ is an inscribed angle of circle O.

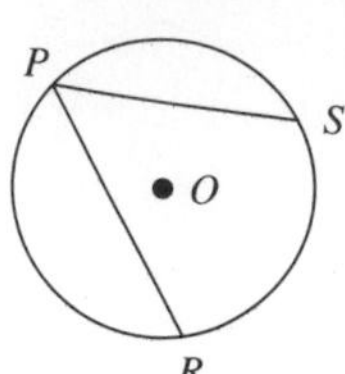

Integers (p. 294)

The integers are the set of whole numbers and their opposites.

Example The numbers -45, 0, and 289 are all integers.

Inverse variation (p. 275)

Inverse variation is a relationship described by an equation of the form $xy = k$, where $k \neq 0$ and k is the constant of variation. We say that y varies inversely as x.

Example The length x and the width y of a rectangle of a given area vary inversely. If the area $= 40$, $xy = 40$.

Irrational number (p. 327)

A number that is represented by a nonrepeating, nonterminating decimal is called an irrational number.

Example The number π, 3.141592653 . . . , is an irrational number.

Isosceles triangle (p. 66)

An isosceles triangle is a triangle with at least two congruent sides.

Example $\overline{LM} \cong \overline{LB}$.

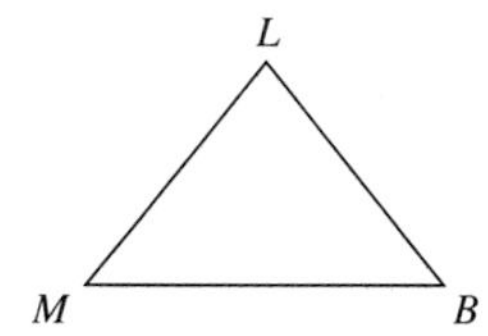

L

Least common denominator (p. 299)

The least common denominator (LCD) of two or more fractions is the least common multiple (LCM) of their denominators.

Example The LCD for the fractions $\frac{3}{8}$ and $\frac{7}{10}$ is $2 \times 2 \times 2 \times 5$, or 40.

Least common multiple (p. 299)

The smallest number that is a common multiple of two or more numbers is the least common multiple (LCM).

Example The LCM of 15 and 6 is 30.

Like terms (p. 145)

Terms with the same variable(s) are like terms.

Example $3b$ and $12b$ are like terms. Like terms can be combined because of the distributive property:

$3b + 12b = 3 \cdot b + 12 \cdot b = (3 + 12)b = 15b$

Line of symmetry (p. 231) When the reflection of a figure coincides with the original figure, the line of reflection is called a line of symmetry.

Example Line l is a line of symmetry.

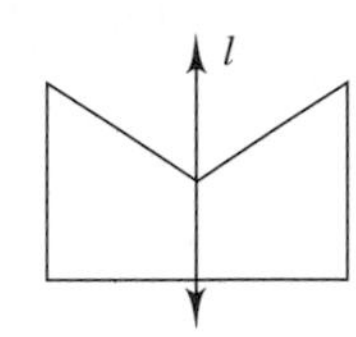

Line plot (p. 12) A line plot shows data on a number line by placing an x for each response above the category of the response.

Example The line plot shows the heights in inches of a classroom of girls.

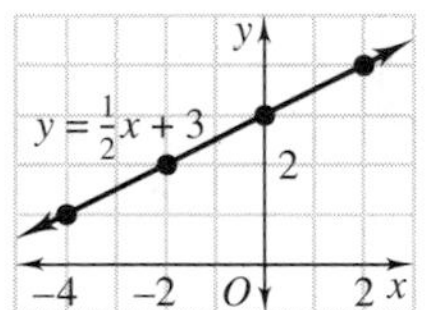

Linear equation (p. 199) An equation is a linear equation when the graphs of all of its solutions lie on a line.

Example $y = \frac{1}{2}x + 3$ is linear because the graphs of its solutions lie on a line.

Linear function (p. 254) A linear function is a function whose points lie on a line.

Example $f(x) = \frac{1}{2}x + 2$

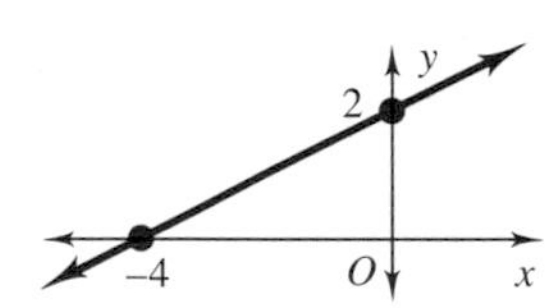

M

Multiple (p. 299) A multiple of a number is the product of that number and any nonzero whole number.

Example The multiples of 13 are 13, 26, 39, 52, and so on.

Multiple line graph (p. 7) A multiple line graph displays more than one category changing over time.

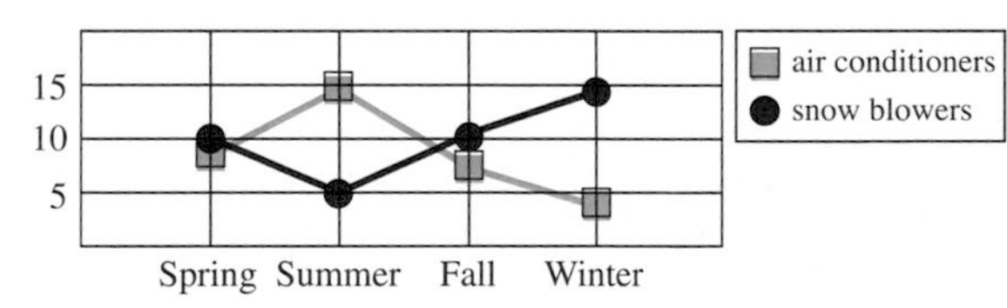

Example This multiple line graph represents seasonal air conditioner and snow blower sales (in thousands) for a large chain of stores.

Student Study Guide

Multiplication properties for inequalities (p. 179)

When multiplying each side of an inequality by the same positive number, the direction of the inequality stays the same. When multiplying each side by the same negative number, change the direction of the inequality symbol.

Example If $a < b$ and $c > 0$, then $ac < bc$. If $a < b$ and $c < 0$, then $ac > bc$.

Multiplication property of equality (p. 155)

If both sides of an equation are multiplied by the same number, the results are equal.

Example If $a = b$, then $a \cdot c = b \cdot c$.

Multiplicative inverse (p. 309)

The reciprocal of a number is also called its multiplicative inverse.

Example The multiplicative inverse of $\frac{4}{9}$ is $\frac{9}{4}$.

N

Nonagon (p. 68)

A polygon that has nine sides is a nonagon.

Example

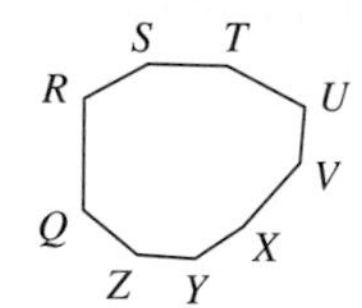

O

Obtuse triangle (p. 66)

An obtuse triangle is a triangle with one obtuse angle.

Example $90° < m\angle J < 180°$

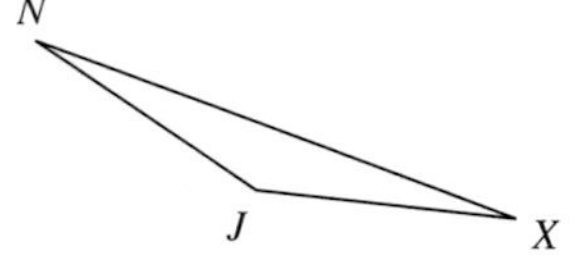

Octagon (p. 68)

A polygon that has eight sides is an octagon.

Example

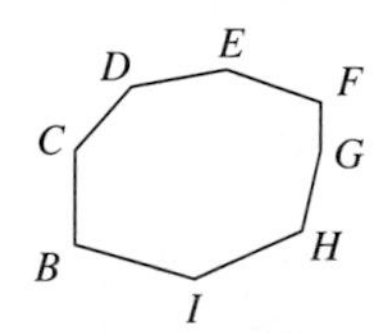

Odds (p. 393)

Odds are used to compare favorable outcomes to unfavorable outcomes. The odds in favor of an event is given by:

$$\frac{\text{number of favorable outcomes}}{\text{number of unfavorable outcomes}}$$

Example The odds in favor of getting a 4 when spinning the wheel are $\frac{1}{7}$.

Opposite numbers (p. 103) Numbers that are the same distance from zero on the number line but in opposite directions are opposite numbers.

Example -17 and 17 are opposite numbers because they are both 17 units from zero on the number line.

Ordered pair (p. 195) An ordered pair is a pair of numbers that describe the location of a point on a coordinate plane. The first value is called the x-coordinate and the second value is called the y-coordinate.

Example The ordered pair of coordinates $(-2, 1)$ identifies the point that is 2 units to the left, and 1 unit above the origin.

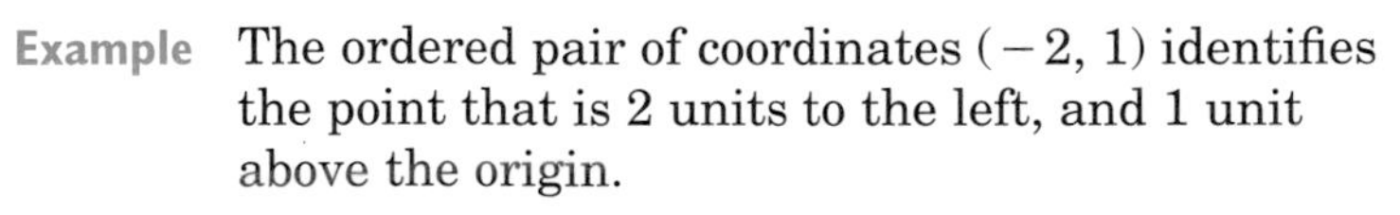

Origin (p. 196) The origin is the intersection point of the x- and y-axes in a coordinate plane.

Example O is the origin. The coordinates of the origin are (0, 0).

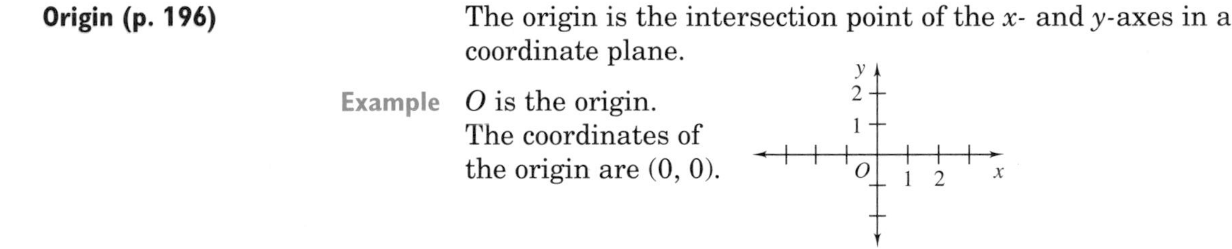

Outlier (p. 16) An item of data that is much higher or lower than the rest of the data is an outlier.

Example An outlier in the list 1, 1, 2, 3, 4, 4, 6, 7, 7, 52 is 52.

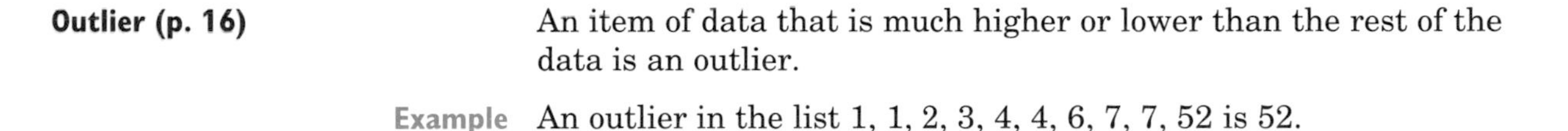

P

Parallel lines (p. 79) Parallel lines are lines in the same plane that do not intersect.

Example $\overleftrightarrow{EF} \parallel \overleftrightarrow{HI}$

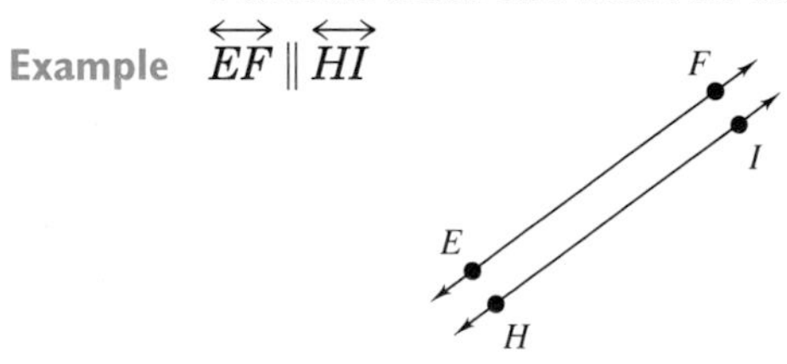

Parallelogram (p. 65) A parallelogram is a quadrilateral with two pairs of opposite sides parallel.

Example $KVDA$ is a parallelogram.

Pentagon (p. 68) A polygon that has five sides is a pentagon.

Example

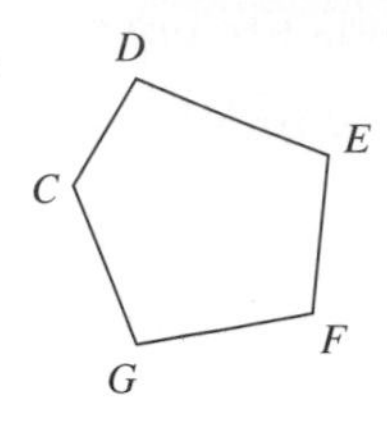

Percent (p. 423) A percent is a ratio that compares a number to one hundred. The symbol for percent is %.

Example $\frac{50}{100} = 50\%$

Percent of change (p. 442) Percent of change is the percent something increases or decreases from its original measure or amount.

Example If a school's population increased from 500 to 520 students, the percent of change would be $\frac{520 - 500}{500} = 4\%$.

Perfect square (p. 86) The square of a whole number is a perfect square.

Example $3^2 = 9$. 9 is a perfect square.

Perimeter (p.168) The perimeter of a polygon is the sum of the lengths of all its sides.

Example The perimeter of *ABCD* is 12 ft.

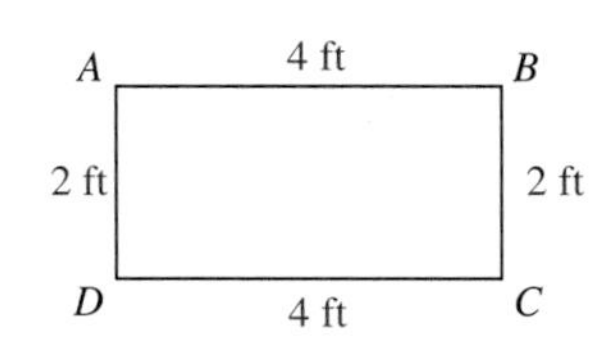

Permutation (p. 384) A permutation is an arrangement of a set of objects in a particular order.

Example The seating plans (Judith, Ann, Adrian) and (Ann, Judith, Adrian) are two different permutations.

Perpendicular lines (p. 76) Perpendicular lines are lines that intersect to form right angles.

Example $\overleftrightarrow{DE} \perp \overleftrightarrow{RS}$

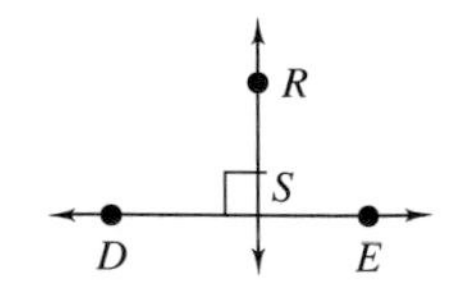

Prime factorization (p. 288) Writing a composite number as the product of its prime factors is called prime factorization.

Example The prime factorization of 30 is $2 \times 3 \times 5$.

Prime numbers (p. 288)

A whole number greater than 1 that has exactly two factors, 1 and the number itself, is a prime number.

Example 13 is a prime number because its only factors are 1 and 13.

Prism (p. 465)

A prism is a three-dimensional figure with two parallel and congruent polygonal faces, called bases. A prism is named by the shape of its base.

Example

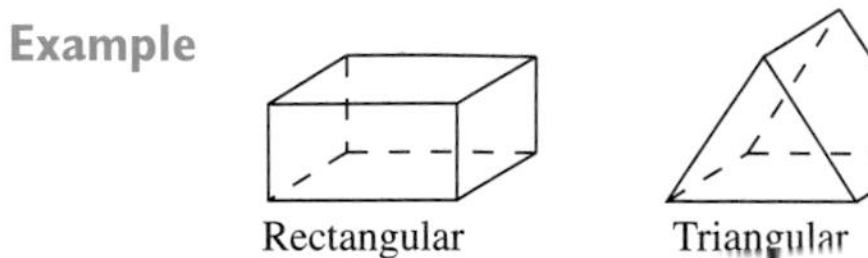

Probability (p. 392)

When all outcomes are equally likely, the probability that an event E will happen is $P(E) = \frac{\text{number of favorable outcomes}}{\text{number of possible outcomes}}$.

Example The probability of getting a 4 on a number cube is $\frac{1}{6}$.

Proportion (p. 346)

A proportion is an equation stating that two ratios are equal.

Example $\frac{3}{12} = \frac{12}{48}$ is a proportion.

Pyramid (p. 465)

A pyramid is a space figure with triangular sides and one base that is a polygon.

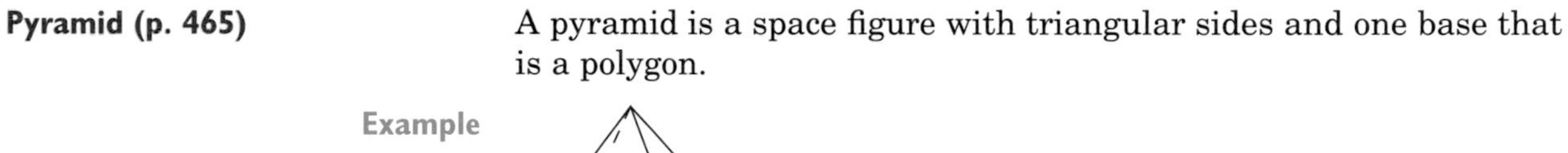

Example

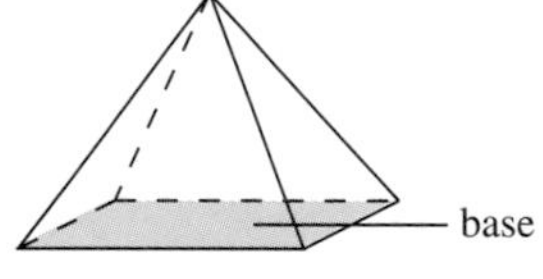

Pythagorean theorem (p. 89)

In any right triangle the square of the length of the hypotenuse is equal to the sum of the squares of the lengths of the legs.

Example $c^2 = a^2 + b^2$

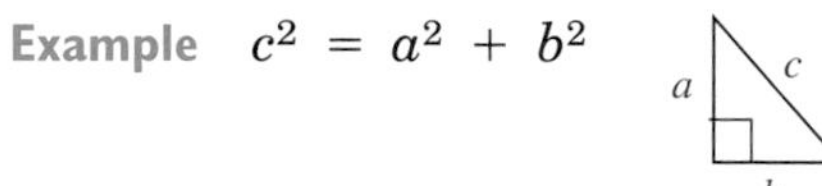

Q

Quadrants (p. 196)

The x- and y-axes divide the coordinate plane into four quadrants.

Example

Quadratic function (p. 266) In a quadratic function, the greatest power of the variable is 2. The graph of a quadratic function is a curve.

Example $f(x) = -\frac{1}{2}x^2 + 2x$

R

Range (p. 13) The range of a set of numerical data is the difference between the greatest and least values in the set.

Example A group of students spent the following number of hours a week exercising: 7 9 15 3 18 2 16 14 14 20

The range of the data is $20 - 2 = 18$.

Ratio (p. 339) A ratio is a comparison of two numbers by division.

Example A ratio can be written in three different ways: 72 to 100, 72 : 100, and $\frac{72}{100}$.

Rational numbers (p. 291) A rational number is a number that can be written in the form $\frac{a}{b}$ where a is an integer and b is any nonzero integer.

Example $\frac{3}{5}$, -8, 8.7, 0.333 . . . , $-5\frac{3}{11}$, 0, $\frac{17}{4}$ are all rational numbers.

Real numbers (p. 328) The rational numbers and irrational numbers together form the set of real numbers.

Example 3, -5.25, 3.141592653 . . . , and $\frac{7}{8}$ are real numbers.

Reciprocal (p. 309) Two numbers whose product is 1 are called reciprocals.

Example $-\frac{4}{9}$ and $-\frac{9}{4}$ are reciprocals. $-\frac{4}{9} \cdot (-\frac{9}{4}) = 1$

Rectangle (p. 65) A rectangle is a parallelogram with four right angles.

Example $RSWH$ is a rectangle.

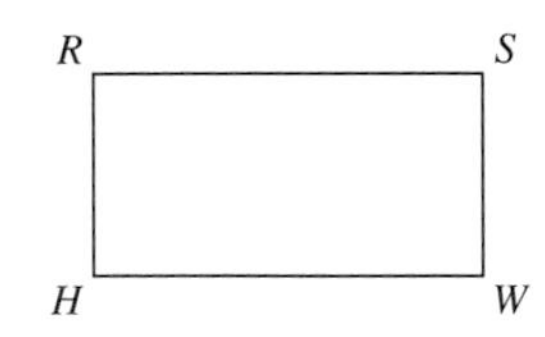

Reflection (p. 229) A reflection flips a figure across a line.

Example $K'L'M'N'$ is a reflection of $KLMN$ over the y-axis.

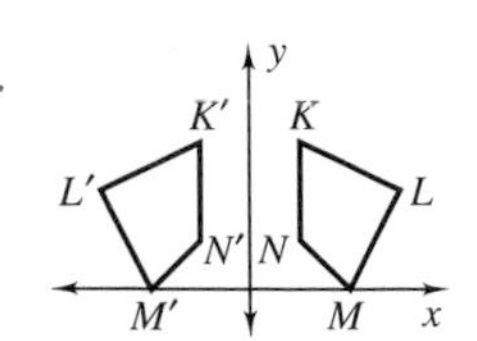

Repeating decimal (p. 295)

A repeating decimal is a decimal in which a digit or a sequence of digits keeps repeating. The symbol for a repeating decimal is a bar drawn over the digit or digits that repeat.

Example $0.8888\ldots$, or $0.\overline{8}$

Rhombus (p. 65)

A rhombus is a parallelogram with four congruent sides.

Example *GHJI* is a rhombus.

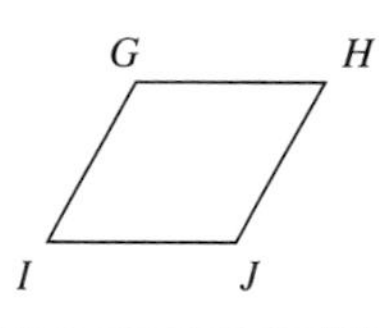

Right triangle (p. 66)

A right triangle is a triangle with one right angle.

Example $m\angle B = 90°$

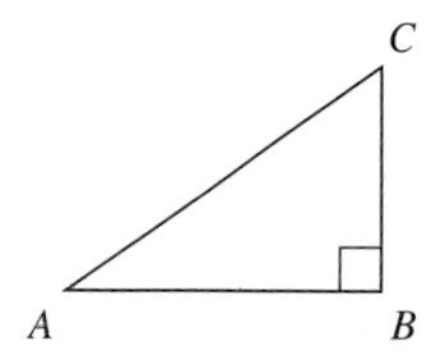

Rotation (p. 233)

A rotation is a transformation that turns a figure about a fixed point, called the center of rotation.

Example The image of $\triangle STR$ after a 180° rotation about the origin is $\triangle S'T'R'$. The origin is the center of rotation.

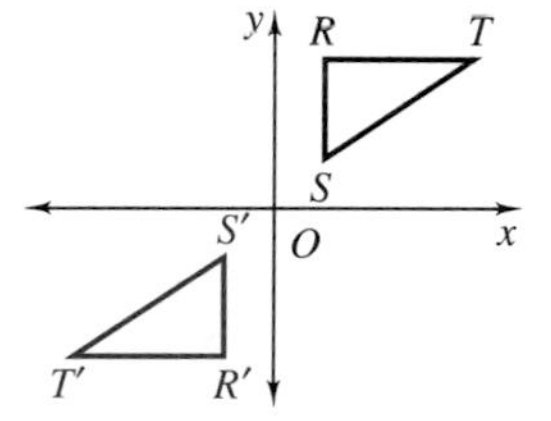

Rotational symmetry (p. 234)

A figure has rotational symmetry when an image after a rotation fits exactly on top of the original figure.

Example This figure has a 60° rotational symmetry.

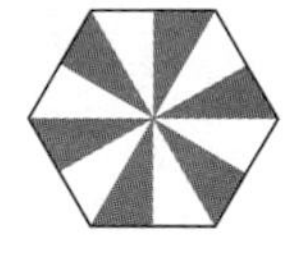

Rule of exponents for division (p. 315)

To divide numbers with the same base, subtract the exponents.

Example $\frac{8^7}{8^2} = 8^5$; $\frac{a^m}{a^n} = a^{m-n}$ for $a \neq 0$

S

Sample (p. 21)

A sample is a small subset of the population, which is any collection of objects. The number of objects in the sample is called the sample size. A sample is random if each object in the population has an equal chance of being included.

Example A class of 25 students is a sample of a school population. The sample size is 25.

Scale factor (p. 351)

In similar polygons, the ratio of the lengths of corresponding sides is the scale factor of similarity.

Example $\triangle ABC \sim \triangle RTS$. If $AB = 8$ and $RT = 4$, the scale factor is $\frac{2}{1}$.

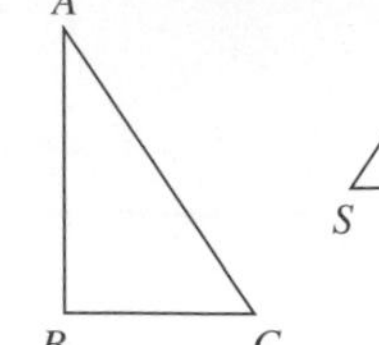

Scalene triangle (p. 66)

A scalene triangle is a triangle with no congruent sides.

Example

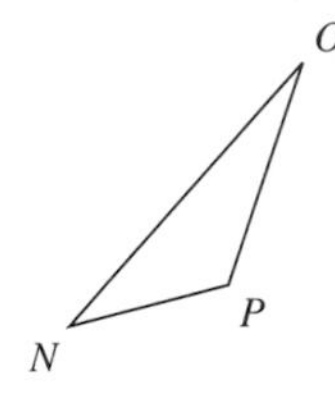

Scatter plot (p. 24)

A scatter plot displays data from two sets as ordered pairs.

Example The scatter plot at the right displays the amount spent on advertising (in dollars) versus product sales (in thousands of dollars).

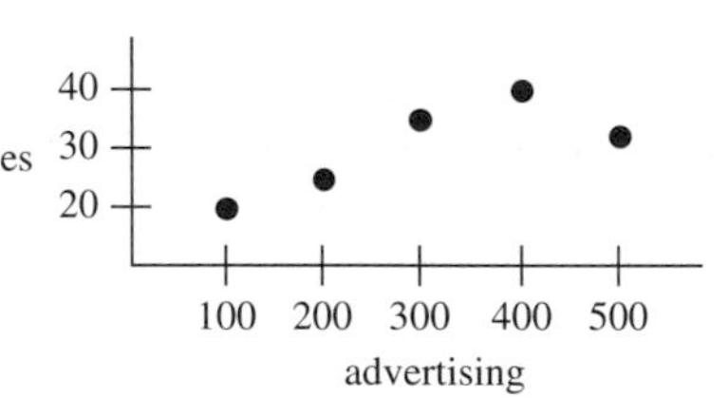

Scientific notation (p. 318)

A number is expressed in scientific notation when it is written as the product of a number greater than or equal to 1 and less than 10, and a power of 10.

Example 37,000,000 is written as 3.7×10^7 in scientific notation.

Self-similar figures (p. 369)

Each part of a self-similar figure is similar, at each stage, to the whole figure.

Example

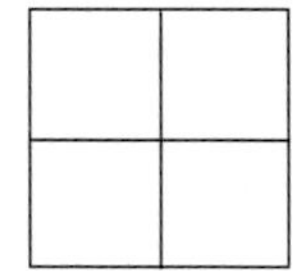

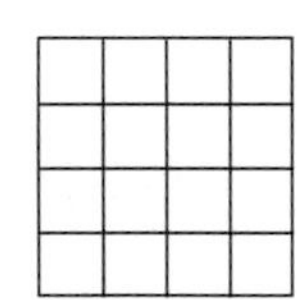

Semicircle (p. 52)

A semicircle is an arc whose endpoints are the endpoints of a diameter of the circle.

Example $\overparen{ABC}$ is a semicircle of $\odot O$.

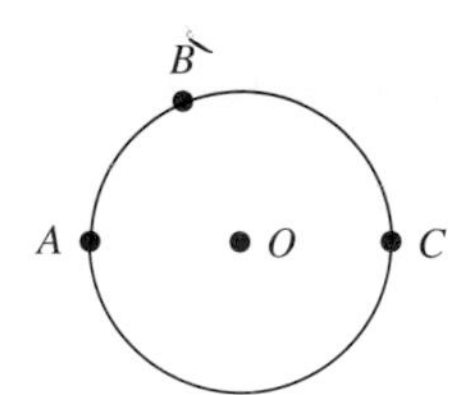

Simple interest (p. 448)

Simple interest is interest calculated on the principal, the initial amount of money invested or borrowed.

Example: The simple interest on \$1,000 at 5% for 2 years is \$100.

Simplest form of a fraction (p. 292)

A fraction is in simplest form when the greatest common factor (GCF) of the numerator and the denominator is 1.

Example: $\frac{3}{4}$ is the simplest form of the fraction $\frac{15}{20}$.

Sine (p. 364)

In $\triangle ABC$ with right $\angle C$,

$$\sin A = \frac{\text{length of side opposite } \angle A}{\text{hypotenuse}}$$

Example: $\sin A = \frac{CB}{AB} = \frac{4}{5} = 0.8$

Sliding bar graph (p. 5)

A sliding bar graph displays two categories as bars graphed in opposite directions. Sliding bar graphs can be used to compare amounts or frequencies.

Example: The sliding bar graph represents class sizes for grades 6, 7, and 8 for both boys and girls.

Slope (p. 206)

Slope is a number that describes the steepness of a line.

$$\text{slope} = \frac{\text{vertical change}}{\text{horizontal change}}$$

Example: The slope of the given line $= \frac{2}{4} = \frac{1}{2}$.

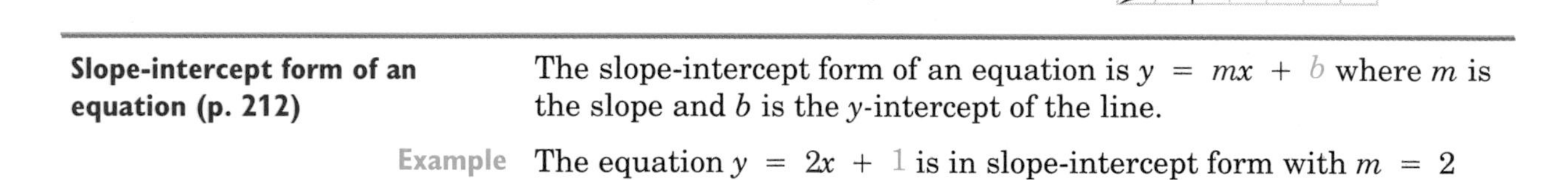

Slope-intercept form of an equation (p. 212)

The slope-intercept form of an equation is $y = mx + b$ where m is the slope and b is the y-intercept of the line.

Example: The equation $y = 2x + 1$ is in slope-intercept form with $m = 2$ and $b = 1$.

Solution of a system of linear equations (p. 217)

The solution of a system of linear equations is any ordered pair(s) that make(s) all the equations true.

Example (1, 3) is the solution of the system of linear equations $y = 2x + 1$ and $y = -x + 4$.

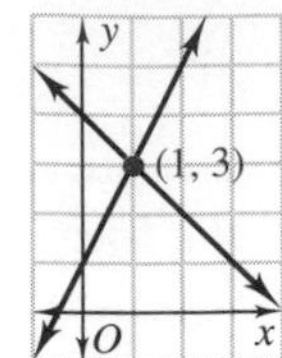

Solution of an equation (p. 149)

A value of the variable that makes the equation true is called a solution of the equation.

Example The solution of $2y - 5 = -7$ is -1.

Solution of an equation in two variables (p. 198)

An ordered pair that makes an equation in two variables a true statement is a solution of the equation.

Example (8, 4) is a solution of $y = -1x + 12$ because $4 = -1(8) + 12$.

Sphere (p. 466)

A sphere is the set of all points in space that are the same distance from a given point called the center.

Example

Square (p. 65)

A square is a parallelogram with four right angles and four congruent sides.

Example *QRTS* is a square.

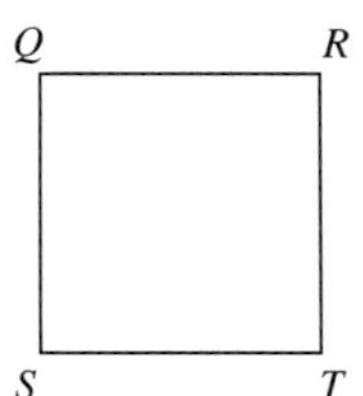

Square root (p. 86)

The opposite of squaring a number is finding its square root. The symbol for a square root is $\sqrt{}$.

Example $\sqrt{25} = 5$ because $5^2 = 25$.

Stacked bar graph (p. 5)

A stacked bar graph has bars divided into categories. Each bar represents a total. Stacked bar graphs can be used to compare amounts or frequencies.

Example This stacked bar graph represents class sizes for grades 6, 7, and 8.

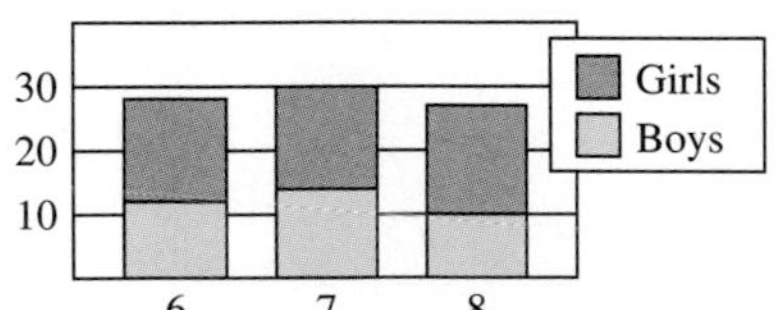

Stem-and-leaf plot (p. 28) A display that shows data in order of place value is a stem-and-leaf plot. A leaf is a data item's last digit on the right. A stem represents the digits to the left of the leaf.

Example This stem-and-leaf plot displays recorded times in a race. The stem records the whole number of seconds. The leaves represent tenths of a second. So, 27|7 represents 27.7.

stem	leaves
27	7
28	568
29	69
30	8

Subtraction properties for inequalities (p. 178) If the same number is subtracted from both sides of an inequality, the order of the inequality will remain the same.

Example $10 > 7$, so $10 - 3 > 7 - 3$; if $a > b$, then $a - c > b - c$. $2 < 7$, so $2 - 3 < 7 - 3$; if $a < b$, then $a - c < b - c$.

Subtraction property of equality (p. 149) If the same number is subtracted from each side of an equation, the results will be equal.

Example If $a = b$, then $a - c = b - c$.

Surface area (pp. 474, 477) The surface area of a three-dimensional figure is the number of square units needed to cover the outside of the figure.

Example The surface area of a prism is the sum of the areas of the faces.

$4 \times 12 + 2 \times 9 = 66$ in.^{2}

Each square = 1 in.^{2}

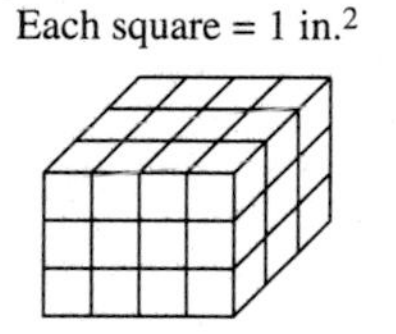

System of linear equations (p. 217) Two or more linear equations using the same variables form a system of linear equations.

Example $y = 2x + 1$ and $y = -x + 4$ form a system of linear equations.

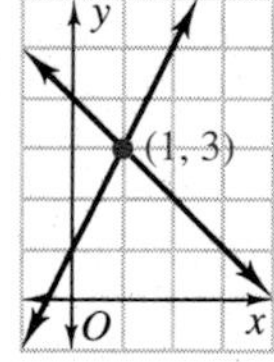

T

Tangent (p. 364) In $\triangle ABC$ with right $\angle C$,

$$\tan A = \frac{\text{length of side opposite } \angle A}{\text{length of side adjacent to } \angle A}.$$

Example $\tan A = \frac{BC}{AC} = \frac{4}{3} = 1.\overline{3}$

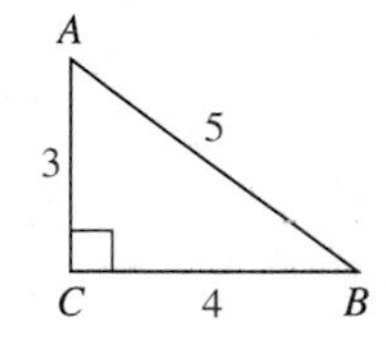

Term (p. 145)	A term is a part of a variable expression.
Example	The expression $7x + 12 + (-9y)$ has three terms: $7x$, 12, and $-9y$.
Terminating decimal (p. 295)	A terminating decimal is a decimal that stops, or terminates.
Example	Both 0.6 and 0.7265 are terminating decimals.
Tessellation (p. 72)	A tessellation is a repeated geometric design that covers a plane without gaps or overlaps.
Example	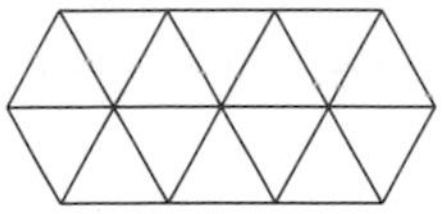
Transformations (p. 225)	Movements of figures on a plane are transformations. A transformation can be a translation, reflection, or rotation.
Example	$K'L'M'N'$ is a reflection of $KLMN$ over the y-axis.
Translation (p. 225)	A translation slides a figure.
Example	$ABCD$ has been translated to $A'B'C'D'$.
Transversal (p. 79)	A transversal is a line that intersects two other coplanar lines in different points.
Example	$\overleftrightarrow{RI}$ is a transversal of $\overleftrightarrow{QS}$ and $\overleftrightarrow{HJ}$.
Trapezoid (p. 65)	A trapezoid is a quadrilateral with exactly one pair of parallel sides.
Example	$UVYW$ is a trapezoid.
Trigonometric ratios (p. 364)	*See* cosine, sine, and tangent.

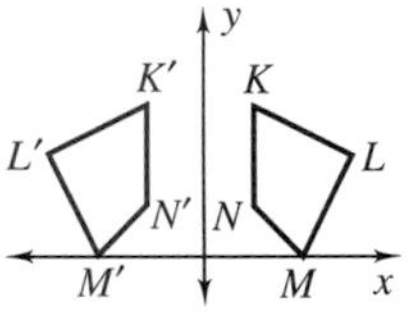

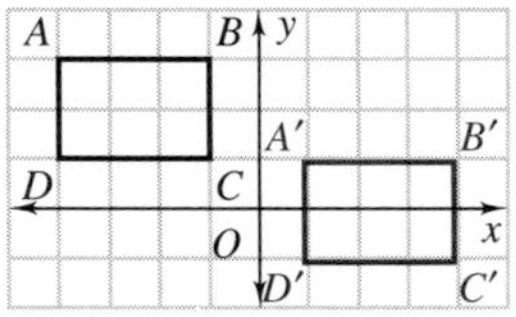

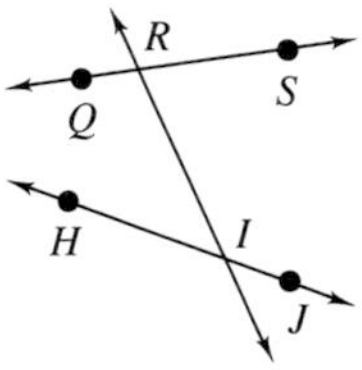

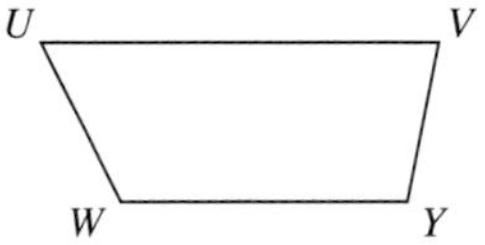

U

Unit rate (p. 340) A unit rate is the rate for one unit of a given quantity.

Example: If you drive 165 mi in 3 h, your unit rate of travel is $\frac{165 \text{ mi}}{3 \text{ h}} =$ 55 mi/h.

V

Variable expression (p. 106) A variable expression is an expression that contains a variable.

Example: $7 + x$ is a variable expression.

Volume (p. 481) The volume of a three-dimensional figure is the number of cubic units needed to fill the space inside the figure.

Example: The volume of the rectangular prism is 36 in.^{3}.

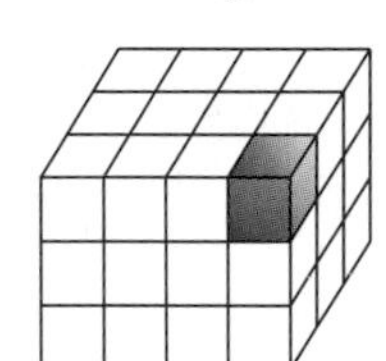

each cube = 1 in.^{3}

W

Whole numbers (p. 294) The whole numbers are 0, 1, 2, 3, . . .

Example: The number 165 is a whole number.

X

x-intercept (p. 211) The x-intercept of a line is the x-coordinate of the point where the line crosses the x-axis.

Example: To find the x-intercept, substitute 0 for y.
$6x - 4y = 12;$
$6x - 4(\ ) = 12;$
$x = 2$
The x-intercept is 2.

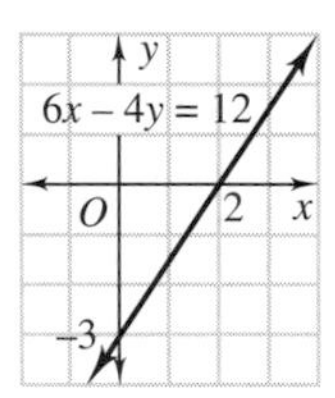

Y

y-intercept (p. 211) The y-intercept of a line is the y-coordinate of the point where the line crosses the y-axis.

Example: To find the y-intercept, substitute 0 for x.
$6x - 4y = 12; 6(\ ) - 4y = 12;$
$y = -3$
The y-intercept is -3.

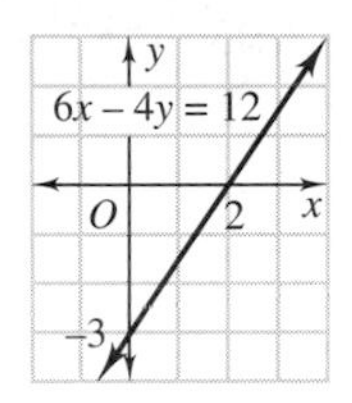

Index

Index

Tables

Math You May Need to Know

Working with Decimals

Each digit in a whole number or a decimal has both a place and a value. The value of any place is one-tenth the value of the place to its left. A place value chart like the one below can help you read and write decimals.

millions	hundred thousands	ten thousands	thousands	hundreds	tens	ones	.	tenths	hundredths	thousandths	ten-thousandths	hundred-thousandths	millionths
1	2	6	2	8	3	0	•	7	5	0	1	9	4

Examples

a. What is the value of the digit 8?
The digit 8 is in the hundreds place.
So, its value is 8 hundreds.

b. Write 2.006 in words.
The digit 6 is in the thousandths place.
So, 2.006 is read two and six thousandths.

c. Write five and thirty-four ten-thousandths as a decimal.
Ten-thousandths is 4 places to the right of the decimal point.
So, the decimal will have 4 places after the decimal point.
The answer is 5.0034.

EXERCISES

Use the chart above. Write the value of each digit.

1. the digit 9
2. the digit 7
3. the digit 5
4. the digit 6
5. the digit 4
6. the digit 3

Write a decimal for the given words.

7. forty-one ten-thousandths
8. eighteen and five hundred four thousandths
9. eight millionths
10. seven and sixty-three hundred-thousandths
11. twelve thousandths
12. sixty-five and two hundred one thousandths

Write each decimal in words.

13. 0.06
14. 4.7
15. 0.00011
16. 0.9
17. 0.012
18. 0.000059
19. 0.0042
20. 6.029
21. 5.000186

Comparing and Ordering Decimals

To compare two decimals, use the symbol $>$ (is greater than) and $<$ (is less than). When you compare, start at the left and compare the digits.

Examples

Use $>$ or $<$ to compare the decimals.

a. 0.1 ■ 0.06
1 tenth $>$ 0 tenths, so
0.1 $>$ 0.06

b. 2.4583 ■ 2.48
5 hundredths $<$ 8 hundredths, so
2.4583 $<$ 2.48

c. 0.30026 ■ 0.03026
3 tenths $>$ 0 tenths, so
0.30026 $>$ 0.03026

You can also use number lines to help you compare decimals.

More Examples

Draw number lines to compare the decimals.

d. 0.1 ■ 0.06

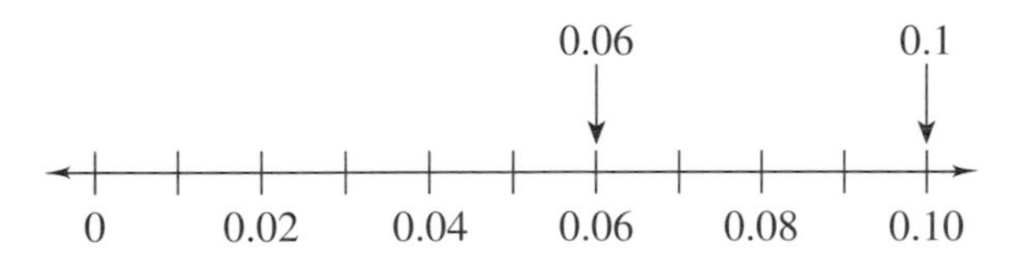

0.1 $>$ 0.06

e. 2.4583 ■ 2.48

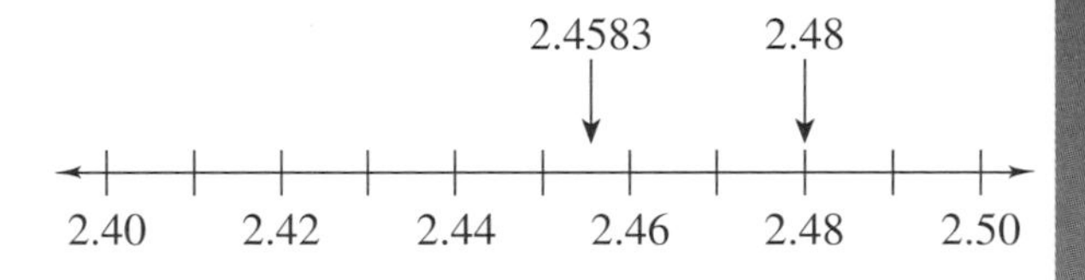

2.4583 $<$ 2.48

EXERCISES

Use $>$ or $<$ to compare the decimals. Draw number lines if you wish.

1. 0.003 ■ 0.02
2. 84.2 ■ 842
3. 0.162 ■ 0.106
4. 0.0659 ■ 0.6059
5. 2.13 ■ 2.99
6. 3.53 ■ 3.529
7. 0.7562 ■ 0.7559
8. 0.00072 ■ 0.07002
9. 0.458 ■ 0.4589
10. 8.627 ■ 8.649
11. 0.0019 ■ 0.0002
12. 0.19321 ■ 0.19231

Write the decimals in order from greatest to least.

13. 2.31, 0.231, 23.1, 0.23, 3.21
14. 1.02, 1.002, 1.2, 1.11, 1.021
15. 0.02, 0.002, 0.22, 0.222, 2.22
16. 55.5, 555.5, 55.555, 5.5555
17. 0.07, 0.007, 0.7, 0.71, 0.72
18. 2.78, 2.7001, 2.701, 2.71, 2.7
19. 7, 7.3264, 7.3, 7.3246, 7.0324
20. 0.0101, 0.0099, 0.011, 0.00019

Rounding Decimals

You can draw number lines to help you round decimals.

Examples

a. Round 1.627 to the nearest whole number.

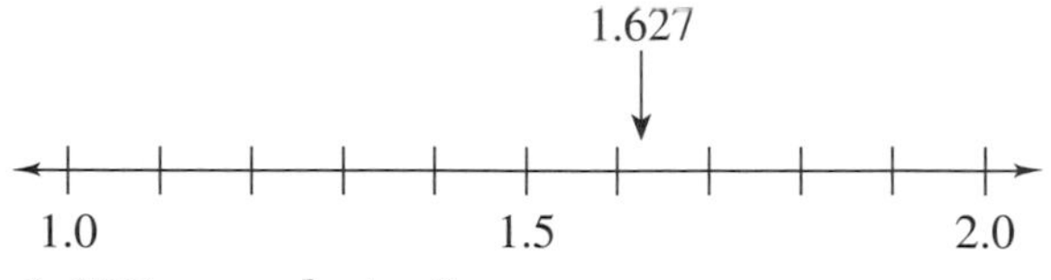

1.627 rounds to 2.

b. Round 0.3092 to the nearest tenth.

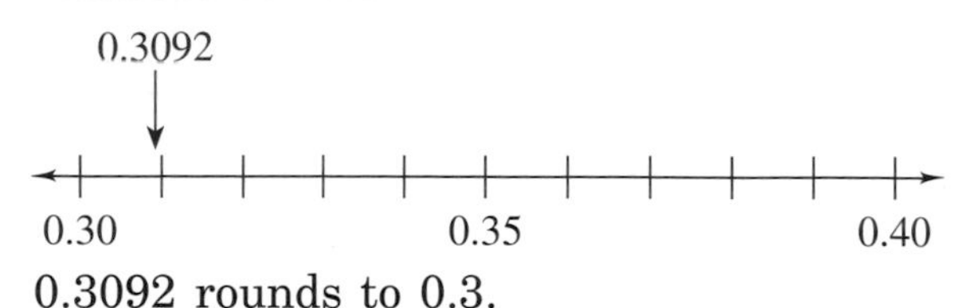

0.3092 rounds to 0.3.

c. Round 2.0195 to the nearest hundredth.

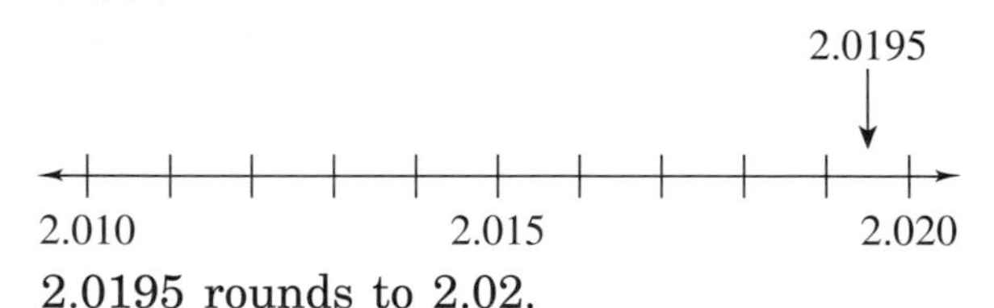

2.0195 rounds to 2.02.

d. Round 0.060521 to the nearest thousandth.

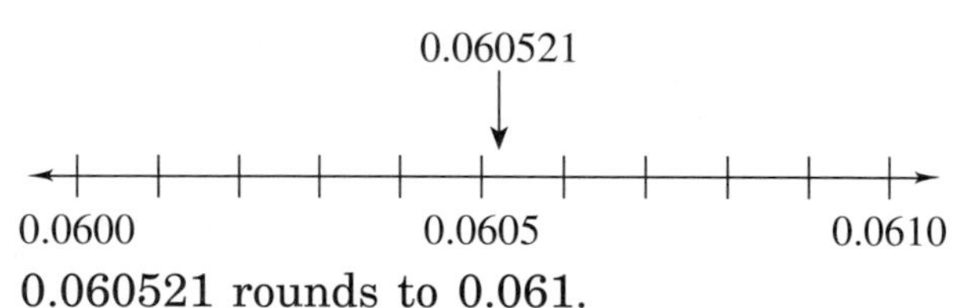

0.060521 rounds to 0.061.

EXERCISES

Round to the nearest whole number.

1. 135.91　**2.** 3.001095　**3.** 96.912　**4.** 101.167　**5.** 299.9

6. 823.54　**7.** 10.4　**8.** 79.527826　**9.** 105.3002　**10.** 431.2349

Round to the nearest tenth.

11. 82.01　**12.** 4.67522　**13.** 20.397　**14.** 399.95　**15.** 129.98

16. 9.754　**17.** 3.816303　**18.** 19.72　**19.** 401.1603　**20.** 499.491

Round to the nearest hundredth.

21. 13.458　**22.** 96.4045　**23.** 0.699　**24.** 4.23　**25.** 12.09531

26. 8.091　**27.** 14.869　**28.** 1.78826　**29.** 0.111982　**30.** 736.941

Round to the nearest thousandth.

31. 7.0615　**32.** 5.77125　**33.** 125.66047　**34.** 0.9195　**35.** 4.003771

36. 6.0004　**37.** 0.0649　**38.** 3.495366　**39.** 8.07092　**40.** 0.6008

Adding and Subtracting Decimals

You add or subtract decimals just as you do whole numbers. You line up the decimal points and then add or subtract. If you wish, you can use zeros to make the columns even.

Examples

Find each sum or difference.

a. 37.6 + 8.431

$$\begin{array}{r} 37.6 \\ +\ 8.431 \\ \hline \end{array} \rightarrow \begin{array}{r} 37.600 \\ +\ 8.431 \\ \hline 46.031 \end{array}$$

b. 8 − 4.593

$$\begin{array}{r} 8 \\ -4.593 \\ \hline \end{array} \rightarrow \begin{array}{r} 8.000 \\ -4.593 \\ \hline 3.407 \end{array}$$

c. 8.3 + 2.99 + 17.5

$$\begin{array}{r} 8.3 \\ 2.99 \\ +17.5 \\ \hline \end{array} \rightarrow \begin{array}{r} 8.30 \\ 2.99 \\ +17.50 \\ \hline 28.79 \end{array}$$

EXERCISES

Find each sum or difference.

1. $\begin{array}{r} 39.7 \\ -36.03 \\ \hline \end{array}$ **2.** $\begin{array}{r} 1.08 \\ -0.9 \\ \hline \end{array}$ **3.** $\begin{array}{r} 6.784 \\ +0.528 \\ \hline \end{array}$ **4.** $\begin{array}{r} 5.01 \\ -0.87 \\ \hline \end{array}$ **5.** $\begin{array}{r} 13.02 \\ +23.107 \\ \hline \end{array}$

6. $\begin{array}{r} 8.634 \\ +1.409 \\ \hline \end{array}$ **7.** $\begin{array}{r} 2.1 \\ -0.5 \\ \hline \end{array}$ **8.** $\begin{array}{r} 8.23 \\ -3.1 \\ \hline \end{array}$ **9.** $\begin{array}{r} 1.05 \\ +12.9 \\ \hline \end{array}$ **10.** $\begin{array}{r} 2.6 \\ +0.003 \\ \hline \end{array}$

11. $\begin{array}{r} 0.1 \\ 58.21 \\ +\ 1.9 \\ \hline \end{array}$ **12.** $\begin{array}{r} 12.2 \\ 3.06 \\ +\ 0.5 \\ \hline \end{array}$ **13.** $\begin{array}{r} 9.42 \\ 3.6 \\ +21.003 \\ \hline \end{array}$ **14.** $\begin{array}{r} 15.22 \\ 7.4 \\ +\ 8.125 \\ \hline \end{array}$ **15.** $\begin{array}{r} 3.7 \\ 20.06 \\ +16.19 \\ \hline \end{array}$

16. 76.39 − 8.47 **17.** 8.7 + 17.03 **18.** 32.403 + 12.06 **19.** 20.5 − 11.45

20. 8.9 − 4.45 **21.** 1.245 + 5.8 **22.** 3.9 + 6.57 **23.** 14.81 − 8.6

24. 11.9 − 2.06 **25.** 3.45 + 4.061 **26.** 8.29 + 4.3 **27.** 7.06 − 4.235

28. 6.02 + 4.005 **29.** 7.05 − 3.5 **30.** 1.18 + 3.015 **31.** 2.304 − 0.87

32. 5.002 − 3.45 **33.** 6.8 + 3.57 **34.** 0.23 + 0.091 **35.** 0.5 − 0.18

36. 8.3 + 2.99 + 17.52 **37.** 9.5 + 12.32 + 6.4 **38.** 4.521 + 1.8 + 3.07

39. 3.602 + 9.4 + 24 **40.** 11.6 + 8.05 + 5.13 **41.** 7.023 + 1.48 + 3.9

42. 57 + 0.6327 + 189.007 **43.** 741 + 6.08 + 0.0309 **44.** 0.045 + 16.32 + 8.6

45. 4.27 + 6.18 + 0.91 **46.** 3.856 + 14.01 + 1.72 **47.** 11.45 + 3.79 + 23.861

Multiplying Decimals

Multiply decimals as you would whole numbers. Then place the decimal point in the product. To do this, add the number of decimal places in the factors.

Example

Multiply 0.068 × 2.3

Step 1	Step 2	
0.068	0.068	← **three decimal places**
×2.3	×2.3	← **one decimal place**
204	204	
+1360	+1360	
1564	0.1564	← **four decimal places**

More Examples

Find each product.

a. 3.12 × 0.9

$$\begin{array}{r} 3.12 \\ \times\ 0.9 \\ \hline 2.808 \end{array}$$

b. 5.75 × 42

$$\begin{array}{r} 5.75 \\ \times\ 42 \\ \hline 11\ 50 \\ +230\ 00 \\ \hline 241.50 \end{array}$$

c. 0.964 × 0.28

$$\begin{array}{r} 0.964 \\ \times\ 0.28 \\ \hline 7712 \\ +19280 \\ \hline 0.26992 \end{array}$$

EXERCISES

Multiply.

1. $\begin{array}{r} 1.48 \\ \times\ 3.6 \\ \hline \end{array}$ **2.** $\begin{array}{r} 191.2 \\ \times\ 3.4 \\ \hline \end{array}$ **3.** $\begin{array}{r} 0.05 \\ \times\ 43 \\ \hline \end{array}$ **4.** $\begin{array}{r} 0.27 \\ \times\ 5 \\ \hline \end{array}$ **5.** $\begin{array}{r} 1.36 \\ \times\ 3.8 \\ \hline \end{array}$

6. $\begin{array}{r} 6.23 \\ \times 0.21 \\ \hline \end{array}$ **7.** $\begin{array}{r} 0.512 \\ \times\ 0.76 \\ \hline \end{array}$ **8.** $\begin{array}{r} 0.04 \\ \times\ 7 \\ \hline \end{array}$ **9.** $\begin{array}{r} 0.136 \\ \times\ 8.4 \\ \hline \end{array}$ **10.** $\begin{array}{r} 3 \\ \times 0.05 \\ \hline \end{array}$

11. 2.07 × 1.004 **12.** 0.12 × 6.1 **13.** 3.2 × 0.15 **14.** 0.74 × 0.23

15. 2.6 × 0.14 **16.** 0.77 × 51 **17.** 9.3 × 0.706 **18.** 71.13 × 0.4

19. 0.42 × 98 **20.** 6.3 × 85 **21.** 45 × 0.028 **22.** 76 × 3.3

23. 9 × 1.35 **24.** 4.56 × 7 **25.** 5 × 2.41 **26.** 704 × 0.3

27. 8.003 × 0.6 **28.** 42.2 × 0.9 **29.** 0.6 × 30.02 **30.** 0.05 × 11.8

31. 15.1 × 0.02 **32.** 0.04 × 2.5 **33.** 6.6 × 0.3 **34.** 0.901 × 0.802

Zeros in the Product

When you multiply with decimals, you may have to write one or more zeros to the left of a product before you can place the decimal point.

Example

Multiply 0.06 × 0.015

Step 1	Step 2	
0.015	0.015	
× 0.06	× 0.06	
90	0.00090	← **Write three zeros before placing the decimal point.**

More Examples

Find each product.

a. 0.02 × 1.3

$$\begin{array}{r} 1.3 \\ \times 0.02 \\ \hline 0.026 \end{array}$$

b. 0.012 × 2.4

$$\begin{array}{r} 2.4 \\ \times\ 0.012 \\ \hline 48 \\ +240 \\ \hline 0.0288 \end{array}$$

c. 0.022 × 0.051

$$\begin{array}{r} 0.051 \\ \times 0.022 \\ \hline 102 \\ +1020 \\ \hline 0.001122 \end{array}$$

EXERCISES

Multiply.

1. 0.03 × 0.9

2. 0.06 × 0.5

3. 2.4 × 0.03

4. 7 × 0.01

5. 0.05 × 0.05

6. 0.016 × 0.12

7. 0.031 × 0.08

8. 0.03 × 0.2

9. 0.27 × 0.033

10. 0.014 × 0.25

11. 0.003 × 0.55 **12.** 0.01 × 0.74 **13.** 0.47 × 0.08 **14.** 0.76 × 0.1

15. 0.3 × 0.27 **16.** 0.19 × 0.05 **17.** 0.018 × 0.04 **18.** 0.43 × 0.2

19. 0.03 × 0.03 **20.** 4.003 × 0.02 **21.** 0.5 × 0.08 **22.** 0.06 × 0.7

23. 0.047 × 0.008 **24.** 0.05 × 0.06 **25.** 0.03 × 0.4 **26.** 0.05 × 0.036

27. 0.4 × 0.23 **28.** 0.3 × 0.017 **29.** 0.3 × 0.24 **30.** 0.67 × 0.09

31. 3.02 × 0.006 **32.** 0.31 × 0.08 **33.** 0.14 × 0.05 **34.** 0.07 × 0.85

Dividing a Decimal by a Whole Number

When you divide a decimal by a whole number, the decimal point in the quotient goes directly above the decimal point in the dividend. Sometimes you need to use extra zeros to place the decimal point.

Example

Divide 2.432 ÷ 32

Step 1

$$\begin{array}{r} 76 \\ 32\overline{)2.432} \\ -2\ 24 \\ \hline 192 \\ -192 \\ \hline 0 \end{array}$$

Step 2

$$\begin{array}{r} 0.076 \\ 32\overline{)2.432} \\ -2\ 24 \\ \hline 192 \\ -192 \\ \hline 0 \end{array}$$

← **You need two extra zeros to get the decimal point in the correct place.**

More Examples

Find each quotient.

a. 37.6 ÷ 8

$$\begin{array}{r} 4.7 \\ 8\overline{)37.6} \\ -32 \\ \hline 5\ 6 \\ -5\ 6 \\ \hline 0 \end{array}$$

b. 39.33 ÷ 69

$$\begin{array}{r} 0.57 \\ 69\overline{)39.33} \\ -34\ 5 \\ \hline 4\ 83 \\ -4\ 83 \\ \hline 0 \end{array}$$

c. 4.482 ÷ 54

$$\begin{array}{r} 0.083 \\ 54\overline{)4.482} \\ -4\ 32 \\ \hline 162 \\ -162 \\ \hline 0 \end{array}$$

EXERCISES

Divide.

1. $7\overline{)17.92}$ **2.** $5\overline{)16.5}$ **3.** $9\overline{)6.984}$ **4.** $6\overline{)91.44}$ **5.** $4\overline{)35.16}$

6. $56\overline{)8.848}$ **7.** $22\overline{)2.42}$ **8.** $26\overline{)1{,}723.8}$ **9.** $83\overline{)15.272}$ **10.** $39\overline{)26.91}$

11. 14.49 ÷ 7 **12.** 10.53 ÷ 9 **13.** 17.52 ÷ 2 **14.** 37.14 ÷ 6

15. 0.1352 ÷ 8 **16.** 0.0324 ÷ 9 **17.** 0.0882 ÷ 6 **18.** 0.8682 ÷ 6

19. 12.342 ÷ 22 **20.** 29.792 ÷ 32 **21.** 22.568 ÷ 26 **22.** 11.340 ÷ 36

23. 45.918 ÷ 18 **24.** 79.599 ÷ 13 **25.** 59.7 ÷ 15 **26.** 74.664 ÷ 12

27. 2.1 ÷ 84 **28.** 89.378 ÷ 67 **29.** 0.0672 ÷ 48 **30.** 171.031 ÷ 53

Powers of Ten

You can use shortcuts when multiplying and dividing by powers of ten.

When you multiply by:	Move the decimal point:	When you divide by:	Move the decimal point:
10,000	4 places to the right	10,000	4 places to the left
1,000	3 places to the right	1,000	3 places to the left
100	2 places to the right	100	2 places to the left
10	1 place to the right	10	1 place to the left
0.1	1 place to the left	0.1	1 place to the right
0.01	2 places to the left	0.01	2 places to the right
0.001	3 places to the left	0.001	3 places to the right

Examples

Multiply or divide.

a. 0.7×0.001
Move the decimal point 3 places to the left.
$0.7 \rightarrow 0.0007$
$0.7 \times 0.001 = 0.0007$

b. $0.605 \div 100$
Move the decimal point 2 places to the left.
$0.605 \rightarrow 0.00605$
$0.605 \div 100 = 0.00605$

EXERCISES

Multiply or divide.

1. $10{,}000 \times 0.056$
2. 0.001×0.09
3. 5.2×10
4. $0.03 \times 1{,}000$
5. $236.7 \div 0.1$
6. $45.28 \div 10$
7. $0.9 \div 1{,}000$
8. $1.07 \div 0.01$
9. 100×0.08
10. $1.03 \times 10{,}000$
11. 1.803×0.001
12. 4.1×100
13. $13.7 \div 0.001$
14. $203.05 \div 0.01$
15. $4.7 \div 10$
16. $0.05 \div 100$
17. 23.6×0.01
18. $1{,}000 \times 0.12$
19. 0.41×0.001
20. 0.01×6.2
21. $42.3 \div 0.1$
22. $0.4 \div 10{,}000$
23. $5.02 \div 0.01$
24. $16.5 \div 100$
25. $0.27 \div 0.01$
26. 1.05×0.001
27. 10×0.04
28. $2.09 \div 100$
29. 0.65×0.1
30. $0.03 \div 100$
31. $2.6 \div 0.1$
32. $12.6 \times 10{,}000$
33. $0.3 \div 1{,}000$
34. 0.01×6.7
35. 100×0.158
36. $23.1 \div 10$

Dividing a Decimal by a Decimal

To divide with a decimal divisor, multiply it by the smallest power of ten that will make the divisor a whole number. Then multiply the dividend by that same power of ten.

Examples

Find each quotient.

a. 3.348 ÷ 6.2
Multiply by 10.

$$\begin{array}{r} 0.54 \\ 6.2.\overline{)3.3.48} \\ -3\,1\,0 \\ \hline 2\,48 \\ -2\,48 \\ \hline 0 \end{array}$$

b. 2.4885 ÷ 0.35
Multiply by 100.

$$\begin{array}{r} 7.11 \\ 0.35.\overline{)2.48.85} \\ -2\,45 \\ \hline 3\,8 \\ -3\,5 \\ \hline 35 \\ -35 \\ \hline 0 \end{array}$$

c. 0.0576 ÷ 0.012
Multiply by 1,000.

$$\begin{array}{r} 4.8 \\ 0.012.\overline{)0.057.6} \\ -48 \\ \hline 9\,6 \\ -9\,6 \\ \hline 0 \end{array}$$

EXERCISES

Divide.

1. $3.2\overline{)268.8}$ **2.** $1.9\overline{)123.5}$ **3.** $0.3\overline{)135.6}$ **4.** $2.3\overline{)170.2}$ **5.** $7.9\overline{)252.8}$

6. $5.7\overline{)10.26}$ **7.** $2.3\overline{)71.53}$ **8.** $3.1\overline{)16.12}$ **9.** $7.8\overline{)24.18}$ **10.** $6.3\overline{)14.49}$

11. 134.42 ÷ 5.17 **12.** 89.96 ÷ 3.46 **13.** 160.58 ÷ 5.18 **14.** 106.59 ÷ 6.27

15. 62.4 ÷ 3.9 **16.** 260.4 ÷ 8.4 **17.** 316.8 ÷ 7.2 **18.** 162.4 ÷ 2.9

19. 1.512 ÷ 0.54 **20.** 3.225 ÷ 0.43 **21.** 2.484 ÷ 0.69 **22.** 511.5 ÷ 5.5

23. 0.992 ÷ 0.8 **24.** 4.53 ÷ 0.05 **25.** 3.498 ÷ 0.06 **26.** 59.2 ÷ 0.8

27. 2.198 ÷ 0.07 **28.** 14.28 ÷ 0.7 **29.** 1.98 ÷ 0.5 **30.** 26.36 ÷ 0.04

31. 3.922 ÷ 7.4 **32.** 23.52 ÷ 0.98 **33.** 71.25 ÷ 7.5 **34.** 114.7 ÷ 3.7

35. 0.832 ÷ 0.52 **36.** 1.125 ÷ 0.09 **37.** 9.666 ÷ 2.7 **38.** 1.456 ÷ 9.1

39. 0.4374 ÷ 1.8 **40.** 2.3414 ÷ 0.46 **41.** 0.07224 ÷ 0.021 **42.** 0.1386 ÷ 0.18

43. 0.16926 ÷ 0.091 **44.** 0.6042 ÷ 5.3 **45.** 2.3374 ÷ 0.62 **46.** 1.0062 ÷ 0.078

Zeros in Decimal Division

When you are dividing by a decimal, sometimes you need to use extra zeros in the dividend or the quotient, or both.

Example

Divide 0.045 ÷ 3.6

Step 1

Multiply by 10.

$3.6.\overline{)0.0.45}$

Step 2

Divide.

```
          125
3.6.)0.0.4500
      -36
        90
       -72
       180
      -180
         0
```

Step 3

Place the decimal point.

```
       0.0125
3.6.)0.0.4500
      -36
        90
       -72
       180
      -180
         0
```

More Examples

Find each quotient.

a. 0.04428 ÷ 8.2
Multiply by 10.

```
       0.0054
8.2.)0.4.4280
```

b. 0.00434 ÷ 0.07
Multiply by 100.

```
            0.062
0.07.)0.00.434
```

c. 0.00306 ÷ 0.072
Multiply by 1,000.

```
               0.0425
0.072.)0.003.0600
```

EXERCISES

Divide.

1. $0.05\overline{)0.0023}$
2. $0.02\overline{)0.000162}$
3. $0.12\overline{)0.009}$
4. $2.5\overline{)0.021}$
5. 0.0019 ÷ 0.2
6. 0.9 ÷ 0.8
7. 0.000175 ÷ 0.07
8. 0.142 ÷ 0.04
9. 0.0017 ÷ 0.02
10. 0.003 ÷ 0.6
11. 0.0105 ÷ 0.7
12. 0.034 ÷ 0.05
13. 0.00056 ÷ 0.16
14. 0.0612 ÷ 7.2
15. 0.177 ÷ 3.1
16. 0.052 ÷ 0.8
17. 0.000924 ÷ 0.44
18. 0.05796 ÷ 0.63
19. 0.00123 ÷ 8.2
20. 0.0954 ÷ 0.09
21. 0.0084 ÷ 1.4
22. 0.259 ÷ 3.5
23. 0.00468 ÷ 0.52
24. 0.104 ÷ 0.05
25. 0.00063 ÷ 0.18
26. 0.011 ÷ 0.25
27. 0.3069 ÷ 9.3
28. 0.00045 ÷ 0.3
29. 0.6497 ÷ 8.9
30. 0.00246 ÷ 0.06
31. 0.00168 ÷ 0.3
32. 0.00816 ÷ 3.4

Working with Integers

Quantities less than zero can be written using negative integers. For example, a temperature of 5 degrees below zero can be written as -5. Positive integers are used for quantities greater than zero.

Examples

Write an integer for each situation.

a. 10 degrees above zero
10

b. a loss of \$20
-20

c. 15 yards lost
-15

A number line can be used to compare integers. The integer to the right is greater.

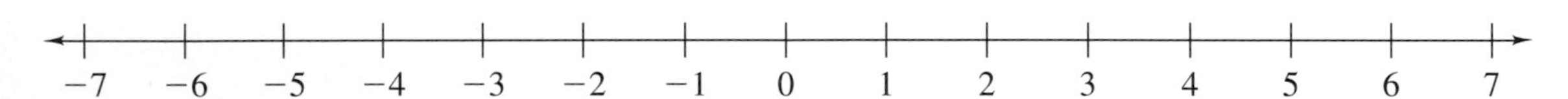

More Examples

Compare. Use > or <.

d. $0 \blacksquare -3$
0 is to the right, so it is greater.
$0 > -3$

e. $-2 \blacksquare -6$
-2 is to the right, so it is greater.
$-2 > -6$

f. $-7 \blacksquare 3$
-7 is to the left, so it is less.
$-7 < 3$

EXERCISES

Write an integer for each situation.

1. 6 yards gained
2. 10 yards lost
3. 5 steps forward
4. 4 steps backward
5. find \$3
6. lose \$8
7. 12 floors up
8. 4 floors down

Compare. Use > or <.

9. $0 \blacksquare -1$
10. $-9 \blacksquare 0$
11. $-3 \blacksquare 3$
12. $7 \blacksquare -3$
13. $0 \blacksquare 1$
14. $3 \blacksquare 0$
15. $1 \blacksquare -4$
16. $-2 \blacksquare -9$
17. $6 \blacksquare -1$
18. $3 \blacksquare -10$
19. $-7 \blacksquare 3$
20. $4 \blacksquare 6$
21. $-16 \blacksquare -25$
22. $-15 \blacksquare -12$
23. $7 \blacksquare -8$
24. $2 \blacksquare 3$
25. $-7 \blacksquare -8$
26. $35 \blacksquare -40$
27. $-30 \blacksquare -20$
28. $25 \blacksquare -25$
29. $9 \blacksquare -9$
30. $-6 \blacksquare -5$
31. $-23 \blacksquare -15$
32. $-17 \blacksquare -19$
33. $-15 \blacksquare -25$

Working with Fractions

To compare fractions with like denominators, compare the numerators. If the denominators are different, first write equal fractions with a common denominator. To compare mixed numbers, compare the whole-number parts first.

Examples

Compare. Use $>$ or $<$.

a. $4\frac{5}{7}$ ■ $4\frac{4}{7}$

The whole numbers are the same.
The denominators are the same.
Compare the numerators.

$5 > 4$, so $4\frac{5}{7} > 4\frac{4}{7}$

b. $\frac{3}{4}$ ■ $\frac{5}{6}$

12 is a common denominator.

Write $\frac{3}{4}$ as $\frac{9}{12}$, and $\frac{5}{6}$ as $\frac{10}{12}$.

$9 < 10$, so $\frac{3}{4} < \frac{5}{6}$

To estimate with fractions, decide if a fraction is closest to 0, $\frac{1}{2}$, or 1. To estimate with mixed numbers, you can round to the nearest whole number.

More Examples

Estimate.

c. Is $\frac{6}{15}$ closest to 0, $\frac{1}{2}$, or 1?

One-half of 15 is 6.5, so $\frac{6}{15}$ is closest to $\frac{1}{2}$.

d. Round $5\frac{5}{6}$ to the nearest whole number.

$\frac{5}{6}$ is greater than $\frac{1}{2}$, so $5\frac{5}{6}$ rounds to 6.

EXERCISES

Compare. Use $>$ or $<$.

1. $\frac{5}{12}$ ■ $\frac{1}{3}$ **2.** $\frac{5}{8}$ ■ $\frac{19}{24}$ **3.** $\frac{1}{6}$ ■ $\frac{3}{4}$ **4.** $\frac{2}{3}$ ■ $\frac{1}{4}$ **5.** $\frac{9}{10}$ ■ $\frac{3}{5}$

6. $\frac{3}{8}$ ■ $\frac{9}{16}$ **7.** $5\frac{1}{6}$ ■ $5\frac{2}{3}$ **8.** $4\frac{7}{12}$ ■ $1\frac{5}{8}$ **9.** $2\frac{5}{9}$ ■ $2\frac{2}{9}$ **10.** $4\frac{5}{8}$ ■ $2\frac{1}{4}$

Is each fraction closest to 0, $\frac{1}{2}$, or 1?

11. $\frac{7}{8}$ **12.** $\frac{5}{9}$ **13.** $\frac{1}{12}$ **14.** $\frac{11}{20}$ **15.** $\frac{3}{7}$ **16.** $\frac{9}{11}$ **17.** $\frac{3}{25}$

Round each mixed number to the nearest whole number.

18. $2\frac{5}{10}$ **19.** $1\frac{5}{9}$ **20.** $7\frac{8}{16}$ **21.** $8\frac{3}{8}$ **22.** $1\frac{3}{7}$ **23.** $3\frac{3}{4}$ **24.** $5\frac{7}{8}$

25. $6\frac{7}{8}$ **26.** $3\frac{1}{3}$ **27.** $5\frac{1}{12}$ **28.** $2\frac{11}{20}$ **29.** $6\frac{5}{12}$ **30.** $7\frac{5}{6}$ **31.** $8\frac{9}{10}$

Adding and Subtracting Fractions with Like Denominators

When you add or subtract fractions with the same denominator, add or subtract the numerators and then write the answer over the denominator.

Examples

Add or subtract. Write the answers in simplest form.

a. $\frac{5}{8} + \frac{7}{8}$

$\frac{5}{8} + \frac{7}{8} = \frac{5 + 7}{8} = \frac{12}{8} = 1\frac{4}{8} = 1\frac{1}{2}$

b. $\frac{11}{12} - \frac{2}{12}$

$\frac{11}{12} - \frac{2}{12} = \frac{11 - 2}{12} = \frac{9}{12} = \frac{3}{4}$

To add or subtract mixed numbers, add or subtract the fractions first. Then add or subtract the whole numbers.

More Examples

Add or subtract. Write the answers in simplest form.

c. $3\frac{4}{6} + 2\frac{5}{6}$

$$\begin{array}{r} 3\frac{4}{6} \\ +2\frac{5}{6} \\ \hline 5\frac{9}{6} \end{array} = 5 + 1 + \frac{3}{6} = 6\frac{1}{2}$$

d. $6\frac{1}{4} - 1\frac{3}{4}$

$$\begin{array}{r} 6\frac{1}{4} \\ -1\frac{3}{4} \\ \hline \end{array} \rightarrow \begin{array}{r} 5\frac{5}{4} \\ -1\frac{3}{4} \\ \hline 4\frac{2}{4} \end{array} = 4\frac{1}{2}$$

EXERCISES

Add or subtract. Write the answers in simplest form.

1. $\frac{4}{5} + \frac{3}{5}$ **2.** $\frac{2}{6} - \frac{1}{6}$ **3.** $\frac{2}{7} + \frac{2}{7}$ **4.** $\frac{7}{8} + \frac{2}{8}$ **5.** $1\frac{2}{5} - \frac{1}{5}$

6. $\frac{3}{6} - \frac{1}{6}$ **7.** $\frac{6}{8} - \frac{3}{8}$ **8.** $\frac{2}{9} + \frac{1}{9}$ **9.** $\frac{4}{5} - \frac{1}{5}$ **10.** $\frac{5}{9} + \frac{7}{9}$

11. $9\frac{1}{3} - 8\frac{1}{3}$ **12.** $8\frac{6}{7} - 4\frac{2}{7}$ **13.** $3\frac{1}{10} + 1\frac{3}{10}$ **14.** $2\frac{2}{9} + 3\frac{4}{9}$

15. $4\frac{5}{12} - 3\frac{1}{12}$ **16.** $9\frac{5}{9} + 6\frac{7}{9}$ **17.** $5\frac{7}{8} + 2\frac{3}{8}$ **18.** $4\frac{4}{7} - 2\frac{1}{7}$

19. $9\frac{3}{4} + 1\frac{3}{4}$ **20.** $8\frac{2}{3} - 4\frac{1}{3}$ **21.** $8\frac{7}{10} + 2\frac{3}{10}$ **22.** $1\frac{4}{5} + 3\frac{3}{5}$

23. $7\frac{1}{5} - 2\frac{3}{5}$ **24.** $4\frac{1}{3} - 1\frac{2}{3}$ **25.** $4\frac{3}{8} - 3\frac{5}{8}$ **26.** $5\frac{1}{12} - 2\frac{7}{12}$

Writing Equivalent Fractions

If you multiply or divide both terms of a fraction by the same number, you get an equivalent fraction.

Examples

a. Find the missing number in $\frac{5}{6} = \frac{20}{\blacksquare}$.

Notice that 5 has been multiplied by 4.

$$\frac{5}{6} = \frac{5 \times 4}{6 \times 4} = \frac{20}{24}$$

$$\frac{5}{6} = \frac{20}{24}$$

b. Find the missing number in $\frac{12}{30} = \frac{\blacksquare}{15}$.

Notice that 30 has been divided by 2.

$$\frac{12}{30} = \frac{12 \div 1}{30 \div 2} = \frac{6}{15}$$

$$\frac{12}{30} = \frac{6}{15}$$

To write a fraction in simplest form, divide both terms by the greatest common factor.

More Examples

c. Write $\frac{6}{15}$ in simplest form.

3 is the greatest common factor.

$$\frac{6}{15} = \frac{6 \div 3}{15 \div 3} = \frac{2}{5}$$

The simplest form of $\frac{6}{15}$ is $\frac{2}{5}$.

d. Write $\frac{36}{42}$ in simplest form.

6 is the greatest common factor.

$$\frac{36}{42} = \frac{36 \div 6}{42 \div 6} = \frac{6}{7}$$

The simplest form of $\frac{36}{42}$ is $\frac{6}{7}$.

EXERCISES

Find each missing number.

1. $\frac{1}{3} = \frac{\blacksquare}{6}$ **2.** $\frac{3}{4} = \frac{\blacksquare}{16}$ **3.** $\frac{18}{30} = \frac{6}{\blacksquare}$ **4.** $\frac{2}{3} = \frac{\blacksquare}{21}$ **5.** $\frac{3}{4} = \frac{9}{\blacksquare}$

6. $\frac{3}{10} = \frac{9}{\blacksquare}$ **7.** $\frac{4}{5} = \frac{\blacksquare}{30}$ **8.** $\frac{2}{3} = \frac{8}{\blacksquare}$ **9.** $\frac{33}{55} = \frac{\blacksquare}{5}$ **10.** $\frac{27}{72} = \frac{9}{\blacksquare}$

11. $\frac{2}{3} = \frac{\blacksquare}{24}$ **12.** $\frac{11}{12} = \frac{55}{\blacksquare}$ **13.** $\frac{3}{5} = \frac{18}{\blacksquare}$ **14.** $\frac{60}{72} = \frac{10}{\blacksquare}$ **15.** $\frac{7}{8} = \frac{\blacksquare}{24}$

Write each fraction in simplest form.

16. $\frac{12}{36}$ **17.** $\frac{25}{30}$ **18.** $\frac{14}{16}$ **19.** $\frac{27}{36}$ **20.** $\frac{21}{35}$ **21.** $\frac{40}{50}$ **22.** $\frac{24}{40}$

23. $\frac{32}{64}$ **24.** $\frac{15}{45}$ **25.** $\frac{27}{63}$ **26.** $\frac{44}{77}$ **27.** $\frac{45}{75}$ **28.** $\frac{60}{72}$ **29.** $\frac{77}{84}$

30. $\frac{12}{24}$ **31.** $\frac{24}{32}$ **32.** $\frac{7}{21}$ **33.** $\frac{18}{42}$ **34.** $\frac{35}{49}$ **35.** $\frac{18}{81}$ **36.** $\frac{6}{18}$

37. $\frac{28}{56}$ **38.** $\frac{10}{25}$ **39.** $\frac{16}{28}$ **40.** $\frac{30}{48}$ **41.** $\frac{22}{55}$ **42.** $\frac{80}{100}$ **43.** $\frac{16}{88}$

Adding and Subtracting Fractions with Unlike Denominators

To add or subtract fractions with different denominators, use the least common denominator to rewrite one or both of the fractions. In subtracting mixed numbers, you may also need to regroup. If necessary, change the answers to simplest form.

Examples

Add or subtract. Write the answers in simplest form.

a. $\frac{2}{5} + \frac{1}{10}$

$$\begin{array}{r} \frac{2}{5} \\ +\frac{1}{10} \\ \hline \end{array} \rightarrow \begin{array}{r} \frac{4}{10} \\ +\frac{1}{10} \\ \hline \frac{5}{10} \end{array} = \frac{1}{2}$$

b. $\frac{3}{5} - \frac{1}{4}$

$$\begin{array}{r} \frac{3}{5} \\ -\frac{1}{4} \\ \hline \end{array} \rightarrow \begin{array}{r} \frac{12}{20} \\ -\frac{5}{20} \\ \hline \frac{7}{20} \end{array}$$

c. $3\frac{3}{4} + 2\frac{7}{12}$

$$\begin{array}{r} 3\frac{3}{4} \\ +2\frac{7}{12} \\ \hline \end{array} \rightarrow \begin{array}{r} 3\frac{9}{12} \\ +2\frac{7}{12} \\ \hline 5\frac{16}{12} \end{array} = 6\frac{4}{12} = 6\frac{1}{3}$$

d. $3\frac{7}{10} - 1\frac{4}{5}$

$$\begin{array}{r} 3\frac{7}{10} \\ -1\frac{4}{5} \\ \hline \end{array} \rightarrow \begin{array}{r} 3\frac{7}{10} \\ -1\frac{8}{10} \\ \hline \end{array} \rightarrow \begin{array}{r} 2\frac{17}{10} \\ -1\frac{8}{10} \\ \hline 1\frac{9}{10} \end{array}$$

EXERCISES

Add or subtract. Write the answers in simplest form.

1. $\frac{5}{12} - \frac{1}{3}$ **2.** $\frac{1}{2} + \frac{2}{3}$ **3.** $\frac{2}{9} + \frac{3}{4}$ **4.** $\frac{2}{3} - \frac{1}{4}$ **5.** $\frac{5}{8} + \frac{2}{3}$

6. $\frac{2}{5} + \frac{3}{10}$ **7.** $\frac{19}{24} - \frac{5}{8}$ **8.** $\frac{1}{2} + \frac{2}{5}$ **9.** $\frac{1}{5} + \frac{3}{7}$ **10.** $\frac{5}{9} + \frac{3}{4}$

11. $\frac{9}{16} + \frac{3}{8}$ **12.** $\frac{3}{10} + \frac{2}{15}$ **13.** $\frac{3}{4} - \frac{1}{6}$ **14.** $\frac{1}{4} - \frac{5}{20}$ **15.** $\frac{9}{10} - \frac{3}{5}$

16. $6\frac{3}{4} + 1\frac{2}{3}$ **17.** $4\frac{7}{12} - 1\frac{5}{8}$ **18.** $5\frac{4}{5} + 2\frac{3}{10}$ **19.** $5 - 3\frac{3}{4}$

20. $4\frac{11}{12} + 3\frac{1}{5}$ **21.** $2\frac{5}{8} - 1\frac{1}{4}$ **22.** $9\frac{5}{18} - 2\frac{1}{3}$ **23.** $7\frac{4}{9} + 1\frac{5}{6}$

24. $5\frac{2}{3} - 2\frac{1}{6}$ **25.** $4\frac{5}{6} + 1\frac{3}{4}$ **26.** $4\frac{5}{8} - 2\frac{1}{4}$ **27.** $7\frac{2}{3} + 4\frac{4}{5}$

Multiplying Fractions and Mixed Numbers

To multiply fractions, first multiply the numerators. Then multiply the denominators. Sometimes you can simplify before multiplying.

To multiply mixed numbers, first change each mixed number to a fraction. Then multiply the fractions.

Examples

Multiply. Write the answers in simplest form.

a. $\frac{2}{3} \times \frac{4}{5}$

$$\frac{2}{3} \times \frac{4}{5} = \frac{2 \times 4}{3 \times 5} = \frac{8}{15}$$

b. $\frac{8}{9} \times \frac{3}{10}$

$$\frac{8}{9} \times \frac{3}{10} = \frac{\overset{4}{\cancel{8}}}{\underset{3}{\cancel{9}}} \times \frac{\overset{1}{\cancel{3}}}{\underset{5}{\cancel{10}}} = \frac{4}{15}$$

c. $3\frac{1}{8} \times 1\frac{3}{4}$

$$3\frac{1}{8} \times 1\frac{3}{4} = \frac{25}{8} \times \frac{7}{4} = \frac{175}{32} = 5\frac{15}{32}$$

d. $1\frac{5}{6} \times \frac{2}{3}$

$$1\frac{5}{6} \times \frac{2}{3} = \frac{11}{6} \times \frac{2}{3} = \frac{11}{\underset{3}{\cancel{6}}} \times \frac{\overset{1}{\cancel{2}}}{3} = \frac{11}{9} = 1\frac{2}{9}$$

EXERCISES

Multiply. Write the answers in simplest form.

1. $\frac{3}{4} \times \frac{3}{5}$
2. $\frac{2}{3} \times \frac{3}{4}$
3. $6 \times \frac{2}{3}$
4. $\frac{3}{4} \times \frac{5}{6}$
5. $\frac{5}{8} \times \frac{2}{3}$

6. $\frac{2}{5} \times \frac{3}{10}$
7. $\frac{4}{9} \times \frac{3}{8}$
8. $\frac{1}{2} \times \frac{2}{5}$
9. $\frac{1}{6} \times \frac{3}{7}$
10. $\frac{5}{9} \times \frac{3}{4}$

11. $\frac{9}{16} \times \frac{2}{3}$
12. $\frac{3}{10} \times \frac{2}{15}$
13. $\frac{3}{4} \times \frac{1}{6}$
14. $\frac{1}{4} \times \frac{5}{20}$
15. $\frac{9}{10} \times \frac{1}{3}$

16. $\frac{4}{9} \times \frac{3}{5}$
17. $\frac{5}{9} \times \frac{2}{3}$
18. $\frac{3}{10} \times \frac{2}{9}$
19. $\frac{4}{5} \times \frac{3}{8}$
20. $\frac{5}{12} \times \frac{2}{3}$

21. $1\frac{1}{3} \times 2\frac{2}{3}$
22. $\frac{3}{5} \times 2\frac{3}{4}$
23. $2\frac{1}{4} \times 3\frac{1}{3}$
24. $\frac{1}{4} \times 3\frac{1}{3}$

25. $6\frac{1}{4} \times 7$
26. $1\frac{3}{4} \times 2\frac{1}{5}$
27. $2\frac{3}{4} \times \frac{1}{2}$
28. $3\frac{4}{5} \times 2\frac{1}{3}$

29. $2\frac{1}{2} \times 1\frac{2}{3}$
30. $4 \times 2\frac{3}{11}$
31. $5\frac{3}{4} \times 6\frac{3}{8}$
32. $3\frac{4}{5} \times \frac{2}{3}$

Dividing Fractions and Mixed Numbers

To divide fractions, multiply by the reciprocal of the divisor. Two numbers are reciprocals if their product is 1.

To divide mixed numbers, first change each mixed number to a fraction. Then divide the fractions.

Examples

Divide. Write the answers in simplest form.

a. $\frac{2}{3} \div \frac{4}{5} = \frac{2}{3} \times \frac{5}{4} = \frac{\overset{1}{\cancel{2}}}{3} \times \frac{5}{\underset{2}{\cancel{4}}} = \frac{5}{6}$

b. $3\frac{1}{8} \div 1\frac{3}{4} = \frac{25}{8} \div \frac{7}{4} = \frac{25}{8} \times \frac{4}{7} = \frac{25}{\underset{2}{\cancel{8}}} \times \frac{\overset{1}{\cancel{4}}}{7} = \frac{25}{14} = 1\frac{11}{14}$

c. $2\frac{1}{4} \div 3 = \frac{9}{4} \div 3 = \frac{9}{4} \times \frac{1}{3} = \frac{\overset{3}{\cancel{9}}}{4} \times \frac{1}{\underset{1}{\cancel{3}}} = \frac{3}{4}$

EXERCISES

Divide. Write the answers in simplest form.

1. $\frac{5}{8} \div \frac{5}{7}$ **2.** $\frac{5}{7} \div \frac{5}{8}$ **3.** $\frac{3}{4} \div \frac{6}{11}$ **4.** $\frac{1}{9} \div \frac{1}{9}$ **5.** $\frac{1}{9} \div 9$

6. $\frac{3}{5} \div \frac{3}{4}$ **7.** $\frac{8}{9} \div \frac{2}{3}$ **8.** $\frac{1}{16} \div \frac{1}{2}$ **9.** $\frac{4}{5} \div \frac{7}{10}$ **10.** $\frac{4}{9} \div \frac{4}{7}$

11. $\frac{9}{10} \div \frac{3}{5}$ **12.** $\frac{2}{3} \div \frac{1}{9}$ **13.** $\frac{4}{5} \div \frac{5}{6}$ **14.** $\frac{1}{5} \div \frac{8}{9}$ **15.** $\frac{7}{8} \div \frac{1}{3}$

16. $\frac{2}{3} \div \frac{3}{7}$ **17.** $\frac{5}{6} \div \frac{3}{4}$ **18.** $\frac{2}{5} \div \frac{4}{5}$ **19.** $\frac{3}{10} \div \frac{3}{5}$ **20.** $4 \div \frac{2}{3}$

21. $4\frac{1}{5} \div 2\frac{2}{5}$ **22.** $6\frac{1}{4} \div 4\frac{3}{8}$ **23.** $2\frac{1}{3} \div 5\frac{5}{6}$ **24.** $1\frac{1}{2} \div 4\frac{1}{2}$

25. $2\frac{1}{12} \div 4\frac{1}{6}$ **26.** $4\frac{1}{2} \div \frac{3}{4}$ **27.** $3\frac{1}{8} \div 2\frac{2}{3}$ **28.** $14 \div 5\frac{1}{4}$

29. $15\frac{2}{3} \div 1\frac{1}{3}$ **30.** $10\frac{1}{3} \div 2\frac{1}{5}$ **31.** $6\frac{1}{4} \div 1\frac{3}{4}$ **32.** $6\frac{2}{3} \div 3\frac{1}{8}$

33. $15\frac{1}{2} \div 4$ **34.** $12\frac{3}{5} \div \frac{3}{10}$ **35.** $1\frac{2}{3} \div 2\frac{1}{12}$ **36.** $3\frac{1}{8} \div 1\frac{1}{4}$

37. $5\frac{1}{4} \div 1\frac{1}{6}$ **38.** $10 \div 2\frac{2}{3}$ **39.** $7\frac{1}{3} \div \frac{2}{3}$ **40.** $4\frac{1}{5} \div 2\frac{1}{5}$

Acknowledgments

Cover Design
Martucci Studio and Bruce Bond

Front Cover Photo Martucci Studio

Book Design DECODE, Inc.

Technical Illustration ANCO/Outlook

Illustration

Anco/OUTLOOK: 34 T, 57, 58, 61, 63, 64, 68, 72, 81, 82, 92, 108, 115, 147, 148, 162, 172, 173, 174, 236, 248, 250, 298, 302, 314, 325 R, 339, 341, 348, 350, 354, 357 R, 358, 359, 361, 362, 363, 367, 371, 398, 399, 408, 409, 410, 467, 469, 473, 474, 479, 483, 484 TR, 486, 489

Eliot Bergman: xii B, 272, 387

Arnold Bombay: 11, 19, 27, 32, 34 B, 107, 176, 347, 428, 450

DECODE, Inc.: vii TL, viii TL, ix TL, x TL, xi T, xii TL, xiii T, xiv TL, xv T, xvi TL, xvii TL, 2 TL, 4, 44 B, 45 B, 45 TL, 45, TR, 48 TL, 96 B, 97 CL, 97 BL, 97 T, 100 TL, 138 B, 139 B, 139 TL, 139 TR, 142 TL, 188 B, 189 CL, 189 CR, 189 T, 192 TL, 240 B, 241 B, 241 TL, 241 TR, 244 TL, 246, 280 CR, 281 B, 281 TL, 281 TR, 284 L, 332 B, 333 B, 333 TL, 333 TR, 336 TL, 374 B, 375 B, 375 TL, 375 TR, 378, 416 B, 417 B, 417 TL, 417 TR, 420 TL, 458 B, 459 B, 459 TL, TR, 462 TL, 504 B, 505 B, 505 TL, 505 TR

Tamar Haber-Schaim: 26, 27 B, 154,

Horizon Design/John Sanderson: 197, 264 T, 355, 357 L

Steve Moscowitz: 433, 492

Matthew Pippin: 18, 264 C, 311, 440, 444, 497

Precision Graphics: vii TR, xiv TR, xvii TR, 2, 3, 49, 65, 73, 79, 80, 192–193, 285, 336 B, 337 L, 337 R, 379, 421, 462–463

Schneck-DePippo Graphics: 231, 232

Schneck-DePippo Graphics and Anco/OUTLOOK: 195, 198, 214, 215 T, 221 L, 227 R, 233 TR

Rob Schuster: 8, 15, 23, 36, 38, 105, 127, 200, 215, 290

Ned Shaw: 7, 78, 125, 167, 181, 277, 340

Photography

Front Matter: i, ii, iii, Martucci Studio; **iv–v,** Bill DeSimone Photography; **vii L,** Jim Commentucci/Allsport; **viii TR,** Pacific Northwest Laboratories; **viii L,** Bob Daemmrich Photography; **ix TR,** K. Stepmell/Bruce Coleman Inc.; **x TR,** Mark Thayer Photography; **x L,** Antonio Rosario/The Image Bank; **xii TR,** Steve Greenberg Photography; **xv L,** Joe Carini/The Image Works; **xvi TR,** Bob Winsett/Tom Stack & Assoc.; **xvii BL,** Photo by Russ Lappa.

Chapter One: 2–3, © Alese & Mort Pechter/ The Stock Market; **6,** Daniel S. Brody/Stock Boston; **9,** Bob Daemmrich/The Image Works; **10 T,** Bill Horsman/Stock Boston; **10 B,** Porterfield-Chickering/Photo Researchers, Inc.; **13,** Lawrence Migdale/Stock Boston; **14,** © duomo; **16,** W.B. Spunbarg/The Picture Cube; **20,** Pam Elness/Comstock; **23,** G. Rose/Gamma Liaison; **28,** M. Antman/The Image Works; **29,** Jim Commentucci/Allsport USA; **33,** Doug Pensinger/Allsport USA; **37,** Comstock; **40,** Ned Haines/Photo Researchers, Inc.; **41,** Courtesy, Levi Strauss; **44,** Bob Daemmrich/The Image Works.

Chapter Two: 48–49, © Mugshots/The Stock Market; **49,** Pacific Northwest Laboratories; **50,** Ken O'Donoghue; **52,** Chris Michaels/FPG International; **55,** Bob Daemmrich/Stock Boston; **56,** Ken O'Donoghue; **59,** John Elk III/Stock Boston; **61,** Alan Becker/The Image Bank; **63,** Renate Hiller/Monkmeyer Press; **67,** Allsport; **70,** Bob Daemmrich Photography; **71,** Ken O'Donoghue; **72,** © Igno Cuypers; **74,** Courtesy, Ken Sharkey; **75 T,** Phil Degginger; **75 B,** Francois Gohier/Photo Researchers, Inc.; **79,** Lifetime Products; **83,** © Annie Hunter; **87,** Comstock; **91,** The Granger Collection; **94,** Pacific Northwest Laboratories; **96,** Robert Fried/Stock Boston.

Chapter Three: 100–101, © Dave Bartruff/Stock Boston; **102,** File Photo; **108,** Grant Faint/The Image Bank; **109,** Joe Azzara/The Image Bank; **110,** Courtesy, Benji Zimmerman; **111 T,** Ken O'Donoghue; **111 B,** Russ Lappa; **112,** Lee Foster/Bruce Coleman, Inc.; **113,** Robert Fried/Stock Boston; **115,** David Breashears/Adventure Photo; **120,** Bob Abraham/Pacific Stock; **124,** M. Veale Hay/Bob Daemmrich Photography; **126,** Hans Reinhard/Bruce Coleman, Inc.; **130,** Rick Stott/The Picture Cube; **133,** Pat Rogers/Sportschrome; **134,** Annie Hunter; **138,** Skjold/The Image Works.

Chapter Four: 142–143, © Bob Daemmrich; **144,** Ellis Herwig/The Picture Cube; **146,** The Granger Collection; **147,** G. Randall/FPG International; **151,**

Debra Herschkowitz/Bruce Coleman, Inc.; **152,** Bob Daemmrich/Stock Boston; **155,** Katherine Lambert; **156,** Courtesy, Maureen Murray; **157,** George Haling/ Science Source/Photo Researchers, Inc.; **158,** The Granger Collection; **164,** Ken O'Donoghue; **169,** NASA; **173,** E.R. Degginger/Bruce Coleman, Inc.; **176,** Herb Snitzer/Stock Boston; **178,** Antonio Rosario/The Image Bank; **180,** Erwitt/Magnum Photos; **183,** V. Wilkinson/Valan Photos; **184,** The Image Bank; **185,** David Phillip/Wide World Photos; **186,** Mark Thayer; **188,** Tony Freeman/PhotoEdit.

Chapter Five: 192–193, © Mark Hunt/Light Sources Stock; **194,** Tom Bean/The Stock Market; **205,** C. Kuhn/ The Image Bank; **206,** Larry Dale Gordon/The Image Bank; **208,** John Elk III; **209,** Jim Harrison/Stock Boston; **211,** Rick Stewart/Allsport; **213,** Tom Lynch/Stock Boston; **219,** Ken O'Donoghue; **223,** Donna H. Chiarelli; **225,** © 1955 M.C. Escher Foundation - Baarn - Holland. All rights reserved.; **226,** Hans Pfletschinger/Peter Arnold, Inc.; **230,** G&J Images/The Image Bank; **232 L,** Rod Williams/Bruce Coleman, Inc.; **232 R,** Nuridsany Et Perennou/Science Source/Photo Researchers, Inc.; **234,** Richard Parker/Photo Researchers, Inc.; **237,** G.E. Kidder Smith; **240,** Lawrence Migdale/Stock Boston.

Chapter Six: 244–245, Owen Franken/Stock Boston; **247,** The Granger Collection; **251,** Carl Bigras/Valan Photos; **253,** Chris Johns/Allstock; **257,** Ron & Valerie Taylor/Bruce Coleman, Inc.; **261,** Charles Gupton/Stock Boston; **262,** Vince Streano/The Stock Market; **267,** Phyllis Picardi/Stock Boston; **274,** Michael Newman/ PhotoEdit; **278,** Steve Greenberg; **280,** Skjold/The Image Works.

Chapter Seven: 284–285, © Bob Daemmrich, **286,** UPI/Bettmann Newsphotos; **287,** Forsythe/Monkmeyer Press; **291,** Courtesy The Bun Boy Restaurant; **293,** Jay Franklin; **295,** UPI/Bettmann; **297,** Thomas Long/Earth Scenes; **301,** Jose Carrillo/PhotoEdit; **305,** Dan McCoy/Rainbow; **306,** Roger Du Buisson/The Stock Market; **308,** George F. Mobley, copyright National Geographic Society; **316,** Stephen Dalton/Photo Researchers, Inc.; **318,** E.R. Degginger, FPSA; **320 T,** Lick Observatory; **320 B,** Courtesy, Anthony Beale; **321,** Dr. Fred Espenak/Science Photo Library/Photo Researchers, Inc.; **323,** Harry Hartman/Bruce Coleman, Inc.; **332,** Alan Carey/The Image Works.

Chapter Eight: 336–337, NASA; **338,** Tom McCarthy/ PhotoEdit; **339,** Bob Daemmrich/Stock Boston; **340,** © Oakland Tribune; **341,** Gregory MacNicol/Photo Researchers, Inc.; **344,** Courtesy, April Lott; **345,** Shelley Gazin/The Image Works; **346,** Nick Pavloff/The Image Bank; **349,** Roland Garros/Allsport; **356,** Greenlar/The Image Works; **365,** Peter Miller/The Image Bank; **366,** David Madison/Bruce Coleman, Inc.; **369,** Homer Smith/Bruce Coleman, Inc.; **375,** Robert Fried/Stock Boston.

Chapter Nine: 378–379, Gayna Hoffman; **380,** Kennan Ward/Bruce Coleman, Inc.; **381,** Bill Horsman/ Stock Boston; **383,** Joe Carini/The Image Works; **384,** The Granger Collection; **388,** Carl Roessler/Bruce Coleman, Inc.; **390,** Joe McDonald/Bruce Coleman, Inc.; **396,** Boston Globe Photo; **405,** Henryk T. Kaiser/The Picture Cube; **412,** Courtesy, Moneet Kohlii; **413,** Ken O'Donoghue; **416,** John Eastcott/The Image Works.

Chapter Ten: 420–421, © Lawrence Migdale; **422,** Dennis Brack/Black Star; **425,** Laurence Hughes/The Image Bank; **431,** Bryan Yablonsky/© duomo; **434,** S. Gazin/The Image Works; **435,** Jessica Ehlers/Bruce Coleman, Inc.; **436,** Bob Daemmrich/Stock Boston; **439,** Lee Foster/Bruce Coleman, Inc.; **442,** David Madison/ Bruce Coleman, Inc. **445,** Myrleen Ferguson/PhotoEdit; **446,** Courtesy, Ben Combetta; **447,** Richard Pasley/ Stock Boston; **449,** Mary Kate Denny/Photo Edit; **455,** Dennis MacDonald/The Picture Cube; **456,** Bob Winsett/Tom Stack & Associates; **458,** Peter Menzel.

Chapter Eleven: 462–463, © Gayna Hoffman; **464,** Steve Krongard/The Image Bank; **465,** Alfred Pasieka/Peter Arnold, Inc.; **467, 470,** PH Photo; **471,** © Peter A. Smith; **474,** Breck P. Kent/Earth Scenes; **476,** Andrea Pistolesi/The Image Bank; **480,** Burnett H. Moody/Bruce Coleman, Inc.; **482,** Ed Bock/The Stock Market; **484,** Russ Lappa; **485,** Annie Hunter; **493,** Rhoda Sidney/PhotoEdit; **494,** Stephen Frisch/Stock Boston; **495,** Wendy Watriss/Woodfin Camp & Associates; **498,** Robert Frerck/Woodfin Camp & Associates; **499,** David Lawrence/The Stock Market; **504,** Renee Lynn/ Photo Researchers, Inc.

Photo Research: Toni Michaels

Contributing Author: Paul Curtis, Hollis Public Schools, Hollis NH

Editorial, Design, and Electronic Prepress Production, for the Teaching Resources: The Wheetley Company

Editorial Services for the Teacher's Edition: Publishers Resource Group, Inc.